# Case Studies

# on Women's

# Employment and

# Pay in Latin America

# Case Studies

# on Women's

# Employment and

# Pay in Latin America

**EDITED BY**

**GEORGE PSACHAROPOULOS**

**AND**

**ZAFIRIS TZANNATOS**

The World Bank
*Washington, D.C.*

This volume is a companion to the World Bank Regional and Sectoral Study *Women's Employment and Pay in Latin America: Overview and Methodology*. The World Bank Regional and Sectoral Studies series provides an outlet for work that is relatively limited in its subject matter or geographical coverage but that contributes to the intellectual foundations of development operations and policy formulation. These studies have not necessarily been edited with the same rigor as Bank publications that carry the imprint of a university press.

The findings, interpretations, and conclusions expressed in this publication are those of the authors and should not be attributed in any manner to the World Bank, to its affiliated organizations, or to the members of its Board of Executive Directors or the countries they represent.

The material in this publication is copyrighted. Requests for permission to reproduce portions of it should be sent to the Office of the Publisher at the address shown in the copyright notice above. The World Bank encourages dissemination of its work and will normally give permission promptly and, when the reproduction is for noncommercial purposes, without asking a fee. Permission to copy portions for classroom use is granted through the Copyright Clearance Center, 27 Congress Street, Salem, Massachusetts 01970, U.S.A.

The complete backlist of publications from the World Bank is shown in the annual *Index of Publications*, which contains an alphabetical title list and indexes of subjects, authors, and countries and regions. The latest edition is available free of charge from Distribution Unit, Office of the Publisher, The World Bank, 1818 H Street, N.W., Washington, D.C. 20433, U.S.A., or from Publications, The World Bank, 66, avenue d'Iéna, 75116 Paris, France.

George Psacharopoulos is the senior human resources adviser to the World Bank's Latin America and Caribbean Technical Department. He previously taught at the London School of Economics. Zafiris Tzannatos is a labor economist with the Population and Human Resources Department at the World Bank. He is an honorary research fellow at the Universities of Nottingham and St. Andrews in the United Kingdom.

*Cover design by Sam Ferro*

*Library of Congress Cataloging-in-Publication Data*

Case studies on women's employment and pay in Latin America / edited
    by George Psacharopoulos and Zafiris Tzannatos.
        p.  cm.
    Includes bibliographical references.
    ISBN 0-8213-2308-3
    1. Women—Employment—Latin America—Case studies.  2. Wages—
Latin America—Case studies.  3. Discrimination in employment—
Latin America—Case studies.  4. Sex discrimination against women—
Latin America—Case studies.    I. Psacharopoulos, George.
II. Tzannatos, Zafiris, 1953.
HD6100.5.C37    1992
331.4'098—dc20
                                                    92-40880
                                                      CIP

# Contents

# Acknowledgments

We have benefited from comments and encouragement from many people who read earlier versions of this study and participated in seminars given at the World Bank, the University of St. Andrews, and conferences organized by the Comparative and International Education Society, the International Union for the Scientific Study of Population, and the European Society for Population Economics. In particular we would like to thank Ana-María Arriagada, Alessandro Cigno, Deborah DeGraff, Barbara Herz, David Huggart, Emmanuel Jimenez, Philip Musgrove, and Michelle Riboud for their helpful comments, Professor William Greene for providing purpose built routines for LIMDEP which facilitated the estimation procedures used in the country studies; Diane Steele and Carolyn Winter for their reviews of the book; Hongyu Yang for preparing the graphics; and Donna Hannah for typing and preparing the earlier versions of this book and Marta Ospina for taking these tasks over and eventually putting the book into its present form. The completion of the present study would have not been possible without the generous support of the Norwegian Trust Fund.

# Foreword

Women's role in economic development can be examined from many different perspectives, including the feminist, anthropological, sociological, economic and legislative. This study employs an economic perspective and focuses on how women behave and are treated in the work force in a number of Latin American economies. It specifically considers the determinants of women's labor force participation and male-to-female earnings differentials. Understanding the reasons for "low" labor market participation rates among women, or "high" wage discrimination against women, can lead to policies that will improve the efficiency and equity with which human resources are utilized in a particular country.

The study is in two volumes. The companion volume presents aggregate data on the evolution of female labor force participation in Latin America over time, showing that in some countries twice as many women (of comparable age groups) work in the market relative to twenty years ago. This volume uses household survey data to analyze labor force participation rates and wages earned by men and women in similar positions, paying special attention to the role of education as a factor influencing women's decision to work. The results show that, overall, the more years of schooling a woman has, the more likely she is to participate in the labor force. In addition, more educated women earn significantly more than less educated women. The book also attempts analyses of the common factors which determine salaries paid to men and women in an effort to identify what part of the male/female earnings differential can be attributed to different human capital endowments between the sexes, and what part is due to unexplained factors such as discrimination. Differences in human capital endowments explain only a small proportion of the wage differential in most of the country studies. The remaining proportion thus represents the upper bound to discrimination.

It is our hope that this work will be followed up by a more careful look at labor legislation and the role it plays in preventing women from reaching their full productive potential.

S. Shahid Husain
Vice President
Latin America and the Caribbean Region
The World Bank

# Female Labor Force Participation and Gender Earnings Differentials in Argentina

*Ying Chu Ng*

## 1. Introduction

In this study we estimate earnings functions for Argentinian males and females using the 1985 Buenos Aires Household Survey data. Our purpose is two-fold. First, we seek to investigate the income differentials between male and female workers. Second, we examine the existence of earnings discrimination by gender. In the following section we provide a brief overview of the Argentine economy and the operation of the labor market. In the third section we discuss the data base used in the analysis and present the main characteristics of male and female labor force participants. Female labor force participation and the factors influencing women's decision to participate are discussed in Section 4. In Section 5 we present the results from earnings functions estimates for male and female workers, and Section 6 provides an analysis and discussion of the extent to which male/female earnings differentials can be attributed to differences in human capital endowments and to discriminatory practices by employers in the labor market. The paper concludes with a discussion of these findings in Section 7.

## 2. The Argentine Economy and Labor Market

Since the 1940s political events in Argentina have had a considerable impact on the functioning of the economy, the structure of the labor market, and the earnings structure of workers. Government policies favoring import-substitution and the introduction of a wage setting mechanism meant that the growth of relative wages from the 1940s to the 1980s was highest in non-tradable activities. This, plus the fact that wage determination was increasingly influenced by collective bargaining, has led to a concentration of resources, including human resources, in urban areas. More than 30 percent (in 1987) of the total population was concentrated in the capital, Buenos Aires.

In general, labor force participation rates in the urban markets in Argentina are above 40 percent of the resident population (Sanchez, 1987). However, the Argentine labor market is characterized by cyclical periods in which labor is either scarce or relatively abundant. Two factors explain this. First, there are substantial fluctuations in terms of domestic and foreign migration. Second, the fact that unemployment and underemployment rates remain relatively low regardless of whether there is an excess or scarcity of labor suggests that there may be a strong "added worker" effect operating. Riveros and Sanchez (1990) provide evidence that this is the case. They report that the "added worker" effect resulted in substantial increases in female labor force participation rates, particularly among women aged 35 to 49 years, during the economic crisis of the early 1980s.

In Argentina there is not only a higher labor force participation rate relative to other Latin American countries, but workers also tend to work longer hours.  Dieguez (n.d.) reported that among 3.9 million employed individuals in May 1985, 37.6 percent worked between 35 and 45 hours weekly, and 31.4 percent worked over 45 hours per week, while only 17.5 percent worked less than 35 hours per week.

*Female workers.*  Among female workers de Lattes (1983) found that in both 1960 and 1970 there was a higher participation rate among single and divorced women aged between 25 and 59 years than among married women of the same age. Wainerman (1979) and de Lattes (1983) found similar results:  The probability of single female participation in the work force was at least three times that of married females.   Education is an important variable determining female participation rates. Wainerman (1979) found that more educated women were more likely to participate in the labor force.  Data collected from the Instituto Nacional de Estadistica y Censos (n.d.) showed that in Buenos Aires in 1970 the proportion of working females with less than primary education was substantially lower than women with higher educational attainment. Women with secondary or university education made up the largest portion of the female work force (de Lattes, 1983).

Female migrants constitute an important proportion of the female labor force in urban areas (Marshall, 1977; de Lattes, 1983) and especially in Buenos Aires.

Female workers are concentrated in non-agricultural activities.  More than 65 percent of workers in the non-tradable sector were females in the 1960s, and this figure increased to 79 percent of workers in 1980.

## 3.    Data Characteristics

The data used in this study are drawn from the 1985 Buenos Aires Household Survey which was undertaken by the National Institute of Statistics (INDEC) and surveyed 15,580 individuals. Though the survey covers only Buenos Aires, it represents more than 30 percent of the total population of the country. In the present study, we extract females (working and non-working) and working males aged 15 to 65, resulting in a sample of 7,097 individuals.

The descriptive statistics and the definitions of the main variables are presented in Table 1.1. The female participation rate is 36 percent.  The average education level of the sample is nearly 9 years of schooling for both sexes.  Working females average over 9 years of schooling but have less work experience than males.  The overall sample characteristics are very similar for both males and females. A very large portion of the working population is employed in the dependent employment sector -- 80 percent of females and 78 percent of males. Females work fewer hours than males on average and the number of part-time female workers is about twice that of part-time males. The average earnings of females is about 64.5 percent that of males, and other income (defined as the difference between family income and the respondent's labor income) is 1.75 times as much for females as it is for males.

In order to have a closer look at the earning differentials, information on earnings among different employment sectors and employment types by educational level is presented in Tables 1.2A and 1.2B. Regardless of the differences in sector and employment type, the higher the

## Table 1.1
### Buenos Aires, Argentina
### Means (and Standard Deviations) of Sample Variables

| Variable | Working Males | Working Females | All Females |
|---|---|---|---|
| Age | 37.99 | 35.71 | 37.95 |
| | (12.39) | (12.42) | (14.68) |
| Years of Schooling | 8.80 | 9.41 | 8.23 |
| | (3.87) | (4.17) | (3.73) |
| Less than Primary | 0.01 | 0.02 | 0.03 |
| | (0.11) | (0.13) | (0.16) |
| Primary | 0.51 | 0.44 | 0.53 |
| | (0.50) | (0.50) | (0.50) |
| Secondary | 0.34 | 0.35 | 0.34 |
| | (0.47) | (0.48) | (0.47) |
| University | 0.14 | 0.19 | 0.10 |
| | (0.35) | (0.39) | (0.30) |
| Experience | 24.19 | 21.30 | |
| | (13.46) | (14.06) | |
| Experience Squared | 766.36 | 651.14 | |
| | (711.62) | (712.08) | |
| Monthly Income | 98483.48 | 63558.97 | |
| | (73274.89) | (52861.05) | |
| Weekly Hours Worked | 46.31 | 37.48 | |
| | (13.62) | (15.04) | |
| Employee | 0.78 | 0.80 | |
| | (0.42) | (0.40) | |
| Public | 0.17 | 0.28 | |
| | (0.38) | (0.45) | |
| Part-time | 0.12 | 0.35 | |
| | (0.88) | (0.48) | |
| Overtime | 0.41 | 0.22 | |
| | (0.49) | (0.41) | |
| Married | 0.74 | 0.55 | 0.65 |
| | (0.44) | (0.50) | (0.48) |
| Size of the Family | 7.50 | 7.28 | 7.35 |
| | (4.28) | (4.36) | (4.23) |
| Number of Children | 0.84 | 0.70 | 0.77 |
| | (1.13) | (1.04) | (1.09) |
| House/Land Ownership | 0.79 | 0.76 | 0.80 |
| | (0.41) | (0.43) | (0.40) |
| Head of Household | 0.73 | 0.13 | 0.09 |
| | (0.44) | (0.34) | (0.29) |
| Number of Income Earners | 4.43 | 4.14 | 4.27 |
| | (2.02) | (2.07) | (1.99) |
| Other Income | 61348.40 | 104887.52 | 106560.65 |
| | (79903.70) | (102931.38) | (100092.14) |
| Foreign Born | 0.11 | 0.08 | 0.11 |
| | (0.31) | (0.28) | (0.32) |
| N | 2,397 | 1,338 | 4,700 |

Note:    Female Labor Force Participation Rate = 36%

Source:    Buenos Aires Household Survey, 1985

**Table 1.2A**
Mean Earnings by Educational Level and Type of Employment
(Pesos per month)

|  | Females | | Males | |
| --- | --- | --- | --- | --- |
|  | Employee | Self-employed | Employee | Self-employed |
| **Education** | | | | |
| Less than primary | 40,506 | 25,233 | 51,409 | 80,000 |
| Primary | 45,026 | 40,268 | 74,379 | 82,629 |
| Secondary | 72,721 | 56,969 | 100,513 | 113,068 |
| University | 97,229 | 106,813 | 174,427 | 159,484 |
| **Employment Sector** | | | | |
| Private | 59,957 | 52,231 | 94,916 | 102,787 |
| Public | 79,539 | 50,654 | 105,894 | 113,962 |
| Overall | 66,399 | 52,060 | 97,100 | 103,333 |
| N | (1,073) | (265) | (1,865) | (532) |

**Table 1.2B**
Mean Earnings by Education and Sector of Employment
(Pesos per month)

|  | Females | | Males | |
| --- | --- | --- | --- | --- |
|  | Private | Public | Private | Public |
| **Education** | | | | |
| Less than primary | 36,109 | 50,000 | 62,269 | 38,000 |
| Primary | 41,679 | 57,345 | 75,461 | 80,018 |
| Secondary | 70,150 | 71,459 | 103,282 | 106,174 |
| University | 108,056 | 92,611 | 180,918 | 152,179 |
| Overall | 58,027 | 77,558 | 96,908 | 106,422 |
| N | (959) | (379) | (2,000) | (397) |

education level the more the individual earns. Males earn about 50 percent more than females with the same education, except where employees have less than primary education or where they are self-employed with less than primary education.

Within employment type, different patterns are seen for males and females. Self-employed males earn more than wage employees at all levels except males with university education. The exact opposite pattern is seen for females: Employees earn more than the self-employed at all levels except females with university education. There is no clear pattern for male earnings by public and private sector. However, female workers in the public sector earn more than those in the private sector for all education levels except for university education.

From the sample statistics, there is obviously a wage gap between males and females. In economic theory, wage differentials come from two broad sources : (1) differences in "skill" (attributes) and (2) differences in "treatment" (wage structure), i.e., from discrimination by employers. The upper bound of this discrimination can be computed by using the Oaxaca (1973) decomposition technique. This requires estimating earnings functions for females and males.

## 4.    Determinants of Female Labor Force Participation

In this section, we discuss the determinants of female labor force participation. Important factors determining women's propensity to participate in the labor force are marital status and presence of young children. It is common for women to withdraw from the labor force during child-bearing and when their children are young. Obviously, the presence of young children increases the value of non-market activities, particularly in developing countries where childcare services are very limited. In certain economic groups it is also common for women to cease working when they marry. Hence, single females have a relatively high probability of participating in the work force.

Age is also a key variable in explaining the probability of female participation. Greenhalgh (1980) and Mohan (1985) use the quadratic form to demonstrate that the participation rate of women increases at a decreasing rate as they age. On the other hand, some researchers argue that the labor force participation of women is expected to follow a U-shaped profile with age, indicating changes over their life cycle (Sheehan, 1978; Layard, Barton and Zabalza, 1980; King, 1990). Hence entry wages and potential market wages of women are associated with age, which in turn exerts effects on female labor force participation.

Aside from demographic characteristics, economic factors are found to be highly correlated with the labor force participation of women. Standing (1978) suggests that in the participation function the "need" for income is the dominant force in explaining the participation decision of women, other things being equal. He argues that the "need" for income can be measured by several variables, namely husband's income, family income excluding female's earning, assets or wealth possessions, the number of income earners in the family and the household status of women. All of the above, excepting women's household status, are expected to have a negative impact on female labor force participation. Evidence from empirical studies in the United States supports the fact that female participation is negatively related to the husband's wage, other family income and other family income per equivalent adult (Sweet, 1973).

As a determinant of labor supply, investment in human capital cannot be ignored. Individuals invest in human capital either through schooling or training to obtain higher future earnings. Thus, the higher an individual's educational level, the higher the opportunity cost of being out of the labor force. The expected positive association between education and labor force participation of women is usually found.

Studies of female labor force participation find that the decision to participate can also be influenced by area of residence and by migration. In Latin America, it is common for non-urban residents to migrate to urban cities to look for better opportunities. Standing (1982) points out that "more women than men [traditionally] have gone to the towns and cities and these women have been predominantly young and single ... getting into labor force activities or finding better, higher-paying work, or access to training for employment." There is also, however, evidence of non-significant effects of migration on the labor force participation decision in Standing (1978) and Behrman and Wolfe (1984).

In summary, the probability of participation is affected by personal characteristics, family composition, educational attainment, and economic factors related to income "need."

An abundant literature has been written on the issue of selectivity bias when estimating wages using only working females (Gronau, 1974; Heckman, 1979). It has been argued that an estimation based only on working females gives rise to biased estimates. The bias is mainly due to the fact that the sample of workers in the labor market is self-selected, having lower reservation prices than otherwise similar non-workers. For those non-working females, their wages are unobserved. To correct for such a censoring problem, Heckman (1979) proposed a two-step method. First, a probit equation is used to estimate the probability of a woman being in the work force. The inverse Mill's ratio is computed (denoted here by Lambda) and is added to the earning function as an additional regressor in the second step. The empirical work in this study follows the Heckman procedure and the definitions of the variables used are discussed in the following paragraphs.

The dummy variable that defines the labor force participation decision of females is set to 1 if the female is economically active, looking for a job, or temporarily unemployed due to sickness and job search, and 0 otherwise. Personal characteristics such as age, marital status and education are important explanatory variables. To capture the non-linear relationship between age and the probability of labor force participation, age splines of 5-year intervals are used and the omitted category is the 60 to 65 age group. A dichotomous variable for marital status is used. Similarly, to examine how differences in educational levels affect the female participation decision, dummy variables are created for less than primary education (the reference group), primary education, commercial secondary education, technical secondary education, other secondary education, and higher education.

Several other variables that measure the wealth, income, and household production demands are also included in the analysis. A dummy variable for the proxy of wealth, is assigned the value 1 if the respondent owns the house and/or the land and 0 otherwise. Likewise, information about family income other than the female respondent's is another independent variable. Total number of income earners within the same household is added to capture the household's division of labor between the home and the market. A dummy variable for a female headed household is used to proxy the financial responsibility of the female and other socio-economic differences in family types. The size of the family and number of young children under 6 years in the family are used to account for the effect of household production on the labor force participation decision. Finally, the probit equation also includes a variable to see whether being foreign-born affects the participation decision positively since a large portion of the population is non-Argentinean. Owing to data limitations, migration status and regional residence are not considered.

The results of the probit function are shown in Table 1.3. As expected, age is found to be an important determinant in explaining female labor force participation. The probability of participation appears to have a concave profile and peaks between ages 25 to 29 years. In addition, married females are less likely to be in the labor force; the probability of labor force participation is reduced by 31 percent as compared to non-married females. Moreover, the estimates for family size and the number of children aged under 6 are consistent with the literature.

Regarding the "need" for income, two out of the four variables are statistically significant at conventional levels. Having owned a house and/or land reduces the probability of being in the labor force of women by 10 percent. Possession of other income (from husband and/or other family members) leads to a 0.1 percent decline in the labor force participation probability. The insignificance of the two other variables may be due to the high correlation between them and the proxy for wealth. Being foreign-born, however, is insignificant in explaining labor force participation among females.

**Table 1.3**
Probit Regression Results for Female Labor Force Participation

| Variable | Coefficient | t-ratio | Partial Derivative |
|---|---|---|---|
| Constant | -0.783 | (-4.62) | |
| Age 19 or less | 0.145 | (1.24) | 0.053 |
| Age 20 to 24 | 1.137 | (9.98) | 0.418 |
| Age 25 to 29 | 1.292 | (11.65) | 0.475 |
| Age 30 to 34 | 1.247 | (11.62) | 0.459 |
| Age 35 to 39 | 1.225 | (11.38) | 0.451 |
| Age 40 to 44 | 1.198 | (10.96) | 0.441 |
| Age 45 to 49 | 1.182 | (10.87) | 0.435 |
| Age 50 to 54 | 0.909 | (8.38) | 0.334 |
| Age 55 to 59 | 0.629 | (5.75) | 0.231 |
| Married | -0.840 | (-13.22) | -0.309 |
| Own house/land | -0.271 | (-5.43) | -0.099 |
| Other Income | -0.004 | (-1.87) | -0.001 |
| Head of Household | 0.002 | (0.02) | 0.000 |
| Number of Earners | -0.018 | (-1.43) | -0.006 |
| Family Size | 0.011 | (1.88) | 0.004 |
| Children under 6 years | -0.095 | (-4.11) | -0.035 |
| Primary Education | 0.299 | (2.29) | 0.110 |
| Regular Secondary | 0.333 | (2.40) | 0.122 |
| Technical Secondary | 0.700 | (3.22) | 0.257 |
| Commercial Secondary | 0.378 | (2.75) | 0.139 |
| University | 0.976 | (6.74) | 0.359 |
| Foreign born | -0.063 | (-0.96) | -0.023 |

Notes:  Sample size = 4,700.
Log-Likelihood = -2666.9

Similar to findings in other Latin American countries, primary education exerts a significant effect on female labor force participation when compared to less than primary eduction (the omitted category). Note that the probability of participation increases with increasing educational attainment. The highest probability of participation is found for those with completed higher education (36 percent). The participation probability varies by type of secondary education. According to our estimates, of the three types of secondary education, having technical secondary education gives the highest probability of participating (26 percent) while commercial secondary education only increases the participation probability by 14 percent.

Using the above probit results, we examine the effect of changes in certain characteristics on female labor force participation by simulation. Given that other sample characteristics remain unchanged, we predict the probability of labor force participation for different educational levels, marital status, the number of young children, the size of the family, the ownership of house and/or land, and age groups. The predicted probabilities are found in Table 1.4. As one might expect, increases in educational levels lead to an increase in participation probability. It is also interesting to find that the predicted probabilities for primary education and academic (regular) secondary education differ by only 1 percent. This interesting finding may reflect the impact of compulsory primary education which reduces the reward differences between primary and secondary education (as shown in Table 1.1 over 50 percent of females in the sample have primary education). Commercial secondary education, on the other hand, does not increase the participation probability as much as technical secondary education does with respect to academic secondary education.

The probability of participation for non-married women is twice that for married women. The number of young children is another constraint on the participation decision. In Table 1.4, predicted probability drops from 37 percent to 23 percent when the number of young children increases from none to 4, other things being equal. Consequently, household responsibilities of women are important factors affecting the participation decision. In contrast, the size of the family increases the probability of participation with a flat rate of 0.4 percentage point. This interesting result may demonstrate the fact that as the size of the family increases, the time needed for childcare and home production from the women is overcome by the "need' for income to support the family. Owning a house and/or the land causes the probability of participation to decline from 42 percent to 32 percent. Finally, predicted probabilities from the age splines demonstrate an inverted U-shaped profile with the highest probability for women aged 25 to 29 years.

## 5. Earnings Functions

Mincer's basic model for estimating earnings functions regresses hourly earnings (wage rates) on schooling, experience and experience squared. The standard way of incorporating education is to use a continuous variable to measure the years of schooling so estimates of private rates of return to additional year of schooling can be obtained. According to economic theory, the earnings profile appears to be increasing at a decreasing rate with years of market attachment. Labor market experience and its square are used to test for this. In most cases, significant quadratic effects with eventual diminishing marginal returns to experience have been found (Shields, 1980; Behrman and Wolfe, 1984). In the absence of actual experience information, potential experience was calculated as age minus years of schooling minus six.

We estimate a Mincer-type earnings function in which years of schooling, experience, experience squared and the natural logarithm of hours worked are included as regressors. A separate earnings function is estimated for females and males to account for any wage differences due to sectoral and industrial differences.

**Table 1.4**
Predicted Participation Probabilities by Characteristic

| Characteristic | Predicted Probability |
|---|---|
| **Education** | |
| Less than primary | 21.7 |
| Primary | 31.4 |
| Regular secondary | 32.6 |
| Commercial secondary | 34.3 |
| Technical secondary | 46.7 |
| University | 57.6 |
| **Marital Status** | |
| Non-married | 55.9 |
| Married | 24.5 |
| **Number of Young Children** | |
| None | 37.2 |
| One | 33.6 |
| Two | 30.2 |
| Three | 26.9 |
| Four | 23.8 |
| **Size of the Family** | |
| One | 31.9 |
| Two | 32.3 |
| Three | 32.7 |
| Four | 33.1 |
| Five | 33.5 |
| Six | 33.9 |
| **Ownership of House and/or Land** | |
| No | 42.7 |
| Yes | 32.4 |
| **Age** | |
| 15-19 | 12.7 |
| 20-24 | 44.0 |
| 25-29 | 50.2 |
| 30-34 | 48.4 |
| 35-39 | 47.5 |
| 40-44 | 46.4 |
| 45-49 | 45.8 |
| 50-54 | 35.2 |
| 55-59 | 25.5 |
| 60-65 | 1.0 |
| **Actual mean participation** | 36.0 |

Note: Based on the results reported in Table 1.3.

For both males and females, the standard Mincer-type regression function includes independent variables measuring the years of schooling (S), potential labor market experience (defined as AGE-S-6)[1] and its square and the natural logarithm of weekly hours work. The dependent variable of the earnings functions is the natural logarithm of monthly earnings.

In order to account for any structural difference in the labor market that affects the "treatment" component of wage differentials, separate earnings functions for males and females are estimated. With the exception of a change in the schooling variable (which is replaced by categorical educational levels as described in the probit equation), several independent variables that measure sectoral employment and types of employment are included. In addition to potential experience, several dichotomous variables indicating whether individuals have received on-the-job training are added to capture the impact of specific training.[2]

Similarly, dummy variables for being employed in the public sector or not, working in the dependent employment sector or not, and whether weekly hours of work is less than 35 or over 45[3] are included.

Earnings differences due to any intra-industrial differentials are taken into account by various industrial sector dummy variables. Finally, being married and/or being a foreign-born individual (FOREIGN) may affect earnings as well. In the case of females, earning functions are estimated by ordinary least squares (OLS) and are presented for the purpose of comparison with respect to the equation with selectivity adjustment.

Table 1.5 shows the results for earnings functions of males and females that are consistent with the theory. The inverse Mill's ratio (Lambda) in the female earnings function in column 3 of Table 1.5 is marginally significant and negative. Consequently, it is not surprising to find that results of the Heckman procedure are little different from those in the regular OLS. For both types of estimation, an additional year of schooling increases earnings by about 11 percent. Likewise, potential labor market experience and its square reveal a non-linear earnings profile for females, increasing at an decreasing rate.

For males, the earnings elasticity with respect to hours of work is 0.3905 and for females is 0.6589 (uncorrected for selectivity) or 0.6607 (corrected for selectivity). Moreover, the returns to education for males is lower than for females, 9 percent compared to 11 percent. The reward of potential market experience among males is higher than that of females.

A different specification of the earnings function, which includes information associated with labor market structure and training produces slightly different results for each earnings function. Table 1.6 presents earnings functions for both males and females, with female earnings functions estimated using regular OLS and OLS with selectivity adjustment. As shown in the table, the

---

[1]    Though the definition has been criticized by various scholars, a more accurate measure is unavailable from this data set. As a result, the reader should be cautious in the interpretation of the estimates.

[2]    See Kugler and Psacharopoulos (1989).

[3]    The purpose of the hours of work variable is to account for any effect of working overtime and moonlighting since there is a large proportion of respondents working more than 45 hours per week.

**Table 1.5**
Earnings Functions

| Variable | Men | Women (uncorrected for selectivity) | Women (corrected for selectivity) |
|---|---|---|---|
| Constant | 8.3429 (63.245) | 7.0701 (48.300) | 6.9662 (52.276) |
| Schooling (years) | 0.0908 (30.006) | 0.1067 (22.875) | 0.1092 (24.747) |
| Experience | 0.0491 (15.505) | 0.0384 (9.185) | 0.0394 (9.540) |
| Experience squared | -0.0007 (-11.482) | -0.0005 (-6.472) | -0.0006 (-7.050) |
| ln (hours) | 0.3905 (11.647) | 0.6589 (21.055) | 0.6607 (21.066) |
| Lambda | | | -0.0837 (-1.695) |
| R-Squared | 0.3463 | 0.4527 | 0.4515 |
| N | 2,397 | 1,338 | 1,338 |

Notes:   Figures in parentheses are t-ratios.

The mean of the dependent variable, log-monthly earnings, for men and working women are 11.29 and 10.79, respectively.

effects of potential experience, its squared term and hours of work for both sexes are similar but with slightly different magnitudes than those in Table 1.5.

The Lambda (inverse Mill's ratio), is again negative but highly significant. The correction for censoring leads to two main differences in the estimation results. First, the dummy variable for marital status is highly significant with a greater effect (17 percent versus 7 percent). Second, the return to higher education is substantially lower in the case of the selectivity result. These changes reflect (1) biased estimates obtained from regressing working females alone without controlling for selectivity and (2) the importance of higher education and marital status in affecting the self-selection process (participation decision).

Since both estimates in the females earnings functions are quite similar (with the exceptions mentioned above), the following discussion is based on the results of the selectivity equation (Column 1 of Table 1.6) unless otherwise specified. Notice that the returns to education increase with educational level (average returns of 5 percent to secondary and 9 percent to higher education) except for primary education.[4] The insignificant effect of primary education on female's earnings might indicate the "deflation value" effect which results from compulsory primary education.

The experience profile appears to be concave, peaking at 34.33 years calculated at the mean value of the working female sample. A one percent increase in weekly hours worked leads to a 0.73 percent increase in earnings.

The consequence of having any work-related training has an interesting impact on earnings. In the case of females, having one training course enhances female earnings by 15 percent while having two or three training courses makes no difference to earnings compared to those having no training at all. Earnings increase by 56 percent if a female has four training courses, while having five or more training courses has a negative impact on earnings, compared to the reference group (no training). This result is puzzling but also likely to be imprecise -- less than one percent of the females in the sample fell into the latter two groups.

For females, earnings do not differ between the public and private sectors, other things equal. On the other hand, if they are an employee (dependent employment) they will earn 10 percent more than the self-employed, holding other factors constant. This is not surprising given the wage determination system in Argentina.

Earnings of part-timers are not statistically different from those of full-time workers. Those who work more than 45 hours weekly, however, earn about 22 percent less than full-time workers, holding hours of work constant.

In the female labor market, ethnicity does not affect earnings. A working married female earns 17 percent more than a non-married woman, though the probability of participation is negatively associated with marital status. Those who work after marriage tend to have a higher educational attainment or more investment in human capital.

Across different types of industry, only finance and services industries exert effects on female earnings. Working in the finance industry allows females to earn 22 percent more while service female workers are paid 37 percent less than other types of industry (the omitted group). The latter result is as expected since the relative overcrowding and the low skill requirement in that sector lowers average earnings.

For males, the alternate specification shows a different picture. The rate of return to different levels of education increases with each successive level of education, with the exception of secondary education (an average of 6.6 percent return to primary education, 5.3 percent to secondary education and 11.6 percent to university level).

The experience profile is concave in shape and has a lower decreasing rate than that of women. Males' earnings are less sensitive with respect to the number of hours worked per week (elasticity of 0.332).

---

[4]   The average returns to each educational level is calculated by dividing the change in coefficients of the compared educational levels by the difference in years of schooling between the compared educational levels.

## Table 1.6
Earnings Functions with Alternative Specification (t-ratios in parentheses)
and Sample Means of Selected Variables (standard deviations in parentheses)

| Variable | Women | | | Males | |
| --- | --- | --- | --- | --- | --- |
| | Corrected for Selectivity | Uncorrected for Selectivity | Mean | OLS | Mean |
| Constant | 7.6189 (26.779) | 7.3687 (27.532) | | 8.8320 (35.086) | |
| **Education** | | | | | |
| Primary | 0.1252 (0.997) | 0.1463 (1.221) | | 0.3946 (4.070) | |
| Secondary | 0.4384 (3.320) | 0.4796 (3.817) | | 0.7126 (7.208) | |
| University | 0.7899 (5.435) | 0.9115 (6.093) | | 1.1753 (11.367) | |
| Experience | 0.0302 (5.571) | 0.0376 (8.278) | | 0.0396 (10.946) | |
| Experience squared | -0.0004 (-4.143) | -0.0006 (-6.913) | | -0.0006 (-9.284) | |
| ln (hours) | 0.7289 (13.398) | 0.7372 (13.398) | | 0.3321 (5.573) | |
| **Training** | | | | | |
| One course | 0.1522 (3.899) | 0.1531 (3.880) | 0.22 (0.42) | 0.1006 (3.311) | 0.16 (0.36) |
| Two courses | 0.0025 (0.040) | 0.00002 (0.000) | 0.07 (0.25) | 0.1917 (3.421) | 0.04 (0.20) |
| Three courses | 0.0867 (1.039) | 0.0826 (0.981) | 0.04 (0.19) | 0.3109 (2.624) | 0.01 (0.09) |
| Four courses | 0.5565 (2.431) | 0.5495 (2.372) | 0.004 (0.07) | 0.3463 (1.744) | 0.003 (0.05) |
| Five or more courses | -0.7796 (-1.961) | -0.7865 (-1.972) | 0.002 (0.04) | -0.1193 (-0.504) | 0.002 (0.05) |
| Public Sector Employee | -0.0188 (-0.203) | -0.0160 (-0.172) | | -0.0042 (-0.105) | |
| Employee | 0.1042 (2.481) | 0.1075 (2.562) | | -0.0509 (-0.177) | |

- continued

### Table 1.6 (continued)
Earnings Functions with Alternative Specification (t-ratios in parenthesis)
and Sample Means of Selected Variables (standard deviations in parenthesis)

| Variable | Women | | | Males | |
| --- | --- | --- | --- | --- | --- |
| | Corrected for Selectivity | Uncorrected for Selectivity | Mean | OLS | Mean |
| Industry Group | | | | | |
| Manufacturing | -0.1010 | -0.1083 | 0.21 | -0.0447 | 0.31 |
| | (-1.007) | (-1.068) | (0.41) | (-0.851) | (0.46) |
| Construction | 0.2287 | 0.2112 | 0.004 | -0.1739 | 0.11 |
| | (0.929) | (0.849) | (0.07) | (-2.894) | (0.31) |
| Commerce | -0.0804 | -0.0850 | 0.14 | -0.0331 | 0.16 |
| | (-0.777) | (-0.881) | (0.35) | (-0.592) | (0.37) |
| Transport | 0.1461 | 0.1400 | 0.01 | 0.0796 | 0.10 |
| | (0.875) | (0.830) | (0.12) | (1.335) | (0.30) |
| Finance | 0.2231 | 0.2119 | 0.09 | 0.1226 | 0.09 |
| | (2.060) | (1.936) | (0.28) | (2.014) | (0.28) |
| Public Sector | 0.0248 | 0.0158 | 0.27 | -0.0321 | 0.10 |
| | (0.188) | (0.118) | (0.45) | (-0.463) | (0.29) |
| Recreation | -0.2971 | -0.3010 | 0.01 | 0.1437 | 0.02 |
| | (-1.592) | (-1.595) | (0.09) | (1.482) | (0.13) |
| Service | -0.3674 | -0.3745 | 0.24 | -0.2438 | 0.08 |
| | (-3.583) | (-3.607) | (0.43) | (-3.891) | (0.27) |
| Married | 0.1734 | 0.0786 | | 0.1867 | |
| | (3.392) | (2.285) | | (6.262) | |
| Foreign | -0.0795 | -0.0897 | | -0.0645 | |
| | (-1.354) | (-1.582) | | (-1.832) | |
| Part-time worker | -0.0334 | -0.0254 | | -0.1248 | |
| | (-0.642) | (-0.483) | | (-2.742) | |
| Works over 45 hours | -0.2151 | -0.2206 | | -0.0292 | |
| | (-4.756) | (-4.824) | | (-0.939) | |
| Lambda | -0.1945 | | | | |
| | (-2.555) | | | | |
| R-squared | 0.4867 | 0.4840 | | 0.3572 | |
| N | 1,338 | 1,338 | | 2,397 | |

Note: The mean of the dependent variable, log-monthly earnings, for men and working women are 11.29 and 10.79, respectively.

Unlike females, the returns to training increase as the number of training courses received increases, except where the individual has five or more training courses.

Sectoral differences have no impact on earnings for males. According to the result, other things equal, part-time male workers earn 12 percent less than full-timers. Like females, married men earn about 19 percent more than non-married males. On the other hand, males who were not born in Argentina earn less, by 6 percent.

In addition to finance and services sectors, the construction sector affects males' earnings relative to the omitted category (other industries). Earnings in the service and construction industries are lower by 24 percent and 17 percent, respectively. On the other hand, males working in the finance sector have an advantage and earn 12 percent more. Both sexes gain more by working in the finance sector and this reflects the profitability of the sector.

## 6. Discrimination

The actual average earnings differential between working females and working males is 35 percent. The Oaxaca (1973) "upper bound" decomposition can be obtained by the following methods :

$$
\ln(\text{Earnings}_m) - \ln(\text{Earnings}_f) = X_f(b_m-b_f) + b_m(X_m-X_f) \tag{1}
$$
$$
= X_m(b_m-b_f) + b_f(X_m-X_f), \tag{2}
$$

where $X_i$s denote variables of the earnings functions, $b_i$s are the corresponding parameter estimates, and $i=f$ (female) or $m$ (male). The first term of the right hand side of equations 1 and 2 is the difference in earnings due to differences in the wage structure while the second term refers to the difference due to differences in endowments. Note that the upper bound decomposition can be done both ways. This gives rise to the so-called index-number problem. Since economic theory provides little guidance on this, Table 1.7 summarizes both methods' results, denoted 1 and 2 accordingly, for regular OLS and OLS with selectivity adjustment.

Using the uncorrected OLS regression estimates (columns 1 and 2 of Table 1.5), if females have the same wage structure as males, differences in endowments between males and females explain 22 percent of the total earnings differential and 78 percent of the total earnings differential is due to differences in the wage structure. Using equation 2, difference in endowments and differences in the wage structure account for 32 percent and 68 percent of differences, respectively.

Taking selectivity bias into account, the first decomposition method shows 26 percent and 74 percent of differences being due to endowments and the wage structure, respectively. When females are assumed to have the same characteristics as males, differences in the wage structure account for 62 percent of the total earnings differential. Differences in endowments, on the other hand, explain 38 percent of the total earnings differential when the second decomposition method is used.

The upper bound of decomposition attributes all of the unexplained earnings gap to discrimination. Since the regressors do not capture all attributes that affect earnings, any left-out variables lead to an upward bias in measuring discrimination.[5] On the other hand, if any

---

[5] The decomposition is calculated for the alternate specification (Table 7.5). The results show that the unexplained portion of the earnings differentials differs by 10 percent.

**Table 1.7**
Decomposition of the Sex Earnings Differential

| | Percentage of the differential due to differences in | |
| --- | --- | --- |
| Specification | Endowments | Wage Structure |
| Not Corrected for Selectivity | | |
| Equation 1 | 22 | 78 |
| Equation 2 | 32 | 68 |
| Corrected for Selectivity | | |
| Equation 1 | 26 | 74 |
| Equation 2 | 38 | 62 |

$(\text{Wage}_m/\text{Wage}_f = 154\%)$

Notes:   The decomposition is based on the results of Table 1.5, above.
Wage$_m$/Wage$_f$ is the ratio of the corresponding mean monthly earnings.

explanatory variables are affected by discrimination such as education, sector of employment etc., the measure of discrimination obtained could be biased downwards instead.

Regardless of which upper bound decomposition method we use, part of the gender earnings differentials come from unexplained sources other than individual's initial endowments. In other words, discrimination appears to exist in the Argentine labor market.

## 7.   Discussion

The analysis of female labor force participation indicates a future change in the socio-economic structure. The highest probability of female labor force participation is found in the prime age group. Moreover, married status and number of young children are the key social determinants in the participation decision, which further supports the fact that there is a tendency among women to postpone marriage and/or childbearing. As these cohorts age we can expect much higher levels of female labor force participation in the future.

Educational attainment is found to be an important factor affecting the participation decision. Better opportunities in education, especially technical secondary education and higher education, stimulate females to enter the labor market. Combining the effects of higher educational attainment with lower fertility, we expect a marked increase in female labor force participation in the near future. In order to facilitate married women in joining the labor market, a greater demand for extensive childcare services provided by the private and/or the public sector is likely to occur.

With respect to earnings differentials between males and females, the upper bound decomposition technique provides an institutional idea on the subject. The following arguments are based on the second decomposition method described in the previous section. For working females alone (the uncorrected OLS estimates), increases in endowments will allow females to earn about 76 percent of male earnings. On the other hand, if females are treated as males, the earnings differential drops to 10 percent. Hence, to bring about greater equality between working males and working females, more emphasis should be placed on the treatment of females in the labor market, occupations and job mobility.

# References

Behrman, J.R. and B.L. Wolfe. "Labor Force Participation and Earnings Determinants for Women in the Special Conditions of Developing Countries." *Journal of Development Economics*, Vol 15 (1984). pp. 259-288.

de Lattes, Z.R. *Dynamics of the Female Labor Force in Argentina*. Paris: The United Nations Educational, Scientific and Cultural Organization, 1983.

Dieguez, H.L. "Social Consequences of the Economic Crisis: Argentina." Mimeograph. Washington, D.C.: World Bank, not dated.

Greenhalgh, C. "Participation and Hours of Work for Married Women in Great Britain." *Oxford Economic Papers*, Vol. 32, no. 2 (1980). pp. 296-318.

Gronau, R. "The Effect of Children on the Housewife's Value of Time" in T.W. Schultz (ed.). *Economics of the Family*. Chicago: University of Chicago Press, 1974.

Heckman, J. "Sample Selection as a Specification Error." *Econometrica*, Vol. 47, no. 1 (1979). pp. 153-161.

King, E.M. "Does Education Pay in the Labor Market? The Labor Force Participation, Occupation and Earnings of Peruvian Women." Living Standards Measurement Study Working Paper No. 67. Washington, D.C.: World Bank, 1990.

Kugler, B. and G. Psacharopoulos. "Earnings and Education in Argentina: An Analysis of the 1985 Buenos Aires Household Survey." *Economics of Education Review*, Vol. 8, no. 4 (1989). pp. 353-365.

Layard, R., M. Barton, and A. Zabalza. "Married Women's Participation and Hours." *Economica*, Vol.47 (1980). pp. 51-72.

Marshall, A. "Inmigración, demanda de fuerza de trabajo y estructura ocupacional en el área metropolitana argentina." *Desarrollo Económico*, Vol. 17, no. 65 (1977).

Mincer, J. *Schooling, Experience and Earnings*. New York: Columbia University Press, 1974.

Mohan, R. "Labor Force Participation in a Developing Metropolis: Does Sex Matter?" World Bank Staff Working Paper No. 749. Washington, D.C.: World Bank, 1985.

Oaxaca, R.L. "Male-female Wage Differentials in Urban Labor Markets." *International Economic Review,* Vol. 14, no. 1 (1973). pp. 693-709.

Riveros, L.A. and C.E. Sanchez. "Argentina's Labor Markets in an Era of Adjustment." Working Paper No. 386. Washington, D.C.: World Bank, 1990.

Sanchez, C.E. "Characteristics and Operation of Labor Markets in Argentina." Development Research Department Discussion Paper Report No. DRD272. Washington, D.C.: World Bank, 1987.

Sheehan, G. "Labor Force Participation in Papua, New Guinea" in G. Standing and G. Sheehan (eds.). *Labor Force Participation in Low-income Countries.* Geneva: International Labor Organization, 1978.

Shields, N. "Women in the Urban Labor Markets of Africa: The Case of Tanzania." World Bank Staff Working Paper No. 380. Washington, D.C.: World Bank, 1980.

Standing, G. "Female Labor Supply in an Urbanising Economy" in G. Standing and G. Sheehan (eds.). *Labor Force Participation in Low-income Countries.* Geneva: International Labor Organization, 1978.

-----. *Labor Force Participation and Development.* Geneva: International Labor Organization, 1982.

Sweet, J.A. *Women in the Labor Force.* New York: Seminar Press, 1973.

Wainerman, C.H. "Educación, familia y participación económica femenina en la Argentina." *Desarrollo Económico,* Vol. 72, no. 18 (1979). pp. 511-537.

# 2

## Women in the Labor Force in Bolivia: Participation and Earnings

*Katherine MacKinnon Scott*

### 1. Introduction

In 1989, ten years after the United Nations approved the Agreement on the Elimination of all Forms of Discrimination against Women, the Honorable National Congress of Bolivia ratified the agreement, joining close to one hundred other countries in pledging to analyze existing laws and legislation to determine where changes needed to be made to bring the legal codes into alignment with the United Nations' Agreement.

In the same year that the Agreement was ratified, weekly earnings for women in Bolivia were, on average, only 63 percent of male earnings, female-headed households were more likely to be below the poverty line than male-headed households and the female illiteracy rate was twice the male rate. It is not at all clear that existing labor law is responsible for the gender-based differential in earnings and living standards observed in Bolivia, especially when there is some agreement that existing laws are not always enforced. It appears that there are other factors which affect the earnings of men and women in Bolivia. This study focuses on the determinants of earnings and those factors which explain the observed wage differential between genders in Bolivia. By decomposing the earnings functions of the two groups it will be possible to identify that part of earnings which is explained by different endowment levels and that part which is due to different market values being placed on male and female labor. A better understanding of labor markets in Bolivia will assist in the formulation of policies which can complement the legislative changes being envisioned and serve to include women in the economic activities of the country on a more equal footing.

The following section of the study presents background information on Bolivia, its economy, and labor force characteristics. Information on the data used in the study is provided in Section 3. Several limitations on the degree to which the data can be used to extrapolate to the country as a whole are discussed in that section. The fourth section contains the labor force participation function for women. This participation function provides the means by which the female earnings function can be corrected for selectivity. Section 5 contains the description and results of the male and female earnings functions and the decomposition of these is carried out in Section 6. In the final section the overall results of the analysis are discussed and recommendations for improving the situation of working women in Bolivia are presented.

## 2.   The Bolivian Economy and the Labor Market

Bolivia is a landlocked country with three distinct geographic regions (highlands, valleys and tropical plains), several ethnic groups speaking different languages (Aymara, Quechua, Guarani, Spanish) and an economy heavily dependent on the export of primary products. The country is poor, especially compared to the other countries in the Latin American region. Per capita Gross National Product was US$570 in 1988 (World Bank, 1990b). Various social indicators also reveal the degree of poverty in the country. In 1988, adult illiteracy was 25 percent (World Bank, 1990b). Rural illiteracy rates were much higher than urban ones (31.3 percent versus 7.7 percent) and, of the illiterate population, 65 percent were women (World Bank, 1990a). Life expectancy at birth, in 1988, was 53 years, infant mortality was 108 per 1000 live births, and the maternal mortality rate (per 100,000 live births) was 480 in 1980 (World Bank, 1990b). The people most likely to live in poverty in Bolivia are those who live in rural areas, own little land, are female, are of Indian origin, are from the central Andean Region, and work in agriculture or household industries.

The physical characteristics of Bolivia (low population density, distinct geographical regions) which have hindered the integration of the economy (Horton, 1989), and the dependence of the economy on primary products has made Bolivia very vulnerable to external shocks. During the economic crisis, which began in the late 1970s and continued through the first half of the 1980s, inflation reached 24,000 percent, GDP fell by 15 percent between 1976 and 1985 and per capita GDP fell by 30 percent in the same period (Arteaga, 1987).

In 1976 (the year of the last national census), 80 percent of the population was considered to be poor and 20 percent was considered to be extremely poor[1]. Concentrations of poverty were found in the rural areas, especially in the Altiplano. GDP per capita has fallen steadily throughout the 1980s and, in 1988, stood at only 72.7 percent of its 1980 level (World Bank, 1990c). Recent data collected from a variety of sources[2] lead to the conclusion that the state of poverty in the country has not improved and, in fact, may be worse in rural areas (World Bank, 1990a).

*The labor force.* The economic crisis has led to a substantial decline in real wages and salaries in Bolivia. (See Table 2.1 for estimates of the fall in real earnings.) While there is some discrepancy in the data, both sources used in Table 2.1 show wages in commerce to have been particularly hard hit by the economic crisis. Wages in the service and manufacturing sectors were also among those which lost more of their real value. Wages in the financial sector also fell although there is some discrepancy in the data about the extent of the decline. Of specific interest to the present study is the fact that the commercial and service sectors, where the real value of wages eroded most, are the two sectors where female employment is concentrated: 81

---

[1]   A household was considered to be poor if its income covered 70 percent or less of the basic needs basket developed by PREALC. It was extremely poor if its income covered only 30 percent or less of the basic needs basket.

[2]   The National Institute of Statistics of Bolivia has carried out, in the 1980s, a series of surveys, some of the most important of which are, Encuesta Permanente de Establecimientos Economicos (1983 and other years), Encuesta Nacional de Poblacion y Vivienda (1988), Encuesta Permanente de Hogares (annual since 1980), and the Encuesta Integrada de Hogares (EIH) which combines the old labor force survey with parts of a Living Standards Measurement Survey. The EIH was started in 1989.

percent of the female economically active population (EAP) was in these sectors in 1985 (Arteaga, 1987).

The distribution of employment by sector of economic activity and occupational type has also changed during the economic crisis.   Prior to 1980, the share of the EAP in agriculture was declining and the share in manufacturing was increasing.  These standard development trends have been reversed in the 1980s as labor has shifted out of industry and into agriculture (Horton, 1989).  (See Table 2.2).

### Table 2.1
Bolivia: Evolution of Real Salaries

| A. | | | |
|---|---|---|---|
| Growth Rates of Real Salaries By Sector: 1971-85 | | | |

| Sector | 1971-76 | 1976-85 | 1971-85 |
|---|---|---|---|
| Agriculture | 0 | -39 | -39 |
| Mining | -18 | -26 | -40 |
| Petroleum | 85 | -30 | 29 |
| Industry | 0 | -39 | -39 |
| Commerce | -7 | -60 | -63 |
| Transport | -2 | -36 | -37 |
| Finance & Insurance | -57 | -51 | -79 |
| Services | -25 | -53 | -64 |
| TOTAL | -13 | -44 | -51 |

Source: Centro de Promocion del Laicado, 1986.

| B. | | | |
|---|---|---|---|
| Evolution of Real Wages By Sector 1982-1987 (March 1982=100) | | | |

| Sector | Dec. 1982 | Dec. 1984 | Dec. 1986 | Dec. 1987 |
|---|---|---|---|---|
| Mining | 162 | 117 | 100 | 68 |
| Hydrocarbons | 74 | 200 | 66 | – |
| Manufacturing | 81 | 136 | 59 | 43 |
| Construction | 52 | 93 | 74 | 85 |
| Utilities | 83 | 89 | 74 | 64 |
| Transport | 57 | 56 | 58 | 71 |
| Commerce | 69 | 76 | 63 | 44 |
| Financial | 90 | 109 | 130 | 65 |
| Services | 63 | 104 | 72 | – |

Source: Horton, 1989. Table 6, p. 35.

### Table 2.2
Industrial Distribution of Total Employment, 1970-1986
(in percent)

| Sector | 1970 | 1976 | 1980 | 1986 |
|---|---|---|---|---|
| Agriculture | 50.6 | 48.1 | 46.5 | 49.9 |
| Mining | 4.0 | 3.3 | 4.0 | 3.1 |
| Hydrocarbons | 0.3 | 0.3 | 0.4 | 0.5 |
| Manufacturing | 9.7 | 10.1 | 10.3 | 8.9 |
| Construction | 3.7 | 5.7 | 5.5 | 2.6 |
| Utilities | 0.2 | 0.2 | 0.4 | 0.5 |
| Transport. & Communic. | 4.0 | 3.9 | 5.4 | 5.6 |
| Commerce | 7.2 | 7.4 | 7.4 | 8.2 |
| Finance | 0.6 | 0.6 | 0.6 | 0.8 |
| Services | 19.7 | 19.6 | 19.3 | 20.0 |

Source: Horton, 1989, Table 4, p. 33

The other major change in employment distribution has been the growth of the informal sector. This sector has always been large, but the early 1980s saw a rapid increase in the number of self-employed and unpaid family workers.  A 1983 study of the self-employed showed that these workers as a percent of the urban labor force had increased from 29 percent in 1976 to 34 percent in 1983. The annual rate of growth of employment in the self-employed sector averaged 5.95 percent and that of unpaid family workers grew by 7.66 percent. In contrast, the salaried labor force grew only 2.25 percent annually during the same period. (Casanovas, 1984). A recent World Bank report (1990a) indicates that another cause of the fall in income has been the movement of large segments of the working force out of the formal sector and into the informal one.

Unemployment rose in the 1980s, with the highest rates found in areas where mining had been a significant industry (Potosi and Oruro). While figures provided by various sources differ, there is consensus that the increase was quite high; the lowest estimate is an increase of 26 percent between 1980 and 1987 (Horton, 1989). It is argued however, that unemployment rates really reflect the fall in formal sector employment and those that appear as unemployed are actually working in the informal sector (Horton, 1989; and World Bank, 1990a).

*Women in the labor force.*  Female participation in the labor force in 1988 was estimated at almost 29 percent (i.e., 29 percent of all women aged 10 and up participated in the labor force). In the eje central[3], women's labor force participation was estimated at 35 percent in 1987, up from the 1976 level of 20 percent (World Bank, 1989; and Horton, 1989). The rate of participation of women has not, however, changed significantly since 1980. Female unemployment rates have been lower than male rates in the 1980s although female underemployment is higher.[4] As has been noted above, women have lower levels of education than men, are more heavily concentrated in the unpaid and family businesses, and are found primarily in commerce and service industries and the informal sector (World Bank, 1990a; and Horton, 1989).

Legally, there are still various statutes in Bolivia limiting women's full participation in the labor force. First, with some exceptions (nurses, domestic servants) women are not permitted to work at night. Second, the 1942 legal code limits the work week of women to only 40 hours, in contrast to men's legal work week of 48 hours. Third, except in cases where "the work requires a higher proportion," women are only allowed to make up 45 percent of the wage and/or salary earners in any given establishment (United States Bureau of Labor Statistics, 1962). Moreover, the labor code bars women from carrying out jobs considered to be dangerous, unhealthy or hard-labor.[5]

The significance of these laws is not clear since it appears that they are not enforced (World Bank, 1989). Since the National Congress of Bolivia ratified the United Nations' "Convencion sobre la eliminacion de todas formas de discriminacion contra la mujer" in 1988, several commissions have been formed to review the existing legislation and recommend changes in those statutes which discriminate against women.

---

[3]    Includes the cities of La Paz, Santa Cruz, Cochabamba and Oruro.

[4]    Underemployment is defined as working less than 12 hours in the reference week (Horton, 1989).

[5]    See: World Bank, 1989; and Romero de Aliaga, 1975.

## 3. The Data

The data for the analysis come from the second round of the 1989 Integrated Household Survey (EIH), a bi-annual survey carried out by the National Statistical Institute of Bolivia (INE). The survey is essentially a living standards measurement survey. Unlike the 1988 survey, The EIH only covers the capital cities of eight departments of the country (Cobija, the capital of Pando was not included), the city of El Alto, and all other cities with populations greater than 10,000. Little or no information on the rural population of the country is contained in the data. It should be remembered that the results of the analysis contained in the present study are applicable only to the urban labor force. The way in which labor markets function on a national level and in rural areas may be quite different.

The EIH data used here were collected in November of 1989. Included in the survey are 7,267 households with data on 36,126 individuals. Of these, a total of 13,842 cases were used. This sample included all people of prime working age range (15 to 54) for whom relevant data were available.[6] Table 2.3 shows some of the characteristics of the total sample used as well as the characteristics of the working population. Working men and women are defined as all those people who worked for more than one hour in the reference week for pay. This definition excludes unpaid family workers but includes the self-employed.[7] Excluding unpaid family workers from the definition of the employed will underestimate both male and female participation rates. Female participation rates will be underestimated more than male rates as more women are unpaid family workers than men. Excluding domestic servants will also lower participation rates of women more than men.

Of the total of 13,842 individuals included in the sample, 7,786 people, or 56 percent, are classified as working, i.e., receive pay. Participation rates for women (44 percent) are significantly lower than for men (65 percent).

The average age of the sample is almost 32 years. Working women and men are more likely to be married than the sample as a whole. Eighteen percent of working women are heads of households as compared to 75 percent of working men.

Working women have, on average, one-half year less schooling than their male counterparts. While this overall gap in education is not large, the distribution of men and women by highest level of education completed shows some sharp differences. Only one quarter of working men ended their schooling at the primary school level compared to more than one-third of working women. The largest gap in educational achievement occurs at the university level; only 7 percent of working women have a university degree compared to 15 percent of the men. Proportionally more women than men have attended a teacher training or normal school and greater percentages of women have attended some form of technical school, especially at secondary level.

---

[6] While the prime working age is usually considered to be between ages 20 and 60, the limits used here reflect more accurately the reality of Bolivia. The survey itself collects labor data for ages 10 and up. School attendance rates, however, are still fairly high until age 15. After age 15, attendance is low and the percentage of working individuals increases. Thus the lower bound of the working age population has been set at 15 in this study.

[7] Domestic servants have been eliminated from the analysis due, in part, to the difficulties of determining actual income and also because of the limited data in this survey on such workers.

## Table 2.3
### Bolivia: Means (and Standard Deviations) of Sample Variables

| Variable | Total Sample[a] | Working Men | Working Women |
|---|---|---|---|
| Age | 31.70 | 33.94 | 35.46 |
| | (10.42) | (9.78) | (8.41) |
| Married | 0.66 | 0.76 | 0.73 |
| | (0.46) | (0.43) | (0.44) |
| Head of Household | 0.36 | 0.75 | 0.18 |
| | (0.48) | (0.43) | (0.38) |
| Years of Schooling | 9.28 | 9.50 | 8.97 |
| | (4.34) | (4.45) | (5.05) |
| No Education | 0.00 | 0.00 | 0.00 |
| | (0.01) | (0.01) | (0.01) |
| Incomplete Primary | 0.16 | 0.14 | 0.23 |
| | (0.37) | (0.35) | (0.42) |
| Finished Primary | 0.09 | 0.10 | 0.11 |
| | (0.29) | (0.30) | (0.32) |
| Incomplete Middle School | 0.10 | 0.11 | 0.10 |
| | (0.30) | (0.31) | (0.29) |
| Finished Middle School | 0.06 | 0.06 | 0.06 |
| | (0.24) | (0.24) | (0.23) |
| Incomplete Secondary | 0.21 | 0.19 | 0.12 |
| | (0.41) | (0.39) | (0.33) |
| Finished Secondary | 0.13 | 0.14 | 0.10 |
| | (0.33) | (0.35) | (0.30) |
| Secondary Technical | 0.04 | 0.03 | 0.06 |
| | (0.19) | (0.18) | (0.24) |
| Higher Technical | 0.02 | 0.02 | 0.03 |
| | (0.14) | (0.15) | (0.16) |
| Normal School | 0.05 | 0.04 | 0.12 |
| | (0.22) | (0.20) | (0.33) |
| University | 0.14 | 0.15 | 0.07 |
| | (0.35) | (0.36) | (0.26) |
| Home Ownership | 0.61 | 0.58 | 0.59 |
| | (0.49) | (0.49) | (0.49) |
| Language: | | | |
| Spanish only | 0.71 | 0.67 | 0.68 |
| | (0.45) | (0.47) | (0.47) |
| Aymara/Quechua/Guarani | 0.00 | 0.00 | 0.00 |
| | (0.06) | (0.06) | (0.06) |
| Bilingual: Span. & Amerind. | 0.28 | 0.31 | 0.31 |
| | (0.45) | (0.46) | (0.46) |
| Bilingual: Span. & other | 0.01 | 0.01 | 0.01 |
| | (0.09) | (0.10) | (0.09) |
| Experience | 17.80 | 19.88 | 21.96 |
| | (11.66) | (10.78) | (10.00) |
| Hours Worked Per Week | — | 51.30 | 44.12 |
| | | (18.18) | (23.00) |
| Weekly Earnings[b] | — | 110.51 | 68.89 |
| | | (181.52) | (85.38) |
| N | 13,842 | 5,314 | 2,472 |

a.  Total sample refers to all people aged 15 to 54.  Working population consists of all those working for pay (aged 15 to 54).  Excludes unpaid family workers.
b.  In current Bolivianos
Notes:  Labor force participation rate was .65 for men, .44 for women, and .56 overall.
Standard deviations in parentheses.
Source:  Bolivia: Integrated Household Survey, 1989.

Only two people in the sample (both males) have no education of any sort. This is somewhat surprising given the levels of illiteracy found in Bolivia. Urban illiteracy was calculated by INE in 1988 to be almost 11 percent with 13.8 percent of the population having no formal schooling. Given the exclusion of people over 55 from the sample, one would expect illiteracy rates to be lower in the sample than the population. This cannot be the full explanation, however, as 11 percent of those aged 20-55 years have had no formal schooling (Instituto Nacional de Estadistica, 1989). It is not clear why people with no formal schooling are so underrepresented in this sample. The underrepresentation of people with no formal schooling biases the level of female educational achievement more than men as a greater proportion of women are illiterate.

Slightly more than 70 percent of the sample speak only Spanish while 28 percent speak both Spanish and an Amerindian language (Aymara, Quechua or Guarani). One percent speaks Spanish and another non-indigenous language.

The most striking difference in the sample is the large gap between the earnings of working men and women. Average weekly earnings for men are Bs.110.5 and Bs.68.9 for females. These figures are consistent with previous estimates.[8] On average, women earn slightly more than 60 percent of men's earnings on a weekly basis. Women also work fewer hours, on average 7 hours a week less than men. If women worked the same number of hours per week as their male counterparts they would earn 80.1 bolivianos, less than average male earnings.

## 4.    The Determinants of Female Labor Force Participation

Whether women participate or not depends on their reservation wage -- i.e., the value of their labor in the home. When this reservation wage is below the market wage women will participate in the labor force. If a woman's reservation wage is higher than that found in the market, she will not participate.

This unobserved reservation wage means that female earnings functions estimates using ordinary least squares (OLS) will be biased. Only the market wage is observed and thus the OLS earnings function will suffer from the problems inherent in using censored samples. Heckman (1979) provides an estimation technique to correct for this selectivity bias. First, a labor force participation function for women is estimated. The inverse Mill's ratio (Lambda) from this equation is then entered on the right-hand side of the earnings function equation. This corrects for selectivity. Thus, the first step in estimating female earnings function is to specify a model of female labor force participation.

Labor force participation among women in Bolivia is low. Only 44 percent of the present sample of women work for pay. As noted above, the definition of working women may underestimate the real female work force as unpaid family workers are excluded from the definition. Also excluded from this definition are the unemployed. This is not a significant number of people (Instituto Nacional de Estadistica in 1988, calculated urban unemployment rates for women to be

---

[8]    Horton (1989) provides estimates of male and female labor earnings as a percent of the average earnings for all workers. In 1982, male earnings were 102.6 percent of the average and female earnings were 95 percent. The equivalent percentages in 1987 were 120.2 and 68.6 percent for men and women respectively. Similar calculations based on the data used here show men earning 118.4 percent of average earnings and women 70.5 percent.

less than 2 percent of the labor force).  The advantage of excluding the unemployed is that there are definitional problems involved in the measurement of this group.[9]

The dependent variable in the participation function is a dichotomous variable which takes the value of one if the woman is working for pay and zero otherwise.  A probit function is used to estimate participation rates.  The regressors measure personal characteristics of the individual woman, her family and socio-economic characteristics, and area of residence.

Personal characteristics include educational level, age, health and fertility patterns.  Schooling is entered as a series of dummy variables for each level of schooling.  Note that for secondary technical, post-secondary technical, teacher's college, and university, no data were available for the number of years of the level completed by individuals who are still students.  Hence the dummy variable for these four education categories takes on the value of one if a person has completed the level or is presently a student in that level of education.  The education coefficients are expected to be positive as it has been shown that, while increased schooling increases both the asking and the offered wage, the latter increases more (Heckman, 1979) .

Age is entered in the participation function as a series of dummy variables (in five year ranges) to take into account any non-linearity in the relationship of age to participation.  It is not a clear a priori what the signs of the coefficients of these age variables will be.  Some evidence exists showing that younger women are more likely to be unemployed (Instituto Nacional de Estadistica, 1988) which would decrease the probability of this group's participation.  Where enrollment in higher education is high, labor force participation will also be lower.  Given the extremely low rate of higher education enrollment among women this will have little effect.

Ethnic origin may be an important variable since different cultures have different attitudes towards paid employment for women and have different opportunities in the society.[10]  A proxy variable for ethnicity, language(s) spoken, is used here.  Four dummy variables are used for language indicating whether the person speaks; (1) only Spanish; (2) only Amerindian languages; (3) both Spanish and one or more Amerindian languages and; (4) Spanish and another language. It is expected that those who do not speak Spanish will have a lower probability of participation.

Health will affect a woman's decision to participate in the labor market (Behrman and Wolfe, 1984).  The proxy for health status used here is number of days (out of the previous month) that a person has been incapacitated, i.e., physically unable to carry out her regular activities. Fertility is especially important in the Bolivian context.  Given the high infant mortality rate in Bolivia, the number of pregnancies a women has had will not be strictly correlated with the number of children she is raising. Hence, fertility is measured by two variables, the number of children that the woman has given birth to, and whether the woman has been pregnant in the last year (measured by a dummy variable).  It is expected that women who are, or have been, pregnant recently will be less likely to be in the labor force.  It is argued that women tend to leave the labor force in order to have children, returning when their children are grown or at least able to take care of themselves.  Thus, the number of children under age 6 (preschool age)

---

[9]   For example: One measurement of the unemployed counts as unemployed only those actively searching for work (McFarlane, 1988; and ILO, 1982), while another includes as unemployed all those who say they want to work.  Obviously, the definition used will affect one's results.

[10]   A recent World Bank study (1990a) argues that there is evidence of ethnically based discrimination in Bolivia.

is expected to lower a woman's probability of participating. This especially true where there are inadequate childcare facilities, as is the case in Bolivia (World Bank, 1989). Also included in the equation is a variable measuring number of children between the ages of 6 and 14 a woman has who are living in her household. Given the lack of universal participation in primary school in Bolivia (net primary enrollment in 1988 was only 83 percent (World Bank, 1990b)) the number of children a woman has to care for in this group is also expected to lower her probability of participating. Total family size has also been included in the equation. The sign of the coefficient on this variable may be either positive or negative. On the one hand, a larger household may have a positive impact on participation because of greater demands for income or the presence of non-working adults who can provide childcare. On the other hand, the size of the household may raise the value of the woman's household production activities and reduce the probability that she will participate in the labor force.

A woman who heads a household is more likely to work for pay. Married women will be expected to have a lower probability of participation than unmarried women. The income of a married woman's spouse is also included in the equation. It is expected to have a negative impact on participation. The final regressors in the equation are those having to do with geographic location and socio-economic status. It is expected that different areas of the country (highlands, valleys and tropical plains) are associated with different probabilities of participation. The tropical plains area of the country is experiencing the greatest growth in population though immigration and participation rates will be higher in this region.

To capture the effect of socio-economic status, variables measuring home ownership (a proxy for family wealth), total family income and access to public water and sewage disposal are included. (The latter two are, to some extent, proxies for the value of the home.) The effect of wealth on participation can be either positive or negative. There is less need to earn income if one's family has a certain level of wealth. But, also, it has been shown in other countries that relatively better-off women are more likely to work outside the home than lower-income women.

The results of the participation function are presented in Table 2.4. The age category omitted from the equation is from 15 to 19 years. As can be seen in the table, all other age groups are more likely to participate than this youngest group. All of the age variables are significant. As can be seen from the simulations presented in Table 2.5, the participation rate for women peaks in the 35 to 39 age range. The 40 to 44 age group has similar participation rates but the probability of participation declines for older women, possibly because retirement for women covered by social security is age 50.

Other personal characteristics are also significant. Married women are less likely to work than non-married women and those who are heads of households are more likely to work. Interestingly, the number of children under six that a woman has does not have a significant impact on labor force participation. This may be because women in the informal sector are able to either arrange their work schedule to fit childcare needs or are able to take their children with as them they work.

A woman's health status does have a significant negative impact on the probability of participation. The effect, however, is quite small.

As expected, women who are presently students are less likely to participate in the labor force than non-students. Unexpectedly, however, educational attainment at the primary, middle and secondary school levels does not have a significant impact on participation. There are two

## Table 2.4
### Probit Estimates for Female Participation

| Variable | Coefficient | t-ratio | Partial Derivative |
|---|---|---|---|
| Constant | -0.360 | -2.37 | |
| Age 20 to 24 | 0.290 | 2.35 | 0.115 |
| Age 25 to 29 | 0.506 | 4.10 | 0.199 |
| Age 30 to 34 | 0.650 | 5.12 | 0.256 |
| Age 35 to 39 | 0.756 | 5.81 | 0.298 |
| Age 40 to 44 | 0.742 | 5.43 | 0.293 |
| Age 45 to 49 | 0.600 | 4.22 | 0.237 |
| Age 50 to 54 | 0.381 | 2.54 | 0.150 |
| Married | -0.390 | -6.15 | -0.154 |
| Student | -0.249 | -2.92 | -0.098 |
| Household Size | -0.019 | -1.55 | -0.008 |
| Finished Primary | 0.017 | 0.27 | 0.007 |
| Some Middle School | -0.002 | -0.04 | -0.001 |
| Finished Middle School | 0.062 | 0.75 | 0.246 |
| Some Secondary | -0.096 | -1.57 | -0.038 |
| Finished Secondary | -0.094 | -1.41 | -0.037 |
| Secondary Technical | 0.225 | 2.55 | 0.089 |
| Higher Technical | 0.424 | 3.27 | 0.167 |
| Teacher College | 0.729 | 9.13 | 0.288 |
| University | 0.279 | 3.24 | 0.110 |
| Incapacity | -0.007 | -2.01 | -0.003 |
| Live Births | -0.001 | -0.18 | -0.001 |
| Home owned | -0.003 | -0.08 | -0.001 |
| Head of Household | 0.660 | 7.80 | 0.260 |
| Valley | 0.025 | 0.57 | 0.010 |
| Tropical | 0.068 | 1.35 | 0.027 |
| Public Water Supply | -0.080 | -1.68 | -0.032 |
| Public Sewer | 0.044 | 1.01 | 0.018 |
| Pregnant | -0.178 | -3.65 | -0.070 |
| Aymara/Quechua | -0.570 | -2.31 | -0.225 |
| Bilingual | 0.156 | 3.47 | 0.062 |
| Bilingual Other | -0.074 | -0.35 | -0.029 |
| Children under 6 | -0.028 | -1.18 | -0.011 |
| Children 6 to 14 | 0.026 | 1.06 | 0.010 |
| Income of spouse | -0.000 | -1.81 | -0.0002 |
| Family income | 0.000 | 0.53 | 0.00004 |
| Household size | -0.019 | -1.55 | -0.008 |

Notes:   Sample is women aged 15 to 55 years
Participation Rate: 44.0%

Log-Likelihood = -3488.2
N = 5624

## Table 2.5
### Predicted Participation Probabilities by Characteristic

| Characteristic | Predicted Probability |
|---|---|
| **Age:** | |
| 15 to 19 | 23.6 |
| 20 to 24 | 33.4 |
| 25 to 29 | 41.5 |
| 30 to 34 | 47.2 |
| 35 to 39 | 51.4 |
| 40 to 44 | 50.9 |
| 45 to 49 | 45.2 |
| 50 to 54 | 36.7 |
| | |
| **Family status:** | |
| Married | 41.0 |
| Unmarried | 56.5 |
| Head of household | 67.0 |
| Not head of household | 41.3 |
| | |
| **Language Spoken:** | |
| Only Spanish | 42.2 |
| Only Indigenous | 22.2 |
| Bilingual Span/indig | 48.4 |
| Bilingual Span/other | 39.4 |
| | |
| **Schooling:** | |
| Secondary Technical | 50.0 |
| Higher Technical School | 57.8 |
| Teacher College | 69.2 |
| University | 52.1 |
| | |
| **Student Status:** | |
| Is a student | 34.8 |
| Not a student | 44.4 |
| | |
| **Pregnancy:** | |
| Pregnant this year | 38.5 |
| Not pregnant this year | 45.4 |
| | |
| **Days incapacitated:** | |
| Zero days incapacitated | 44.3 |
| Number of days = .5*mean | 44.1 |
| Number of days = mean | 43.9 |
| Number of days = 1.5*mean | 43.7 |
| Number of days = 2*mean | 43.5 |

Notes:    Mean Participation Rate = 44.0%
Simulations based on probit results in Table 2.4.

possible explanations for this. First, women are concentrated in the informal sector where the value of education credentials are limited. Second, and perhaps more importantly, Bolivia maintains two separate school systems, one rural and one urban. The curriculum and the quality of the two systems are very different (World Bank, 1989b). Hence, women who have been educated in rural areas will have received very different training. It is not possible to determine the type of schooling a person received and the education variables for these levels may reflect differences in quality which confound the analysis.

In contrast, attendance in, or completion of, technical school (either secondary or post-secondary), teachers' colleges, or university has a highly significant, positive effect on probability of participation. The type of schooling with the greatest impact is that of teacher training. As can be seen in Table 2.5, all else being equal, a woman who attends a teachers' college has a probability of participating close to 70 percent, over 25 percentage points higher than that for a woman with the average level of education. Interestingly, technical education at the post-secondary level has a greater impact on participation than does a university education (57.8 percent probability versus 52.1 percent, respectively).

Pregnancy has the expected negative impact on participation. Women who were pregnant in the given year had a probability of participation of 38.5 percent. Women who had not been pregnant in the preceding twelve months had a probability of participating of 45.4 percent. The number of children a woman has given birth to has an insignificant impact on participation rates.

Ethnicity also proves to have a significant impact on labor force participation with those women who speak no Spanish having the lowest participation rates (22.2 percent, all else held constant). Bilingual women participate at a higher rate than women who speak only Spanish. It should be noted that ethnicity and income levels are highly correlated in Bolivia (World Bank, 1990a) and the effects of ethnic origin are probably partly reflecting economic status.

The variables measuring family wealth and socio-economic status (own home, public water and public sewage) have insignificant effects on the probability of labor force participation. On the one hand, this may reflect the contradictory effects of wealth on participation indicated above. On the other hand, home ownership may not be a good proxy for wealth in Bolivia and access to public water and sewage may be more a function of urban living than socio-economic status. Neither the total family income nor the spouse's income have a significant impact on participation.

Contrary to expectations, the regional variables are not significant. Like the variables for source of water and sewage disposal, the fact that the sample is urban may account for this lack of impact of geography on labor force participation.

In summary, the most important effects on female labor force participation in Bolivia are schooling, student status, age, language spoken, marital status, pregnancy, and number of children between ages 6 and 14. Women between the ages of 35 and 39, those who are unmarried, and/or bilingual, and/or highly educated are the most likely to participate in the labor market.

## 5.   Earnings Functions

The standard earnings function is the Mincerian (1974) formulation of schooling, experience and experience squared regressed on the natural log of earnings:

$$LnY = b_0 + b_1S + b_2EX + b_3EX^2 \qquad (1)$$

Where:

LnY = the natural log of weekly earnings
S   = years of schooling
EX  = experience
$EX^2$ = experience squared

To standardize for hours worked, the natural log of hours (LNH) was entered on the right hand side of the equation. It should be kept in mind that the experience variable used here is actually *potential* experience (i.e., age - years of schooling - 5). Potential experience will closely approximate real experience for any person who has worked steadily since s/he left school. However, as women are more likely to move in and out of the labor force, the potential experience variable may overestimate women's actual experience.

For female earnings, can the model answer the questions about the effect of human capital on earnings for women in the labor force? The sample used in the earnings functions includes the entire male and female working population (i.e., those working for pay). Three separate specifications were used: One for males, one for females not correcting for selectivity and one for females correcting for the selectivity bias. The results of the three earnings functions are shown in Table 2.6.

All of the variables have a significant effect on earnings for both men and women. The impact of schooling is less for women than men although the difference is not great. Experience and experience squared have much less of an impact on earnings for women than men. The number of hours worked, however, has a greater impact on women's earnings than on men's.

The returns to schooling are significant, but not as high as those found in other Latin American countries[11]. To some extent this reflects the size of the informal sector in the economy where education has less of an impact than in the private formal and/or public sector. Returns to experience and experience squared are also low, perhaps for the same reason. Only hours has a high return (relative to men) impact. The inverse Mill's ratio is not significant.

## 6.    Discrimination

As the sample characteristics presented in Table 2.3 demonstrate, there is a substantial gender-based difference in average weekly earnings. By subtracting the two earnings equations (the male and female (uncorrected) equations) it is possible to determine what percent of this difference is due to the different endowment levels of the two groups and what is due to the way in which each groups' endowments are valued in the market place (Oaxaca, 1973).

The initial difference between the earnings of men and women can be expressed as:

$$LnY_m - LnY_f = X_m b_m - X_f b_f \qquad (2)$$

Algebraic manipulations give the following equation:

$$LnY_m - LnY_f = b_m(X_m - X_f) + X_f(b_m - b_f) \qquad (2a)$$

---

[11]    See other chapters in this volume.

**Table 2.6**
Earnings Functions

| Variable | Working Men | Working Women (uncorrected for selectivity) | Working Women (corrected for selectivity) |
|---|---|---|---|
| Constant | 1.575 | 1.346 | 1.235 |
|  | (14.36) | (10.31) | (7.69) |
| Schooling (years) | 0.071 | 0.063 | 0.065 |
|  | (26.23) | (17.08) | (16.16) |
| Experience | 0.050 | 0.028 | 0.031 |
|  | (13.10) | (4.06) | (4.22) |
| Experience Squared | -0.001 | -0.0003 | -0.0004 |
|  | (-7.24) | (-2.39) | (-2.61) |
| Ln(weekly hours) | 0.354 | 0.424 | 0.424 |
|  | (13.91) | (17.18) | (17.17) |
| Lambda | --- | --- | 0.069 |
|  | --- | --- | (1.19) |
| R-squared | 0.179 | 0.176 | 0.176 |
| N | 5,314 | 2,472 | 2,472 |

Notes:   Numbers in parentheses are t-ratios
Dependent variable is Ln(weekly earnings)

An index problem arises here. There is no theoretical reason to prefer the above specification to the following:

$$LnY_m - LnY_f = b_f(X_m - X_f) + X_m(b_m - b_f) \qquad (2b)$$

Both specifications were used and the results are presented in Table 2.7.

The first term measures the actual difference in endowment levels between the two groups. The second term on the right-hand side measures the difference in the market evaluation of endowments. Typically, the value of the second term is considered to be a measure of discrimination in the market place. The first term is considered to be the explained difference in wages due to unequal endowments.[12]

The unexplained difference in wages calculated here is the upper bound of labor market discrimination. In other words, this is the maximum level of discrimination. Controlling for unobserved productive characteristics of the two groups could lower this "unexplained" segment of the equation.[13] It should be remembered, however, that the upper bound calculated here may

---

[12]   It should be noted that the difference in endowments may, in fact, reflect pre-market discrimination.

[13]   Schultz (1989) argues that these unobserved characteristics will create substantial uncertainty in intergroup comparisons of earnings.

*underestimate* discrimination if pre-market discrimination keeps women from obtaining human capital.

As can be seen in Table 2.7, of the total earnings differential, approximately 15 percent is due to women having lower levels of human capital endowments than men. The remainder of the observed wage differential is due to men's endowments receiving a higher price in the labor market. This is the upper bound of discrimination. Depending on the specification used, around four-fifths of the observed wage differential between men and women is due to unexplained market pricing mechanisms.

**Table 2.7**
Decomposition of the Male-Female
Earnings Differential

|  | Percentage Due to | |
| --- | --- | --- |
|  | Endowments | Rewards |
| Equation 2a | 14.9 | 85.1 |
| Equation 2b | 24.1 | 75.9 |
| (Wage$_m$/Wage$_f$ = 160.4%) | | |

## 7. Conclusions and Recommendations

The results of this study show that there are many personal and family characteristics which affect the probability of a woman participating in the labor force. Schooling, age, marital status, status as head of household, pregnancy, and ethnic origin are some of the characteristics which most affect the decision to participate.

Proportionally fewer women than men participate in the labor force. Those women who do participate earn substantially less per week than their male counterparts, even when hours worked are equal. Part of this difference in earnings is attributable to lower endowments of human capital among women. Yet most of the observed differential is due to unexplained differences in the way in which the market values the two genders' labor.

Clearly, the legal efforts underway in Bolivia to eliminate gender discrimination are a necessary step to improve women's position in the labor market. The results of the labor force participation function and the earnings functions provide information on further areas where government policies can have an impact on the labor market activities of women. The obvious first step to decreasing the earnings gap is to increase women's access to human capital formation. Increasing female education levels will have a twofold effect -- it will tend to increase the labor participation rates of woman and it will raise the incomes of women who work outside the home. It should be remembered here that increasing women's earnings will not only assist individual women but also their families. As evidence exists that single-headed households are becoming more common this takes on added importance.

Further increases in female earnings could come about from policies designed to increase productivity in the informal sector. This sector typically has access to very little capital and is constrained by the low levels of technology used. Programs designed to increase credit availability for small businesses in the informal sector and provide technical assistance would benefit the economy as a whole. In the process, the specific benefits to women could be large since a sizeable percentage of women working in urban areas are in this sector.

Without further information about the reasons why male labor is valued so much more highly than female labor it will be difficult to affect the remainder of the observed wage differential in Bolivia. But policies aimed at improving the legal environment in which women work, increasing their access to education, and assisting the informal sector can all have a significant impact on women's participation rates and earnings.

# References

Arteaga, V. "La Crisis Económica y sus efectos sobre la mujer en Bolivia." Paper presented at the United Nations' Childrens' Fund Simposio Nacional sobre Mujer y Necesidades Basicas. Bolivia, June 1987.

Behrman, J. R. and B. Wolfe. "Labor Force participation and Earnings Determinants for Women in the Special Conditions of Developing Countries", *Journal of Development Economics*, Vol 46 (1984). pp. 259-288.

Casanovas, R. "Los Trabajadores pro Cuenta Propia en el mercado de Trabajo: El Caso de la ciudad de La Paz, Boliva." Paper presented at the International Seminar "El Sector Informal Urbano en América Latina y el Ecuador". Quito: ILDIS/CEPESIU, 1984.

Heckman, J. "Sample Selection Bias as a Specification Error." *Econometrica,* Vol.47, no. 1 (1979). pp. 153-161.

Horton, S. "Labour Markets in an era of Adjustment: Bolivia." (Incomplete draft). University of Toronto, 1989.

Mincer, J. *Schooling, Experience, and Earnings.* New York: Columbia University Press, 1974.

Oaxaca, R.L. "Male-female Wage Differentials in Urban Labor Markets." *International Economic Review,* Vol. 14, no. 1 (1973). pp. 693-709.

Romero de Aliaga, N. "The Legal Situation of the Bolivian Woman." Fletcher School of Law and Diplomacy, La Paz, Bolivia: International Advisory Committee on Population and Law, 1975.

United States' Bureau of Labor Statistics, "Labor Law and Practice in Bolivia." 1962. Report No. 218. Washington, D.C.: United States Department of Labor, 1962.

World Bank. "Bolivia: Poverty Report." Report No. 8643-BO. Latin America and Caribbean Region, Country Operations Division I. Washington, D.C.: World Bank, 1990a.

World Bank. *World Development Report,* 1990. Washington, D.C.: World Bank, 1990b.

World Bank. "Social Spending in Latin America: The Story of the 1980s." World Bank: Discussion Paper Series No. 88. Washington D.C.: World Bank, 1990c.

World Bank. "Country Assessment of Women's Role in Development: Proposed Bank Approach and Plan of Action." R.N. 8064-BO. Latin America and Caribbean Region, Country Operations Division 1. Washington, D.C.: The World Bank, 1989.

# 3

---

# Labor Force Behavior and Earnings of Brazilian Women and Men, 1980

*Morton Stelcner, J. Barry Smith, Jon A. Breslaw and Georges Monette*[1]

## 1.    Introduction

Interest in the role of women in the development process of Third World countries increased during the last decade.  A major concern is the status of women in what Behrman and Wolfe (1984) term the "special conditions" of labor markets in developing countries.[2]  Increasing attention is being given to analyzing the labor force behavior of women and to their returns to human capital, especially education.  However, the volume of research on these women is considerably less than that for men in developing countries and for women in industrialized countries.  This study reduces this gap by examining labor force patterns among married and single women, and compares these with their male counterparts.

We present an analysis of the labor force behavior of Brazilian women and men using a sample of 53,000 drawn from the 1980 Census.  The specific concerns of the study are the determinants of labor force status (employee, self-employed, or no market work) and earnings of workers.  We pay particular attention to the impact of education on labor market outcomes.  Four population groups are considered: wives and husbands, single (never married) women and men.

## 2.    Brazil: Economic Background

An analysis of the labor force behavior of Brazilian men and women is important because it is representative of a developing country experiencing severe economic problems.  As for most of its neighbors, the 1980s for Brazil, the largest and most populous country in Latin America, were a "lost decade" in terms of the severity and duration of the economic progress in the 1970s when per capita GDP grew on average by 1.4 percent per year in 1970-1973 and by 7.1 percent in 1974-1980.  Brazil started the 1980s with much economic compromise and many successes, but

---

[1]    The authors thank Ana-Maria Arriagada for her invaluable help in providing the data base and clarifying its contents, and Linda Bonin for her editorial advice.  Brenda Butler, a computer science student at Concordia University, provided competent programming assistance.  We also thank Daniel M. Shapiro, Department of Economics, Concordia University, for providing helpful comments and criticisms that shaped the final version of the paper.

[2]    As Behrman and Wolfe (1984, p. 260) aptly state, the special conditions include "regional and sectoral pluralism, the relevance of human capital investments in health and nutrition, and distinctive determinants of opportunity costs for labor force participation."

early in the decade its economic performance began to deteriorate rapidly and dramatically, and has not yet ended.   In 1981 per capita GDP fell by 4.3 percent, while for the rest of the decade the average annual (erratic) growth rate was about 1 percent.   The economic prospects for the 1990s are not encouraging: in 1990 gross domestic product shrank by 4.3 percent, reflecting a decline of 8 percent in industrial production.

A question that has been receiving increasing attention is:  How have the worsening economic conditions, on top of persistent poverty, affected peoples' welfare in Latin America?   Since market work is the most important income source, an analysis of the labor force behavior of Brazilian men and women, just prior to the onset of the economic difficulties, should shed light on how the economic crisis will affect structural changes in the labor markets and provide insights about the role of factors such as education in this process.   This chapter examines the situation in 1980, while the next chapter considers the conditions in 1989.

The vastness and diversity of Brazil and its well-documented substantial regional economic disparities led us to perform the analysis for six distinct economic regions as well as the entire country.  We thus reexamine the issue of "geographical aggregation bias" or "regional pluralism" in assessing returns to human capital, and how they differ by types of employment and by gender.[3]

A novelty of this study is that it examines the determinants of wages[4] by explicitly incorporating the selection (self or otherwise) of persons into three types of labor force status.  As cogently argued by Schultz (1988), it is important to assess whether work-status effects bias the parameter estimates of wage functions.  Few studies of labor markets in developing countries analyze the impact of sample selectivity and adjustments in earnings regressions, especially when three types of labor force status are involved.

The structure of the paper is as follows.  Section 3 discusses the data used in the study.  Sections 4 and 5 summarize the model of labor force status and wage determinants, and include discussions of the theoretical characterizations and econometric specifications.  Section 6 reports the empirical findings and their interpretation.  The final section contains the conclusions.

## 3.   Data and Stylized Facts

The models used in this study are applied to data originally taken from a public use sample tape (PUST) of the 1980 Brazilian Census.  The tape, which represents a 3 percent sample, contains 3,526,000 individuals and about 800,000 households.  The PUST was used to extract a subsample of 200,000 individuals and about 40,000 households.  From these data, we culled samples of

---

[3]   The issue of regional pluralism is examined for Brazil by Birdsall and Behrman (1984) with 1970 Census data, for Nicaragua by Behrman and Birdsall (1984), and for Panama by Heckman and Hotz (1986).  Unfortunately, there are very few studies that examine male-female differences in labor market outcomes for developing countries, especially in the context of regional pluralism.

[4]   We use the terms "wages" and "earnings" interchangeably throughout the paper.  Also, "hourly earnings," "wage" or "wage rate" are considered to be synonymous, as are "employee" and "wage earner."

individuals who were generally between the ages of 15 and 65 years.[5] This resulted in a sample of 28,926 wives and husbands, 11,225 single (never married) women, and 12,974 single men.[6]

Although the Census data provides much useful information, it has a principal disadvantage: Incomplete information on the number of hours worked.[7] Data are provided on monthly earnings, but not on monthly hours worked, nor hourly earnings. Instead, we are given data on weekly hours of work in intervals: 0 hours (non-workers), 1-14 hours, 15-29 hours, 30-39 hours, 40-48 hours and 49 or more hours. An index of continuous hours worked is desirable before applying standard statistical techniques in estimating the wage function.

The study uses hourly earnings as the principal measure of remuneration because, as discussed in detail by Behrman (1990), Blinder (1976), and Schultz (1988), it is inappropriate (especially for women and the self-employed) to use monthly earnings (monthly hours times hourly earnings) as the dependent variable. To do so may confound wage rate effects and labor supply effects which, in turn, may bias the parameter estimates of the returns to wage-determining characteristics. The direction of the bias depends on whether the labor supply curve is normal or backward-bending. Moreover, as stated by Blinder (1976), the expedient of adding the log of hours as a regressor leads to "strained interpretations" of the parameter estimates of the earnings function.

The hourly earnings measure we use, however, is marred by incomplete information on hours worked. The data provided no direct measure of hourly earnings, but we could calculate the hourly rate from monthly earnings and hours worked during the week of enumeration. As mentioned above, there was, however, a problem -- information on weekly hours worked was available in intervals only, and no information was provided on the number of weeks per month that a person worked. In earlier studies of Brazilian labor markets, Birdsall and Fox (1985) and Dabos and Psacharopoulos (1991) used the 1970 and 1980 census data, respectively, to construct a continuous hours variable by assigning values (usually mid-point) to each work interval.[8] This procedure is likely to create a measurement error and the problem can be thought of as an errors in variables problem in which parameter estimates are likely to be inconsistent and biased. The direction of this bias is not known. Nevertheless, we use their mid-point values, but note the caveat in interpreting the results below.[9]

---

[5]    An exception is made for married men. There were 1,441 married men over the age of 65; about 40 percent of them worked, usually over 30 hours per week.

[6]    The single (never married) men and women in the sample are relatively young. The average age of single men and women is 25 years and 21 years, respectively. About 35 percent of single men are under 20 years, and 40 percent are between 20 and 35 years of age; the corresponding proportions for women are 58 percent and 30 percent. Also, 38 percent of women reported that they were still attending school on a part- or full-time basis, as did 28 percent of the men.

[7]    Unfortunately, the data base also omitted information on migration for married and single men. In addition, for single men it failed to include information on household characteristics, non-labor income, and whether the person worked in the public sector.

[8]    Birdsall and Behrman (1984), who also used the 1970 Census data in their study of Brazilian men, make no mention of this issue. They do not indicate whether they use hourly or monthly earnings.

[9]    As pointed out by Ham and Hsiao (1984), labor economists and econometricians have given insufficient attention this important question.

*Important Characteristics of the Data*

To provide a background for the study, we present detailed descriptive statistics in Appendix Tables 3A.1 to 3A.6. There are substantial regional disparities, gender and work-status differences, and differences between married and single people in the summary information. These features, as well as results from other studies of Brazil, strongly indicated that the study should treat each of the economic regions separately: the Northwest (North plus Central-West), Northeast, South, the Southeast (the states of Rio de Janeiro and Guanabara, Sao Paulo), and Other Southeast states (Minas Gerias and Espirito Santo).[10] For each region, we estimate the models of labor force status and wage determination for four demographic groups, married women, married men, single women and single men. This approach allows one not only to detect regional differences, but also to draw comparisons among the demographic groups.

While a complete discussion of the information in the Appendix tables would be too lengthy to present here, we do examine the more important stylized (i.e., abstracted for the purpose of the analysis) facts about Brazilian labor markets. These stylized facts provide a useful background for the empirical analysis.

*Regional disparities.*[11]   There are acute economic disparities in Brazil which had a population of about 121.3 million in 1980. There are sharp differences among the highly industrialized and modern southern regions (Rio de Janeiro, Sao Paulo, Other Southeast, and the South), the Northwest (where the capital city is located), and the Northeast, which is heavily dependent on agricultural activities. The southern regions have about 60 percent of the population, and 17 percent of the land mass; the Northeast accounts for 30 percent of the population and 19 percent of total area, while the vast Northwest has about 10 percent of the population. Although there are pockets of poverty in the southern regions (in Rio de Janeiro, Minas Gerias, Espirito Santo, and Santa Catarina), they are the relatively prosperous parts of Brazil, while the Northeast is the poorest area, whatever indicators one wishes to use.

Looking at Appendix Tables 3A.1 and 3A.2 (data for married people), we obtain a good indication of the intensity of these regional disparities. All monetary units are in 1980 cruzeiros.[12] Total monthly employment earnings of husbands in the Northeast is $8,020 compared to $12,790 in the Northwest, $11,730 in Other Southeast, $18,970 in Rio, $20,170 in Sao Paulo, and $13,020 in the South. The pattern for monthly asset and transfer income is similar -- $2,650 in the Northeast, $3,620 in the Northwest, $4,440 in Other Southeast, $8,900

---

[10]   The states in each region are:

North:            Rondonia, Acre, Amazonas, Roraima, Para, Amapa
Central-West: Mato Grosso, Goias, Distrito Federal
Northeast:      Maranhao, Piaui, Ceara, Rio Grande do Norte, Paraiba, Pernambuco, Alagoas, Sergipe and Bahia
South:           Parana, Rio Grande do Sul, Santa Catarina
Southeast:     Rio de Janeiro and Guanabara, Sao Paulo, Minas Gerais and Espirito Santo

[11]   We caution the reader that we did not take spatial price variations into account when making regional comparison because we were unable to obtain geographical price indices. For further discussion of this issue see Birdsall and Behrman (1984) and Thomas (1980).

[12]   In 1980 the official exchange rate was about 40 cruzeiros = $ 1 (US). The monetary units used are cruzeiros expressed with the symbol $.

in Rio, $8,760 in Sao Paulo, $4,280 in the South. In brief, family income is much lower in the Northeast than in the rest of Brazil.

A similar pattern is revealed when education is examined. In the Northeast, the average years of schooling for husbands and wives are 2.2 and 2.3 years, respectively. The corresponding values for the other regions are: Northwest: 3.5 and 3.4 years; Other Southeast: 3.4 and 3.4; Rio: 6.1 and 5.4 years; Sao Paulo: 5.0 and 4.5 years; and South: 4.1 and 3.9 years.

There are also some noteworthy regional differences in labor force participation patterns. In the Northeast, Northwest, and Other Southeast, wives' labor force participation rates are in the 82-85 percent range, while in the remaining regions they are in the 76-78 percent range. As regards market work activities, in the Northeast just over one-half of working wives are self-employed. In the Northwest, the fraction is one-third, and it is about 37 percent in the Other Southeast and the South. In the urbanized regions of Rio and Sao Paulo, only 20 percent of working wives are self-employed. This pattern is similar for husbands. Over 60 percent of working husbands in the Northeast are self-employed. The proportion drops to 53 percent in the Northwest, to 45 percent in the Other Southeast and in the South, to 29 percent in Sao Paulo, and to 23 percent in Rio.

The above regional configuration for earnings, education and labor force participation also prevails among singles. For example, consider the data on single women (Appendix 3A.4). In the Northeast, the average monthly earnings of employees and the (paid) self-employed are about $4,900 and $2,000, respectively. The corresponding values for the other regions: Northwest: $5,200 and $4,400; Other Southeast: $4,600 and $4,100; Rio: $8,300 and $12,200; Sao Paulo $7,800 and $11,100; and South: $9,200 and $4,500. As regards education, the average years of schooling among single women is 4.1 years in the Northeast; 5.2 years in the Northwest; 5.4 years in the Other Southeast; 7.4 years in Rio; 7.1 years in Sao Paulo; and 5.9 years in the South. Finally, we note regional differences in labor force participation. In the Northeast, only 30 percent of single women are in the labor force. This compares with 33 percent in the Northwest, 37 percent in the Other Southeast, 41 percent in Rio, 59 percent in Sao Paulo, and 44 percent in the South. The types of market work performed by single women also differs among regions. In the Northeast, 63 percent of working women are employees. This proportion rises considerably in the other regions -- 87 percent in the Northwest, 90 percent in the Other Southeast, 93 percent in Rio and in Sao Paulo, and 77 percent in the South. Much the same story can be told about single men (Appendix Table 3A.5).

*Gender and marital status differences.* It should come as no surprise to find that there are notable gender and marital status differences in labor force activities and outcomes. First, as noted above, the labor force participation rate of men is much higher than that of women. The participation rate of single women exceeds that of married women. There are also interesting differences in the types of jobs, and, among workers, in earnings, hours of work, and wage-determining characteristics (education, experience). Bearing in mind regional differences, the main features are as follows.

*Job composition.* The job composition of men and women differs. The proportion of women workers who are employees generally exceeds that of men. Nationally, about 65 percent of working wives and 83 percent of single women are employees compared to 43 percent of husbands and 75 percent of single men. A regional breakdown shows that this pattern is largely sustained. In the Northeast, 39 percent of working husbands and 44 percent of single men are employees compared to 48 percent of working wives and 63 percent of single women. The proportions for the Northwest are: husbands, 47 percent; single men, 66 percent; wives, 67 percent; and single women, 87 percent. The male-female differences are somewhat smaller in the remaining regions. In the Other Southeast, 64 percent of working wives and 90 percent of single women are employees, while 56 percent of husbands and 77 of single men are employees. In Rio, the proportions for wives and husbands are about the same, about 80 percent, while for single men and women, the proportions are 86 percent and 93 percent, respectively. In Sao Paulo, about 80 percent of wives and 70 percent of husbands are employees, as are 93 percent of single women and 87 percent of single men. In the South, 63 percent of working wives and 54 percent of husbands are wage earners, while the proportions for single men and women are about the same at 75 percent.

*Earnings.* Looking at Appendix Table 3A.3 (for married people) and Appendix Table 3A.6 (for singles), we see that women, on average, earn less than men, and also work fewer hours. Nationally, the average monthly wage of husbands who are employees is $15,100 and $9,200 for wives; the values for single men and women are $7,800 and $6,400, respectively. Thus, the wife-husband earnings ratio is 0.61, while the single female-male ratio is 0.82. Among the (paid) self-employed, monthly earnings of husbands and wives are $14,600 and $7,900, respectively, yielding a ratio of 0.54. Single self-employed men earn $7,500, while their female counterparts earn $4,500, for a ratio of 0.60.

These indicators of female-male earnings disparities must be treated with caution because women tend to work fewer hours than men. Accordingly, it would be useful to take labor supply differences into account by examining differences in hourly earnings between men and women. This changes the story somewhat. The average hourly wage for employee husbands and wives is $84 and $63, respectively, yielding a ratio of 0.75. The corresponding values for self-employed workers is $84 for husbands and $55 for wives, for a ratio of 0.65. The hourly wage for single male and female employees is almost the same, $45 for men and $40 for women, so that the ratio is 0.89. Paid self-employed women earn about two-thirds the hourly earnings of self-employed men ($43).

These summary statistics on the male-female hourly earnings gap suggest that working wives (employees or self-employed) are, on average, worse off than their husbands. However, the gap between single men and women employees is much smaller, but the earnings differential among the self-employed remains large. We also note that the observed wage may differ from the wage offer, which takes into account labor force status decisions. In the econometric analysis we concentrate on male-female differences in wage offers.

One should also note the regional differences in the male-female hourly earnings gap. For employees, the wife-husband wage ratio ranges from a low of 0.65 in Sao Paulo to a high of 0.92 in the Other Southeast. The ratio is 0.72 in the Northeast, 0.76 in the South, 0.80 in Rio, and 0.85 in the Northwest. Regional differences in the female-male earnings ratio of roughly 0.60 among self-employed spouses are much less pronounced.

As shown in Appendix Table 3A.6 for singles, the average hourly wage of women employees is about equal to that of men. In most regions, the female-male wage ratio is similar to the national average (0.89). In the Other Southeast, the ratio is 0.77, while in Sao Paulo and the Northwest, it is 0.81 and 0.85, respectively. In the Northeast and Rio, the average wage of single women exceeds that of single men. Worst off are single self-employed women whose hourly earnings are about 70 percent those of men.

*Education.* We now turn to a brief summary of the differences in the principal variables that are likely to affect labor force status and wages. Nationally, as well as within specific regions and labor force status, education levels of working women are generally higher than those of men. For Brazil as a whole, the mean years of schooling for wives who are employees is 7.0, while for husbands it is 4.9 years. Single women employees have 7.4 years, while single men have 5.7 years. Similarly, self-employed wives have 3.4 years of schooling and their husband counterparts 2.9 years. The means for self-employed single women and men are 3.3 years and 3.1 years, respectively. In each region, with few exceptions, the education levels of women employees exceed those of men employees by 2 to 3 years of school. Among the self-employed, women have an education advantage of less than a year.

The relationship between education and labor force status is as expected. Generally, the educational attainment of employees is higher than that of the self-employed, and the latter have more years of schooling than those not working. For example, the average years of school of non-working wives is 3.2 years compared to 3.4 years for self-employed wives and 7.0 years for employees. With minor variations this pattern prevails for men and single women in all regions.

*Age.* As regards age, regional differences are relatively small. However, in all regions, wives and married and single men who are employees tend to be younger than their self-employed counterparts. For example, the average age of a married male employee is 38 years, and that of the self-employed man, 42 years. The corresponding values for wives are 36 years and 38 years, while for single men they are 24 years and 28 years. The pattern for single women differs. Nationally, the average ages of employees and the self-employed are about the same, 23 years and 22 years, respectively. However, in some regions (Northwest, Sao Paulo) self-employed single women are older (25 years) than employees (22 years). In the Northeast, the Other Southeast, and Rio, the average ages are the same (22-23 years), while in the South self-employed single women are younger than employees (19 years and 21 years). It should also be noted that single women and men are much younger than married women and men.

*Fertility and child composition.* We next consider past fertility and the child composition of the household, which are particularly relevant to the analysis of married women. First we note that well over 80 percent of the married households in the sample are comprised of nuclear families that consist only of a father, a mother, and children. The proportions are slightly lower for employee wives than for non-working or self-employed wives. The two exceptions are in the Northeast and the Northwest, where the proportion of nuclear families is about 70 percent.

A Brazilian wife in our sample, on average, gave birth to about 4 (live or dead) children. The average is lowest among employee wives (3.0) and, surprisingly, highest among self-employed wives (4.7); for non-working wives it is 4.2 births. As expected, these numbers mask important regional differences. Fertility is highest in the Northeast and lowest in the three southern regions. In the Northeast, the averages for non-working, self-employed, and employee wives are 5.2, 6.1, and 3.9, respectively. The corresponding values for the Northwest are 4.2, 4.6, and 3.3, while for the Other Southeast they are 4.4, 4.9, and 3.3. Fertility in the southern regions is lower. In Rio and Sao Paulo, the averages are almost the same: 3.4 for non-working wives, 3.2 for self-employed wives, and 2.5 for employees. The values in the South are 3.9 for non-working and self-employed wives, and 2.8 for wives who are employees.

Now, we comment on child composition. The average number of each type of child -- babies, toddlers, and school-age children -- in the household is highest in the Northwest and Northeast. In these regions the average number of babies is about 0.56, which is much higher than that in the other regions--0.33 in Rio, 0.38 in Sao Paulo and the South, and 0.46 in Other Southeast. This pattern generally repeats itself for each child type and labor force status. It is noteworthy that the average number of babies among non-working wives is much higher than among workers. For each type of working wife the average number of babies is roughly the same in most regions.

The average number of toddlers in the household (0.40) is about the same for non-working and self-employed wives, but lower for employees (0.30). Of course, there are regional differences. For example, in the Northeast and Northwest, the average number of toddlers is 0.50, while in the remaining regions it is about 0.34.

The profile of school-age children is different. The national average of self-employed wives (1.30) exceeds that of employees (0.93) and non-workers (1.04). As expected, there are regional differences. In Rio, Sao Paulo, and the South, the average for self-employed wives is 0.84, 1.10, and 1.19, respectively; for employees, 0.68, 0.88, and 0.88, respectively, and for non-working wives, 0.79, 0.85, and 0.96. The corresponding averages for the remaining three regions are: Northeast, 1.24, 1.52, and 1.14; Northwest, 1.16, 1.59, 1.11; and the Other Southeast, 1.14, 1.21, and 1.00.

In contrast to married women, Appendix Table 3A.4 shows that the child composition for single women is different. Single women may live alone and may have children, or live in households with children. However, in our sample of relatively young women, over 90 percent are daughters or daughters-in-law of a male household head. The average number of babies is about one-half that for married women (0.20). With a few exceptions (Northwest, Other Southeast, and Rio), there is little discernible difference in this magnitude between non-working and self-employed workers. However, the value for employees tends to be smaller than that for self-employed, especially in the Northeast, the Other Southeast, and Rio. As regards toddlers, the national average is 0.24, and the mean is lower for employees (0.19) than for non-working (0.25) or self-employed (0.32) women. However, in the Northeast, Rio, Sao Paulo, and the South, the average is higher for self-employed women than that for non-working women, while in the remaining regions, the average is the same. The average number of school-age children present in the household is lower for married women (1.04) than for single women (1.35). There are fewer such children among women who are employees (1.17) than among non-working (1.43) or self-employed women (1.17). As expected, these values are higher in the Northeast, the Northwest, and the Other Southeast than in the remaining three regions. Also, with the exception of the Northeast, the average for self-employed women are 1.02 and 1.15, respectively; in the South, the corresponding values are 1.23 and 1.69.

Overall, the salient features presented above and the details provided in the tables indicate that there are important regional, labor force status, gender and marital status differences in the data. This suggests a stratification of the sample by region, work status, gender and marital status. Such an approach provides the opportunity to explore the extent to which the descriptive profiles are reflected in the empirical analysis of labor market outcomes.

## 4. Female Labor Force Participation

Before proceeding with the models, it should be noted that only 20 percent of married women and 41 percent of single women performed market work (i.e. reported positive hours of work).[13] Of the working women a negligible fraction (1.5 percent) were employers, and about 8 percent of married and 10 percent of single women workers reported that they did not receive remuneration for their market work (unpaid family workers). Among working wives, 65 percent were employees and 35 percent were self-employed; the corresponding figures for single women were 83 percent and 17 percent. As regards men, 90 percent of married men were employed, and of this group, 4 percent were employers, 40 percent were self-employed, and 56 percent were employees. All single men in our sample were in the labor force; 75 percent were employees and 25 percent were self-employed. A negligible fraction of men were unpaid family workers.

This information on Brazil, discussed more fully later, indicates that the labor force status choice model should be characterized by a three-way choice (employee, self-employment, and non-work) for women and married men, while a two-way choice (wage work and self-employment) should suffice for single men. This is the approach we adopt.

The econometric specifications of the models were carefully considered given the data at our disposal. Table 3.1 below displays the definitions and measurement of the variables used in the analysis. In specifying the models we tried to maintain uniformity as much as possible across regions, gender, marital and labor force status.[14] However, because of small cell counts or insufficient information (especially for single men) it was necessary to be flexible.

While we analyze the data for single (never married) women and men, most of our attention is given to the labor force behavior of married women. Wives are usually secondary workers who also bear the responsibility for household maintenance and child raising. We note that, for analysis and policy purposes, the labor force behavior of wives is of considerable current interest.

The explanatory variables in the labor force status model are straightforward and standard in the literature. For single and married women, these are age, age squared (divided by 100), years of education, child composition (the number of babies, toddlers, and school-age children),[15] household size, asset and transfer income of the household, home ownership, number of rooms

---

[13]    The low participation rates of Brazilian women should not be surprising. We note that at the turn of the century women comprised 45 percent of the reported labor force, mainly in agriculture, home-based textiles, and domestic-servant activities. Two decades later the proportion fell to 20 percent, and has since remained in the 20-25 percent range. A possible reason for the relatively low participation rate is the manner in which statistical information on women's activities is collected. Most census and survey practices in developing countries typically exclude unpaid family and intermittent workers (especially in home-based market activities) from the labor force. For further discussion, see Boulding (1983).

[14]    Considerable effort and resources were devoted to ensuring that data inconsistencies were removed and to experimenting with alternative specifications. Generally, the estimates were not sensitive to alternative specifications.

[15]    Since over 80 percent of married households are nuclear families, the children variables generally reflect the fertility of the wife. This is certainly the case for the sample of relatively young single women, 90 percent of whom are daughters or daughters-in-law of a male household head.

**Table 3.1**
Definition of Variables Used in the Analysis

| VARIABLE | DESCRIPTION | Married | | Single | |
|---|---|---|---|---|---|
| | | WOMEN | MEN | WOMEN | MEN |
| **LABOR FORCE STATUS ANALYSES** | | | | | |
| KIDS 0-2 | Number of children in household under 3 (Babies) | x | x | | |
| KIDS 3-5 | Number of children in household 3-5 (Toddlers) | x | x | | |
| KIDS 6-14 | Number of children in household 6-14 | x | x | | |
| HSIZNFAM | Number of persons in household | x | x | x | |
| AGE | Age in years | x | x | x | x |
| AGESQ2 | Age squared/100 | x | x | x | x |
| YRSEDUC | Years of education | x | x | x | x |
| HSLEVNON | = 1 if no schooling completed, 0 otherwise | | | | x |
| HEMPLYE | = 1 if husband is an employee, 0 otherwise | x | | | |
| WYESWRK | = 1 if wife works, 0 otherwise | | x | | |
| ASSETINC | Asset + Transfer income of household/100,000 | x | | x | |
| OTHERINC | ASSETINC + wife's total earnings/100,000 | | x | | |
| HUSEARN | Husband's total earnings/100,000 | x | | | |
| OWN HOME | = 1 if homeowner, 0 otherwise | x | x | x | |
| ROOMS | Number of rooms in the home | x | x | | |
| URBAN | = 1 if urban resident, 0 otherwise | x | x | x | x |
| **REGION VARIABLES** | | | | | |
| NORTHWEST | = 1 if lives in Northwest, 0 otherwise (reference) | x | x | x | x |
| NORTHEAST | = 1 if lives in Northeast, 0 otherwise | x | x | x | x |
| MARANE | = 1 if lives in Maranhoa or Piaui, 0 otherwise | x | x | x | x |
| BAHIANE | = 1 if lives in Bahia or Sergipe, 0 otherwise | x | x | x | x |
| OTHERNE | = 1 if lives in Other Northeast states, 0 otherwise (reference) | x | x | x | x |
| RIO | = 1 if lives in state of Rio de Janeiro, 0 otherwise | x | x | x | x |
| SAO PAULO | = 1 if lives in state of Sao Paulo, 0 otherwise | x | x | x | x |
| OTHERSE | = 1 if lives in Other Southeast states, 0 otherwise | x | x | x | x |
| SOUTH | = 1 if lives in South, 0 otherwise | x | x | x | x |
| **WAGE ANALYSES** | | | | | |
| LNWAGE | Natural log of hourly wage in main job | x | x | x | x |
| MILLS 1,2 | Inverse of Mills' ratio (1 employee, 2 self-employed) | x | x | x | x |
| SECPUB | = 1 if government employee, 0 otherwise | x | x | x | |
| SOCSEC | = 1 if social security contributor, 0 otherwise | x | x | x | x |
| EXPR | Potential work experience = (age - 6 - years of schooling) | x | x | x | x |
| EXPSQ2 | Experience squared | x | x | x | x |
| YRSEDUC | Years of education | x | x | x | x |
| BIRTOT | Number of children ever born | x | | x | |
| URBAN | = 1 if urban resident, 0 otherwise | x | x | x | x |
| **REGION VARIABLES** | | | | | |
| NORTHWEST | = 1 if lives in Northwest, 0 otherwise (reference) | x | x | x | x |
| NORTHEAST | = 1 if lives in Northeast, 0 otherwise | x | x | x | x |
| MARANE | = 1 if lives in Maranhoa or Piaui, 0 otherwise | x | x | x | x |
| BAHIANE | = 1 if lives in Bahia or Sergipe, 0 otherwise | x | x | x | x |
| OTHERNE | = 1 if lives in Other Northeast states, 0 otherwise (reference) | x | x | x | x |
| RIO | = 1 if lives in state of Rio de Janeiro, 0 otherwise | x | x | x | x |
| SAO PAULO | = 1 if lives in state of Sao Paulo, 0 otherwise | x | x | x | x |
| OTHERSE | = 1 if lives in Other Southeast states, 0 otherwise | x | x | x | x |
| SOUTH | = 1 if lives in South, 0 otherwise | x | x | x | x |

in the house, and urban residence. In the analysis of wives, we also include the husband's monthly earnings, and a dummy variable if he is a wage and salary worker.

For married men, the variables are age and its square, years of education, home ownership, asset and transfer income plus the wife's earnings, whether the wife worked, and urban residence. For single men, the data base did not provide information on household characteristics, and the following variables were used: age and its square, years of education, urban residence, and a dummy variable indicating whether the person completed any schooling.

For the entire Brazil sample we also estimated the model with and without regional dummy variables (the excluded category is Northwest). This was also done for the Northeast, for which the state dummy variables are Bahia/Sergipe and Maranhao/Piaui (the excluded category is Other Northeast states).[16] The results did not change in any significant way.

*Labor Force Status Choice Model*

Our analysis uses the standard one-period static labor supply framework in which preferences are defined by a utility function whose arguments are the Hicksian composite of all goods, non-market time, and a vector of exogenous variables that affect labor force decisions.[17] Rational decision making is reflected in the maximization of the utility function subject to time and budget constraints.[18] One of an individual's decisions is to select amongst three mutually exclusive alternatives: employee, self-employment, and no work.[19] These choices are indexed by 1, 2, and 3, and choices 1 and 2 have reported hours of work. The alternative chosen is the one that yields the highest utility. In other words, the individual compares the pecuniary and nonpecuniary costs and benefits of each labor force status and chooses the one that yields the largest gain.

More formally, let $V_j$ be the maximum utility attainable for an individual if alternative $j = 1, 2, 3$ is chosen. Assuming that this indirect utility function is linear for estimation purposes: $V_j = x\gamma_j + \epsilon_j$, where x is a (row) vector of observed explanatory variables (the non-stochastic component or measured individual characteristics), $\gamma_j$ is a vector of unknown parameters, and $\epsilon_j$ is a random disturbance corresponding to unobserved individual differences in tastes.

Thus, the probability that alternative j is chosen is just the probability that the individual characteristics (x) "pay off" more in the jth alternative than in any other choice:

---

[16]   We also estimated the model with state dummy variables for the remaining regions, and found that the results did not change in any significant way. The results are available from the authors.

[17]   In keeping with the standard assumptions, the labor force behavior of other household members is assumed to be exogenous. For instance, wives make labor supply decisions without reference to those of the husband, and likewise husbands. A future research topic is the issue of joint decision-making and household labor supply.

[18]   For fuller discussions of the model see Greene (1990), Hill (1988) and Trost and Lee (1984).

[19]   This assumption, of course, precludes concurrent multiple job holdings, but this is of little concern in this study. Almost no women in the sample reported that they held a second job. About 5 percent of the men reported second jobs.

$P_j = \text{prob}[V_j > V_k]$ for $k \neq j$, $j, k = 1, 2, 3$
  $= \text{prob}[x\gamma_j - x\gamma_k > \epsilon_k - \epsilon_j]$ for $k \neq j$, $j, k = 1, 2, 3$

If disturbances are independently and identically randomly distributed, the difference between the error terms (and hence between payoffs) follows a logistic distribution in what is commonly referred to as the multinomial choice model of McFadden (1973):

$$P_j = \frac{\exp(x\gamma_j)}{\displaystyle\sum_{k=1}^{3} \exp(x\gamma_k)}, \quad j = 1, 2, 3; \quad \gamma_3 \equiv 0\,(normalization).$$

The estimates of the multinomial logit model can be used to obtain the partial derivative or marginal effect of an explanatory variable (m) on the probabilities of being in a given labor force status:

$$\frac{\partial P_j}{\partial x_m} = P_j[\gamma_{jm} - \sum_{k=1}^{3} P_k\gamma_{km}], \quad j = 1, 2, 3$$

It should be noted that the signs of the partial derivatives of the probabilities need not correspond to the partial derivatives of utility. That is, $\partial P_j/\partial x_m$ may differ from $\partial V_j/\partial x_m = \gamma_{jm}$. Even though, for example, $V_j$ increases as $x_m$ increases, $P_j$ may decline because the increase in $x_m$ raises the payoff in another alternative (say $V_k$) by more. The estimates can also be used to evaluate the impact of a change in one variable, holding the remaining ones constant at their mean values, on the probability of choosing among the types of labor force status. We consider these simulation exercises below.

After estimating the choice models for women and men, we construct the selectivity correction variable (the inverse of Mills' ratio, $\lambda$) for each type of worker, and include it as regressor in the ordinary least squares (OLS) estimations of the earnings functions. Since the selectivity correction procedure for the two-choice model developed by Heckman (1987) is well-known, we do not review the details here.[20]   Instead, we summarize the salient features of the less familiar three-choice model and review the procedure of Maddala (1983) and Lee (1983) for obtaining the selectivity bias correction terms.  This is presented when we consider the wage equations below.

*Empirical Estimates – Logit Estimates of Labor Force Status*

*Married women* (Tables 3.2 and 3.3).  Turning first to the effect of children, we see that young children reduce the propensity to perform market work, a result that is commonly found in participation studies of married women.  Children effects are slightly stronger for employees than for the self-employed.  As expected, babies and toddlers have the strongest negative effects, while the impact diminishes for school-age children. The derivatives and the simulations also show that children are stronger deterrents in the southern than the northern regions.

A larger household (the average size is 7-8 people) has a strong positive effect on labor force participation. A reasonable interpretation of this finding is that household members other than the

---

[20]   See also Dubin and Rivers (1989).

wife serve as childcare alternatives and share house-keeping chores, thereby releasing the wife's time for labor market activities. Household size effects appear to be stronger in Rio, Sao Paulo and the South than in the remaining regions.

As regards the housing characteristics variables, in most instances home ownership (a proxy for wealth) does not have a statistically significant impact on labor force status. In only two cases is the coefficient significant and negative -- for employees in Rio and Sao Paulo. The coefficient is unexpectedly positive and significant for self-employed wives in the Northeast. This may simply reflect the poor quality of housing in the region. The number of rooms, which proxies the burden of housework, has the expected negative impact in all regions, except Rio, where the coefficient is not statistically significant.[21]

If the husband is an employee, this increases the probability that the wife will work as an employee, but reduces the probability that she will be self-employed. This may reflect selective mating in which relatively better educated men marry more highly educated women. We note that wives who are employees tend to have husbands who are wage earners, and that employees have more schooling than the self-employed. Income effects are captured by two variables: husband's earnings and asset plus transfer income. In most cases, the higher the husband's earnings the lower the probability that a wife will work as an employee, but this variable has little effect on the self-employment choice. Overall, husband's earnings has a small significant negative effect. The other variable used to approximate income effects (asset plus transfer income, but not husband's earnings) also has the expected negative effect on the propensity to work, particularly on the probability of working as an employee. However, with the exception of Rio and Sao Paulo, it generally has a small impact.

The dummy variable for urbanization presumably reflects a mix of demand-side and taste effects, which are likely to work in the same direction. An urban area may provide more plentiful job opportunities and a more congenial environment for a wife to perform market work, and thus encourage greater participation than in rural areas.[22] We see that living in an urban area has a positive effect on labor force participation, especially as an employee. In most regions, however, the urban variable has no significant impact on self-employment. In the Northeast and South, the urban variable has a negative effect on being self-employed, while in the Other Southeast and Rio (which also encompasses rural areas) the impact is positive.

The age of the wife is significantly related to labor force status, but in a non-linear fashion. This is readily seen by glancing at the coefficients, the marginal effects, and the predicted probabilities. Younger wives (under 25 years) and older wives (over 40 years) are less likely to participate than wives in the 25-40 years age range, yielding an inversely U-shaped age conditional profile, which accords with prior expectations and other empirical results for developing countries.[23] This pattern is generally repeated for both employees and the self-employed.

---

[21]    The number of rooms in a house may also be a surrogate for wealth, depending on the quality of the dwelling, which is not known. As regards the finding for Rio, one hypothesis, though not testable with these data, is that there is better access to domestics in Rio than in the other regions.

[22]    The same reasoning can be used in interpreting the effects of regional dummy variables.

[23]    See, for instance, Psacharopoulos and Tzannatos (1989), Mohan (1988), and Standing and Sheehan (1978).

## Table 3.2
### Multinational Logit Estimates of the Labor Force Participation - Married Women

| REGION | CONSTANT | KIDS 0-2 | KIDS 3-5 | KIDS 6-14 | FAMILY SIZE | AGE | AGESQ /100 | YEARS SCHOOL | HUSBAND EMPLOYEE | ASSET INCOME '0000 | HUSBANDS EARNINGS '00000 | OWN HOME | ROOMS IN HOME | URBAN |
|---|---|---|---|---|---|---|---|---|---|---|---|---|---|---|
| **ALL BRAZIL** Non-work n= 28926 | -2LLKFULL = 30481.1 | -2LLKRESTR = 36175.0 | | | | | | | | | | | | |
| Employee n = 3741 | -8.591 | -0.921 | -0.583 | -0.354 | 0.332 | 0.249 | -0.345 | 0.251 | 0.371 | -2.796 | -1.040 | -0.119 | -0.080 | 0.638 |
| | (32.48) | (22.91) | (15.72) | (16.02) | (29.96) | (17.14) | (17.62) | (41.17) | (8.39) | (11.72) | (9.33) | (2.83) | (7.44) | (10.41) |
| derivative x 100 | | -6.290 | -3.990 | -2.370 | 2.220 | 1.670 | -2.320 | 1.740 | 2.950 | -19.150 | -7.370 | -0.890 | -0.540 | 4.670 |
| Self-employed n = 1985 | -6.929 | -0.533 | -0.322 | -0.294 | 0.282 | 0.201 | -0.259 | 0.084 | -0.656 | -1.489 | -0.020 | 0.090 | -0.065 | -0.300 |
| | (23.23) | (11.84) | (7.83) | (12.33) | (23.01) | (12.66) | (12.91) | (9.99) | (12.08) | (6.05) | (0.22) | (1.68) | (5.07) | (5.38) |
| derivative x 100 | | -2.660 | -1.600 | -1.540 | 1.490 | 1.050 | -1.350 | 0.370 | -4.000 | -7.330 | 0.380 | 0.580 | -0.340 | -2.050 |
| **NORTHEAST** Non-work n = 6027 | -2LLKFULL = 7503.9 | -2LLKRESTR = 8875.2 | | | | | | | | | | | | |
| Employee n = 639 | -8.929 | -0.713 | -0.515 | -0.298 | 0.286 | 0.264 | -0.351 | 0.310 | 0.433 | -4.600 | -0.775 | -0.111 | -0.052 | 0.093 |
| | (14.41) | (8.16) | (6.19) | (6.20) | (11.63) | (7.78) | (7.75) | (20.70) | (4.25) | (4.87) | (2.92) | (1.10) | (2.13) | (0.77) |
| derivative x 100 | | -2.990 | -2.110 | -1.190 | 1.150 | 1.090 | -1.450 | 1.340 | 2.110 | -18.320 | -3.230 | -0.620 | -0.210 | 0.520 |
| Self-employed n = 708 | -6.600 | -0.389 | -0.399 | -0.307 | 0.286 | 0.187 | -0.242 | 0.060 | -0.497 | -4.959 | -0.479 | 0.337 | -0.052 | -0.268 |
| | (13.45) | (5.81) | (6.16) | (7.88) | (12.95) | (7.27) | (7.38) | (3.32) | (4.82) | (4.88) | (1.30) | (3.42) | (2.29) | (2.83) |
| derivative x 100 | | -2.760 | -2.920 | -2.280 | 2.130 | 1.360 | -1.750 | 0.340 | -4.050 | -36.950 | -3.440 | 2.680 | -0.390 | -2.130 |
| **NORTHWEST** Non-work n = 2522 | -2LLKFULL = 2589.0 | -2LLKRESTR = 3242.6 | | | | | | | | | | | | |
| Employee n = 325 | -10.066 | -0.598 | -0.460 | -0.250 | 0.275 | 0.278 | -0.367 | 0.332 | 0.349 | -2.508 | -0.740 | 0.164 | -0.110 | 0.973 |
| | (11.05) | (4.95) | (3.92) | (3.60) | (7.93) | (5.43) | (5.26) | (15.06) | (2.33) | (3.08) | (1.98) | (1.09) | (3.13) | (4.89) |
| derivative x 100 | | -2.820 | -2.220 | -1.180 | 1.300 | 1.310 | -1.740 | 1.610 | 1.810 | -12.150 | -3.650 | 0.820 | -0.520 | 4.740 |
| Self-employed n = 155 | -8.666 | -0.581 | -0.222 | -0.219 | 0.246 | 0.260 | -0.326 | 0.130 | -0.373 | -1.080 | -0.049 | -0.042 | -0.112 | 0.292 |
| | (8.05) | (3.88) | (1.65) | (2.83) | (6.26) | (4.44) | (4.29) | (4.38) | (1.95) | (1.25) | (0.13) | (0.22) | (2.48) | (1.49) |
| derivative x 100 | | -2.370 | -0.850 | -0.890 | 1.000 | 1.060 | -1.320 | 0.480 | -1.690 | -4.070 | -0.040 | -0.220 | -0.460 | 1.030 |
| **OTHER SOUTHEAST** Non-work n = 3103 | -2LLKFULL = 3177.6 | -2LLKRESTR = 3889.6 | | | | | | | | | | | | |
| Employee n = 357 | -10.873 | -0.927 | -0.537 | -0.429 | 0.372 | 0.346 | -0.476 | 0.297 | 0.244 | -2.469 | -1.411 | -0.036 | -0.070 | 0.526 |
| | (11.98) | (7.31) | (4.48) | (6.12) | (10.10) | (6.92) | (6.97) | (14.89) | (1.78) | (3.12) | (3.26) | (0.27) | (2.08) | (2.76) |
| derivative x 100 | | -4.400 | -2.560 | -2.000 | 1.740 | 1.640 | -2.270 | 1.440 | 1.320 | -11.570 | -7.040 | -0.140 | -0.330 | 2.490 |
| Self-employed n = 207 | -9.884 | -0.756 | -0.379 | -0.527 | 0.402 | 0.295 | -0.370 | 0.106 | -0.496 | -2.654 | 0.317 | -0.166 | -0.095 | 0.468 |
| | (9.77) | (4.97) | (2.77) | (6.76) | (9.81) | (5.55) | (5.49) | (4.16) | (3.09) | (3.02) | (1.44) | (1.02) | (2.38) | (2.46) |
| derivative x 100 | | -3.000 | -1.490 | -2.140 | 1.620 | 1.170 | -1.460 | 0.380 | -2.160 | -10.710 | 1.680 | -0.700 | -0.390 | 1.870 |
| **RIO DE JANEIRO** Non-work n = 2223 | -2LLKFULL = 3406.5 | -2LLKRESTR = 3949.6 | | | | | | | | | | | | |
| Employee n = 553 | -6.907 | -1.076 | -0.639 | -0.410 | 0.310 | 0.191 | -0.272 | 0.203 | 0.294 | -2.118 | -0.646 | -0.195 | -0.019 | 0.209 |
| | (9.51) | (8.80) | (5.99) | (6.21) | (10.76) | (5.69) | (5.57) | (13.30) | (2.34) | (4.41) | (2.88) | (1.75) | (0.60) | (0.89) |
| derivative x 100 | | -12.530 | -7.570 | -4.780 | 3.610 | 2.170 | -3.110 | 2.430 | 3.780 | -25.830 | -8.150 | -2.140 | -0.190 | 2.160 |
| Self-employed n = 149 | -7.526 | -0.822 | -0.292 | -0.299 | 0.238 | 0.210 | -0.281 | 0.049 | -0.319 | 0.125 | 0.441 | -0.349 | -0.067 | 0.581 |
| | (6.19) | (4.01) | (1.81) | (3.03) | (5.75) | (3.44) | (3.67) | (1.88) | (1.73) | (0.32) | (1.58) | (1.92) | (1.31) | (1.43) |
| derivative x 100 | | -2.990 | -0.890 | -1.080 | 0.860 | 0.820 | -1.090 | 0.080 | -1.640 | 1.930 | 2.420 | -1.440 | -0.290 | 2.480 |
| **SAO PAULO** Non-work n = 5339 | -2LLKFULL = 7657.6 | -2LLKRESTR = 8908.2 | | | | | | | | | | | | |
| Employee n = 1170 | -7.219 | -1.061 | -0.641 | -0.357 | 0.402 | 0.203 | -0.281 | 0.223 | 0.237 | -3.722 | -0.890 | -0.290 | -0.142 | 0.338 |
| | (14.51) | (14.06) | (9.38) | (8.54) | (17.92) | (7.61) | (7.82) | (19.97) | (2.86) | (8.44) | (4.32) | (3.75) | (6.39) | (2.38) |
| derivative x 100 | | -10.660 | -6.630 | -3.650 | 4.070 | 2.020 | -2.810 | 2.270 | 2.880 | -38.580 | -9.310 | -2.880 | -1.460 | 3.500 |
| Self-employed n = 352 | -7.137 | -0.843 | -0.165 | -0.172 | 0.251 | 0.188 | -0.234 | 0.111 | -0.729 | -0.793 | -0.038 | -0.298 | -0.057 | 0.074 |
| | (9.20) | (6.32) | (1.60) | (2.93) | (8.56) | (4.69) | (4.70) | (6.48) | (6.21) | (2.25) | (0.25) | (2.45) | (1.87) | (0.38) |
| derivative x 100 | | -3.090 | -0.370 | -0.560 | 0.870 | 0.700 | -0.870 | 0.360 | -3.300 | -1.430 | 0.320 | -1.140 | -0.170 | 0.140 |
| **SAO PAOLO** Non-work n = 3986 | -2LLKFULL = 5529.2 | -2LLKRESTR = 6812.3 | | | | | | | | | | | | |
| Employee n = 697 | -10.215 | -1.179 | -0.706 | -0.462 | 0.412 | 0.302 | -0.428 | 0.257 | 0.395 | -4.039 | -1.806 | 0.088 | -0.058 | 1.227 |
| | (15.55) | (11.32) | (7.72) | (8.09) | (13.97) | (8.38) | (8.66) | (16.55) | (3.68) | (5.46) | (4.96) | (0.85) | (2.33) | (8.80) |
| derivative x 100 | | -7.650 | -4.520 | -2.920 | 2.590 | 1.930 | -2.740 | 1.680 | 3.050 | -26.010 | -12.140 | 0.510 | -0.350 | 8.490 |
| Self-employed n = 414 | -7.076 | -0.570 | -0.458 | -0.376 | 0.349 | 0.206 | -0.272 | 0.107 | -0.781 | -2.327 | -0.026 | 0.168 | -0.078 | -0.454 |
| | (10.64) | (5.12) | (4.51) | (6.59) | (11.54) | (5.78) | (6.00) | (5.30) | (6.05) | (3.17) | (0.12) | (1.33) | (2.66) | (3.68) |
| derivative x 100 | | -3.100 | -2.610 | -2.200 | 2.050 | 1.180 | -1.540 | 0.560 | -5.260 | -13.030 | 0.740 | 1.040 | -0.480 | -3.560 |

Notes: The numbers in parentheses are t-statistics.

The numbers below the t-statistics are the partial derivatives x 100 evaluated at the sample means.

## Table 3.3
### Logit Simulations:  Probabilities of Labor Force Participation % - Married Women
### E = Employee;  S = Self-employed;  N = Non-worker

| REGION / WORK STATUS | ALL BRAZIL E | S | N | NORTHEAST E | S | N | NORTHWEST E | S | N | OTHER SOUTHEAST E | S | N | RIO E | S | N | SAO PAULO E | S | N | SOUTH E | S | N |
|---|---|---|---|---|---|---|---|---|---|---|---|---|---|---|---|---|---|---|---|---|---|
| KIDS 0-2  0 | 11 | 7 | 82 | 7 | 10 | 83 | 7 | 6 | 87 | 8 | 6 | 86 | 19 | 6 | 75 | 16 | 6 | 78 | 11 | 8 | 81 |
| 1 | 5 | 5 | 90 | 3 | 7 | 89 | 4 | 4 | 92 | 3 | 3 | 94 | 8 | 3 | 89 | 7 | 3 | 90 | 4 | 5 | 91 |
| 2 | 2 | 3 | 95 | 2 | 5 | 93 | 2 | 2 | 96 | 1 | 2 | 97 | 3 | 1 | 96 | 2 | 1 | 96 | 1 | 3 | 96 |
| KIDS 3-5  0 | 9 | 7 | 84 | 6 | 10 | 84 | 6 | 5 | 89 | 6 | 5 | 89 | 17 | 5 | 78 | 14 | 5 | 81 | 9 | 8 | 83 |
| 1 | 6 | 5 | 89 | 4 | 7 | 89 | 4 | 4 | 92 | 4 | 4 | 93 | 10 | 4 | 86 | 8 | 4 | 88 | 5 | 5 | 90 |
| 2 | 3 | 4 | 93 | 2 | 5 | 93 | 3 | 3 | 94 | 2 | 3 | 95 | 5 | 3 | 91 | 5 | 4 | 92 | 2 | 4 | 94 |
| 3 | 2 | 3 | 95 | 1 | 3 | 95 | 2 | 3 | 96 | 1 | 2 | 97 | 3 | 3 | 94 | 2 | 3 | 94 | 1 | 2 | 96 |
| KIDS 6-14  0 | 11 | 8 | 81 | 6 | 12 | 82 | 7 | 6 | 88 | 8 | 8 | 85 | 18 | 6 | 76 | 15 | 5 | 80 | 11 | 9 | 80 |
| 1 | 8 | 6 | 86 | 5 | 9 | 86 | 5 | 4 | 90 | 5 | 5 | 90 | 13 | 4 | 82 | 11 | 4 | 84 | 7 | 7 | 86 |
| 2 | 6 | 5 | 89 | 4 | 7 | 89 | 5 | 4 | 92 | 4 | 3 | 93 | 9 | 4 | 87 | 8 | 4 | 88 | 5 | 5 | 90 |
| 3 | 4 | 4 | 92 | 3 | 5 | 92 | 3 | 3 | 93 | 2 | 2 | 96 | 6 | 3 | 91 | 6 | 3 | 91 | 3 | 4 | 93 |
| FAMILY SIZE  2 | 1 | 2 | 97 | 1 | 2 | 97 | 1 | 1 | 98 | 1 | 1 | 99 | 4 | 2 | 95 | 2 | 1 | 97 | 1 | 1 | 98 |
| 4 | 3 | 3 | 95 | 2 | 3 | 95 | 2 | 2 | 96 | 2 | 1 | 97 | 7 | 3 | 91 | 4 | 2 | 94 | 2 | 3 | 95 |
| 6 | 5 | 4 | 90 | 3 | 6 | 92 | 3 | 3 | 93 | 3 | 3 | 94 | 11 | 4 | 85 | 8 | 4 | 88 | 5 | 5 | 90 |
| 8 | 9 | 7 | 83 | 5 | 9 | 86 | 6 | 5 | 89 | 6 | 6 | 88 | 19 | 6 | 76 | 16 | 5 | 79 | 10 | 9 | 81 |
| 10 | 16 | 11 | 73 | 8 | 15 | 77 | 9 | 8 | 83 | 12 | 11 | 77 | 29 | 8 | 63 | 29 | 7 | 64 | 19 | 15 | 67 |
| AGE  15 | 3 | 2 | 95 | 1 | 4 | 95 | 1 | 1 | 97 | 1 | 1 | 98 | 8 | 2 | 90 | 6 | 2 | 93 | 3 | 3 | 95 |
| 20 | 5 | 4 | 91 | 3 | 6 | 92 | 3 | 2 | 95 | 3 | 2 | 95 | 12 | 3 | 85 | 9 | 3 | 88 | 5 | 5 | 90 |
| 25 | 8 | 6 | 86 | 5 | 8 | 87 | 5 | 4 | 91 | 6 | 4 | 91 | 16 | 5 | 80 | 12 | 4 | 84 | 9 | 7 | 85 |
| 30 | 11 | 7 | 82 | 6 | 10 | 84 | 7 | 6 | 87 | 8 | 5 | 87 | 18 | 6 | 76 | 15 | 5 | 80 | 12 | 8 | 80 |
| 35 | 12 | 8 | 80 | 7 | 11 | 81 | 8 | 7 | 85 | 9 | 7 | 84 | 19 | 6 | 74 | 16 | 6 | 78 | 13 | 9 | 78 |
| 40 | 11 | 9 | 80 | 7 | 12 | 81 | 8 | 7 | 84 | 9 | 7 | 84 | 18 | 6 | 75 | 16 | 6 | 78 | 12 | 10 | 79 |
| 45 | 9 | 8 | 83 | 6 | 11 | 83 | 7 | 7 | 86 | 7 | 7 | 86 | 16 | 6 | 79 | 14 | 6 | 80 | 9 | 9 | 82 |
| 50 | 7 | 7 | 87 | 5 | 9 | 86 | 5 | 6 | 89 | 4 | 5 | 90 | 12 | 5 | 84 | 10 | 5 | 84 | 6 | 7 | 87 |
| 55 | 4 | 5 | 91 | 3 | 7 | 90 | 3 | 4 | 93 | 2 | 4 | 94 | 8 | 3 | 89 | 7 | 4 | 89 | 3 | 5 | 92 |
| 60 | 2 | 3 | 95 | 1 | 5 | 94 | 2 | 2 | 96 | 1 | 2 | 97 | 4 | 2 | 94 | 4 | 3 | 93 | 1 | 3 | 96 |
| 65 | 1 | 2 | 97 | 1 | 3 | 97 | 1 | 1 | 98 | 0 | 1 | 99 | 2 | 1 | 97 | 2 | 2 | 96 | 0 | 2 | 98 |
| SCHOOL YRS  0 | 3 | 5 | 92 | 2 | 8 | 90 | 2 | 3 | 95 | 2 | 3 | 95 | 5 | 4 | 91 | 5 | 3 | 92 | 3 | 5 | 92 |
| 1 | 4 | 5 | 91 | 3 | 8 | 89 | 2 | 3 | 94 | 3 | 4 | 94 | 6 | 4 | 89 | 6 | 3 | 91 | 4 | 5 | 91 |
| 2 | 5 | 6 | 89 | 4 | 8 | 87 | 3 | 4 | 93 | 3 | 4 | 93 | 8 | 4 | 88 | 7 | 4 | 89 | 5 | 6 | 89 |
| 3 | 7 | 6 | 87 | 6 | 9 | 86 | 5 | 4 | 91 | 5 | 4 | 91 | 9 | 4 | 86 | 9 | 4 | 87 | 6 | 6 | 88 |
| 4 | 8 | 6 | 85 | 8 | 9 | 83 | 6 | 5 | 89 | 6 | 5 | 89 | 11 | 5 | 84 | 11 | 4 | 85 | 7 | 7 | 86 |
| 5 | 10 | 7 | 83 | 10 | 9 | 81 | 9 | 5 | 86 | 8 | 5 | 87 | 13 | 5 | 82 | 13 | 5 | 82 | 9 | 8 | 83 |
| 6 | 13 | 7 | 80 | 13 | 10 | 78 | 12 | 6 | 83 | 10 | 5 | 84 | 16 | 5 | 80 | 16 | 5 | 79 | 12 | 8 | 80 |
| 7 | 16 | 7 | 77 | 17 | 10 | 74 | 15 | 6 | 78 | 13 | 6 | 81 | 18 | 5 | 77 | 19 | 5 | 76 | 14 | 9 | 77 |
| 8 | 19 | 8 | 73 | 21 | 10 | 69 | 20 | 7 | 73 | 17 | 6 | 77 | 22 | 5 | 74 | 22 | 6 | 72 | 18 | 9 | 73 |
| 9 | 23 | 8 | 69 | 27 | 9 | 64 | 25 | 7 | 68 | 22 | 6 | 72 | 25 | 5 | 70 | 26 | 6 | 68 | 22 | 10 | 69 |
| 10 | 28 | 8 | 64 | 33 | 9 | 58 | 32 | 7 | 61 | 27 | 7 | 66 | 29 | 5 | 66 | 30 | 6 | 63 | 26 | 10 | 64 |
| 11 | 33 | 8 | 59 | 40 | 8 | 51 | 39 | 7 | 54 | 33 | 7 | 60 | 33 | 5 | 62 | 35 | 7 | 58 | 31 | 10 | 59 |
| 12 | 39 | 8 | 54 | 48 | 8 | 45 | 47 | 7 | 46 | 40 | 7 | 54 | 38 | 5 | 57 | 40 | 7 | 53 | 36 | 10 | 53 |
| 13 | 45 | 8 | 48 | 55 | 7 | 38 | 55 | 7 | 39 | 46 | 6 | 47 | 43 | 4 | 53 | 45 | 7 | 48 | 42 | 10 | 48 |
| 14 | 50 | 7 | 42 | 62 | 6 | 31 | 62 | 6 | 31 | 54 | 6 | 40 | 48 | 4 | 48 | 50 | 7 | 43 | 48 | 10 | 42 |
| 15 | 56 | 7 | 37 | 69 | 5 | 26 | 69 | 6 | 25 | 60 | 6 | 34 | 53 | 4 | 43 | 56 | 7 | 38 | 54 | 10 | 37 |
| HUSB EMPLOYEE  NO | 6 | 9 | 85 | 4 | 10 | 86 | 4 | 5 | 90 | 5 | 6 | 90 | 12 | 6 | 82 | 10 | 7 | 83 | 6 | 10 | 84 |
| YES | 9 | 5 | 86 | 6 | 6 | 88 | 6 | 4 | 90 | 6 | 4 | 91 | 15 | 4 | 80 | 13 | 4 | 84 | 9 | 5 | 86 |
| ASSET $ 0 | 9 | 7 | 85 | 5 | 10 | 85 | 6 | 5 | 90 | 6 | 5 | 89 | 17 | 5 | 79 | 16 | 5 | 80 | 8 | 8 | 84 |
| INCOME  500 | 9 | 7 | 85 | 5 | 9 | 86 | 6 | 5 | 90 | 6 | 5 | 89 | 16 | 5 | 79 | 15 | 5 | 80 | 8 | 7 | 84 |
| 1000 | 9 | 7 | 85 | 5 | 9 | 86 | 6 | 5 | 90 | 6 | 5 | 90 | 16 | 5 | 79 | 15 | 5 | 80 | 8 | 7 | 84 |
| 1500 | 8 | 7 | 85 | 5 | 9 | 86 | 5 | 5 | 90 | 6 | 5 | 90 | 16 | 5 | 79 | 15 | 5 | 80 | 8 | 7 | 85 |
| 2500 | 8 | 6 | 85 | 5 | 9 | 87 | 5 | 5 | 90 | 5 | 5 | 90 | 16 | 5 | 80 | 15 | 5 | 81 | 8 | 7 | 85 |
| 5000 | 8 | 6 | 86 | 4 | 8 | 88 | 5 | 4 | 90 | 5 | 4 | 90 | 15 | 5 | 80 | 13 | 5 | 82 | 7 | 7 | 86 |
| 10000 | 7 | 6 | 87 | 3 | 6 | 90 | 4 | 4 | 91 | 5 | 4 | 92 | 14 | 5 | 81 | 11 | 5 | 84 | 6 | 6 | 88 |
| 15000 | 6 | 6 | 88 | 3 | 5 | 92 | 4 | 4 | 92 | 4 | 3 | 92 | 13 | 5 | 82 | 10 | 4 | 86 | 5 | 6 | 89 |
| HUSBANDS $ 0 | 9 | 6 | 85 | 5 | 9 | 86 | 6 | 5 | 90 | 6 | 4 | 90 | 16 | 4 | 80 | 14 | 4 | 82 | 9 | 7 | 84 |
| EARNINGS  500 | 9 | 6 | 85 | 5 | 9 | 86 | 6 | 5 | 90 | 6 | 4 | 90 | 16 | 4 | 80 | 14 | 4 | 82 | 9 | 7 | 84 |
| 1000 | 9 | 6 | 85 | 5 | 9 | 86 | 6 | 5 | 90 | 6 | 4 | 90 | 16 | 4 | 80 | 14 | 4 | 82 | 9 | 7 | 84 |
| 1500 | 9 | 6 | 85 | 5 | 9 | 86 | 6 | 5 | 90 | 6 | 4 | 90 | 16 | 4 | 80 | 14 | 4 | 82 | 9 | 7 | 84 |
| 2500 | 9 | 6 | 85 | 5 | 9 | 86 | 6 | 5 | 90 | 6 | 4 | 90 | 16 | 4 | 80 | 14 | 4 | 82 | 9 | 7 | 84 |
| 5000 | 8 | 6 | 85 | 5 | 9 | 87 | 6 | 5 | 90 | 6 | 4 | 90 | 15 | 5 | 80 | 13 | 5 | 82 | 8 | 7 | 85 |
| 10000 | 8 | 6 | 86 | 5 | 8 | 87 | 5 | 5 | 90 | 5 | 4 | 90 | 15 | 5 | 81 | 13 | 5 | 83 | 8 | 7 | 85 |
| 15000 | 8 | 6 | 86 | 4 | 8 | 87 | 5 | 5 | 90 | 5 | 5 | 90 | 14 | 5 | 81 | 12 | 5 | 83 | 7 | 7 | 86 |
| OWN HOME NO | 8 | 6 | 86 | 5 | 7 | 88 | 5 | 5 | 91 | 5 | 5 | 90 | 15 | 6 | 79 | 13 | 5 | 81 | 7 | 6 | 87 |
| OWN HOME YES | 7 | 6 | 86 | 4 | 9 | 86 | 6 | 4 | 90 | 5 | 4 | 91 | 13 | 4 | 83 | 11 | 4 | 85 | 7 | 7 | 85 |
| ROOMS IN HOME  1 | 10 | 8 | 82 | 6 | 10 | 84 | 7 | 6 | 86 | 7 | 7 | 87 | 15 | 6 | 79 | 19 | 5 | 76 | 9 | 9 | 82 |
| 2 | 10 | 7 | 83 | 5 | 10 | 85 | 7 | 6 | 87 | 6 | 6 | 87 | 15 | 6 | 79 | 17 | 5 | 78 | 8 | 9 | 83 |
| 3 | 9 | 7 | 84 | 5 | 9 | 86 | 6 | 5 | 89 | 6 | 6 | 88 | 15 | 5 | 80 | 15 | 5 | 80 | 8 | 8 | 84 |
| 4 | 8 | 7 | 85 | 5 | 9 | 86 | 6 | 5 | 90 | 6 | 5 | 89 | 14 | 5 | 80 | 13 | 5 | 82 | 8 | 8 | 85 |
| 5 | 8 | 6 | 86 | 5 | 9 | 87 | 5 | 5 | 91 | 5 | 5 | 90 | 14 | 5 | 81 | 12 | 5 | 84 | 7 | 7 | 86 |
| 6 | 7 | 6 | 87 | 4 | 8 | 87 | 5 | 4 | 92 | 5 | 4 | 91 | 14 | 5 | 81 | 11 | 4 | 85 | 7 | 7 | 86 |
| 7 | 7 | 6 | 88 | 4 | 8 | 88 | 4 | 4 | 92 | 5 | 4 | 91 | 14 | 4 | 82 | 9 | 4 | 86 | 7 | 6 | 87 |
| 8 | 6 | 5 | 88 | 4 | 7 | 89 | 4 | 3 | 93 | 4 | 4 | 92 | 14 | 4 | 82 | 8 | 4 | 88 | 6 | 6 | 88 |
| 9 | 6 | 5 | 89 | 4 | 7 | 89 | 3 | 3 | 94 | 4 | 3 | 93 | 13 | 4 | 83 | 7 | 4 | 89 | 6 | 5 | 89 |
| 10 | 5 | 5 | 90 | 4 | 7 | 90 | 3 | 3 | 94 | 4 | 3 | 93 | 13 | 4 | 83 | 6 | 4 | 90 | 6 | 5 | 89 |
| RURAL | 5 | 8 | 87 | 4 | 10 | 86 | 3 | 4 | 93 | 4 | 3 | 93 | 12 | 3 | 85 | 9 | 4 | 86 | 3 | 9 | 87 |
| URBAN | 9 | 6 | 85 | 5 | 5 | 88 | 7 | 5 | 88 | 6 | 5 | 89 | 14 | 5 | 81 | 12 | 5 | 83 | 11 | 6 | 83 |
| AT MEANS $ | 8 | 6 | 86 | 5 | 9 | 87 | 5 | 5 | 90 | 5 | 4 | 90 | 14 | 5 | 81 | 12 | 5 | 84 | 7 | 7 | 86 |
| ACTUAL $ | 9 | 9 | 80 | 9 | 10 | 82 | 11 | 5 | 76 | 10 | 6 | 85 | 15 | 19 | 5 | 78 | | 14 | 8 | 78 |
| OBS | 3741 | 1985 | 23200 | 639 | 706 | 6027 | 325 | 155 | 2522 | 357 | 207 | 3103 | 553 | 149 | 2223 | 1170 | 352 | 5339 | 697 | 414 | 3986 |

The role of education as a determinant of labor force status is of special interest. The effect of education reflects both non-pecuniary factors ("tastes" for market work versus work at home) and pecuniary ones (potential market earnings). It is expected that education would not only be positively related to labor force participation, but would also play an important role in "sorting" working wives between wage work and self-employment. The estimates show that this is indeed the case. In all regions, increasing educational attainment monotonically increases the probability of working and, especially, of working as an employee.

It is important to draw attention to the difference in the effect of schooling on the probabilities of working as an employee and on self-employment. The effect of education is considerably stronger on the former than the latter. Although the education effect is significant in all regions, there are regional variations, particularly on the probability of working as an employee. For example, in Rio and Sao Paulo, the marginal effects of the education variable for employees are 0.024 and 0.020, respectively, suggesting that an additional year of schooling increases the probability of being an employee by about 2 percent. For the self-employed, an additional year of schooling increases the probability by 0.8 and 0.4 percent in Rio and Sao Paulo, respectively. In the other regions, the partial derivatives of education for employees range from 0.013 to .016, while those for the self-employed (0.003 to 0.005) are similar to Sao Paulo.

A better picture of the prominent role of education in determining labor market status can be obtained by looking at the predicted probabilities in Table 3.3. A cursory examination shows that an additional year of schooling (especially in excess of 5 years) not only increases the probability of participation, but more importantly, the probability of working as an employee. For example, nationally, an increase in schooling from 5 to 6 years increases the participation probability by 3 percentage points, but only as an employee. Similarly, an increase from 10 to 11 years raises the probability by 5 percentage points, again as an employee. In sum, the principal effect of education is to increase the propensity of wives to work as employees. The schooling effects on self-employment are very small. Of course, the force of schooling effects on labor market status is linked to the role of education in determining the market wage, which is a major incentive for a woman to enter the labor force.

*Married men* (Tables 3.4 and 3.5). The estimated parameters of the logit function for married men look reasonable and most variables are significant determinants of labor force status.

In most instances (Rio is the exception), having a working wife does not have a statistically significant effect on the work-status of the husband. We also see that household size affects the husband's work-status in selected regions -- the Northeast, Other Southeast, Sao Paulo and the South. The larger the household the more likely it is that a married man will be an employee. The effects of living in an urban area on work status are significant in most cases. Generally, a husband who lives in an urban area is more likely to be an employee, and less likely to be self-employed. This may reflect the more plentiful wage work opportunities in urban areas. The strength of the effects of the urban variable, however, is not uniform across regions. As expected, home ownership and his non-labor income have retarding effects on working either as an employee or a self-employed worker.

Age generally has the expected effect in most cases. Exceptions are in Rio, where the coefficient of age is not statistically significant for both types of workers, in the Other Southeast, where it is not significant for employees, and in Sao Paulo where it is not significant for the self-employed.

## Table 3.4
### Multinational Logit Estimates of Labor Force Participation by Region - Married Men

| REGION | CONSTANT | AMIL SIZE | AGE | AGESQ /100 | YEARS CHOO | WIFE WORKS | OTHER INCOME /100000 | OWN HOME | URBAN |
|---|---|---|---|---|---|---|---|---|---|
| **ALL BRAZIL** Non-work n = 2920 | -2LLKFULL = 43838.9 | | -2LLKRESTR = 54587.5 | | | | | | |
| Employee | 3.720 | 0.031 | 0.027 | -0.143 | 0.110 | 0.019 | -1.989 | -0.535 | -0.160 |
| n = 14596 | (11.17) | (3.72) | (1.96) | (10.09) | (14.38) | (0.30) | (14.42) | (10.07) | (2.57) |
| derivative x 100 | | 0.270 | -0.020 | -0.870 | 1.690 | 0.900 | -18.710 | -20.990 | 30.440 |
| Self-employed | 3.612 | 0.022 | 0.032 | -0.122 | 0.047 | -0.020 | -1.399 | 0.347 | -1.560 |
| n = 11410 | (11.08) | (2.75) | (2.36) | (9.16) | (6.08) | (0.30) | (10.54) | (6.43) | (26.05) |
| derivative x 100 | | -0.130 | 0.170 | 0.190 | -1.270 | -0.890 | 9.870 | 20.250 | -34.420 |
| **NORTHEAST** Non-work n = 758 | -2LLKFULL = 10897.1 | | -2LLKRESTR = 13741.8 | | | | | | |
| Employee | 1.824 | 0.030 | 0.078 | -0.182 | 0.141 | -0.162 | -3.279 | -0.431 | 0.034 |
| n = 2590 | (3.21) | (1.92) | (3.20) | (7.22) | (7.33) | (1.27) | (6.62) | (4.02) | (0.31) |
| derivative x 100 | | 0.230 | 0.310 | -1.000 | 2.740 | -0.750 | 0.590 | -19.430 | 25.040 |
| Self-employed | 2.429 | 0.021 | 0.071 | -0.152 | 0.021 | -0.142 | -3.660 | 0.481 | -1.197 |
| n = 4026 | (4.54) | (1.45) | (3.21) | (6.94) | (1.05) | (1.17) | (6.70) | (4.59) | (11.87) |
| derivative x 100 | | -0.090 | 0.130 | 0.020 | -2.360 | -0.150 | -21.650 | 20.320 | -29.520 |
| **NORTHWEST** Non-work n = 202 | -2LLKFULL = 4283.7 | | -2LLKRESTR = 5349.7 | | | | | | |
| Employee | 1.359 | -0.015 | 0.156 | -0.273 | 0.145 | 0.037 | -2.742 | -0.654 | -0.291 |
| n = 1307 | (1.28) | (0.57) | (3.25) | (5.41) | (4.59) | (0.14) | (5.07) | (3.30) | (1.36) |
| derivative x 100 | | -0.090 | 0.230 | -0.940 | 2.890 | 3.590 | -25.540 | -29.190 | 24.270 |
| Self-employed | 1.398 | -0.012 | 0.156 | -0.251 | 0.029 | -0.117 | -1.821 | 0.570 | -1.365 |
| n = 1493 | (1.36) | (0.49) | (3.42) | (5.35) | (0.93) | (0.45) | (3.65) | (2.88) | (6.66) |
| derivative x 100 | | 0.040 | 0.310 | 0.020 | -2.600 | -3.760 | 17.690 | 29.250 | -27.340 |
| **OTHER SOUTHEAST** Non-work n = 362 | -2LLKFULL = 5670.6 | | -2LLKRESTR = 6891.4 | | | | | | |
| Employee | 2.795 | 0.092 | 0.049 | -0.152 | 0.159 | -0.032 | -3.464 | -0.478 | -0.525 |
| n = 1863 | (3.07) | (3.73) | (1.26) | (3.90) | (5.66) | (0.16) | (6.36) | (3.18) | (2.96) |
| derivative x 100 | | 0.850 | -0.600 | -0.280 | 0.350 | -0.360 | -16.910 | -19.220 | 28.760 |
| Self-employed | 1.879 | 0.065 | 0.082 | -0.159 | 0.162 | -0.019 | -3.128 | 0.330 | -1.888 |
| n = 1442 | (2.08) | (2.65) | (2.16) | (4.21) | (5.75) | (0.10) | (5.77) | (2.15) | (10.87) |
| derivative x 100 | | -0.460 | 0.910 | -0.480 | 0.430 | 0.240 | 0.760 | 18.610 | -34.230 |
| **RIO DE JANEIRO** Non-work n = 416 | -2LLKFULL = 4298.7 | | -2LLKRESTR = 5096.0 | | | | | | |
| Employee | 4.659 | 0.030 | -0.026 | -0.085 | 0.108 | 0.450 | -1.762 | -0.374 | -0.325 |
| n = 1933 | (4.67) | (1.29) | (0.64) | (2.08) | (6.52) | (2.69) | (5.93) | (2.70) | (1.37) |
| derivative x 100 | | 0.650 | -0.070 | -0.970 | 1.320 | 7.190 | -33.360 | -6.950 | 2.320 |
| Self-employed | 3.552 | -0.002 | -0.031 | -0.052 | 0.061 | 0.145 | -0.229 | -0.058 | -0.594 |
| n = 576 | (3.43) | (0.08) | (0.74) | (1.25) | (3.45) | (0.79) | (0.92) | (0.38) | (2.36) |
| derivative x 100 | | -0.490 | -0.130 | 0.410 | -0.620 | -4.440 | 23.190 | 4.770 | -5.150 |
| **SAO PAULO** Non-work n = 680 | -2LLKFULL = 10019.9 | | -2LLKRESTR = 11848.0 | | | | | | |
| Employee | 7.982 | 0.047 | -0.112 | -0.015 | 0.085 | 0.012 | -1.672 | -0.343 | -0.781 |
| n = 4405 | (8.97) | (2.62) | (3.20) | (0.43) | (6.16) | (0.09) | (7.96) | (3.18) | (4.06) |
| derivative x 100 | | 0.840 | -1.670 | 0.890 | 0.410 | 1.370 | -23.340 | -8.660 | 9.280 |
| Self-employed | 5.569 | 0.010 | -0.040 | -0.064 | 0.075 | -0.059 | -0.673 | 0.065 | -1.374 |
| n = 1776 | (6.19) | (0.53) | (1.12) | (1.81) | (5.35) | (0.44) | (4.15) | (0.58) | (7.12) |
| derivative x 100 | | -0.700 | 1.330 | -0.990 | -0.110 | -1.400 | 18.320 | 7.840 | -12.740 |
| **SOUTH** Non-work n = 502 | -2LLKFULL = 7402.2 | | -2LLKRESTR = 9614.9 | | | | | | |
| Employee | 2.945 | 0.054 | 0.074 | -0.201 | 0.106 | 0.117 | -3.928 | -0.820 | 0.064 |
| n = 2498 | (3.42) | (2.29) | (2.02) | (5.34) | (5.03) | (0.73) | (8.39) | (5.61) | (0.43) |
| derivative x 100 | | 0.280 | -0.110 | -0.910 | 0.740 | -1.030 | -4.240 | -23.570 | 38.530 |
| Self-employed | 2.475 | 0.047 | 0.087 | -0.182 | 0.084 | 0.175 | -4.150 | 0.137 | -1.634 |
| n = 2097 | (2.94) | (2.02) | (2.46) | (5.14) | (3.96) | (1.09) | (8.46) | (0.92) | (11.55) |
| derivative x 100 | | -0.060 | 0.460 | 0.070 | -0.320 | 1.660 | -13.440 | 21.910 | -41.690 |

Notes: The numbers in parentheses are t-statistics.

The numbers below the t-statistics are the partial derivatives x 100 evaluated at the sample means.

**Table 3.5**
**Logit Simulations: Probabilities of Labor Force Participation (%) - Married Men**
E = Employee; S = Self-employed; N = Non-worker

| REGION | | ALL BRAZIL | | | NORTH-EAST | | | NORTH-WEST | | | OTHER SOUTHEAST | | | RIO | | | SAO PAULO | | | SOUTH | | |
|---|---|---|---|---|---|---|---|---|---|---|---|---|---|---|---|---|---|---|---|---|---|---|
| WORK STATUS | | E | S | N | E | S | N | E | S | N | E | S | N | E | S | N | E | S | N | E | S | N |
| FAMILY SIZE | 2 | 51 | 43 | 6 | 33 | 60 | 7 | 44 | 52 | 3 | 49 | 44 | 8 | 67 | 24 | 9 | 64 | 32 | 4 | 50 | 44 | 6 |
| | 4 | 52 | 42 | 6 | 33 | 60 | 7 | 44 | 53 | 3 | 50 | 43 | 7 | 68 | 23 | 8 | 66 | 30 | 4 | 50 | 44 | 5 |
| | 6 | 52 | 42 | 6 | 34 | 60 | 7 | 44 | 53 | 4 | 52 | 42 | 6 | 70 | 22 | 8 | 67 | 29 | 4 | 51 | 44 | 5 |
| | 8 | 53 | 42 | 5 | 34 | 60 | 6 | 44 | 53 | 4 | 54 | 41 | 5 | 71 | 21 | 8 | 69 | 27 | 4 | 52 | 44 | 4 |
| | 10 | 53 | 41 | 5 | 35 | 59 | 6 | 43 | 53 | 4 | 55 | 40 | 4 | 72 | 20 | 7 | 71 | 26 | 3 | 52 | 44 | 4 |
| AGE | 15 | 66 | 33 | 1 | 43 | 54 | 3 | 52 | 45 | 3 | 72 | 26 | 2 | 82 | 17 | 1 | 88 | 12 | 0 | 67 | 31 | 2 |
| | 20 | 64 | 34 | 1 | 43 | 55 | 3 | 52 | 46 | 2 | 69 | 29 | 2 | 81 | 17 | 1 | 84 | 16 | 0 | 65 | 33 | 2 |
| | 25 | 63 | 36 | 2 | 42 | 56 | 3 | 50 | 48 | 2 | 66 | 32 | 2 | 80 | 18 | 2 | 80 | 19 | 1 | 63 | 35 | 2 |
| | 30 | 60 | 37 | 2 | 41 | 57 | 3 | 49 | 49 | 2 | 62 | 35 | 2 | 79 | 19 | 3 | 76 | 23 | 1 | 60 | 38 | 2 |
| | 35 | 58 | 39 | 3 | 39 | 58 | 3 | 47 | 51 | 2 | 59 | 39 | 3 | 76 | 20 | 4 | 72 | 26 | 2 | 57 | 41 | 2 |
| | 40 | 55 | 41 | 4 | 37 | 59 | 4 | 45 | 53 | 2 | 55 | 42 | 4 | 73 | 21 | 6 | 67 | 29 | 3 | 53 | 44 | 3 |
| | 45 | 51 | 43 | 6 | 34 | 60 | 6 | 42 | 55 | 3 | 51 | 44 | 5 | 69 | 22 | 9 | 62 | 32 | 6 | 49 | 46 | 5 |
| | 50 | 47 | 44 | 9 | 31 | 60 | 8 | 39 | 56 | 5 | 46 | 46 | 7 | 63 | 23 | 14 | 57 | 33 | 10 | 44 | 48 | 8 |
| | 55 | 41 | 44 | 15 | 27 | 60 | 13 | 35 | 56 | 9 | 41 | 47 | 12 | 55 | 23 | 22 | 50 | 32 | 17 | 38 | 49 | 13 |
| | 60 | 34 | 42 | 25 | 23 | 57 | 21 | 29 | 54 | 17 | 35 | 46 | 19 | 45 | 22 | 33 | 42 | 30 | 28 | 30 | 47 | 23 |
| | 65 | 25 | 36 | 39 | 17 | 50 | 33 | 22 | 46 | 32 | 28 | 42 | 30 | 33 | 19 | 47 | 33 | 25 | 42 | 21 | 39 | 40 |
| | 70 | 16 | 27 | 57 | 11 | 39 | 50 | 13 | 32 | 55 | 20 | 33 | 47 | 22 | 15 | 63 | 24 | 18 | 58 | 12 | 27 | 61 |
| | 75 | 8 | 17 | 75 | 6 | 25 | 69 | 6 | 16 | 78 | 12 | 22 | 66 | 13 | 11 | 76 | 15 | 12 | 73 | 5 | 15 | 80 |
| SCHOOL YEARS | 0 | 46 | 47 | 7 | 28 | 64 | 7 | 34 | 61 | 5 | 52 | 40 | 9 | 61 | 26 | 13 | 66 | 28 | 6 | 48 | 45 | 7 |
| | 1 | 48 | 45 | 7 | 31 | 62 | 7 | 37 | 59 | 4 | 52 | 40 | 7 | 63 | 25 | 12 | 67 | 28 | 5 | 49 | 45 | 6 |
| | 2 | 50 | 44 | 6 | 34 | 60 | 6 | 39 | 56 | 4 | 53 | 41 | 6 | 64 | 24 | 11 | 67 | 28 | 5 | 50 | 45 | 6 |
| | 3 | 51 | 43 | 6 | 36 | 58 | 6 | 42 | 54 | 4 | 53 | 41 | 5 | 66 | 24 | 10 | 67 | 28 | 4 | 51 | 44 | 5 |
| | 4 | 53 | 42 | 5 | 39 | 55 | 6 | 45 | 51 | 3 | 53 | 42 | 5 | 67 | 23 | 10 | 68 | 28 | 4 | 51 | 44 | 5 |
| | 5 | 55 | 40 | 5 | 42 | 53 | 5 | 48 | 49 | 3 | 54 | 42 | 4 | 69 | 23 | 9 | 68 | 28 | 4 | 52 | 44 | 4 |
| | 6 | 56 | 39 | 5 | 45 | 50 | 5 | 51 | 46 | 3 | 54 | 43 | 3 | 70 | 22 | 8 | 69 | 28 | 4 | 53 | 43 | 4 |
| | 7 | 58 | 38 | 4 | 48 | 47 | 5 | 54 | 43 | 3 | 54 | 43 | 3 | 71 | 21 | 7 | 69 | 28 | 3 | 53 | 43 | 4 |
| | 8 | 60 | 37 | 4 | 51 | 45 | 4 | 57 | 41 | 2 | 54 | 43 | 3 | 73 | 21 | 7 | 69 | 28 | 3 | 54 | 43 | 3 |
| | 9 | 61 | 35 | 4 | 54 | 42 | 4 | 60 | 38 | 2 | 54 | 43 | 2 | 74 | 20 | 6 | 70 | 27 | 3 | 55 | 42 | 3 |
| | 10 | 63 | 34 | 3 | 57 | 39 | 4 | 63 | 35 | 2 | 55 | 44 | 2 | 75 | 20 | 6 | 70 | 27 | 3 | 56 | 42 | 3 |
| | 11 | 64 | 33 | 3 | 60 | 37 | 3 | 65 | 33 | 2 | 55 | 44 | 2 | 76 | 19 | 5 | 71 | 27 | 2 | 56 | 41 | 2 |
| | 12 | 66 | 31 | 3 | 63 | 34 | 3 | 68 | 31 | 2 | 55 | 44 | 1 | 77 | 18 | 5 | 71 | 27 | 2 | 57 | 41 | 2 |
| | 13 | 67 | 30 | 3 | 66 | 31 | 3 | 70 | 28 | 1 | 55 | 44 | 1 | 78 | 18 | 4 | 71 | 27 | 2 | 57 | 41 | 2 |
| | 14 | 69 | 29 | 2 | 69 | 29 | 2 | 73 | 26 | 1 | 55 | 44 | 1 | 79 | 17 | 4 | 71 | 27 | 2 | 58 | 40 | 2 |
| | 15 | 70 | 28 | 2 | 71 | 27 | 2 | 75 | 24 | 1 | 55 | 45 | 1 | 80 | 16 | 3 | 72 | 27 | 2 | 59 | 40 | 2 |
| WIFE WORKS | NO | 53 | 42 | 5 | 34 | 60 | 6 | 43 | 53 | 4 | 53 | 42 | 5 | 68 | 23 | 9 | 68 | 28 | 4 | 52 | 44 | 5 |
| WIFE WORKS | YES | 53 | 41 | 5 | 33 | 59 | 7 | 47 | 50 | 4 | 53 | 42 | 5 | 75 | 19 | 6 | 69 | 27 | 4 | 51 | 45 | 4 |
| OTHER $ INCOME | 0 | 54 | 41 | 5 | 34 | 60 | 6 | 45 | 52 | 3 | 54 | 42 | 4 | 74 | 19 | 7 | 71 | 26 | 3 | 52 | 45 | 4 |
| | 500 | 54 | 41 | 5 | 34 | 60 | 6 | 45 | 52 | 3 | 54 | 42 | 4 | 74 | 19 | 7 | 71 | 26 | 3 | 52 | 45 | 4 |
| | 1000 | 54 | 41 | 5 | 34 | 60 | 6 | 45 | 52 | 3 | 54 | 42 | 4 | 74 | 19 | 7 | 71 | 26 | 3 | 52 | 45 | 4 |
| | 1500 | 54 | 41 | 5 | 34 | 60 | 6 | 45 | 52 | 3 | 54 | 42 | 5 | 74 | 19 | 7 | 71 | 26 | 3 | 52 | 45 | 4 |
| | 2500 | 54 | 41 | 5 | 34 | 60 | 6 | 44 | 52 | 3 | 54 | 42 | 5 | 73 | 20 | 7 | 70 | 26 | 3 | 52 | 44 | 4 |
| | 5000 | 53 | 42 | 5 | 34 | 59 | 7 | 44 | 53 | 4 | 53 | 42 | 5 | 72 | 20 | 7 | 70 | 27 | 3 | 51 | 44 | 4 |
| | 7500 | 53 | 42 | 5 | 34 | 59 | 7 | 43 | 53 | 4 | 53 | 42 | 5 | 72 | 21 | 7 | 69 | 27 | 4 | 51 | 44 | 5 |
| | 10000 | 52 | 42 | 6 | 34 | 58 | 8 | 42 | 54 | 4 | 53 | 42 | 6 | 71 | 21 | 8 | 69 | 28 | 4 | 51 | 43 | 5 |
| | 12500 | 52 | 42 | 6 | 34 | 57 | 9 | 42 | 54 | 4 | 52 | 42 | 6 | 70 | 22 | 8 | 68 | 28 | 4 | 51 | 43 | 6 |
| | 15000 | 51 | 43 | 6 | 34 | 57 | 9 | 41 | 54 | 5 | 52 | 42 | 7 | 69 | 23 | 8 | 67 | 29 | 4 | 51 | 43 | 7 |
| OWN HOME | NO | 65 | 30 | 5 | 48 | 45 | 7 | 62 | 35 | 3 | 64 | 31 | 5 | 74 | 19 | 7 | 73 | 24 | 3 | 66 | 30 | 3 |
| OWN HOME | YES | 45 | 50 | 6 | 28 | 66 | 6 | 33 | 63 | 4 | 45 | 49 | 5 | 67 | 24 | 9 | 64 | 32 | 4 | 43 | 51 | 5 |
| RURAL | | 32 | 65 | 3 | 23 | 73 | 4 | 30 | 68 | 2 | 34 | 64 | 2 | 67 | 27 | 6 | 58 | 40 | 2 | 28 | 69 | 3 |
| URBAN | | 62 | 31 | 7 | 47 | 44 | 9 | 53 | 42 | 5 | 62 | 30 | 7 | 70 | 21 | 8 | 69 | 26 | 4 | 65 | 29 | 6 |
| AT MEANS % | | 53 | 42 | 5 | 34 | 60 | 6 | 44 | 53 | 4 | 53 | 42 | 5 | 70 | 22 | 8 | 68 | 28 | 4 | 51 | 44 | 5 |
| ACTUAL % | | 50 | 39 | 10 | 35 | 55 | 10 | 44 | 50 | 7 | 51 | 39 | 10 | 66 | 20 | 14 | 64 | 26 | 10 | 49 | 41 | 10 |
| OBS | | 14596 | 11410 | 2920 | 2590 | 4026 | 758 | 1307 | 1493 | 202 | 1863 | 1442 | 362 | 1933 | 576 | 416 | 4405 | 1776 | 680 | 2498 | *** | 502 |

As was the case for wives, the estimates show that schooling proves to be an effective explanatory variable in sorting husbands between wage work and self-employment. Looking at the predicted probabilities (Table 3.5), we see that additional years of schooling result in consistent increases in the probability that a working husband is an employee. This is usually matched by decreases in the probability that he is self-employed. Of course, the strength of the schooling effects varies from region to region.

*Single women*[24] (Table 3.6 and Table 3.7). The logit estimates for single women show that the children variables play a minor role in determining labor force status. The coefficient on the babies variable is statistically significant in only two regions (Northwest and South) and for employees only. Similarly, the coefficient on the toddlers variable is not significant in most regions, but it is puzzlingly significant and positive for employees in the Northeast. The presence of school-age children makes participation more likely as an employee in Rio and as a self-employed worker in Sao Paulo. Household size generally does not have a significant (positive) impact, except in the South and in Sao Paulo for wage work only. Age effects are generally present, as expected, for both employees and self-employed women. The coefficients of asset/transfer income and of home ownership have the predicted negative coefficients, but only in determining work as an employee. However, these tend to have a positive effect on the probability of self-employment. Overall, however, the strength of the effects is small. The proxy for housework and number of rooms tends to discourage working, especially as an employee. Living in an urban area has a strong positive impact on working as an employee, and a negative effect on self-employment.

Finally, we remark on the important role of education in determining labor force status. As was the case for married women, increasing school attainment increases the probability of working, but mostly as an employee. Only in the Northeast does education have a positive effect on self-employment. It is interesting to note that regional differences in schooling effects are not as strong among single women as among married women. For example, in Rio and Sao Paulo, the marginal effects of the education variable for employees are 0.029 and 0.031, respectively, suggesting that an additional year of schooling increases the probability of being an employee by about 3 percent. In the other regions, the partial derivatives of education for employees range from 0.025 to 0.039. The predicted probabilities in Table 3.7 show that an additional year of schooling in excess of 5 years increases the probability of working as an employee from 28 percent to 32 percent. Similarly, an increase from 10 to 11 years raises the probability from 48 percent to 52 percent. In sum, the main effect of education is to increase the propensity of single women to work as employees.

*Single men* (Tables 3.8 and 3.9). The estimates for single men reflect the choice between working as an employee or being self-employed. Unfortunately, the set of regressors excludes household characteristics and, perhaps more important, migrant status because no information was provided in the data set. Nationally, 41 percent of the men did not complete any schooling, especially those who were self-employed -- 64 percent versus 33 percent for employees. In the Northeast the respective proportions rise to 84 percent and 53 percent, while in Rio and Sao Paulo they are 37 percent and 25 percent.

---

[24]   The reader should note the small number of self-employed single women in the Northwest, the Other Southeast, and Rio. We do not comment on these results for obvious reasons.

## Table 3.6
### Multinominal Logit Estimates of Labor Force Participation by Region - Single Women

| REGION | CONSTAN | KIDS 0-2 | KIDS 3-5 | KIDS 6-14 | FAMILY SIZE | AGE | AGESQ /100 | YEARS SCHOOL | OTHER INCOME '00000 | OWN HOME | ROOMS N HOME | URBAN |
|---|---|---|---|---|---|---|---|---|---|---|---|---|
| ALL BRAZIL | -2LLKFULL = 16074.74   -2LLKRESTR = 19320.57 | | | | | | | | | | | |
| Non-work n = 6601 | | | | | | | | | | | | |
| Employee | -7.493 | -0.199 | -0.042 | 0.055 | 0.067 | 0.424 | -0.634 | 0.167 | -0.531 | -0.291 | -0.176 | 1.258 |
| n = 3871 | (27.22) | (3.66) | (0.81) | (2.24) | (4.62) | (20.70) | (17.25) | (21.50) | (6.21) | (5.71) | (14.47) | (18.41) |
| derivative x 100 | | -4.190 | -1.190 | 1.060 | 1.410 | 8.610 | -12.960 | 3.620 | -11.310 | -6.760 | -3.630 | 28.340 |
| Self-employed | -5.010 | -0.017 | 0.187 | 0.059 | 0.002 | 0.242 | -0.313 | -0.048 | 0.031 | 0.375 | -0.067 | -1.048 |
| n = 753 | (12.32) | (0.20) | (2.37) | (1.46) | (0.08) | (8.57) | (6.64) | (3.19) | (0.23) | (3.78) | (3.20) | (11.38) |
| derivative x 100 | | 0.230 | 0.990 | 0.200 | -0.100 | 0.520 | -0.530 | -0.500 | 0.990 | 2.300 | -0.050 | -7.130 |
| NORTHEAST | -2LLKFULL = 3987.47   -2LLKRESTR = 4848.33 | | | | | | | | | | | |
| Non-work n = 2156 | | | | | | | | | | | | |
| Employee | -8.832 | -0.114 | 0.229 | 0.102 | 0.028 | 0.437 | -0.616 | 0.213 | -1.042 | -0.285 | -0.088 | 0.849 |
| n = 561 | (14.06) | (1.01) | (2.18) | (1.98) | (0.89) | (9.93) | (8.18) | (12.26) | (3.71) | (2.34) | (3.19) | (5.90) |
| derivative x 100 | | -1.300 | 2.410 | 1.250 | 0.270 | 4.730 | -6.690 | 2.510 | -10.770 | -3.800 | -0.950 | 10.420 |
| Self-employed | -4.731 | 0.006 | 0.169 | -0.085 | 0.048 | 0.202 | -0.260 | -0.092 | -0.941 | 0.540 | -0.039 | -0.762 |
| n = 328 | (7.63) | (0.05) | (1.46) | (1.48) | (1.28) | (4.77) | (3.72) | (3.37) | (1.45) | (3.13) | (1.15) | (5.02) |
| derivative x 100 | | 0.170 | 1.040 | -0.760 | 0.330 | 1.070 | -1.310 | -0.930 | -6.040 | 4.420 | -0.200 | -6.720 |
| NORTHWEST | -2LLKFULL = 1176.68   -2LLKRESTR = 1497.97 | | | | | | | | | | | |
| Non-work n = 646 | | | | | | | | | | | | |
| Employee | -9.259 | -0.329 | -0.276 | 0.055 | 0.086 | 0.501 | -0.760 | 0.196 | -0.980 | -0.536 | -0.087 | 1.303 |
| n = 287 | (7.82) | (1.91) | (1.53) | (0.68) | (1.66) | (5.35) | (4.27) | (6.58) | (2.65) | (2.82) | (2.03) | (5.41) |
| derivative x 100 | | -5.890 | -5.150 | 0.670 | 1.660 | 8.860 | -13.530 | 3.680 | -18.330 | -9.420 | -1.590 | 24.150 |
| Self-employed | -8.853 | -0.230 | 0.152 | 0.540 | -0.160 | 0.516 | -0.650 | -0.158 | 0.660 | -0.662 | -0.015 | -0.468 |
| n = 42 | (4.37) | (0.60) | (0.46) | (3.08) | (1.43) | (3.42) | (2.48) | (2.42) | (1.63) | (1.70) | (0.20) | (1.26) |
| derivative x 100 | | -0.360 | 0.530 | 1.280 | -0.440 | 0.950 | -1.120 | -0.500 | 2.190 | -1.290 | 0.020 | -1.920 |
| OTHER SOUTHEAST | -2LLKFULL = 2261.91   -2LLKRESTR = 2709.81 | | | | | | | | | | | |
| Non-work n = 1086 | | | | | | | | | | | | |
| Employee | -7.687 | 0.150 | -0.019 | 0.083 | 0.037 | 0.430 | -0.643 | 0.144 | -0.835 | -0.208 | -0.170 | 1.688 |
| n = 581 | (11.19) | (1.07) | (0.14) | (1.34) | (0.96) | (8.56) | (7.17) | (6.96) | (2.98) | (1.56) | (5.62) | (9.48) |
| derivative x 100 | | 2.590 | -0.380 | 1.480 | 0.890 | 8.590 | -12.870 | 2.940 | -17.150 | -4.610 | -3.320 | 35.270 |
| Self-employed | -4.410 | 0.571 | -0.009 | 0.257 | -0.153 | 0.243 | -0.331 | -0.002 | 0.079 | 0.427 | -0.174 | -0.902 |
| n = 65 | (3.19) | (2.09) | (0.03) | (1.75) | (1.63) | (2.48) | (1.99) | (0.03) | (0.16) | (1.36) | (2.39) | (2.97) |
| derivative x 100 | | 1.500 | -0.010 | 0.660 | -0.470 | 0.330 | -0.400 | -0.120 | 0.930 | 1.390 | -0.350 | -3.970 |
| RIO DE JANIERO | -2LLKFULL = 1490.41   -2LLKRESTR = 1836.19 | | | | | | | | | | | |
| Non-work n = 697 | | | | | | | | | | | | |
| Employee | -10.629 | -0.092 | 0.077 | 0.266 | -0.007 | 0.729 | -1.097 | 0.126 | -0.432 | -0.181 | -0.192 | 0.389 |
| n = 453 | (11.12) | (0.48) | (0.47) | (3.12) | (0.14) | (10.34) | (8.75) | (5.09) | (1.72) | (1.19) | (4.58) | (1.18) |
| derivative x 100 | | -2.440 | 1.540 | 5.690 | -0.080 | 16.130 | -24.370 | 2.860 | -10.230 | -4.410 | -4.340 | 9.050 |
| Self-employed | -10.014 | 0.393 | 0.213 | 0.386 | -0.071 | 0.472 | -0.617 | -0.009 | 0.455 | 0.334 | -0.014 | -0.243 |
| n = 32 | (5.03) | (1.08) | (0.56) | (1.94) | (0.59) | (3.62) | (2.95) | (0.15) | (1.46) | (0.76) | (0.15) | (0.36) |
| derivative x 100 | | 1.080 | 0.470 | 0.740 | -0.170 | 0.540 | -0.570 | -0.140 | 1.550 | 1.010 | 0.140 | -0.970 |
| SAO PAULO | -2LLKFULL = 3614.49   -2LLKRESTR = 4224.22 | | | | | | | | | | | |
| Non-work n = 1043 | | | | | | | | | | | | |
| Employee | -7.237 | -0.186 | -0.153 | 0.070 | 0.153 | 0.467 | -0.706 | 0.123 | -0.971 | -0.179 | -0.192 | 0.911 |
| n = 1391 | (13.06) | (1.51) | (1.30) | (1.32) | (5.03) | (11.33) | (9.56) | (7.67) | (5.84) | (1.78) | (7.28) | (5.57) |
| derivative x 100 | | -4.690 | -4.180 | 1.130 | 3.850 | 10.580 | -16.210 | 3.090 | -23.820 | -4.880 | -4.630 | 24.390 |
| Self-employed | -8.383 | 0.055 | 0.209 | 0.309 | -0.034 | 0.480 | -0.615 | -0.027 | -0.056 | 0.242 | -0.044 | -1.014 |
| n = 109 | (7.88) | (0.20) | (0.82) | (2.59) | (0.49) | (6.80) | (5.40) | (0.85) | (0.23) | (0.99) | (0.84) | (3.91) |
| derivative x 400 | | 0.540 | 0.990 | 0.890 | -0.410 | 0.690 | -0.680 | -0.330 | 1.690 | 1.150 | 0.220 | -5.130 |
| SOUTH | -2LLKFULL = 2684.34   -2LLKRESTR = 3233.61 | | | | | | | | | | | |
| Non-work n = 973 | | | | | | | | | | | | |
| Employee | -7.262 | -0.310 | -0.087 | -0.002 | 0.159 | 0.368 | -0.550 | 0.175 | -0.484 | -0.088 | -0.174 | 1.246 |
| n = 598 | (9.65) | (2.04) | (0.59) | (0.03) | (3.80) | (6.58) | (5.28) | (8.24) | (2.63) | (0.65) | (5.54) | (8.62) |
| derivative x 100 | | -6.190 | -2.420 | -0.040 | 3.190 | 7.620 | -11.310 | 3.920 | -9.040 | -2.540 | -3.650 | 29.630 |
| Self-employed | -3.408 | -0.250 | 0.305 | -0.001 | 0.119 | 0.154 | -0.275 | -0.089 | -0.737 | 0.361 | -0.053 | -1.545 |
| n = 177 | (3.04) | (1.16) | (1.71) | (0.01) | (1.84) | (1.78) | (1.67) | (2.19) | (1.37) | (1.59) | (0.99) | (6.90) |
| derivative x 100 | | -0.820 | 1.850 | 0.000 | 0.370 | 0.170 | -0.510 | -0.820 | -3.190 | 2.160 | 0.030 | -10.840 |

Notes:   The numbers in parentheses are t-statistics.
The numbers below the t-statistics are the partial derivatives x 100 evaluated at the sample means.

**Table 3.7**
**Logit Simulations: Probabilities of Labor Force Participation (%) - Single Women**
**E = Employee; S = Self-employed; N = Non-worker**

| REGION / WORK STATUS | | ALL BRAZIL | | | NORTHEAST | | | NORTHWEST | | | OTHER SOUTHEAST | | | RIO | | | SAO PAULO | | | SOUTH | | |
|---|---|---|---|---|---|---|---|---|---|---|---|---|---|---|---|---|---|---|---|---|---|---|
| | | E | S | N | E | S | N | E | S | N | E | S | N | E | S | N | E | S | N | E | S | N |
| KIDS 0-2 | 0 | 31 | 5 | 64 | 13 | 8 | 78 | 26 | 3 | 72 | 28 | 3 | 69 | 35 | 2 | 62 | 57 | 3 | 40 | 32 | 6 | 62 |
| | 1 | 27 | 5 | 67 | 12 | 8 | 80 | 20 | 2 | 78 | 31 | 4 | 65 | 33 | 4 | 63 | 52 | 4 | 44 | 26 | 5 | 69 |
| | 2 | 24 | 6 | 71 | 11 | 9 | 81 | 15 | 2 | 83 | 33 | 7 | 60 | 30 | 6 | 64 | 47 | 5 | 48 | 21 | 4 | 75 |
| KIDS 3-5 | 0 | 31 | 5 | 64 | 12 | 8 | 80 | 26 | 2 | 72 | 29 | 3 | 68 | 35 | 3 | 63 | 57 | 3 | 40 | 32 | 6 | 63 |
| | 1 | 30 | 6 | 64 | 15 | 9 | 76 | 21 | 3 | 76 | 28 | 3 | 69 | 36 | 3 | 61 | 52 | 4 | 43 | 29 | 8 | 63 |
| | 2 | 28 | 7 | 64 | 18 | 10 | 72 | 16 | 4 | 80 | 28 | 3 | 69 | 38 | 4 | 59 | 48 | 6 | 46 | 27 | 10 | 63 |
| | 3 | 27 | 9 | 64 | 21 | 11 | 68 | 13 | 4 | 83 | 28 | 3 | 69 | 39 | 4 | 57 | 44 | 8 | 49 | 24 | 14 | 62 |
| KID 6-14 | 0 | 29 | 5 | 66 | 11 | 10 | 79 | 23 | 1 | 76 | 27 | 2 | 71 | 30 | 2 | 68 | 55 | 3 | 43 | 31 | 6 | 63 |
| | 1 | 30 | 5 | 65 | 12 | 9 | 79 | 24 | 2 | 75 | 28 | 3 | 69 | 35 | 3 | 62 | 56 | 3 | 41 | 31 | 6 | 63 |
| | 2 | 31 | 5 | 63 | 13 | 8 | 79 | 24 | 3 | 73 | 30 | 3 | 67 | 41 | 3 | 56 | 57 | 4 | 39 | 31 | 6 | 63 |
| | 3 | 32 | 6 | 62 | 15 | 7 | 78 | 25 | 5 | 70 | 31 | 4 | 65 | 47 | 4 | 49 | 58 | 6 | 37 | 31 | 6 | 63 |
| FAMILY SIZE | 1 | 22 | 6 | 72 | 11 | 6 | 83 | 14 | 8 | 78 | 22 | 8 | 69 | 35 | 4 | 61 | 33 | 6 | 61 | 15 | 4 | 81 |
| | 2 | 23 | 6 | 71 | 11 | 6 | 82 | 15 | 7 | 78 | 23 | 7 | 69 | 35 | 4 | 61 | 36 | 6 | 58 | 17 | 4 | 79 |
| | 4 | 26 | 6 | 69 | 12 | 7 | 81 | 18 | 5 | 77 | 25 | 5 | 69 | 35 | 3 | 62 | 44 | 5 | 51 | 22 | 5 | 73 |
| | 6 | 28 | 5 | 66 | 12 | 8 | 80 | 21 | 4 | 76 | 27 | 4 | 69 | 35 | 3 | 62 | 52 | 4 | 44 | 28 | 5 | 67 |
| | 8 | 31 | 5 | 64 | 13 | 8 | 79 | 24 | 3 | 74 | 29 | 3 | 68 | 35 | 2 | 63 | 59 | 3 | 38 | 34 | 6 | 60 |
| | 10 | 34 | 5 | 61 | 13 | 9 | 78 | 27 | 2 | 71 | 31 | 2 | 67 | 35 | 2 | 63 | 67 | 2 | 31 | 41 | 7 | 53 |
| AGE | 15 | 17 | 4 | 80 | 6 | 6 | 89 | 12 | 1 | 87 | 15 | 2 | 83 | 11 | 1 | 88 | 35 | 2 | 64 | 19 | 6 | 75 |
| | 20 | 34 | 5 | 60 | 15 | 9 | 77 | 29 | 3 | 68 | 32 | 3 | 65 | 41 | 3 | 57 | 60 | 3 | 36 | 36 | 6 | 58 |
| | 25 | 50 | 6 | 44 | 27 | 11 | 63 | 46 | 6 | 48 | 48 | 4 | 48 | 67 | 4 | 29 | 73 | 6 | 21 | 50 | 5 | 45 |
| | 30 | 58 | 7 | 35 | 36 | 12 | 52 | 53 | 11 | 36 | 57 | 4 | 39 | 78 | 4 | 18 | 77 | 8 | 15 | 58 | 5 | 37 |
| | 35 | 58 | 8 | 33 | 40 | 13 | 47 | 51 | 16 | 34 | 58 | 4 | 37 | 78 | 6 | 17 | 75 | 11 | 14 | 60 | 4 | 37 |
| | 40 | 52 | 10 | 38 | 37 | 14 | 49 | 41 | 21 | 38 | 52 | 5 | 43 | 68 | 8 | 23 | 68 | 15 | 17 | 55 | 3 | 42 |
| | 45 | 38 | 12 | 50 | 28 | 15 | 58 | 26 | 23 | 51 | 38 | 5 | 57 | 45 | 12 | 43 | 54 | 19 | 27 | 43 | 3 | 54 |
| | 50 | 21 | 12 | 67 | 16 | 14 | 70 | 12 | 19 | 69 | 20 | 5 | 75 | 16 | 11 | 73 | 34 | 19 | 47 | 26 | 2 | 71 |
| | 55 | 8 | 9 | 83 | 7 | 12 | 82 | 3 | 10 | 86 | 7 | 3 | 89 | 2 | 6 | 92 | 13 | 13 | 73 | 11 | 1 | 87 |
| | 60 | 2 | 6 | 92 | 2 | 8 | 90 | 1 | 4 | 96 | 2 | 2 | 97 | 0 | 2 | 98 | 3 | 5 | 92 | 3 | 1 | 96 |
| | 65 | 0 | 3 | 97 | 0 | 5 | 95 | 0 | 1 | 99 | 0 | 1 | 99 | 0 | 0 | 100 | 0 | 1 | 98 | 1 | 0 | 99 |
| SCHOOL YEARS | 0 | 14 | 8 | 78 | 6 | 13 | 82 | 10 | 6 | 84 | 16 | 3 | 81 | 17 | 4 | 79 | 34 | 6 | 59 | 13 | 12 | 75 |
| | 1 | 17 | 8 | 76 | 7 | 11 | 82 | 12 | 5 | 83 | 18 | 3 | 79 | 19 | 3 | 77 | 37 | 6 | 57 | 16 | 11 | 74 |
| | 2 | 19 | 7 | 74 | 9 | 10 | 81 | 14 | 5 | 81 | 20 | 3 | 77 | 21 | 3 | 75 | 40 | 5 | 54 | 18 | 10 | 72 |
| | 3 | 22 | 7 | 72 | 10 | 9 | 80 | 17 | 4 | 79 | 22 | 3 | 75 | 24 | 3 | 73 | 43 | 5 | 52 | 21 | 9 | 70 |
| | 4 | 25 | 6 | 69 | 13 | 8 | 79 | 20 | 3 | 77 | 25 | 3 | 72 | 26 | 3 | 71 | 46 | 5 | 49 | 24 | 8 | 68 |
| | 5 | 28 | 6 | 66 | 15 | 7 | 77 | 23 | 3 | 74 | 28 | 3 | 69 | 28 | 3 | 69 | 50 | 4 | 46 | 28 | 7 | 65 |
| | 6 | 32 | 5 | 63 | 19 | 7 | 75 | 27 | 2 | 71 | 31 | 3 | 67 | 31 | 3 | 66 | 53 | 4 | 43 | 32 | 6 | 62 |
| | 7 | 36 | 5 | 60 | 22 | 6 | 72 | 31 | 2 | 67 | 34 | 3 | 64 | 34 | 3 | 64 | 56 | 3 | 41 | 36 | 5 | 59 |
| | 8 | 40 | 4 | 56 | 26 | 5 | 69 | 36 | 1 | 63 | 37 | 3 | 60 | 37 | 3 | 61 | 59 | 3 | 38 | 40 | 4 | 56 |
| | 9 | 44 | 4 | 53 | 31 | 4 | 65 | 41 | 1 | 58 | 40 | 2 | 57 | 40 | 2 | 58 | 62 | 3 | 35 | 45 | 4 | 52 |
| | 10 | 48 | 3 | 49 | 35 | 4 | 61 | 45 | 1 | 54 | 44 | 2 | 54 | 43 | 2 | 55 | 65 | 3 | 33 | 49 | 3 | 48 |
| | 11 | 52 | 3 | 45 | 41 | 3 | 56 | 50 | 1 | 49 | 47 | 2 | 50 | 46 | 2 | 52 | 68 | 2 | 30 | 53 | 3 | 44 |
| | 12 | 56 | 2 | 41 | 46 | 3 | 52 | 55 | 1 | 44 | 51 | 2 | 47 | 49 | 2 | 49 | 70 | 2 | 28 | 58 | 2 | 40 |
| | 13 | 60 | 2 | 37 | 51 | 2 | 47 | 60 | 0 | 40 | 55 | 2 | 44 | 52 | 2 | 46 | 73 | 2 | 25 | 62 | 2 | 36 |
| | 14 | 64 | 2 | 34 | 57 | 2 | 42 | 65 | 0 | 35 | 58 | 2 | 40 | 55 | 2 | 43 | 75 | 2 | 23 | 66 | 1 | 32 |
| | 15 | 68 | 2 | 30 | 62 | 1 | 37 | 69 | 0 | 31 | 62 | 2 | 37 | 58 | 2 | 40 | 77 | 1 | 21 | 70 | 1 | 29 |
| OTHER $ INCOME | 0 | 33 | 5 | 62 | 15 | 9 | 76 | 29 | 2 | 69 | 33 | 3 | 65 | 38 | 2 | 60 | 64 | 3 | 33 | 33 | 7 | 60 |
| | 500 | 33 | 5 | 62 | 15 | 9 | 76 | 28 | 2 | 69 | 33 | 3. | 65 | 38 | 2 | 60 | 64 | 3 | 33 | 33 | 7 | 60 |
| | 1000 | 33 | 5 | 62 | 15 | 9 | 76 | 28 | 2 | 70 | 33 | 3 | 65 | 38 | 2 | 60 | 64 | 3 | 33 | 33 | 7 | 60 |
| | 1500 | 33 | 5 | 62 | 15 | 9 | 76 | 28 | 2 | 70 | 32 | 3 | 65 | 38 | 2 | 60 | 64 | 3 | 33 | 33 | 7 | 60 |
| | 2500 | 33 | 5 | 62 | 14 | 9 | 77 | 28 | 2 | 70 | 32 | 3 | 65 | 38 | 2 | 60 | 64 | 3 | 33 | 33 | 7 | 60 |
| | 5000 | 33 | 5 | 62 | 14 | 9 | 77 | 28 | 2 | 70 | 32 | 3 | 65 | 38 | 2 | 60 | 63 | 3 | 34 | 33 | 7 | 60 |
| | 7500 | 33 | 5 | 62 | 14 | 9 | 77 | 27 | 2 | 71 | 31 | 3 | 66 | 37 | 2 | 60 | 63 | 3 | 34 | 33 | 6 | 61 |
| | 10000 | 32 | 5 | 63 | 14 | 9 | 78 | 27 | 2 | 71 | 31 | 3 | 66 | 37 | 2 | 61 | 62 | 3 | 35 | 33 | 6 | 61 |
| | 12500 | 32 | 5 | 63 | 13 | 8 | 78 | 26 | 2 | 72 | 30 | 3 | 67 | 37 | 2 | 61 | 61 | 3 | 35 | 32 | 6 | 61 |
| | 15000 | 32 | 5 | 63 | 13 | 8 | 79 | 26 | 2 | 72 | 30 | 3 | 67 | 37 | 2 | 61 | 61 | 3 | 36 | 32 | 6 | 62 |
| OWN HOME | NO | 36 | 4 | 61 | 16 | 6 | 78 | 32 | 4 | 65 | 32 | 2 | 66 | 38 | 2 | 60 | 59 | 3 | 38 | 33 | 4 | 62 |
| OWN HOME | YES | 29 | 6 | 65 | 12 | 9 | 78 | 22 | 2 | 76 | 27 | 3 | 69 | 33 | 3 | 64 | 54 | 4 | 42 | 31 | 6 | 63 |
| ROOMS IN HOME | 1 | 51 | 5 | 44 | 18 | 9 | 72 | 32 | 2 | 66 | 49 | 5 | 46 | 58 | 2 | 40 | 76 | 2 | 22 | 52 | 5 | 42 |
| | 2 | 47 | 5 | 48 | 17 | 9 | 74 | 30 | 2 | 68 | 45 | 5 | 50 | 54 | 2 | 45 | 72 | 3 | 25 | 48 | 5 | 46 |
| | 3 | 42 | 5 | 52 | 16 | 9 | 75 | 28 | 2 | 69 | 42 | 4 | 54 | 49 | 2 | 49 | 68 | 3 | 29 | 44 | 6 | 50 |
| | 4 | 38 | 5 | 56 | 15 | 9 | 76 | 27 | 2 | 71 | 38 | 4 | 58 | 44 | 2 | 54 | 64 | 3 | 33 | 40 | 6 | 54 |
| | 5 | 34 | 5 | 60 | 14 | 8 | 78 | 25 | 2 | 73 | 34 | 4 | 62 | 39 | 2 | 58 | 60 | 3 | 37 | 36 | 6 | 58 |
| | 6 | 31 | 5 | 64 | 13 | 8 | 79 | 23 | 3 | 74 | 31 | 3 | 66 | 35 | 3 | 62 | 55 | 3 | 41 | 32 | 6 | 62 |
| | 7 | 27 | 5 | 68 | 12 | 8 | 80 | 22 | 3 | 76 | 27 | 3 | 70 | 31 | 3 | 67 | 50 | 4 | 46 | 29 | 6 | 66 |
| | 8 | 24 | 5 | 71 | 11 | 8 | 81 | 20 | 3 | 77 | 24 | 2 | 73 | 27 | 3 | 70 | 46 | 4 | 50 | 25 | 6 | 69 |
| | 9 | 21 | 5 | 74 | 10 | 8 | 82 | 19 | 3 | 79 | 21 | 2 | 77 | 23 | 3 | 74 | 41 | 4 | 55 | 22 | 6 | 72 |
| | 10 | 18 | 5 | 77 | 10 | 7 | 83 | 18 | 3 | 80 | 19 | 2 | 80 | 20 | 3 | 77 | 37 | 4 | 59 | 19 | 6 | 75 |
| RURAL | | 14 | 13 | 73 | 8 | 13 | 79 | 11 | 4 | 85 | 10 | 7 | 83 | 27 | 4 | 69 | 33 | 12 | 55 | 16 | 17 | 68 |
| URBAN | | 39 | 3 | 58 | 18 | 6 | 76 | 32 | 2 | 66 | 39 | 2 | 59 | 35 | 3 | 62 | 58 | 3 | 39 | 43 | 3 | 54 |
| AT MEANS % | | 31 | 5 | 64 | 13 | 8 | 79 | 24 | 2 | 73 | 29 | 3 | 68 | 35 | 3 | 62 | 56 | 3 | 41 | 31 | 6 | 63 |
| ACTUAL % | | 34 | 7 | 59 | 18 | 11 | 71 | 29 | 4 | 66 | 34 | 3 | 63 | 38 | 3 | 59 | 55 | 4 | 41 | 34 | 10 | 56 |
| OBS | | 3871 | 753 | 6601 | 561 | 328 | 2156 | 287 | 42 | 646 | 581 | 65 | 1086 | 453 | 32 | 697 | 1391 | 109 | 1043 | 598 | 177 | 973 |

**Table 3.8**
Logit Estimates of Labor Force Participation by Region – Single Men

| VARIABLE | ALL BRAZIL | NORTHEAST | NORTHWES | OTHER SOUTHEAST | RIO | SAO PAULO | SOUTH |
|---|---|---|---|---|---|---|---|
| CONSTANT | 1.280 | -0.258 | 1.864 | 2.922 | 3.431 | 2.737 | 1.464 |
| | (7.31) | (0.71) | (3.61) | (6.35) | (4.86) | (6.67) | (3.28) |
| AGE | -0.054 | -0.011 | -0.080 | -0.134 | -0.090 | -0.070 | -0.072 |
| | (4.97) | (0.50) | (2.58) | (4.69) | (2.11) | (2.81) | (2.52) |
| | -0.930 | -0.260 | -1.730 | -2.220 | -0.990 | -0.710 | -1.230 |
| AGESQ/100 | 0.036 | -0.021 | 0.068 | 0.143 | 0.064 | 0.035 | 0.049 |
| | (2.34) | (0.67) | (1.55) | (3.61) | (1.09) | (1.01) | (1.21) |
| | 0.620 | -0.500 | 1.460 | 2.360 | 0.710 | 0.350 | 0.840 |
| YEARS SCHOOL | 0.071 | 0.119 | 0.086 | 0.042 | 0.024 | 0.046 | 0.054 |
| | (7.52) | (5.30) | (2.83) | (1.73) | (0.90) | (2.60) | (2.25) |
| | 1.230 | 2.890 | 1.850 | 0.690 | 0.260 | 0.460 | 0.920 |
| NO SCHOOL COMPLETED | -0.380 | -0.110 | -0.638 | -0.214 | -0.093 | 0.042 | -0.029 |
| | (5.51) | (0.65) | (3.13) | (1.27) | (0.38) | (0.28) | (0.17) |
| | -6.550 | -2.690 | -13.810 | -3.540 | -1.020 | 0.420 | -0.500 |
| URBAN | 1.186 | 1.243 | 0.598 | 0.897 | 0.256 | 0.534 | 1.406 |
| | (24.31) | (13.52) | (4.42) | (7.00) | (0.94) | (3.55) | (11.50) |
| | 20.460 | 30.310 | 12.930 | 14.820 | 2.820 | 5.400 | 24.050 |
| Employees | 9673 | 1609 | 929 | 1472 | 1147 | 3072 | 1444 |
| Self-Employed | 3301 | 1261 | 486 | 445 | 182 | 443 | 484 |
| -2LLKFULL | 12719.7 | 3333.1 | 1575.0 | 1888.4 | 1012.9 | 2518.1 | 1882.4 |
| -2LLKREST | 14716.5 | 3936.4 | 1820.6 | 2077.4 | 1061.6 | 2662.8 | 2172.8 |

Notes: Numbers in parentheses are t-statistics.

The numbers below the t-statistics are the partial derivatives x 100 evaluated at the sample means.

**Table 3.9**
Logit Simulations: Probabilities of Labor Force Participation (%) - Single Men
E = Employee; S = Self-employed

| REGION | | ALL BRAZIL | | NORTHEAST | | NORTHWEST | | OTHER SOUTHEAST | | RIO | | SAO PAULO | | SOUTH | |
|---|---|---|---|---|---|---|---|---|---|---|---|---|---|---|---|
| WORK STATUS | | E | S | E | S | E | S | E | S | E | S | E | S | E | S |
| AGE | 15 | 83 | 17 | 63 | 37 | 77 | 23 | 88 | 12 | 93 | 7 | 93 | 7 | 85 | 15 |
| | 20 | 80 | 20 | 61 | 39 | 72 | 28 | 82 | 18 | 90 | 10 | 90 | 10 | 81 | 19 |
| | 25 | 77 | 23 | 58 | 42 | 67 | 33 | 76 | 24 | 87 | 13 | 88 | 12 | 77 | 23 |
| | 30 | 74 | 26 | 55 | 45 | 62 | 38 | 71 | 29 | 84 | 16 | 85 | 15 | 72 | 28 |
| | 35 | 71 | 29 | 52 | 48 | 58 | 42 | 67 | 33 | 81 | 19 | 82 | 18 | 68 | 32 |
| | 40 | 68 | 32 | 49 | 51 | 54 | 46 | 64 | 36 | 77 | 23 | 78 | 22 | 64 | 36 |
| | 45 | 65 | 35 | 46 | 54 | 51 | 49 | 62 | 38 | 74 | 26 | 74 | 26 | 61 | 39 |
| | 50 | 63 | 37 | 42 | 58 | 49 | 51 | 62 | 38 | 71 | 29 | 71 | 29 | 58 | 42 |
| | 55 | 61 | 39 | 38 | 62 | 48 | 52 | 64 | 36 | 69 | 31 | 67 | 33 | 55 | 45 |
| | 60 | 60 | 40 | 34 | 66 | 48 | 52 | 67 | 33 | 67 | 33 | 64 | 36 | 53 | 47 |
| | 65 | 59 | 41 | 30 | 70 | 49 | 51 | 72 | 28 | 66 | 34 | 61 | 39 | 52 | 48 |
| SCHOOL | 0 | 71 | 29 | 48 | 52 | 60 | 40 | 76 | 24 | 86 | 14 | 85 | 15 | 73 | 27 |
| YEARS | 1 | 73 | 27 | 51 | 49 | 62 | 38 | 77 | 24 | 86 | 14 | 86 | 14 | 74 | 26 |
| | 2 | 74 | 26 | 54 | 46 | 64 | 36 | 77 | 23 | 86 | 14 | 87 | 13 | 75 | 25 |
| | 3 | 75 | 25 | 57 | 43 | 66 | 34 | 78 | 22 | 86 | 14 | 87 | 13 | 76 | 24 |
| | 4 | 77 | 23 | 60 | 40 | 68 | 32 | 79 | 21 | 87 | 13 | 88 | 12 | 77 | 23 |
| | 5 | 78 | 22 | 63 | 37 | 70 | 30 | 79 | 21 | 87 | 13 | 88 | 12 | 78 | 22 |
| | 6 | 79 | 21 | 66 | 34 | 71 | 29 | 80 | 20 | 87 | 13 | 89 | 11 | 79 | 21 |
| | 7 | 80 | 20 | 68 | 32 | 73 | 27 | 81 | 19 | 88 | 13 | 89 | 11 | 80 | 20 |
| | 8 | 81 | 19 | 71 | 29 | 75 | 25 | 81 | 19 | 88 | 12 | 89 | 11 | 80 | 20 |
| | 9 | 82 | 18 | 73 | 27 | 76 | 24 | 82 | 18 | 88 | 12 | 90 | 10 | 81 | 19 |
| | 10 | 83 | 17 | 75 | 25 | 78 | 22 | 83 | 17 | 88 | 12 | 90 | 10 | 82 | 18 |
| | 11 | 84 | 16 | 78 | 22 | 79 | 21 | 83 | 17 | 89 | 11 | 91 | 9 | 83 | 17 |
| | 12 | 85 | 15 | 80 | 20 | 81 | 19 | 84 | 16 | 89 | 11 | 91 | 9 | 84 | 16 |
| | 13 | 86 | 14 | 81 | 19 | 82 | 18 | 84 | 16 | 89 | 11 | 91 | 9 | 84 | 16 |
| | 14 | 87 | 13 | 83 | 17 | 83 | 17 | 85 | 15 | 89 | 11 | 92 | 8 | 85 | 15 |
| | 15 | 88 | 12 | 85 | 15 | 84 | 16 | 85 | 15 | 89 | 11 | 92 | 8 | 86 | 14 |
| COMPLETED SCHOOL | YES | 80 | 20 | 60 | 40 | 75 | 25 | 81 | 19 | 88 | 12 | 88 | 12 | 78 | 22 |
| | NO | 74 | 26 | 57 | 43 | 61 | 39 | 77 | 23 | 87 | 13 | 89 | 11 | 78 | 22 |
| RURAL | | 60 | 40 | 41 | 59 | 60 | 40 | 67 | 33 | 85 | 15 | 83 | 17 | 58 | 42 |
| URBAN | | 83 | 17 | 71 | 29 | 73 | 27 | 83 | 17 | 88 | 12 | 89 | 11 | 85 | 15 |
| AT MEANS % | | 78 | 22 | 58 | 42 | 68 | 32 | 79 | 21 | 87 | 13 | 89 | 11 | 78 | 22 |
| ACTUAL % | | 75 | 25 | 56 | 44 | 66 | 34 | 77 | 23 | 86 | 14 | 87 | 13 | 75 | 25 |
| OBS | | 9673 | 3301 | 1609 | 1261 | 929 | 486 | 1472 | 445 | 1147 | 182 | 3072 | 443 | 1444 | 484 |

The results show that the probability of holding a wage job decreases with age, but the coefficient on age squared is generally not significant. In all regions, living in an urban area strongly increases the probability of being an employee. The urban effect is especially strong in the Northeast and the South.

Once again, the education effects are interesting. In most instances, (the Northwest is the exception), uncompleted schooling is not an important factor in determining the type of job.[25] The amount of schooling, however, does play a role in the Northwest, the Northeast, and the Other Southeast. In the remaining regions, the coefficient of the schooling is not significant. The simulations generally reflect the pattern found for single women. For example, an extra year of schooling raises the probability of being an employee by about 3 percentage points.

## 5.   Wage Determinants

The analysis of wage determinants is based on the human capital framework developed by Becker (1964) and Mincer (1974). This provides the theoretical base for the study of wages as a function of productivity-enhancing variables. We estimate a wage function where the dependent variable is the natural log of the hourly earnings (including cash in-kind payments) which is obtained by dividing monthly earnings by weekly hours times 4.33. In doing so, we assumed that the individual worked for the entire month.

The regressors are the inverse of the Mills' ratio, potential work experience (age - 6 - years of schooling), experience squared (divided by 100), years of education, dummy variables indicating public sector employment, contributions to social security, urban and state residence. Since data on actual work experience are not reported, the set of regressors in the female wage equations also include the number of babies ever born, which is used to reflect interruptions in potential work experience.

### *Wage Functions - The Issue of Selectivity Bias*

Now, we consider the specification of the wage function:

Let:   $C_1 = 1$, if the person is an employee (1), 0 otherwise;
$C_2 = 1$, if the person is self-employed (2), 0 otherwise;
$C_3 = 1$, if the person does not work (3), 0 otherwise;

The wage function in the jth work-status is given by:

$$\ln W_j = \begin{cases} z\alpha_j + \psi_j & \text{if } C_j = 1, \ j = 1, 2 \\ 0 & \text{otherwise} \end{cases}$$

where $\ln W_j$ is natural log of the wage, z is a (row) vector of wage-determining characteristics, which has some elements in common with x, $\alpha_j$ is a vector of estimated parameters and $\psi_j$ is the error term. If the individual does not work (j = 3), then no market wage function is observed.

Traditional OLS estimation of the wage function may produce biased and inconsistent parameter estimates owing to selectivity bias because the observations on earnings by job alternative are not

---

[25]   The data showed that the proportion of single men who did not complete any schooling was much higher than that of single women.

randomly distributed. The selectivity bias correction term ($\lambda$) for the multinomial logit choice case is derived using the transformation of Maddala (1983, p.275). That is, $\lambda_j = \phi[J_i(x\gamma_j)] / F(x\gamma_j)$, where $\phi$ is the standard normal distribution function, F is the logistic distribution function, and the transformation $J = \phi^{-1}F$. Thus, for each work-status wage regression (j= 1, 2) $\lambda$ can be included as a regressor.

$$\ln W_j = z\beta_j + \kappa_j\hat{\lambda}_j + \mu_j$$

In sum, because decisions about labor force status as well as wage offers influence the observed wage structure, corrections for selectivity bias are needed to obtain consistent parameter estimates of the wage determinants.

## Empirical Estimates

*Married women.* Table 3.10 shows that the effect of the selectivity correcting variable among wives varies across regions and work status. At the national level, both the employee and self-employment wage regressions are subject to selectivity bias. However, a region by region comparison seems to tell a different story. In three regions, the Northeast, the Northwest, and the Other Southeast, the coefficient of Lambda is not statistically significant in either of the wage regressions. Both wage regressions for Rio are subject to sample selection bias -- the coefficient on Lambda is positive and significant in the wage function of employees, and negative and significant in that of the self-employed. In Sao Paulo and the South, the coefficient of Lambda is negative and significant only in the wage regression for employees.

The coefficients of the best available work experience variables in the data are generally as expected, but there are regional variations. Experience effects do not appear to be present in the two wage regressions for the Northwest, and in that of the self-employed in all regions, except the Northeast where the coefficients on all experience variables are statistically significant. In the national wage regressions, all experience coefficients are statistically significant, suggesting that there may be geographical aggregation bias" in assessing returns to work experience. Moreover, there are also some regional differences in the magnitudes of the coefficients of the experience variables (especially experience squared) of employees.

Because the measure of work experience for wives is imperfect we also included the number of children ever-born in an attempt to capture interruptions in potential work experience. Nationally, the coefficient on this variable is statistically significant and negative (-0.033 for employees and -0.036 for self-employed). However, this proxy for discontinuity in work experience met with limited success in the region-specific regressions. The parameter estimates are significant only in wage regression of employees the Northeast (-0.025) and in Sao Paulo (-0.021).

In most regions the coefficient estimates of the effects of having a job in the public sector are not significant and, in one case (the Northeast) it is unexpectedly significantly negative (-0.286). Only in Rio does public sector employment have a positive effect of about 16 percent on wages.

## Table 3.10
### Wage Regressions by Region - Married Men and Women
(The dependent variable is: LN WAGE)

| REGION | ALL BRAZIL | | | | NORTHEAST | | | | NORTHWEST | | | | OTHER SOUTHEAST | | | | RIO DE JANEIRO | | | | SAN PAULO | | | | SOUTH | | | |
|---|---|---|---|---|---|---|---|---|---|---|---|---|---|---|---|---|---|---|---|---|---|---|---|---|---|---|---|---|
| | EMPLOYEES | | SELF-EMPLOYED | | EMPLOYEES | | SELF-EMPLOYED | | EMPLOYEES | | SELF-EMPLOYED | | EMPLOYEES | | SELF-EMPLOYED | | EMPLOYEES | | SELF-EMPLOYED | | EMPLOYEES | | SELF-EMPLOYED | | EMPLOYEES | | SELF-EMPLOYED | |
| VARIABLE | MEN | WOMEN | MEN | WOMEN | MEN | WOMEN | MEN | WOMEN | MEN | WOMEN | MEN | WOMEN | MEN | WOMEN | MEN | WOMEN | MEN | WOMEN | MEN | WOMEN | MEN | WOMEN | MEN | WOMEN | MEN | WOMEN | MEN | WOMEN |
| OBS | 14596 | 3741 | 11410 | 1518 | 2590 | 639 | 4026 | 547 | 1307 | 325 | 1493 | 117 | 1863 | 357 | 1442 | 173 | 1933 | 553 | 576 | 143 | 4405 | 1170 | 1776 | 311 | 2498 | 697 | 2097 | 227 |
| CONSTANT | 2.395 (56.5) | 1.752 (27.3) | 2.133 (34.3) | 1.822 (12.4) | 2.354 (24.4) | 1.311 (8.1) | 2.142 (19.4) | 1.527 (6.1) | 2.285 (19.8) | 2.094 (8.5) | 2.646 (16.7) | 3.118 (5.2) | 2.489 (20.2) | 1.659 (9.7) | 2.051 (14.5) | 1.884 (3.7) | 3.255 (14.9) | 2.138 (12.1) | 2.282 (10.8) | 3.014 (7.3) | 3.870 (23.4) | 2.293 (20.5) | 2.569 (19.2) | 2.039 (5.8) | 2.605 (26.9) | 1.870 (14.4) | 2.354 (16.7) | 2.343 (7.6) |
| LAMBDA | -0.195 (6.9) | -0.297 (6.5) | 0.247 (4.5) | 0.515 (1.8) | -0.117 (1.5) | -0.222 (1.6) | 0.181 (2.2) | 0.166 (0.4) | 0.027 (0.4) | -0.122 (0.7) | 0.092 (1.0) | -0.072 (0.1) | -0.204 (2.6) | -0.262 (1.7) | 0.324 (2.0) | 0.714 (1.2) | -0.622 (4.9) | -0.285 (2.2) | 1.271 (3.6) | 3.440 (2.6) | -0.884 (10.3) | -0.438 (7.1) | 1.779 (6.4) | 0.851 (1.0) | -0.282 (4.7) | -0.226 (2.8) | 0.171 (1.3) | -0.279 (0.4) |
| SECPUB | -0.070 (4.7) | -0.107 (4.0) | - | - | -0.094 (2.5) | -0.286 (4.2) | - | - | 0.150 (3.1) | -0.025 (0.3) | - | - | 0.022 (0.5) | 0.120 (1.7) | - | - | -0.056 (1.5) | 0.155 (2.4) | - | - | -0.078 (3.0) | 0.049 (1.1) | - | - | -0.002 (0.1) | 0.078 (1.4) | - | - |
| SOCSEC | 0.272 (18.3) | 0.334 (11.1) | 0.465 (22.3) | 0.608 (9.9) | 0.263 (8.4) | 0.441 (5.3) | 0.487 (11.6) | 0.743 (5.0) | 0.061 (1.4) | 0.266 (2.6) | 0.303 (5.2) | 0.642 (3.2) | 0.349 (9.6) | 0.394 (4.5) | 0.421 (7.2) | 0.622 (3.0) | 0.086 (1.8) | 0.182 (2.5) | 0.517 (7.3) | 0.258 (1.7) | 0.321 (10.6) | 0.318 (7.7) | 0.375 (8.7) | 0.529 (4.8) | 0.228 (6.5) | 0.415 (6.5) | 0.415 (8.4) | 0.521 (3.9) |
| EXPR | 0.042 (22.9) | 0.059 (9.9) | 0.032 (10.3) | 0.027 (2.5) | 0.032 (6.7) | 0.041 (3.3) | 0.020 (3.8) | 0.041 (2.2) | 0.049 (8.2) | 0.005 (0.3) | 0.031 (3.7) | -0.013 (0.3) | 0.034 (6.7) | 0.032 (2.7) | 0.036 (4.1) | 0.012 (0.3) | 0.041 (7.8) | 0.034 (3.8) | 0.012 (1.1) | -0.044 (1.7) | 0.029 (8.3) | 0.032 (6.1) | 0.001 (0.2) | 0.036 (1.7) | 0.036 (8.9) | 0.039 (4.4) | 0.032 (4.1) | 0.027 (1.5) |
| EXPSQ/100 | -0.063 (22.6) | -0.048 (6.2) | -0.038 (8.9) | -0.033 (2.0) | -0.044 (6.1) | -0.052 (2.2) | -0.023 (3.1) | -0.062 (2.1) | -0.069 (7.5) | 0.016 (0.5) | -0.041 (3.5) | 0.015 (0.2) | -0.051 (7.0) | -0.041 (1.7) | -0.042 (3.7) | 0.002 (0.0) | -0.077 (8.5) | -0.040 (2.4) | -0.011 (0.7) | 0.082 (1.8) | -0.072 (15.8) | -0.044 (4.9) | -0.007 (0.6) | -0.045 (1.3) | -0.060 (9.7) | -0.055 (3.0) | -0.037 (3.3) | -0.037 (1.3) |
| YRSEDUC | 0.147 (94.1) | 0.156 (39.1) | 0.138 (47.0) | 0.128 (14.5) | 0.149 (29.7) | 0.170 (13.1) | 0.131 (16.4) | 0.193 (5.9) | 0.138 (22.1) | 0.152 (9.5) | 0.120 (13.8) | 0.135 (4.5) | 0.134 (27.3) | 0.154 (10.7) | 0.136 (14.9) | 0.132 (4.9) | 0.154 (41.8) | 0.166 (18.0) | 0.116 (13.6) | 0.131 (6.4) | 0.118 (38.5) | 0.138 (25.9) | 0.095 (15.2) | 0.127 (7.3) | 0.130 (31.4) | 0.129 (14.4) | 0.128 (16.6) | 0.097 (4.8) |
| URBAN | 0.326 (17.3) | 0.347 (8.2) | 0.457 (12.2) | 0.467 (7.4) | 0.145 (3.5) | 0.214 (2.6) | 0.449 (8.0) | 0.321 (3.1) | 0.138 (2.8) | 0.209 (1.6) | 0.320 (5.3) | -0.315 (1.4) | 0.214 (4.6) | 0.178 (1.7) | 0.392 (3.8) | 0.379 (1.6) | 0.287 (5.8) | 0.016 (0.1) | 0.341 (2.8) | 0.026 (0.1) | 0.426 (13.2) | 0.288 (3.4) | 0.408 (4.8) | 0.367 (1.9) | 0.347 (8.1) | 0.157 (2.7) | 0.322 (3.1) | 0.270 (1.7) |
| BIRTOT | - | -0.033 (7.1) | - | -0.036 (4.7) | - | -0.025 (2.5) | - | -0.014 (1.3) | - | -0.008 (0.5) | - | -0.018 (0.7) | - | -0.007 (0.5) | - | -0.041 (1.5) | - | -0.016 (1.3) | - | -0.037 (1.5) | - | -0.021 (3.1) | - | -0.025 (1.3) | - | -0.013 (1.3) | - | -0.024 (1.3) |
| R-SQUARED | 0.551 | 0.569 | 0.414 | 0.449 | 0.515 | 0.530 | 0.300 | 0.297 | 0.494 | 0.541 | 0.292 | 0.334 | 0.545 | 0.644 | 0.369 | 0.421 | 0.576 | 0.654 | 0.460 | 0.510 | 0.580 | 0.643 | 0.373 | 0.436 | 0.502 | 0.563 | 0.278 | 0.349 |
| F-STAT | 2553.3 | 615.3 | 1341.4 | 175.6 | 392.2 | 88.9 | 287.5 | 31.8 | 181.1 | 46.5 | 102.1 | 7.8 | 317.6 | 78.5 | 140.0 | 17.1 | 373.4 | 128.3 | 80.9 | 20.0 | 867.8 | 261.4 | 175.2 | 33.4 | 358.2 | 110.9 | 134.3 | 16.8 |
| STD.ERR | 0.599 | 0.633 | 0.820 | 0.891 | 0.635 | 0.752 | 0.783 | 0.918 | 0.615 | 0.621 | 0.761 | 0.907 | 0.542 | 0.588 | 0.807 | 0.885 | 0.606 | 0.605 | 0.722 | 0.790 | 0.542 | 0.511 | 0.781 | 0.819 | 0.536 | 0.515 | 0.858 | 0.814 |
| LN WAGE | 3.9533 (0.89) | 3.6679 (0.96) | 3.674 (1.07) | 3.1979 (1.20) | 3.5551 (0.91) | 3.1646 (1.09) | 3.1369 (0.94) | 2.55 (1.08) | 3.8333 (0.86) | 3.6896 (0.90) | 3.7592 (0.90) | 3.2359 (1.08) | 3.697 (0.80) | 3.5592 (0.97) | 3.7239 (1.01) | 3.2589 (1.14) | 4.2411 (0.93) | 3.9782 (1.02) | 4.3186 (0.98) | 3.7513 (1.10) | 4.261 (0.84) | 3.8515 (0.85) | 4.424 (0.98) | 3.8646 (1.08) | 3.855 (0.76) | 3.6204 (0.77) | 3.8086 (1.01) | 3.4245 (0.99) |
| WAGE/HOUR | 83.9 (119.6) | 63.1 (79.8) | 80.1 (194.5) | 54.7 (110.2) | 60.1 (109.9) | 43.1 (62.8) | 43.3 (140.2) | 26.6 (62.5) | 72.4 (98.4) | 61.4 (69.4) | 72.4 (155.5) | 46.1 (70.9) | 59.9 (78.4) | 55.2 (59.6) | 78.8 (160.9) | 51.7 (83.0) | 115.4 (155.6) | 92.8 (120.8) | 126.8 (184.1) | 93.3 (182.6) | 106.4 (129.7) | 69.4 (76.2) | 151.5 (313.3) | 90.9 (148.5) | 68.6 (100.0) | 52.1 (62.9) | 84.0 (181.8) | 55.5 (91.5) |
| WAGE$/MONTH '000 | 15.1 (20.5) | 9.2 (11.0) | 14.6 (33.6) | 7.9 (18.1) | 10.4 (16.0) | 6.3 (9.7) | 7.5 (21.5) | 3.6 (9.4) | 13.2 (17.5) | 9.7 (11.6) | 13.4 (31.3) | 6.8 (11.4) | 10.9 (13.6) | 7.6 (9.3) | 14.6 (30.7) | 7.6 (13.5) | 20.6 (27.4) | 13.0 (16.0) | 23.0 (33.6) | 13.2 (30.0) | 19.5 (23.1) | 10.3 (10.1) | 27.8 (51.9) | 13.3 (24.8) | 12.4 (16.4) | 7.6 (7.6) | 15.7 (32.5) | 8.1 (16.5) |
| HOURS/WEEK | 47.0 (6.7) | 39.6 (7.8) | 46.9 (7.8) | 37.6 (12.9) | 45.9 (7.1) | 37.5 (12.1) | 44.7 (7.2) | 36.5 (11.6) | 47.2 (7.2) | 40.0 (10.4) | 46.8 (7.5) | 37.5 (12.4) | 47.4 (6.5) | 37.5 (11.6) | 48.0 (7.7) | 37.4 (13.4) | 46.4 (7.2) | 39.7 (11.1) | 47.5 (9.2) | 37.9 (14.3) | 47.3 (6.0) | 41.1 (10.1) | 48.5 (7.7) | 39.0 (13.2) | 47.5 (6.7) | 39.9 (11.1) | 48.8 (7.9) | 38.2 (14.2) |

Notes: Numbers in parentheses are t-statistics or standard deviations.

We note, however, that the national wage regression displays a disadvantage of 11 percent, which obscures regional differences.[26]

Access to social security (SOCSEC) has a strong effect on hourly earnings of both types of workers in all regions. This dummy variable, as discussed in Dabos and Psacharopoulos (1991), reflects unmeasurable job quality characteristics and conditions of employment, including health care, pensions, and other fringe benefits. Nationally, about 80 percent of employees and 30 percent of the self-employed in the sample reported that they contribute to social security. Of course, there are regional variations in these magnitudes and in the parameter estimates.[27] The estimated positive effects of SOCSEC on hourly earnings among the self-employed are usually in excess of 50 percent, and range from 75 percent in the Northeast to 53 percent in the South. Only in Rio is the impact relatively small and statistically weak. In the employee wage regression, the estimated wage gain from contributing to social security is smaller. It varies from 18 percent in Rio, 27 percent in the Northwest, and 38 percent in Sao Paulo, to over 40 percent in the remaining regions. Nationally, the estimate is 33 percent.

Urban residence is generally associated with higher hourly earnings especially for employees, but less so for the self-employed. The coefficient of the urban variable for self-employed wives is statistically significant and positive only in the Northeast and Sao Paulo, while in the national wage regression it is strongly significant.

The relationship between education and hourly earnings is indeed interesting. The parameter estimates and the low standard errors show that schooling proves to be the most consistently effective variable determining hourly earnings. Table 3.10 shows that the wage gains from schooling among both employees and the self-employed are striking. Self-employed wives have somewhat lower estimated (private) returns to schooling than employees. The national wage regressions imply a return to schooling of 16 percent for employees and 13 percent for the self-employed. These magnitudes, however, are undoubtedly affected by regional heterogeneity.[28]

Consider first the region-specific wage regressions of employees. The estimates indicate that there are regional differences. In Rio and the Northeast, the estimated return to education is about 17 percent; in the Northwest and Other Southeast it is 15 percent, while in Sao Paulo and the South, the returns are 14 percent and 13 percent, respectively. There is also regional variation in the estimated returns among self-employed wives. In the Northeast and the South the return is about 10 percent, about 14 percent in the Northwest, and about 13 percent in the remaining areas. In sum, our estimates of returns to schooling in Brazil are much in line with those obtained in recent studies of women's earnings in other Latin American countries.[29]

---

[26]     A high proportion of employee wives work in the public sector -- over one-half in the Northeast, Northwest, and Other Southeast; just over one-third in Rio and the South, and about one-quarter in Sao Paulo. We recognize that public versus private sector employment is subject to a selection process. This is a topic for future research.

[27]     Since enrollment in a social security scheme is voluntary, this variable also may be subject to a selection process, especially among the self-employed.

[28]     The inclusion of regional dummy variables in the national wage function slightly altered the point estimates: 0.15 for employees and 0.12 for the self-employed.

[29]     See Arriagada (1990) on Peru; Behrman and Wolfe (1984) on Nicaragua; Khandker (1990) and King (1990) on Peru; and Terrell (1989) on Guatemala.

*Married men.*   The estimated wage functions for husbands in Table 3.10 show that there is evidence of selectivity bias. In most instances the coefficient of Lambda is significantly negative for employees and significantly positive for the self-employed. In the Northwest, however, we can detect no evidence of selectivity bias for either type of worker, while in the South, the coefficient of Lambda is significant only in the employee regression and in the Northeast, only in the wage function of the self-employed.

The effects of experience on hourly earnings are generally as expected, though there are variations across regions and work status. All coefficients are statistically significant in the employee regressions, as are most coefficients in the self-employed regressions (the exceptions are Rio and Sao Paulo). The effect of public sector employment in most regions is either negative (Northeast and Sao Paulo) or not statistically significant.   Only in the Northwest is there a significant positive impact of 15 percent. In all regions, working in an urban area generally has a strong positive effect on hourly earnings, especially of employees, in all regions. Contributing to social security generally has a significantly strong positive effect on hourly earnings for both employees and the self-employed. The exceptions are among employees in Rio and the Northwest where the coefficient on this variable is not statistically significant.

As in the regressions for wives, the coefficients of the education variable stand out, and in all instances there are statistically significant returns to schooling. Nationally, the returns for employees and the self-employed are similar: 15 percent and 14 percent, respectively. A regional comparison shows the following pattern. Among employees, the returns are highest in Rio and the Northeast (about 15 percent), followed by the Northwest (14 percent), the Other Southeast and the South (about 13 percent), and Sao Paulo (12 percent). The regional pattern among self-employed workers is: Other Southeast, 14 percent; the Northeast, 13 percent; the Northwest and Rio, about 12 percent; and Sao Paulo and the South, just under 10 percent. Finally, we note that married women tend to have higher returns to schooling (and more schooling) than their husbands. This seems to be the case for both wage and self-employed workers.

*Single men and women* (Table 3.11).   Looking only at the regressions for which there is a sufficient sample size (ie. ignoring those for self-employed women in the Northwest, the Other Southeast, Rio, and the South), we see that selectivity effects are found in both the male and female employee equations. In all regions, the Lambda correction terms are significantly negative for female employees, but not for the self-employed. The male regressions tell a somewhat different story. For employees, the coefficient of Lambda is significantly negative in the Northeast, and significantly positive in Sao Paulo and the South, while in the remaining regions it is not. For self-employed men, there is evidence of selectivity bias only in Rio, where the coefficient of Lambda is negative.

The results for the remaining regressors are generally consistent with a priori expectations. Living in an urban area makes a smaller contribution to expected earnings of employees among singles than among married people. (The urban coefficient is not statistically significant for the self-employed.) Moreover, urban residence has a positive impact among female wage earners only in the Other Southeast and in Sao Paulo, and for males only in the Northeast. Unexpectedly, in the state of Sao Paulo urban residence has a negative effect on earnings for male employees, 10 percent of whom worked in rural areas. Access to social security strongly enhances earnings of men and women in both work activities; the effects tend to be stronger for women than men. The public sector employment variable (which is relevant only for women because of missing information for men) shows a positive and significant effect on earnings only in the southern regions (Other Southeast, Rio, Sao Paulo, and the South).

## Table 3.11
### Wage Regression by Region - Single Men and Women
(The dependent variable is: LN WAGE)

| REGION | ALL BRAZIL | | | | NORTHEAST | | | | NORTHWEST | | | | OTHER SOUTHEAST | | | | RIO DE JANEIRO | | | | SAN PAULO | | | | SOUTH | | | |
|---|---|---|---|---|---|---|---|---|---|---|---|---|---|---|---|---|---|---|---|---|---|---|---|---|---|---|---|---|
| | EMPLOYEES | | SELF-EMPLOYED | | EMPLOYEES | | SELF-EMPLOYED | | EMPLOYEES | | SELF-EMPLOYED | | EMPLOYEES | | SELF-EMPLOYED | | EMPLOYEES | | SELF-EMPLOYED | | EMPLOYEES | | SELF-EMPLOYED | | EMPLOYEES | | SELF-EMPLOYED | |
| VARIABLE | MEN | WOMEN | MEN | WOMEN | MEN | WOMEN | MEN | WOMEN | MEN | WOMEN | MEN | WOMEN | MEN | WOMEN | MEN | WOMEN | MEN | WOMEN | MEN | WOMEN | MEN | WOMEN | MEN | WOMEN | MEN | WOMEN | MEN | WOMEN |
| OBS | 9675 | 3671 | 3301 | 439 | 1609 | 561 | 1261 | 222 | 929 | 287 | 486 | 29 | 1472 | 581 | 445 | 37 | 1147 | 453 | 182 | 31 | 3072 | 1391 | 443 | 79 | 1444 | 598 | 484 | 41 |
| CONSTANT | 1.501 (18.7) | 1.291 (24.5) | 1.842 (7.1) | 1.760 (8.0) | 0.611 (1.4) | 1.031 (7.0) | 1.526 (2.9) | 1.510 (5.1) | 1.649 (10.2) | 1.036 (4.6) | 2.311 (4.9) | | 1.764 (14.3) | 1.042 (6.8) | 2.049 (2.0) | | 1.591 (6.8) | 1.325 (6.4) | 10.528 (2.7) | | 1.854 (12.4) | 1.556 (20.6) | 3.563 (0.9) | 2.116 (8.1) | 2.367 (8.0) | 1.394 (14.0) | 3.705 (0.9) | |
| LAMBDA | -0.423 (3.6) | -0.274 (5.8) | -0.189 (0.8) | -0.351 (0.5) | -1.186 (2.7) | -0.353 (2.3) | 0.847 (1.1) | -0.768 (0.9) | -0.361 (1.4) | -0.545 (3.0) | -0.181 (0.4) | | 0.321 (0.9) | -0.326 (2.4) | 0.185 (0.3) | | -0.461 (0.3) | -0.386 (3.9) | -4.426 (2.2) | | 4.322 (3.9) | -0.274 (5.1) | -0.757 (0.4) | -0.963 (0.8) | 0.907 (1.8) | -0.303 (2.4) | -1.329 (0.4) | |
| SECPUB | | 0.023 (0.8) | | | | -0.106 (1.4) | | | | 0.086 (1.0) | | | | 0.259 (3.9) | | | | 0.257 (3.2) | | | | 0.128 (2.5) | | | | 0.144 (2.2) | | |
| SOCSEC | 0.387 (26.8) | 0.627 (26.6) | 0.394 (9.5) | 0.665 (4.8) | 0.393 (12.3) | 0.456 (6.4) | 0.362 (4.0) | 0.621 (2.2) | 0.199 (5.0) | 0.340 (3.8) | 0.415 (3.1) | | 0.327 (9.8) | 0.559 (9.8) | 0.438 (4.7) | | 0.289 (5.9) | 0.464 (6.8) | 0.497 (4.5) | | 0.357 (12.9) | 0.582 (17.1) | 0.155 (1.6) | 0.202 (1.0) | 0.446 (11.0) | 0.736 (13.0) | 0.382 (4.1) | |
| EXPR | 0.074 (30.9) | 0.075 (14.4) | 0.055 (8.4) | 0.042 (2.1) | 0.066 (10.9) | 0.071 (4.7) | 0.045 (4.9) | 0.064 (2.1) | 0.081 (9.1) | 0.089 (4.1) | 0.064 (3.9) | | 0.090 (9.5) | 0.077 (5.5) | 0.042 (1.4) | | 0.078 (4.4) | 0.109 (6.5) | -0.075 (1.2) | | 0.111 (12.8) | 0.089 (11.3) | 0.047 (0.8) | 0.074 (1.8) | 0.080 (10.5) | 0.074 (7.4) | 0.004 (0.0) | |
| EXPSQ/100 | -0.118 (25.9) | -0.134 (9.2) | -0.072 (8.6) | -0.070 (1.8) | -0.116 (8.2) | -0.109 (2.8) | -0.052 (4.4) | -0.104 (1.7) | -0.130 (9.3) | -0.162 (2.6) | -0.087 (3.6) | | -0.130 (10.6) | -0.130 (4.1) | -0.056 (1.4) | | -0.123 (4.8) | -0.216 (3.8) | 0.014 (0.3) | | -0.094 (8.4) | -0.178 (7.2) | -0.094 (3.1) | -0.110 (1.5) | -0.110 (8.1) | -0.137 (5.4) | -0.019 (0.3) | |
| YRSEDUC | 0.129 (46.5) | 0.153 (29.5) | 0.121 (12.7) | 0.113 (7.4) | 0.143 (10.2) | 0.033 (0.4) | 0.066 (1.8) | 0.104 (3.7) | 0.131 (13.5) | 0.209 (8.8) | 0.135 (5.6) | | 0.133 (21.1) | 0.153 (10.2) | 0.100 (7.9) | | 0.134 (13.3) | 0.177 (14.8) | 0.082 (3.5) | | 0.135 (30.5) | 0.135 (24.3) | 0.152 (8.7) | 0.119 (5.3) | 0.101 (17.4) | 0.138 (11.2) | 0.132 (6.2) | |
| URBAN | 0.260 (5.3) | 0.195 (4.9) | 0.153 (1.2) | 0.129 (0.7) | 0.539 (2.5) | 0.033 (0.4) | -0.244 (0.7) | -0.172 (0.8) | 0.090 (1.4) | 0.205 (1.4) | 0.207 (1.5) | | -0.029 (0.3) | 0.241 (2.1) | 0.193 (0.7) | | 0.141 (1.5) | 0.037 (0.2) | 0.823 (2.9) | | -0.365 (3.2) | 0.270 (4.2) | 0.350 (0.7) | 0.261 (1.0) | -0.290 (1.5) | 0.067 (0.9) | 1.085 (0.5) | |
| BIRTOT | | -0.038 (5.3) | | 0.003 (0.1) | | -0.020 (1.1) | | 0.046 (1.5) | | 0.007 (0.3) | | | | 0.009 (0.3) | | | | -0.062 (2.5) | | | | -0.010 (0.8) | | -0.039 (0.5) | | -0.019 (1.0) | | |
| R-SQUARED | 0.470 | 0.586 | 0.389 | 0.357 | 0.451 | 0.589 | 0.233 | 0.164 | 0.347 | 0.583 | 0.314 | | 0.487 | 0.617 | 0.351 | | 0.486 | 0.633 | 0.468 | | 0.487 | 0.618 | 0.404 | 0.391 | 0.426 | 0.631 | 0.330 | |
| F-STAT | 1430.4 | 682.1 | 349.7 | 34.2 | 218.9 | 98.9 | 63.5 | 6.0 | 81.8 | 48.6 | 36.6 | | 232.1 | 115.1 | 39.5 | | 179.8 | 95.8 | 25.7 | | 483.9 | 279.4 | 49.2 | 6.5 | 177.6 | 125.9 | 39.1 | |
| STD.ERR | 0.552 | 0.568 | 0.716 | 0.904 | 0.566 | 0.648 | 0.664 | 0.952 | 0.586 | 0.564 | 0.703 | | 0.517 | 0.565 | 0.694 | | 0.561 | 0.555 | 0.711 | | 0.511 | 0.466 | 0.673 | 0.804 | 0.490 | 0.459 | 0.767 | |
| LN WAGE | 3.4491 (0.76) | 3.2744 (0.88) | 3.2087 (0.91) | 2.7003 (1.12) | 3.0829 (0.76) | 2.9235 (1.00) | 2.7861 (0.76) | 2.2047 (1.02) | 3.3308 (0.72) | 3.1231 (0.86) | 3.4152 (0.84) | 2.9553 (0.79) | 3.2680 (0.72) | 2.9948 (0.91) | 3.3051 (0.86) | 2.9028 (0.84) | 3.6145 (0.78) | 3.5575 (0.91) | 3.8335 (0.96) | 3.1751 (1.04) | 3.7189 (0.71) | 3.5172 (0.75) | 3.7517 (0.87) | 3.6709 (0.99) | 3.9918 (0.65) | 3.2197 (0.75) | 3.2817 (0.93) | 2.7916 (0.77) |
| WAGE/HOUR | 44.4 (59.8) | 39.5 (47.6) | 43.3 (116.8) | 29.4 (50.9) | 30.8 (39.4) | 32.4 (55.9) | 22.5 (27.5) | 15.6 (24.6) | 38.7 (60.0) | 32.9 (36.3) | 48.8 (84.4) | 27.5 (31.2) | 37.0 (45.8) | 28.6 (32.2) | 42.0 (58.1) | 26.5 (30.0) | 53.8 (69.1) | 54.9 (58.4) | 89.5 (285.0) | 40.0 (46.4) | 56.4 (74.7) | 45.7 (44.8) | 68.2 (119.5) | 69.1 (91.8) | 37.5 (37.6) | 33.7 (37.6) | 53.0 (186.6) | 23.8 (34.9) |
| WAGES/MONTH '000 | 7.8 (9.6) | 6.4 (6.8) | 7.5 (16.9) | 4.5 (7.8) | 5.3 (6.1) | 4.9 (7.1) | 3.9 (5.1) | 2.0 (2.6) | 6.9 (10.3) | 5.2 (5.0) | 8.5 (13.4) | 4.4 (4.6) | 6.6 (7.8) | 4.6 (4.9) | 7.9 (11.7) | 4.1 (4.5) | 9.4 (11.6) | 8.3 (8.4) | 12.2 (16.2) | 5.9 (6.3) | 10.0 (11.5) | 7.8 (7.3) | 12.4 (23.8) | 11.1 (14.1) | 6.8 (6.4) | 5.4 (4.6) | 9.2 (30.0) | 4.5 (7.7) |
| HOURS/WEEK | 45.9 (8.8) | 43.5 (8.1) | 45.2 (8.1) | 39.9 (10.9) | 44.8 (7.3) | 41.4 (10.1) | 43.5 (7.8) | 37.4 (10.1) | 46.0 (7.1) | 43.0 (10.0) | 45.4 (7.7) | 42.2 (10.6) | 46.3 (7.1) | 44.1 (9.5) | 47.0 (7.1) | 40.3 (10.6) | 45.6 (7.4) | 42.6 (10.0) | 43.6 (10.5) | 38.7 (12.9) | 46.0 (6.4) | 44.3 (6.8) | 46.7 (8.0) | 43.5 (9.9) | 46.4 (7.0) | 43.8 (8.9) | 47.1 (8.2) | 45.6 (11.4) |

Notes: Numbers in parentheses are t-statistics or standard deviations.

The results for the experience variables are in line with the concave earnings-experience profiles. The coefficients for experience and experience squared are significant in all the employee regressions, but less so for the self-employed. The coefficient of the fertility variable in the female regressions is significantly negative (-0.06) only in Rio for employees.

Education makes a large positive contribution to expected hourly earnings; the estimated schooling coefficients are consistently strong. Table 3.11 shows that women employees have higher returns to education than men, while among the self-employed they are about the same. Nationally, the returns to schooling among male and female employees are 13 percent and 15 percent, respectively. The corresponding values for the self-employed are 12 percent and 11 percent.

As might be expected, there are important regional differences. In the Northeast, the return for female employees is 18 percent, but only 14 percent for men. In the Northwest, the return is 21 percent for women, and 13 percent for men, while in Rio the values are 18 percent and 13 percent. In the Other Southeast the female advantage is 2 percentage points (15 percent versus 13 percent), and in the South the advantage is 4 percentage points (14 percent and 10 percent). In Sao Paulo, the schooling returns are the same for male and female employees (14 percent). As regards the self-employed, the estimated returns to education for women is higher than that for men in the Northeast (10 percent versus 7 percent), but slightly lower in Sao Paulo (13 percent versus 12 percent).

## 6.    Accounting For Male-Female Earnings Differentials

The usual strategy in analyzing male-female wage differentials is to partition the observed wage gap between an "endowments" component and a "coefficients" component. The latter is derived as an unexplained residual and is called "discrimination." We use the popular "decomposition approach," first developed by Oaxaca (1973), and extend its implementation to incorporate selectivity bias (Reimers, 1985) and the approach of Cotton (1988) that addresses the "index number" problem.

The decomposition analysis is based on observed mean characteristics (eg. education, work experience) and the parameter estimates of the selectivity-bias corrected wage equations. These regressions yield estimated wage structures of men and women in each work status. That is, the regression coefficients indicate the way in which the labor market rewards the background attributes. The basic question addressed by the decomposition method is: How much would the male-female wage gap change if men and women were paid according to a common wage structure, but their work-related attributes remained as they are? We now summarize the method.[30]

The decomposition analysis typically involves a logarithmic scale which can be transformed into monetary units. For each group of workers, the difference in the observed geometric mean wages between males (m) females (f) can be written as:

---

[30]    The limitations of the technique in measuring discrimination are discussed by   Cain (1986), Shapiro and Stelcner (1987), and Gunderson (1989).

$$\overline{lnW_m} - \overline{lnW_f} = (\overline{Z}_m\hat{\beta}_m - \overline{Z}_f\hat{\beta}_f) + (\overline{\lambda}_m\hat{k}_m - \overline{\lambda}_f\hat{k}_f)$$

where the $\overline{Z}s$ are the average background characteristics, and the $\hat{\beta}s$ and the $\hat{k}s$ are the estimated parameters.

As discussed by Reimers (1985), the observed wage differential has two components -- differences in mean wage offers (based on selectivity-corrected estimates) and differences in average selectivity bias between men and women. Depending on the magnitudes and direction of selectivity bias, the differences in observed mean wages may under- or over-state the difference in mean wage offers. Hence, the decomposition of the male-female wage differential should be based on wage offers, and not on observed wages.

The difference in average wage offers is given by:

$$\overline{lnW_m^0} - \overline{lnW_f^0} = (\overline{Z}_m\hat{\beta}_m - \overline{Z}_f\hat{\beta}_f)$$

*where*:

$$\overline{lnW_m^0} = \overline{lnW_m} - \overline{\lambda}_m\hat{k}_m$$

$$\overline{lnW_f^0} = \overline{lnW_f} - \overline{\lambda}_f\hat{k}_f$$

The decomposition method is straightforward and focuses on the issue of "unequal pay for equal productivity-generating characteristics," or wage discrimination. The decomposition of the gap in wage offers centers on differences in mean characteristics and differences in the estimated returns to these characteristics. In other words, if the estimated returns to the characteristics are the same for men and women, the wage offer gap would be solely attributable to differences in productivity-generating traits.

There is an index number problem in applying the technique: Which common wage structure (estimated coefficients) should be used as the non-discriminating norm? Since there is no clear cut solution to this problem we perform the analysis with three norms: (1) the male coefficients, (2) the female coefficients, and (3) a weighted average of the male and female coefficients based on the proportions of men and women in the sample.

The difference in average wage offers can now be decomposed into two components: A portion that is attributable to differences in regression coefficients, and a part that can be attributed to differences in endowments. There are at least three ways to compute these magnitudes.

1.    If the male wage function is used as the non-discriminatory norm:

$$\overline{lnW_m^0} - \overline{lnW_f^0} = \overline{Z}_f(\hat{\beta}_m - \hat{\beta}_f) + \hat{\beta}_m(\overline{Z}_m - \overline{Z}_f)$$

The term on the right is the endowments component and that on the left the coefficients or residual component.

2.    If the female wage function is used as the non-discriminatory norm:

$$\overline{lnW_m^0} - \overline{lnW_f^0} = \overline{Z}_m(\hat{\beta}_m - \hat{\beta}_f) + \hat{\beta}_f(\overline{Z}_m - \overline{Z}_f)$$

Again, the term on the right is the endowments component and that on the left the coefficients component.

3.    A third alternative suggested by Cotton (1988) is to define the non-discriminatory norm as the weighted average of the male and female coefficients where the weights are proportions of men $(P_m)$ and women $(P_f)$.

$$Let \quad \beta^* = P_m\hat{\beta}_m + P_f\hat{\beta}_f$$

$$\overline{lnW_m^0} - \overline{lnW_f^0} = \overline{Z}_m(\hat{\beta}_m - \beta^*) + \overline{Z}_f(\beta^* - \hat{\beta}_f) + \beta^*(\overline{Z}_m - \overline{Z}_f)$$

As before, the third term represents the portion attributable to differing endowments. The first and second terms divide the "unexplained" residual into two parts: A "premium" or higher than expected returns for men (the first term) and a "penalty" or lower than expected returns for women (the second term).

In the decomposition analysis we analyze wage differentials first between married men and women, and then between single men and women. This is done separately for employees and the self-employed.

### Estimates of Discrimination

It should be noted that the decomposition analysis is carried out using a logarithmic scale which can then be transformed into monetary units -- cruzeiros.[31] Since we are flexible regarding the choice of a non-discriminatory norm we present three estimates: using male coefficient weights, female coefficient weights, and a weighted average of the two. The endowments and coefficients components are reported in terms of logarithms, cruzeiros, and percentage of the gap in wage offers (expressed in logarithms). Before proceeding with the findings, we emphasize that there are some important limitations of the method, which include missing variables and errors in measurement problems. These shortcomings of the technique should be borne in mind.

*Married employees*[32] (Table 3.12).   Looking at Table 3.12 we see that the national observed wage gap (row 3) is 29 percent, but the magnitude varies across regions. It is highest in Sao Paulo (41 percent), followed by the Northeast (39 percent), Rio and the South (about 25 percent). The lowest value is in the Northwest (15 percent). After removing selectivity bias effects, there is quite a dramatic change in the gap in average wage offers when compared to the observed differential. At the national level the gap in wage offers rises to 33 percent (row 13). However, in Sao Paulo and Rio the gap in wage offers increases to 122 and 88 percent, respectively; in the Northwest it falls to only 5 percent, and in the Northeast it remains unchanged at 38 percent. In the South the mean wage offer of husbands is about 40 percent higher than that of wives, while in the Other Southeast it is 22 percent higher. This suggests that in most cases the observed wage

---

[31]    In 1980 the official exchange rate was about 40 cruzeiros = $ 1 US.

[32]    See Zabalza and Arrufat (1985) for a similar comparison of hourly earnings for British married men and women.

differential understates the disparity in wage offers due, of course, to differences in selectivity bias effects in the wage equations of husbands and wives.

The decomposition of the gap in wage offers shows that the "endowments" component favors wives, but this is far outweighed by the "coefficients" component, which penalizes wives in favor of husbands. Using the proportional weights (rows 18-21), we see that, for the entire country, the endowments portion favors wives by 70 percent of the wage offer gap, but husbands have coefficient advantages of 170 percent. In monetary terms, the endowment component translates into $15/hour while the "discrimination" component reflects $33/hour. This pattern -- endowments favoring wives and coefficients favoring husbands -- is similar in the other regions where the wage offer gap is large, and it seems not to make much of a difference which weights are chosen as the non-discriminating norm. In each case, the coefficients component, as an estimate of discrimination, is in excess of 100 percent of the wage offer differential.

There are several possible reasons for this large unexplained residual, and the attempt to measure "discrimination" is fraught with well-known difficulties and limitations. First, the presence of missing variables and errors-in-measurement bias may have unpredictable effects on the decomposition. Unobserved factors originating outside the labor market (e.g., household responsibilities, quality of education, ability, motivation, and aspirations) and imperfectly measured observed productivity traits (e.g. work experience) have, no doubt, influenced our estimate of "discrimination." Second, we note that the decomposition of the wage gap is based on the "average" man and woman, so that the entire weight is placed on mean observed characteristics which have a large dispersion. Recent work by Kuhn (1987) suggests that an improvement could be made by examining individual-specific measures of the "unexplained" component. This implies that it may be desirable to examine the distribution properties of the residual portion among individual women and men. Third, there is some evidence that the OLS estimator used by conventional analyses such as ours may result in upwardly-biased estimates of the unexplained male-female wage gap.[33] Finally, in examining the regression coefficients and mean characteristics we see that the intercept differences account for the largest part of the unexplained wage gap.[34] We caution the reader, however, that no importance should be given to this. For, as Jones (1983) has shown, a further division of the unexplained gap between intercept and slope effects is not independent of the arbitrary measurement of the explanatory variables, so that it is impossible to uniquely disentangle the portion of the wage gap between coefficient and intercept differences.

With the above qualifications, our decomposition of the wage gap between husbands and wives suggests an interesting conclusion: If married women and men wage earners were paid according to a common wage structure, the wages of wives would be at least as high as that of husbands (compare rows 11 and 12).

*The married self-employed* (Table 3.13). The decomposition analysis of the earnings gap for the self-employed is shown in Table 3.13. Two versions are presented. We present the analysis of

---

[33]     Evidence on this point is given in Ohsfeldt and Culler (1986) who show that a nonparametric "smearing" estimator yields a lower measure of the unexplained portion than does traditional OLS.

[34]     When we examined the contribution of each variable to the "discrimination" component (not reported here), we found that, in most cases, the returns to background characteristics tended to favor women rather than men, and thus contributed to narrowing the wage gap. The difference in the male-female intercepts far outweighed the coefficient differences of the explanatory variables.

**Table 3.12**

**Decomposition of Wage Differential - Employees - Married Men and Women**

| | | | All Brazil | Northeast | Northwest | Other Southeast | Rio | Sao Paulo | South |
|---|---|---|---|---|---|---|---|---|---|
| | Men | OBS | 14596 | 2590 | 1307 | 1863 | 1933 | 4405 | 2498 |
| | | % | 80 | 80 | 80 | 84 | 78 | 79 | 78 |
| | Women | OBS | 3741 | 639 | 325 | 357 | 553 | 1170 | 697 |
| | | % | 20 | 20 | 20 | 16 | 22 | 21 | 22 |
| (1) | Observed Male Wage | Log | 3.953 | 3.555 | 3.833 | 3.697 | 4.241 | 4.261 | 3.855 |
| | | | (0.89) | (0.91) | (0.86) | (0.80) | (0.93) | (0.84) | (0.76) |
| | | $ | 52.1 | 35.0 | 46.2 | 40.3 | 69.5 | 70.9 | 47.2 |
| (2) | Observed Female Wage | Log | 3.668 | 3.165 | 3.690 | 3.559 | 3.978 | 3.852 | 3.620 |
| | | | (0.96) | (1.09) | (0.90) | (0.06) | (1.02) | (0.85) | (0.77) |
| | | $ | 39.2 | 23.7 | 40.0 | -9.0 | 53.4 | 47.1 | 37.4 |
| (3) | Observed Gap | Log | 0.285 | 0.391 | 0.144 | 0.138 | 0.263 | 0.410 | 0.235 |
| | | $ | 12.9 | 11.3 | 6.2 | 5.2 | 16.1 | 23.8 | 9.9 |
| (4) | Selection Bias Male | Log | -0.201 | -0.096 | 0.025 | -0.201 | -0.779 | -1.051 | -0.291 |
| | | | (0.07) | (0.04) | (0.01) | (0.06) | (0.18) | (0.26) | (0.10) |
| | | $ | -11.6 | -3.5 | (1.2) | -9.0 | -81.9 | -131.9 | -16.0 |
| (5) | Selection Bias Female | Log | -0.151 | -0.107 | -0.067 | -0.122 | -0.157 | -0.228 | -0.130 |
| | | | (0.10) | 0.09 | (0.05) | (0.9) | (0.09) | (0.14) | (0.09) |
| | | $ | -6.4 | -2.7 | -2.8 | -4.6 | -9.1 | -12.0 | -5.2 |
| (6) | Selection Bias Gap | Log | -0.050 | 0.012 | 0.092 | -0.079 | -0.622 | -0.823 | -0.161 |
| | | $ | -5.2 | -0.8 | 3.9 | -4.4 | -72.8 | -119.8 | -10.8 |
| (7) | Male Wage Offer | Log | 4.154 | 3.651 | 3.808 | 3.898 | 5.020 | 5.312 | 4.146 |
| | | | (0.70) | (0.69) | (0.60) | (0.61) | (0.76) | (0.69) | (0.58) |
| | | $ | 63.7 | 38.5 | 45.1 | 49.3 | 151.4 | 202.8 | 63.2 |
| (8) | Female Wage Offer | Log | 3.819 | 3.272 | 3.757 | 3.681 | 4.135 | 4.080 | 3.750 |
| | | | (0.80) | (0.86) | (0.70) | (0.85) | (0.89) | (0.76) | (0.64) |
| | | $ | 45.5 | 26.4 | 42.8 | 39.7 | 62.5 | 59.1 | 42.5 |
| (9) | Male Wage Offer Female Weights | Log | 3.677 | 3.015 | 3.403 | 3.215 | 3.985 | 4.018 | 3.555 |
| | | | (0.72) | (0.80) | (0.68) | (0.68) | (0.76) | (0.64) | (0.56) |
| | | $ | 39.5 | 20.4 | 30.i | 24.9 | 53.8 | 42.5 | 35.0 |
| (10) | Female Wage Offer Male Weights | Log | 4.413 | 4.027 | 4.170 | 4.311 | 5.232 | 5.470 | 4.405 |
| | | | (0.74) | (0.73) | (0.62) | (0.72) | (0.81) | (0.73) | (0.62) |
| | | $ | 82.5 | 56.1 | 64.7 | 74.5 | 187.1 | 237.5 | 81.9 |
| (11) | Male Offer Frop. Weights | Log | 4.057 | 3.525 | 3.727 | 3.788 | 4.790 | 5.040 | 4.017 |
| | | | (0.70) | (0.71) | (0.61) | (0.62) | (0.76) | (0.68) | (0.57) |
| | | $ | 57.8 | 33.9 | 41.6 | 44.2 | 120.2 | 154.5 | 55.5 |
| (12) | Female Wage Offer Prop. Weights | Log | 4.291 | 3.878 | 4.088 | 4.210 | 4.988 | 5.178 | 4.262 |
| | | | (0.75) | (0.76) | (0.63) | (0.74) | (0.82) | (0.73) | (0.62) |
| | | $ | 73.1 | 48.3 | 59.6 | 67.3 | 146.6 | 177.4 | 71.0 |
| (13) | Wage Offer Gap | Log | 0.336 | 0.379 | 0.051 | 0.217 | 0.885 | 1.233 | 0.396 |
| | | $ | 18.2 | 12.1 | 2.3 | 9.6 | 88.9 | 143.6 | 20.7 |
| | | % | 100 | 100 | 100 | 100 | 100 | 100 | 100 |
| | **Male Weights** | | | | | | | | |
| (14) | Endowments | Log | -0.259 | -0.377 | -0.362 | -0.413 | -0.212 | -0.158 | -0.259 |
| | | $ | -18.8 | -17.6 | -19.7 | -25.2 | -35.7 | -34.8 | -18.7 |
| | | % | -77 | -99 | -707 | -191 | -24 | -13 | -65 |
| (15) | Coefficients | Log | 0.594 | 0.755 | 0.413 | 0.630 | 1.097 | 1.391 | 0.655 |
| | | | (0.11) | (0.17) | (0.19) | (0.14) | (0.19) | (0.17) | (0.10) |
| | | $ | 36.9 | 29.7 | 21.9 | 34.8 | 124.6 | 178.4 | 39.4 |
| | | % | 177 | 199 | 807 | 291 | 124 | 113 | 165 |
| | **Female Weights** | | | | | | | | |
| (16) | Endowments | Log | -0.142 | -0.257 | -0.354 | -0.466 | -0.150 | -0.062 | -0.195 |
| | | $ | -6.0 | -6.0 | -12.8 | -14.8 | -8.7 | -3.5 | -7.5 |
| | | % | -42 | -68 | -690 | -215 | -17 | -5 | -49 |
| (17) | Coefficients | Log | 0.477 | 0.636 | 0.405 | 0.683 | 1.035 | 1.294 | 0.591 |
| | | | (0.08) | (0.14) | (0.21) | (0.09) | (0.21) | (0.23) | (0.10) |
| | | $ | 24.2 | 18.1 | 15.0 | 24.4 | 97.6 | 147.2 | 28.2 |
| | | % | 142 | 168 | 790 | 315 | 117 | 105 | 149 |
| | **Proportional Weights** | | | | | | | | |
| (18) | Endowments | Log | -0.235 | -0.353 | -0.360 | -0.422 | -0.198 | -0.138 | -0.245 |
| | | $ | -15.3 | -14.4 | -18.0 | -23.2 | -26.4 | -22.9 | -15.4 |
| | | % | -70 | -93 | -703 | -195 | -22 | -11 | -62 |
| (19) | Coefficients | Log | 0.570 | 0.732 | 0.412 | 0.639 | 1.083 | 1.371 | 0.641 |
| | | $ | 33.4 | 26.5 | 20.3 | 32.8 | 115.2 | 166.5 | 36.1 |
| | | % | 170 | 193 | 803 | 295 | 122 | 111 | 162 |
| (20) | Male Premium | Log | 0.097 | 0.126 | 0.081 | 0.110 | 0.230 | 0.272 | 0.129 |
| | | | (0.02) | (0.03) | (0.04) | (0.01) | (0.05) | (0.05) | (0.02) |
| | | $ | 5.9 | 4.6 | 3.5 | 5.1 | 31.1 | 48.2 | 7.6 |
| | | % | 29 | 33 | 157 | 51 | 26 | 22 | 33 |
| (21) | Female Penalty | Log | 0.473 | 0.606 | 0.331 | 0.529 | 0.853 | 1.099 | 0.512 |
| | | | (0.09) | (0.14) | (0.16) | (0.11) | (0.15) | (0.14) | (0.08) |
| | | $ | 27.5 | 22.0 | 16.8 | 27.7 | 84.1 | 118.3 | 28.5 |
| | | % | 141 | 160 | 646 | 244 | 96 | 89 | 129 |

Notes: Calculated from regression coefficients and mean values. Numbers in parentheses are standard deviations.

In rows (1), (2), and (7) through (12) monetary values are the anit-logs of the logarithms.

For the other rows, monetary values are obtained by subtraction. For example, (3)=(1)-(2), and (13) = (7)-(8).

the husband-wife wage gap for paid self-employed workers. Then, since some wives (and a small number of husbands) are unpaid self-employed workers, we impute a fitted wage for them and decompose the wage offer differential between **all** self-employed wives and husbands. The two versions yield a similar set of results.

The observed hourly earnings gap for Brazil between paid self-employed husbands and wives is 48 percent (row 3, right panel). It is lowest in the South (39 percent), and highest in the Northeast, Rio and Sao Paulo (56-59 percent). The values for the Northwest and the Other Southeast are 53 percent and 47 percent respectively. We also see that the wage offer differential (row 13) tends to be smaller than the observed gap. Nationally, the wage offer gap falls to 37 percent. Similarly, in the Northeast and Northwest it drops to about 42 percent; in the Other Southeast to 36 percent, and to only 17 and 18 percent in Sao Paulo and the South, respectively. Only in Rio does the wage offer gap (59 percent) exceed slightly the observed differential (57 percent).

The decomposition of the wage offer gap yields results similar to that obtained for employees. The differential attributable to coefficient differences (the "discrimination" component) is strongly in favor of husbands, and this portion outweighs the "endowment" component, which usually favors wives. With the exception of Rio, the coefficients component is in excess of 100 percent of the gap in offers of hourly earnings. Unlike employees, an examination of the contribution of the explanatory variables to the earnings differential showed that the coefficient differences of the work experience variables was a consistent major contributor to widening the gap.

The conclusion we reach for self-employed wives and husbands is the same as that for employees: If productivity-generating traits of self-employed wives were rewarded on the same basis as those of self-employed husbands, the hourly earnings of wives would be at least equal to that of their husbands (compare row 11 and 12).

*Single employees* (Table 3.14). With a few exceptions, the observed male-female pay differential is smaller for single than for married people. Nationally, the gap is 18 percent, but the magnitude varies across regions, from 6 percent in Rio to 34 percent in the Other Southeast. However, looking at the gap in wage offers, we see that in three regions (the Northeast, the Northwest, and Rio) single women fare better than do men, while in the remaining regions the average wages offered to men exceed those offered to women.[35]

First consider the differential in the three regions where male wage offers exceed those of females. Looking at row 18 (proportional weights), we see that the men are strongly favored in terms of the coefficients component, implying that women tend to be paid less than men who are otherwise comparable in terms of background characteristics. The male advantage translates into a cruzeiro gain of $9/hour in the Other Southeast, $11/hour in the South, and $60/hour in Sao Paulo.

The story is different in the Northeast, the Northwest and Rio, where female wage offers exceed those of men. In the Northeast women have average wage offers that are 77 percent higher, while in the Northwest and Rio the female advantage is about 40 percent (row 13). The decomposition of the wage differentials shows that in each region women are favored in terms of the

---

[35]    We also performed the decomposition for employees based on the regressions that excluded the public sector dummy variable in the female equation. The results did not change in any significant way.

## Table 3.13
### Decomposition of Wage Differential - Self Employed - Married Men and Women

| | | All Brazil | Northeast | Northwest | Other Southeast | Rio | Sao Paulo | South | All Brazil | Northeast | Northwest | Other Southeast | Rio | Sao Paulo | South |
|---|---|---|---|---|---|---|---|---|---|---|---|---|---|---|---|
| Men | OBS | 11491 | 4078 | 1497 | 1445 | 578 | 1787 | 2106 | 11410 | 4026 | 1492 | 1442 | 576 | 1776 | 2097 |
| | % | 85 | 85 | 87 | 87 | 80 | 84 | 84 | 88 | 88 | 93 | 89 | 80 | 85 | 90 |
| Women | OBS | 1985 | 708 | 207 | 207 | 149 | 352 | 414 | 1518 | 547 | 117 | 173 | 143 | 311 | 227 |
| | % | 15 | 15 | 13 | 13 | 21 | 16 | 16 | 12 | 12 | 7 | 11 | 20 | 15 | 10 |
| (1) Observed Male Wage | Log | 3.673 | 3.759 | 3.724 | 3.724 | 4.317 | 4.422 | 3.807 | 3.676 | 3.137 | 3.759 | 3.724 | 4.319 | 4.424 | 3.809 |
| | | (1.13) | (1.02) | (0.93) | (1.03) | (1.02) | (1.06) | (1.05) | (1.07) | (0.94) | (0.90) | (1.01) | (0.98) | (0.98) | (1.01) |
| | s | 39.4 | 23.0 | 42.9 | 41.4 | 75.0 | 83.3 | 45 | 39.5 | 23.0 | 42.9 | 41.4 | 83.4 | 83.4 | 45.1 |
| (2) Observed Female Wage | Log | 3.053 | 2.471 | 3.186 | 3.151 | 3.767 | 3.806 | 3.161 | 3.198 | 2.553 | 3.234 | 3.259 | 3.865 | 3.865 | 3.425 |
| | | (1.93) | (1.66) | (1.92) | (1.74) | (1.39) | (1.77) | (2.12) | (1.20) | (1.08) | (1.08) | (1.14) | (1.10) | (1.08) | (0.99) |
| | s | 21.2 | 11.8 | 24.2 | 23.4 | 43.3 | 45.0 | 23.6 | 24.5 | 12.8 | 25.4 | 26.0 | 42.6 | 47.1 | 30.7 |
| (3) Observed Gap | Log | 0.621 | 0.664 | 0.573 | 0.573 | 0.550 | 0.616 | 0.646 | 0.478 | 0.584 | 0.525 | 0.465 | 0.567 | 0.559 | 0.384 |
| | s | 18.2 | 11.1 | 18.7 | 18.1 | 31.7 | 38.3 | 21.4 | 15.0 | 10.2 | 17.5 | 15.4 | 32.5 | 35.7 | 14.4 |
| (4) Selection Bias Male | Log | 0.202 | 0.195 | 0.091 | 0.253 | 0.464 | 0.847 | 0.150 | 0.202 | 0.195 | 0.091 | 0.253 | 0.464 | 0.847 | 0.150 |
| | | (0.09) | (0.06) | (0.03) | (0.10) | (0.12) | (0.25) | (0.06) | (0.09) | (0.06) | (0.03) | (0.10) | (0.13) | (0.25) | (0.06) |
| | s | 7.2 | 4.1 | 3.7 | 9.2 | 27.8 | 47.6 | 6.3 | 7.2 | 4.1 | 3.7 | 9.3 | 27.9 | 47.7 | 6.3 |
| (5) Selection Bias Female | Log | 0.098 | 0.041 | -0.011 | 0.140 | 0.478 | 0.126 | -0.070 | 0.091 | 0.039 | -0.012 | 0.147 | 0.483 | 0.122 | -0.052 |
| | | (0.05) | (0.02) | (0.01) | (0.10) | (0.24) | (0.06) | (0.04) | (0.05) | (0.02) | (0.01) | (0.10) | (0.24) | (0.06) | (0.03) |
| | s | 2.0 | 0.5 | -0.3 | 3.0 | 16.4 | 5.3 | -1.7 | 2.1 | 0.5 | -0.3 | 3.6 | 16.3 | 5.5 | -1.6 |
| (6) Selection Bias Gap | Log | 0.104 | 0.154 | 0.113 | 0.113 | -0.014 | 0.722 | 0.220 | 0.111 | 0.156 | 0.103 | 0.106 | -0.019 | 0.725 | 0.202 |
| | s | 5.2 | 3.6 | 6.2 | 6.2 | 11.4 | 42.3 | 8.0 | 5.1 | 3.6 | 4.0 | 5.7 | 11.6 | 42.2 | 7.9 |
| (7) Male Wage Offer | Log | 3.472 | 2.939 | 3.668 | 3.471 | 3.853 | 3.575 | 3.657 | 3.474 | 2.942 | 3.668 | 3.471 | 3.855 | 3.577 | 3.659 |
| | | (0.74) | (0.56) | (0.51) | (0.66) | (0.66) | (0.60) | (0.57) | (0.74) | (0.56) | (0.51) | (0.66) | (0.66) | (0.60) | (0.57) |
| | s | 32.2 | 18.9 | 39.2 | 32.2 | 47.1 | 35.7 | 38.7 | 32.3 | 18.9 | 39.2 | 32.2 | 47.2 | 35.8 | 38.8 |
| (8) Female Wage Offer | Log | 2.954 | 2.430 | 3.197 | 3.011 | 3.290 | 3.681 | 3.231 | 3.107 | 2.514 | 3.246 | 3.112 | 3.268 | 3.743 | 3.476 |
| | | (0.79) | (0.55) | (0.59) | (0.72) | (0.73) | (0.71) | (0.53) | (0.81) | (0.59) | (0.56) | (0.72) | (0.71) | (0.70) | (0.58) |
| | s | 32.2 | 11.4 | 24.5 | 20.3 | 26.8 | 39.7 | 25.3 | 22.4 | 12.4 | 25.6 | 22.4 | 26.3 | 42.2 | 32.3 |
| (9) Male Wage Offer Female Weights | Log | 3.093 | 2.473 | 3.241 | 3.136 | 3.566 | 3.898 | 3.385 | 3.096 | 2.477 | 3.960 | 3.136 | 3.569 | 3.901 | 3.387 |
| | | (0.77) | (0.56) | (0.56) | (0.71) | (0.66) | (0.73) | (0.53) | (0.77) | (0.56) | (0.51) | (0.71) | (0.66) | (0.73) | (0.53) |
| | s | 22.0 | 11.9 | 25.6 | 23 | 35.4 | 29.5 | 29.5 | 22.1 | 11.9 | 52.4 | 26.3 | 35.5 | 49.4 | 29.6 |
| (10) Female Wage Offer Male Weights | Log | 3.516 | 2.983 | 3.836 | 3.612 | 3.702 | 3.516 | 3.604 | 3.661 | 3.075 | 3.637 | 3.569 | 3.696 | 3.572 | 3.868 |
| | | (0.73) | (0.59) | (0.54) | (0.65) | (0.67) | (0.58) | (0.57) | (0.75) | (0.63) | (0.51) | (0.66) | (0.67) | (0.56) | (0.61) |
| | s | 33.6 | 19.8 | 46.3 | 37.1 | 40.5 | 33.7 | 36.8 | 38.9 | 21.7 | 52.4 | 35.5 | 40.3 | 35.6 | 47.8 |
| (11) Male Offer Prop. Weights | Log | 3.416 | 2.870 | 3.628 | 3.429 | 3.794 | 3.628 | 3.612 | 3.430 | 2.886 | 3.637 | 3.696 | 3.798 | 3.625 | 3.632 |
| | | (0.75) | (0.55) | (0.50) | (0.66) | (0.55) | (0.62) | (0.56) | (0.75) | (0.56) | (0.51) | (0.67) | (0.65) | (0.62) | (0.61) |
| | s | 30.4 | 17.6 | 37.6 | 30.8 | 44.4 | 37.6 | 37.1 | 30.9 | 17.9 | 38.0 | 40.3 | 44.6 | 37.5 | 46.0 |
| (12) Female Wage Offer Prop. Weights | Log | 3.433 | 2.901 | 3.776 | 3.537 | 3.617 | 3.544 | 3.543 | 3.596 | 3.008 | 3.908 | 3.798 | 3.611 | 3.598 | 3.829 |
| | | (0.74) | (0.59) | (0.54) | (0.65) | (0.67) | (0.62) | (0.56) | (0.75) | (0.62) | (0.51) | (0.65) | (0.67) | (0.58) | (0.61) |
| | s | 31.0 | 18.2 | 43.6 | 34.4 | 37.2 | 34.6 | 34.6 | 36.4 | 20.3 | 49.8 | 38.4 | 37.0 | 36.5 | 46.0 |
| (13) Wage Offer Gap | Log | 0.517 | 0.509 | 0.471 | 0.460 | 0.563 | -0.106 | 0.426 | 0.367 | 0.428 | 0.422 | 0.359 | 0.587 | -0.166 | 0.182 |
| | s | 13.0 | 7.5 | 14.7 | 11.9 | 20.3 | -4.0 | 13.4 | 9.9 | 6.6 | 13.5 | 9.7 | 20.9 | -6.4 | 6.5 |
| | % | 100 | 100 | 100 | 100 | 100 | 100 | 100 | 100 | 100 | 100 | 100 | 100 | 100 | 100 |
| **Male Weights** | | | | | | | | | | | | | | | |
| (14) Endowments | Log | -0.045 | -0.044 | -0.168 | -0.142 | 0.152 | 0.058 | 0.053 | -0.187 | -0.134 | -0.292 | -0.241 | 0.159 | 0.005 | -0.209 |
| | s | -1.5 | -0.9 | -7.2 | -4.9 | 6.6 | 2.0 | 2.0 | -6.6 | -2.7 | -13.3 | -8.8 | 6.9 | 0.2 | -9.0 |
| | % | -9 | -9 | -36 | -31 | 27 | 12 | 12 | -51 | -31 | -69 | -67 | 27 | -3 | -115 |
| (15) Coefficients | Log | 0.562 | 0.554 | 0.639 | 0.602 | 0.412 | 0.412 | 0.373 | 0.554 | 0.562 | 0.714 | 0.600 | 0.428 | -0.171 | 0.391 |
| | | (0.15) | (0.15) | (0.32) | (0.17) | (0.26) | (0.26) | (0.12) | (0.15) | (0.15) | (0.29) | (0.17) | (0.24) | (0.19) | (0.12) |
| | s | 14.5 | 8.4 | 21.9 | 16.7 | 13.7 | 13.7 | 11.4 | 16.5 | 9.3 | 26.8 | 18.5 | 14.0 | -6.6 | 15.5 |
| | % | 109 | 109 | 136 | 131 | 73 | 73 | 88 | 151 | 131 | 169 | 167 | 73 | 103 | 215 |
| **Female Weights** | | | | | | | | | | | | | | | |
| (16) Endowments | Log | 0.138 | 0.044 | 0.044 | 0.125 | 0.277 | 0.217 | 0.154 | -0.011 | -0.037 | -0.004 | 0.025 | 0.301 | 0.158 | 0.391 |
| | s | 2.8 | 0.5 | 1.1 | 2.7 | 8.6 | 9.6 | 4.2 | -0.3 | -0.4 | -0.1 | 0.6 | 9.2 | 7.2 | -2.8 |
| | % | 27 | 9 | 9 | 27 | 49 | 36 | 36 | -3 | -9 | -1 | 7 | 51 | -96 | -49 |
| (17) Coefficients | Log | 0.379 | 0.466 | 0.427 | 0.335 | 0.287 | -0.324 | 0.272 | 0.379 | 0.464 | 0.427 | 0.335 | 0.286 | -0.324 | 0.271 |
| | | (0.6) | (0.17) | (0.33) | (0.15) | (0.29) | (0.18) | (0.09) | (0.06) | (0.17) | (0.33) | (0.15) | (0.29) | (0.18) | (0.09) |
| | s | 10.1 | 7.0 | 13.6 | 9.1 | 11.7 | -13.6 | 9.2 | 10.2 | 7.0 | 13.6 | 9.1 | 11.7 | -13.7 | 9.2 |
| | % | 73 | 91 | 91 | 73 | 51 | 304 | 64 | 103 | 109 | 101 | 93 | 49 | 196 | 149 |
| **Proportional Weights** | | | | | | | | | | | | | | | |
| (18) Endowments | Log | -0.018 | -0.031 | -0.148 | -0.108 | 0.177 | 0.084 | 0.069 | -0.166 | -0.122 | -0.271 | -0.213 | 0.187 | 0.028 | -0.197 |
| | s | -0.5 | -0.6 | -6.0 | -3.5 | 7.2 | 3.0 | 2.5 | -5.6 | -2.3 | 11.8 | -7.3 | 7.6 | 1.0 | -8.2 |
| | % | -3 | -6 | -23 | -23 | 31 | 16 | 16 | -45 | -29 | -64 | -59 | 32 | -17 | -108 |
| (19) Coefficients | Log | 0.535 | 0.541 | 0.619 | 0.568 | 0.386 | -0.191 | 0.356 | 0.533 | 0.550 | 0.693 | 0.572 | 0.400 | -0.193 | 0.380 |
| | s | 13.5 | 8.1 | 20.7 | 15.4 | 13.1 | -7.0 | 10.9 | 15.5 | 8.9 | 25.3 | 17.1 | 13.4 | -7.5 | 14.7 |
| | % | 103 | 106 | 132 | 123 | 69 | 179 | 84 | 145 | 129 | 164 | 159 | 68 | 117 | 208 |
| (20) Male Premium | Log | 0.056 | 0.069 | 0.040 | 0.042 | 0.059 | -0.053 | 0.045 | 0.045 | 0.056 | 0.031 | 0.036 | 0.057 | -0.048 | 0.027 |
| | | (0.01) | (0.03) | (0.03) | (0.02) | (0.06) | (0.03) | (0.02) | (0.01) | (0.02) | (0.02) | (0.02) | (0.06) | (0.03) | (0.01) |
| | s | 1.7 | 1.3 | 1.5 | 1.3 | 2.7 | -2.0 | 1.7 | 1.4 | 1.0 | 1.2 | 1.1 | 2.6 | -1.8 | 1.0 |
| | % | 11 | 14 | 9 | 9 | 10 | 50 | 10 | 12 | 13 | 7 | 10 | 10 | 29 | 15 |
| (21) Female Penalty | Log | 0.479 | 0.472 | 0.579 | 0.526 | 0.327 | -0.137 | 0.312 | 0.489 | 0.495 | 0.662 | 0.536 | 0.343 | -0.145 | 0.353 |
| | | (0.13) | (0.13) | (0.29) | (0.15) | (0.21) | (0.16) | (0.10) | (0.14) | (0.14) | (0.27) | (0.15) | (0.19) | (0.16) | (0.11) |
| | s | 11.8 | 6.8 | 19.2 | 14.1 | 10.4 | -5.1 | 9.3 | 14.1 | 7.9 | 24.1 | 15.9 | 10.7 | -5.7 | 13.7 |
| | % | 93 | 93 | 123 | 114 | 58 | 129 | 73 | 133 | 116 | 157 | 149 | 58 | 88 | 194 |

Not Calculated from regression coefficients and mean values. Numbers in parentheses are standard deviations.

In rows (1), (2), and (7) through (12) monetary values are the anit-logs of the logarithms.

For the other rows, monetary values are obtained by subtraction. For example, (3)=(1)-(2), and (13)=(7)-(8).

**Table 3.14**
**Decomposition of Wage Differential - Employees - Single Men and Women**

| | | All Brazil | Northeast | Northwest | Other Southeast | Rio | Sao Paulo | South |
|---|---|---|---|---|---|---|---|---|
| Men | OBS | 9673 | 1609 | 929 | 1472 | 1147 | 3072 | 1444 |
| | % | 71 | 74 | 76 | 72 | 72 | 69 | 71 |
| Women | OBS | 3871 | 561 | 287 | 581 | 453 | 1391 | 598 |
| | % | 29 | 26 | 24 | 28 | 28 | 31 | 29 |
| (1) Observed Male Wage | Log | 3.449 | 3.083 | 3.331 | 3.288 | 3.615 | 3.719 | 3.392 |
| | | (0.76) | (0.76) | (0.72) | (0.72) | (0.78) | (0.71) | (0.65) |
| | $ | 31.5 | 21.8 | 28.0 | 26.8 | 37.1 | 41.2 | 29.7 |
| (2) Observed Female Wage | Log | 3.275 | 2.924 | 3.123 | 2.945 | 3.558 | 3.517 | 3.220 |
| | | (0.88) | (1.00) | (0.86) | (0.91) | (0.91) | (0.75) | (0.75) |
| | $ | 26.4 | 18.6 | 22.7 | 19.0 | 35.1 | 33.7 | 25 |
| (3) Observed Gap | Log | 0.174 | 0.160 | 0.208 | 0.343 | 0.057 | 0.202 | 0.172 |
| | $ | 5.0 | 3.2 | 5.2 | 7.8 | 2.1 | 7.5 | 4.7 |
| (4) Selection Bias Male | Log | 0.156 | 0.697 | 0.174 | -0.116 | 0.112 | -0.970 | -0.333 |
| | | (0.10) | (0.39) | (0.10) | (0.06) | (0.05) | (0.45) | (0.20) |
| | $ | 4.6 | 11.0 | 4.5 | -3.3 | 3.9 | -67.5 | -11.7 |
| (5) Selection Bias Female | Log | -0.228 | -0.233 | -0.437 | -0.259 | -0.349 | -0.293 | -0.246 |
| | | (0.11) | (0.15) | (0.22) | (0.11) | (0.15) | (0.10) | (0.11) |
| | $ | -6.8 | -4.9 | -12.4 | -5.6 | -14.7 | -11.5 | -7.0 |
| (6) Selection Bias Gap | Log | 0.385 | 0.930 | 0.610 | 0.143 | 0.461 | -0.676 | -0.086 |
| | $ | 11.3 | 15.8 | 16.9 | 2.3 | 18.6 | -56.0 | -4.7 |
| (7) Male Wage Offer | Log | 3.293 | 2.386 | 3.157 | 3.404 | 3.503 | 4.688 | 3.725 |
| | | (0.57) | (0.78) | (0.46) | (0.49) | (0.54) | (0.65) | (0.40) |
| | $ | 26.9 | 10.9 | 23.5 | 30.1 | 33.2 | 108.7 | 41.5 |
| (8) Female Wage Offer | Log | 3.503 | 3.157 | 3.560 | 3.204 | 3.907 | 3.180 | 3.466 |
| | | (0.75) | (0.90) | (0.83) | (0.79) | (0.82) | (0.65) | (0.67) |
| | $ | 33.2 | 23.5 | 35.1 | 24.6 | 49.7 | 45.2 | 32.0 |
| (9) Male Wage Offer Female Weights | Log | 3.316 | 2.728 | 3.112 | 2.952 | 3.719 | 3.709 | 3.332 |
| | | (0.73) | (0.82) | (0.80) | (0.70) | (0.75) | (0.62) | (0.61) |
| | $ | 27.6 | 15.3 | 22.5 | 19.2 | 41.2 | 40.8 | 28.0 |
| (10) Female Wage Offer Male Weights | Log | 3.450 | 2.837 | 3.362 | 3.481 | 3.614 | 4.581 | 3.715 |
| | | (0.60) | (0.82) | (0.52) | (0.58) | (0.57) | (0.64) | (0.46) |
| | $ | 31.5 | 17.1 | 28.8 | 32.5 | 37.1 | 97.6 | 41.1 |
| (11) Male Offer Prop. Weights | Log | 3.299 | 2.474 | 3.146 | 3.276 | 3.564 | 4.383 | 3.610 |
| | | (0.61) | (0.79) | (0.54) | (0.54) | (0.59) | (0.57) | (0.43) |
| | $ | 27.1 | 11.9 | 23.3 | 26.5 | 35.3 | 80.1 | 37.0 |
| (12) Female Wage Offer Prop. Weights | Log | 3.465 | 2.919 | 3.408 | 3.403 | 3.697 | 4.341 | 3.642 |
| | | (0.64) | (0.84) | (0.59) | (0.63) | (0.64) | (0.63) | (0.51) |
| | $ | 32.0 | -0.771 | 30.2 | 30.0 | 40.3 | 76.8 | 38.2 |
| (13) Wage Offer Gap | Log | -0.210 | -12.6 | -0.403 | 0.2 | -0.404 | 0.878 | 0.259 |
| | $ | -6.3 | 12.1 | -11.6 | 5.5 | -16.5 | 63.5 | 9.4 |
| | % | 100 | 100 | 100 | 100 | 100 | 100 | 100 |
| **Male Weights** | | | | | | | | |
| (14) Endowments | Log | -0.157 | -0.451 | -0.205 | -0.077 | -0.111 | 0.107 | 0.01 |
| | $ | -4.6 | -6.2 | -5.3 | -2.4 | -3.9 | 11.1 | 0.4 |
| | % | 75 | 58 | 51 | -39 | 27 | 12 | 4 |
| (15) Coefficients | Log | -0.053 | -0.32 | -0.198 | 0.277 | -0.293 | 0.771 | 0.249 |
| | | (0.19) | (0.20) | (0.34) | (0.28) | (0.28) | (0.33) | (0.32) |
| | $ | -1.7 | -6.4 | -6.3 | 7.9 | -12.6 | 52.4 | 9.0 |
| | % | 25 | 42 | 49 | 139 | 73 | 88 | 96 |
| **Female Weights** | | | | | | | | |
| (16) Endowments | Log | -0.187 | -0.429 | -0.448 | -0.252 | -0.188 | -0.102 | -0.134 |
| | $ | -5.7 | -8.2 | -12.7 | -5.5 | -8.5 | -4.4 | -4.0 |
| | % | 89 | 56 | 111 | -126 | 46 | -12 | -52 |
| (17) Coefficients | Log | -0.023 | -0.342 | 0.045 | 0.452 | -0.216 | 0.980 | 0.392 |
| | | (0.19) | (0.23) | (0.39) | (0.31) | (0.27) | (0.65) | (0.40) |
| | $ | -0.6 | -4.4 | 1.0 | 10.9 | -8.0 | 67.9 | 13.4 |
| | % | 11 | 44 | -11 | 226 | 54 | 112 | 152 |
| **Proportional Weights** | | | | | | | | |
| (18) Endowments | Log | -0.166 | -0.445 | -0.062 | -0.127 | -0.133 | 0.042 | -0.032 |
| | $ | -4.9 | -6.7 | -7.0 | -3.6 | -5 | 3.3 | -1.2 |
| | % | 79 | 58 | 65 | -63 | 33 | 5 | -13 |
| (19) Coefficients | Log | -0.045 | -0.326 | -0.141 | 0.327 | -0.271 | 0.836 | 0.291 |
| | $ | -1.4 | -6.0 | -4.7 | 9 | -11.5 | 60.2 | 10.7 |
| | % | 21 | 42 | 35 | 163 | 67 | 95 | 113 |
| (20) Male Premium | Log | -0.007 | -0.089 | 0.011 | 0.128 | -0.061 | 0.305 | 0.115 |
| | | (0.06) | (0.06) | (0.09) | (0.09) | (0.08) | (0.20) | (0.12) |
| | $ | -0.2 | -1.0 | 0.2 | 3.6 | -2.1 | 28.6 | 4.5 |
| | % | 3 | 22 | -3 | 64 | 15 | 35 | 44 |
| (21) Female Penalty | Log | -0.038 | -0.237 | 0.151 | 0.199 | -0.21 | 0.530 | 0.176 |
| | | (0.14) | (0.15) | (0.26) | (0.20) | (0.20) | (0.22) | (0.23) |
| | $ | -1.2 | -5.0 | -4.9 | 5.4 | -9.4 | 31.6 | 6.2 |
| | % | 18 | 31 | 38 | 99 | 52 | 60 | 68 |

Notes: Calculated from regression coefficients and mean values. Numbers in parentheses are standard deviations.
In rows (1), (2), and (7) through (12) monetary values are the anti-logs of the logarithms.
For the other rows, monetary values are obtained by subtraction. For example, (3)=(1)-(2), and (13)=(7)-(8).

endowments and coefficients components. In the Northwest, the residual component is 35 percent of the wage offer gap; it is 42 percent in the Northeast, and 67 percent in Rio.

*The single self-employed* (Table 3.15). Finally, we come to the results for the self-employed shown in Table 3.15. The analysis of the hourly earnings gap that shows the observed earnings differential (row 3, right panel) differs from the gap in offered wages (row 13). For example, nationally and in the Northeast the observed hourly wage is about one-half that of men. However, the offered wages of women are only 23 percent less than those offered to men for the entire country, and in the Northeast women have an earnings advantage of 28 percent. The decomposition results show that nationally men are strongly favored in terms of coefficient differences, while in the Northeast the reverse is the case -- the coefficients component strongly penalizes men. The pattern is similar when the analysis is performed for all (paid and unpaid) self-employed workers (see left panel).

In sum, the decomposition analysis for single men and women yields a much lower measure of "discrimination" than that for wives and husbands. This suggests that factors outside the labor market (household responsibilities, fertility, and work interruptions) probably play an important role in the earnings disadvantage of married women.

## 7.    Discussion

In this study we have used data from the 1980 Census of Brazil to investigate determinants of labor force status and earnings in samples of married and single men and women. Unlike most studies on labor markets in developing countries, we analyzed labor force status in terms of a three-choice model (employee, self-employed, no work). Moreover, our analysis of earnings determinants among employees and the self-employed explicitly incorporates the selection of individuals among the three types of labor force status. National and region-specific selectivity corrected wage regressions were then used to examine the effects of human capital and other wage-determining characteristics, and to explore the issue of male-female wage differentials among wage and self-employed workers.

### Main Findings

1.    The regional diversity of Brazil is clearly reflected in the estimated models of labor force status and earnings. This pluralism leads us to concur with Birdsall and Behrman (1984) that much care must be taken in reaching conclusions from estimates for Brazil "as a whole." Nation-wide estimates of policy-relevant considerations such as returns to human capital and gender disparities may be misleading.

2.    It is important to analyze the labor force status, especially of single and married women, in terms of a three-choice context. For example, although education plays an important role in determining overall labor market participation, the principal effect is to increase the propensity to perform wage work; the schooling effects on self-employment are generally small. Our empirical results suggest that modeling labor force behavior in developing countries in terms of only a "work or no-work" choice is likely to mask important aspects of the underlying determining factors. This point is especially relevant for women, and, during periods of prolonged recession, for men as well.

3.    Our results reflect the well-documented findings that the presence of young children in the home and more advanced age discourages married women's labor market participation.

**Table 3.15**
Decomposition of Wage Differential - Self-Employed - Single Men and Women

| | | | All Brazil | Northeast | Sao Paulo | South | All Brazil | Northeast | Sao Paulo | South |
|---|---|---|---|---|---|---|---|---|---|---|
| | Men | OBS | 3301 | 1261 | 443 | 484 | 3301 | 1261 | 443 | 484 |
| | | % | 81 | 79 | 80 | 73 | 88 | 85 | 85 | 92 |
| | Women | OBS | 753 | 328 | 109 | 177 | 439 | 222 | 79 | 41 |
| | | % | 19 | 21 | 20 | 27 | 12 | 15 | 15 | 8 |
| (1) | Observed Male Wage | Log | 3.209 | 2.786 | 3.752 | 3.282 | 3.209 | 2.786 | 3.752 | 3.282 |
| | | | (0.91) | (0.76) | (0.87) | (0.93) | (0.91) | (0.76) | (0.87) | (0.93) |
| | | $ | 24.7 | 16.2 | 42.6 | 26.6 | 24.7 | 16.2 | 42.6 | 26.6 |
| (2) | Observed Female Wage | Log | 2.553 | 2.154 | 3.501 | 2.692 | 2.700 | 2.205 | 3.671 | 2.792 |
| | | | (1.88) | (1.60) | (2.13) | (1.52) | (1.12) | (1.02) | (0.99) | (0.77) |
| | | $ | 12.8 | 8.6 | 33.1 | 14.8 | 14.9 | 9.1 | 39.3 | 16.3 |
| (3) | Observed Gap | Log | 0.656 | 0.632 | 0.251 | 0.590 | 0.508 | 0.581 | 0.081 | 0.490 |
| | | $ | 11.9 | 7.6 | 9.4 | 11.9 | 9.9 | 7.1 | 3.3 | 10.3 |
| (4) | Selection Bias Male | Log | 0.204 | 0.635 | -1.176 | -1.448 | 0.204 | 0.635 | -1.176 | -1.448 |
| | | | (0.07) | (0.29) | (0.22) | (0.52) | (0.07) | (0.29) | (0.22) | (0.52) |
| | | $ | 4.6 | 7.6 | -95.5 | -86.6 | 4.6 | 7.6 | -95.5 | -86.6 |
| (5) | Selection Bias Female | Log | -0.086 | -0.245 | -0.172 | -0.705 | -0.077 | -0.230 | -0.166 | -0.484 |
| | | | (0.05) | (0.12) | (0.13) | (0.33) | (0.06) | (0.13) | (0.13) | (0.48) |
| | | $ | -1.1 | -2.4 | -6.2 | -15.1 | -1.2 | -2.3 | -7.1 | -10.2 |
| (6) | Selection Bias Gap | Log | 0.289 | 0.880 | -1.004 | -0.743 | 0.281 | 0.864 | -1.010 | -0.963 |
| | | $ | 5.7 | 10.0 | -89.2 | -71.5 | 5.8 | 10.0 | -88.4 | -76.4 |
| (7) | Male Wage Offer | Log | 3.005 | 2.151 | 4.928 | 4.729 | 3.005 | 2.151 | 4.928 | 4.729 |
| | | | (0.53) | (0.26) | (0.62) | (0.91) | (0.53) | (0.26) | (0.62) | (0.91) |
| | | $ | 20.2 | 8.6 | 138.1 | 113.2 | 20.2 | 8.6 | 138.1 | 113.2 |
| (8) | Female Wage Offer | Log | 2.638 | 2.399 | 3.673 | 3.396 | 2.778 | 2.434 | 3.837 | 3.276 |
| | | | (0.54) | (0.34) | (0.61) | (0.24) | (0.64) | (0.38) | (0.61) | (0.30) |
| | | $ | 14.0 | 11.0 | 39.4 | 29.9 | 16.1 | 11.4 | 46.4 | 26.5 |
| (9) | Male Wage Offer Female Weights | Log | 2.702 | 2.337 | 3.742 | 3.770 | 2.702 | 2.337 | 3.742 | 3.770 |
| | | | (0.59) | (0.36) | (0.52) | (1.16) | (0.59) | (0.36) | (0.52) | (1.16) |
| | | $ | 14.9 | 10.4 | 42.2 | 43.4 | 14.9 | 10.4 | 42.2 | 43.4 |
| (10) | Female Wage Offer Male Weights | Log | 2.885 | 2.122 | 4.988 | 4.437 | 3.031 | 2.133 | 5.143 | 4.981 |
| | | | (0.51) | (0.24) | (0.66) | (0.63) | (0.59) | (0.26) | (0.67) | (0.97) |
| | | $ | 17.9 | 8.3 | 146.6 | 84.5 | 20.7 | 8.4 | 171.2 | 145.7 |
| (11) | Male Offer Prop. Weights | Log | 2.949 | 2.190 | 4.694 | 4.473 | 2.969 | 2.179 | 4.748 | 4.654 |
| | | | (0.53) | (0.26) | (0.59) | (0.64) | (0.53) | (0.26) | (0.60) | (0.81) |
| | | $ | 19.1 | 8.9 | 109.2 | 87.6 | 19.5 | 8.8 | 115.4 | 105.0 |
| (12) | Female Wage Offer Prop. Weights | Log | 2.839 | 2.179 | 4.728 | 4.159 | 3.001 | 2.178 | 4.945 | 4.848 |
| | | | (0.51) | (0.25) | (0.65) | (0.48) | (0.59) | (0.27) | (0.66) | (0.90) |
| | | $ | 17.1 | 8.8 | 113.1 | 64.0 | 20.1 | 8.8 | 140.5 | 127.5 |
| (13) | Wage Offer Gap | Log | 0.367 | -0.248 | 1.255 | 1.333 | 0.227 | -0.283 | 1.091 | 1.453 |
| | | $ | 6.2 | -2.4 | 98.7 | 83.4 | 4.1 | -2.8 | 91.7 | 86.8 |
| | | % | 100 | 100 | 100 | 100 | 100 | 100 | 100 | 100 |
| | **Male Weights** | | | | | | | | | |
| (14) | Endowments | Log | 0.120 | 0.030 | -0.060 | 0.292 | -0.026 | 0.019 | -0.215 | -0.252 |
| | | $ | 2.3 | 0.3 | -8.6 | 28.7 | -0.5 | 0.2 | -33.1 | -32.5 |
| | | % | 33 | -12 | -5 | 22 | -11 | -7 | -20 | -17 |
| (15) | Coefficients | Log | 0.247 | -0.278 | 1.315 | 1.041 | 0.253 | -0.302 | 1.306 | 1.706 |
| | | | (0.12) | (0.18) | (0.22) | (0.64) | (0.14) | (0.20) | (0.24) | (0.90) |
| | | $ | 3.9 | -2.7 | 107.3 | 54.7 | 4.6 | -3.0 | 124.8 | 119.2 |
| | | % | 67 | 112 | 105 | 78 | 111 | 107 | 120 | 117 |
| | **Female Weights** | | | | | | | | | |
| (16) | Endowments | Log | 0.064 | -0.062 | 0.069 | 0.374 | -0.076 | -0.097 | -0.095 | 0.494 |
| | | $ | 0.9 | -0.7 | 2.8 | 13.5 | -1.2 | -1.1 | -4.2 | 16.9 |
| | | % | 17 | 25 | 5 | 28 | -33 | 34 | -9 | 34 |
| (17) | Coefficients | Log | 0.303 | -0.186 | 1.186 | 0.959 | 0.303 | -0.186 | 1.186 | 0.959 |
| | | | (0.18) | (0.23) | (0.28) | (1.69) | (0.18) | (0.23) | (0.28) | (1.69) |
| | | $ | 5.3 | -1.8 | 95.9 | 69.8 | 5.3 | -1.8 | 95.9 | 69.8 |
| | | % | 83 | 75 | 95 | 72 | 133 | 66 | 109 | 66 |
| | **Proportional Weights** | | | | | | | | | |
| (18) | Endowments | Log | 0.109 | 0.011 | -0.035 | 0.314 | -0.032 | 0.001 | -0.197 | -0.194 |
| | | $ | 2.0 | 0.1 | -3.9 | 23.6 | -0.6 | 0.1 | -25.1 | -22.5 |
| | | % | 30 | 4 | -3 | 24 | -14 | 0 | -18 | -13 |
| (19) | Coefficients | Log | 0.257 | -0.259 | 1.289 | 1.019 | 0.259 | -0.284 | 1.288 | 1.647 |
| | | $ | 4.2 | -2.5 | 102.5 | 59.8 | 4.7 | -2.8 | 116.8 | 109.2 |
| | | % | 70 | 104 | 103 | 76 | 114 | 100 | 118 | 113 |
| (20) | Male Premium | Log | 0.056 | -0.038 | 0.234 | 0.257 | 0.036 | -0.028 | 0.179 | 0.075 |
| | | | (0.03) | (0.05) | (0.06) | (0.45) | (0.02) | (0.03) | (0.04) | (0.13) |
| | | $ | 1.1 | -0.3 | 28.8 | 25.7 | 0.7 | -0.2 | 22.7 | 8.2 |
| | | % | 15 | 15 | 19 | 19 | 16 | 10 | 16 | 5 |
| (21) | Female Penalty | Log | 0.201 | -0.220 | 1.055 | 0.762 | 0.223 | -0.257 | 1.109 | 1.572 |
| | | | (0.09) | (0.15) | (0.17) | (0.47) | (0.12) | (0.17) | (0.20) | (0.83) |
| | | $ | 3.1 | -2.2 | 73.7 | 34.1 | 4.0 | -2.6 | 94.1 | 101 |
| | | % | 55 | 89 | 84 | 57 | 98 | 91 | 102 | 108 |

Notes: See notes to Table 20. A value of 0.000001 was assigned to the observed earnings of unpaid family workers.

The analyses for the remaining regions are excluded because of too small sample sizes for women.

Brazil does not differ in these respects from other countries. To some extent, a larger household and having a spouse who is an employee mitigates these deterrent effects.

4.    Urban residence is conducive for both men and women to work as employees and also enhances their earnings. The effects, however, on being self-employed and on earnings are generally weak.

5.    Our estimates show that education is an important, perhaps the most important, determinant of labor force status and earnings. We found that education not only enhances earnings, but plays an important role in "sorting" individuals among the alternative labor force activities. These indirect "sorting effects" of schooling strongly suggest the importance of incorporating them in an analysis of earnings determinants. Schooling effects remain strong in the selectivity-corrected wage regressions for males and females, especially for employees, but less so among the self-employed. We also note that our estimated returns to schooling are generally bracketed by those obtained for other Latin American countries.

6.    Finally, we comment about male-female earnings differentials. The decomposition analyses revealed that the gap in wage offers between husbands and wives could not be accounted for by differences in earnings-determining traits. This residual could be attributed, with caution, to labor market "discrimination." Our results show that if the given wage-determining characteristics of wives were rewarded on the same basis as those of husbands, the (hypothetical) average hourly earnings of married women would be at least equal to those of their spouses. What makes us uneasy about calling this result "discrimination" is mainly that it is based on data and estimation methods that are subject to well-known limitations, including husband-wife (life-cycle) productivity differences that are not easily measurable or observable. An indication that this is likely to be the case is revealed by the findings for the samples of the relatively young men and women. The "unexplained" wage gap was generally not an issue; in fact, the decomposition analysis showed that the labor market tended to "favor" single women. An important question, however, is will the "premium" persist after they marry?

### *Policy Implications*

A decade has passed since the 1980 Census of Brazil and it might be asked how the findings of the study are relevant today? As stated in the introduction, after a period of relatively high growth in the 1970s, the 1980s were a "lost decade" for Brazil. The prospects are not encouraging. The statistics for 1990 show that Brazil experienced its sharpest recession in a decade. Gross domestic product declined by 4.3 percent (US$12 billion), the monthly inflation rate was 20 percent, industrial production shrank by 8 percent, and over 250,000 workers lost their jobs in the state of Sao Paulo alone. Moreover, little progress has been made in reducing the massive debt of $125 billion.

The reduced household incomes and prospects for wage employment will dramatically alter the structure of labor markets. More single and married women as well as children, who previously did not perform market work, will continue to join the labor force, probably as self-employed workers. Men who held wage jobs will either become unemployed or self-employed. Large groups of young people are unlikely to complete their schooling and those who do will find it increasingly difficult to find wage jobs corresponding to their qualification. Both groups, no doubt, will resort to self-employment. At the same time, the sharp reductions in federal and state social expenditures on health and education in the 1980s is likely to continue.

While our study provides several vital insights into how policy, such as extended support for education resulting in a more highly-skilled labor force, may be expected to influence work status and earnings, any conclusions and policy implications are made based on our cross-sectional (static) data. It is quite reasonable to expect that the magnitudes of the responses we have estimated may differ between 1980 and the present due to the business cycle. However, it is unlikely that the direction of the results would change. This is confirmed in the next chapter. Nonetheless, it is important to study with some care the dynamic (including stability) dimensions of work status and earnings determinants. One, and perhaps the only, way now available to do this would be to redo the analysis using a more recent data set. Adopting our approach for the 1990 Census or other recent data would be particularly useful given that 1990 stands in stark contrast to 1980 in Brazil. Knowledge of the determinants of work status and earnings in both expansionary and recessionary periods suggests that policy can be conditioned on current and expected aggregate economic activity.

The overall effects on the development process of the structural changes in the labor market and the budgetary squeezes on education are not yet well understood. This study provides a benchmark by which the consequences of the Brazilian economic crisis may be compared. The next chapter examines the relevant issues using data for 1989.

### Appendix Table 3A.1
### Means and Variables Used in Logits - Married Women

| REGION | OBS | KIDS 0-2 | KIDS 3-5 | KIDS 6-14 | FAMILY SIZE | AGE | AGESQ /100 | YEARS SCHOOL | HUSBAND EMPLOYER | ASSET INCOME | HUSBAND EARNINGS | OWN HOME | ROOMS IN HOME | URBAN |
|---|---|---|---|---|---|---|---|---|---|---|---|---|---|---|
| **ALL BRAZIL** | | | | | | | | | | | | | | |
| Total | 28926 | 0.45 | 0.40 | 1.04 | 7.33 | 36.19 | 14.55 | 3.68 | 0.51 | 5,350 | 13,860 | 0.61 | 5.12 | 0.68 |
| | 100.0% | (0.67) | (0.65) | (1.39) | (2.81) | (12.08) | (9.56) | (3.86) | (0.50) | (15,350) | (27,010) | (0.49) | (2.32) | (0.47) |
| Non-workers | 23200 | 0.48 | 0.42 | 1.04 | 7.22 | 36.38 | 14.80 | 3.18 | 0.49 | 5,380 | 13,120 | 0.61 | 5.07 | 0.65 |
| | 80.20% | (0.68) | (0.66) | (1.39) | (2.73) | (12.50) | (9.93) | (3.35) | (0.50) | (15,370) | (26,190) | (0.49) | (2.26) | (0.48) |
| Self-employed | 1985 | 0.38 | 0.40 | 1.30 | 8.36 | 38.04 | 15.64 | 3.38 | 0.33 | 5,890 | 13,740 | 0.68 | 5.22 | 0.60 |
| | 6.9% | (0.63) | (0.65) | (1.54) | (3.08) | (10.80) | (8.60) | (3.85) | (0.47) | (20,680) | (28,550) | (0.47) | (2.41) | (0.49) |
| Employees | 3741 | 0.31 | 0.30 | 0.93 | 7.45 | 33.97 | 12.45 | 6.96 | 0.70 | 4,830 | 18,480 | 0.55 | 5.38 | 0.89 |
| | 12.9% | (0.55) | (0.57) | (1.32) | (2.98) | (9.56) | (7.11) | (5.08) | (0.46) | (11,460) | (30,500) | (0.50) | (2.58) | (0.31) |
| **NORTHEAST** | | | | | | | | | | | | | | |
| Total | 7374 | 0.56 | 0.50 | 1.26 | 7.72 | 36.45 | 14.81 | 2.30 | 0.35 | 2,650 | 8,020 | 0.67 | 5.00 | 0.50 |
| | 100.0% | (0.75) | (0.73) | (1.58) | (3.11) | (12.35) | (9.82) | (3.39) | (0.48) | (8,440) | (19,220) | (0.47) | (2.17) | (0.50) |
| Non-workers | 6027 | 0.58 | 0.52 | 1.24 | 7.61 | 36.51 | 14.94 | 1.91 | 0.34 | 2,680 | 7,530 | 0.67 | 4.94 | 0.48 |
| | 81.7% | (0.75) | (0.74) | (1.57) | (3.01) | (12.70) | (10.13) | (2.89) | (0.48) | (8,830) | (17,910) | (0.47) | (2.10) | (0.50) |
| Self-employed | 708 | 0.53 | 0.49 | 1.52 | 8.74 | 37.85 | 15.59 | 1.77 | 0.22 | 2,360 | 6,090 | 0.77 | 4.91 | 0.41 |
| | 9.6% | (0.74) | (0.71) | (1.64) | (3.25) | (11.26) | (8.91) | (2.93) | (0.42) | (6,390) | (10,070) | (0.42) | (2.17) | (0.49) |
| Employees | 639 | 0.39 | 0.34 | 1.14 | 7.60 | 34.33 | 12.71 | 6.59 | 0.60 | 2,680 | 14,770 | 0.60 | 5.64 | 0.78 |
| | 8.7% | (0.64) | (0.63) | (1.56) | (3.62) | (9.61) | (7.20) | (4.94) | (0.49) | (6,420) | (32,780) | (0.49) | (2.71) | (0.42) |
| **NORTHWEST** | | | | | | | | | | | | | | |
| Total | 3002 | 0.56 | 0.48 | 1.18 | 7.60 | 34.05 | 12.97 | 3.35 | 0.44 | 3,620 | 12,790 | 0.62 | 4.61 | 0.61 |
| | 100.0% | (0.74) | (0.69) | (1.51) | (3.10) | (11.74) | (9.01) | (3.60) | (0.50) | (11,610) | (25,700) | (0.48) | (2.30) | (0.49) |
| Non-workers | 2522 | 0.59 | 0.49 | 1.16 | 7.50 | 34.04 | 13.06 | 2.81 | 0.42 | 3,450 | 12,020 | 0.62 | 4.53 | 0.57 |
| | 84.0% | (0.76) | (0.70) | (1.48) | (2.95) | (12.12) | (9.32) | (3.07) | (0.49) | (11,590) | (25,550) | (0.48) | (2.25) | (0.50) |
| Self-employed | 155 | 0.43 | 0.48 | 1.59 | 8.90 | 36.68 | 14.47 | 3.58 | 0.36 | 5,300 | 13,280 | 0.65 | 4.62 | 0.68 |
| | 5.2% | (0.60) | (0.66) | (1.76) | (3.54) | (10.11) | (7.99) | (3.64) | (0.48) | (15,170) | (26,370) | (0.48) | (2.61) | (0.47) |
| Employees | 325 | 0.42 | 0.35 | 1.11 | 7.76 | 32.86 | 11.60 | 7.41 | 0.65 | 4,200 | 18,570 | 0.60 | 5.19 | 0.89 |
| | 10.8% | (0.64) | (0.60) | (1.52) | (3.77) | (8.95) | (6.50) | (4.66) | (0.48) | (9,580) | (25,880) | (0.49) | (2.44) | (0.31) |
| **OTHER SOUTHEAST** | | | | | | | | | | | | | | |
| Total | 3667 | 0.46 | 0.40 | 1.13 | 7.40 | 36.25 | 14.57 | 3.43 | 0.51 | 4,440 | 11,730 | 0.58 | 5.58 | 0.66 |
| | 100.0% | (0.66) | (0.63) | (1.43) | (2.80) | (11.97) | (9.46) | (3.62) | (0.50) | (11,500) | (22,910) | (0.49) | (2.43) | (0.47) |
| Non-workers | 3103 | 0.49 | 0.41 | 1.14 | 7.30 | 36.26 | 14.66 | 2.98 | 0.50 | 4,250 | 10,860 | 0.58 | 5.50 | 0.62 |
| | 84.6% | (0.67) | (0.64) | (1.45) | (2.74) | (12.32) | (9.76) | (3.12) | (0.50) | (11,410) | (20,140) | (0.49) | (2.39) | (0.48) |
| Self-employed | 207 | 0.31 | 0.36 | 1.21 | 8.58 | 39.13 | 16.36 | 3.77 | 0.41 | 6,820 | 17,000 | 0.61 | 5.87 | 0.77 |
| | 5.6% | (0.60) | (0.62) | (1.38) | (2.91) | (10.27) | (8.26) | (3.92) | (0.49) | (11,600) | (42,960) | (0.49) | (2.43) | (0.42) |
| Employees | 357 | 0.32 | 0.32 | 1.00 | 7.53 | 34.54 | 12.77 | 7.14 | 0.64 | 4,740 | 16,210 | 0.59 | 6.11 | 0.88 |
| | 9.7% | (0.55) | (0.55) | (1.31) | (3.03) | (9.21) | (6.74) | (5.07) | (0.48) | (12,110) | (27,580) | (0.49) | (2.68) | (0.32) |
| **RIO DE JANEIRO** | | | | | | | | | | | | | | |
| Total | 2925 | 0.33 | 0.33 | 0.77 | 6.87 | 37.56 | 15.50 | 5.44 | 0.66 | 8,900 | 18,970 | 0.55 | 5.30 | 0.91 |
| | 100.0% | (0.57) | (0.59) | (1.12) | (2.59) | (11.80) | (9.50) | (4.31) | (0.47) | (21,200) | (29,260) | (0.50) | (2.18) | (0.29) |
| Non-workers | 2223 | 0.37 | 0.35 | 0.79 | 6.79 | 37.92 | 15.89 | 4.79 | 0.65 | 9,150 | 17,280 | 0.57 | 5.22 | 0.90 |
| | 76.0% | (0.60) | (0.61) | (1.14) | (2.60) | (12.28) | (9.96) | (3.75) | (0.48) | (19,680) | (26,800) | (0.50) | (2.11) | (0.30) |
| Self-employed | 149 | 0.21 | 0.31 | 0.84 | 7.52 | 38.56 | 15.92 | 5.60 | 0.59 | 12,920 | 23,900 | 0.52 | 5.40 | 0.95 |
| | 5.1% | (0.43) | (0.59) | (1.16) | (2.55) | (10.28) | (8.24) | (4.60) | (0.49) | (44,690) | (46,150) | (0.50) | (2.14) | (0.21) |
| Employees | 553 | 0.22 | 0.24 | 0.68 | 7.05 | 35.81 | 13.80 | 8.00 | 0.76 | 6,800 | 24,470 | 0.51 | 5.56 | 0.95 |
| | 18.9% | (0.47) | (0.50) | (1.02) | (2.54) | (9.90) | (7.58) | (5.28) | (0.43) | (16,700) | (32,010) | (0.50) | (2.42) | (0.21) |
| **SAO PAULO** | | | | | | | | | | | | | | |
| Total | 6861 | 0.38 | 0.34 | 0.87 | 7.09 | 36.24 | 14.54 | 4.53 | 0.64 | 8,760 | 20,170 | 0.53 | 5.02 | 0.88 |
| | 100.0% | (0.60) | (0.59) | (1.23) | (2.54) | (11.84) | (9.39) | (4.08) | (0.48) | (22,220) | (34,360) | (0.50) | (2.40) | (0.32) |
| Non-workers | 5339 | 0.40 | 0.35 | 0.85 | 6.95 | 36.71 | 14.98 | 4.05 | 0.64 | 9,230 | 19,910 | 0.54 | 5.04 | 0.87 |
| | 77.8% | (0.62) | (0.60) | (1.20) | (2.46) | (12.26) | (9.79) | (3.59) | (0.48) | (23,010) | (34,380) | (0.50) | (2.36) | (0.34) |
| Self-employed | 352 | 0.22 | 0.34 | 1.10 | 7.85 | 38.49 | 15.88 | 4.93 | 0.47 | 11,610 | 22,980 | 0.54 | 5.40 | 0.89 |
| | 5.1% | (0.49) | (0.60) | (1.40) | (2.88) | (10.33) | (8.44) | (4.41) | (0.50) | (32,840) | (30,050) | (0.50) | (2.73) | (0.31) |
| Employees | 1170 | 0.29 | 0.28 | 0.88 | 7.51 | 33.42 | 12.10 | 6.61 | 0.74 | 5,800 | 20,510 | 0.45 | 4.83 | 0.94 |
| | 17.1% | (0.53) | (0.56) | (1.29) | (2.68) | (9.66) | (7.19) | (5.26) | (0.44) | (12,020) | (35,470) | (0.50) | (2.45) | (0.24) |
| **SOUTH** | | | | | | | | | | | | | | |
| Total | 5097 | 0.39 | 0.35 | 0.97 | 7.11 | 36.15 | 14.58 | 3.90 | 0.49 | 4,280 | 13,020 | 0.66 | 5.31 | 0.61 |
| | 100.0% | (0.59) | (0.59) | (1.30) | (2.53) | (12.30) | (9.73) | (3.51) | (0.50) | (10,040) | (25,210) | (0.47) | (2.35) | (0.49) |
| Non-workers | 3986 | 0.42 | 0.36 | 0.96 | 6.96 | 36.48 | 14.95 | 3.42 | 0.48 | 4,330 | 12,620 | 0.65 | 5.24 | 0.58 |
| | 78.2% | (0.61) | (0.60) | (1.28) | (2.44) | (12.80) | (10.19) | (2.98) | (0.50) | (10,100) | (25,900) | (0.48) | (2.28) | (0.49) |
| Self-employed | 414 | 0.33 | 0.33 | 1.19 | 8.14 | 37.79 | 15.50 | 3.73 | 0.27 | 4,310 | 13,850 | 0.74 | 5.42 | 0.43 |
| | 8.1% | (0.55) | (0.59) | (1.51) | (2.87) | (11.06) | (8.70) | (3.37) | (0.44) | (11,400) | (28,580) | (0.44) | (2.41) | (0.50) |
| Employees | 697 | 0.27 | 0.29 | 0.88 | 7.34 | 33.31 | 11.96 | 6.75 | 0.70 | 3,960 | 14,840 | 0.65 | 5.64 | 0.89 |
| | 13.7% | (0.50) | (0.57) | (1.21) | (2.64) | (9.31) | (6.81) | (4.81) | (0.46) | (8,730) | (17,960) | (0.48) | (2.64) | (0.32) |

Note: Numbers in parentheses are standard deviations.

**Appendix Table 3A.2**
**Means and Variables Used in Logits - Married Men**

| REGION | OBS | FAMILY SIZE | AGE | AGESQ /100 | YEARS SCHOOL | WIFE WORKS | OTHER INCOME | OWN HOME | URBAN |
|---|---|---|---|---|---|---|---|---|---|
| **ALL BRAZIL** | | | | | | | | | |
| Total | 28926 | 7.33 | 40.96 | 18.53 | 3.89 | 0.20 | 6,950 | 0.61 | 0.68 |
| | 100.0% | (2.81) | (13.24) | (11.98) | (4.15) | (0.40) | (17,100) | (0.49) | 0.47 |
| Non-workers | 2920 | 7.19 | 57.45 | 34.67 | 2.94 | 0.17 | 18,170 | 0.73 | 0.80 |
| | 10.1% | (3.16) | (12.91) | (14.11) | (3.56) | (0.37) | (25,400) | (0.45) | 0.40 |
| Self-employed | 11410 | 7.53 | 41.58 | 18.87 | 2.90 | 0.17 | 5,370 | 0.71 | 0.49 |
| | 39.4% | (2.92) | (12.57) | (11.17) | (3.62) | (0.38) | (17,990) | (0.45) | 0.50 |
| Employees | 14596 | 7.19 | 37.17 | 15.03 | 4.86 | 0.22 | 5,940 | 0.50 | 0.81 |
| | 50.5% | (2.63) | (11.02) | (9.10) | (4.41) | (0.42) | (13,010) | (0.50) | 0.39 |
| **NORTHEAST** | | | | | | | | | |
| Total | 7374 | 7.72 | 41.85 | 19.48 | 2.19 | 0.18 | 3,460 | 0.67 | 0.50 |
| | ·100.0% | (3.11) | (14.02) | (13.02) | (3.47) | (0.39) | (9,640) | (0.47) | 0.50 |
| Non-workers | 758 | 7.52 | 58.47 | 36.34 | 1.72 | 0.18 | 9,640 | 0.73 | 0.63 |
| | 10.3% | (3.41) | (14.70) | (16.17) | (2.99) | (0.38) | (18,750) | (0.44) | 0.48 |
| Self-employed | 4026 | 7.88 | 41.43 | 18.88 | 1.34 | 0.17 | 2,240 | 0.76 | 0.33 |
| | 54.6% | (3.05) | (13.11) | (11.79) | (2.47) | (0.37) | (6,380) | (0.43) | 0.47 |
| Employees | 2590 | 7.54 | 37.64 | 15.48 | 3.66 | 0.21 | 3,540 | 0.53 | 0.71 |
| | 35.1% | (3.10) | (11.43) | (9.50) | (4.34) | (0.41) | (9,240) | (0.50) | 0.45 |
| **NORTHWEST** | | | | | | | | | |
| Total | 3002 | 7.60 | 39.38 | 17.15 | 3.47 | 0.16 | 4,940 | 0.62 | 0.61 |
| | 100.0% | (3.10) | (12.79) | (11.30) | (3.90) | (0.37) | (13,190) | (0.48) | 0.49 |
| Non-workers | 202 | 7.98 | 56.35 | 33.79 | 2.45 | 0.14 | 13,490 | 0.72 | 0.78 |
| | 6.7% | (3.81) | (14.31) | (14.98) | (3.42) | (0.35) | (21,780) | (0.45) | 0.41 |
| Self-employed | 1493 | 7.78 | 40.14 | 17.63 | 2.47 | 0.13 | 3,870 | 0.75 | 0.46 |
| | 49.7% | (3.23) | (12.34) | (10.70) | (3.12) | (0.33) | (12,860) | (0.43) | 0.50 |
| Employees | 1307 | 7.35 | 35.90 | 14.02 | 4.78 | 0.20 | 4,840 | 0.46 | 0.74 |
| | 43.5% | (2.78) | (10.64) | (8.66) | (4.35) | (0.40) | (11,180) | (0.50) | 0.44 |
| **OTHER SOUTHEAST** | | | | | | | | | |
| Total | 3667 | 7.40 | 41.45 | 18.94 | 3.43 | 0.15 | 5,540 | 0.58 | 0.66 |
| | 100.0% | (2.80) | (13.24) | (12.04) | (3.63) | (0.36) | (12,770) | (0.49) | 0.47 |
| Non-workers | 362 | 7.33 | 57.14 | 34.39 | 2.33 | 0.15 | 15,770 | 0.72 | 0.81 |
| | 9.9% | (3.07) | (13.19) | (14.41) | (2.58) | (0.36) | (22,950) | (0.45) | 0.40 |
| Self-employed | 1442 | 7.47 | 42.56 | 19.69 | 3.04 | 0.14 | 4,590 | 0.67 | 0.48 |
| | 39.3% | (2.90) | (12.54) | (11.32) | (3.37) | (0.34) | (10,870) | (0.47) | 0.50 |
| Employees | 1863 | 7.35 | 37.54 | 15.35 | 3.95 | 0.17 | 4,290 | 0.49 | 0.76 |
| | 50.8% | (2.66) | (11.20) | (9.29) | (3.90) | (0.37) | (10,230) | (0.50) | 0.43 |
| **RIO DE JANEIRO** | | | | | | | | | |
| Total | 2925 | 6.87 | 42.05 | 19.34 | 6.14 | 0.24 | 12,000 | 0.55 | 0.91 |
| | 100.0% | (2.59) | (12.89) | (11.75) | (4.70) | (0.43) | (24,180) | (0.50) | 0.29 |
| Non-workers | 416 | 6.86 | 56.43 | 33.27 | 4.75 | 0.17 | 24,050 | 0.69 | 0.92 |
| | 14.2% | (2.86) | (11.93) | (12.93) | (4.34) | (0.37) | (25,980) | (0.46) | 0.27 |
| Self-employed | 576 | 6.88 | 43.29 | 20.23 | 5.86 | 0.22 | 14,980 | 0.62 | 0.89 |
| | 19.7% | (2.67) | (12.24) | (11.11) | (4.67) | (0.41) | (36,940) | (0.49) | 0.32 |
| Employees | 1933 | 6.87 | 38.58 | 16.08 | 6.52 | 0.26 | 8,520 | 0.51 | 0.92 |
| | 66.1% | (2.51) | (10.93) | (9.14) | (4.73) | (0.44) | (16,950) | (0.50) | 0.28 |
| **SAO PAULO** | | | | | | | | | |
| Total | 6861 | 7.09 | 40.34 | 17.87 | 5.04 | 0.22 | 11,130 | 0.53 | 0.88 |
| | 100.0% | (2.54) | (12.61) | (11.19) | (4.46) | (0.42) | (23,950) | (0.50) | 0.32 |
| Non-workers | 680 | 7.03 | 57.19 | 33.90 | 3.56 | 0.17 | 28,180 | 0.70 | 0.94 |
| | 9.9% | (2.97) | (10.95) | (12.07) | (3.77) | (0.38) | (32,020) | (0.46) | 0.24 |
| Self-employed | 1776 | 7.09 | 42.23 | 19.19 | 4.99 | 0.21 | 12,770 | 0.61 | 0.84 |
| | 25.9% | (2.55) | (11.63) | (10.26) | (4.58) | (0.41) | (32,980) | (0.49) | 0.37 |
| Employees | 4405 | 7.10 | 36.98 | 14.86 | 5.28 | 0.23 | 7,830 | 0.47 | 0.89 |
| | 64.2% | (2.45) | (10.87) | (8.98) | (4.47) | (0.42) | (15,490) | (0.50) | 0.31 |
| **SOUTH** | | | | | | | | | |
| Total | 5097 | 7.11 | 40.43 | 18.08 | 4.10 | 0.22 | 5,670 | 0.66 | 0.61 |
| | 100.0% | (2.53) | (13.18) | (11.79) | (3.63) | (0.41) | (11,690) | (0.47) | 0.49 |
| Non-workers | 502 | 6.79 | 57.78 | 34.91 | 3.07 | 0.16 | 16,200 | 0.79 | 0.75 |
| | 9.8% | (2.91) | (12.38) | (13.47) | (3.19) | (0.37) | (20,410) | (0.41) | 0.43 |
| Self-employed | 2097 | 7.27 | 41.19 | 18.51 | 3.50 | 0.20 | 4,080 | 0.75 | 0.39 |
| | 41.1% | (2.69) | (12.40) | (10.83) | (3.11) | (0.40) | (9,720) | (0.43) | 0.49 |
| Employees | 2498 | 7.05 | 36.30 | 14.34 | 4.82 | 0.24 | 4,900 | 0.56 | 0.77 |
| | 49.0% | (2.29) | (10.79) | (8.82) | (3.96) | (0.43) | (9,530) | (0.50) | 0.42 |

Note: Numbers in parentheses are standard deviations.

**Appendix Table 3A.3**

**Means and Variables Used in Wage Regressions**

| REGION | ALL BRAZIL | | | | NORTHEAST | | | | NORTHWEST | | | | OTHER SOUTHEAST | | | | RIO DE JANEIRO | | | | SAO PAULO | | | | SOUTH | | | |
|---|---|---|---|---|---|---|---|---|---|---|---|---|---|---|---|---|---|---|---|---|---|---|---|---|---|---|---|---|
| | EMPLOYERS | | SELF EMPLOYED | | EMPLOYERS | | SELF EMPLOYED | | EMPLOYERS | | SELF EMPLOYED | | EMPLOYERS | | SELF EMPLOYED | | EMPLOYERS | | SELF EMPLOYED | | EMPLOYERS | | SELF EMPLOYED | | EMPLOYERS | | SELF EMPLOYED | |
| VARIABLE | MEN | WOMEN | MEN | WOMEN | MEN | WOMEN | MEN | WOMEN | MEN | WOMEN | MEN | WOMEN | MEN | WOMEN | MEN | WOMEN | MEN | WOMEN | MEN | WOMEN | MEN | WOMEN | MEN | WOMEN | MEN | WOMEN | MEN | WOMEN |
| OBS | 14596 | 3741 | 11410 | 1518 | 2590 | 639 | 4026 | 547 | 1307 | 325 | 1493 | 117 | 1863 | 357 | 1442 | 173 | 1933 | 553 | 576 | 143 | 4405 | 1170 | 1776 | 311 | 2498 | 697 | 2097 | 227 |
| LAMBDA | 1.03 (0.35) | 0.51 (0.35) | 0.82 (0.35) | 0.18 (0.09) | 0.82 (0.38) | 0.48 (0.40) | 1.08 (0.35) | 0.24 (0.11) | 0.94 (0.39) | 0.55 (0.39) | 1.00 (0.37) | 0.16 (0.09) | 0.99 (0.31) | 0.47 (0.36) | 0.78 (0.31) | 0.21 (0.14) | 1.25 (0.30) | 0.55 (0.32) | 0.69 (0.10) | 0.14 (0.07) | 1.19 (0.29) | 0.52 (0.32) | 0.48 (0.14) | 0.14 (0.07) | 1.03 (0.37) | 0.57 (0.39) | 0.88 (0.37) | 0.19 (0.12) |
| SECPUB | 0.15 (0.34) | 0.38 (0.49) | – | – | 0.17 (0.38) | 0.52 (0.50) | – | – | 0.21 (0.41) | 0.54 (0.50) | – | – | 0.13 (0.33) | 0.52 (0.50) | – | – | 0.21 (0.41) | 0.37 (0.48) | – | – | 0.12 (0.33) | 0.26 (0.44) | – | – | 0.14 (0.34) | 0.34 (0.47) | – | – |
| SOCSEC | 0.81 (0.39) | 0.78 (0.42) | 0.34 (0.48) | 0.28 (0.45) | 0.70 (0.46) | 0.76 (0.43) | 0.18 (0.38) | 0.14 (0.35) | 0.69 (0.46) | 0.82 (0.39) | 0.26 (0.44) | 0.22 (0.42) | 0.73 (0.44) | 0.70 (0.46) | 0.37 (0.48) | 0.29 (0.45) | 0.91 (0.29) | 0.78 (0.41) | 0.69 (0.46) | 0.45 (0.50) | 0.88 (0.33) | 0.76 (0.43) | 0.62 (0.49) | 0.42 (0.49) | 0.86 (0.35) | 0.86 (0.35) | 0.38 (0.49) | 0.36 (0.48) |
| EXPR | 26.31 (12.4) | 21.01 (11.5) | 32.68 (13.4) | 28.31 (11.8) | 27.99 (12.7) | 21.74 (11.5) | 34.09 (13.5) | 29.65 (11.7) | 25.11 (12.1) | 19.45 (10.6) | 31.67 (13.0) | 26.38 (10.6) | 27.59 (12.6) | 21.39 (11.2) | 33.52 (13.6) | 29.33 (11.6) | 26.06 (12.1) | 21.81 (11.7) | 31.42 (13.4) | 27.27 (11.0) | 25.70 (12.3) | 20.82 (11.7) | 31.24 (13.1) | 27.34 (12.2) | 25.48 (12.2) | 20.56 (11.3) | 31.70 (13.4) | 27.26 (12.4) |
| EXPSQ/100 | 8.43 (7.61) | 5.73 (5.75) | 12.49 (9.59) | 9.40 (7.12) | 9.44 (8.14) | 6.05 (5.86) | 13.45 (10.19) | 10.16 (7.30) | 7.76 (7.27) | 4.91 (5.08) | 11.73 (9.11) | 8.07 (6.20) | 9.20 (7.99) | 5.83 (5.37) | 13.09 (9.81) | 9.94 (7.06) | 8.26 (7.18) | 6.11 (5.87) | 11.67 (8.97) | 8.63 (6.26) | 8.12 (7.48) | 5.71 (5.99) | 11.48 (8.71) | 8.95 (7.04) | 7.97 (7.32) | 5.50 (5.61) | 11.85 (9.24) | 8.96 (7.15) |
| YRSEDUC | 4.86 (4.41) | 6.96 (5.08) | 2.90 (3.62) | 3.78 (4.08) | 3.66 (4.34) | 6.59 (4.94) | 1.34 (2.47) | 2.07 (3.14) | 4.78 (4.35) | 7.41 (4.66) | 2.47 (3.12) | 4.09 (3.67) | 3.95 (3.90) | 7.14 (5.07) | 3.04 (3.37) | 4.10 (4.08) | 6.52 (4.73) | 8.00 (5.28) | 5.86 (4.67) | 5.49 (4.54) | 5.28 (4.47) | 6.61 (5.26) | 4.99 (4.58) | 5.14 (4.47) | 4.82 (3.96) | 6.75 (4.81) | 3.50 (3.11) | 4.56 (3.99) |
| URBAN | 0.81 (0.39) | 0.89 (0.31) | 0.49 (0.50) | 0.74 (0.44) | 0.71 (0.45) | 0.78 (0.42) | 0.33 (0.47) | 0.50 (0.50) | 0.74 (0.44) | 0.89 (0.31) | 0.46 (0.50) | 0.85 (0.36) | 0.76 (0.43) | 0.88 (0.32) | 0.48 (0.50) | 0.87 (0.34) | 0.92 (0.28) | 0.95 (0.21) | 0.89 (0.32) | 0.95 (0.22) | 0.89 (0.31) | 0.94 (0.24) | 0.84 (0.37) | 0.95 (0.23) | 0.77 (0.42) | 0.89 (0.32) | 0.39 (0.49) | 0.75 (0.43) |
| BIRTOT | – | 3.00 (2.89) | – | 4.67 (3.77) | – | 3.91 (3.62) | – | 5.99 (4.41) | – | 3.33 (2.88) | – | 4.73 (3.60) | – | 3.31 (3.20) | – | 4.95 (3.52) | – | 2.54 (2.43) | – | 3.34 (2.69) | – | 2.65 (2.54) | – | 3.39 (2.68) | – | 2.80 (2.64) | – | 3.82 (3.10) |
| HOURS/WEEK | 47.0 (6.7) | 39.6 (11.0) | 46.9 (7.4) | 37.6 (12.9) | 45.9 (7.1) | 37.5 (12.1) | 44.7 (7.2) | 36.5 (11.6) | 47.2 (7.2) | 40.0 (10.4) | 46.8 (7.5) | 37.5 (12.4) | 47.4 (6.5) | 37.5 (11.6) | 48.0 (7.7) | 37.4 (13.4) | 46.4 (7.2) | 39.7 (11.1) | 47.5 (9.2) | 37.9 (14.3) | 47.3 (6.0) | 41.1 (10.1) | 48.5 (7.7) | 39.0 (13.2) | 47.5 (6.7) | 39.9 (11.1) | 48.8 (7.9) | 38.2 (14.2) |
| 1-14 HRS % | 0.3 | 2.7 | 0.6 | 6.7 | 0.3 | 4.4 | 0.5 | 5.1 | 0.6 | 2.5 | 0.3 | 6.8 | 0.3 | 2.8 | 0.5 | 8.1 | 0.3 | 2.4 | 1.6 | 8.4 | 0.1 | 2.4 | 0.7 | 7.1 | 0.3 | 2.2 | 0.7 | 7.5 |
| 15-29 HRS % | 1.1 | 16.9 | 2.0 | 18.2 | 1.7 | 22.5 | 2.3 | 19.2 | 1.3 | 13.8 | 1.5 | 14.5 | 0.8 | 23.2 | 1.7 | 17.9 | 2.0 | 17.2 | 3.1 | 19.6 | 0.5 | 11.8 | 1.7 | 15.4 | 1.1 | 18.2 | 1.8 | 21.1 |
| 30-39 HRS % | 4.2 | 13.6 | 8.1 | 24.6 | 7.2 | 15.6 | 11.9 | 31.6 | 4.7 | 16.0 | 9.2 | 30.8 | 3.7 | 15.9 | 6.5 | 23.1 | 5.0 | 15.0 | 6.1 | 20.3 | 2.7 | 10.9 | 4.2 | 18.3 | 3.4 | 10.6 | 5.0 | 16.7 |
| 40-48 HRS % | 60.6 | 53.1 | 50.9 | 31.9 | 62.4 | 44.8 | 63.5 | 32.4 | 55.7 | 55.4 | 52.0 | 31.6 | 59.3 | 41.7 | 44.9 | 31.2 | 60.8 | 50.5 | 41.0 | 25.9 | 63.1 | 60.9 | 43.3 | 36.7 | 57.9 | 54.5 | 39.1 | 28.6 |
| 49+ HRS % | 33.7 | 13.7 | 38.5 | 18.6 | 28.1 | 12.7 | 21.8 | 11.7 | 37.6 | 12.3 | 36.9 | 16.2 | 36.0 | 12.3 | 44.4 | 19.7 | 31.7 | 15.0 | 48.3 | 25.9 | 33.6 | 14.0 | 50.2 | 22.5 | 37.3 | 14.5 | 53.5 | 26.0 |
| WAGE/MONTH | 15.1 (20.5) | 9.2 (11.0) | 14.6 (33.6) | 7.9 (18.1) | 10.4 (16.0) | 6.3 (9.7) | 7.5 (21.5) | 3.6 (9.4) | 13.2 (17.5) | 9.7 (11.6) | 13.4 (31.3) | 6.8 (11.4) | 10.9 (13.6) | 7.6 (9.3) | 14.6 (30.7) | 7.6 (13.5) | 20.6 (27.4) | 13.0 (16.0) | 23.0 (33.6) | 13.2 (30.0) | 19.5 (23.1) | 10.3 (10.1) | 27.8 (51.9) | 13.3 (24.8) | 12.4 (16.4) | 7.6 (7.6) | 15.7 (32.5) | 8.1 (16.5) |
| WAGE/HOUR | 83.9 (119.6) | 63.1 (79.8) | 80.1 (194.5) | 54.7 (110.2) | 60.1 (109.9) | 43.1 (62.8) | 43.3 (140.2) | 26.6 (62.5) | 72.4 (96.4) | 61.4 (69.4) | 72.4 (155.5) | 46.1 (70.9) | 59.9 (78.4) | 55.2 (59.6) | 90.7 (160.9) | 51.7 (33.0) | 115.4 (155.6) | 92.8 (120.8) | 124.8 (184.1) | 93.3 (182.6) | 106.4 (129.7) | 69.4 (76.2) | 151.5 (313.3) | 90.9 (148.3) | 48.6 (100.0) | 52.1 (82.9) | 84.0 (181.8) | 55.5 (91.5) |
| LN WAGE | 3.9933 (0.89) | 3.6779 (0.96) | 3.6760 (1.07) | 3.1979 (1.20) | 3.3551 (0.91) | 3.1646 (1.09) | 3.1369 (0.94) | 2.5530 (1.08) | 3.8333 (0.86) | 3.6496 (0.90) | 3.7592 (0.90) | 3.2239 (1.06) | 3.6970 (0.80) | 3.5592 (0.97) | 3.7729 (1.01) | 3.2349 (1.14) | 4.2411 (0.93) | 3.9782 (1.02) | 4.3186 (0.98) | 3.7513 (1.10) | 4.2610 (0.94) | 3.8515 (0.85) | 4.4240 (0.98) | 3.8646 (1.08) | 3.8550 (0.76) | 3.6204 (0.77) | 3.8066 (1.01) | 3.4245 (0.99) |
| **FEMALE/MALE RATIOS** | | | | | | | | | | | | | | | | | | | | | | | | | | | | |
| WAGE/MONTH | 0.61 | 0.54 | | | 0.60 | 0.48 | | | 0.74 | 0.51 | | | 0.70 | 0.52 | | | 0.63 | 0.57 | | | 0.53 | 0.48 | | | 0.61 | 0.51 | | |
| WAGE/HOUR | 0.75 | 0.68 | | | 0.72 | 0.62 | | | 0.85 | 0.64 | | | 0.92 | 0.66 | | | 0.80 | 0.74 | | | 0.65 | 0.60 | | | 0.76 | 0.66 | | |
| HOURS/WEEK | 0.84 | 0.80 | | | 0.82 | 0.82 | | | 0.85 | 0.80 | | | 0.79 | 0.78 | | | 0.86 | 0.80 | | | 0.87 | 0.80 | | | 0.84 | 0.78 | | |

Note: Numbers in parentheses are standard deviations.

### Appendix Table 3A.4
### Means and Variables Used in Logits - Single Women

| REGION | OBS | KIDS 0-2 | KIDS 3-5 | KIDS 6-14 | FAMILY SIZE | AGE | AGESQ /100 | YEARS SCHOOL | OTHER INCOME | OWN HOME | ROOMS IN HOME | URBAN |
|---|---|---|---|---|---|---|---|---|---|---|---|---|
| **ALL BRAZIL** | | | | | | | | | | | | |
| Total | 11225 | 0.20 | 0.24 | 1.35 | 7.64 | 20.54 | 4.65 | 5.68 | 24,870 | 0.71 | 6.02 | 0.73 |
| | 100.0% | (0.49) | (0.52) | (1.47) | (2.68) | (6.55) | (3.77) | (3.87) | (38,860) | (0.45) | (2.39) | (0.45) |
| Non-workers | 6601 | 0.22 | 0.25 | 1.43 | 7.73 | 19.44 | 4.18 | 4.96 | 25,310 | 0.73 | 6.17 | 0.66 |
| | 58.8% | (0.51) | (0.53) | (1.51) | (2.70) | (6.29) | (3.69) | (3.45) | (42,370) | (0.44) | (2.52) | (0.47) |
| Self-employed | 753 | 0.23 | 0.32 | 1.51 | 7.84 | 22.49 | 5.74 | 3.31 | 16,300 | 0.80 | 5.62 | 0.35 |
| | 6.7% | (0.54) | (0.60) | (1.55) | (2.78) | (8.24) | (4.93) | (3.45) | (35,600) | (0.40) | (2.00) | (0.48) |
| Employees | 3871 | 0.15 | 0.19 | 1.17 | 7.45 | 22.02 | 5.24 | 7.38 | 25,780 | 0.67 | 5.86 | 0.91 |
| | 34.5% | (0.44) | (0.48) | (1.37) | (2.62) | (6.24) | (3.52) | (3.99) | (32,510) | (0.47) | (2.20) | (0.29) |
| **NORTHEAST** | | | | | | | | | | | | |
| Total | 3045 | 0.27 | 0.33 | 1.67 | 8.26 | 20.91 | 4.90 | 4.09 | 15,160 | 0.76 | 5.94 | 0.57 |
| | 100.0% | (0.56) | (0.60) | (1.66) | (2.99) | (7.27) | (4.26) | (3.85) | (25,920) | (0.43) | (2.43) | (0.50) |
| Non-workers | 2156 | 0.28 | 0.33 | 1.73 | 8.30 | 19.86 | 4.40 | 3.63 | 15,360 | 0.76 | 5.93 | 0.55 |
| | 70.8% | (0.58) | (0.60) | (1.67) | (2.94) | (6.72) | (3.91) | (3.31) | (27,090) | (0.43) | (2.43) | (0.50) |
| Self-employed | 328 | 0.27 | 0.36 | 1.50 | 8.00 | 23.22 | 6.17 | 1.91 | 8,260 | 0.86 | 5.34 | 0.26 |
| | 10.8% | (0.57) | (0.65) | (1.64) | (3.12) | (8.82) | (5.36) | (2.71) | (14,930) | (0.35) | (2.02) | (0.44) |
| Employees | 561 | 0.21 | 0.30 | 1.50 | 8.25 | 23.61 | 6.10 | 7.16 | 18,390 | 0.68 | 6.34 | 0.84 |
| | 18.4% | (0.51) | (0.59) | (1.63) | (3.10) | (7.28) | (4.45) | (4.57) | (25,690) | (0.47) | (2.54) | (0.37) |
| **NORTHWEST** | | | | | | | | | | | | |
| Total | 975 | 0.29 | 0.30 | 1.68 | 8.15 | 19.81 | 4.24 | 5.18 | 22,930 | 0.75 | 5.47 | 0.71 |
| | 100.0% | (0.58) | (0.59) | (1.57) | (2.69) | (5.60) | (2.88) | (3.50) | (36,160) | (0.43) | (2.44) | (0.45) |
| Non-workers | 646 | 0.32 | 0.34 | 1.76 | 8.24 | 18.58 | 3.68 | 4.46 | 22,670 | 0.77 | 5.44 | 0.64 |
| | 66.3% | (0.61) | (0.61) | (1.58) | (2.61) | (4.76) | (2.40) | (3.16) | (40,390) | (0.42) | (2.62) | (0.48) |
| Self-employed | 42 | 0.21 | 0.33 | 1.81 | 7.93 | 24.57 | 6.77 | 2.76 | 21,490 | 0.71 | 5.17 | 0.40 |
| | 4.3% | (0.52) | (0.75) | (1.81) | (3.14) | (8.67) | (4.82) | (2.80) | (37,720) | (0.46) | (2.04) | (0.50) |
| Employees | 287 | 0.21 | 0.21 | 1.47 | 7.99 | 21.90 | 5.13 | 7.15 | 23,740 | 0.71 | 5.59 | 0.90 |
| | 29.4% | (0.51) | (0.48) | (1.50) | (2.81) | (5.81) | (3.10) | (3.47) | (23,880) | (0.45) | (2.06) | (0.30) |
| **OTHER SOUTHEAST** | | | | | | | | | | | | |
| Total | 1732 | 0.19 | 0.23 | 1.42 | 7.82 | 20.62 | 4.68 | 5.37 | 22,800 | 0.72 | 6.57 | 0.72 |
| | 100.0% | (0.47) | (0.50) | (1.47) | (2.62) | (6.58) | (3.79) | (3.54) | (37,580) | (0.45) | (2.44) | (0.45) |
| Non-workers | 1086 | 0.19 | 0.24 | 1.48 | 7.87 | 19.74 | 4.32 | 4.82 | 24,000 | 0.73 | 6.76 | 0.63 |
| | 62.7% | (0.47) | (0.50) | (1.50) | (2.68) | (6.46) | (3.79) | (3.17) | (43,010) | (0.44) | (2.49) | (0.48) |
| Self-employed | 65 | 0.29 | 0.25 | 1.66 | 7.63 | 21.97 | 5.40 | 3.51 | 14,200 | 0.77 | 5.82 | 0.37 |
| | 3.8% | (0.58) | (0.47) | (1.46) | (2.51) | (7.62) | (4.45) | (3.46) | (20,770) | (0.42) | (2.05) | (0.49) |
| Employees | 581 | 0.18 | 0.22 | 1.29 | 7.74 | 22.10 | 5.29 | 6.59 | 21,510 | 0.70 | 6.31 | 0.91 |
| | 33.5% | (0.46) | (0.52) | (1.42) | (2.53) | (6.38) | (3.63) | (3.85) | (26,320) | (0.46) | (2.34) | (0.28) |
| **RIO DE JANEIRO** | | | | | | | | | | | | |
| Total | 1182 | 0.14 | 0.19 | 0.96 | 7.10 | 20.80 | 4.75 | 7.40 | 31,750 | 0.66 | 6.00 | 0.94 |
| | 100.0% | (0.45) | (0.50) | (1.25) | (2.46) | (6.53) | (3.80) | (3.70) | (41,060) | (0.47) | (2.06) | (0.24) |
| Non-workers | 697 | 0.16 | 0.21 | 1.02 | 7.23 | 19.15 | 4.04 | 6.68 | 33,330 | 0.68 | 6.14 | 0.92 |
| | 59.0% | (0.46) | (0.52) | (1.25) | (2.44) | (6.12) | (3.68) | (3.27) | (37,130) | (0.47) | (2.06) | (0.27) |
| Self-employed | 32 | 0.22 | 0.25 | 1.22 | 7.53 | 23.66 | 6.38 | 6.81 | 41,520 | 0.75 | 6.38 | 0.91 |
| | 2.7% | (0.75) | (0.62) | (1.43) | (2.99) | (9.02) | (6.11) | (4.50) | (104,610) | (0.44) | (2.27) | (0.30) |
| Employees | 453 | 0.09 | 0.17 | 0.87 | 6.87 | 23.13 | 5.73 | 8.55 | 28,630 | 0.62 | 5.76 | 0.96 |
| | 38.3% | (0.39) | (0.44) | (1.23) | (2.44) | (6.16) | (3.51) | (3.98) | (38,870) | (0.49) | (2.04) | (0.18) |
| **SAO PAULO** | | | | | | | | | | | | |
| Total | 2543 | 0.13 | 0.16 | 1.05 | 7.12 | 20.59 | 4.64 | 7.05 | 35,930 | 0.64 | 5.83 | 0.90 |
| | 100.0% | (0.39) | (0.42) | (1.26) | (2.45) | (6.34) | (3.63) | (3.76) | (45,250) | (0.48) | (2.41) | (0.30) |
| Non-workers | 1043 | 0.12 | 0.16 | 1.02 | 6.96 | 19.08 | 4.02 | 6.59 | 43,170 | 0.66 | 6.32 | 0.86 |
| | 41.0% | (0.38) | (0.42) | (1.24) | (2.39) | (6.18) | (3.76) | (3.34) | (57,610) | (0.47) | (2.82) | (0.35) |
| Self-employed | 109 | 0.14 | 0.19 | 1.15 | 7.15 | 24.65 | 6.92 | 5.72 | 35,210 | 0.68 | 6.06 | 0.70 |
| | 4.3% | (0.35) | (0.46) | (1.44) | (2.13) | (9.23) | (5.72) | (4.50) | (54,480) | (0.47) | (1.94) | (0.46) |
| Employees | 1391 | 0.13 | 0.16 | 1.07 | 7.23 | 21.41 | 4.93 | 7.50 | 30,550 | 0.63 | 5.44 | 0.94 |
| | 54.7% | (0.40) | (0.42) | (1.25) | (2.51) | (5.89) | (3.19) | (3.93) | (30,930) | (0.48) | (2.01) | (0.23) |
| **SOUTH** | | | | | | | | | | | | |
| Total | 1748 | 0.16 | 0.20 | 1.21 | 7.22 | 19.94 | 4.33 | 5.88 | 24,180 | 0.76 | 6.22 | 0.62 |
| | 100.0% | (0.42) | (0.47) | (1.32) | (2.32) | (5.95) | (3.42) | (3.42) | (43,640) | (0.43) | (2.29) | (0.49) |
| Non-workers | 973 | 0.16 | 0.19 | 1.23 | 7.13 | 19.35 | 4.12 | 5.38 | 25,690 | 0.76 | 6.36 | 0.57 |
| | 55.7% | (0.41) | (0.44) | (1.33) | (2.32) | (6.17) | (3.68) | (3.09) | (47,480) | (0.43) | (2.44) | (0.50) |
| Self-employed | 177 | 0.19 | 0.36 | 1.69 | 8.08 | 19.31 | 3.97 | 3.86 | 14,550 | 0.81 | 5.78 | 0.16 |
| | 10.1% | (0.49) | (0.58) | (1.41) | (2.36) | (4.95) | (2.54) | (2.29) | (17,160) | (0.39) | (1.81) | (0.37) |
| Employees | 598 | 0.15 | 0.17 | 1.05 | 7.13 | 21.08 | 4.77 | 7.27 | 24,580 | 0.73 | 6.14 | 0.84 |
| | 34.2% | (0.42) | (0.46) | (1.23) | (2.27) | (5.68) | (3.17) | (3.69) | (42,230) | (0.44) | (2.14) | (0.36) |

Note: Numbers in parentheses are standard deviations.

**Appendix Table 3A.5**
**Means and Variables Used in Logits - Single Men**

| REGION | OBS | AGE | AGESQ /100 | YEARS SCHOOL | NO SCHOOL COMPLETED | URBAN |
|---|---|---|---|---|---|---|
| **ALL BRAZIL** | | | | | | |
| Total | 12974 | 24.76 | 7.13 | 5.00 | 0.41 | 0.72 |
| | 100.0% | (10.01) | (6.99) | (4.16) | (0.49) | (0.45) |
| Self-employed | 3301 | 27.93 | 9.38 | 3.05 | 0.64 | 0.47 |
| | 25.4% | (12.56) | (9.18) | (3.63) | (0.48) | (0.50) |
| Employees | 9673 | 23.68 | 6.37 | 5.67 | 0.33 | 0.81 |
| | 74.6% | (8.72) | (5.87) | (4.12) | (0.47) | (0.39) |
| **NORTHEAST** | | | | | | |
| Total | 2870 | 24.68 | 7.17 | 3.21 | 0.67 | 0.54 |
| | 100.0% | (10.37) | (7.32) | (4.03) | (0.47) | (0.50) |
| Self-employed | 1261 | 26.22 | 8.34 | 1.66 | 0.84 | 0.32 |
| | 43.9% | (12.11) | (8.83) | (2.87) | (0.37) | (0.47) |
| Employees | 1609 | 23.48 | 6.25 | 4.42 | 0.53 | 0.72 |
| | 56.1% | (8.57) | (5.70) | (4.37) | (0.50) | (0.45) |
| **NORTHWEST** | | | | | | |
| Total | 1415 | 25.21 | 7.45 | 4.25 | 0.50 | 0.62 |
| | 100.0% | (10.45) | (7.34) | (3.82) | (0.50) | (0.49) |
| Self-employed | 486 | 28.86 | 9.89 | 2.55 | 0.73 | 0.43 |
| | 34.3% | (12.51) | (9.17) | (3.15) | (0.44) | (0.50) |
| Employees | 929 | 23.30 | 6.17 | 5.14 | 0.38 | 0.72 |
| | 65.7% | (8.60) | (5.78) | (3.84) | (0.49) | (0.45) |
| **OTHER SOUTHEAST** | | | | | | |
| Total | 1917 | 24.90 | 7.24 | 4.67 | 0.40 | 0.69 |
| | 100.0% | (10.21) | (7.23) | (3.81) | (0.49) | (0.46) |
| Self-employed | 445 | 28.88 | 9.91 | 3.39 | 0.58 | 0.48 |
| | 23.2% | (12.54) | (9.24) | (3.57) | (0.49) | (0.50) |
| Employees | 1472 | 23.70 | 6.44 | 5.05 | 0.35 | 0.75 |
| | 76.8% | (9.05) | (6.29) | (3.80) | (0.48) | (0.43) |
| **RIO DE JANEIRO** | | | | | | |
| Total | 1329 | 26.23 | 7.88 | 6.66 | 0.27 | 0.90 |
| | 100.0% | (10.01) | (6.92) | (4.28) | (0.44) | (0.29) |
| Self-employed | 182 | 31.13 | 11.25 | 5.89 | 0.36 | 0.88 |
| | 13.7% | (12.53) | (8.99) | (4.41) | (0.48) | (0.33) |
| Employees | 1147 | 25.45 | 7.35 | 6.78 | 0.25 | 0.91 |
| | 86.3% | (9.32) | (6.38) | (4.25) | (0.44) | (0.29) |
| **SAO PAULO** | | | | | | |
| Total | 3515 | 24.29 | 6.77 | 6.10 | 0.26 | 0.90 |
| | 100.0% | (9.35) | (6.43) | (4.13) | (0.44) | (0.30) |
| Self-employed | 443 | 29.24 | 10.22 | 5.02 | 0.37 | 0.82 |
| | 12.6% | (12.95) | (9.59) | (4.13) | (0.48) | (0.38) |
| Employees | 3072 | 23.57 | 6.28 | 6.26 | 0.25 | 0.91 |
| | 87.4% | (8.48) | (5.66) | (4.11) | (0.43) | (0.29) |
| **SOUTH** | | | | | | |
| Total | 1928 | 24.26 | 6.88 | 5.41 | 0.31 | 0.66 |
| | 100.0% | (10.00) | (6.95) | (3.70) | (0.46) | (0.47) |
| Self-employed | 484 | 28.19 | 9.60 | 4.01 | 0.48 | 0.39 |
| | 25.1% | (12.89) | (9.48) | (3.30) | (0.50) | (0.49) |
| Employees | 1444 | 22.94 | 5.97 | 5.88 | 0.26 | 0.76 |
| | 74.9% | (8.42) | (5.58) | (3.70) | (0.44) | (0.43) |

Note:  Numbers in parentheses are standard deviations.

**Appendix Table 3A.6**

**Means and Variables Used in Wage Regressions - Single Men and Women**

| REGION | ALL BRAZIL | | | | NORTHEAST | | | | NORTHWEST | | | | OTHER SOUTHEAST | | | | RIO DE JANEIRO | | | | SAO PAULO | | | | SOUTH | | | |
|---|---|---|---|---|---|---|---|---|---|---|---|---|---|---|---|---|---|---|---|---|---|---|---|---|---|---|---|---|
| | EMPLOYEES | | SELF EMPLOYED | | EMPLOYEES | | SELF EMPLOYED | | EMPLOYEES | | SELF EMPLOYED | | EMPLOYEES | | SELF EMPLOYED | | EMPLOYEES | | SELF EMPLOYED | | EMPLOYEES | | SELF EMPLOYED | | EMPLOYEES | | SELF EMPLOYED | |
| VARIABLE | MEN | WOMEN | MEN | WOMEN | MEN | WOMEN | MEN | WOMEN | MEN | WOMEN | MEN | WOMEN | MEN | WOMEN | MEN | WOMEN | MEN | WOMEN | MEN | WOMEN | MEN | WOMEN | MEN | WOMEN | MEN | WOMEN | MEN | WOMEN |
| OBS | 9675 | 3671 | 3391 | 439 | 1609 | 561 | 1261 | 222 | 929 | 287 | 486 | 29 | 1472 | 581 | 445 | 37 | 1147 | 433 | 182 | 31 | 3072 | 1391 | 443 | 79 | 1444 | 598 | 484 | 41 |
| LAMBDA | -0.37 | 0.83 | 1.08 | 0.22 | -0.39 | 0.66 | 0.75 | 0.30 | -0.48 | 0.80 | 0.92 | 0.30 | -0.36 | 0.80 | 1.19 | 0.14 | -0.24 | 0.90 | 0.80 | 0.09 | -0.22 | 1.07 | 1.55 | 0.17 | -0.37 | 0.81 | 1.09 | 0.26 |
| | (0.23) | (0.39) | (0.39) | (0.17) | (0.33) | (0.44) | (0.34) | (0.17) | (0.27) | (0.41) | (0.35) | (0.26) | (0.19) | (0.35) | (0.32) | (0.11) | (0.10) | (0.40) | (0.27) | (0.07) | (0.10) | (0.35) | (0.29) | (0.14) | (0.23) | (0.38) | (0.39) | (0.25) |
| SECPUB | - | 0.17 | - | - | - | 0.27 | - | - | - | 0.25 | - | - | - | 0.21 | - | - | - | 0.16 | - | - | - | 0.11 | - | - | - | 0.14 | - | - |
| | | (0.37) | | | | (0.44) | | | | (0.44) | | | | (0.41) | | | | (0.36) | | | | (0.31) | | | | (0.34) | | |
| SOCSEC | 0.64 | 0.71 | 0.18 | 0.19 | 0.51 | 0.64 | 0.07 | 0.06 | 0.51 | 0.63 | 0.11 | 0.14 | 0.59 | 0.57 | 0.24 | 0.22 | 0.78 | 0.75 | 0.43 | 0.32 | 0.79 | 0.78 | 0.32 | 0.48 | 0.75 | 0.76 | 0.26 | 0.27 |
| | (0.47) | (0.45) | (0.38) | (0.39) | (0.50) | (0.48) | (0.25) | (0.24) | (0.50) | (0.48) | (0.31) | (0.35) | (0.49) | (0.50) | (0.43) | (0.42) | (0.41) | (0.44) | (0.50) | (0.48) | (0.41) | (0.42) | (0.47) | (0.50) | (0.43) | (0.43) | (0.44) | (0.45) |
| EXPR | 12.02 | 8.65 | 18.88 | 14.82 | 13.06 | 10.45 | 18.56 | 15.73 | 12.16 | 8.75 | 20.32 | 17.86 | 12.66 | 9.50 | 19.49 | 14.03 | 12.65 | 8.59 | 19.24 | 10.94 | 11.32 | 7.92 | 18.22 | 14.46 | 11.08 | 7.81 | 18.18 | 12.07 |
| | (9.96) | (6.37) | (13.37) | (9.72) | (9.57) | (7.22) | (12.58) | (9.72) | (9.99) | (5.77) | (13.30) | (9.52) | (10.36) | (6.85) | (13.67) | (9.50) | (10.55) | (6.28) | (13.74) | (9.38) | (9.09) | (5.87) | (14.22) | (10.63) | (9.65) | (6.07) | (14.15) | (7.12) |
| EXPSQ/100 | 2.44 | 1.15 | 5.35 | 3.14 | 2.62 | 1.61 | 5.05 | 3.41 | 2.47 | 1.10 | 5.89 | 4.06 | 2.67 | 1.37 | 5.66 | 2.85 | 2.72 | 1.13 | 5.58 | 2.05 | 2.24 | 0.97 | 5.34 | 3.21 | 2.16 | 0.98 | 5.30 | 1.95 |
| | (4.61) | (1.99) | (7.52) | (4.15) | (4.48) | (2.59) | (7.54) | (4.32) | (4.68) | (1.69) | (7.58) | (3.64) | (5.19) | (2.38) | (7.74) | (4.05) | (4.83) | (1.82) | (6.62) | (4.32) | (4.39) | (1.64) | (7.63) | (4.43) | (4.31) | (1.84) | (7.88) | (2.28) |
| YREDUC | 5.67 | 7.38 | 3.05 | 3.66 | 4.42 | 7.16 | 1.66 | 2.26 | 5.14 | 7.15 | 2.55 | 3.14 | 5.05 | 6.59 | 3.39 | 4.00 | 6.78 | 8.55 | 5.89 | 6.65 | 6.26 | 7.50 | 5.02 | 6.20 | 5.88 | 7.27 | 4.01 | 4.17 |
| | (3.63) | (3.99) | | | (4.37) | (4.57) | (2.87) | (3.01) | (3.47) | (3.15) | | | (3.80) | (3.85) | | | (4.25) | (3.98) | | | (4.11) | (3.93) | | | (3.70) | (3.69) | (3.30) | (3.71) |
| URBAN | 0.81 | 0.91 | 0.47 | 0.54 | 0.72 | 0.84 | 0.32 | 0.37 | 0.72 | 0.90 | 0.43 | 0.55 | 0.75 | 0.91 | 0.48 | 0.57 | 0.91 | 0.96 | 0.88 | 0.90 | 0.91 | 0.94 | 0.82 | 0.86 | 0.76 | 0.84 | 0.39 | 0.56 |
| | (0.39) | (0.29) | (0.50) | (0.50) | (0.45) | (0.37) | (0.47) | (0.48) | (0.45) | (0.30) | (0.50) | (0.51) | (0.43) | (0.28) | (0.33) | (0.50) | (0.29) | (0.18) | (0.33) | (0.30) | (0.29) | (0.23) | (0.38) | (0.35) | (0.43) | (0.36) | (0.49) |  |
| BRTOT | | | | 1.31 | | | | 1.51 | | | | 1.52 | | 1.06 | | 1.32 | | 0.77 | | 1.13 | | 0.76 | | 1.20 | | 0.74 | | 1.22 |
| | | | | (1.71) | | | | (1.74) | | | | (1.60) | | (1.46) | | (2.14) | | (1.15) | | (1.91) | | (1.24) | | (1.67) | | (1.13) | | (1.44) |
| HOURS/WEEK | 45.9 | 43.5 | 45.2 | 39.9 | 44.8 | 41.4 | 43.5 | 37.4 | 46.0 | 43.0 | 45.4 | 42.2 | 46.3 | 44.1 | 47.0 | 40.3 | 45.6 | 42.6 | 43.6 | 38.7 | 46.0 | 44.3 | 46.7 | 43.5 | 47.1 | 43.8 | 45.6 | 45.6 |
| | (7.0) | (8.8) | (8.1) | (10.9) | (7.3) | (10.1) | (7.8) | (10.1) | (7.1) | (10.9) | (10.6) | (10.6) | (7.1) | (9.5) | (7.1) | (10.6) | (7.4) | (10.0) | (10.5) | (12.9) | (6.4) | (6.8) | (8.0) | (9.9) | (7.0) | (8.9) | (8.2) | (11.4) |
| 1-14 HRS % | 0.4 | 1.0 | 0.7 | 2.5 | 0.3 | 1.1 | 0.8 | 3.6 | 0.3 | 1.4 | 0.6 | 0.0 | 0.3 | 0.9 | 0.0 | 2.7 | 0.6 | 2.0 | 2.7 | 3.2 | 0.4 | 0.4 | 0.7 | 0.0 | 0.5 | 1.5 | 0.6 | 2.4 |
| 15-29 HRS % | 2.2 | 7.1 | 2.9 | 13.4 | 3.7 | 13.9 | 3.5 | 14.0 | 1.7 | 9.1 | 1.6 | 17.2 | 2.1 | 8.1 | 1.6 | 10.8 | 3.1 | 9.3 | 6.6 | 3.2 | 1.3 | 3.2 | 2.3 | 10.1 | 2.1 | 6.0 | 2.9 | 9.8 |
| 30-39 HRS % | 5.3 | 9.1 | 12.1 | 24.1 | 8.0 | 10.9 | 16.0 | 34.2 | 8.5 | 13.2 | 13.8 | 3.4 | 6.0 | 9.3 | 8.1 | 24.3 | 4.8 | 10.6 | 13.7 | 19.4 | 3.7 | 7.5 | 8.1 | 15.5 | 3.3 | 8.2 | 6.6 | 2.4 |
| 40-48 HRS % | 65.1 | 62.9 | 55.6 | 42.6 | 66.0 | 57.6 | 62.1 | 41.0 | 59.7 | 51.9 | 55.1 | 58.6 | 60.4 | 54.4 | 53.7 | 45.9 | 64.8 | 57.8 | 47.3 | 32.3 | 69.2 | 72.4 | 51.0 | 44.3 | 63.8 | 63.0 | 48.1 | 41.5 |
| 49+ HRS % | 27.0 | 19.9 | 28.7 | 17.3 | 22.1 | 16.6 | 17.6 | 7.2 | 29.7 | 24.4 | 28.8 | 20.7 | 31.3 | 27.4 | 36.6 | 16.2 | 26.8 | 20.3 | 29.7 | 22.6 | 25.4 | 16.5 | 37.9 | 29.1 | 30.4 | 21.2 | 41.7 | 43.9 |
| WAGE/MONTH | 7.8 | 6.4 | 7.5 | 4.5 | 5.3 | 4.9 | 3.9 | 2.0 | 6.9 | 5.2 | 8.5 | 4.4 | 6.6 | 4.6 | 7.9 | 4.1 | 9.4 | 8.3 | 12.2 | 5.9 | 10.0 | 7.8 | 12.4 | 11.1 | 6.8 | 5.4 | 9.2 | 4.5 |
| | (9.6) | (6.4) | (16.9) | (7.8) | (6.1) | (7.1) | (5.1) | (2.6) | (10.3) | (5.0) | (13.4) | (4.6) | (7.8) | (4.9) | (11.7) | (4.5) | (11.6) | (8.4) | (16.2) | (6.3) | (11.5) | (7.3) | (23.8) | (14.1) | (6.4) | (4.6) | (30.0) | (7.7) |
| WAGE/HOUR | 44.4 | 39.5 | 43.3 | 29.4 | 30.8 | 32.4 | 22.5 | 15.6 | 38.7 | 32.9 | 48.8 | 27.5 | 37.0 | 28.6 | 42.0 | 26.5 | 53.8 | 54.9 | 99.5 | 40.0 | 56.4 | 45.7 | 64.2 | 69.1 | 37.5 | 33.7 | 53.0 | 23.8 |
| | (59.8) | (47.6) | (116.8) | (50.9) | (39.4) | (55.9) | (27.5) | (24.6) | (60.0) | (36.3) | (84.4) | (30.0) | (45.8) | (34.4) | (58.1) | (30.0) | (69.1) | (68.4) | (285.0) | (46.4) | (74.7) | (44.8) | (119.5) | (91.8) | (37.6) | (37.6) | (186.6) | (34.9) |
| LN WAGE | 3.4491 | 3.3748 | 3.2007 | 2.7003 | 3.0029 | 2.9735 | 2.7861 | 2.2047 | 3.3308 | 3.1231 | 3.4152 | 2.9553 | 3.2280 | 2.948 | 3.3051 | 2.9028 | 3.6145 | 3.5575 | 3.8335 | 3.1751 | 3.7189 | 3.5172 | 3.7517 | 3.6709 | 3.3918 | 3.2197 | 3.2817 | 2.7916 |
| | (0.76) | (0.80) | (0.91) | (1.12) | (0.76) | (1.00) | (0.76) | (1.02) | (0.72) | (0.86) | (0.84) | (0.79) | (0.72) | (0.91) | (0.86) | (0.84) | (0.78) | (0.91) | (0.96) | (1.04) | (0.71) | (0.75) | (0.87) | (0.99) | (0.65) | (0.75) | (0.93) | (0.77) |
| FEMALE/MALE RATIOS | | | | | | | | | | | | | | | | | | | | | | | | | | | | |
| WAGE/MONTH | 0.82 | | 0.60 | | 0.93 | | 0.52 | | 0.76 | | 0.52 | | 0.70 | | 0.49 | | 0.88 | | 0.49 | | 0.78 | | 0.89 | | 0.49 | | | |
| WAGE/HOUR | 0.89 | | 0.64 | | 1.05 | | 0.69 | | 0.83 | | 0.56 | | 0.77 | | 0.63 | | 1.02 | | 0.45 | | 0.81 | | 1.01 | | 0.45 | | | |
| HOURS/WEEK | 0.95 | | 0.88 | | 0.92 | | 0.86 | | 0.94 | | 0.93 | | 0.95 | | 0.86 | | 0.93 | | 0.89 | | 0.96 | | 0.93 | | 0.97 | | | |

Note: Numbers in parentheses are standard deviations.

# References

Arriagada, A-M. "Labor Market Outcomes of Non-formal Training for Male and Female Workers in Peru." *Economics of Education Review,* Vol. 9, no. 1 (1990). pp. 331-342.

Becker, G.S. *Human Capital.* New York: Columbia University Press, 1964.

Behrman, J.R. "The Action of Human Resources and Poverty on One Another: What We have Yet to Learn." Living Standards Measurement Study Working Paper No. 74. Washington, D.C.: World Bank, Population and Human Resources Department, 1990.

Behrman, J.R. and B. Wolfe. "Labor Force Participation and Earnings Determinants for Women in the Special Conditions of Developing Countries." *Journal of Development Economics,* Vol. 46 (1984). pp. 259-288.

Birdsall, J. and J.R. Behrman. "Does Geographical Aggregation Cause Overestimates of the Returns to Schooling?" *Oxford Bulletin of Economics and Statistics,* Vol. 46, no. 1 (1984). pp. 55-72.

Birdsall, J. and L.M. Fox. "Why Males Earn More: Location and Training of Brazilian School Teachers." *Economic Development and Cultural Change,* Vol. 33, no. 3 (1985). pp. 533-556.

Blinder, A.S. "On Dogmatism in Human Capital Theory." *Journal of Human Resources,* Vol. 11, no.1 (1976). pp. 8-22.

Boulding, E. "Measurement of Women's Work in the Third World: Problems and Suggestions" in M. Buvinic, M.A. Lycette and W.P. McGreevey (eds.). *Women and Poverty in the Third World.* Cambridge, Baltimore: Johns Hopkins University Press, 1983.

Cain, G.G. "The Economic Analysis of Labor Market Discrimination: A Survey" in O. Ashenfelter and R. Layard (eds.). *Handbook of Labor Economics.* New York: Elsevier, 1986.

Cotton, J. "On the Decomposition of Wage Differentials." *Review of Economics and Statistics,* Vol. 70, no. 2 (1988). pp. 236-243.

Dabos, M. and G. Psacharopoulos. "An Analysis of the Sources of Earnings Variation Among Brazilian Males." *Economics of Education Review,* 1991 (forthcoming).

Dubin, J.A. and D. Rivers. "Selection Bias in Linear Regression, Logit and Probit Models." Social Science Working Paper No. 698. Pasadena,California: California Institute of Technology, Division of Humanities and Social Sciences, 1989.

Greene, W.H. *Econometric Analysis*. New York: Macmillan, 1990.

Gunderson, M. "Male-Female Wage Differentials and Policy Responses." *Journal of Economic Literature,* Vol. 27 (1989). pp. 46-72.

Ham, J. and C. Hsiao. "Two-stage Estimation of Structural Labor Supply Parameters Using Interval Data from the 1971 Canadian Census." *Journal of Econometrics,* Vol. 24 (1984). pp. 133-158.

Heckman, J.J. "Selection Bias and Self-selection" in J. Eatwell, M. Milgate and P. Newman (eds.). *The New Palgrave: A Dictionary of Economics.* New York: Stockton Press, 1987.

Heckman, J.J. and V.J. Hotz. "An Investigation of the Labor Market Earnings of Panamanian Males." *Journal of Human Resources,* Vol. 21, no. 4 (1986). pp. 507-542.

Hill, M.A. "Female Labor Supply in Japan: Implications of the Informal Sector for Labor Force Participation and Hours of Work." *Journal of Human Resources,* Vol. 24, no. 1 (1988). pp. 459-468.

Jones, F.L. "On Decomposing the Wage Gap: A Critical Comment on Blinder's Method." *Journal of Human Resources,* Vol. 18 (1983). pp. 126-130.

King, E.M. "Does Education Pay in the Labor Market? The Labor Force Participation, Occupation and Earnings of Peruvian Women." Living Standards Measurement Study Working Paper No. 67.  Washington, D.C.: World Bank, Population and Human Resources Department, 1990.

Khandker, S.R. "Labor Market Participation, Returns to Education, and Male-female Wage Differences in Peru." PRE Working Paper Series No. 461. Washington, D.C.: World Bank, Population and Human Resources Department, 1990.

Kuhn, P. "Sex Discrimination in Labor Markets: The Role of Statistical Evidence." *American Economic Review,* Vol. 77 (1987). pp. 567-583.

Lee, F.L. "Generalized Econometric Models with Selectivity." *Econometrica,* Vol. 51, no. 2 (1983). pp. 126-130.

Maddala, G.S. *Limited-dependent and Qualitative Variables in Econometrics.* Cambridge: Cambridge University Press, 1983.

McFadden, D. "Conditional Logit Analysis of Qualitative Choice Behavior" in P. Zarembka (ed.). *Frontiers in Econometrics.* New York: Academic Press, 1973.

Mincer, J. *Schooling, Experience and Earnings.* New York: Columbia University Press, 1974.

Mohan, R. *Work, Wage, and Welfare in a Developing Metropolis: Consequences of Growth in Bogota, Colombia.* New York: Oxford University Press, 1988.

Oaxaca, R. "Male-female Wage Differentials in Urban Labor Markets." *International Economic Review,* Vol. 14 (1973). pp. 693-709.

Ohsfeldt, R.L. and S.D. Culler. "Differences in Income Between Male and Female Physicians." *Journal of Health Economics,* Vol. 5 (1986). pp. 335-346.

Psacharopoulos, G. and Z. Tzannatos. "Female Labor Force Participation: An International Perspective." *The World Bank Research Observer,* Vol. 4, no. 2 (1989). pp. 187-201.

Reimers, C.W. "A Comparative Analysis of the Wages of Hispanics, Blacks and Non-Hispanic Whites" in G.J. Borjas and M. Tienda (eds.). *Hispanics in the U.S.Economy.* New York: Academic Press, 1985.

Schultz, T.P. "Education Investments and Returns" in H. Chenery and T.N. Srinivasan (eds.). *Handbook of Development Economics.* Amsterdam: Elsevier Science Publishers, 1988.

Shapiro, D.M. and M. Stelcner. "The Persistence of the Male-female Earnings Gap in Canada, 1970-1980: The Impact of Equal Pay Laws and Language Policies." *Canadian Public Policy/Analyse de Politique,* Vol. 13, no. 4 (1987). pp. 462-476.

Standing, G. and G. Sheenhan (eds.). *Labour Force Participation in Low-Income Countries.* Geneva: International Labor Office, 1978.

Terrell, T. "An Analysis of the Wage Structure in Guatemala City." *Journal of Developing Areas,* Vol.23 (1989). pp. 405-424.

Thomas, V. "Spatial Differences in the Cost of Living." *Journal of Urban Economics,* Vol. 8 (1980).

Trost, R. and L.F. Lee. "Technical Training and Earnings: A Polychotomous Choice Model with Selectivity." *Review of Economics and Statistics,* Vol. 66 (1984). pp. 151-156.

Zabalza, A. and J.L. Arrufat. "The Extent of Sex Discrimination in Great Britain" in A. Zabalza and Z. Tzannatos. *Women and Equal Pay: The Effects of Legislation on Female Employment and Wages in Britain.* Cambridge: Cambridge University Press, 1985.

# 4

# Female Labor Force Participation
# and Wage Determination in Brazil, 1989

*Jill Tiefenthaler*

## 1.    Introduction

Over the past two decades, many countries have experienced drastic increases in female labor force participation.  However, participation rates, in general, are still lower for women than men and women's wages are significantly lower than men's in most countries.  These differentials have spurred an interest in the determinants of both women's participation decisions and women's wages.

While studies on women's work in developed countries are generally based on a single sector model, there has been a growing interest among development economists in the effects of more complex labor markets in developing countries on modeling and estimating women's decisions to work and women's earnings functions.  The importance of accounting for the large informal sector in many developing countries was recognized over 30 years ago by Jaffe and Azumi (1960).  They observed that women engaged in informal or "cottage-industry" work had higher fertility rates than women who worked in the formal sector.  Results from several more recent studies,  using more rigorous empirical analysis, have supported Jaffe and Azumi's supposition that women's costs of participation are not equivalent across sectors.[1]

In this study, a multi-sector model of female labor force participation and wage determination in Brazil is estimated.  In analyzing the Brazilian labor market it is important to distinguish between the formal sector and the large informal sector.  However, it is also important to account for the distinction between the unregistered workers and the self-employed within the informal sector. The characteristic that distinguishes formal sector wage-earners from informal sector wage-earners is that formal sector employees carry a work booklet.  Under Brazilian labor law, employers are obligated to sign the employee's work booklet when contracting a worker.  Unregistered employment is illegal with the exception of self-employment.

In Section 2, the distinctions between these three identified sectors are more rigorously explored, the data are discussed, and some sample characteristics are presented and discussed.  Section 3 briefly outlines the theoretical polychotomous choice model that underlies the empirical analysis. In Section 4, the empirical model is specified.  The results from estimating the multi-sector

---

[1]    See, for example, Hill (1980, 1983, 1988), Smith (1981), Blau (1984), and Tiefenthaler (1991).

briefly outlines the theoretical polychotomous choice model that underlies the empirical analysis. In Section 4, the empirical model is specified. The results from estimating the multi-sector participation equations for both single women and married women are presented in Section 5, and Section 6 contains the results from estimating the sectoral wage equations. The potential existence of sex differentials in the earnings functions is discussed in Section 7. The conclusions of this research are outlined in Section 8.

## 2.    Data and Sample Characteristics

*Sector definitions and characteristics.*   Most studies of labor markets in developing (and developed) countries prior to 1980 regarded the labor market as one sector and the labor force participation decision as simply a decision to work or not to work. However, several more recent studies have attempted to construct more accurate multi-sector models of the participation decision in more complex labor markets.   The common sectoral decomposition is to increase the participation decision from two choices (work or don't work) to three choices - non-participation, work in the formal sector or work in the informal sector.  In these models, non-participants are considered to be those who do not work for pay.  The formal sector is defined as comprising all individuals who work for a wage while the informal sector is made up of the self-employed.

In this study, following Alderman and Kozel's (1989) study of multi-sector participation and wage determination in Pakistan, the sectoral decomposition is taken a step further.  As Alderman and Kozel found in urban Pakistan, in Brazil a formal sector exists parallel to an informal wage-earning sector as well as a self-employment sector.  Therefore, the participation decision presents four distinct labor market alternatives: non-participation (N), working for a wage in the formal sector (F), working for a wage in the informal sector (I), and self-employment (S).  While non-participation and self-employment continue to be defined as they are in the preceding paragraph, there is an important distinction between formal and informal sector employees.

The informal sector employees are easily distinguished from their formal sector counterparts because informal workers do not carry booklets required by Brazilian labor law and, therefore, are not registered with the government.  Employers must sign all employees' work booklets and then register the employees. Unregistered work is illegal with the exception of self-employment. When an employer signs an individual's booklet, the employer gets access to all information on that individual's former employment because the booklet, by law, is a record of the employee's work history including wages.

There are both pros and cons to being officially registered as a worker in Brazil.  The benefits include eligibility for unemployment compensation, social security (27 percent of the total 37 percent is paid by the employer), protection of labor law including minimum wage legislation, benefits of labor negotiations and union membership.  However, unregistered workers do not have to pay payroll taxes and their wages are not regulated by official wage indexations.  In addition, people who are collecting various government transfers can continue to collect them while working in the informal sector.

The employer faces many added costs when registering employees including the 27 percent social security payment and other payroll taxes, the possibility of dismissal fines, union bargaining, and the regulation of Brazilian labor law.  Employers must weigh these costs against the probability of being caught and fined for employing unregistered workers (see Table 4.1 for the sectoral decomposition of the work force for the Brazilian sample).

***Data.*** The data for this study were collected from 70,777 Brazilian households (301,088 individuals) in the fourth quarter of 1989 by the National Statistical Service. Data collection was organized according to four distinct regions: Rio de Janeiro and Sao Paulo, the rest of the South (Parana, Santa Catarina, Rio Grande do Sul, Minas Gerais, and Espirito Santo), the Northeast (Maranhao, Piaui, Ceara, Rio Grande do Norte, Paraiba, Pernambuco, Alagoas, Sergipe, and Bahia), and the Northwest/Central (Distrito Federal, Rondonia, Acre, Amazonas, Roraima, Para, Amapa, Mato Grosso do Sul, Mato Grosso, and Goias). These four regions comprise the strata used in a modified stratified random sampling scheme based on the 1980 demographic census. Information was collected on household demographics, individual characteristics of all household members, educational histories of all school-aged (5 years and older) household members, and labor and income details of all household members over age nine.

The final sample, used for both data and regression analyses, includes 9,973 single women, 50,452 married women, and 58,000 men. The male subsample includes all married men whose spouse is under age 65 and all single male heads of households.[2] The 50,452 married women are comprised of all married women under age 65 and the subsample of single women includes all female single heads of households.

***Sample characteristics.*** Brazil experienced rapid rises in employment and productivity in the 1960s and the 1970s. However, during the 1980s, the world recession and debt problems contributed to a resurgence in unemployment rates and an average annual growth rate of only one percent. Although recovery was under way by 1989, when the data employed in this study were collected, the backdrop of this study is an economy worn by a decade of recession and adjustment.

In this section, statistics describing Brazilian women's labor market opportunities in 1989 are discussed. Women's participation rates, earnings, and wages are presented and compared with men's. It is often suggested that women bear a disproportionate share of the burden of adjustment. By comparing the data from this study with those from a study by Stelcner et al. (1991) which uses Brazilian data from 1980, this hypothesis is evaluated. In addition, regional disparities in participation rates and wages will also be discussed.

***Sex differentials.*** As outlined in the introduction, although women are increasingly entering the labor force, men's participation rates are still higher and men earn higher wages than women. In this sample, 86.4 percent of men participate in the paid labor force compared with only 57.4 percent of women. Single women are more likely to participate in the labor force than married women. Sixty-two percent of single women categorized themselves as paid laborers while only 34 percent of married women worked for pay. Men who work make more than their female counterparts. Male workers' average earnings are 1430.36 cruzados (C) per month while single women and married women make, on average, 811.54C and 762.53C per month, respectively. One source of the deviation in total earnings is the number of hours worked. The average man spends approximately 46 hours in a primary job per week while women, on average, work around 37 hours in a primary job. The six percent of men who hold two jobs work, on average, 20 hours per week in their second jobs while the average woman who holds two jobs (5.5 percent) spends approximately 18 hours at her second job.

---

[2]   Some men over retirement age, 65, had to be included in the male subsample in order that husbands' wages could be predicted for all females under 65.

Another source of the sex differential in total earnings is a sex differential in hourly wages. Men, in this study, earned an average hourly wage of 8.34C per hour while the average employed woman made only 5.74C per hour. The result that women are making only 70 percent of the average male wage may be contributed to several factors, including differences in education and experience or job tenure and the sectoral composition of the work force. If education and experience are important determinants of wages and men are significantly better educated and have accumulated more experience than women, we would expect men to earn higher wages. However, the mean male has received 5.68 years of formal education while the mean female has received only slightly less formal education, 5.05 years. No data on work experience are available in this data set.

The wage differential may, in part, be due to the sectoral distribution of male and female employees within the paid labor force. As presented in the following chart, women are more likely to work as employees in the informal sector while men are more likely to work as employees in the formal sector. Women's preferences for informal sector work may be due to easier entry and exit and more flexibility in the informal sector than in the formal sector. Paes de Barros and Varandas (1987) find that there is both a higher degree of flexibility in the number of hours worked and a shorter duration in employment in the informal sector than in the formal sector in Brazil. Flexibility in work schedule is often deemed to be more important to women than to men due to women's household responsibilities of household production and childcare.

**Figure 4.1**

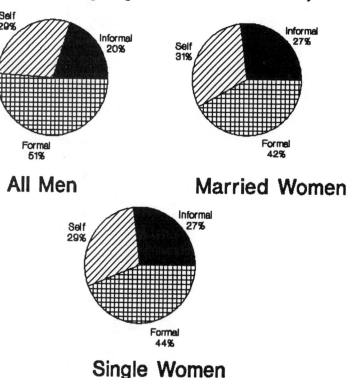

# Sectoral Employment in Brazil, 1989

All Men

Married Women

Single Women

An alternative explanation for the disproportionate number of women working as informal employees is a shortage of jobs in the formal sector. If such a shortage exists, formal sector employers may discriminate against women who are then forced to work in the informal sector. However, Sedlacek, Paes de Barros, and Varandas (1989) conclude that no such mobility barriers between formal and informal sector employment exist.

As shown in the table below, wages are, on average, higher for both men and women in the formal sector than in the informal sectors. However, it is also important to note that the sex differential is greater among formal employees (women earn 70.3 percent of men's wages) and the self-employed (70.5 percent) than in the informal sector (85.2 percent).

**Table 4.1**
Sectoral Wages by Sex Group in Brazil (Cruzados/hour), 1989.

|  | Men | Married Women | Single Women |
| --- | --- | --- | --- |
| Formal Employees | 10.93 | 7.68 | 7.46 |
| Informal Employees | 5.28 | 4.51 | 4.46 |
| Self-Employed | 5.96 | 4.17 | 4.37 |

By reviewing the information in the chart and the table, the interpretation is that a contributing factor to relatively low wages for women is that women are disproportionately represented as employees in the lower wage sector. These data suggest that if the proportion of women working in the formal sector increases, the sex differential in wages would be expected to decrease.

***Changes in women's economic opportunities - 1980 to 1989.*** It is often suggested that disadvantaged groups - the rural poor, women, children, minorities - bear a disproportional amount of the burden of economic adjustment programs (see, for example, Cornia et al. (1987)). The 1980s was a decade of adjustment for Brazil as she recovered from the world recession and began to deal with the problems of a bulging foreign debt. Although there are many measures of welfare, comparing women's economic opportunities in 1980 with those in 1989 will provide some insight into the effects of the adjustment programs on the well-being of Brazilian women.

Participation rates of both single women and married women increased from 1980 to 1989. According to Stelcner et al. (1991), 20 percent of the married women and 41 percent of the single women in their sample reported to be working for pay. In the sample taken in 1989, used in this study, over 34 percent of married women and 62 percent of single women were wage earners. This comparison is consistent with Edwards' (1991) study of economy-wide trends in the Brazilian labor market in the 1980s as she finds that "labor force participation has continued to increase significantly during the decade of the 1980s."

Although participation has increased among both married and single women, the increases have not been proportionally distributed across sectors. In 1980, from the Stelcner et al. sample, 65 percent of working married women were employees (either with or without an employment booklet) while the remaining 35 percent were self-employed. In 1989, slightly more married women classified themselves as employees at 69 percent while the percentage of self-employed fell to 31. The opposite transition occurred among single working women. In the 1980 sample, 83 percent said they were employees and only 17 percent were self-employed. In 1989, the number of employees fell to 71 percent of working single women while more women classified themselves as self-employed, 29 percent.

Although earnings are not directly comparable across years, the female/male earnings ratio is comparable and provides evidence of women's relative position in the economy. In the Stelcner et al. 1980 sample, the female/male earnings ratio was 59 percent (61 percent for married women and 54 percent for single women). This number fell slightly to 56 percent in the 1989 sample (55 percent for married women and 57 percent for single women). Single women made a relative gain in total earnings throughout the decade while married women lost ground to men.

The female/male ratio of hourly wages is a better measure for comparing women's relative economic strength across time. In the 1980 sample, the female/male wage ratio was 75 percent for employees while self-employed women were making only 68 percent of their male counterparts' wages. There was little change in this statistic over the decade. In the 1989 sample, employed women were making 76 percent of employed men's wages while self-employed women were making 69 percent of self-employed men's wages. Women gained little in their economic power relative to men in the 1980s as the sex ratio of wages improved by only one percent in both sectors over the decade.

*Regional differentials.* Brazil is a large and diverse country. Studies which have accounted for its size and diversity by treating distinct regions separately and including regional dummy variables have found that regional differences should not be ignored. Stelcner et al. (1991), using data from 1980, extensively analyze regional differences in labor market conditions in Brazil. They note important differences between the highly industrialized and modern regions in the South (Rio de Janeiro, Sao Paulo, Other Southeast, and the South) and the Northeast which is heavily dependent on agricultural activities. Their data analysis, most notably, points to much lower incomes, wages, and education in the Northeast region than in the rest of Brazil. The conclusion is that significant barriers to migration exist which prevent the equalization of wages across regions.

**Table 4.2**
Regional Wages in Brazil, 1989.

|  | Male | Female | Female/Male[a] |
|---|---|---|---|
|  | (Cruzados/hour) | | (percent) |
| Rio de Janeiro | 10.89 | 8.47 | 77.8 |
| Sao Paulo | 11.18 | 8.23 | 73.6 |
| South | 9.00 | 6.68 | 74.2 |
| Other Southeast | 7.87 | 5.15 | 65.4 |
| Northeast | 5.61 | 3.56 | 63.5 |
| Northwest/Central | 9.19 | 6.43 | 70.0 |

a. The ratio of the average woman's wage to the average man's wage.

These regional wage differentials continue to persist in 1989. As the following table shows, mean wages are not equal across regions. (It is important to note, however, that these wages have not been adjusted to reflect any cost of living discrepancies which may exist across regions.) Wages are notably lowest in the Northeast for both men and women. The ratio of female/male wages is also lowest in the Northeast while this ratio is highest in Rio de Janeiro. A relationship appears to exist between high wages and more favorable female/male wage ratios.

There are few noteworthy regional differences in the labor force participation patterns of women, as shown in Table 4.3. Participation of married women varies by less than four percent across the seven regions while the participation of single women jumps over seven percent from a low of 59.1 percent in the Northeast to over 66 percent in the Northwest/Central. Participation rates are the lowest in the Northeast for both married women and single women followed closely by Sao Paulo. One striking figure in male participation rates is the relatively low participation of men in Rio de Janeiro. While this city definitely has the lowest male participation rate, the female participation rates for Rio are relatively moderate.

**Table 4.3**
**Regional Participation Rates in Brazil, 1989**
**(percent)**

|  | Male | Female | Ratio[a] |
|---|---|---|---|
| Rio de Janeiro | 81.0 | 36.8 | 61.2 |
| Sao Paulo | 85.2 | 33.3 | 59.4 |
| South | 86.8 | 35.6 | 64.3 |
| Southeast | 86.2 | 33.3 | 61.3 |
| Northeast | 85.5 | 33.1 | 59.1 |
| Northwest/Central | 90.5 | 35.8 | 66.7 |

a.  Note that the male participation rates are lower than expected because the male sample includes some men over age 65. Men 65 with wives under 65 were included in the sample because wages had to be predicted for these men so the women could be included in the female sample.

## 3.   Theoretical Model

Assume that a woman must choose among the four mutually exclusive alternatives discussed in the previous sections - working in the formal sector (F), working for a wage in the informal sector (I), being self-employed in the informal sector (S), and not working in the labor force (N). The problem that the woman faces is to choose the labor force alternative which maximizes household utility. Assuming that the household observes the offered wages the woman could earn in each sector, the value of her time in household production, and the time and money costs of participation in each sector, the household maximizes the household utility function subject to the household time and budget constraints under each alternative. The household then compares the levels of indirect utility obtainable from the various choices and chooses the participation status that maximizes household indirect utility.

Following Maddala (1983), the indirect utility function is decomposed into a nonstochastic component and a stochastic component where the nonstochastic component is a linear function of the observable variables in the indirect utility functions and the stochastic component is a function of unobservables. The probability that individual i will participate in sector k is the probability that the indirect utility yielded in sector k is greater than that derived from the other sectors. This implies that the probability of individual i participating in sector k is the probability that the difference between the stochastic components is greater than the difference between the nonstochastic components.

This analysis implies that the offered wage in sector k for individual i is observed if the individual participates in sector k and the condition for participation in k is that the difference between the stochastic components is greater than the difference in the nonstochastic components. Therefore, this is the selection rule for the multi-sector model. Consistent estimates of the three sector wage equations can be obtained by accounting for this selection rule in the estimations.

The form of the participation equation, the method of estimation, and the calculation of the selection correction will depend upon the distributional assumption on the errors. Assume that the errors of the linear indirect utility functions are independently and identically distributed with the type I extreme-value distribution (also called the Weibull distribution). Given this distribution of the errors, the difference between the errors has a logistic distribution (see McFadden (1973)).

Because the difference between the errors is assumed to follow a logistic distribution, the participation equation must be estimated with the multinomial logit model. The probabilities of participation in each sector, given that the nonstochastic component of indirect utility is a linear function, under the multinomial model are written as:

$$P_{ik} = \frac{\exp(\delta_k D_i)}{\sum \exp(\delta_j D_i)}, \qquad k=F,I,S \qquad j=F,I,S,N. \tag{1}$$

The above expression requires some normalization. Using a commonly used and simple normalization, that the coefficients of the nonparticipation alternative $\delta_N = 0$, together with the three probability equations uniquely determines the selection probabilities and guarantees that they sum to one for each individual. The multinomial logit model can then be estimated using maximum likelihood methods.

As mentioned in the previous section, it is also interesting to estimate the sectoral wage equations. Because of the existence of selection bias (those women from whom wages are observed all have an offered wage above the reservation wage), a Heckman-type method must to used to correct for the selectivity. Hay (1980) adapted Heckman's (1979) inverse Mill's ratio correction for probit models so that it is applicable to both binary and multinomial logit models. In the multinomial logit model, the correction is:

$$\lambda_{ik} = (\frac{6}{\pi^2})(-1)^{j+1}(\sum_{j \neq k} \frac{1}{J}(\frac{P_x}{1-P_x})\log(P_x) + (\frac{J-1}{J})\log(P_{ik})) \tag{2}$$

where J = the total number of alternative choices, in this case J equals four.

The procedure for estimating the three sector wage equations free from selection bias is then to first estimate the maximum likelihood participation equation. By using the results to calculate the probabilities of participation, Hay's inverse Mill's ratio for the multinomial logit participation model can be calculated. Then, given the inverse Mill's ratio, the wage equations can be estimated. It is important to note that the derivation of the multinomial logit model of participation did not require any assumption about the distribution of the errors in the wage equations. Consequently, they can be assumed to be normally distributed and the wage equations can be estimated using ordinary least squares (OLS).

## 4.   Empirical Specification

As pointed out in Section 3, three wage equations will be estimated, one for each sector.  The offered wages in each sector are hypothesized to be a function of a vector of the individual's human capital variables and labor market conditions. Consequently, the wage equations are set up as standard Mincer equations (see Mincer (1974)) with formal education, predicted experience, experience-squared, regional dummies, and racial dummies included as regressors.  Formal education is included to pick up wage increases resulting from human capital investment. Experience is believed to have important positive effects on both productivity and earnings but at a declining rate.   The racial dummies are included to account for the possibility of discrimination (white or of European descent is the omitted category) and the regional dummies are included to reflect differing employment opportunities across regions.

The wage variable for each sector is measured as total income in cruzados per month divided by the average number of hours worked per month (the number of hours worked in a week multiplied by four).  The reference period is the September 24 through September 30, 1989. Formal education is measured as six dummy variables - (1) if the woman received any formal schooling, (2) if the woman completed the first four years of primary school[3], (3) if the women finished primary school (eight years), (4) if the woman finished secondary school, (5) if the woman finished college, and (6) if the woman did any graduate work.  The survey question asked was "highest grade completed" and this variable was converted into the six dummy variables specified.  The dummy variables are specified such that all six will be equal to one for a woman who has attained post-graduate work (the first five will be equal to one for a woman who completed college and stopped, etc.).  Therefore, the coefficients on all six variables have to added up to get the total premium paid to education for a woman who has achieved higher education (the first five added up for the total returns to finishing college, etc.).

Labor market experience is measured in years.  However, because no data were collected on experience, this variable was constructed using the standard formula:  age - education - 6. Although this formula has worked well as a proxy for male work experience, it has not performed as well as a predictor of female labor market experience because women are more likely to take additional time off work due to childbirth and childcare. However, this proxy will be used for a lack of a better alternative.  The regional dummy variables are specified as follow: Rio de Janeiro, Sao Paulo, Other South (Parana, Santa Catarina, Rio Grande do Sul, Minas Gerais, and Espirito Santo), Northeast (Maranhao, Piaui, Cerara, Rio Grande do Norte, Paraiba, Pernambuco, Alagoas, Sergipe, and Bahia), and Northwest/Central (Distrito Federal, Rondonia, Acre, Amazonas, Roraima, Para, Amapa, Mato Grosso do Sul, Mato Grosso, and Goias).  The Other South is the omitted category in the regressions.

From the theoretical derivation in Section 3, it is clear that the variables included as regressors in the participation equation should reflect the offered wages across sectors and the differing costs of employment in the three sectors as well as other factors that influence the reservation wage. Age and the formal education dummy variables are included in the participation equation to proxy for the offered wages (wages across sectors cannot be included because they are not observed for all women and because of endogeneity) and because they will affect the reservation wage.  The

---

[3]   A distinction was made between finishing the first four years of primary school and completing primary school because prior to 1971 grades 1-4 were considered compulsory and entrance into the next levels (grades 5-8 and grades 9-11) was controlled by examination.

number of children in the household disaggregated into four different groups (children under age 2, children 3 to 5, children 6 to 12, daughters over 13, and sons over 13) are included to reflect childcare costs. The total number of children is disaggregated into these groups because the presence of some groups may increase childcare costs (children under 2) while others may decrease these costs (daughters over 13). A dummy for whether or not the husband is self-employed is included in the married women's regression to reflect other opportunity costs of participating in the labor force. The household head being self-employed in an activity in which the woman can help is expected to raise the shadow value of the woman's time in non-market activities and reduce the probability that she will be a wage earner.

Monthly unearned income (includes both cash and in-kind unearned income from all sources) and the husband's hourly wage are hypothesized to increase the reservation wage. Both of these variables are measured in current cruzados. Because not all husbands work, the husbands' wages are predicted from selectivity-corrected wage equations (see Appendix). A dummy for whether or not the household owns the home in which they are living is included as a measure of household wealth. Therefore, owning a home is also expected to increase the reservation wage. The racial dummies are included to pick up any variance in ideas about women and work across ethnic cultures and the regional dummies are included to reflect differing labor market opportunities and values across regions.

Table 4.4 shows the means and standard deviations (in parenthesis) of all of independent variables included in the participation and wage equations. The means and characteristics of the dependent variables were discussed in Section 2. Because separate regressions will be undertaken for married women and single women in the following sections, the means and standard deviations are presented by these subsamples.

## 5.   The Determinants of Female Labor Force Participation

*Single women.* Table 4.5 presents the results from estimating the multi-sector participation equation for single women using maximum likelihood multinomial logit methods. Statistical tests of pooling the five regions specified in the previous section were accepted for the subsample of single women as well as for the married women and male subsamples. Consequently, the regional data were pooled and dummies were included to account for intercept regional effects. The partial derivatives are in bold, the logit coefficients follow and the t-ratios are the numbers in parenthesis. The log likelihood from estimation of this equation is -11,191.

Age is included in the participation equation to reflect the effects of human capital investments on wages which will effect participation. As expected, age has a positive and significant effect on work in all three sectors. An interpretation is that as age increases, the level of human capital acquired increases and the offered wage goes up. An increasing wage, holding all else constant, will increase the probability of participation. Age-squared is included as a regressor to pick up possible nonlinearities in this relationship. The significance of the squared terms in all three sectors supports the hypothesis of curvature in the effects of age on the probability of participation.

Education has stronger effects in increasing the participation of single women in the formal sector than in the informal and self-employed sectors. In fact, additional education decreases the probability of participation in the informal and self-employed sectors in many instances. Attaining each of the first three levels of education increases the probability of formal sector participation by between eight to nine percentage points. Finishing secondary school and college

**Table 4.4**
Means (and Standard Deviations) of Independent Variables

| Variables | Married Women | | Single Women | |
|---|---|---|---|---|
| Age | 37.09 | (11.53) | 44.69 | (11.89) |
| Age-squared | 1508.9 | (922.3) | 2138.7 | (1044.5) |
| Some Primary | .820 | (.386) | .749 | (.433) |
| Primary - Level 4 | .617 | (.486) | .551 | (.497) |
| Primary - Level 8 | .291 | (.454) | .279 | (.448) |
| Secondary | .181 | (.385) | .194 | (.395) |
| College | .067 | (.250) | .091 | (.87) |
| Graduate Work | .002 | (.039) | .003 | (.055) |
| Own Home | .667 | (.471) | .657 | (.478) |
| Black | .042 | (.201) | .070 | (.255) |
| Mulatto/Indian | .395 | (.489) | .427 | (.495) |
| Asian | .004 | (.066) | .003 | (.056) |
| Unearned Income | 173.75 | (879.34) | 280.31 | (701.55) |
| Husband's Wage | 1.488 | (6.338) | | |
| Husband Self-Employed | .263 | (.440) | | |
| # Children 0-2 | .342 | (.578) | .089 | (.317) |
| # Children 3-5 | .314 | (.555) | .134 | (.394) |
| # Children 6-12 | .831 | (1.063) | .465 | (.830) |
| # Daughters > 13 | .504 | (.899) | .561 | (.887) |
| # Sons > 13 | .428 | (.794) | .634 | (.966) |
| Experience | 23.728 | (11.50) | 29.487 | (12.89) |
| Experience-Squared | 695.23 | (625.7) | 1035.4 | (788.3) |
| Sao Paulo | .128 | (.334) | .110 | (.313) |
| Rio de Janeiro | .072 | (.258) | .092 | (.289) |
| Northwest/Central | .208 | (.406) | .205 | (.404) |
| Northeast | .287 | (.452) | .303 | (.460) |

each increase it an additional 13 percentage points while attaining some higher education increases the probability of being a formal sector employee another 22 percentage points. Education is included in the participation equation to reflect the effects of wages on the probability of participation. Given the results, it is expected that education has the highest returns in the formal sector because women with more education are more likely to choose to work in this sector.

The dummy variable for owning a home and the continuous variable for unearned income are included in the estimated equation to proxy for wealth. These proxies for wealth are expected to have negative effects on the probability of participation in all three sectors. Owning a home does have a negative and significant effect on participation in all three sectors. Unearned income also has a negative and strongly significant effect on the probability of participation in all three sectors. Increasing income by 1000 cruzados per month decreases participation by 11 percentage points in the formal sector and 6 to 7 percentage points in the other two sectors.

The racial dummy variables are included in the participation equation to reflect different ethnic and cultural values about women and work across races. The reference group is white single women. The results show that black single women are more likely to be employees in both the formal and informal sectors than white single women but less likely to be self-employed. Indian and mulatto women are more likely to participate in all three sectors than white women. Asian women are 19 percentage points more likely to participate as self-employed than white women.

**Table 4.5**
Multi-Sector Participations Results, Single Women N=9,973

|  | Formal Employees | Informal Employees | Self- Employed |
|---|---|---|---|
| Constant | -4.012 | -2.224 | -3.154 |
|  | (8.800) | (4.629) | (6.517) |
| Age | .0338 | .0042 | .0109 |
|  | .2511 | .1546 | .1892 |
|  | (11.748) | (6.854) | (8.545) |
| Age-Squared | -.0006 | -.0001 | -.0001 |
|  | -.0027 | -.0024 | -.0025 |
|  | (14.989) | (9.22) | (10.167) |
| Some Primary School | .0823 | -.022 | .0143 |
|  | .4943 | .0626 | .2767 |
|  | (5.047) | (.662) | (3.28) |
| Primary - Level 4 | .0812 | -.0178 | -.0162 |
|  | .4185 | .0149 | .0329 |
|  | (4.864) | (.156) | (.387) |
| Primary - Level 8 | .0946 | -.0159 | .0113 |
|  | .5793 | .1390 | .2995 |
|  | (5.178) | (.9680) | (2.371) |
| Finished Secondary | .1312 | .1127 | -.0449 |
|  | .9977 | 1.210 | .2716 |
|  | (6.947) | (7.024) | (1.587) |
| College | .1319 | .1484 | .0002 |
|  | 1.214 | 1.641 | .7368 |
|  | (6.439) | (8.177) | (3.194) |
| Graduate Education | .224 | .0352 | -.0464 |
|  | 1.370 | .7731 | .2996 |
|  | (1.118) | (.612) | (.195) |
| Own Home | -.0338 | -.034 | -.0008 |
|  | -.3034 | -.3882 | -.1854 |
|  | (4.660) | (5.517) | (2.728) |
| Black | .0423 | .07 | -.0061 |
|  | .4323 | .7063 | .2447 |
|  | (3.499) | (5.641) | (1.974) |
| Indian/Mulatto | .0291 | .0291 | .0095 |
|  | .2828 | .3551 | .2314 |
|  | (4.102) | (4.729) | (3.338) |
| Asian | .0083 | -.0889 | .1926 |
|  | .3245 | -.2481 | 1.369 |
|  | (.5300) | (.3190) | (2.46) |
| Unearned Income (1000s of cruzados) | -.11 | -.062 | -.068 |
|  | -1.4 | -1.3 | -1.1 |
| # Children 0-2 | -.0937 | -.0209 | -.0078 |
|  | -.6614 | -.4486 | -.3649 |
|  | (6.577) | (4.364) | (3.628) |
| # Children 3-5 | -.0378 | .0095 | .012 |
|  | -.1803 | .0152 | .0244 |
|  | (2.183) | (.1080) | (.295) |
| # Children 6-12 | -.0148 | .0097 | .0194 |
|  | -.0165 | .0972 | .1456 |
|  | (.411) | (2.323) | (3.672) |
|  | (18.128) | (14.628) | (11.878) |

-continued

**Table 4.5 (continued)**
Multi-Sector Participations Results, Single Women N=9,973

|  | Formal Employees | Informal Employees | Self- Employed |
|---|---|---|---|
| # Daughters over 13 | **-.0045** | **-.0035** | **-.0065** |
|  | -.0539 | -.0591 | -.0748 |
|  | (1.469) | (1.5) | (2.123) |
| # Sons over 13 | **-.024** | **-.0102** | **-.0118** |
|  | -.2080 | -.1829 | -.1871 |
|  | (5.961) | (4.96) | (5.712) |
| Northeast | **-.1095** | **.0064** | **.0405** |
|  | -.5611 | -.125 | .0617 |
|  | (6.687) | (1.385) | (.756) |
| Sao Paulo | **.0266** | **.0253** | **-.0753** |
|  | .0348 | .093 | -.4825 |
|  | (.34) | (.792) | (3.874) |
| Rio de Janeiro | **-.0546** | **.0059** | **.0014** |
|  | -.3221 | -.0883 | -.1161 |
|  | (2.859) | (.693) | (.966) |
| Northwest | **-.0464** | **.0372** | **.0007** |
|  | -.1895 | .2051 | -.0182 |
|  | (2.140) | (2.115) | (.195) |

Note: Absolute t-ratios in parenthesis.

As outlined in Section 3, the varying costs of participating in the three sectors are important determinants of a woman's work decision. The number of children in each of five age groups are included in the participation equation to reflect the costs of working. The number of children in the three youngest age groups reflect costs associated with childcare. These costs appear to be the highest in the formal sector as the number of children in the 0-2 and the 3-5 age groups have significant negative effects on participation. An additional child under age two decreases the probability of formal sector participation by nine percentage points while an additional child in the 3-5 age group decreases the participation probability by four points. Childcare costs seem to be lower in the other two sectors. Among informal employees and the self-employed, an additional child under age two decreases the probability of participation by 2 points and less than one point, respectively. Additional children in the 3-5 age group have no significant effect on participation in the informal and self-employment sectors.

The number of daughters and the number of sons over age 13 are included in the participation equation because older children can decrease the childcare costs of labor force participation by taking care of their siblings while mother is at work. Therefore, the number of children in each of these two groups (but especially the number of daughters) is expected to increase participation in high childcare cost sectors. However, daughters have a significant effect only in the self-employed sector (less than one percentage point) and sons have a negative and significant effect in all three sectors, decreasing the probability of participation by one to two percentage points. It appears that teenage children are not replacing their mother as childcaretaker but are instead replacing mother in earning income. Older children can go to work and, therefore, their presence decreases the probability of mother having to work for pay.

The regional dummy variables are included in the equation to pick up differing values and opportunities across regions in Brazil. Since a test of pooling across regions without including these dummy variables was rejected, some significance is expected. The relative region is the "other South" (see the previous section). The results confirm that there are differences across regions. In Rio de Janeiro, the Northeast, and the Northwest, women are less likely to be formal sector workers than women who live in the more industrial South. The only significance difference between the South and Sao Paulo is that women in Sao Paulo are approximately eight percentage points less likely to be self-employed.

Table 4.6 presents logit simulations to help to interpret the participation results. The independent variables are set equal to their sample means and a single variable is varied for each simulation exercise. The constant term has been adjusted so that the predicted probabilities of participation, evaluated at the means of the independent variables, are equal to the actual means of the dependent variable.

The age simulations are adjusted to reflect both changes in age and age-squared. As the other variables are held constant at their means, the probability of being a formal employee increases from 20 to 30 years but then decreases after the age of 30. In the other two sectors, the probability of participation continues to increase with age through age 50. All else held constant, a 20-year-old single woman, a 30-year-old, and a 40-year-old are all most likely to be in the formal sector while a 50-year-old is most likely to be at home.

The next simulation is education. As education increases, the probability of being a non-participant continually falls. A woman with no formal schooling is most likely not to participate while the probability of being a non-participant for a woman with a graduate education is less than two percent. As schooling increases, the probability of being a formal sector employee increases with each level. A woman with a graduate degree has a 72 percent probability of being a formal employee. The effects of education on participation in the other two sectors are not as strong. In fact, in the self-employed sector, additional levels of education generally lead to decreases in the participation probability. A woman with a graduate degree is almost as likely to not participate as she is likely to be self-employed.

Those women who own homes are more likely to be non-participants than those who do not own homes and less likely to work as either formal or informal employees. Owning a home has no effect on the probability of self-employment. The most striking result from the simulations with the racial dummy variables is the relatively high probability that an Asian woman is self-employed and the relatively low probability than she is an informal employee.

The most interesting results from the child variable simulations is for the youngest age groups. The probability of being a non-participant increases with each additional child 0-2. A woman with no young children has a 37 percent probability of staying home while the probability for a woman with two small children increases to over 62 percent. The probability of being in all three sectors decreases with each additional child but the greatest decreases are in the formal sector - the probability decreases approximately nine percentage points for the first child and seven points for the second child. The number of children aged 3-5 also increases the probability of being a non-participant and decreases the probability of being in the formal sector but at much smaller changes than with the 0-2 age group.

**Table 4.6**
Multinomial Logit Simulations, Single Women N=9,973
(percent)

|  | Non-Participant | Formal Employee | Informal Employee | Self-Employed |
|---|---|---|---|---|
| Age=20 | 33.5 | 57.7 | 10.2 | 4.6 |
| Age=30 | 22.6 | 58.0 | 11.8 | 7.6 |
| Age=40 | 24.6 | 47.2 | 14.7 | 13.4 |
| Age=50 | 36.9 | 23.8 | 17.1 | 22.1 |
| No Schooling | 55.4 | 13.7 | 14.4 | 16.3 |
| Some Primary | 47.3 | 19.6 | 13.3 | 18.8 |
| Primary -4 | 43.5 | 26.8 | 12.3 | 17.5 |
| Primary -8 | 33.7 | 37.1 | 10.9 | 18.3 |
| Secondary | 17.3 | 51.6 | 18.8 | 12.3 |
| College | 5.5 | 55.4 | 30.9 | 8.2 |
| Graduate | 1.8 | 72.3 | 22.2 | 3.7 |
| Own Home - Yes | 40.9 | 26.6 | 15.1 | 17.4 |
| Own Home - No | 34.1 | 30.0 | 18.5 | 17.4 |
| Black | 31.6 | 30.2 | 22.1 | 16.2 |
| Mulatto | 25.4 | 29.2 | 17.4 | 17.9 |
| Asian | 26.9 | 23.1 | 7.3 | 42.6 |
| White | 42.2 | 26.2 | 14.6 | 17.0 |
| Kids 0-2 = 0 | 37.4 | 28.7 | 16.4 | 17.5 |
| Kids 0-2 = 1 | 50.0 | 19.8 | 14.0 | 16.2 |
| Kids 0-2 = 2 | 62.2 | 12.7 | 11.0 | 14.0 |
| Kids 3-5 = 0 | 38.3 | 28.3 | 16.1 | 17.3 |
| Kids 3-5 = 1 | 39.9 | 24.7 | 17.0 | 18.4 |
| Kids 3-5 = 2 | 41.3 | 21.3 | 17.9 | 19.5 |
| Kids 6-12 = 0 | 37.2 | 28.5 | 15.8 | 16.6 |
| Kids 6-12 = 1 | 37.7 | 27.0 | 16.8 | 18.5 |
| Kids 6-12 = 2 | 36.2 | 25.5 | 17.7 | 20.5 |
| Daughters>13=0 | 37.7 | 28.1 | 16.4 | 17.8 |
| Daughters>13=1 | 39.1 | 26.9 | 16.1 | 17.2 |
| Sons > 13 = 0 | 35.6 | 29.4 | 16.9 | 18.2 |
| Sons > 13 = 1 | 40.2 | 26.9 | 15.9 | 17 |
| Northeast | 41.7 | 21.8 | 15.4 | 21.1 |
| Northwest | 36.5 | 27.6 | 18.8 | 17.1 |
| South | 35.6 | 32.5 | 14.9 | 16.9 |
| Sao Paulo | 37.0 | 35.1 | 17.0 | 10.9 |
| Rio | 40.5 | 26.8 | 15.5 | 17.1 |
| Sample Means | 38 | 27.6 | 16.4 | 17.9 |

The regional simulations show that, as in the total sample, single women in each region are most likely to be non-participants. However, women in the Northeast are the most likely to be non-participants and to be self-employed, women in Sao Paulo are the most likely to be in the formal sector, and women in the Northwest are the most likely to be informal employees.

*Married women.* The multinomial logit results from estimating the participation equation using data on 50,452 married women are presented in Table 4.7. The same maximum likelihood methods used to estimate the participation equation for single women are employed here. The log likelihood function for this participation equation is -46,165. The results from estimating the participation equation for married women are very similar to the results presented previously for single women. Age, again, has a positive and significant effect on participation in all three sectors. The education variables continue to have the strongest effects in the formal sector (however, all of these effects are weaker than those for single women). Unearned income continues to have a significantly negative effect on participation in all three sectors. Children in the 0-2 age group significantly decrease the probability of participation in all sectors and children in the 3-5 age group decrease the probability of being a formal sector employee.

The regional results, again, show that women in the Northeast, the Northwest, and Rio are less likely to be in the formal sector than women in the South and that women in Sao Paulo are less likely to work in formal sector. While most of the racial results found for single women hold true for married women, an important difference is that the high increase in the probability of an Asian single woman being self-employed does not hold for married Asian women. In fact, there is no significant difference between the probability of Asian women and white women being self-employed (this difference was close to 20 percentage points for single women). This result likely reflects that married Asian women are helping their husband's with their businesses (they are unpaid family workers) rather than being self-employed themselves.

There are two additional variables included in the married women's participation equation - the husband's wage and the husband's self-employment status. The husband's wage (expected to increase the reservation wage and decrease the probability of participation) has a strongly significant and negative effect on participation in all three sectors. If her husband is self-employed, the probability of a woman being an employee in both the formal and informal sectors falls while the probability of being self-employed increases by two percentage points.

The Table 4.8 presents the results from replicating the simulations for single women using the results from estimating the married women's participation equation.

The probability of participation increases until age 40 in the formal and informal sectors and then begins to fall while in the self-employment sector, the probability continuously increases with age through age 50. Formal education, again, has strong negative effects on the probability of being a non-participant and strong positive effects on the probability of being a formal employee. While a woman with no formal education has a 77 percent probability of being a non-participant and a six percent chance of being a formal employee, a woman with a graduate education has a three percent probability of being a non-participant and a 48 percent change of working in the formal sector. Higher levels of education also have significant effects in increasing informal employment. However, the effects are relatively negligible in self-employment.

Among married women, mulatto women are the most likely to be non-participants. Black women have the highest probability of the four racial groups of working in both the formal and informal sectors while Asian women still have the highest probability of being self-employed (however,

## Table 4.7
### Participation Results, Married Women N=50,452

|  | Formal Employees | Informal Employees | Self-Employed |
|---|---|---|---|
| Constant | -6.387 | -4.853 | -5.943 |
|  | (31.297) | (21.28) | (27.583) |
| Age | .0254 | .0097 | .0127 |
|  | .2505 | .1774 | .1933 |
|  | (23.029) | (14.739) | (17.81) |
| Age-Squared | -.0004 | -.0001 | -.0001 |
|  | -.0034 | -.0023 | -.0023 |
|  | (24.302) | (15.204) | (17.258) |
| Some Primary School | .0638 | -.0102 | .0001 |
|  | .5277 | -.0280 | .0830 |
|  | (8.163) | (.4960) | (1.741) |
| Primary - Level 4 | .0334 | .0048 | .0107 |
|  | .3082 | .1255 | .1757 |
|  | (6.676) | (2.481) | (4.175) |
| Primary - Level 8 | .0579 | -.0021 | .006 |
|  | .4992 | .0715 | .1506 |
|  | (10.753) | (1.100) | (2.889) |
| Finished Secondary | .1091 | .0944 | -.0274 |
|  | 1.031 | 1.283 | .0097 |
|  | (20.744) | (18.256) | (.140) |
| College | .0908 | .1001 | .0196 |
|  | .9552 | 1.397 | .5050 |
|  | (17.075) | (21.277) | (5.328) |
| Graduate Education | .1749 | .1282 | .1509 |
|  | 1.913 | 2.069 | 2.113 |
|  | (3.583) | (3.797) | (3.409) |
| Husband Self-Employed | -.0482 | -.034 | .0191 |
|  | -.4331 | -.4640 | .0842 |
|  | (11.795) | (11.130) | (2.481) |
| Husband's Wage (predicted) | -.0316 | -.028 | -.0225 |
|  | -.3456 | -.4260 | -.3365 |
|  | (14.216) | (17.515) | (13.838) |
| Own Home | -.0005 | -.0163 | .0061 |
|  | -.0202 | -.1913 | .0410 |
|  | (.652) | (5.433) | (1.193) |
| Black | .0502 | .0473 | .0072 |
|  | .5106 | .6678 | .2275 |
|  | (7.215) | (9.002) | (3.101) |
| Indian/Mulatto | .0039 | .0219 | .0091 |
|  | .0800 | .2890 | .1388 |
|  | (2.381) | (7.565) | (4.019) |
| Asian | 0.0104 | -.0533 | .0084 |
|  | -.1568 | -.6574 | -.0052 |
|  | (.795) | (2.284) | (.021) |

--continued

**Table 4.7 (continued)**
Participation Results, Married Women N=50,452

|  | Formal Employees | Informal Employees | Self-Employed |
|---|---|---|---|
| Unearned Income | -.017 | -.014 | -.0049 |
|  | -.24 | -.22 | -.101 |
|  | (7.626) | (6.781) | (4.266) |
| # Children 0-2 | -.053 | -.0293 | -.0164 |
|  | -.5206 | -.4654 | -.3048 |
|  | (16.817) | (13.005) | (9.077) |
| # Children 3-5 | -.0339 | .0002 | .0001 |
|  | -.2879 | -.0483 | -.0494 |
|  | (10.459) | (1.632) | (1.749) |
| # Children 6-12 | -.0209 | .0051 | .0066 |
|  | -.1599 | .0406 | .0486 |
|  | (9.913) | (2.428) | (3.215) |
| # Daughters over 13 | -.0001 | .0024 | -.0008 |
|  | .0014 | .0281 | -.0050 |
|  | (.063) | (1.220) | (.253) |
| # Sons over 13 | -.0099 | .0007 | -.0035 |
|  | -.0881 | -.0114 | -.0518 |
|  | (4.275) | (.547) | (2.896) |
| Northeast | -.0154 | -.0135 | .0207 |
|  | -.1204 | -.1572 | .1824 |
|  | (2.965) | (3.381) | (4.368) |
| Sao Paulo | .0023 | .0256 | -.0302 |
|  | -.0268 | .2639 | -.2957 |
|  | (.583) | (4.992) | (5.171) |
| Rio de Janeiro | -.041 | -.0057 | .0117 |
|  | -.3376 | -.1143 | -.0571 |
|  | (5.899) | (1.713) | (.94) |
| Northwest | -.0084 | .0001 | .002 |
|  | -.0688 | -.0093 | .0091 |
|  | (1.695) | (.195) | (.201) |

Note: Absolute t-ratios in parenthesis.

while single Asian women have 43 percent probability of being self-employed, this probability is less than 11 percent for married Asian women).

If a woman's husband is self-employed, the probability of her being a non-participant increases from 64 to 70 percent. While a self-employed husband decreases the probability of being a formal or informal sector worker (from 15 percent to 11 percent and from 10 percent to 7 percent, respectively), it increases the probability of a woman herself being self-employed (from 10 percent to 12 percent). Married women from Rio de Janeiro are the most likely regional group not to participate in the labor force; women from the South have the highest probability of being formal sector workers; women from Sao Paulo have the highest probability of working in the informal sector; and women in the Northeast are the most likely group to be self-employed.

### Table 4.8
Multinomial Logit Simulations, Married Women N=50,452

|  | Non-Participant | Formal Employee | Informal Employee | Self-Employed |
|---|---|---|---|---|
| Age=20 | 77.5. | 10.2 | 6.8 | 5.5 |
| Age=30 | 61.9 | 18.3 | 10.1 | 9.7 |
| Age=40 | 57.2 | 19.2 | 11.0 | 12.7 |
| Age=50 | 65.2 | 12.5 | 9.3 | 12.9 |
|  |  |  |  |  |
| No Schooling | 77.3 | 6.1 | 7.3 | 9.3 |
| Some Primary | 73.7 | 9.9 | 6.8 | 9.6 |
| Primary - 4 | 69.3 | 12.7 | 7.2 | 10.8 |
| Primary - 8 | 62.7 | 18.9 | 7.0 | 11.3 |
| Secondary | 41.1 | 34.8 | 16.6 | 7.5 |
| College | 19.5 | 42.8 | 31.8 | 5.9 |
| Graduate | 3.2 | 47.5 | 41.3 | 8.0 |
|  |  |  |  |  |
| Own Home - Yes | 66.2 | 14.5 | 8.8 | 10.4 |
| Own Home - No | 65.1 | 14.6 | 10.5 | 9.8 |
|  |  |  |  |  |
| Black | 56.4 | 19.7 | 13.6 | 10.3 |
| Mulatto | 72.1 | 12.9 | 4.6 | 10.5 |
| Asian | 64.1 | 14.5 | 10.6 | 10.7 |
| White | 67.6 | 14.2 | 8.4 | 9.9 |
|  |  |  |  |  |
| Husband Self-Employed - Yes | 70.1 | 11.2 | 7.1 | 11.6 |
| Husband Self-Employed - No | 64.1 | 15.9 | 10.3 | 9.8 |
|  |  |  |  |  |
| Kids 0-2 = 0 | 62.7 | 16.3 | 10.3 | 10.7 |
| Kids 0-2 = 1 | 72.3 | 11.2 | 7.5 | 9.1 |
| Kids 0-2 = 2 | 80.0 | 7.3 | 5.2 | 7.4 |
| Kids 3-5 = 0 | 64.7 | 15.8 | 9.3 | 10.2 |
| Kids 3-5 = 1 | 68.0 | 12.4 | 9.4 | 10.2 |
| Kids 3-5 = 2 | 70.9 | 9.7 | 9.3 | 10.2 |
| Kids 6-12 = 0 | 65.0 | 16.4 | 8.9 | 9.7 |
| Kids 6-12 = 1 | 66.0 | 14.2 | 9.4 | 10.4 |
| Kids 6-12 = 2 | 66.8 | 12.2 | 10.0 | 11.0 |
|  |  |  |  |  |
| Northeast | 65.9 | 13.9 | 8.2 | 12.1 |
| Northwest | 65.8 | 14.6 | 9.5 | 10.1 |
| South | 65.1 | 15.5 | 9.5 | 9.9 |
| Sao Paulo | 65.1 | 15.1 | 12.3 | 7.4 |
| Rio | 68.5 | 11.6 | 8.9 | 11.0 |
|  |  |  |  |  |
| Sample Means | 65.8 | 14.3 | 9.3 | 10.6 |

The probability of being a formal sector worker falls from 16 percent to 11 percent with the first child aged 0-2 in the household and to seven percent with the second child. The number of children aged 0-2 also decreases the probabilities of informal and self-employment but at a much smaller rate. The number of children aged 3-5 also decreases the probability of formal sector participation (from 16 percent to 12 percent for the first child and to 10 percent for the second child) but have no significant effects on the probability of being in the informal sector or self-employed. While the number of children aged 6-12 had little effect on single women's employment, their presence again decreases the probability of a married woman working in the formal sector. However, children in this age group also have a positive effect on informal sector participation and self-employment.

## 6.   Earnings Functions

Table 4.9 presents the results from estimating the earnings functions for single women and married women. The earnings functions are estimated as Mincer equations with the natural log of wages regressed on levels of the independent variables. The first three columns are results from estimating the sectoral wage equations for single women and columns four through six are the results from estimating the sectoral wage equations for married women. These results are corrected for selectivity using the inverse Mill's ratio for the multinomial logit model presented in Section 3. The standard errors have been corrected for the use of an estimated inverse Mill's ratio. The OLS results are presented in Appendix Table 4A.3 for comparison. Because the selection term is significant in most of the equations, the selectivity corrected results are used for discussion and the calculations of discrimination to follow.

The selection term is strongly significant in the formal and self-employment sectors for single women and in both the formal and informal sectors for married women. Consequently, in these cases, the selection correction was needed to get consistent estimates of the earnings functions. Predicted experience has a positive and significant effect on wages in all three sectors for both single and married women (except self-employed single women). For single women, the rate of return of a year of experience is approximately three percent in the formal sector, four percent in the informal sector, and one percent in self-employment. Married women enjoy slightly higher returns to experience at five percent in the formal sector, four percent in the informal, and three percent in self-employment. The relationship between experience, however, is not linear as the squared terms are negative and significant in each equation.

The racial variables are also significant in many cases. Among married women, black women make 16 percent less than white women in the formal sector, eight percent less in the informal sector, and 15 percent less in self-employment. The results are similar for single black women as they make 23 percent, three percent, and 16 percent less, respectively, than white single women. These results suggest that there appears to be more discrimination against black women in the formal and self-employed sectors than in the informal employee sector. Mulatto women also make significantly less than white women in all three sectors (21 percent, nine percent, and 14 percent less, respectively, for married women and 15 percent, eight percent, and 10 percent less, respectively, for single women). While married Asian women make significantly more than white women in self-employment (56 percent), this results does not hold among single Asian women.

There also are regional differences in the earnings functions for both single and married women. In the Northeast, both groups make less in all three sectors than in the South (the reference region). In the formal sector, married women in the Northeast make 35 percent less and single women make 27 percent less and in the informal sector, married women make 46 percent less and single women make 36 percent less. Both groups make 39 percent less in self-employment in the Northeast than in the South. However, in Sao Paulo, women make more (from 23 to 47 percent more) in all three sectors than they would in the "other South." In Rio de Janeiro and in the Northwest, there are some regional differences but they are not across the board as in the

**Table 4.9**
Sectoral Wage Equations (Corrected for Selectivity)

| | Single Women | | | Married Women | | |
|---|---|---|---|---|---|---|
| | Formal | Informal Wage | Self-Employed | Formal | Informal Wage | Self-Employed |
| Constant | -.5521 | -1.146 | -.6178 | -1.17 | -1.57 | -.682 |
| | (3.33) | (4.96) | (2.11) | (6.42) | (8.01) | (2.84) |
| Selection Term (Lambda) | .3314 | .1411 | .6092 | .3382 | .3585 | .0889 |
| | (3.74) | (1.11) | (4.32) | (4.45) | (4.56) | (1.63) |
| Experience (age-educ-6) | .0268 | .0407 | .0069 | .0567 | .0427 | .0320 |
| | (5.17) | (5.56) | (.669) | (12.9) | (10.2) | (5.34) |
| Some Primary | .2533 | .3347 | .2222 | .1298 | .2486 | .2180 |
| | (4.21) | (5.33) | (3.48) | (2.67) | (6.10) | (4.94) |
| Primary - 4 | .2294 | .2779 | .2737 | .2928 | .3240 | .3659 |
| | (4.85) | (4.45) | (4.41) | (8.77) | (9.06) | (9.68) |
| Primary - 8 | .5124 | .5836 | .5416 | .4891 | .5913 | .4180 |
| | (10.31) | (6.66) | (6.17) | (14.8) | (12.7) | (8.76) |
| Finished Secondary | .5530 | .6492 | .2390 | .6169 | .6372 | .5337 |
| | (10.64) | (6.80) | (2.08) | (17.5) | (12.7) | (8.48) |
| College | .8455 | .726 | .6407 | .7987 | .7815 | .7751 |
| | (17.83) | (9.96) | (4.36) | (27.0) | (20.5) | (9.39) |
| Graduate | .3202 | .2863 | -.2158 | .7144 | .2779 | -.1126 |
| | (2.01) | (.903) | (.454) | (5.56) | (1.89) | (.380) |
| Black | -.2253 | -.0291 | -.1605 | -.1563 | -.0843 | -.1498 |
| | (3.73) | (.385) | (1.79) | (3..32) | (1.67) | (2.32) |
| Asian | .5215 | .2205 | -.4822 | .0954 | -.041 | .5566 |
| | (2.42) | (.477) | (1.05) | (.803) | (.213) | (2.52) |
| Indian/Mulatto | -.1465 | -.0778 | -.1043 | -.2060 | -.0938 | -.1372 |
| | (4.47) | (1.66) | (2.03) | (9.41) | (3.73) | (4.89) |
| Northeast | -.2710 | -.3642 | -.3887 | -.3447 | -.4645 | -.3919 |
| | (6.50) | (6.39) | (6.24) | (10.0) | (15.1) | (10.5) |
| Northwest | .1281 | .0270 | -.0367 | .1178 | .0431 | .1827 |
| | (3.18) | (.464) | (.540) | (4.45) | (1.35) | (4.62) |
| Sao Paulo | .3501 | .3924 | .4663 | .2326 | .2835 | .2541 |
| | (7.591) | (4.575) | (4.806) | (7.91) | (8.19) | (5.03) |
| Rio de Janeiro | .02726 | .0473 | .0012 | -.0260 | .0260 | -.1142 |
| | (.530) | (.080) | (.014) | (.699) | (.587) | (2.16) |
| F-Statistic | 190.14 | 139.44 | 51.73 | 408.94 | 397.95 | 165.99 |

Note: Absolute t-ratios in parenthesis

other two sectors. The regional results indicate that labor demand conditions differ across regions and that barriers to migration do exist which are preventing the equalization of wage rates across regions.

Because of the manner in which the education dummy variables are constructed (see Section 4), the total effects of education earnings are presented in Table 4.10 for single women and married women.

**Table 4.10**
Percentage increase in earnings by education

| | Formal Employees | Informal Employees | Self-Employed |
|---|---|---|---|
| Single Women | | | |
| | | | |
| Some Primary School | .253 | .335 | .222 |
| Primary - Level 4 | .482 | .613 | .496 |
| Primary - Level 8 | .994 | 1.197 | 1.038 |
| Finished Secondary | 1.547 | 1.846 | 1.277 |
| Finished College | 2.393 | 2.572 | 1.918 |
| Graduate Work | 2.713 | 2.858 | 1.702 |
| | | | |
| Married Women | | | |
| | | | |
| Some Primary School | .13 | .25 | .22 |
| Primary - Level 4 | .42 | .57 | .58 |
| Primary - Level 8 | .91 | 1.16 | 1.00 |
| Finished Secondary | 1.53 | 1.80 | 1.54 |
| Finished College | 2.33 | 2.58 | 2.31 |
| Graduate Work | 3.04 | 2.85 | 2.20 |

Education has strong effects on earnings in all three sectors. A married woman who finished primary school makes 91 percent more than her uneducated counterpart in the formal sector, 116 percent more than an uneducated co-worker in the informal sector, and 100 percent more than an uneducated competitor in self-employment. These effects continue to increase, in most cases, through graduate work and a woman (married or single) who does graduate work can make approximately 200 to 300 percent more in each sector than if she had no education.

Surprisingly, the effects of education are highest in the informal sector. The incremental returns in the formal sector do not overtake those in the informal sector until the college level is reached. The total effects in the formal sector do not exceed those in the informal sector for married women until the graduate work level is reached and they never do for single women. This is largely due to relatively low returns to the introductory levels of education in the formal sector.

There are two important points to note when comparing the effects of education across sectors. First, women who work in the formal sector are more likely to receive benefits and social security. Consequently, some of the effects of education in the formal sector may be in the form of benefits (i.e., a promotion includes health benefits or increased vacation time) and these additional effects are not captured by the earnings functions. Secondly, wages in the formal sector are subject to government regulations such as minimum wage laws and wage indexation. Consequently, the wage paid in the formal sector to an educated woman may still be higher than the wage in the informal sector because the base wage is higher in the formal sector.

## 7.   Discrimination

As discussed in Section 2, there are earnings differentials between men and women in this Brazilian sample. Married women make 70 percent of the male wage in the formal sector, 85 percent of it in the informal sector, and 70 percent of the male wage in self-employment. These differentials are similar to the racial differentials in that the highest racial differentials for black and mulatto women compared with white women were in the formal and self-employment sectors. It would be interesting to explain how much of the sex earnings differential is explained by different endowments and how much is unexplained or due to labor market structures.

The standard Oaxaca (1973) decomposition permits us to estimate these two components of the sex wage differential. The decomposition is written as:

$$\ln(wage_m) - \ln(wage_f) = X_f(b_m - b_f) + b_m(X_m - X_f) \qquad (3)$$
$$= X_m(b_m - b_f) + b_f(X_m - X_f) \qquad (4)$$

where the Xs are the endowments and the bs are the coefficients from the estimated earnings functions. The two equations are alternative representations of the decomposition and neither is preferred over the other. However, because we are dealing with index numbers, the two equations will not produce equivalent results. The first term in the decompositions is the amount of the differential attributed to the labor market rewards or unexplained factors. This term is often interpreted as the amount of the differential due to discrimination. The second term is the amount of the differential attributable to differences in endowments.

Table 4.11 presents the decompositions of the sex earnings differentials into the percentage points attributable to differences in endowments and the percentage points due to discrimination. The numbers in parenthesis are the percentages of the total explained by each component. Discrimination appears to be slightly higher in the formal and self-employment sectors than in the informal sector.

**Table 4.11**
Decomposition of the Earnings Differentials

|  | Rewards | | Endowments | |
|---|---|---|---|---|
| Formal Sector | | | | |
| Equation 3 | 24.3 | (81%) | 5.7 | (19%) |
| Equation 4 | 26.7 | (89%) | 3.3 | (11%) |
| Informal Sector | | | | |
| Equation 3 | 10.8 | (72%) | 4.2 | (28%) |
| Equation 4 | 11.3 | (75%) | 3.7 | (25%) |
| Self-Employment | | | | |
| Equation 3 | 24.8 | (83%) | 5.2 | (17%) |
| Equation 4 | 35.2 | (84%) | 4.8 | (16%) |

(100% of differential)

## 8.   Conclusions

Labor force participation rates of both single and married women have increased since the Stelcner et al. (1991) study using 1980 data. In 1989, 34 percent of married women were working for pay and 62 percent of single women were wage earners. However, the increases in participation have not been proportionally distributed across the three identified market sectors. Between 1980 and 1989, the percentage of married women who classified themselves as employees increased while the percentage who considered themselves to be self-employed fell.

The opposite occurred among single women.  The number of single woman employees fell and the number of self-employed single women increased.

The results from estimating the multi-sector participation equation reinforce many of the hypotheses concerning the determinants of the probability of participation.  The theoretical model shows that the important determinants are those variables which influence the wage, the variables which affect the reservation wage and the proxies for the costs of participation across sectors. Age and education, human capital variables expected to increase the offered wages, were found to have positive effects on participation in all sectors.  The effects of education are the strongest in the formal sector.  The proxies for wealth - unearned income, owning a home, and the husband's wage - which increase the reservation wages are found to have, as expected, negative effects on participation across sectors.  The most important costs of participation, childcare costs, have the strongest negative effects on formal sector participation.  This result supports the hypothesis that formal sector work and childcare are less compatible than work in self-employment or the informal sector.

In estimating the sectoral wage equations, it is necessary to correct for sample selectivity.  The selection correction is significant in many cases indicating that OLS results will be biased. Education and predicted experience have significant and positive effects on earnings for men, single women, and married women.  Although, it was expected from the participation results, that the highest returns would be paid to education in the formal sector, the highest returns are paid in the informal sector especially at lower levels of education.  Despite the high returns to education in the informal sector, women with more education are more likely to participate in the formal sector. It is important to note that although the returns are higher in the informal sector, the overall wage paid to a highly educated woman may still be higher in the formal sector because the returns in the formal sector may be added to a higher starting base wage.  The base wage may be higher in the formal sector because of the existence of labor unions, minimum wage laws, and other government regulations in the formal sector.  It is also important to note that this discrepancy in returns may be due to non-monetary returns to education in the formal sector such as increases in benefits and better working conditions.

As discussed in Section 3, the differentials between male and female wages changed little between 1980 and 1989.  In 1989, the sample indicates that women in the formal and self-employed sectors make 70 percent of their male counterparts.  In the informal sector, the differential is less as women make 85 percent of the male wage.  The decompositions of the wage rates in Section 7 suggest that discrimination is a more important source of the earnings differentials between men and women than differences in male and female endowments.  In the formal and self-employed sectors, between 81 and 89 percent of the wage differential is attributable to discrimination while in the informal sector 72 to 75 percent of the differential is due to discrimination.

## Appendix 4A

## Male Participation Equation and Earnings Functions

As discussed in the text, a husband's wage is assumed to be a determining factor in a woman's participation decision. However, because not all husbands in the sample work for pay and because of endogeneity problems, husbands' wages must be predicted before estimating married women's participation decisions. Consistently estimating wage equations to be used for prediction requires several steps:

1. Estimate the multi-sector participation equations for males. The sectoral definitions are assumed to be the same for men and women and are outlined in Section 2.

2. Calculate the inverse Mill's ratios - one for each individual for each sector. See the equation for the inverse Mill's ratio in Section 3.

3. Estimate the wage equations including the appropriate inverse Mill's ratios as regressors.

4. Use the resulting coefficients to predict a wage for each individual in each of the three sectors.

5. Use the wage of the sector in which the individual is most likely to participate as that individual's wage or market value of time.

The following tables present the results from estimating a multinomial logit participation equation and the results from estimating the three sectoral wage equations for the male subsample (with and without a selectivity correction) respectively. The log likelihood from estimating the participation equation for men is -61,829.

**Appendix Table 4A.1**
Sectoral Participation Equation, Men N=58,000

|  | Formal Employees | Informal Employees | Self-Employed |
|---|---|---|---|
| Constant | 1.458 | 2.950 | 1.504 |
|  | (7.599) | (14.86) | (7.892) |
| Age | .1048 | .0412 | .0956 |
|  | (13.401) | (5.096) | (12.573) |
| Age-Squared | -.0020 | -.0013 | -0.0017 |
|  | (25.567) | (15.382) | (22.519) |
| Some Primary School | .3652 | -.2666 | .0968 |
|  | (7.46) | (5.159) | (2.045) |
| Primary - Level 4 | .1335 | -.2605 | -.1318 |
|  | (2.957) | (5.060) | (2.848) |
| Finished Secondary | .4433 | .3936 | .0121 |
|  | (5.297) | (4.161) | (.13) |
| College | 1.029 | 1.249 | .8338 |
|  | (9.845) | (10.976) | (7.219) |
| Graduate Education | 3.396 | 3.335 | 2.553 |
|  | (3.817) | (3.673) | (2.675) |
| Urban | .4657 | -1.163 | -1.456 |
|  | (9.700) | (23.687) | (31.675) |
| Own Home | -.2201 | -.5645 | .3131 |
|  | (5.799) | (13.845) | (7.812) |
| Black | -.0783 | .1442 | -.4906 |
|  | (1.129) | (1.919) | (6.616) |
| Indian/Mulatto | -.0089 | .1392 | -.0753 |
|  | (.238) | (3.398) | (1.975) |
| Asian | .3009 | -.5276 | .6385 |
|  | (1.273) | (1.552) | (2.638) |
| Unearned Income | -.0006 | -.0006 | -.0006 |
|  | (25.337) | (17.318) | (19.753) |
| Northeast | -.2742 | .1616 | .2009 |
|  | (6.083) | (3.266) | (4.414) |
| Sao Paulo | .0297 | -.2411 | -.2930 |
|  | (.579) | (3.896) | (5.244) |
| Rio de Janeiro | -.2836 | -.1182 | -.4737 |
|  | (4.72) | (1.684) | (7.042) |
| Northwest | .1689 | .6624 | .4931 |
|  | (3.333) | (12.002) | (9.517) |

Note: Absolute t-ratios in parentheses.

## Appendix Table 4A.2
### Multi-Sector Wage Equations, Men N=58,000

| | Selectivity Corrected[a] | | | OLS | | |
|---|---|---|---|---|---|---|
| | Formal | Informal Wage | Self-Employed | Formal | Informal Wage | Self-Employed |
| Constant | -.6264 | -.7638 | -.1548 | -.0331 | -.3945 | -.0529 |
| | (9.96) | (5.70) | (1.33) | (.994) | (8.91) | (1.03) |
| Selection Term | .5097 | .302 | .1571 | | | |
| | (11.1) | (2.92) | (1.98) | | | |
| Experience (age-educ-6) | .0458 | .0421 | .0332 | .0399 | .0375 | .0298 |
| | (26.7) | (15.5) | (11.1) | (24.5) | (16.9) | (12.3) |
| Experience$^2$ | -.0006 | -.0006 | -.0005 | -.0004 | -.0005 | -.0004 |
| | (19.6) | (13.21) | (10.1) | (16.3) | (16.1) | (12.7) |
| Some Primary | .3142 | .2454 | .2821 | .3177 | .2467 | .2826 |
| | (15.1) | (10.8) | (12.9) | (15.3) | (10.9) | (13.0) |
| Primary - 4 | .3341 | .3399 | .2082 | .3441 | .3426 | .2101 |
| | (21.1) | (14.4) | (9.78) | (21.7) | (14.6) | (9.88) |
| Primary - 8 | .4316 | .501 | .4683 | .4344 | .4985 | .4681 |
| | (25.4) | (16.3) | (14.3) | (25.6) | (16.3) | (14.4) |
| Finished Secondary | .5456 | .4938 | .3089 | .5448 | .4926 | .3062 |
| | (27.8) | (13.2) | (6.92) | (27.7) | (13.2) | (6.86) |
| College | .7457 | .7539 | .678 | .7451 | .7538 | .6837 |
| | (37.1) | (19.8) | (12.8) | (37.1) | (19.8) | (12.9) |
| Graduate | .2447 | .0704 | .2613 | .2389 | .0596 | .2599 |
| | (2.91) | (.432) | (.746) | (2.84) | (.366) | (.742) |
| Black | -.3071 | -.1083 | -.2453 | -.3078 | -.1086 | -.2441 |
| | (12.8) | (3.4) | (6.22) | (12.8) | (3.40) | (6.19) |
| Asian | .1625 | .2634 | .137 | .1801 | .2576 | .1315 |
| | (2.48) | (1.35) | (1.29) | (2.74) | (1.32) | (1.24) |
| Indian/Mulatto | -.1944 | -.0731 | -.1884 | -.1963 | -.0735 | -.1885 |
| | (16.3) | (4.25) | (10.7) | (16.4) | (4.28) | (10.8) |
| Northeast | -.1626 | -.216 | -.178 | -.256 | -.3207 | -.1746 |
| | (10.8) | (10.2) | (8.4) | (10.4) | (9.97) | (8.27) |
| Sao Paulo | .2401 | .2426 | .3457 | .2390 | .2644 | .3448 |
| | (15.5) | (8.70) | (11.5) | (15.4) | (8.69) | (11.4) |
| Rio de Janeiro | -.1479 | .0011 | -.0717 | -.1446 | .0068 | -.0699 |
| | (7.50) | (.031) | (1.83) | (7.32) | (.202) | (1.78) |
| Northwest | .1098 | .109 | .1651 | .1056 | .1076 | .1627 |
| | (7.42) | (4.98) | (7.23) | (7.12) | (4.92) | (7.14) |

a.   Standard errors corrected for use of an estimated inverse Mill's ratio.

Note:   Absolute t-ratios in parenthesis

## Appendix Table 4A.3
### OLS Estimates of Women's Multi-Sector Earnings Functions

| | Single Women | | | Married Women | | |
| | Formal | Informal Wage | Self-Employed | Formal | Informal Wage | Self-Employed |
|---|---|---|---|---|---|---|
| Constant | -.0731 | -.9355 | -.3957 | -.4124 | -.7261 | -.4540 |
| | (.694) | (7.18) | (2.25) | (6.28) | (11.08) | (4.91) |
| Experience (age-educ-6) | .0208 | .0376 | -.0125 | .0398 | .0342 | .0288 |
| | (4.20) | (5.58) | (1.05) | (12.19) | (9.15) | (5.59) |
| Experience$^2$ | -.0002 | -.0004 | -.0002 | -.0006 | -.0004 | -.0004 |
| | (2.07) | (3.90) | (1.31) | (8.72) | (5.83) | (4.92) |
| Some Primary | .2330 | .3278 | .1922 | .0824 | .2034 | .2051 |
| | (3.88) | (5.25) | (3.01) | (1.74) | (5.14) | (4.84) |
| Primary - 4 | .2231 | .2735 | .2621 | .2708 | .2939 | .3576 |
| | (4.71) | (4.39) | (4.21) | (8.19) | (8.35) | (9.68) |
| Primary - 8 | .5064 | .5824 | .5353 | .4508 | .5418 | .4048 |
| | (10.18) | (6.64) | (6.07) | (14.08) | (11.92) | (8.809) |
| Finished Secondary | .5433 | .6439 | .1986 | .5436 | .5570 | .5130 |
| | (10.44) | (6.75) | (1.72) | (17.38) | (11.79) | (8.598) |
| College | .8302 | .7622 | .6644 | .7566 | .7383 | .7601 |
| | (17.3) | (9.78) | (4.47) | (26.93) | (19.96) | (9.35) |
| Graduate | .3158 | .2854 | -.3378 | .6883 | .2444 | -.0970 |
| | (1.95) | (.868) | (.360) | (5.35) | (1.66) | (.283) |
| Black | -.2439 | -.0401 | -.2067 | -.2067 | -.144 | -.1649 |
| | (4.04) | (.537) | (2.31) | (4.51) | (2.96) | (2.62) |
| Asian | .5097 | .2663 | -.4771 | .1101 | .0084 | .5743 |
| | (2.37) | (.578) | (1.43) | (.85) | (.044) | (2.61) |
| Indian/Mulatto | -.1556 | -.0857 | -.1324 | -.2156 | -.1058 | -.1395 |
| | (4.75) | (1.85) | (2.59) | (9.88) | (4.218) | (4.57) |
| Northeast | -.2478 | -.3517 | -.3174 | -.3299 | -.4480 | -.3871 |
| | (5.99) | (6.30) | (5.26) | (12.53) | (14.66) | (10.45) |
| Sao Paulo | .3475 | .3320 | .4617 | .2429 | .2890 | .2568 |
| | (7.52) | (4.61) | (4.74) | (8.274) | (8.338) | (5.089) |
| Rio de Janeiro | .0355 | .0537 | .0283 | -.0043 | -.0005 | -.1079 |
| | (.690) | (.688) | (.318) | (.116) | (.11) | (2.054) |
| Northwest | .1401 | .0321 | -.0173 | .1324 | .0536 | .1870 |
| | (3.47) | (4.61) | (.253) | (5.03) | (1.68) | (4.75) |
| F-Statistic | 188.8 | 139.36 | 51.73 | 432.14 | 419.76 | 176.29 |

Note:  Absolute t-ratios in parenthesis.

# References

Alderman, H. and V. Kozel. "Formal and Informal Sector Wage Determination in Urban Low-Income Neighborhoods in Pakistan," Living Standards Measurement Study Working Paper No. 65, World Bank, 1989.

Blau, D.M. "A Model of Child Nutrition, Fertility, and Women's Time Allocation," *Research in opulation Economics* 5:113-135, 1984.

Cornia, G.A., R. Jolly, and F. Stewart. *Adjustment with a Human Face*. Oxford: Clarendon Press, 1987.

Edwards, A. Cox. "Brazil: The Brazilian Labor Market in the 1980s," World Bank, Country Operations Division, Country Department 1, Latin America and Caribbean Regional, 1991. Office, mimeo.

Hay, J.W. "Occupational Choice and Occupational Earnings: Selectivity Bias in a Simultaneous Logit-OLS Model," unpublished Ph.D. dissertation, Yale University, 1980.

Heckman, J.J. "Sample Selection Bias as a Specification Error," *Econometrica* 47,1:153-161 1979.

Hill, M.A. "Labor Force Participation of Married Women in Urban Japan," Ph.D. dissertation, Duke University 1980.

Hill, M.A. "Female Labor Force Participation in Developing and Developed Countries - Consideration of the Informal Sector," *Review of Economics and Statistics* 63,3:459-468, 1983.

Hill, M.A. "Female Labor Supply in Japan: Implications of the Informal Sector For Labor Force Participation and Hours of Work," *The Journal of Human Resources* 24:143-161, 1988.

Jaffe, A.J. and K. Azumi. "The Birth Rate and Cottage Industries in Underdeveloped Countries," *Economics Development and Cultural Change* 9:52-63, 1960.

Lee, L.F. "Generalized Econometric Models with Selectivity," *Econometrica* 51:507-512, 1983.

Maddala, G.S. *Limited-Dependent and Qualitative Variables in Econometrics*. Cambridge: Cambridge University Press, 1983.

McCabe, J.L. and M.R. Rosenzweig. "Female Employment Creation and Family Size," in R. Ridker, ed., *Population and Development: The Search for Selective Interventions*. Baltimore: The Johns Hopkins University Press, 1976.

McFadden, D. "Conditional Logit Analysis of Qualitative Choice Behavior," in P. Zarembka (ed.), *Frontiers in Econometrics*. New York: Academic Press 1973.

Mincer, J. *Schooling, Experience, and Earnings*. New York: Columbia University Press, 1974.

Oaxaca, R. "Male-female Wages Differenctians in Urban Labor Markets," *International Economic Review* 14:693-709, 1973.

Paes de Barros, R. and S. Varandas. "A Carteira de Trabalho e, as Condicoes de Trabalho e Remuneracao dos Chefes de Familia no Brasil," IPEA, 1987.

Sedlacek, G.L., R. Paes de Barros, and S. Varandas. "Segmentacao Mobilidade No Mercado de Trabalho Brasileiro: Uma Analise Da Regiao Metropolitana De Sao Paulo," in *Perspectivas Da Economia Brasileira - 1989* IPEA/INPES, 1989.

Smith, S.K. "Determinants of Female Labor Force Participation and Family Size in Mexico City," *Economic Development and Cultural Change* 30,1:129-152, 1981.

Stelcner, M., J.B. Smith, J.A. Brelaw, and G. Monette. "Labor Force Behavior and Earnings of Brazilian Women and Men," in this volume, 1991.

Tiefenthaler, J.M. "A Multi-Sector Model of Female Labor Force Participation and Wage Determination: Empirical Evidence from Cebu Island, Philippines," unpublished Ph.D. dissertation, Duke University, 1991.

Trost, R. and L.F. Lee. "Technical Training and Earnings: A Polychotomous Choice Model with Selectivity," *Review of Economics and Statistics* 66:151-156, 1984.

# 5

# Is There Sex Discrimination in Chile?
# Evidence from the CASEN Survey

*Indermit S. Gill*

## 1.    Introduction

The aim of this study is to determine the extent of and components of the earnings differential between men and women in Chile's formal sector.  We hesitate to call this earnings differential "labor market discrimination" since the study does not seriously attempt to explain this gap.[1] But there is little doubt that this gap exists. Figures 5.1, 5.2 and 5.3 graph the schooling-, age- and tenure- earnings profiles of Chilean men and women in 1987. These graphs reveal the existence of significant male-female earnings differentials across all schooling, age, and tenure levels.

These figures are a graphic but inaccurate representation of the  true earnings differentials between men and women. They are inaccurate because: First, there may be interactions between the various components of human capital--schooling, job tenure and general work experience-- so that simple correlations between any one of these components and earnings may be misleading, especially for purposes of comparison across sexes.   Second, the numbers are based upon earnings reported by working men and women, who may  not be unbiased samples of their respective populations. As a result of this  sampling bias, calculations of returns to human capital (of working men and women) cannot be generalized to all men and women, hence limiting the

---

[1]    The word "discrimination" is fraught with misunderstanding.  Boulding (1976) writes:

"The history of the word itself is a strange one as it has two almost entirely opposite meanings, one very good and one very bad.  On the good side, it means a correct appraisal of complex issues and valuations, as in the expression "a discriminating taste."  A person who has a discriminating taste is supposed to be able to reject what is meretricious and to discount what is only superficially either attractive or repellant, and is thus able to exercise true judgment...

At the other end of the scale the word discrimination in a bad sense means precisely the opposite of the discriminating taste, that is, a failure to make correct judgments, especially of other people.  The consequence of discrimination in the bad sense, then, is illegitimate differences, that is, differences in the treatment or rewards of different individuals which are not in accord with some standard of equity."

The definition of a standard of equity is essential for any study that attempts to measure discrimination.  In the case of gender discrimination, given the biological differences between the sexes, it is particularly difficult to agree upon a sensible standard.

**Figure 5.1**
Schooling and Primary Income
Chile 1987

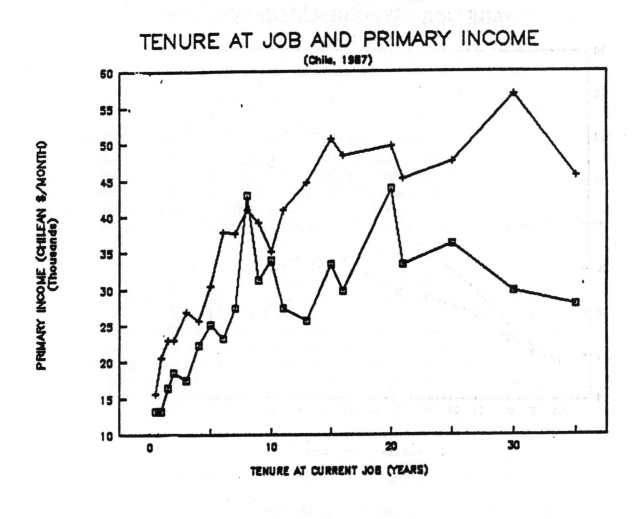

## TENURE AT JOB AND PRIMARY INCOME
### (Chile, 1987)

□ Females   + Males

**Figure 5.2**
Age and Primary Income
Chile 1987

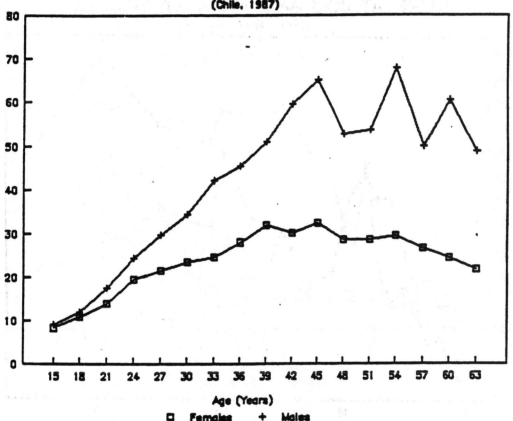

AGE AND PRIMARY INCOME
(Chile, 1987)

Age (Years)
□ Females    + Males

**Figure 5.3**
Tenure at Job and Primary Income
Chile, 1987

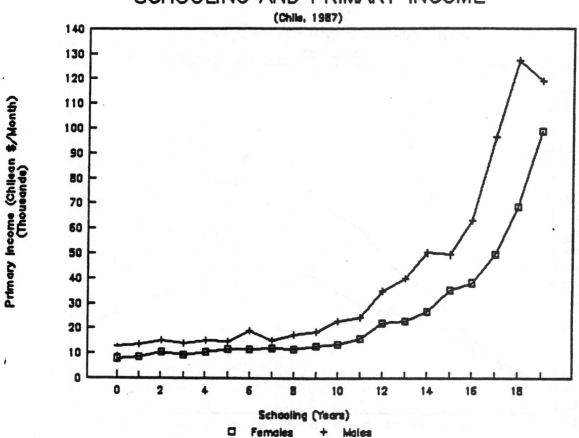

## SCHOOLING AND PRIMARY INCOME
### (Chile, 1987)

applicability of studies relying on rates of return calculations to propose subsidization of schooling or job training.[2]

Later sections of this chapter correct for both these problems. Human capital earnings functions using all three measures of skill are estimated to calculate returns to each of these components (see Mincer 1974). The sample selectivity bias is corrected using a now familiar method proposed by Heckman (1979). The male-female earnings differential is then divided into two components: The segment due to lower endowments of human capital of women, and the segment due to lower returns to the human capital of women (See Oaxaca, 1973 for details).

Schooling levels are lower for working men than women, the gender gap in job tenure is small, but working men are older than working women, and hence men have greater (potential) work experience. Thus composite human capital endowments are roughly the same for men and women. Much of the earnings differentials then must be explained by differential returns and/or unobserved ability.

The plan of this chapter is as follows. The next section provides a brief overview of the labor market in Chile. Section 3 discusses the characteristics of the data used in this study: Information from the National Socioeconomic Survey (Encuesta de Caracterizacion Socioeconomica Nacional, or CASEN) of Chilean households conducted in 1987. Section 4 examines the determinants of female and male work participation. Section 5 uses the results of work participation regressions to adjust for sample selectivity in analyzing the determinants of earnings of workers. Section 6 uses these earnings regressions to compute the components of the earnings differential between men and women, dividing it into the part due to market structure and the part due to observable human capital differences. Section 6 also offers partial explanations for the gender differential in returns to human capital based on male-female differences in the industrial and occupational distribution of employment. Section 7 concludes the paper.

## 2.    The Chilean Labor Market

Chile is a relatively developed labor market in terms of life expectancy, degree of urbanization (usually associated with advanced health and education systems), and literacy rates. Table 5.1 shows some key indicators of development for Chile, Latin America and the Caribbean, and the United States. Chilean health and schooling levels seems to lie about halfway between Latin American and United States' levels. Paradoxically, this is not reflected in corresponding differences in per capita income.[3]

For the purposes of this study, the interesting comparisons are those of male-female differences in schooling enrollments and labor force participation. There are almost no gender differences in schooling investments. However, women constitute only about 28 percent of the labor force,

---

[2]    There are other problems with these graphs. Reported earnings do not represent true returns to human capital where part or all of output is self-consumed. These skill-earnings profiles can also be interpreted as approximating unobserved ability-earnings relationships: see Willis & Rosen (1979). These problems are not addressed here.

[3]    Such discrepancies between human capital and income is the subject of the "Human Development Report" (UNDP 1990), which proposes an average of indicators of income, health and education as an index of development. For some theoretical shortcomings of this index and their resolution, see Gill and Bhalla (1990).

**Table 5.1**
Indicators of Development:
Chile, Latin America & Caribbean, and the USA

| Source[a] | Indicator | USA | Latin America & Caribbean | Chile |
|---|---|---|---|---|
| W | GNP Per Capita (1988 US$) | 19,840 | 1,840 | 1,510 |
| H | Human Development Index (1987)[b] | 0.96 | 0.84 | 0.93 |
| W | Urbanization (1988 %) | 74 | 71 | 85 |
| H | Life Expectancy at Birth (1988 Years) | 76 | 67 | 72 |
|   | Males | 72 | 64 | 68 |
|   | Females | 79 | 70 | 75 |
| H | Literacy Rates (1985 %) | 96 | 83 | 98 |
|   | Males |   | 85 | 97 |
|   | Females | 81 | 97 |   |
| W | Secondary School Enrollment (1988) | 98 | 49 | 70 |
|   | Males | 97 | 47 | 69 |
|   | Females | 99 | 53 | 71 |
| H | Women in Labor Force (1988, % of LF) | 41.5 | 26.3 | 28.3 |
| W | Share in GDP (1988 %) |   |   |   |
|   | - Agriculture | 2 | 10 | 9 |
|   | - Industry (Manufacturing) | 33(22) | 39(27) | 39(24) |
|   | - Services | 65 | 52 | 52 |
| H | Share in Employment (1985-87 %) |   |   |   |
|   | - Agriculture | 3 | 25 | 20 |
|   | - Industry | 19 | 17 | 17 |
|   | - Services | 78 | 57 | 63 |

a.   H denotes Human Development Report, UNDP (1990).
     W denotes World Development Report, World Bank (1990).
b.   The Human Development Index consists (roughly) of an equally weighted average of per capita income (top-coded), adult literacy and life expectancy at birth. The index varies between 0 and 1. GDP shares  for Chile are for 1965.

so female labor force participation is less than half of the male  participation rate. These numbers highlight a peculiarity of the Latin American labor market: Female work participation rates have not increased in  step with education, as they have in other parts of the world. Female labor force participation rates are, however, closely correlated with the share of the services sector in GDP and employment, a pattern observed globally.

The question posed by these correlations are: Why, in the face of  rapid equalization of education and health levels across the sexes, have  female labor force participation rates not increased to levels observed in  industrialized countries? The correlations between the share of services and participation rates may be key to designing policies that aim to improve the  status of women in developing countries.

## 3.    The Data

Table 5.2 lists means and standard deviations of the key variables  used in the study. The sample consists of about 63,000 individuals aged 14 to 65 years in 1987.

Provincial variations in most variables are almost entirely accounted for by the degree of urbanization, with the possible exception of Santiago.[4] This is in sharp contrast to the patterns described for Brazil in Stelcner, Smith, Breslaw and Monette (1992). In this study, therefore, the rural-urban divide will be used (in one form or another) in both the work participation and the earnings regressions. No decomposition by province is necessary if rural-urban differences have already been taken into consideration.

As expected, male participation rates are higher than female rates. Rural women participate less than urban women, urban men participate less than rural men. The result for males can be explained simply by the higher school enrollment rates for urban areas. Schooling levels are higher in urban areas, which is not surprising. Marriage rates are the same in both rural and urban areas and across sexes. But more women are heads of household in urban areas, chiefly due to the larger fraction of separated women in urban areas. Both household size and number of workers per household are higher in rural areas, the latter probably due to the production structure of family farms. Fertility rates, reflected by the ratio of the number of children to household size, are also higher in rural areas.

Comparisons across age groups indicate that rural-urban gaps in schooling have narrowed over time: For both males and females, rural-urban schooling ratios are about 50 percent for people aged 51 to 65 years, and increase progressively to about 80 percent for the youngest age group (14 to 20 years). The rural-urban age distribution is relatively constant over time, so that there seems to be no age bias in migration to urban areas.

Male-female schooling gaps have narrowed over time, to the extent that women aged 14 to 30 years are marginally more schooled than males in 1987. There does not seem to be much difference between the sexes in the trends in the type of schooling. This makes Chile an interesting case study for examining whether work participation and wage differentials persist even when pre-employment human capital endowments are the same across sexes. Tenure levels (number of years spent working at the current job) continue to be higher for males. The rural-urban difference between tenure for working women is greater than for working men, probably reflecting differences in industrial composition of employment both between sexes and region of residence.

## 4. Determinants of Work Participation

The decision on whether to work in the market depends on both market wage, W, and reservation wage, W* . If W > W* , the person works. Thus,

$$P = f(W, W*) \qquad (1)$$
$$\phantom{P = f(} + \quad -$$

where P takes on the value 1 if the person participates in the labor market, and 0 if the person does not.

---

[4] The data were analyzed for each of 3 provinces. Work participation, income, schooling, tenure levels, age, and household characteristics (marital status, size, dependency ratio, etc.) seem to vary proportionately with the degree of urbanization of the labor force in the province.

## Table 5.2
### Means (and Standard Deviations) of Variables: By Region

| Variable | FEMALES | | | MALES | | |
|---|---|---|---|---|---|---|
| | Total | Urban | Rural | Total | Urban | Rural |
| LF Participation Rate (Fraction) | 0.272 (0.45) | 0.296 (0.46) | 0.138 (0.35) | 0.663 (0.47) | 0.642 (0.48) | 0.760 (0.43) |
| Primary Income (Chilean $/Month) | 20045 (26553) | 20885 (27332) | 11142 (1316900) | 30673 (50684) | 34498 (53646) | 14885 (31363) |
| Household Income (Chilean $/Month) | 55548 (79187) | 60232 (83087) | 28903 (42846) | 53566 (73657) | 58656 (77997) | 30259 (41845) |
| Schooling (Years) | 8.811 (4.09) | 9.272 (3.98) | 6.190 (3.72) | 9.050 (4.20) | 9.711 (4.04) | 6.024 (3.52) |
| Age (Years) | 33.653 (14.17) | 33.821 (14.13) | 32.693 (14.33) | 33.296 (14.14) | 33.418 (14.14) | 32.737 (14.14) |
| Tenure (Years on Current Job) | 5.267 (7.17) | 5.403 (7.19) | 3.558 (6.44) | 6.421 (8.43) | 6.592 (8.47) | 5.733 (8.24) |
| Fraction Married | 0.478 (0.50) | 0.473 (0.50) | 0.508 (0.50) | 0.504 (0.50) | 0.515 (0.50) | 0.451 (0.50) |
| Fraction Cohabiting | 0.036 (0.19) | 0.035 (0.18) | 0.043 (0.20) | 0.036 (0.19) | 0.035 (0.18) | 0.039 (0.19) |
| Fraction Separated | 0.045 (0.20) | 0.048 (0.22) | 0.021 (0.14) | 0.020 (0.13) | 0.021 (0.14) | 0.014 (0.12) |
| Fraction Widowed | 0.050 (0.22) | 0.052 (0.22) | 0.040 (0.20) | 0.014 (0.12) | 0.015 (0.12) | 0.013 (0.11) |
| Fraction Single | 0.391 (0.49) | 0.392 (0.49) | 0.389 (0.49) | 0.427 (0.50) | 0.414 (0.49) | 0.484 (0.50) |
| Fraction Hshold Head | 0.105 (0.31) | 0.111 (0.31) | 0.068 (0.25) | 0.507 (0.50) | 0.512 (0.50) | 0.482 (0.50) |
| Household Size (Number of Members) | 5.107 (2.18) | 5.054 (2.15) | 5.607 (2.47) | 5.222 (2.19) | 5.117 (2.14) | 5.584 (2.48) |
| Workers in Household (Number) | 1.627 (1.12) | 1.626 (1.11) | 1.637 (1.17) | 1.738 (1.16) | 1.702 (1.13) | 1.903 (1.29) |
| # Children: 0-5 Yrs (Number) | 0.626 (0.85) | 0.601 (0.82) | 0.764 (0.98) | 0.589 (0.83) | 0.572 (0.81) | 0.668 (0.92) |
| # Children: 6-13 Yrs (Number) | 0.615 (0.84) | 0.582 (0.81) | 0.806 (0.99) | 0.606 (0.84) | 0.575 (0.80) | 0.744 (0.97) |

Note: Primary income is monthly income from main job.

Market wage W depends upon stocks of productive skills -- human capital -- such as schooling and job market experience, and the state of the labor market -- regional and infrastructural factors -- which determines the reward to these skills. Reservation wage W* depends upon the productivity in activities other than labor market work. For both men and women, it may depend upon the returns to further investment in human capital, which may require full time school attendance. Thus, for example, reservation wage rates will be higher for students who have begun studies toward a degree but have not yet obtained a diploma. W* also depends upon household characteristics such as the number of (young) children and other dependent relatives, and on household wealth.

Table 5.3 reports the results of probit estimations for the work participation functions (equation 1 above) of women and men aged 14 to 65 years.[5] Table 5.3 also reports the percentage change in the probability of participation ("%Deriv"), evaluated at the means of the right-hand-side variables. The results indicate that:

1. Higher schooling levels are positively associated with the probability of participation, except when the years of schooling indicate incomplete programs of study (8 to 11 years for both females and males, and 13 to 15 years for males).

2. The age profile of participation is inverted U-shaped. The profile for males is more curved than for females.

3. Married and cohabiting women are less likely to work than those who are single or separated. Married and cohabiting men are more likely to work than separated or single men. This result is consistent with the theory that marriage allows males and females to specialize in tasks, and females have a comparative advantage over men in household production.

4. Being a household head is positively correlated with the probability of participation for both men and women.

5. Higher household income (total income of other members of the household) increases the likelihood of work for women, but decreases it for men. The result for women is somewhat puzzling.

6. Holding constant household size and the number of children, increases in the number of workers increase the probability of participation for both women and men. Holding constant the total number of household workers and children, increases in household decrease the probability of participation for both women and men.

7. The more young children there are in the household, the lower the likelihood of participation of women, but the greater the probability of men working. Older

---

[5] Many functional forms were fitted. The results do not change significantly, so the most easily interpretable form is reported.

children have similar but weaker effects on decisions to work.[6]   There is no evidence that older female children are substitutes for adult females in household tasks.

8.   Rural women participate less than urban women; urban men participate less than rural men.

Using the probit regressions in Table 5.3 and Appendix Table 5A.2, we conducted simulations of the effects of schooling, age, marital status, and household characteristics on female participation probabilities.  Results of the simulation exercises are reported in Table 5.4 below.

*Reasons for not working.*  Table 5.5 reports the reasons for not working.  Naturally, the sample consists of those individuals for whom $W^* > W$.  A short description of the table is that women who do not work cite working at home, in school, and retired (in that order) as the most important reasons, and men who do not work are in school, unemployed, or are retired (in that order).

Appendix Table 5A.1 reports the reasons for not working by sex, marital status, and age group.  Married, cohabiting and widowed women overwhelmingly cite household work as the reason for not working in the market (with "Retired" being the only other important reason for about 25 percent of  non-workers aged more than 50 years).  Single and separated women do not work because they are in school (when they are young), or because of household work (for all ages).  More than 10 percent of single women aged 21 to 40 years also list unemployment as a reason for not working.

Prime aged men who are married, cohabiting and widowed and who do  not work are generally unemployed (actively looking for work). Older non-workers are pensioners. Single men who do not work are in school (age  groups 14-20 and 21-30 years), or unemployed (age groups 21-30, 31-40 and  41-50 years), or physically unable to work (age groups 31-40, 41-50 and 51-65 years).

Following Killingsworth and Heckman (1986), the error term in the  work participation equation can be divided into three components:  The error  term due to differences in tastes (utility function errors), the errors due  to unaccounted-for differences in budget constraints, and the errors due to  discrepancies between observed and optimal decisions. This last error is more important for men, since "Unemployed" as a reason for not working is more  important for men than for women. Such differences between the sexes make it  inadvisable to attach a uniform interpretation to the sample selectivity  correction terms (inverse of the Mill's ratio) for men and women, since these  are derived from the error term in their respective participation functions. This problem is discussed further in the next section.

---

[6]   To further examine the effects of children on the decision to work, examine the probit estimates of men and women by marital status listed in Table A11.2  in the Appendix.  For married and cohabiting women, increases in the number of children lowers the probability of participation, especially if the number of children are 0 to 5 years old.  For single and separated women, the number of children in the household increases the likelihood of working.  The number of children has no effect on the participation decision of men, holding constant household size and number of workers in the household.

**Table 5.3**
**Work Participation Probit Estimates: All Males & Females**
**Dependent Variable: Do you work? (Yes=1, No=0)**

| | Females | | | Males | | |
|---|---|---|---|---|---|---|
| | Coeff. | Standard Error | %Deriv. | Coeff. | Standard Error | %Deriv. |
| Schooling: 8-11 Years† | -0.0145 | 0.0219 | -0.5 | -0.0759** | 0.0225 | -2.6 |
| Schooling: 12 Years | 0.2699*** | 0.0235 | 8.4 | 0.1176*** | 0.0263 | 4.1 |
| Schooling: 13-15 Years | 0.2841*** | 0.0315 | 8.9 | -0.1885*** | 0.0352 | -6.5 |
| Schooling: 16+ Years | 0.9990*** | 0.0376 | 31.2 | 0.1828*** | 0.0392 | -6.4 |
| Age: 21-30 Years† | 0.0046*** | 0.0270 | 31.4 | 1.2882*** | 0.0255 | 44.7 |
| Age: 31-40 Years | 1.2750*** | 0.0321 | 39.8 | 1.5186*** | 0.0359 | 52.7 |
| Age: 41-50 Years | 1.1497*** | 0.0350 | 35.9 | 1.2059*** | 0.0391 | 41.9 |
| Age: 51-65 Years | 0.5966*** | 0.0377 | 18.6 | 0.4275*** | 0.0382 | 14.8 |
| Married† | -0.6920*** | 0.0228 | 21.6 | 0.6077*** | 0.0322 | 21.1 |
| Cohabiting | -0.6223*** | 0.0468 | -19.4 | 0.6285*** | 0.0548 | 21.8 |
| Widowed | 0.3843*** | 0.0436 | -12.0 | -0.1697*** | 0.0695 | 5.9 |
| Separated | 0.0662* | 0.0408 | 2.1 | 0.4798*** | 0.0630 | 16.7 |
| Household Head | 0.3262*** | 0.0319 | 10.2 | 0.2503*** | 0.0324 | 8.7 |
| Household Income | 7.5e-7*** | 1.1e-7 | 0.0 | -2.2e-6*** | 2.0e-7 | 0.0 |
| # Household Members | -0.0262*** | 0.0062 | -0.8 | -0.0441*** | 0.0066 | -1.5 |
| # Household Workers | 0.0618*** | 0.0104 | 1.9 | 0.1479*** | 0.0107 | 5.1 |
| Boys: 0-5 Yrs | -0.0247* | 0.0157 | -0.8 | 0.0631*** | 0.0177 | 2.2 |
| Girls: 0-5 Yrs | -0.0034 | 0.0160 | -0.1 | 0.0507*** | 0.0177 | 1.8 |
| Boys: 6-13 Yrs | -0.0053 | 0.0160 | -0.2 | 0.0368** | 0.0173 | 1.3 |
| Girls: 6-13 Yrs | 0.0016 | 0.0158 | 0.1 | 0.0289* | 0.0173 | 1.0 |
| Rural Dummy | -0.3701*** | 0.0261 | -11.9 | 0.4906*** | 0.0245 | 17.0 |
| Constant | -1.2090*** | 0.0363 | -37.8 | -0.8458*** | 0.0363 | -29.4 |
| Log Likelihood | -16277.6 | | | -14215.4 | | |
| Chi-Square | 5811.1 | | | 11025.2 | | |
| Sample Size | 32765 | | | 30887 | | |
| Mean of Dependent Variable | 0.2722 | | | 0.6635 | | |

† The omitted schooling group is "0-7 years," the omitted age group is "14-20 years," and the omitted marital status class is "Single."

* Indicates significance at 10 percent level.

** Indicates significance at 5 percent level.

*** Indicates significance at 1 percent level.

**Table 5.4**
Predicted Probability of Female Labor Force Participation
(Results of Simulation Exercises)

| Characteristic | Predicted Probability (Percentage) |
|---|---|
| **0.** Mean Participation Rate | |
| All Women | 27.22 |
| Married Women Only | 22.70 |
| **1.** Completed Schooling | |
| 0 to 7 Years | 23.37 |
| 8 to 11 Years | 22.93 |
| 12 Years | 32.47 |
| 13 to 15 Years | 32.90 |
| 16 and More Years | 60.73 |
| **2.** Age | |
| 14 to 20 Years | 8.00 |
| 21 to 30 Years | 34.49 |
| 31 to 40 Years | 44.84 |
| 41 to 50 Years | 39.95 |
| 51 to 65 Years | 20.99 |
| **3.** Marital Status | |
| Married | 13.91 |
| Single | 40.77 |
| **4.** Female Head of Household | 37.78 |
| **5.** Number of Children Aged 0 to 5 Years[a] | |
| 0 Children | 28.59 |
| 1 Child | 22.97 |
| 2 Children | 18.03 |
| **6.** Number of Children Aged 6 to 13 Years[a] | |
| 0 Children | 28.59 |
| 1 Child | 25.75 |
| 2 Children | 23.07 |
| **7.** Rural Residence | 17.93 |

a. Simulation based on results for probit regressions for Married, Cohabiting and Widowed Women reported in Appendix Table 5A.2.

Note: Intercept is adjusted to make predicted probability equal to mean probability.

**Table 5.5**
**Reasons for not Working: By Sex and Marital Status (%)**

| | | Married, Cohabiting & Widowed | | Separated & Single | | Total | |
|---|---|---|---|---|---|---|---|
| | | Women | Men | Women | Men | Women | Men |
| 1. | Looking for First Job | 0.16 | 0.60 | 3.91 | 8.49 | 1.62 | 6.36 |
| 2. | Unemployed | 1.06 | 30.35 | 5.17 | 10.35 | 2.66 | ·15.75 |
| 3. | Household Work | 88.38 | 3.78 | 35.24 | 1.57 | 67.71 | 2.17 |
| 4. | Studying | 0.55 | 2.17 | 48.35 | 64.15 | 19.14 | 47.40 |
| 5. | Retired (Pensions, etc) | 7.36 | 45.00 | 2.69 | 2.12 | 5.55 | 13.71 |
| 6. | Rentier | 0.13 | 0.34 | 0.09 | 0.06 | 0.11 | 0.13 |
| 7. | Unable to Work | 1.56 | 9.78 | 3.52 | 6.12 | 2.32 | 7.11 |
| 8. | Temporarily Inactive | 0.60 | 6.63 | 0.70 | 1.60 | 0.64 | 2.96 |
| 9. | Other Reasons | 0.21 | 1.35 | 0.33 | 5.55 | 0.25 | 4.41 |
| | Total Observations | 14,956 | 2,669 | 9,516 | 7,208 | 24,472 | 9,877 |

## 5.    Earnings Functions

*The problem of sample selectivity.* Earnings data are available only for working women and men, that is, individuals with $W > W^*$. For people who have the same wage, $W$, working men and women have smaller $W^*$ than those who do not work. For individuals with the same reservation wage, $W^*$, working women have relatively high market wages, $W$. Because of both these differences, working men and women are unrepresentative of the male and female populations, and policy inferences derived from regressions for workers may be invalid both for nonworking men and women and for working men and women.

The problem can be interpreted, alternatively, as:

1.    sample selectivity bias, or

2.    a problem of omitted relevant variables in estimating the human capital earnings function (equivalently, of simultaneous equations bias), or

3.    a problem of truncated data, since we do not observe (offered) wages for people who do not work.

Following Killingsworth and Heckman (1986), let the work participation decision be:

$$P = W\omega + R\rho + u \tag{2}$$

where $P = 1$ if the individual works, 0 otherwise, $W$ is the market wage, $R$ is a set of variables that determine the reservation wage $W^*$, and $u$ is the error term. The human capital earnings function, which determines the market wage, is:

$$W = X\beta + v \tag{3}$$

where $X$ is the matrix of observed human capital variables (schooling, tenure, general work experience, etc), $\beta$ is the vector of returns to these variables, and $v$ is the error term.

Estimates of $\beta$ obtained by estimating equation 3 by ordinary least squares will be biased, since some of the factors that make women more likely to work may also be factors that make them extraordinarily high or low wage earners. That is, v is likely to be correlated with X, which also determines wages.

A way out of this problem is to estimate the work participation equation 2, using X as an instrument for W (since W is observed only for workers, but X -- schooling, age, tenure, etc.-- is observed for everybody), and including R to ensure identifiability. Then, the unexplained part of P is a composite index of unobserved characteristics that are relevant for the decision to work. A summary measure of these unobserved attributes is $\lambda$, the inverse of the Mill's ratio. $\lambda$ is then included as a regressor in the earnings equation,

$$W = X\beta + \lambda\alpha + e ,  \tag{4}$$

which provides measures of $\beta$ that are free of selectivity bias.

$\lambda$ is an inverse, monotonic function of the probability of participation. Therefore, the value of $\lambda$ must be greater for non-workers than for workers.[7]  A negative value of $\alpha$ in equation 4 implies that the unobserved attributes that make workers earn unusually high wages are also attributes that make it less likely that the individual will in fact work. A positive value means that unusually high paid workers are those whose reservation wages are low, making it more likely for them to be in the market.

It is commonly argued that sample selectivity is a more serious problem for women. The argument is that while only women who have unusually large amounts of market skills work outside the home, almost all men work in the market. At least in Chile's case, this argument is seriously flawed. To see why, take another look at Table 5.5. The reasons for not working (other than attending school) are chiefly "Unemployment" for men and "Household Work" for women. While the reasons for not working are different, both can result in the samples of workers being unrepresentative of their respective populations. The reasons that make (employed) males highly paid relative to their observed human capital levels may also be those that make them more (or less) likely to be employed in the first place. Just as theory cannot help us predict the sign of $\alpha$ for women, it does not help us predict the sign of $\alpha$ for men.

Because of the above arguments, both female and male earnings functions were estimated using the sample selectivity correction.

*Results of earnings regressions.*  A crippling limitation of the CASEN survey is that there is no information on amount of labor supplied (hours worked per week or weeks worked per year). All workers are assumed to supply the same amount of labor per time period. While this is a patently absurd assumption, there was simply no way out of this problem.

Tables 5.6 and 5.7 report the results of estimating equations 3 and 4 for women and men respectively. Odd-numbered columns report results for equation 3, while even-numbered columns are results of fitting equation 4 to the data. The main results are:

---

[7]   The ratio of average $\lambda$ of workers to that of non-workers must therefore be less than 1. This ratio is about 0.70 for women, and about 0.40 for men.

1.  Returns to schooling for males are about 13 percent, roughly 2 percent higher than those for females. Adjusting for sample selectivity lowers the returns to schooling for females marginally (by 1 or 2 percent), but leaves the returns to schooling of males unchanged.

2.  Returns to potential work experience (Age-Schooling-6) are about 2 percent for women and about 4 percent for men. The reason is that potential work experience is a better proxy of job tenure for men than for women, who have more frequently interrupted careers.

3.  Tenure-earnings profiles are steeper but more curved for women. Evaluating the returns to tenure for women and men at their respective means yields returns of about 5 percent and 3 percent respectively. Due to higher multicollinearity between tenure and potential work experience for men, the more meaningful measure of returns to work experience is the sum of the returns to tenure and potential experience. This is about 7 percent per year for both men and women.[8]

4.  The coefficient for Lambda is significant and negative in all regressions except those including marital status dummies, and is slightly greater in magnitude for males. This implies that sample selectivity is important for both men and women, though one must be careful in interpreting this coefficient. For women, given the information in Table 5.5, it implies that the unobserved characteristics that make women high income-earners relative to their schooling and tenure levels, also make them more likely to stay at home (or attend school). For men, a negative coefficient for Lambda implies that unobserved attributes which make them better earners relative to their schooling and tenure levels, also make them more likely to be unemployed (or attend school).

5.  Rural dummies are insignificant for women, but negative and significant for men. This probably reflects the greater amounts of subsistence production in rural areas. The results remain unchanged when the rural area dummy is dropped from the regressions.

6.  Finally, including marital status in earnings regressions significantly lowers the returns to schooling and to tenure for women, but leaves the coefficients for males unaltered. Including marital status significantly alters the sample selectivity coefficients for both sexes: a for females triples in magnitude while remaining negative, while that for males becomes zero (and statistically insignificant at the 5 percent level). Married men and women earn about 20 and 30 percent more respectively than single workers.

---

[8]    Strictly speaking, tenure should not be included in the earnings regressions since it was not included in the work participation functions, and since it is simultaneously determined with earnings. (Tenure is observed only for workers, so it cannot be included in the work participation regression.) To correct for both these problems, we used instrumental variables technique instead of ordinary least squares, with quadratic forms of schooling and age and their interaction as instruments for tenure. These are poor instruments for tenure, especially for women, but they were the best we could find. The results do not change significantly, so we report only the least squares regressions in the paper.

## Table 5.6
### Female Earnings Regressions

#### Dependent Variable: Log (Primary Income)

| | (1) | (2) | (3) | (4) | (5) | (6) |
|---|---|---|---|---|---|---|
| Schooling | 0.1263 | 0.1187 | 0.1163 | 0.1084 | 0.1120 | 0.0835 |
| | (64.54) | (56.59) | (48.48) | (41.19) | (45.53) | (27.93) |
| Age-School-6 | 0.0292 | 0.0246 | 0.0191 | 0.0144 | 0.0141 | -0.0057 |
| | (16.92) | (13.87) | (8.37) | (6.08) | (5.82) | (-2.14) |
| $(\text{Age-School-6})^2$ | -0.0003 | -0.0003 | -0.0002 | -0.0002 | -0.0002 | 0.0002 |
| | (-10.98) | (-7.77) | (-5.36) | (-3.22) | (-3.91) | (3.15) |
| Tenure | | | 0.0552 | 0.0552 | 0.0535 | 0.0507 |
| | | | (18.34) | (18.39) | (17.75) | (17.07) |
| $\text{Tenure}^2$ | | | -0.0014 | -0.0014 | -0.0013 | -0.0012 |
| | | | (-13.85) | (-13.75) | (-13.23) | (-12.05) |
| Married Dummy | | | | | 0.1571 | 0.3793 |
| | | | | | (8.03) | (16.08) |
| Cohabiting Dummy | | | | | 0.0403 | 0.2287 |
| | | | | | (0.82) | (4.57) |
| Widowed Dummy | | | | | 0.0649 | 0.1658 |
| | | | | | (1.66) | (4.25) |
| Separated Dummy | | | | | 0.0298 | -0.0329 |
| | | | | | (0.97) | (-1.07) |
| Rural Dummy | -0.0889 | -0.0247 | -0.0208 | 0.0359 | -0.0260 | 0.1267 |
| | (-3.42) | (-0.92) | (-0.67) | (1.13) | (-0.84) | (3.98) |
| Lambda $(\lambda)$ | | -0.0824 | | -0.0685 | | -0.1973 |
| | | (-9.85) | | (-7.26) | | (-16.31) |
| Constant | 7.895 | 8.2153 | 7.9706 | 8.2607 | 8.0118 | 8.8962 |
| | (252.86) | (182.78) | (216.47) | (152.26) | (215.46) | (135.96) |
| F-Statistic | 1316.20 | 1081.65 | 759.41 | 662.51 | 466.33 | 461.65 |
| Adjusted R | 0.3253 | 0.3312 | 0.3540 | 0.3580 | 0.3591 | 0.3790 |
| Sample Size | 10,912 | 10,912 | 8,305 | 8,305 | 8,305 | 8,305 |

#### Means of Variables

| | | | | | | |
|---|---|---|---|---|---|---|
| Log (Primary Income) | | 9.4654 | | 9.5668 | | 9.5668 |
| Schooling | | 9.3788 | | 10.1467 | | 10.1467 |
| Age-Schooling-6 | | 22.2929 | | 18.2192 | | 18.2192 |
| Tenure | | | | 5.6325 | | 5.6325 |
| Married & Cohabiting | | | | | | 0.4147 |
| Rural | | 0.0863 | | 0.0738 | | 0.0738 |
| Lambda (Workers/Nonworkers) | | 0.7253 | | 0.6928 | | 0.6928 |

Notes: t-statistics in parentheses. Primary income is monthly income from main job.

Odd numbered columns report results for equation (3) and even numbered columns report results for equation (4).

## Table 5.7
### Male Earnings Regressions

#### Dependent Variable: Log (Primary Income)

|  | (1) | (2) | (3) | (4) | (5) | (6) |
|---|---|---|---|---|---|---|
| Schooling | 0.1366 | 0.1338 | 0.1292 | 0.1262 | 0.1233 | 0.1231 |
|  | (100.60) | (97.77) | (88.26) | (85.13) | (82.46) | (82.11) |
| Age-School | 0.0541 | 0.0426 | 0.0423 | 0.0317 | 0.0314 | 0.0301-6 |
|  | (42.26) | (27.66) | (28.82) | (18.15) | (19.55) | (17.16) |
| (Age-School-6)$^2$ | -0.0006 | -0.0004 | -0.0005 | -0.0003 | -0.0004 | -0.0004 |
|  | (-27.07) | (-15.31) | (-19.33) | (-10.57) | (-13.68) | (-11.25) |
| Tenure |  |  | 0.0356 | 0.0347 | 0.0334 | 0.0333 |
|  |  |  | (20.82) | (20.33) | (19.62) | (19.58) |
| Tenure$^2$ |  |  | -0.0006 | -0.0006 | -0.0006 | -0.0006 |
|  |  |  | (-12.33) | (-11.52) | (-11.18) | (-11.07) |
| Married Dummy |  |  |  |  | 0.2404 | 0.2214 |
|  |  |  |  |  | (17.23) | (13.05) |
| Cohabiting Dummy |  |  |  |  | 0.0976 | 0.0784 |
|  |  |  |  |  | (3.73) | (2.81) |
| Widowed Dummy |  |  |  |  | 0.1181 | 0.1089 |
|  |  |  |  |  | (2.58) | (2.37) |
| Separated Dummy |  |  |  |  | 0.0323 | 0.0169 |
|  |  |  |  |  | (0.92) | (0.47) |
| Rural Dummy | -0.1176 | -0.1581 | -0.1114 | -0.1452 | -0.0980 | -0.1067 |
|  | (-8.81) | (-11.59) | (-8.23) | (-10.50) | (-7.27) | (-7.52) |
| Lambda ($\lambda$) |  | -0.1020 |  | -0.0890 |  | -0.0191 |
|  |  | (-13.35) |  | (-11.13) |  | (-1.96) |
| Constant | 7.8561 | 8.1017 | 7.9531 | 8.1777 | 7.9937 | 8.0397 |
|  | (355.91) | (282.54) | (340.17) | (265.20) | (342.19) | (243.18) |
| F-Statistic | 3419.93 | 2792.49 | 2343.29 | 2037.93 | 1461.12 | 1328.82 |
| Adjusted R$^2$ | 0.371 | 0.376 | 0.400 | 0.404 | 0.409 | 0.409 |
| Sample Size | 23,166 | 23,166 | 21,080 | 21,080 | 21,080 | 21,080 |

#### Means of Variables

|  |  |  |  |  |  |  |
|---|---|---|---|---|---|---|
| Log (Primary Income) |  | 9.8031 |  | 9.8191 |  | 9.8191 |
| Schooling |  | 8.8696 |  | 9.0005 |  | 9.0005 |
| Age-Schooling-6 |  | 22.4708 |  | 21.0874 |  | 21.0874 |
| Tenure |  |  |  | 6.8908 |  | 6.8908 |
| Married & Cohabiting |  |  |  |  |  | 0.6872 |
| Rural |  | 0.1950 |  | 0.2018 |  | 0.2018 |
| Lambda (Workers/Nonworkers) |  | 0.4144 |  | 0.3951 |  | 0.3951 |

Note:  t-statistics in parentheses.  Primary income is monthly income from main job.
Odd numbered columns report results for equation (3) and even numbered columns report results for equation (4).

To understand these results, let us first examine the rationale for including marital status in these regressions. In almost every country, married people are observed to earn more than similarly skilled single workers. One explanation is that attributes that lead to a person marrying and staying married may be correlated with higher unobserved job skills. Another explanation is that men who are high wage earners have greater incentives to marry, due to increased specialization afforded by marriage.[9] Women who are married and nonetheless work may be those with very high market wage, W, relative to their reservation wage, W*.

*The importance of marital status.* In any case, it seems that the interaction between marital status and sample selectivity is not fully captured by marital status dummies. To further examine this issue, we computed separate probit work participation regressions and earnings functions for four groups: Married, cohabiting and widowed ("married") females, and males; and single and separated ("single") females, and males. These results are reported in the Appendix as Table 5A.2 (probit participation results), and Tables 5A.3 and 5A.4 (female and male earnings regressions).

The main results of these earnings regressions are that:

1.  While the returns to schooling, potential work experience, and tenure are roughly the same for married and single women, the returns to all three forms of human capital are higher for married men than for single men.

2.  Selectivity coefficients for women are negative for both groups, but sample selectivity is greater for married women. That is, the same unobserved attributes that make women better earners than their schooling and tenure levels warrant, are more likely to make married women stay away from work than single women.

3.  The selectivity coefficient for married men is negative and significant, while that for single men is positive and small. This implies that the unobserved characteristics that make men higher income-earners than their schooling and tenure would suggest, also make it less likely that married men in fact work, while making it more likely that single men work. These magnitudes can easily be explained: While married men who do not work are either retired or unemployed, single male non-workers are mostly in school.

## 6.   Accounting for the Earning Differential

*The Oaxaca decomposition.* Table 5.8 presents the Oaxaca decomposition of the earnings gap between men and women. The primary result is that all of the higher earnings of men can be explained in terms of higher rates of return to human capital. Women appear to have higher endowments of human capital than men, than their earnings would indicate. Market structure rewards male skills more than seemingly comparable female skills. Some analysts would interpret this as evidence that the "purest" form of discrimination -- that the market rewards females less than males for the same skills -- explains all of the earnings differential. This result is robust to the choice of index type.

---

[9]   See Cornwell and Rupert (1990) for a test of these alternative hypotheses using United States data, and the implications of their results for the treatment of marital status in earnings regressions.

**Table 5.8**
Accounting for Earnings Differentials: The Oaxaca Decomposition
(All Numbers are Percentages)

| Norm: | Male Wage Function | | Female Wage Function | | |
|---|---|---|---|---|---|
| Components: | Coefficients | Endowments | Coefficients | Endowments | $W_f/W_m$ |
| **I. All Women and Men** | | | | | |
| Using Equations without Tenure | 114.9 | -14.9 | 113.7 | -13.7 | 71.3 |
| Using Equations with Tenure | 116.8 | -16.8 | 118.2 | -18.2 | 77.6 |
| Using Equations with Tenure & Marital Status | 102.6 | -2.6 | 93.0 | 7.0 | 77.6 |
| **II. Married Women and Men** | | | | | |
| Using Equations without Tenure | 107.7 | -7.7 | 103.2 | -3.2 | 65.3 |
| Using Equations with Tenure | 112.5 | -12.5 | 111.5 | -11.5 | 77.3 |
| **III. Single Women and Men** | | | | | |
| Using Equations without Tenure | 177.8 | -77.8 | 155.7 | -55.7 | 96.3 |
| Using Equations with Tenure | 152.1 | -52.1 | 136.3 | -36.3 | 98.7 |

Notes:   Male Wage function as Discriminatory Norm:

Coefficients Component = $X_f(\beta_m - \beta_f)$, Endowments Component = $\beta_m(X_m - X_f)$.

Female Wage function as Discriminatory Norm:

Coefficients Component = $X_m(\beta_m - \beta_f)$, Endowments Component = $\beta_f(X_m - X_f)$.

## Table 5.9
### Labor Force and Earnings by Sex and Industry

| Industry | Percentage Labor Force | | | Earnings | | |
|---|---|---|---|---|---|---|
| | Females | Males | F/M | Females | Males | F/M |
| Agriculture & Fishing | 8.02 | 32.37 | 0.25 | 15.56 | 18.11 | 0.86 |
| Mining | 0.40 | 4.28 | 0.09 | 41.07 | 43.95 | 0.93 |
| Maufacturing | 13.00 | 14.38 | 0.90 | 16.88 | 32.84 | 0.51 |
| Construction | 0.98 | 9.57 | 0.10 | 28.53 | 23.36 | 1.22 |
| Commerce | 20.06 | 11.66 | 1.72 | 20.20 | 32.81 | 0.62 |
| Services: Govt. & Financial | 8.04 | 7.71 | 1.04 | 32.56 | 50.52 | 0.64 |
| Services: Hhold & Personal | 25.57 | 5.27 | 4.58 | 9.79 | 21.55 | 0.45 |
| Services: Social & Community | 21.08 | 5.44 | 3.88 | 31.57 | 48.03 | 0.66 |
| Transportation & Utilities | 2.17 | 8.63 | 0.25 | 35.26 | 36.19 | 0.97 |
| Not Elsewhere Classified | 0.67 | 0.68 | 1.00 | 27.73 | 43.49 | 0.64 |
| Total Number in Sample | 9,152 | 22,985 | | 10,912 | 23,166 | |

Note:    Earnings are Monthly Earnings in Thousands of 1987 Chilean Dollars (US$1 approximately equal to C$219).

## Table 5.10
### Average Schooling, Tenure and Age by Industry

| Industry | Schooling | | Tenure | | Age | |
|---|---|---|---|---|---|---|
| | Female | Male | Female | Male | Female | Male |
| Agriculture & Fishing | 7.49 | 6.20 | 2.27 | 5.78 | 29.84 | 34.05 |
| Mining | 11.91 | 9.09 | 8.39 | 7.95 | 35.27 | 36.58 |
| Manufacturing | 9.70 | 9.56 | 5.63 | 6.51 | 34.45 | 35.00 |
| Construction | 11.66 | 7.90 | 6.12 | 5.21 | 31.78 | 37.96 |
| Commerce | 9.93 | 9.67 | 4.98 | 6.55 | 35.40 | 35.82 |
| Services: Govt. & Fincial | 12.14 | 11.36 | 4.89 | 6.82 | 32.82 | 35.94 |
| Services: Hhold & Personal | 7.33 | 8.70 | 3.78 | 7.36 | 32.57 | 36.78 |
| Services: Social & Community | 13.55 | 13.04 | 8.20 | 8.77 | 35.02 | 37.16 |
| Transportation & Utility | 11.68 | 9.69 | 7.48 | 7.06 | 33.50 | 37.02 |
| Not Elsewhere Classified | 10.37 | 10.89 | 5.12 | 5.35 | 32.62 | 32.94 |
| All Workers | 9.38 | 8.87 | 5.63 | 6.89 | 34.37 | 36.09 |
| All Non-Workers | 8.24 | 9.26 | 0.76 | 0.68 | 33.37 | 26.66 |
| Total Number in Sample | 32,676 | 32,078 | 9,249 | 23,035 | 32,675 | 32,078 |

Notes:    Schooling is Highest Grade Attained (in Years).
    Tenure is Number of Years Worked at Current Job.
    Age is in Years.

**Table 5.11**
Labor Force and Earnings by Sex and Occupation

| Industry | Percentage Labor Force | | | Earnings | | |
|---|---|---|---|---|---|---|
| | Females | Males | F/M | Females | Males | F/M |
| Professional & Technical | 17.07 | 7.44 | 2.29 | 39.73 | 73.18 | 0.54 |
| Managers & Proprietors | 0.14 | 0.66 | 0.21 | 180.42 | 168.94 | 1.07 |
| Administrative Personnel | 15.68 | 9.14 | 1.72 | 32.30 | 49.47 | 0.65 |
| Traders & Vendors | 15.24 | 8.62 | 1.77 | 20.91 | 31.58 | 0.66 |
| Service Workers | 32.92 | 7.14 | 4.61 | 11.16 | 17.87 | 0.62 |
| Transport Workers | 1.04 | 11.03 | 0.10 | 28.12 | 23.50 | 1.20 |
| Non-Precision Workers | 14.60 | 35.98 | 0.41 | 12.43 | 14.80 | 0.84 |
| Armed Forces Personnel | 0.02 | 0.99 | 0.04 | 51.56 | 44.66 | 1.15 |
| Not Elsewhere Classified | 0.39 | 0.38 | 1.00 | 26.54 | 23.41 | 1.13 |
| Total Number in Sample | 9,152 | 22,985 | | 10,912 | 23,166 | |

Notes: Earnings are Monthly Earnings in Thousands of 1987 Chilean Dollars (US$1 approximately equal to C$219).

**Table 5.12**
Average Schooling, Tenure and Age by Occupation

| Occupation | Schooling | | Tenure | | Age | |
|---|---|---|---|---|---|---|
| | Female | Male | Female | Male | Female | Male |
| Professional & Technical | 14.78 | 14.85 | 8.62 | 8.68 | 34.68 | 37.08 |
| Managers & Proprietors | 14.42 | 12.59 | 11.55 | 15.25 | 40.26 | 45.32 |
| Administrative Personnel | 12.65 | 11.27 | 5.89 | 7.80 | 32.37 | 35.99 |
| Traders & Vendors | 9.86 | 9.56 | 5.11 | 7.02 | 35.23 | 36.62 |
| Service Workers | 7.57 | 7.95 | 3.98 | 4.92 | 33.96 | 35.78 |
| Transport Workers | 9.87 | 8.31 | 5.10 | 6.25 | 31.31 | 36.04 |
| Non-Precision Workers | 8.20 | 6.22 | 4.88 | 5.86 | 34.37 | 34.16 |
| Precision Workers | 8.99 | 8.11 | 3.22 | 5.91 | 33.49 | 36.03 |
| Armed Forces Personnel | 12.00 | 11.09 | 3.53 | 12.11 | 34.43 | 33.93 |
| Not Elsewhere Classified | 9.55 | 9.85 | 5.60 | 7.11 | 31.92 | 32.06 |
| Non-Workers | 8.24 | 8.88 | 0.76 | 0.65 | 33.48 | 26.51 |
| Total Number in Sample | 32,676 | 32,078 | 92,49 | 23,035 | 32,675 | 32,078 |

Notes: Schooling is Highest Grade Attained (in Years).
Tenure is Number of Years Worked at Current Job.
Age is in Years.

However, the wage differential is entirely due to the differential between the earnings of married men and women. For single men and women, the gender earnings differential is insignificant. This is a stronger finding than other studies which find that "discrimination" (difference in coefficients) is--as expected--much less for single than for married workers. In this paper, because information on hours worked is not available, marital status is likely to pick up some of the effect of differences in hours worked by men and women; it is likely that hours worked in the market differ significantly for married men and women, but are roughly equal across sexes for single workers.

*Possible explanations.* Before this earnings differential between married men and women (of about 6000 Chilean dollars per month) is deemed due to discrimination, it is useful to examine the labor market further. The main argument against the discrimination view is that having the same amount of market skills is not enough to ensure that earnings are the same: It is the use to which these skills are put that determines the returns. To examine this question, a logical first step is to study gender differences in the industrial and occupational composition of employment.

Table 5.9 lists the industrial composition of female and male employment and their mean earnings. Females are concentrated in non-financial services, commerce and manufacturing, out of which only household and personal services is an extraordinarily low paying sector. Males are relatively more dispersed, though about one third of all males work in agriculture and fishing. Except in construction, females earn less than their male counterparts in all sectors, with the largest differentials existing in household services and manufacturing (one dominated by women and the other by men).

Table 5.10 lists industry means of schooling, tenure at current job and age. While working women are generally more schooled than working males, they have less tenure, and are younger. Given these levels of human capital across sectors, the earning differentials in manufacturing, social and community services, and commerce seem particularly unjustified. The diverse nature of these three sectors also rules out production function explanations of gender gaps in earnings.

The occupational distribution of female and male employment ratios and earnings (Table 5.11) clearly shows that occupations in which women are concentrated (Professionals, Administrative Personnel, Traders, and Service Workers) are also those that have the lowest female-to-male earnings ratios. Table 5.12 shows that these occupations have the smallest differences in schooling and the largest male-female differences in tenure and/or age. There is no occupation where the schooling advantage of women is not offset by tenure and age advantage of men.

These tables suggest that there are large positive interactions between schooling and work experience (both job-specific and general). The nature of female human capital seems to prevent it from obtaining market returns that are separately due to either schooling or tenure, since average tenure is generally smaller for women, both across sectors and occupations.

## 7. Discussion

This paper analyzed the determinants of work participation and earnings for women and men in Chile. Chile is an interesting case study since male-female differences in health and the levels and types of schooling are not large, but gender differentials in earnings remain significant: The average female worker earns about 30 percent less than the average male.

The main results are:

1.   Provincial variation in key labor market variables is explained almost entirely by the extent of urbanization of the province.

2.   Sample selectivity bias is important for married and single women and married men. The interpretation of the sample selectivity coefficient in the earnings regressions is,

however, different for these three groups, since this depends upon the reason for not participating in work. For married, cohabitating and widowed women, the reason for non-participation is household work, for single and separated women it is both household work and schooling, and for married men it is unemployment or (premature) retirement.

3. Most of the earnings differential is due to lower returns to the observed components of human capital of women, especially schooling. The rate of return to schooling is about 2 to 4 percent lower than that of males.

4. These results can be interpreted to mean that the Chilean labor market discriminates against women. The occupational and industrial composition of female and male human capital and earnings suggests, however, that the returns to schooling are an increasing function of general and job-specific work experience. Since work histories of females are likely to be different from those of men, the results can also be explained in terms of intrinsic differences between female and male human capital.

This study suggests that in studying labor market phenomena, especially for women, it would be more fruitful to concentrate on the collection and analysis of more refined work experience data, than on the issue of sampling bias of observed work histories.

## Appendix Table 5A.1
### Reasons for Not Working: Females, by Marital Status and Age (percent)

| Age Group (Years) | 14-20 | 21-30 | 31-40 | 41-50 | 51-65 | All |
|---|---|---|---|---|---|---|
| **Married, Cohabiting & Widowed Women** | | | | | | |
| 1. Looking for First Job | 1.04 | 0.34 | 0.03 | 0.07 | 0.03 | 0.16 |
| 2. Unemployed | 0.69 | 1.33 | 1.70 | 0.83 | 0.38 | 1.06 |
| 3. Household Work | 94.10 | 95.33 | 94.69 | 90.93 | 71.46 | 88.38 |
| 4. Studying | 3.82 | 1.14 | 0.14 | 0.23 | 0.05 | 0.55 |
| 5. Retired (Pensions, etc.) | 0.00 | 0.31 | 1.53 | 5.55 | 23.36 | 7.36 |
| 6. Rentier | 0.00 | 0.02 | 0.06 | 0.37 | 0.13 | 0.13 |
| 7. Unable to Work | 0.00 | 0.43 | 0.68 | 1.26 | 4.12 | 1.56 |
| 8. Temporarily Inactive | 0.17 | 0.05 | 0.28 | 0.40 | 0.16 | 0.21 |
| 9. Other Reasons | 0.17 | 0.05 | 0.28 | 0.40 | 0.16 | 0.21 |
| Total Observations | 576 | 4,138 | 3,521 | 3,010 | 3,711 | 14,956 |
| **Single & Separated Women** | | | | | | |
| 1. Looking for First Job | 3.19 | 8.15 | 0.51 | 0.00 | 0.00 | 3.91 |
| 2. Unemployed | 1.60 | 11.66 | 15.62 | 6.20 | 3.42 | 5.17 |
| 3. Household Work | 20.41 | 55.20 | 69.27 | 66.67 | 49.05 | 35.24 |
| 4. Studying | 73.26 | 17.58 | 0.00 | 0.00 | 0.00 | 48.35 |
| 5. Retired (Pensions, etc.) | 0.05 | 0.57 | 4.24 | 13.18 | 31.18 | 2.69 |
| 6. Rentier | 0.00 | 0.04 | 0.17 | 0.26 | 1.14 | 0.09 |
| 7. Unable to Work | 1.17 | 4.78 | 7.98 | 10.59 | 13.50 | 3.52 |
| 8. Temporarily Inactive | 0.14 | 1.32 | 1.70 | 2.84 | 1.52 | 0.70 |
| 9. Other Reasons | 0.17 | 0.70 | 0.51 | 0.26 | 0.19 | 0.33 |
| Total Observations | 5,733 | 2,281 | 589 | 387 | 526 | 9,516 |

**Appendix Table 5A.1** (continued)
Reasons for Not Working: Males, by Marital Status and Age (percent)

| Age Group (Years) | 14-20 | 21-30 | 31-40 | 41-50 | 51-65 | All |
|---|---|---|---|---|---|---|

**Married, Cohabiting & Widowed Women**

| | | 14-20 | 21-30 | 31-40 | 41-50 | 51-65 | All |
|---|---|---|---|---|---|---|---|
| 1. | Looking for First Job | 5.71 | 2.99 | 0.57 | 0.00 | 0.00 | 0.60 |
| 2. | Unemployed | 20.00 | 55.97 | 62.29 | 37.23 | 13.24 | 30.35 |
| 3. | Household Work | 5.70 | 6.47 | 7.14 | 4.11 | 2.04 | 3.78 |
| 4. | Studying | 45.71 | 10.20 | 0.29 | 0.00 | 0.00 | 2.17 |
| 5. | Retired (Pensions, etc.) | 5.71 | 2.49 | 9.43 | 38.96 | 68.73 | 45.00 |
| 6. | Rentier | 0.00 | 0.00 | 0.57 | 0.00 | 0.49 | 0.34 |
| 7. | Unable to Work | 2.86 | 5.97 | 6.29 | 10.82 | 11.55 | 9.78 |
| 8. | Temporarily Inactive | 8.57 | 12.94 | 12.29 | 8.44 | 2.82 | 6.63 |
| 9. | Other Reasons | 5.71 | 2.99 | 1.14 | 0.43 | 1.13 | 1.35 |
| | Total Observations | 35 | 402 | 350 | 462 | 1,420 | 2,669 |

**Single & Separated Men**

| | | 14-20 | 21-30 | 31-40 | 41-50 | 51-65 | All |
|---|---|---|---|---|---|---|---|
| 1. | Looking for First Job | 7.80 | 13.56 | 1.50 | 0.00 | 0.00 | 8.49 |
| 2. | Unemployed | 3.59 | 27.33 | 39.50 | 25.38 | 16.41 | 10.35 |
| 3. | Household Work | 1.20 | 2.03 | 3.50 | 5.38 | 3.08 | 1.57 |
| 4. | Studying | 80.24 | 31.59 | 1.50 | 0.00 | 0.51 | 64.15 |
| 5. | Retired (Pensions, etc.) | 0.02 | 1.31 | 7.50 | 21.54 | 45.64 | 2.12 |
| 6. | Rentier | 0.00 | 0.00 | 0.00 | 1.54 | 1.03 | 0.06 |
| 7. | Unable to Work | 2.00 | 11.14 | 35.00 | 35.38 | 26.67 | 6.12 |
| 8. | Temporarily Inactive | 0.62 | 3.60 | 5.00 | 8.46 | 3.59 | 1.60 |
| 9. | Other Reasons | 4.54 | 9.44 | 6.50 | 2.31 | 3.08 | 5.55 |
| | Total Observations | 5,157 | 1,526 | 200 | 130 | 195 | 7,208 |

### Appendix Table 5A.2
#### Work Participation Probit Estimates: By Marital Status
#### Dependent Variable: Work? (Yes=1, No=0)

| | Females | | Males | |
|---|---|---|---|---|
| | Married, Widowed & Cohabitating | Single & Separated | Married, Widowed & Cohabitating | Single & Separated |
| Schooling: 8-11 Years | 0.4224 | -0.11897*** | 0.00808 | -0.20683*** |
| Schooling: 12 Years | 0.36884*** | 0.16961*** | 0.14062*** | 0.01207 |
| Schooling: 13-15 Years | 0.79838*** | -0.10329*** | 0.14190** | 0.49657*** |
| Schooling: 16+ Years | 1.44259*** | 0.45249** | 0.42136*** | -0.22878*** |
| Age: 21-30 Years | 0.33964*** | 1.15493*** | 0.44959*** | 1.37922*** |
| Age: 31-40 Years | 0.57143*** | 1.48150*** | 0.59082*** | 1.68564*** |
| Age: 41-50 Years | 0.44493*** | 1.22799*** | 0.31934** | 1.26741*** |
| Age: 51-65 Years | -0.02334 | 0.53017*** | -0.46811 | 0.87184*** |
| Household Head | 0.51807*** | 0.26280*** | 0.36315** | 0.24247*** |
| Household Income | -7.40e-7*** | 1.53e-6*** | 1.60e-6** | -3.01e-6*** |
| # Household Members | 0.02613** | -0.08746*** | -0.00976 | -0.06455*** |
| # Household Workers | 0.02693* | 0.10835*** | -0.02105 | 0.22930*** |
| Boys: 0-5 Yrs | -0.17739*** | 0.10984*** | 0.03208 | 0.02884** |
| Girls: 0-5 Yrs | -0.17139*** | 0.17180*** | 0.02820 | 0.04274 |
| Boys: 6-13 Yrs | -0.07520*** | 0.07610** | 0.03875 | 0.02510 |
| Girls: 6-13 Yrs | -0.09593*** | 0.11423*** | 0.02089 | 0.01749 |
| Rural Dummy | -0.44907*** | -0.29074*** | 0.30621*** | 0.056517*** |
| Constant | -1.28960*** | -1.06593*** | 0.39812*** | -0.75933*** |
| | | | | |
| Log Likelihood | -8902.2 | -7030.7 | -6836.9 | -7169.4 |
| Chi-Square | 2376.4 | 3612.8 | 1705.5 | 4701.3 |
| Sample Size | 18,844 | 13,921 | 17,063 | 13,824 |

#### Means of Variables

| | | | | |
|---|---|---|---|---|
| Participation Rate | 0.2270 | 0.3309 | 0.8333 | 0.4527 |
| Schooling | 8.2036 | 9.5988 | 8.8207 | 9.3343 |
| Age | 39.9215 | 25.5275 | 41.2932 | 23.3692 |
| Household Head | 0.0989 | 0.1125 | 0.8667 | 0.0602 |
| # Household Members | 4.8804 | 5.4678 | 4.9116 | 5.5600 |
| # Household Workers | 1.3132 | 1.4105 | 0.7449 | 1.4844 |
| # Children: 0-5 Yrs | 0.7219 | 0.6004 | 0.7482 | 0.3920 |
| # Children: 6-14 Yrs | 0.6413 | 0.5812 | 0.6608 | 0.5369 |
| Rural Dummy | 0.1564 | 0.1406 | 0.1625 | 0.2002 |

* Indicates significance at 10 percent level.
** Indicates significance at 5 percent level.
*** Indicates significance at 1 percent level.

## Appendix Table 5A.3
### Female Earnings Regressions: by Marital Status

#### Dependent Variable: Log (Primary Income)

|  | Married, Widowed & Cohabiting | | | Single & Separated | | |
|---|---|---|---|---|---|---|
|  | (13) | (14) | (15) | (16) | (17) | (18) |
| Schooling | 0.1291 (45.84) | 0.1024 (30.16) | 0.0942 (19.43) | 0.1149 (41.05) | 0.1050 (35.06) | 0.0902 (25.62) |
| Age-School-6 | 0.0161 (5.63) | 0.0112 (3.95) | 0.0015 (0.38) | 0.0282 (11.54) | 0.0130 (4.38) | -0.0003 (-0.08) |
| (Age-School-6)$^2$ | -0.0002 (-3.56) | -0.0001 (-1.62) | 0.0000 (0.63) | -0.0004 (-7.12) | -0.0001 (-1.37) | 0.0001 (0.93) |
| Tenure |  |  | 0.0564 (13.13) |  |  | 0.0463 (11.08) |
| Tenure$^2$ |  |  | -0.0014 (-9.42) |  |  | -0.0011 (-8.28) |
| Rural Dummy | -0.0894 (-2.39) | 0.0613 (1.59) | 0.1508 (2.89) | -0.1036 (-2.91) | -0.0207 (-0.57) | 0.0882 (0.71) |
| Lambda ($\lambda$) |  | -0.2002 (-13.55) | -0.1658 (-8.61) |  | -0.1137 (-8.91) | -0.1246 (-9.14) |
| Constant | 8.1103 (149.02) | 9.0018 (106.11) | 8.9183 (75.10) | 7.9659 (191.20) | 8.4284 (127.01) | 8.6360 (115.19) |
| F-Statistic | 810.88 | 706.32 | 372.55 | 489.14 | 413.06 | 268.43 |
| Adjusted R$^2$ | 0.3633 | 0.3832 | 0.4014 | 0.2717 | 0.2825 | 0.2973 |
| Sample Size | 5,768 | 5,678 | 3,879 | 5,234 | 5,234 | 4,426 |

#### Means of Variables

|  | (13) | (14) | (15) | (16) | (17) | (18) |
|---|---|---|---|---|---|---|
| Log (Primary Income) |  | 9.5496 | 9.7222 |  | 9.3757 | 9.4291 |
| Schooling |  | 9.0533 | 10.2287 |  | 9.7254 | 10.0739 |
| Age-Schooling-6 |  | 27.8991 | 22.6173 |  | 16.3219 | 14.3201 |
| Tenure |  |  | 7.1827 |  |  | 4.2581 |
| Rural |  | 0.0865 | 0.0638 |  | 0.0860 | 0.0828 |
| Lambda (Workers/Nonworkers) |  | .8054 | 0.7552 |  | 0.6038 | 0.5956 |

Notes:  t-statistics in parentheses. Primary income is monthly income from main job.

## Appendix Table 5A.4
### Male Earnings Regressions: by Marital Status

#### Dependent Variable: Log (Primary Income)

| | Married, Widowed & Cohabiting | | | Single & Separated | | |
|---|---|---|---|---|---|---|
| | (19) | (20) | (21) | (22) | (23) | (24) |
| Schooling | 0.1358 | 0.1367 | 0.1283 | 0.1150 | 0.1161 | 0.1166 |
| | (82.40) | (84.16) | (73.88) | (45.60) | (44.51) | (40.73) |
| Age-School-6 | 0.0436 | 0.0334 | 0.0174 | 0.0350 | 0.0377 | 0.0394 |
| | (23.48) | (17.71) | (8.23) | (14.90) | (13.06) | (11.98) |
| $(\text{Age-School-6})^2$ | -0.0005 | -0.0001 | 0.0001 | -0.0004 | -0.0005 | -0.0005 |
| | (-15.66) | (-2.23) | (2.73) | (-9.21) | (-8.72) | (-8.51) |
| Tenure | | | 0.0358 | | | 0.0113 |
| | | | (18.73) | | | (3.03) |
| $\text{Tenure}^2$ | | | -0.0006 | | | -0.0002 |
| | | | (-10.57) | | | (-1.76) |
| Rural Dummy | -0.1567 | -0.3103 | -0.2946 | -0.0231 | -0.0112 | -0.0115 |
| | (-9.15) | (-16.97) | (-15.87) | (-1.13) | (-0.52) | (-0.51) |
| Lambda ($\lambda$) | | -0.5094 | -0.5273 | | 0.0173 | 0.0278 |
| | | (-21.88) | (-21.23) | | (1.62) | (2.47) |
| Constant | 8.0727 | 8.3634 | 8.4987 | 8.0769 | 8.0147 | 7.9883 |
| | (249.75) | (242.32) | (227.92) | (218.35) | (150.17) | (139.00) |
| F-Statistic | 2268.77 | 1964.65 | 1490.19 | 635.94 | 509.39 | 345.42 |
| Adjusted $R^2$ | 0.3604 | 0.3789 | 0.4170 | 0.2643 | 0.2645 | 0.2704 |
| Sample Size | 16,096 | 16,096 | 14,574 | 7,070 | 7,070 | 6,506 |

#### Means of Variables

| | | | | | | |
|---|---|---|---|---|---|---|
| Log (Primary Income) | | 9.9664 | 9.9804 | | 9.4134 | 9.4418 |
| Schooling | | 8.8607 | 9.0152 | | 8.8908 | 8.9661 |
| Age-Schooling-6 | | 26.4388 | 24.8246 | | 13.0072 | 12.3514 |
| Tenure | | | 8.4187 | | | 3.3192 |
| Rural | | 0.1647 | 0.0638 | | 0.2672 | 0.2759 |
| Lambda (Workers/Nonworkers) | | .6933 | 0.6388 | | 0.4922 | 0.4828 |

Notes: t-statistics in parentheses. Primary income is monthly income from main job.

# References

Boulding, K. "Toward a Theory of Discrimination." in P. Wallace (ed.). *Equal Employment Opportunity and the AT&T Case.* Cambridge, Massachusetts: The MIT Press, 1976.

Cornwell, C. and P. Rupert. "Unobservable Individual Effects, Marriage and the Earnings of Young Men." Working Paper. State University of New York at Buffalo, 1990.

Gill, I.S. and S.S. Bhalla. "Income Growth and Improvement in Living Standards." Mimeograph. Washington, D.C.: World Bank, 1990.

Heckman, J.J. "Sample Selection Bias as a Specification Error." *Econometrica, Vol.* 47 (1979). pp. 153-161.

Killingsworth, M.R. and J.J. Heckman. "Female Labor Supply: A Survey" in O. Ashenfelter and R. Layard (eds.). *Handbook of Labor Economics.* Vol. 1. New York: Elsevier Science Publishers, 1986.

Mincer, J. *Schooling, Experience and Earnings.* New York: Columbia University Press, 1974.

Oaxaca, R. "Male-female Wage Differentials in Urban Labor Markets." *International Economic Review.* Vol. 14, no. 1 (1973). pp. 693-701.

Stelcner, M.J., B. Smith, J. Breslaw and G. Monette. "Labor Force Behavior and Earnings of Brazilian Women and Men, 1980." This volume, 1992.

United Nations Development Programme. *Human Development Report.* New York: Oxford University Press, 1990.

Willis, R.J. and S. Rosen. "Education and Self-selection." *Journal of Political Economy* (supplement). Vol. 87 (1979). pp. S7-S36.

World Bank. *World Development Report.* Washington, D.C.: Oxford University Press, 1990.

# 6

# Labor Markets, the Wage Gap and Gender Discrimination:
# The Case of Colombia

*Jaime Tenjo*[1]

## 1.    Introduction

Earnings differentials between men and women have been documented in a large number of studies both for developed and developing countries. However, unlike the case of more advanced countries[2], very little work has been done in developing countries to explain why men are systematically paid more than women. In many earnings functions, for example, the introduction of a dummy variable for sex has produced statistically significant coefficients that indicate sizable differences in pay between men and women[3] but very little effort has been made to investigate more thoroughly the source of this differential[4]. Rather, researchers have been more concerned with explanations of differentials between regions (rural-urban), between sectors (modern-traditional or formal-informal) and between industries (agriculture versus manufacture, etc). As explained below, gender wage differentials can be associated with a number of factors such as differences in productivity, working conditions, discrimination, etc. This paper is an attempt to identify the degree to which these and other factors contribute to the explanation of the wage gap between men and women in Colombia.

The structure of the paper is the following: Section 2 presents a discussion of the reasons for the existence of wage differentials in the labor market and the meaning of various forms of

---

[1]      The author wishes to acknowledge the useful comments and support received from A. Berry, P. Bowles, J. Newton and the participants in the Development Workshop of the University of Toronto. The errors remaining are mine alone.

[2]      A summary of the work done in developed countries in this area can be found in Gunderson (1989).

[3]      For a summary of the most important findings of this type of analysis in the case of Developing Countries see Fields (1980).

[4]      Important exceptions are the contribution by Chapman and Harding (1985), by Gannicott (1986), and Schultz (1989).

discrimination. Section 3 introduces a model to measure the earnings gap between men and women and its composition. Sections 4 and 5 present the results of the estimation of the model with Colombian data. In Section 6 a comparison with other country studies is made. Section 7 investigates some aspects of women's access to high paying occupations. Section 8 summarizes and concludes.

## 2.   Wage Differentials and Discrimination

As explained below, two types of discrimination can be identified: market discrimination and non-market discrimination. Both manifest themselves in wage differentials but are generated in very different ways. A brief discussion of these two forms of discrimination and the way in which they are generated is important at this point.

*Competitive markets.*   It is difficult to explain discrimination in the labor market under competitive conditions. In competitive markets wage differences are either temporary or "compensating differentials" that reflect differences in working conditions, workers' characteristics and preferences, or human capital endowments. If women prefer, say, safer jobs, or have lesser amounts of human capital than men, they will, of course, earn lower wages. However, in this case there is no discrimination in the labor market but compensations for differences in productivity or working conditions[5].

However, discrimination can exist outside the market and the result of it be reflected by the market in the form of wage differentials in favor of men. For example, women could come to the market with smaller human capital endowments than men because they do not have equal access to the educational system[6]. Or it could be that the double role of being home-makers and workers make women's investment in education less profitable than men's. Women can also be victims of social practices and prejudices that crowd them into "feminine" occupations (maids, secretaries, teachers, etc). Wages in these occupations would be lower than if women could compete with men in other occupations. Whatever the case, the competitive market reflects discriminatory practices in the society, but is not the source of them. Discrimination takes place outside of the market sphere.

*Non-competitive markets.*   When non-competitive elements are recognized, the possibility of discrimination in the market arises. The following are some examples of market generated wage discrimination:

1.   Market segmentation (formal-informal, modern-traditional, etc.) can occur along sex lines. In this case wage differentials between segments of the market coincides with sex differentials.

---

[5]   Becker's (1957) theory of discrimination allows for the possibility of discrimination in competitive conditions by introducing the assumption that producers maximize their utility which is a function of profits and the sex composition of his labor force. Under this assumption the wage differential against women is the amount necessary to compensate the employer (or groups of influential workers) for the disutility produced by hiring one additional women rather than a man.

[6]   In most developing countries school enrollment ratios and the levels of educational attainment are lower for women than for men. See for example Najafizadeh and Mennerick (1988).

2.   Non-competitive firms may pay wages above the market wage rate in order to lower labor turnover and have a continuous queue of workers available for work. The rationing of these (well paying) jobs can be done on the basis of sex (favoring men over women).

3.   Discrimination can be generated by patriarchal attitudes of non-competitive employers who can decide to pay higher wages to male employees because they adhere to the belief that men have more economic responsibilities than women, or that women are secondary earners.

4.   Information problems may be responsible for discrimination against women. For example, job evaluation procedures can be gender biased or rely heavily on the subjective opinions of male supervisors.

5.   Systemic discrimination against women can exist in the form of gender biased job requirements (height or physical strength[7]) or access to the necessary networks that facilitate the entrance into high paying jobs in the economy.

On the basis of the arguments above, two forms of discrimination can be identified: Market and non-market discrimination. Market discrimination exists when there is a systematic wage differential that cannot be explained in terms of compensating differentials. Non-market discrimination exists when social practices result in women entering the market in conditions of disadvantage relative to men. In both cases discrimination manifests itself as wage differentials but in the case of non-market discrimination the market only reflects the discriminatory treatment of women in other areas of the society. In other words, market discrimination produces a situation in which men and women are remunerated according to different rules while non-market discrimination is more likely to manifest itself in the form of different "productivity factors" (endowments) between sexes.

## 3.   A Model to Measure the Size and Composition of the Wage Differentials

The methodology applied here is well established in the literature[8]. The departure point is the earnings function of the human capital theory. According to this theory the wage rate (W) of a person i can be expressed in the following way:

$$\ln(W_i) = X_iB + E_i \tag{1}$$

where $X_i$ is a vector of explanatory human capital variables representing relevant characteristics of individual i, as well as a set of dummy variables that reflect differences in working conditions and characteristics of occupations; B is a vector of associated parameters and $E_i$ is the error term which is assumed to have mean zero and constant variance across the population. The model can

---

[7]   In some cases these requirements reflect legitimate needs of the job. However, in the modern technological world pure physical attributes have become less important than attributes that can be acquired through training. The retention of these requirements can serve the purpose of limiting the number of job applicants in order to reduce the cost of screening and hiring. The problem is that these procedures, intentionally or not, may restrict the access of women to certain occupations.

[8]   See Gunderson, op cit.

be expanded with the inclusion of other variables (institutions for example) to make it general enough to test the importance of different theoretical explanations of wage rates.

As is well known, the estimation of equation 1 by ordinary least squares (OLS) is likely to produce biased parameter estimates due to the fact that the samples are not random[9]. This problem can be solved by adding to equation 1 the inverse of the Mill's ratio, which is a monotone decreasing function of the probability that an observation is selected into the sample[10]. Equation 1 then becomes

$$Ln(Wi) = XiB + bLi + Ui \qquad (2)$$

where Li is the Mill's ratio and U the error term (assumed to have zero mean and constant variance).

One way of proceeding is to separate men and women and define different wage equations for each group. In this case one has:

$$ln(Wmi) \quad = XmiBm + bmLmi + Umi \quad i = i,...,Nm \qquad (3a)$$

$$ln(Wfj) \quad = XfjBf + bfLfj + Ufj \quad j = 1,...,Nf \qquad (3b)$$

where the subscripts m and f refer to males and females respectively. By doing the necessary transformations, the "corrected" average wage differential between men and women can be expressed in the following way:

$$ln(Wm)-ln(Wf)-(bmLm-bfLf) = (Xm-Xf)Bm + Xf(Bm-Bf) \qquad (4)$$

where ln(Wm) and ln(Wf) are the predicted average wage rates; and Xm, Xf, Lm, and Lf are mean values of the respective variables.

Equation 4 decomposes the wage differential between men and women in two ways: The first term on the right measures the differential due to differences in the amount of human capital and other variables (endowments), while the second term measures the differential due to the application of different remuneration rules (market discrimination). In a competitive market the latter term should be equal to zero and the total differential would reflect only differences in the amount of human capital between men and women or compensating differential between occupations. This difference in endowments, however, can be the result of non-market discrimination. For example, women can have smaller human capital endowments because somehow their access to the educational system is restricted. If market discrimination against women exists, then Xf(Bm-Bf) will be positive[11].

---

[9]     See for example Gronau (1974).

[10]     See Heckman (1979).

[11]     The implicit assumption here is that if no market discrimination existed women would be paid according to the same rules that apply to men (namely Bm). It is possible to argue that this approach overestimates the discrimination component because most likely the parameter of a non-discriminatory situation (call them Be) are between Bm and Bf. In this case the model in the text has to be modified slightly but the essence of the analysis remains the same.

## 4. Wage Equations and Sex Differentials in Colombia

The methodology presented above requires two steps: First the estimation of separate wage equations for men and women, and second, the decomposition of the total differential along the lines of equation 4. This part of the paper deals with the first step while the second step is discussed in Section 5.

The data used in the estimation is a household sample for Bogotá (Colombia) collected by the Colombian Department of Statistics (DANE) in December 1979. The sample includes both labor force participants and non-participants. For the estimation of the wage equations only the sub-sample of wage earners was used, but the selection bias correction is done on the basis of all the sample.

Table 6.1 presents the sample gross earnings per hour differentials between men and women by occupations and types of jobs. According to this table men earn on average 32.7 percent (28 percent in geometric terms[12]) more than women for each hour of work. The differential ranges from 3.23 percent in favor of women in transportation occupations, to 127.8 percent in favor of men among supervisors. In terms of the types of jobs, the highest differential is among white collar workers (32.2 percent in favor of men) while the smallest one is among domestic servants (4.9 percent in favor of women). The special case of domestic servants is analyzed in Section 7. This is a very particular group composed almost exclusively of women (only 2 men versus 349 women in the sample are classified as domestic servants). Serious problems with the quality of the data for this particular group exist.

For the estimation of the model in equations 3a and 3b the following variables were used:

1. Human Capital Variables
   EDUCATION  = Years of Schooling
   EXPERIENCE  = Number of consecutive years in the same economic sector. A quadratic form of this variable was used to allow for the possibility of decreasing returns to experience.
   SENIORITY  = Number of consecutive years in the same firm.
   TRAINING  = 1 if the worker received training in the firm and 0 otherwise.

2. Occupations: a set of dummy variables equal to 1 if the worker is in the respective occupation and 0 otherwise. The occupations are DIRECTOR, SUPERVISOR, PROFESSIONAL, CLERICAL, SALES PERSONAL, and (personal) SERVICE OCCUPATIONS.

3. Other Variables: Another set of dummy variables that are equal to 1 if the worker has the characteristic described.
   UNION =  There is a union in the firm.
   MARRIED =  The worker is married or lives in a common law situation.
   R-MIGR =  The worker has lived in Bogotá for less than three years.

---

[12]    The geometric mean reduces the weight of the extreme positive values, thus producing a lower mean than the arithmetic average. The geometric differential is the difference between the logarithm of the geometric means and is more comparable with the results of the model in sections 3, 4 and 5 than the arithmetic mean.

## Table 6.1
### Average Income per Hour by Occupation and Sex

| | Blue Collar | White Collar | Domestic Servant | Other | Mean (Arithm) | Geometric Mean |
|---|---|---|---|---|---|---|
| **Occupation:** | | | | | | |
| **DIRECTORS** | | | | | | |
| men | | 89.28 | | | 89.28 | 71.90 |
| women | | 76.28 | | | 76.28 | 61.39 |
| % difference | | -17.04 | | | -17.04 | -15.80 |
| **SUPERVISORS** | | | | | | |
| men | 45.39 | 68.49 | | | 59.80 | 40.41 |
| women | 17.52 | 29.75 | | | 26.25 | 32.22 |
| % difference | -159.08 | -130.22 | | | -127.81 | -55.41 |
| **PROFESSIONALS** | | | | | | |
| men | 80.42 | 107.60 | | 155.98 | 190.03 | 79.73 |
| women | | 77.20 | | 755.81 | 81.05 | 59.96 |
| % difference | | -39.38 | | 79.36 | -34.52 | -28.50 |
| **CLERICAL WORKERS** | | | | | | |
| men | 14.70 | 37.53 | | | 37.46 | 24.65 |
| women | | 38.70 | | | 38.70 | 30.69 |
| % difference | | 3.02 | | | 3.20 | 1.26 |
| **SALES PERSONNEL** | | | | | | |
| men | | 37.09 | | | 36.73 | 24.65 |
| women | 11.21 | 19.44 | | | 19.08 | 15.99 |
| % difference | | -90.79 | | | -92.51 | -43.29 |
| **SERVICE WORKERS** | | | | | | |
| men | | 19.20 | 11.76 | | 19.13 | 15.99 |
| women | 18.24 | 17.82 | 12.36 | | 14.51 | 11.75 |
| % difference | | -7.74 | 4.85 | | -31.84 | -30.84 |
| **MACHINE OPERATORS** | | | | | | |
| men | 22.78 | 96.56 | | 16.36 | 25.22 | 20.40 |
| women | 18.64 | 17.84 | | | 18.61 | 15.64 |
| % difference | -22.21 | -441.26 | | | -35.52 | -26.56 |
| **CONST. OPERATORS** | | | | | | |
| men | 19.74 | 13.47 | | | 19.70 | 16.73 |
| women | 12.27 | | | | 12.27 | 11.89 |
| % difference | -60.88 | | | | -60.55 | -34.13 |
| **TRANSPORT WORKERS** | | | | | | |
| men | 18.19 | 22.93 | | | 21.59 | 19.15 |
| women | 19.30 | 43.40 | | | 22.31 | 18.23 |
| % difference | 5.75 | 47.17 | | | 3.23 | -4.90 |
| **OTHER OCCUPATIONS** | | | | | | |
| men | 22.93 | 37.57 | | | 26.38 | 23.57 |
| women | 18.70 | 15.79 | 12.36 | | 17.55 | 16.13 |
| % difference | -22.62 | -137.94 | | | -50.31 | -37.89 |
| **TOTAL** | | | | | | |
| men | 22.92 | 51.17 | 11.75 | 119.72 | 39.73 | 26.35 |
| women | 18.60 | 38.70 | 12.36 | 160.14 | 29.94 | 19.92 |
| % difference | -23.23 | -32.22 | 4.94 | 25.24 | -32.70 | -27.95 |

$$\%difference = \frac{Ywomen - Ymen}{Ywomen}$$

4.    LAMBDA =    The inverse of the Mill's ratio. As indicated above, this variable is introduced to correct the selection bias problem. The details of the estimation of this variable are in the Appendix. In this model the parameters of the variables in (1) can be interpreted as the returns to various forms of "measured" human capital, the parameters in (2) measure a combination of compensating differentials and the effect of some (possible) barriers to entry in some occupations. Finally the parameters of variables in (3), except Lambda, measure the (percentage) wage differential attributable to those variables.

Separate equations were estimated for men, women including servants, and women excluding servants[13] and the results are presented in Table 6.2A and Table 6.2B. For comparison purposes the (selection bias) corrected and uncorrected estimates are included. The statistics are in general good: The adjusted R-squared are above 0.5 (high for cross-section analysis), and most of the parameters are significantly different from zero. Even the parameters with low t-values are interesting because they shed light on important aspects of the functioning of the labor markets.

It is interesting to note that the t-values of Lambda are below the 5 percent significance level for men but not in the case of women, indicating that there is not a serious selection bias problem in the sample of women. As explained in Section 5, the conclusions about the composition of the wage differential between men and women are not very sensitive to this type of correction. In spite of the low t-values of Lambda in the case of women, the effect of the correction is the expected one: It decreases the values of the coefficients associated with the human capital variables such as Education.

The general results of the estimation are consistent with those obtained in a large number of other studies in developing countries[14]. The returns to education are slightly lower than 10 percent, which is the value usually obtained, but this is not unreasonable given the large number of variables included in the model, not available in other cases. What is more important for the purposes of this paper is that there is a clear difference in the estimated coefficients (corrected and uncorrected) of men and women and that the estimates for women are very sensitive to the inclusion or exclusion of domestic servants. The exclusion of domestic servants makes the estimates for women closer to those for men.

In general men have higher returns to education than women and the quadratic form of experience indicates that the returns to additional years of experience decline faster for women than for men. Women receive higher returns to seniority and on-the-job training. Some occupation premiums are higher for men than for women. Such is the case of Directors and professional occupations. Unions benefit both men and women but the exclusion of servants decreases the contribution of this variable. The premium to variables like recent migration (R-migr) and service occupations are not significantly different from zero.

---

[13]    There are two reasons to exclude domestic servants: One is that their measured wage rate is less reliable than in the case of other workers, because a proportion of this payment is in kind (food and shelter). Two, that domestic servants constitute a very particular group of individuals (young, uneducated, female, immigrants) that are not comparable with the rest of the women in the sample. The case of domestic servants will be analyzed in Section 7.

[14]    Good reviews of these studies can be found in Fields (1980) and Psacharopoulos (1981).

## 5.   Size and Composition of the Wage Gap

The average wage gap and its composition, as expressed in equation 4 can be computed directly from the information given in Table 6.2A. Endowments are measured by the mean values of the variables in the model and discrimination by the difference in the coefficients. A summary of these results is presented in Table 6.3.

The most obvious implication of these results is that a large part of the wage differential between men and women is due to the existence of domestic servants and to the fact that they are particularly poorly endowed: When domestic servants are excluded, not only does the total differential drop by about 64 percent, but the endowment component also is significantly reduced (by about 90 percent).

*Contribution of human capital variables.*   It is important to notice that when endowments are measured by the mean values of the variables in the model (Table 6.2A), women (excluding servants) are not at a great disadvantage relative to men: On average they have higher levels of education than men but smaller amounts of other human capital variables. On balance this results in a small negative contribution of human capital endowments to the gross differential. The greatest disadvantage for women in terms of their human capital endowments is their short amount of experience, a result of the double role that they play as homemakers and workers. As indicated above, this can be a result of non-market discrimination, a reflection of individual preferences, or an (endogenous) response to the existence of market discrimination. The lack of better data makes it difficult to carry the analysis any further.

The effect of correcting the selection bias is to increase the total wage differential and the market discrimination component, leaving the endowment component almost unchanged.

Certainly a closer look at the factors that produce these results is of great interest. Table 6.4 presents the contribution of each variable in the model to the total differential in hourly earnings estimated on the basis of the corrected coefficients[15]. The rest of this section considers only the results of the estimations excluding domestic servants (last three columns of Table 6.4). The particular case of domestic servants is analyzed below under "Some International Comparisons."

In contrast with the above results, the contribution of human capital variables to the discrimination component is shockingly large:  The fact that the returns to women's education are lower than those of men is the single largest discriminatory element found in the analysis and has a magnitude larger than the total wage differential between the two groups (10.36 percent versus 9.85 percent).

It is important to notice, however, that given the kind of data used here (the only ones available), not all the measured discrimination component of education can be attributed to actual market discrimination. It is possible that at least one part of it reflects differences in productivity created by differences in the quality and type of education that women receive. If this is the case, the actual market discrimination component is overestimated by the results in Table 6.4, and the non-market discrimination element is underestimated.

---

[15]    The exercise with the uncorrected coefficients was also done and the results do not change dramatically.

## Table 12.2A
### Corrected and Uncorrected Regression Estimates of Wage per Hour Equations

| | MEN | | | WOMEN | | | WOMEN EXCLUDING SERVANTS | | |
|---|---|---|---|---|---|---|---|---|---|
| | MEAN | COEFF | CORRECTED COEFF | MEAN | COEFF | CORRECTED COEFF | MEAN | COEFF | CORRECTED COEFF |
| Intercept | 2.1825 (59.1) | 2.2922 (45.0) | | 2.1675 (41.4) | 2.2712 (24.7) | | 2.1355 (41.5) | 2.2164 (30.9) | |
| Education | 7.547 | 0.0834 (19.7) | 0.0813 (19.3) | 7.141 | 0.0711 (12.0) | 0.0661 (9.59) | 8.161 | 0.0718 (12.0) | 0.0686 (11.0) |
| Experience | 7.038 | 0.0246 (5.82) | 0.0226 (5.33) | 5.557 | 0.0221 (4.21) | 0.0216 (4.09) | 5.412 | 0.0413 (6.19) | 0.0402 (6.00) |
| Experience² | 116.902 | -4.576E-4 (4.21) | -3.656E-4 (3.29) | 76.606 | -4.924E-4 (3.36) | -4.806E-4 (3.25) | 67.389 | -0.0011 (4.87) | -0.0011 (4.72) |
| Seniority | 4.372 | 0.0107 (4.00) | 0.0111 (4.17) | 3.515 | 0.0148 (3.97) | 0.0146 (3.86) | 3.975 | 0.0138 (3.48) | 0.0143 (3.58) |
| Training | 0.228 | 0.0940 (3.13) | 0.0926 (3.11) | 0.141 | 0.1475 (3.33) | 0.1397 (3.11) | 0.179 | 0.1390 (3.35) | 0.1295 (3.08) |
| Director | 0.011 | 0.6288 (5.29) | 0.6400 (5.37) | 0.003 | 0.9858 (3.49) | 0.9817 (3.47) | 0.003 | 1.0112 (3.83) | 1.0075 (3.82) |
| Supervisor | 0.045 | 0.3428 (5.44) | 0.3540 (5.65) | 0.028 | 0.1877 (1.99) | 0.2056 (2.16) | 0.036 | 0.1914 (2.17) | 0.2115 (2.38) |
| Professional | 0.128 | 0.5679 (10.9) | 0.5748 (10.9) | 0.122 | 0.6916 (9.56) | 0.6978 (9.57) | 0.154 | 0.6773 (9.65) | 0.6900 (9.78) |
| Clerical | 0.163 | 0.1387 (3.58) | 0.1475 (3.82) | 0.239 | 0.3054 (5.74) | 0.3070 (5.73) | 0.302 | 0.2942 (5.79) | 0.3000 (5.86) |
| Sales Person | 0.076 | 0.0910 (1.88)a | 0.0818 (1.71)a | 0.078 | -0.0466 (0.73)b | -0.0540 (0.83)b | 0.098 | -0.0485 (0.81)b | -0.0553 (0.91)b |
| Service Workers | 0.090 | -0.2740 (6.12) | -0.2758 (6.25) | 0.358 | -0.1208 (2.66) | -0.1257 (2.75) | 0.188 | -0.0454 (0.94)b | -0.0368 (0.75)b |
| Union | 0.293 | 0.1306 (4.45) | 0.1244 (4.26) | 0.229 | 0.1238 (3.16) | 0.1348 (3.41) | 0.289 | 0.0993 (2.70) | 0.1074 (2.90) |
| Married | 0.627 | 0.2209 (7.65) | 0.1875 (6.13) | 0.318 | 0.0798 (2.39) | 0.0926 (2.60) | 0.398 | 0.0356 (1.10)b | 0.0609 (1.62)a |
| R-migr | 0.109 | -0.0214 (0.54)b | -0.0237 (0.60)b | 0.169 | -0.0454 (1.07)b | -0.0470 (1.09)b | 0.077 | -0.0473 (0.81)b | -0.0461 (0.78)b |
| Lambda | 0.498 | | -0.1426 (2.73) | 0.831 | | -0.0852 (1.31)b | 0.776 | | -0.0892 (1.49)b |
| R² (Adjusted) | | 0.5325 | 0.5316 | | 0.5438 | 0.5417 | | 0.5411 | 0.5389 |
| N. Oserv | | 2,060 | 2,060 | | 1,454 | 1,454 | | 1,151 | 1,151 |

Figures in Brackets are t-values.
a. Significance level between 5 and 10%
b. Significance level above 10%

**Table 6.2B**
Results of the Estimation of a Simple Human Capital Model
(Dependent variable = logarithm of hourly wage)

| | Men | | Women | | Women Excluding Servants | |
|---|---|---|---|---|---|---|
| | Coeff | Corrected Coeff | Coeff | Corrected Coeff | Coeff | Corrected Coeff |
| Intercept | 2.0734 (62.3) | 1.9445 (43.5) | 1.8653 (52.6) | 1.8514 (49.6) | 1.9317 (45.9) | 1.9523 (39.8) |
| Education | 0.1294 (40.6) | 0.1263 (39.6) | 0.1338 (35.3) | 0.1318 (31.0) | 0.1235 (29.8) | 0.1237 (27.9) |
| Experience | 0.1469 (12.8) | 0.0432 (11.7) | 0.0444 (9.36) | 0.0440 (9.20) | 0.0630 (10.4) | 0.0662 (10.1) |
| Experience$^2$ | -0.0008 (7.62) | -0.0006 (6.23) | -0.0009 (5.83) | -0.0009 (5.74) | -0.0014 (6.18) | -0.0014 (6.09) |
| Lambda | | 0.2422 (4.76) | | 0.0430 (0.78) | | -0.0423 (0.55) |
| R$^2$ (adjusted) | 0.453 | 0.455 | 0.479 | 0.473 | 0.476 | 0.471 |
| N. Observ. | 2,144 | 2,144 | 1,489 | 1,489 | 1,177 | 1,177 |

Figures in brackets are t-ratios

*Contribution of occupations.* In this case "endowments" measures the effect of the distribution of men and women across different occupations. The mean values in Table 6.2 indicate that close to two-thirds of the women are concentrated in three occupations: Clerical, Service occupations, and Professionals, and in all three of these occupations women are over-represented. The regression results indicate that clerical and professional occupations receive a premium relative to other occupations, but services are penalized. This indicates that high participation in service occupations is a disadvantage. If women were paid according to the same rules that apply to men, the advantages that women derive from having higher participation than men in clerical and professional occupations is offset by their higher participation in service occupations. This explains why the contribution of "endowments" to the total differential is so small: Two-tenths of one percent in favor of women.

The discrimination component of this group of variables is large and in favor of women (negative sign) indicating that, on average, women receive larger percentage premiums than men in the same occupations. The magnitude of this component is slightly smaller than the total wage differential between men and women which means that if occupational premiums were the same for men and women the total wage differential would roughly double. The large size of the component is due mainly to the difference in premiums in the three occupations where women concentrate.

## Table 6.3
### Decomposition of Sex Wage Gap

| | Market Endowments $(Xm-Xf)Bm$ | Discrimination $Xf(Bm-Bf)$ | Total |
|---|---|---|---|
| **Uncorrected Estimates[a]** | | | |
| Gap Including Servants | 0.2241 | 0.0532 | 0.2774 |
| Composition | (80.8%) | (19.2%) | (100%) |
| | | | |
| Gap Excluding Servants | 0.0716 | 0.0241 | 0.0957 |
| Composition | (74.8%) | (25.2%) | (100%) |
| | | | |
| **Corrected Estimates [a]** | | | |
| Gap Including Servants | 0.2138 | 0.0636 | 0.2774 |
| Composition | (77.1%) | (22.9%) | (100%) |
| | | | |
| Gap Excluding Servants | 0.0184 | 0.0801 | 0.0985 |
| Composition | (18.7%) | (81.3%) | (100%) |

a.   The correction referred to here is the selection bias correction. The estimates are based in results presented in Table 6.2.

Although much more research is necessary in this area, this result is consistent with a situation in which women have (other things equal) higher reservation wages than men and search until they find the job that pays what they expect or drop out of the market. If successful in finding a job, women are likely to receive higher wages than men in similar circumstances. This can be important in occupations such as clerical and service jobs that do not require large amounts of education, and where the actual wage is more closely related to the worker's reservation wage and the amount of experience than to other forms of human capital.

*Contribution of other variables.* The contribution of these variables (Union, Marital Status and Migration) is positive both in terms of endowments and discrimination. The largest effect is that of marital status, indicating that being married represents a higher premium for men than for women, and the proportion of married men is 60 percent higher than the proportion of married women. It should be noted that the variable R-migr is not significantly different from zero in any of the equations.

## 6.   Some International Comparisons

Although the purpose of this paper is not to make  a complete review of the studies on gender discrimination, it is interesting to compare the results of this paper with those for other countries. Table 6.5 presents a summary of selected country studies. The low number of developing countries for which information was found reflects the lack of attention that gender wage differentials have received in these areas. It should also be noted that the methodologies of the studies presented are too different to make them properly comparable and therefore one should be careful not to read too much into these results.

**Table 6.4**
Contribution of the Variables in the Model
to the Wage Differential

| | Including Servants | | | Excluding Servants | | |
|---|---|---|---|---|---|---|
| | Endowments | Discrimination | Total | Endowments | Discrimination | Total |
| Education | 0.0330 | 0.1085 | 0.1415 | -0.0499 | 0.1036 | 0.0537 |
| Experience | 0.0187 | 0.0144 | 0.0331 | 0.0186 | -0.0458 | -0.0272 |
| Seniority | 0.0095 | -0.0123 | -0.0028 | 0.0044 | -0.0127 | -0.0083 |
| Training | 0.0080 | -0.0066 | 0.0014 | 0.0045 | -0.0066 | -0.0021 |
| | | | | | | |
| TOTAL HUMAN CAPITAL | 0.0693 | 0.1040 | 0.1733 | -0.0223 | 0.0386 | 0.0163 |
| | | | | | | |
| Director | 0.0051 | -0.0010 | 0.0041 | 0.0051 | -0.0011 | 0.0040 |
| Supervisor | 0.0060 | 0.0042 | 0.0102 | 0.0032 | 0.0051 | 0.0083 |
| Professionals | 0.0034 | -0.0150 | -0.0116 | -0.0149 | -0.0177 | -0.0327 |
| Clerical | -0.0112 | -0.0381 | -0.0493 | -0.0205 | -0.0461 | -0.0666 |
| Sales Person | -0.0002 | 0.0106 | 0.0104 | -0.0018 | 0.0134 | 0.0116 |
| Service | 0.0739 | -0.0537 | 0.0202 | 0.0270 | -0.0449 | -0.0179 |
| | | | | | | |
| TOTAL OCCUPATIONS | 0.0771 | -0.0931 | -0.0160 | -0.0019 | -0.0913 | -0.0932 |
| | | | | | | |
| Union | 0.0080 | -0.0024 | 0.0056 | 0.0005 | 0.0050 | 0.0055 |
| Married | 0.0579 | 0.0302 | 0.0881 | 0.0429 | 0.0504 | 0.0933 |
| R.migr | 0.0014 | 0.0039 | 0.0053 | -0.0008 | 0.0017 | 0.0009 |
| | | | | | | |
| TOTAL OTHER VAR | 0.0673 | 0.0317 | 0.0990 | 0.0426 | 0.0571 | 0.0997 |
| | | | | | | |
| Intercept | | 0.0210 | 0.0210 | | 0.0758 | 0.0758 |
| Lambda | 0.0475 | -0.0477 | -0.0002 | 0.0396 | -0.0414 | -0.0018 |
| | | | | | | |
| TOTAL | 0.2613 | 0.0159 | 0.2772 | 0.0580 | 0.0387 | 0.0967 |

Note:   Following equation 4, the "corrected" wage gap in Table 6.3 can be obtained by subtracting from the total in this table the values of Lambda.

Source:   Table 6.2.

One of the most interesting observations in the table is that even if domestic servants are included in the comparison, the wage gap estimated for Colombia is one of the smallest by international standards, only the gap in the service industry in the United States is smaller. If servants are excluded, the gap in this paper is by far the smallest. The gap for Malaysia is also lower than most of the differentials for developed countries although slightly higher than the Colombian one. Taiwan presents wage differentials and composition closer to those found in developed countries.

A similar thing happens with the discrimination component. Again developing countries have smaller levels of discrimination than developed ones, whether in absolute or in relative terms.

**7.    Women's Access to High Paying Jobs and the Existence of "Female Ghettoes"**

This part of the chapter deals with two questions: (1) Is there evidence of the existence of dead-end, low paying occupations in which women tend to concentrate ("Female Ghettos")? (2) Do women have equal access to high paying jobs? The answer to the first question is yes and to the second one is no.

*The case of domestic servants.*    The best example of female dead-end occupations that are poorly paid and require long and unregulated hours of work is domestic service. As Table 6.6 shows, domestic servants are almost exclusively women, represent about 18 percent of female employment (23 percent of female wage earners), and almost 60 percent of female employment in service occupations (Table 6.2A). Domestic servants outnumber female blue collar workers. Only clerical occupations employ more women than the occupation of domestic service. A large proportion of domestic servants live with the families for which they work, which means that part of their salary is in kind in the form of room and board[16]. According to one of the few studies of domestic servants done in Colombia[17], this group not only receives the lowest salaries in the market[18] but also has very poor working conditions. Particularly serious is the situation of live-in servants because in practice they do not have a working schedule (basically they are on call all the time) and frequently become victims of physical, psychological, and sexual harassment. The vast majority of women in this occupation are young (frequently in their early teens), uneducated (average schooling 3.3 years) rural immigrants who have little human capital of any type.[19] For many this is their first job and the first time they experience life in an urban location.[20] These characteristics make domestic servants a special case of female occupations that, as explained above, accounts for more than 50 percent of the total wage differential between men and women.

---

[16]    This creates serious interpretation problems with the income figure available, since an arbitrary monetary value is given to the in-kind component of the remuneration of this persons by the families that employ them. Given that it is the employer who "estimates" the value of the in-kind salary and declares the number of hours that she works, the suspicion is that the wage of domestic servants is overestimated. This is an additional reason to present results including and excluding this group of women.

[17]    See Méndez (1985).

[18]    The minimum legal wage for domestic servants is lower that of other workers and they are entitled to fewer legal fringe benefits (for example severance payments and vacation) than the rest of the labor force.

[19]    Even the average educational levels are misleading because in many cases they attended school in rural areas where the quality of education is significantly worse than in cities.

[20]    To my knowledge, no studies have been done to investigate whether domestic service occupations are permanent or temporary. Many people believe that domestic service is a temporary occupation that allows young immigrant women time to acquire the necessary market knowledge to move to other occupations. This, however is not consistent with the fact that domestic servants have higher levels of experience than other women (6.11 versus 5.41 years respectively). Until better information becomes available the best hypothesis to work with is that domestic service occupations are "more permanent" than is believed, or that they are a rather inefficient way of acquiring market knowledge.

**Table 6.5**
**Results from Selected Wage Differential Studies**

| Study | Endowments | Discrim | Total |
|---|---|---|---|
| USA Manufact 1970[a] | 0.320 | 0.389 | 0.709 |
| | (45.0%) | (55.0%) | (100.0%) |
| USA Manufact 1981[b] | 0.129 | 0.283 | 0.412 |
| | (31.5%) | (68.9%) | (100.0%) |
| USA Services 1981[b] | 0.100 | 0.152 | 0.252 |
| | (39.7%) | (60.3%) | (100.0%) |
| Canada 1970[c] | 0.187 | 0.323 | 0.510 |
| | (36.7%) | (63.3%) | (100.0%) |
| Due to: Human Capital | 0.051 | 0.345 | 0.396 |
| Education[d] | (-0.001) | (0.242) | (0.241) |
| Occupations | 0.055 | 0.044 | 0.099 |
| Other Variables | 0.081 | -0.066 | 0.015 |
| Canada 1980[e] | 0.223 | 0.409 | 0.632 |
| | (35.3%) | (64.7%) | (100.0%) |
| Malaysia 1979[f] | 0.280 | 0.046 | 0.326 |
| | (85.9%) | (14.1%) | (100.0%) |
| Taiwan 1982[g] | 0.177 | 0.264 | 0.441 |
| | (40.1%) | (59.9) | (100.0%) |

a.   See Hodson and England (1986).
b.   See Montgomery and Wascher (1987).
c.   Gunderson (1979).
d.   Education is part of the Human Capital variables in the line before. The information in brackets is presented only for comparison purposes.
e.   Miller (1987). This is the only study that corrects for selectivity bias and does it with a methodology similar to the one used here.
f.   Chapman and Harding (1985).
g.   Gannicot (1986).

**Table 6.6**
**Number of Employed Workers in the Sample by Sex and Type of Job**

| | Men | Women |
|---|---|---|
| White Collar Workers | 1,239 | 914 |
| Blue Collar Workers | 890 | 254 |
| Unpaid Family Helpers | 22 | 50 |
| Employers/Owners | 204 | 33 |
| Independent Workers | 673 | 346 |
| Domestic Servants | 2 | 349 |
| Total | 3,030 | 1,946 |

The inclusion of domestic servants in the decomposition of the wage gap has the effect of increasing the total contribution of endowments in a significant manner (from 0.018 to 0.224, Table 6.3) and lowering that of discrimination by less than 2 percentage points. Although these changes are not unexpected, the small decrease in the discrimination component is interesting because it indicates a high degree of stability in this component. Almost all the change in the gross wage gap is due to changes in the endowment component.

The contribution of the human capital variables to the two components of the wage gap (Table 6.4) is also affected by the inclusion of servants. Two points are worth mentioning: One, an increase occurs in the endowments component of human capital variables, almost all of it explained by an increase in the endowments component of education. Two, there is also a large increase in the discrimination component of the same group of variables (about 6.5 percentage points), but in this case the explanatory factor is the increase in the discrimination component of experience (about 6 percentage points).

*Other occupations.* As mentioned above, clerical occupations constitute over 30 percent of the female employment and represents the largest concentration of women in the Bogotá labor market. The definition of this occupation is very broad, including a large number of occupations such as typist, secretaries, receptionists, etc. As in the case of developed countries these are traditional women's occupation that do not offer many advancement opportunities. Something similar can be said about service occupations.

On the other hand, the proportion of women in professional occupations (15.4 percent of the sample excluding servants) is larger than that of men, indicating a significant presence of career oriented occupations available to women. This is consistent with the relative high levels of educational attainment of women and with the relatively low levels of discrimination found in this paper.

One question that arises is whether women have the same access as men do to the high paying jobs within a particular occupation. An answer to this question can be found by estimating the probability that a person receives a wage rate above the average of the occupation as a function of a series of relevant variables, including gender. This was done by estimating a logit equation of the following form:

$$\Pr(W_{ij} > W_j) = h(\text{Education, Experience, M-exper, Seniority, Sex}) \tag{5}$$

where $\Pr(..)$ represents probability, $W_{ij}$ is the hourly wage of worker $i$ in occupation $j$, $W_j$ is the average wage rate in occupation $j$, and M-exper is market experience measured as Age-Education-5. The results of this estimation are presented in Table 6.7.

In general they have the expected sign and are clearly significant from zero. The most relevant conclusion for the purposes of this paper is the negative sign of the coefficient of sex, which indicates that, other things being equal, women have a lower probability of receiving wages above the average in their occupation than men do. In other words, there is a systematic tendency for women to be employed at the bottom of the wage scale in each occupation regardless of their human capital endowments. This implies that although the access of women to high pay occupations is not completely blocked, still women find it harder to move to the top of each occupation.

**Table 6.7**
Logit Estimates of the Probability of receiving
Hourly Wages Above the Occupation Average

| | |
|---|---|
| Intercept | -1.3831 |
| | (11.0) |
| Education | 0.0998 |
| | (9.79) |
| Market Experience | 0.0251 |
| | (5.85) |
| Experience | 0.0077 |
| | (1.20)[a] |
| Seniority | 0.0725 |
| | (8.48) |
| Sex | -0.5725 |
| | (7.85) |

a.    Significance level above 1 percent.
Note:  Figures in brackets are t-values

## 8.    Summary and Conclusions

The analysis above has to be taken as a first approximation to the understanding of the wage differences between men and women in the labor markets of developing countries. The results are interesting and provocative but have to be regarded as tentative until more research can be done. A list of the most important findings is the following:

1.    It was estimated that the total wage gap between men and women is below 30 percent, lower that what has been found in developed countries. If domestic servants (which constitute a very special group) are excluded from the comparison, the differential drops to only 10 percent, indicating a surprising degree of equality between men and women.

2.    As expected, the composition of the gender gap is sensitive to the inclusion of domestic servants. If they are included 77 percent of the gap can be explained by differences in endowments and occupations and only 23 percent by market discrimination. If they are excluded, the market discrimination component constitutes about four-fifths of the total gap, but given that the total gap is only 10 percent, one should conclude that market discrimination is rather small. There is however the possibility that there is a large non-market discrimination component responsible for the large endowment differential.

3.    Although there is evidence of the existence of "female ghettos" such as domestic servants and some clerical occupations, a significant proportion of women have access to occupations that offer advancement opportunities. This is consistent with the relatively small levels of market discrimination and the relatively high educational levels that women have. However, evidence was found that within each occupation men still have better advancement opportunities than women.

## Appendix 6A

### *Selection Bias Correction*

A typical problem faced in the estimation of wage equations such as those in equations 3a and 3b in the text with cross section data is the fact that the sample used is not random. The individuals choose to work as wage-earners on the basis of a number of factors, some of which can be identified. Those individuals who choose not to work as wage-earners do not report wages. In this case, the use of ordinary least squares to estimate the wage equation produces biased estimates.

Heckman (1979) developed a simple methodology to correct the problem which consists of the introduction of the inverse of the Mill's ratio (Lambda) associated with the probability of being in the sample as an explanatory variable in the model. The steps to follow are the following:

1.  Estimate the parameters of the probability that an observation is in the sample using a probit function applied to the whole sample.

2.  Estimate Z according to the following expression:

    $$Z = -Yk \qquad\qquad\qquad (A1)$$

    where Y is the vector of explanatory variables in the probit in point 1, and k is the associated vector of parameters.

3.  Estimate Lambda as:

    $$Lambda = f(Z)/F(-Z) \qquad\qquad\qquad (A2)$$

    where f() is the normal density and F() the cumulative normal distribution.

4.  Use Lambda as a regressor in the wage equations.

*Estimation of probit functions.* Probit estimates of the probability that an observation is in the sample were estimated for each one of the three groups that were compared in the text (men, women, and women excluding servants). Given the differences in the factors that determine the participation of men and women the equations are slightly different. For men:

$$Zm = Gm(lfinc, age, age^2, education, atsh) \qquad\qquad (A3)$$

For women:

$$Zf = Gf(finc, finc^2, age, education, marr, atsh) \qquad\qquad (A4)$$

where lfinc is the natural logarithm of finc, and finc is the income of the rest of the family estimated as the difference between the total family income minus the income of the individual. Atsh is a dummy variable equal to 1 if the individual is attending school and 0 otherwise.

On the basis of the results of the probit estimates equation A2 above becomes:

For men:

$$Zm = 0.9824 + 0.0558lfinc - 0.0902age + 0.0014age^2$$
$$\phantom{Zm = 0.9824 + }(14.8)\phantom{lfinc - }(10.9)\phantom{age - }(12.7)$$

$$- 0.0379education + 1.0248atsh \tag{A4}$$
$$(7.05)\phantom{education + }(17.0)$$

For women (including servants):

$$Zf = 0.8285 + 0.0089finc - 0.0002finc^2 + 0.0102age$$
$$\phantom{Zf = 0.8285 + }(6.39)\phantom{finc - }(4.84)\phantom{finc + }(6.42)$$

$$- 0.1270education + 1.1851atsh + 0.4390marr \tag{A5}$$
$$(21.3)\phantom{education + }(19.5)\phantom{atsh + }(9.72)$$

For women excluding servants:

$$Zfs = -0.1156 - 0.0043finc + 0.00001finc^2 + 0.0198age$$
$$\phantom{Zfs = -0.1156 - }(3.65)\phantom{finc + }(1.99)\phantom{finc + }(13.1)$$

$$-0.0684education + 1.5224atsh + 0.7897marr \tag{A6}$$
$$(12.4)\phantom{education + }(26.2)\phantom{atsh + }(18.1)$$

Lambda can now be calculated and used as a regressor in the wage equations.

# References

Becker, G.S. *The Economics of Discrimination.* Chicago: University of Chicago Press, 1957.

Chapman, B.J. and J.R. Harding. "Sex Differentials in Earnings: An Analysis of Malaysian Wage Data." *Journal of Development Studies,* Vol. 21 (April, 1985). pp. 362-376.

Fields, F. "Education and Income Distribution in Developing Countries: A Review of Literature" in T. King (ed.). *Education and Income.* Washington D.C.: World Bank Staff Paper No. 402, World Bank, 1980.

Gannicot, K. "Women, Wages and Discrimination: Some Evidence from Taiwan." *Economic Development and Cultural Change,* Vol. 34, no. 4 (July, 1986). pp. 721-730.

Gronau, R. "Wage Comparisons - A Selectivity Bias." *Journal of Political Economy,* Vol. 82, no. 6 (1974). pp. 1119-1143.

Gunderson, M. "Male-Female Wage Differential and Policy Responses." *Journal of Economic Literature,* Vol. 27, no. 1 (March, 1989). pp. 46-72.

----- "Decomposition of the Male/Female Earnings Differential: Canada 1970." *Canadian Journal of Economics,* Vol. 12, no. 3 (August, 1979). pp. 479-485.

Heckman, J. "Sample Selection Bias as a Specification Error." *Econometrica,* Vol. 47, no. 1 (January, 1979). pp. 153-161.

Hodson, R. and P. England. "Industrial Structure and Sex Differences in Earnings." *Industrial Relations,* Vol. 25, no.1 (Winter, 1986). pp. 16-32.

Mendez, M. and R. Askew. "The Colombian 'Muchacha del Servicio'". Unpublished mimeograph. Bogota, 1985.

Miller, P.W. "Gender Differences in Observed and Offered Wages in Canada, 1980." *Canadian Journal of Economics,* Vol. 20, no. 2 (May, 1987). pp. 225-244.

Montgomery, E. and W. Wascher. "Race and Gender Wage Inequality in Services and Manufacturing." *Industrial Relations,* Vol. 26, no. 3 (Fall, 1987). pp. 284-290.

Psacharopoulos, G. "Returns to Education: An Updated International Comparison." *Comparative Education,* Vol. 17, no. 3 (1981). pp. 321-341.

Najafizadeh, M. and L.A. Mennerick. "Worldwide Educational Expansion from 1950 to 1980: The Failure of the Expansion of Schooling in Developing Countries." *Journal of Developing Areas,* Vol. 22 (April, 1988). pp. 333-358.

Schultz, T.P. *Returns to Women's Education.* Washington D.C.: World Bank, 1989.

# 7

## Female Labor Market Participation and Wages in Colombia

*Thierry Magnac*[1]

### 1.    Introduction

This paper describes the estimation results of a microeconometric model of female participation in Colombia.  The samples used are drawn from urban household surveys between 1980 and 1985.    The set of exogenous variables includes individual as well as household-related characteristics.  The results are used to assess the power of the modeling strategy in explaining the dramatic increase in female participation rates.  Wage equations are estimated correcting for selectivity biases and compared for males and females.

### 2.    The Colombian Labor Market

The industrialization process in Colombia dates back to the 1930s but a significant increase in the industrial labor force took place in the late 1940s.  Colombia was in those days mainly an agricultural country:  The agricultural sector employed 55.6 percent of the whole labor force in 1951 (Bourguignon, 1986).  GDP growth between 1950 and 1980 had been sizeable despite the "violencia" period in the 1950s and had averaged 5.5 percent in the late 1960s and early 1970s (Sarmiento Palacio, 1984).  This period marked the end of the import-substitution policies, the industrial sector producing 85 percent of consumption goods, 50 percent of intermediate goods and 20 percent of capital goods, consumed in the country (Sarmiento Palacio, 1984).  Export-promoting policies for manufactured goods were then set up but Colombia mostly remained a single-good exporting country where coffee still accounted for 70 percent of exports in 1980, and 50 percent in 1984 (DANE, 1986).

The Colombian economy underwent a crisis in 1974 but quickly recovered because of the booming coffee prices and exports in 1976-86 ("bonanza cafetera").  Inflation soared to 30 percent yearly in 1980.  In this disequilibrium context, the international crisis of 1979-80 hit Colombia very hard.  A severe recession began and lasted at least until 1984 when production got back to its 1980 level although the employment level lagged behind.

---

[1]    I want to thank J. A. Ocampo, Director of Fedesarrollo, Bogota, where I began this work and thank the DANE in Bogota for having given me access to data and computers while I was there.  To be also acknowledged is the help of people in the Laboratoire d'Economie Politique in Paris and especially F. Bourguignon who followed and encouraged this work.  The usual disclaimer applies.

Nevertheless, the history of last twenty years shows that the Colombian labor market has adjusted very quickly. In fact, despite catastrophic predictions by the ILO in 1970 (Misión de Empleo, ILO, 1970) of unemployment rates in the 1980s, the economy and particularly the modern sector succeeded in creating a huge number of jobs in absolute and relative terms. The ILO report correctly predicted the dramatic increase in labor supply but underestimated the labor demand growth. Even if labor demand and supply growth are hardly distinguishable using the aggregate data, some points are worth mentioning. Several factors caused the growth in labor supply. First, the demographic growth rate, though decreasing, was still large because both fecundity and mortality were decreasing. Another factor feeding urban labor supply growth was the continuous flow of migrants from rural to urban areas. Migration only stabilized in the early 1980s when 65 percent of the population was living in towns of 20,000 and above (DANE, 1986). Finally, female labor force participation rates had been increasing in the 1970s and 1980s. The ratio of female to male workers went up from 20 percent in 1964 to 26 percent in 1973 and 31 percent in 1978 (Bourguignon, 1986).

However, the international crisis changed the labor market situation. If the analysis is restricted to the urban labor market (Coyuntura Económica, 1985), it is clear that global participation rate decreased during 1981-82 but went up again in 1983. It shows that the unemployment rate dramatically increased (7.5 percent in 1980 to 7.5 percent in 1985). Labor demand was stagnant or decreasing, particularly in the modern sector, and the number of self-employed soared. The modern sector's wages began to decrease at the end of 1985. High inflation prevailed during this period (20 to 25 percent).

The focus of this study is married women's participation rates, because they seem the most responsive to changing economic conditions. The standard participation microeconomic model (Killingsworth, 1983) is estimated using household data for six consecutive years. Exogenous variables used are individual as well as household-related characteristics. The usual effects are found. Human capital variables positively affect the probability of participation, while the number of children and other household member's incomes act negatively on it. The number of other women in the household have a sizeable impact and capture the likely substitutions in domestic work in the household. The results show that the coefficients are generally stable over time.

The predictions of this model can then be used to assess the power of this participation model in explaining the huge increase in female participation which took place during the period. Even if it explains only 30 percent of the increase, it relates the increase to changes in education and fecundity over the period which corroborates a finding derived from macroeconomic studies. The residual (70 percent) might be attributed either to missing variables determining labor supply or to labor demand factors. Demand and supply are obviously connected to wages. To informally evaluate the impact of the demand factors, some estimation results related to the wage equations during the period are proposed. They are compared to equations for the male household's heads and other members in order to gauge discrimination effects. Some evidence is produced showing that the difference between male and female wages might be biased if the work experience of females is not correctly measured, as is the case in these data.

The plan of the paper is as follows. Section 3 presents a descriptive analysis of female labor participation during the period, a very brief survey of previous studies and the estimation results of the participation models. It concludes by assessing their explanatory power. Section 4 discusses and presents the results of the estimations for the wage equations.

## 3.   Female Labor Force Participation

*Descriptive Analysis.* The data analyzed in this section and the estimation results given in the subsequent sections concern yearly subsamples extracted from urban households surveys undertaken between March 1980 and March 1985 (Encuestas de Hogares, DANE). These surveys are briefly discussed in Appendix 7A along with the method of construction of subsamples which include households composed of a man and a woman aged between 18 and 60, reported as being married or living together.

The labor participation rate of married women, defined as the ratio of those working or currently searching for a job population to the whole population was 22 percent in 1975, 30.5 percent in 1980, decreased to 28.1 percent in 1981 and increased again in 1985 to 35.7 percent (Table 7.1). The decade 1975-85 can clearly be split into two periods, the first being a period of continuous growth (1975-80), the second showing a fall followed by a dramatic increase (1981-85). The married women's participation rate increased much more than the whole population's which went up from 52.5 percent to 57.3 percent between 1981 and 1985. It must also be noted that the married women's unemployment rate, after having decreased between 1975 and 1980, shot up between 1981 and 1985 from 7.5 percent to 15.1 percent. Unemployment expectations apparently did not put off labor market entries between 1981 and 1985. In particular, 1984 saw the largest increase in the two indicators, unemployment and participation, which corresponds with a partial recovery of the Colombian economy after the crisis.

### Table 7.1
#### Participation and Unemployment Rates of Married Women (percent)

| Towns | 1975 | 1980 | 1981 | 1982 | 1983 | 1984 | 1985 |
|---|---|---|---|---|---|---|---|
| **Barranquilla** | | | | | | | |
| P | 15.9 | 21.0 | 22.8 | 21.0 | 25.5 | 26.5 | 24.4 |
| C | - | 5.2 | 7.5 | 7.6 | 6.7 | 9.1 | 10.7 |
| **Bogotá** | | | | | | | |
| P | 25.4 | 34.4 | 27.6 | 33.8 | 32.6 | 40.0 | 41.6 |
| C | - | 9.3 | 6.5 | 8.6 | 8.3 | 15.3 | 17.1 |
| **Medellín** | | | | | | | |
| P | 17.4 | 28.3 | 25.7 | 25.1 | 26.2 | 26.4 | 29.2 |
| | - | 12.4 | 8.9 | 11.2 | 16.4 | 17.4 | 14.4 |
| **Cali** | | | | | | | |
| P | 19.4 | 35.3 | 29.5 | 30.9 | 30.2 | 32.7 | 33.0 |
| C | - | 5.4 | 8.1 | 11.8 | 8.6 | 11.9 | 16.7 |
| **Medium-sized towns** | | | | | | | |
| P | | 26.5 | 37.8 | 28.6 | 38.1 | 41.1 | 40.7 |
| C | | 4.5 | 7.7 | 8.0 | 10.0 | 10.5 | 9.8 |
| **Total** | | | | | | | |
| P | 22.0 | 30.5 | 28.1 | 29.2 | 30.5 | 34.4 | 35.7 |
| C | | 9.4 | 7.5 | 9.5 | 9.5 | 14.5 | 15.4 |

Notes:   P = participation rate (incl. unemployment)
       C = unemployment rate (unemployment/participants)
      Medium-sized towns: Bucaramanga, Manizales, Pasto.

First, differentiating by towns, after a uniform increase of participation rates in every town between 1975 and 1980, the 1981 reduction is quite strong, especially in the three major towns, Bogotá, Cali and Medellín.[2]   Throughout the second period, Table 7.1 shows that the participation rate, which seems unstable in the three medium-sized towns, increased between 2 and 4 percent in Barranquilla, Medellín and Cali, and dramatically in Bogotá.

Thus, Bogotá seems to have been a large generator of employment for married women, even if the 1981 crisis had a strong impact.  It must be recalled that migrations to Bogotá came to a stop in 1975-80.  It might be possible that firms, in particular in the service industry, no longer being able to recruit migrants into their labor force, tried to employ some workers from lower participation groups.  After 1980, labor demand growth is less marked in other large towns because those underwent severe crises, as was the case with the textile industry in Medellín. Bogotá, the commercial, financial and administrative center of Colombia is clearly the one with the greatest potential for growth in the tertiary sector.

Participation rates are clearly positively associated with education level (Figure 7.1).  The two periods are again distinct.  Between 1975 and 1980, labor participation increased uniformly in all groups and the university-degree group's participation rate had risen to 65 percent.  After 1981, the greatest increase in participation rates was among low-level education groups.  Consequently, the participation curve, as a function of education, took on a parabolic form in 1985.

**Figure 7.1**
Married Women's Participation by Education

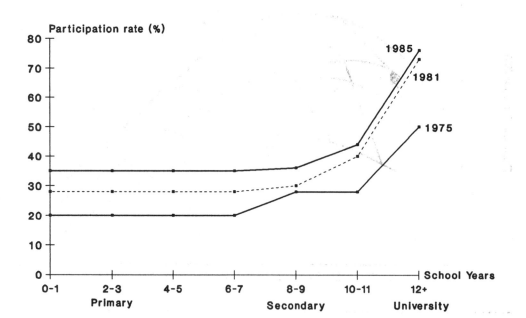

During the second period, the labor supply of different age-groups changed, above all for cohorts aged between 35 and 45 years (in 1985) (Figure 7.2). Arrows in Figure 7.2 show the evolution of participation by age cohorts. If the participation curve as a function of age in 1981 is used to predict the entry-exit flow for cohorts over 30 years, that flow should be negative. In fact, it was positive, as was the case for cohorts aged less than 45 years in 1985. Married women stayed in the labor market longer than previous generations. This evolution was quite similar between 1975 and 1980 when the increase had mainly been noticeable for cohorts between 25 and 35 years. Figure 7.3 clearly shows that the 1980 crisis made young women withdraw from the labor force, but they reentered the market as soon as the crisis waned.

The models estimated in the following sections make use of some exogenous variables related to individual and household characteristics of married women. It is useful to describe the evolution of these variables as presented in Tables 7.2 and 7.3. The most worthy points in Table 7.3 are the following: First, the number of persons per household decreased, mainly because of a diminishing number of children and teenagers. This is a consequence of the decrease in fecundity in Colombia since 1970. At the same time the number of adult men and women remained stable.

**Figure 7.2**
Participation Rate by Age Group and Cohort

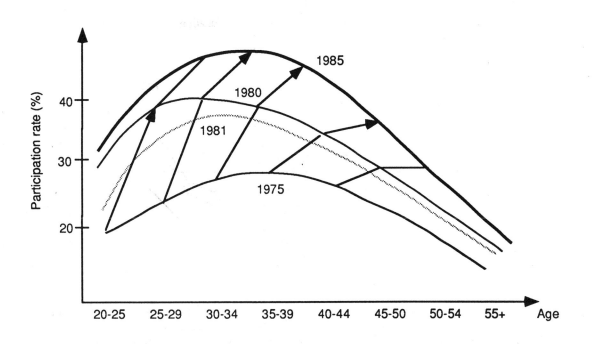

**Figure 7.3**
Potential and Reservation Wages

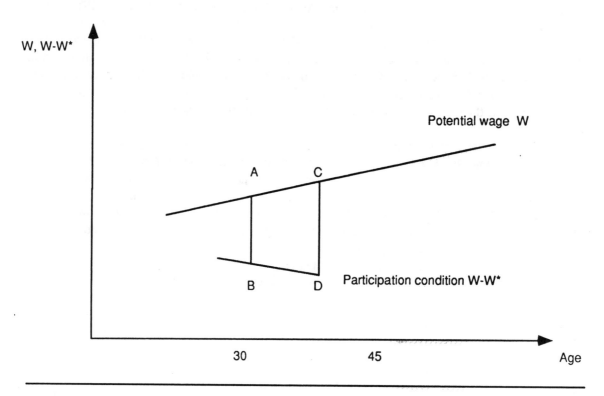

**Table 7.2**
Individual Characteristics

| Variable | 1981 | 1982 | 1983 | 1984 | 1985 |
|----------|------|------|------|------|------|
| EDUC | 10.9 | 11.4 | 11.6 | 11.7 | 11.8 |
|  | (3.6) | (3.0) | (2.9) | (2.9) | (3.3) |
| AGE | 35.4 | 35.4 | 35.4 | 35.6 | 35.8 |
|  | (11.1) | (8.3) | (8.1) | (8.2) | (9.2) |
| AG | 40.9 | 41.0 | 41.1 | 41.3 | 41.2 |
|  | (12.7) | (9.5) | (9.4) | (9.3) | (10.5) |
| EDUM | 11.5 | 12.0 | 12.3 | 12.2 | 12.3 |
|  | (4.3) | (3.5) | (3.4) | (3.4) | (3.8) |

Notes: Standard errors are in parentheses. EDUC, EDUM = years of education (wife and husband), AGE, AGM (wife's and husband's age)

Second, there is a significant increase in the ratio of active to inactive women in the household, from .42 to .51. This is mainly due to the entry of married women into the labor market. Third, the unemployment rate, defined in this case as the ratio of unemployed to active adults in the household, went up from 6 percent in 1981 to 9.5 percent in 1985 for men, and from 10.5 percent to 14.5 percent for women. The unemployment rate in those households reached 10.7 percent in 1985, in comparison to a global unemployment rate in the population equal to 7.1 percent.

Thus, these households were seemingly less affected by unemployment than households headed by a lone person. This confirms the findings of previous studies of unemployed people (Ayala, 1981). However, this effect may also be interpreted as a selectivity effect on household size, because the subsamples under study comprise larger households. Also, other variables may be related to the sample selection rule and be correlated to the unemployment probability.

Concluding, it is clear that the number of active persons remained stable while the unemployment rate had increased, that is to say the labor supply of these families grew without more members being employed. Nevertheless, there is also some substitution between active women and active men. This has, as usual, two possible meanings. First, a supply effect if women begin to work because men are more affected by unemployment (the additional worker effect). Second, a demand effect if firms systematically replace men by women or if firms employing women (e.g. in the service industry) are growing faster than others (e.g. manufacturing). It might also be a consequence of discrimination if women earn less than men with equal productivity. In the subsequent sections we will have the opportunity to confirm the demand effect.

*Estimation of female labor force participation models.* Few studies of female labor supply in Colombia in the literature have been conducted. These include studies by de Gómez et al. (1981), Castañeda (1981), Bourguignon (1981) and Caillavet (1981). The paper by de Gómez et al. (1981) used data from the 1973 Census and data from one of the urban household surveys (December 1980). (Table 7.3)

The estimated model consists of joint labor supply equations for husband and wife with wages as regressors.[3] The study by Castañeda is concerned by the relationship between fecundity and participation. The data used come from one of the urban household surveys (June 1977). The method used is a probit estimation. The third study (Bourguignon, 1981) deals with a simultaneous estimation of married women's participation and use of servants at home. Some regression results of participation on exogenous variables are given although they are not the focus of the paper. The paper by Caillavet (1981) gives the results of the estimation of participation functions for household heads and their spouses using data from the urban household surveys in 1975 and 1978.

Summing up the results across these papers, which investigate different points related to labor supply, it is generally agreed that the own wage effect on labor supply is positive for women while husband's wage has a negative impact. This conforms with the usual income effect and implies that leisure is a normal good. Additionally, the usual effects are found. Human capital variables have a positive impact on labor supply while the effect of children is clearly negative. However, it must be noted that, except in the Castañeda (1981) study, these results are plagued by selectivity biases.

---

[3]    Wages are regressed on the usual human capital variables.

**Table 7.3**
Household Composition

| | 1981 | 1982 | 1983 | 1984 | 1985 |
|---|---|---|---|---|---|
| **Children** | | | | | |
| 0-3 | 0.55 | 0.53 | 0.52 | 0.50 | 0.48 |
| 4-12 | 1.13 | 1.12 | 1.03 | 1.05 | 1.03 |
| **Women** | | | | | |
| Active | 0.38 | 0.39 | 0.40 | 0.41 | 0.42 |
| Unemployed | 0.040 | 0.035 | 0.039 | 0.058 | 0.061 |
| **Students** | | | | | |
| 13-18 | 0.38 | 0.37 | 0.35 | 0.36 | 0.34 |
| 19+ | 0.019 | 0.027 | 0.025 | 0.029 | 0.026 |
| **Inactive** | | | | | |
| 13-18 | 0.057 | 0.060 | 0.048 | 0.048 | 0.046 |
| 19-60 | 0.90 | 0.89 | 0.88 | 0.85 | 0.84 |
| 60+ | 0.042 | 0.041 | 0.041 | 0.045 | 0.043 |
| **Men** | | | | | |
| Active | 1.23 | 1.21 | 1.18 | 1.16 | 1.18 |
| Unemployed | 0.073 | 0.077 | 0.096 | 0.10 | 0.11 |
| **Students** | | | | | |
| 13-18 | 0.34 | 0.32 | 0.32 | 0.30 | 0.29 |
| 18+ | 0.026 | 0.031 | 0.030 | 0.030 | 0.030 |
| **Inactive** | | | | | |
| 13-18 | 0.022 | 0.020 | 0.020 | 0.020 | 0.018 |
| 19-60 | 0.11 | 0.12 | 0.11 | 0.115 | 0.11 |
| 60+ | 0.012 | 0.010 | 0.009 | 0.010 | 0.010 |
| **Total** | 5.32 | 5.26 | 5.10 | 5.09 | 5.04 |
| **N** | 5,585 | 10,505 | 11,535 | 11,526 | 9,741 |

Note:  N = number of observations.

To clarify things, the married women's participation model is briefly presented here. It must be borne in mind that this is a reduced model that can be derived from assumptions on preferences of the agents. The aim here is not to estimate the elasticity of labor supply with respect to wages, but to permit a descriptive analysis of female labor force participation.[4]

---

[4]  Some attempts have been made to estimate hours of work equations (Magnac, 1987) but the results mainly point out that the elasticity is nonsignificantly different from 0 as far as workers are concerned. The main flexibility here comes from participation and non-participation.

The basic model of labor participation (Killingsworth, 1983) states:

Participation if        $w - w^* > 0$
Non-participation if    $w - w^* < 0$

where w is the potential or market hourly wage and $w^*$ the reservation or asked wage.

Two additional equations are specified:

$$\log(w) = X\beta + u$$
$$\log(w^*) = Z\tau + v$$

The first equation, the wage equation, relates the logarithm of the hourly wage rate to human capital variables (X). The second equation, the reservation wage equation, is derived from the preferences of the married women and depends either on personal or household characteristics.[5]

If u and v, conditional on X and Z, are supposed binormally distributed, the estimation strategy to get consistent estimators is Probit and the reduced form model comprises variables X and Z.

This model was estimated using six subsequent years (1980-85) keeping the same set of exogenous variables. The households' characteristics retained in the present specification have been chosen for their significance among a large number of explicative variables (Appendix 7B).

These exogenous variables are the following:

*Human capital variables:*[6]
EDUC completed years of education
EXP work experience which is not reported in the survey and which is approximated here by age minus education
EXP2 work experience squared

*Household's characteristics:*[7]
IMAR husband's income in thousands of pesos (constant 1981)
DM dummy variable equal to 1 in case of non-reported husband's income
IOTR other household members' income in 1,000 pesos
D number of other household members' non-reported incomes

---

[5]    This set-up is called the male chauvinistic model because it assumes that the married woman is the last to choose in the family. Or similarly that she had well-defined preferences conditional on all other variables. The interpretations we are going to propose here assume that household organization and decisions to work by other members is given and that it is not made simultaneously with the married woman's decision to work. This is a disputable assumption but an instrumental variable procedure to correct these biases is out of the scope of the present paper.

[6]    Influence the potential wage function (X) and possibly preferences as well.

[7]    Incomes are real incomes computed by deflating nominal incomes by an aggregate consumption price index (DANE, 1986).

*Household composition.*[8]
>    E1 number of children between 0 and 1 year
>    E2 number of children between 1 and 3 years
>    HST1 number of male students between 12 and 18
>    HST2 number of male students over 18
>    FST2 number of female students over 18
>    HDE number of unemployed male adults
>    MJI number of inactive women between 12 and 18
>    MAI number of inactive women between 18 and 60
>    MVI number of inactive women over 60

In the specification, dummy variables for towns were added to this list in order to correct first for some sampling effects in different years and, secondly, to take into account the fact that female participation depends on the unique economic development and labor demand determinants in each town.

All estimation results are given in Table 7.4. The coefficients of the human capital variables (EDUC, EXP, EXP2) are significant and stable across time. Differences are not significant across years. From these estimates can be deduced that the highest point of the predicted participation curve as a function of age is around 30 years although it varies slightly across time in the interval 28 to 33. It is largely before the highest point in the wage equation function. This implies that the reservation wage increases strongly after 30 as represented in Figure 7.3, since AB > CD. This can be attributed to changes in the domestic production function when the woman ages and acquires a larger relative productivity in comparison to the other members. Specialization in domestic work is important at this age. This can also be related to generation or cohort effects if there are systematic differences in the division of domestic work across generations. Unfortunately, a cross-section analysis does not permit us to distinguish between the two interpretations.

The husband's income effect is significant (except in 1981) and negative as expected. However it is unstable (1981-82) and the differences are significant. Strong interactions with other composition variables might be responsible for this instability. Similarly, the other members' income effect has the expected negative sign. Dummy variables for non-reporting errors are significant and negative only for other members. This confirms that other members' income effect is much larger than the husband's. As the estimated model is a reduced form, this income effect might take into account substitution effects between the married woman's labor supply and other potential workers in the household. The substitution with the household head is *a priori* smaller. Nevertheless, variables such as the number of active members in the household have proved to be nonsignificant (Appendix 7B).

Among the household's composition variables, the effect of children aged between 0 and 3 is largely significant as expected. The opportunity cost of the married woman's time increases when she has young children. Additionally, the influence of the numbers of inactive women on the participation probability is positive and significant. This is clearly related to substitutions in domestic work within the household between women. If the married woman works outside the

---

[8]   The married woman is clearly not included in these comments.

**Table 7.4**
**Probit Estimation Results of the Labor Participation Model**

|           | 1980      | 1981      | 1982      | 1983      | 1984      | 1985      |
|-----------|-----------|-----------|-----------|-----------|-----------|-----------|
| Intercept | -1.09     | -0.94     | -1.15     | -0.74     | -0.68     | -0.90     |
| Educ      | 0.061     | 0.065     | 0.065     | 0.064     | 0.057     | 0.062     |
|           | (9.2)     | (9.9)     | (9.9)     | (15.1)    | ( 7.6)    | (14.0)    |
| Exp       | 0.020     | 0.022     | 0.021     | 0.019     | 0.017     | 0.026     |
|           | (2.5)     | (3.0)     | (3.9)     | (3.9)     | (3.5)     | (4.9)     |
| $Exp^2$   | -0.00058  | -0.00051  | -0.00055  | -0.00051  | -0.00054  | -0.00059  |
|           | (4.2)     | (3.9)     | (5.7)     | (5.8)     | (6.1)     | (6.2)     |
| Imar      | -0.020    | -0.0050   | -0.012    | -0.023    | -0.022    | -0.024    |
|           | (1.9)     | (0.5)     | (2.9)     | (2.5)     | (3.5)     | (4.6)     |
| Dm        | -0.09     | 0.0026    | -0.020    | -0.043    | -0.13     | 0.004     |
|           | (1.9)     | (0.05)    | (0.6)     | (1.2)     | (2.9)     | (0.0)     |
| Iotr      | -0.063    | -0.049    | -0.113    | -0.102    | -0.082    | -0.080    |
|           | (2.9)     | (1.9)     | (5.8)     | (6.1)     | (4.4)     | (5.2)     |
| d         | -         | -0.13     | -0.10     | -0.077    | -0.11     | -0.15     |
|           |           | (2.2)     | (2.9)     | (2.1)     | (2.2)     | (2.3)     |
| E1        | -0.23     | -0.22     | -0.27     | -0.24     | -0.25     | -0.21     |
|           | (5.3)     | (5.0)     | (8.2)     | (7.5)     | (8.0)     | (6.0)     |
| E2        | -0.11     | -0.11     | -0.13     | -0.12     | -0.14     | -0.10     |
|           | (2.7)     | (2.5)     | (4.4)     | (4.4)     | (5.0)     | (3.3)     |
| HST1      | -0.026    | -0.077    | -0.026    | -0.039    | -0.026    | -0.016    |
|           | (0.8)     | (2.6)     | (1.2)     | (1.9)     | (1.3)     | (1.7)     |
| HST2      | -0.03     | -0.21     | -0.17     | -0.21     | -0.22     | -0.17     |
|           | (0.4)     | (1.8)     | (2.4)     | (3.2)     | (3.2)     | (2.4)     |
| MST2      | -0.10     | -0.19     | -0.23     | -0.18     | -0.15     | -0.05     |
|           | (1.6)     | (1.3)     | (2.7)     | (2.6)     | (2.1)     | (0.6)     |
| HDE       | -0.020    | -0.024    | -0.104    | -0.11     | -0.047    | -0.17     |
|           | (0.3)     | (0.3)     | (1.8)     | (2.4)     | (1.1)     | (3.4)     |
| MJI       | 0.26      | 0.22      | 0.16      | 0.29      | 0.29      | 0.25      |
|           | (4.9)     | (3.0)     | (3.3)     | (5.6)     | (5.7)     | (4.3)     |
| MAI       | 0.36      | 0.10      | 0.15      | 0.15      | 0.11      | 0.17      |
|           | (5.0)     | (1.9)     | (3.9)     | (4.3)     | (2.9)     | (4.3)     |
| MVI       | 0.29      | 0.14      | 0.37      | 0.21      | 0.22      | 0.14      |
|           | (3.3)     | (1.7)     | (5.9)     | (3.4)     | (3.8)     | (2.1)     |
| BARRANQ.  | -0.17     | -0.60     | -0.40     | -0.64     | -0.49     | -0.61     |
|           | (1.5)     | (5.7)     | (6.0)     | (10.2)    | (7.8)     | (9.6)     |
| BUCARAM.  | 0.01      | -0.11     | -0.16     | -0.44     | -0.34     | -0.37     |
|           | (0.1)     | (1.0)     | (1.9)     | (5.7)     | (4.4)     | (5.1)     |
| Bogotá    | -0.04     | -0.43     | -0.037    | -0.48     | -0.17     | -0.15     |
|           | (0.3)     | (4.5)     | (0.7)     | (8.9)     | (3.1)     | (2.8)     |

- continued

**Table 7.4** (continued)
Probit Estimation Results of the Labor Participation Model

|  | 1980 | 1981 | 1982 | 1983 | 1984 | 1985 |
|---|---|---|---|---|---|---|
| Manizales | -0.56 | -0.56 | -0.43 | -0.78 | -0.28 | -0.43 |
|  | (3.9) | (4.4) | (4.6) | (8.8) | (3.4) | (5.4) |
| Medellín | -0.17 | -0.52 | -0.27 | -0.62 | -0.50 | -0.47 |
|  | (1.5) | (5.0) | (4.2) | (10.1) | (7.9) | (7.4) |
| Cali | -0.43 | -0.39 | -0.90 | -0.50 | -0.35 | -0.36 |
|  | (3.9) | (3.9) | (1.3) | (8.3) | (5.8) | (5.9) |
| N | 5,215 | 5,585 | 10,505 | 11,535 | 11,526 | 9,741 |
| LOGV | -3014.3 | -3167.8 | -6003.3 | -6735.5 | -7040.5 | -6004.5 |
| LOGV/N | -0.578 | 0.567 | -0.571 | -0.584 | -0.610 | -0.616 |
| SRV | 386.2 | 328.0 | 681.9 | 717.9 | 756.4 | 686.8 |

Notes:   The labor participation status (1,0) is the dependent variable.  Exogenous variables are defined in the text.
N = number of observations
LOGV = log-likelihood
LOGV/N = mean log-likelihood
SRV = likelihood ratio statistic (Ho: all parameters (22) are equal to 0 except the intercept.  SRV distribution is asymptotically $\chi^2(22)$ under Ho.
T-statistics are shown in parentheses.

house, then other women take charge of the domestic work.  The effect of a young or old woman is much stronger.[9]

The negative effect of the number of unemployed men in the household, though unstable, looks as if an expected income interpretation would be needed instead of the usual additional or discouraged worker effects.  Since it is negative, the additional worker interpretation can be discarded.  However, as the presence of an unemployed woman does not matter much, the discouraged worker hypothesis would imply that the married woman assesses her opportunities to get a job by looking at the men's unemployment rate and not at woman's.  This is unlikely.  Moreover, the difference between the coefficients of the dummy variable for non-reported other members' income and of the number of unemployed male adults is not significant.  This effect could then be related to a missing income.  However, this coefficient is the result of these three effects.  Going back to the hypothesis proposed previously to explain the increase in the ratio of active women to active men, the demand effect seems to be the most likely interpretation since the supply effect (additional worker) seems to be hardly noticeable.

It is more difficult to interpret the effect of the presence of students in the family (HST1, HST2, MST2).  These effects are negative and significant in most cases.  It belies the thesis that married

---

[9]   The effect of active men is not significant (Appendix 13.2) which confirms the findings of Caillavet (1981) about men's non-participation in domestic work.

women work in order to pay for their children's education.[10]  These effects can have two economic meanings.[11]  An income-effect (of children), expected in the short run, is real since many students work.  It can be noticed that the presence of girls going to school is not significant although it is for boys.  A tentative explanation would be that for girls two effects are combined: The first one similar to boys which is negative, and the second, a positive substitution effect similar to young inactive women's (MJI).  But the instability of the result makes this interpretation shaky.

The last group of variables are the geographic dummy variables.[12]  Several groups can be distinguished.  Barranquilla, Manizales and Medellín have low participation rates.  Bucaramanga, Bogotá and Cali belong to the medium range below Pasto where participation rates are the highest.  The parallel evolution of global participation rates by towns and the coefficients of dummy variables must be noted.  Table 7.5 presents the results for Bogotá.

**Table 7.5**
Differences in Participation Rates and Dummy Variable Coefficients for Bogotá

|  | 1980 | 1981 | 1982 | 1983 | 1984 | 1985 |
|---|---|---|---|---|---|---|
| Differences in participation rates with Pasto (percent) | 1.1 | -15.4 | 1 | -14.5 | -3.6 | -4.4 |
| Coefficient of Bogotá | -0.04 | -0.43 | -0.04 | -0.48 | -0.17 | -0.15 |

These results show that the estimated model explains very little of the difference between participation rates in different towns.  These variables partly control for sampling biases, above all in a small sample like Pasto, but these effects are very unstable.  They might also show different evolutions of labor demands in the different towns.  For example, the labor market in Pasto depends heavily on the economic relationship with the neighbor country, Ecuador, which tended to deteriorate in 1984 and 1985 after the Andes pact was called off.

To sum up these results, the predicted participation variation as a function of factors can be computed at the mean sample point (Table 7.6).  This table is just another way of presenting Table 7.4 and does not need further comment.  In conclusion, if this model shows some classical and expected effects, such as the influence of human capital variables, children or incomes, it reveals also strong substitution effects within the household and sets forth the importance of the household organization on the probability of the married woman's participation.

---

[10]    In surveys where married women are asked their reasons for working the second most common answer is "to pay for my children's education" (Gutiérrez de Pineda (1975)).

[11]    No doubt the simultaneity of education decisions and the decision to work is likely to play an important role.  For example, the presence of students in the household corresponds to ages when the married woman leaves the labor market.

[12]    The missing dummy is related to Pasto where the participation rate is high.

**Table 7.6**
Participation Probability Variation as a Function of Variables
(for an additional unit with initial probability equal to
the 1983 participation rate)
(in percent)

|         | 1981    | 1982    | 1983    | 1984    | 1985    |
|---------|---------|---------|---------|---------|---------|
| Educ    | +8**    | +7**    | +8**    | +7**    | +7**    |
| Imar    | -0.6    | -14**   | -2.6**  | -2.5**  | -2.8**  |
| Iotr    | -6      | -10**   | -7**    | -9**    | -9**    |
| E1      | -26**   | -31**   | -27**   | -29**   | -24**   |
| E2      | -13*    | -15**   | -14**   | -16**   | -12**   |
| HST1    | -9*     | -3      | -4      | -3      | -2      |
| HST2    | -25     | -19*    | -24**   | -25**   | -20*    |
| MST2    | -22     | -26**   | -21**   | -17*    | -5      |
| HDE     | -3      | -12     | -13*    | -5      | -20*    |
| MJI     | +26**   | +18**   | +33**   | +33**   | +29**   |
| MAI     | +12     | +17**   | +17**   | +13**   | +20**   |
| MVI     | 16      | +42**   | +24**   | +25**   | +16*    |

Note:  Significance of coefficients at 5%(*) or 1%(**)

The data and the estimates cannot be used to assess the explanatory power of this model.  As we could not estimate this model on stacked data for 1980 to 1985, the following subsection proposes a simple decomposition of the various effects of those variables during the period 1981-85.  It will allow us to distinguish more clearly the supply and demand effects.

*Explanatory power of the model in forecasting participation rates.*  The probit results have shown that the model was rather stable during the period.  Despite this fact, the explanatory power of these models are usually low (Killingsworth, 1983).  However, these results can be used for short-term predictions of participation rates.  As our purpose is to test the predictive ability of the model in a context of very large increases in female labor participation, we computed forecasts of the participation rate in every year using the coefficients related to another year. Table 7.7 shows the following values:[13]

$$\hat{p}_{ij} = E_k \left( F(X_{ik} b_j) \right) \cong \frac{1}{N_i} \Sigma^i \sum_{k=1}^{n} F(X_{ik} \, b_j)$$

---

[13]  The analysis here is restricted to years 1981 to 1985 because of the non-simultaneous availability of the 1980 and other surveys.

where i is an index of the year for which the prediction is computed, j is an index of the set of the estimated coefficients, $b_j$, related to year j, $N_i$ is the number of observations in each year, $X_k$ are the exogenous variables for year i and observation K, and F(.) is the cumulative distribution function of a standard normal variate.

It clearly appears that changes in the exogenous variables explain little of the global increase in participation rates. The predicted increase belongs to the interval 1.8 percent (1981) and 2.9 percent (1982) much less than the actual increase of 7.8 percent. It implies that more than 60 percent of this increase may be attributed to changes in the estimated coefficients. Stern and Gomulka (1990) proposed to distinguish the comparative effects upon participation rates of changes in exogenous variables and changes in the coefficients. The difference between the estimated participation rates can be written:

$$
\begin{aligned}
P_{1985} - P_{1981} \quad &= \quad E\ (F(X_{1985}b_{1985})) - E(F(X_{1985}b_{1981})) + E\ (F(X_{1985}b_{1981})) - \\
&\qquad E\ (F(X_{1981}b_{1981})) \\
&= \quad \text{changes in variables} + \text{changes in coefficients}
\end{aligned}
$$

using the same notations as before.

It can be computed by groups of variables and the results appear in Table 7.8.[14] It appears that changes in variables determining the increase in participation are mainly due to increases in mean education and to the decreases of the number of children below 3 years. The income effects are small. On the other hand, changes in the coefficients mainly come from the coef-ficient for Bogotá. This barely explains the sizeable increase of labor participation in that town.

**Table 7.7**
**Predictions of Participation Rates Using Different**
**Sets of Coefficients**

| Coefficients of: | 1981 | 1982 | 1983 | 1984 | 1985 |
|---|---|---|---|---|---|
| Data: | | | | | |
| 1981 | 0.280 | 0.283 | 0.288 | 0.325 | 0.340 |
| 1982 | 0.294 | 0.298 | 0.307 | 0.337 | 0.360 |
| 1983 | 0.297 | 0.301 | 0.310 | 0.342 | 0.361 |
| 1984 | 0.302 | 0.306 | 0.309 | 0.350 | 0.361 |
| 1985 | 0.307 | 0.312 | 0.309 | 0.350 | 0.358 |

Note:   At intersection (i.i) the actual rates are asymptotically close to the predicted rates.

---

[14]   Another (symmetric) decomposition exists. Changes in coefficients are measured using the sample in 1981 instead of 1985, and changes in variables using coefficients of 1985 instead of 1981. It would give approximately the same results (Magnac, 1987).

**Table 7.8**
Decomposition of Changes in Labor Participation Rates over 1981-85
by Variables and Coefficients
(percent)

| Change | in variables | in coefficients |
|---|---|---|
| Variable groups: | | |
| Education (Educ) | +1.7% | -1.3 |
| Experience (Exp. exp²) | 0 | +1.4 |
| Incomes (Imar, Dm, Iotr, D) | +0.5 | -1.3 |
| Children (E1, E2) | +0.4 | +0.2 |
| Inactive Women (MJI, MAI, MVI) | -0.1 | +0.5 |
| Other members (HST1-2, MST2, HDE) | -0.1 | +0.4 |
| Intercept and towns except | -0.2 | +1.0 |
| Bogotá (BOG) | +0.5 | +4.1 |
| Total | 2.7 | 5.1 |

Note:   Computations were done using the method presented in the text for each group, variables and coefficients of other groups have been kept constant and equal to their initial values.

Concluding if 25 percent of the increase in participation rates is correctly predicted by the model, confirmed by the effects of education and fecundity, this is clearly a modification in the "center of gravity" of the model, (intercept and dummy variables) which is implied by the participation evolution between 1981 and 1985.[15]   It should be recalled that if costs of access to the labor market are significant, the participation model does not permit their identification from the reservation wage (Cogan, 1981).   Only an estimation of an equation of hours of work would permit this.   Additionally, productivity gains during the period and/or exogenous growth of real wages are not identifiable from demand variations.   The absence of variables in the model describing labor demand or peculiar economic conditions might explain the residuals of the predictions, here called changes in the coefficients.   These changes in labor demand can be described alternatively by studying the determination of wages over the period since those are related to changes in supply and demand.

---

[15]   This method looks like an analysis of variance by variables groups.   Another procedure could have been used by stacking together the observations.   However, that method would possibly give different results because of the non-linear nature of the model.

## 4.   Wage Functions

Tables 7.9 and 7.10 show the results of such estimates for different groups in the population drawn from different survey studies (Mohan, 1981; Carrizosa, 1982). The dependent variable in those regressions is generally the logarithm of total income or labor income.

Results are rather scattered. The education coefficient, that is to say its mean yield, varies between .14 and .20. These variations can be explained mainly by different survey coverages or by the different sets of variables used. These results imply that income doubles for every 5 additional years of education which roughly correspond to an entire cycle in a primary or secondary school. These yields are much higher than in developed countries, as generally the case is in less developed countries (LDCs) (Psacharopoulos, 1973) but even seem to be quite large by LDCs standards.

The usual long-term interpretation of Mincer (1962) would relate these yields to the interest rates but they may also be related to high costs of education (Magnac, 1987). Given the limited access to the financial markets of many households, the second reason may be the most important. However, in the 1970s large increases in average education took place since primary education became compulsory in the 1960s. Education yields should have shown large short-run variations. This indeed shows up in these results. The question of whether these fluctuations are related to demand or supply shocks remains unsolved.

*Married women's wage equations.* In order to correct for the selectivity bias in the wage equations (Killingsworth, 1983), a Heckman (1979) procedure is used here. The inverse Mill's ratio associated with the participation equations estimated in the previous section is included as a regressor. This method will give consistent estimates of the coefficients but inconsistent estimates of the standard errors.[16]

Table 7.11 shows the estimation results for the following equation, with and without selectivity corrections:

$$\log(w) = Xa + u$$

where w is the hourly wage rate, defined as the ratio of labor income to normal hours of work.

The $R^2$ is relatively high given the number of observations and the coefficients are largely significant, especially for education. The usual positive effect of education and the positive but decreasing effect of experience is corroborated. Without selectivity corrections, an additional year of education increases wages on average by 14 percent and the maximum point for the wage profile as a function of age is reached for experience equal to 30, that is to say around age 40.

Coefficients have a positive trend between 1981 and 1984 but decrease again to their 1981 levels in 1985. On the other hand, 1980 coefficients appear to be very large. This decrease can be partially explained by the evolution of labor participation over the period. In 1983, and above all in 1984, there is a large increase in participation rates and women, with low education and little experience, enter the labor market. This group, with low earnings, make the wage function steeper (Figure 7.4). This phenomenon could be attributed to the modification of the selection rule across time.

---

[16]   These are reported for information purposes. For 1980, a standard complete likelihood method was used but the numerical results were not any different from those given here.

### Table 7.9
#### Income Functions Estimates

| Variables | Int. | Educ | Exp | Exp² | SEX | YP | R2 | N |
|---|---|---|---|---|---|---|---|---|
| Studies | | | | | | | | |
| (1) | 4.8 | 0.173 | 0.121 | -0.0018 | | | 0.881 | 47 |
| | | ( 7.4) | (8.8) | (7.3) | | | | |
| (2) | n.d | 0.151 | 0.135 | | ns | 0.127 | 0.70 | n.d |
| | | (17.8) | (7.2) | | (-0.9) | (4.3) | | |
| (3a) | 5.08 | 0.167 | 0.078 | -0.0011 | | | 0.63 | 1016 |
| | | (38.9) | (17.6) | (12.6) | | | | |
| (3b) | 5.88 | 0.151 | 0.068 | -0.009 | | | 0.51 | 3640 |
| | | (59.2) | (25.8) | (19.3) | | | | |
| (4a) | 4.85 | 0.201 | 0.068 | -0.001 | | | 0.32 | n.d. |
| | | (50.0) | (21.6) | (17.3) | | | | |
| (4b) | 4.86 | 0.219 | 0.066 | -0.001 | | | 0.32 | n.d. |

Notes:   Int = Intercept; EDUC = Education; EXP = Experience; EXP2 = Experience squared;
SEX = Sex; YP = Father's income; N = Number of observations
Student tests in brackets

Source:  Mohan (1981), Carrizosa (1982).

Original Sources:  (1) Schultz (1968): Men, Bogotá in 47 groups (aggregated) in 1965: Dependent variable = log (monthly income).
(2) Kugler (1974): Rural and urban population: dependent variable = log of labor income in 1970.
(3) Bourguignon (1980): Men, Bogotá; Dependent variable = log of monthly income.
   a) in 1971
   b) in 1974
(4) Fields (1977): Dependent variable = log of total income in 1973.
   a) Salaried workers
   b) Self-employed

Selectivity bias corrections have an important influence on estimates. Education yield increases by 15 percent and experience yield by 40 percent. The inverse Mill's ratio is positive and significant. But this correction does not change the conclusions made above on the temporal evolution of the coefficients.[17]

***Comparison with wage equations for other members in the household.*** Wage equations for the years between 1981 and 1985 have been estimated for husbands and results are presented in Table 7.12. Similar results are given in Table 7.13 for other members in the household in two subsamples, salaried workers and self-employed.

---

[17]   The crucial hypothesis for the Heckman method is the binormality of the disturbances. If this hypothesis is not verified then the regressions give inconsistent estimates. This might be the cause of the noncorrections.

**Figure 7.4**
Influence of New Entrants on Education Yields in the Wage Equations

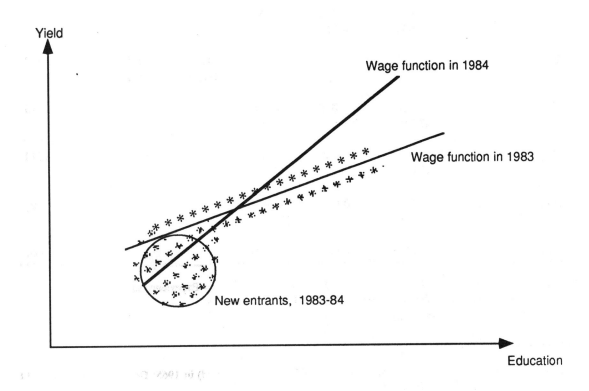

**Table 7.10**
Wage Equations in Bogotá

|        | Intercept | Educ             | Exp             | Exp2              | R2    | N    |
| ------ | --------- | ---------------- | --------------- | ----------------- | ----- | ---- |
| Men    | 4.26      | 0.119<br>(28.9)  | 0.068<br>(18.5) | -0.0010<br>(13.4) | 0.329 | 2216 |
| Women  | 4.29      | 0.099<br>(15.8)  | 0.055<br>(7.6)  | -0.0012<br>(5.5)  | 0.229 | 1047 |
| Total  | 4.23      | 0.114<br>(32.7)  | 0.067<br>(21.7) | -0.0010<br>(14.5) | 0.323 | 3264 |

Notes:   Similar conventions than Table 7.9 note 2.  Dependent variable = log of monthly incomes.
Student tests in brackets.
Source:  Kugler et. al. (1979)

### Table 7.11
#### Married Women's Potential Wage Equations, 1980-85

|  |  | Educ | Exp | Exp² | Mill | R2 | Means |
|---|---|---|---|---|---|---|---|
| 1980 (N=1179) | 2.24 | 0.157 (24.0) | 0.039 (4.7) | -0.00058 (3.6) | - | 0.387 | 4.81 |
|  | 1.49 | 0.174 (20.9) | 0.046 (5.4) | -0.00077 (4.5) | 0.44 (3.4) | 0.393 |  |
| 1981 (N=1165) | 3.09 | 0.135 (20.4) | 0.023 (2.7) | -0.00033 (2.0) | - | 0.330 | 5.01 |
|  | 2.20 | 0.155 (17.6) | 0.031 (3.5) | -0.00052 (3.1) | 0.50 (3.5) | 0.337 |  |
| 1982 (N=2100) | 3.30 | 0.132 (30.2) | 0.030 (5.1) | -0.00046 (4.1) | - | 0.380 | 5.36 |
|  | 2.45 | 0.152 (26.0) | 0.039 (6.4) | -0.00067 (5.7) | 0.44 (5.0) | 0.387 |  |
| 1983 (N=2526) | 3.38 | 0.139 (33.3) | 0.030 (6.2) | -0.00045 (5.1) | - | 0.371 | 5.54 |
|  | 2.40 | 0.161 (30.4) | 0.042 (7.2) | -0.00072 (6.4) | 0.57 (6.7) | 0.381 |  |
| 1984 (N=3067) | 3.44 | 0.144 (37.0) | 0.033 (7.2) | -0.00050 (6.1) | - | 0.365 | 5.72 |
|  | 2.34 | 0.169 (34.2) | 0.046 (8.1) | -0.00083 (7.5) | 0.72 (8.0) | 0.378 |  |
| 1985 (N=2571) | 3.76 | 0.136 (34.3) | 0.029 (6.0) | -0.00040 (4.9) | - | 0.378 | 5.91 |
|  | 3.14 | 0.151 (29.7) | 0.032 (5.6) | -0.00047 (4.3) | 0.40 (4.5) | 0.383 |  |

Notes:   Dependent variable = log (wage), Mean = mean (log wage).
Student test statistics in brackets.

The estimation of husbands' wage equations show that the education yield is less important for men than women but, on average, wage rates seem to be higher. These differences would seem to indicate that "discrimination" between men and women is lower in higher education groups. However, it sets forth the problem of the approximation of the variable work experience by the difference (age-education). Women have not only a lower probability of participation but also lower levels of experience than (age-education). In order to show the importance of this approximation, we develop a very simple model.

Assume that the true model is given by the wage equation where EXP2 was deleted for the sake of simplicity.

$$\log(w) = a + b.EDUC + c.EXP + v$$

**Table 7.12**
Husband's Wage Equations

|  | 1981 | 1982 | 1983 | 1984 | 1985 |
|---|---|---|---|---|---|
| Intercept | 3.33 | 3.43 | 3.54 | 3.68 | 3.72 |
| Educ | 0.121 | 0.126 | 0.129 | 0.132 | 0.133 |
|  | (41.0) | (56.3) | (66.7) | (73.5) | (67.4) |
| Exp | 0.036 | 0.040 | 0.045 | 0.040 | 0.044 |
|  | (9.2) | (12.7) | (16.7) | (15.3) | (15.3) |
| Exp² | -0.00045 | -0.00048 | -0.00055 | -0.00045 | -0.00050 |
|  | (7.2) | (9.2) | (12.3) | (10.5) | (10.4) |
| R² | 0.298 | 0.320 | 0.353 | 0.356 | 0.357 |
| N | 4048 | 6781 | 7698 | 9208 | 7771 |
| Mean | 5.32 | 5.61 | 5.86 | 6.00 | 6.14 |

Notes:  Dependent variable = log of hourly wage rate.
Student tests in brackets

A priori we have $b > 0$, $c > 0$. Estimated wage equations are however given by the approximated model:
$$\log(w) = d + e.EDUC + f.X + u \text{ with } X=AGE\text{-}EDUC$$

but $u=c(EXP\text{-}X) + v$ is clearly correlated to EDUC and X. This endogeneity problem should imply that the estimates of d, e, and f are biased estimates of a,b,c.

So as to estimate the direction of the bias, let us write the auxiliary regression:

$$EXP - X = C + A.EDUC + B.X + t$$

Then if $E(v \mid X) = 0$ is assumed, the estimates of d, e, and f are unbiased estimates of $(a+c.C, b+c.A, c+c.B)$ because the true model can be rewritten:

$$\ln(W)= (a+c.C) + (b+c.A) EDUC + (c+c.B).X + (v+ct)$$

Finally, an heuristic argument shows that $A > 0$ and $B < 0$. As a matter of fact, if X is fixed, the negative difference (EXP-X) describing the opposite of the time spent out of the market increases as education increases because labor participation increases with education, with fixed X. Hence: $Cov(EXP\text{-}X, EDUC \mid X) > 0$ and $A > 0$. Moreover, if EDUC is fixed, the negative difference (EXP-X) decreases as X increases since the participation rate is less than one. Then $Cov(EXP\text{-}X, X \mid EDUC) < 0$ and $B < 0$.

Concluding, the estimator of the education yield in the regressions we used is an upward biased estimator of the true yield and the estimator of the experience yield is a downward biased estimator of the true experience yield. These biases go in the same direction as the differences between male and female wage functions. These differences might thus be a statistically spurious

### Table 7.13
### Other Members' Wage Equations.

|  | Intercept | Educ | Exp | Exp$^2$ | Sex | R2 | N | Means |
|---|---|---|---|---|---|---|---|---|
| **Wage earners** | | | | | | | | |
| 1981 | 3.03 | 0.151 (47.8) | 0.050 (15.5) | -0.00071 (11.6) | -0.392 (18.8) | 0.490 | 2,951 | 4.71 |
| 1982 | 3.27 | 0.151 (63.7) | 0.053 (20.7) | -0.00076 (15.2) | 0.40 (24.6) | 0.507 | 4,835 | 4.97 |
| 1983 | 3.36 | 0.158 (70.0) | 0.052 (19.8) | -0.00068 (12.8) | -0.40 (24.8) | 0.526 | 5,395 | 5.16 |
| 1984 | 3.75 | 0.147 (67.0) | 0.045 (17.4) | -0.00062 (11.8) | -0.40 (26.0) | 0.495 | 5,711 | 5.37 |
| 1985 | 3.67 | 0.156 (70.0) | 0.052 (19.9) | -0.00075 (14.1) | -0.38 (24.2) | 0.543 | 5,062 | 5.52 |
| **Self-employed** | | | | | | | | |
| 1981 | 3.42 | 0.120 (9.3) | 0.050 (5.1) | -0.00065 (4.4) | -0.39 (3.9) | 0.238 | 377 | 4.81 |
| 1982 | 3.53 | 0.129 ( 7.2) | 0.035 (4.2) | -0.00041 (3.2) | -0.23 (2.8) | 0.222 | 651 | 5.14 |
| 1983 | 3.67 | 0.131 (16.2) | 0.033 (4.5) | -0.00040 (3.6) | -0.20 (3.0) | 0.282 | 724 | 5.39 |
| 1984 | 3.74 | 0.129 (15.9) | 0.028 (3.7) | -0.00034 (2.8) | -0.11 (1.6) | 0.250 | 845 | 5.52 |
| 1985 | 3.94 | 0.110 (10.1) | 0.042 (4.4) | -0.00056 (3.6) | -0.17 (1.9) | 0.119 | n.d. | 5.36 |

Notes:   Dependent variable = log of hourly wage rate.
Student tests in brackets.

artifact related to the bad measure of the true market experience.  The education yield for women may in fact be less than 15 percent.  In order to correct for this experience bias several methods are possible but it is necessary to have panel data.

The analysis of the wage functions for other members in the family show that no significant differences appears in the human capital yields.  In contrast, the sex variable is significant and for salaried workers; women earn 40 percent less than men, all other things being equal. Discrimination thus seems to be very important.  But it must be noticed that these results are valid for salaried workers but less so for the self-employed.  Among the latter, wages are explained less by human capital variables.  It is possible that the self-employed wages have larger variations across time than salaried workers' wages.

## 5. Conclusions

In this paper, the results lead to some firm conclusions but also pose some questions about the basic hypothesis of the model. First, the results of the participation model seem robust and stable across time. The results show the importance of the classical effects of human capital variables or incomes on the labor participation of married women. They also permit us to measure the substitution effects within the household. Nevertheless, even if 25 percent of the increase in participation is predicted by supply effects, such as increasing average education of decreasing fecundity, its explanatory power remains quite small in cross-section and rather mild in time-series.

The estimation of wage equations is usual but omits variables related to occupations or to the demand side of the labor market. The latter seem to be an important determinant of the evolution of the labor market (Magnac, 1991). In particular, the segmentation hypothesis of the labor market should be considered. However, in this case the estimation of wage equations by merely including occupational status variables is plagued by major biases since those variables are endogenously determined. Occupational status is chosen at the same time as participation. It is thus necessary to use a more complete model so as to treat it in a more rigorous way.

## Appendix 7A

Household Composition Variables Left Out of the Analysis of Female Participation

Number of persons in the family.

Number of children of the household's head aged between 3 and 12.

Number of children of other members.

Number of active adult men and women.

Number of students aged between 12 and 18.

Number of unemployed women.

These variables were left out of the analysis because they were not significant in all samples except the number of persons and the number of active women which were left out because of a strong colinearity with other members' income (IOTR).

## Appendix 7B
### Presentation of the Data

The data used in the estimations come from the yearly Encuestas de Hogares (EH) from March 1980 to 1985 (EH26 to EH46) collected by the DANE in the four major cities of Colombia, Bogotá, Medellín, Barranquilla, Cali, and in the smaller towns Bucaramanga, Manizales and Pasto. The DANE in recent years aims to include suburbs in the surveys but it was not the case in 1980 to 1985 surveys. The survey methods are homogeneous in the period under study, with the exceptions of March 1981 in Bogotá where the sample is much larger and of March 1982 for the three smaller towns for the same reason (Estudios de Población).

Generally speaking, the main questionnaire consists of questions related to individual characteristics on work, income, etc., but it is easy to construct household variables from the survey.

These surveys or similar ones have been studied by Ayala (1981) who compared the results to a survey undertaken by the CEDE (Universidad de les Andes, Empleo y Pobreza, 1978) in Bogotá. Differences are rather mild, but the Encuestas de Hogares seems to underestimate the number of children in the family and domestic services as well. Similarly, it seems that partial work is underreported, in particular by unemployed people.

Another possible criticism is the sampling strategy based on the 1973 census. The latter is not renowned for its coverage. However, the DANE reactualises these predictions by cartographic methods. Nevertheless, as suburbs are left out, no coverage exists for the districts called barrios de invasion setting up very quickly. The poorest families are surely missed.

The sample that we selected retains the following criteria: The family must be composed of a male household head and his wife or companion, the latter being aged between 18 and 60. The number of households varies between 5,000 and 10,000 (Table 7.6). Generally left out are 20 to 25 percent of the households present in the whole sample. All household's variables have been constructed from individual observations by counting methods.

# References

Aguiar, N. "La mujer en la fuerza de trabajo en la America Latina: un resumen introductorio." *Desarrollo y Sociedad,* Vol. 13, January (1984).

Angulo Novoa, A. and López de Rodríguez, C. *Trabajo y fecundidad de la mujer colombiana. Fedesarrollo: Bogotá,* April 1975.

Ayala, U. *Comparaciones intertemporales de estadísticas sobre fuerza laboral.* Bogotá: Universidad de los Andes, CEDE, 1981.

-----. *El empleo en las grandes ciudades colombianas.* Bogotá: Universidad de los Andes, CEDE, 1981.

Bayona, A. "El descenso de la fecundidad y su impacto sobre la participación de la mujer en la actividad en Colombia" in *Implicaciones socioeconómicas y demográficas del descenso de la fecundidad en Colombia,* Vol. 18, April (1982).

Berry, A. and M. Urrutia, *Income Distribution in Colombia.* New Haven, London: Yale University Press, 1976.

Bonilla de Ramos, E. *La Madre Trabajadora.* Document 66. Bogotá: Universidad de los Andes, 1981.

Bourguignon, F. "Participation, emploi et travail domestiques des femmes mariees." *Consommation,* Vol. 2 (1981). pp. 75-98.

-----. "The Labor Market in Colombia." Washington D.C.: The World Bank, Report No. DRD157, 1986.

Bourguignon, F., F. Gagey and T. Magnac. "On Estimating Female Labor Supply Behavior in Developing Countries." *Doc. LEP,* Vol. 103, January (1985). pp.41.

Cáceres, I. *Algunos aspectos de la situación de la mujer trabajadora en Colombia.* Unpublished Dissertation. Bogotá: Universidad de los Andes, 1977.

Caillavet, F. *Allocation du temps des menages a Bogotá, Colombie.* Unpublished Dissertation. University of Paris, 1981.

Castañeda, IT. "Determinantes del cambio poblacional en Colombia." *Desarrollo y Sociedad,* Vol. 4, July (1980).

-----. "La participación de las madres en el mercado urbano en Colombia." *Desarrollo y Sociedad,* (1981).

Departamento Administrativo Nacional de Estadística (DANE). Boletines de estadística. Bogotá.

-----. *Metodología de las encuestas de hogares.* Bogotá, 1986.

-----. Colombia Estadística 86. Bogotá, 1986.

Fields, G. and T.P. Schultz. "Income Generating Functions in a Low Income Country: Colombia." *Review of Income and Wealth,* Vol. 28, no. 1 (1982). pp. 71-87.

Gómez de, M. I., B. Kugler and A. Reyes. *Determinantes económicos y demográficos de la participación laboral en Colombia.* Bogotá: CCRP, 1981.

Gourieroux, C. *Econometrie des variables qualitatives.* Paris: Economica, 1984.

Gutiérrez de Pineda, V. *Estructura, función y cambio de la familia en Colombia.* Bogotá: ACFM, 1975.

Heckman, J. "Sample Selection Bias as a Specification Erro9r." *Economietrica,* Vol. 47, no. 1 (1979). pp.153-161.

Kugler, B., A. Reyes, and M. I. de Gómez. *Educación y Mercado de Trabajo Urbano en Colombia.* Bogotá: Monografías de la CCPR. Vol. 10, 1979.

Killingsworth, M. *Labor Supply.* New Jersey: Cambridge University Press, 1983.

Kugler, B. "Influencia de la educación en los ingresos de trabajo: el caso colombiano." *Rev. de Planeación y Desarrollo,* (1971).

León de Leal, M. La mujer y el desarrollo en Colombia. Bogotá: ACEP, 1977.

Magnac, T. *Analyse de l'offre de travail sur un marche concurrentiel ou segmente.* Unpublished Dissertation. Paris: EHESS, 1987.

-----. "Competitive or Segmented Labour Markets?" *Econometrica,* Vol 59 (1): 165-187, 1991.

Mohan, R. *The Determinants of Labor Earnings in Developing Metropolis: Estimates from Bogotá and Cali, Colombia.* Washington D.C.: The World Bank, 1981.

Munoz, C. and M. Palacios. *El niño trabajador.* Bogotá: Carlos Valencia Editores, 1980.

Ranis, G. "Distribución del ingreso y crecimiento en Colombia." *Desarrollo y Sociedad,* Vol. 1, January (1980).

Rey de Marulanda, N. *El trabajo de la mujer.* Bogotá: Universidad de los Andes, CEDE, 1981.

Rey de Marulanda, N., U. Ayala, M.C. Niño and F. Durán. *Empleo y pobreza*. Bogotá: Universidad de los Andes, CEDE, 1978.

Reyna, J. V., H. G. Buendía and C. C. Argaez. *Desarrollo social en la década del 70*. Bogotá: UNICEF, 1984.

Stern, N. and J. Gomulka. "The Employment of Married Women in the U.K. 1970-83." *Económica*, Vol. 571 (1990). pp. 171-200.

Urrutia, M. *Winners and Losers in Colombia's Economic Growth of the 70's*. London: Oxford University Press, 1984.

# Chapter 8

# Women's Labor Force Participation and Earnings in Colombia

*Eduardo Velez and Carolyn Winter*

## 1.    Introduction

This chapter contributes to the rather small literature on factors influencing female labor force participation and earnings in Colombia.  The movement of women from the home to the workplace is generally seen to be an indicator of increasing sex equality in society since it implies improved access to education by women and reduced fertility rates.  While women's labor force participation rates have increased substantially in Colombia (from 19 percent in 1951 to 39 percent in 1985)[1] relatively little is known about women's work experience, their occupations, or their earnings relative to men.  In this chapter we address the following questions: What factors influence a women's decision to participate in the labor market?  Are human capital indicators lower for women than men? and, What accounts for the earnings differential between the sexes?

The following section briefly describes the Colombian labor market.  Section 3 describes the characteristics of the sample used in this analysis and Section 4 identifies the most important determinants of women's labor force participation.  Section 5 presents earnings function estimates for male and female workers respectively, allowing us to examine earnings differences while controlling for human capital endowments.  In Section 6 we decompose the earnings differential into the portion attributable to differences in productivity related variables and the portion attributable to "unexplained" factors (largely differences in the way employers reward male and female workers).  A discussion of these findings and their implications for policy formulation is presented in the final section.

## 2.    The Colombian Labor Market

A wealth of resources, extensive industrial diversification, and prudent fiscal management has led to sustained economic growth, averaging close to 5 percent per annum since the 1960s, and the continuing real growth in real incomes.

In the last few decades the country has experienced a rapid social transformation that has affected the structure of the labor force and labor-supply behavior.  In fact, the urban share of the population increased from 31 percent in 1938 to almost 70 percent in 1985; total fertility rates

---

[1]    ILO (1990).

declined by about 45 percent from the early 1960s and are currently estimated at about 3.5 percent; maternal mortality that was 254 per 100,000 live births in 1964 was 107 in 1984; primary education enrollment more than doubled, and secondary education enrollment increased six-fold since the 1960s; and a substantial modification of the sectoral distribution of the labor force occurred -- the agricultural sector accounted for 57.2 percent of the labor force in 1950 and 34.3 percent in 1980, the industrial sector for 17.9 percent in 1950 and 23.5 percent in 1980, and the service sector for 24.9 percent in 1950 and 42.3 percent in 1980.

A significant change in the Colombian labor market over the last few decades has been the increase in women's labor force participation from 19 percent in 1950 to 39 percent in 1985. Women continue, however, to be heavily represented in the informal sector and it is estimated (Federico de Alonso, 1990) that 64 percent of working women were in the informal sector in 1990.

In terms of educational achievement, gross enrollment ratios at primary and secondary education are about the same for boys and girls. Even in higher education women show good standing relative to men; in 1986 the enrollment ratio for higher education as a whole was 13.1, and was 12.6 for women. Since the end of the 1970s more women than men have been attending higher education (DANE, 1985). However, field of study varies significantly by gender, with women being found in educational tracks that lead to low-paying careers. The average education of labor force participants has increased substantially over the past 30 years; more than 40 percent had no education in 1951, only 8 percent had gone beyond primary education, and the illiteracy rate was around 10 percent. The average educational level of the labor force has more than doubled since the 1960s; an impressive change.

## 3.   Sample Characteristics

The data used in this analysis are from the June 1988 National Household Survey conducted by the Departamento Administrativo Nacional de Estadística (DANE) in the largest Colombian cities.[2] The survey covers about 75,000 individuals aged twelve years or older in more than 20,000 households and provides detailed data on individual socio-economic and labor status. A 10 percent random sample of households was selected for use in this analysis. As we were primarily interested in prime-age workers, we retained in our subsample individuals aged 15 to 60 years.

Table 8.1 shows the mean characteristics of the sample by gender and, for women, by work status. Individuals were classified as working if they were employed in the formal sector, reported positive earnings and worked more than 2 hours a week. Within the sample of working males and females, individuals who reported earning less than 10 percent of the mean hourly wage or more than 15 times the mean hourly wage for their sex were excluded. This procedure resulted in our dropping nine cases from the sample in which reported earnings were over three standard deviations from the mean. The sample used in the analysis was composed of 3,163 working males, 1,748 working females and 5,735 non-working females. The female participation rate in the sample was 25 percent.

---

[2]   The sample is representative of Colombia's urban population and the socio-economic composition of each city. The cities and metropolitan areas included in the sample are: Bogotá, Medellín, Cali, Barranquilla, Bucaramanga, Cartagena, Cucuta, Manizales, Pasto, Ibague, Pereira and Villavicencio.

**Table 8.1**
Colombia Means (and Standard Deviations) of Sample Variables

| Characteristics | Working Males | Working Females | Non-Working Females |
|---|---|---|---|
| Age | 34.2 | 32.7 | 31.4 |
| | (11.16) | (9.59) | (11.39) |
| Married (%) | 64.2 | 38.4 | 47.4 |
| | (0.48) | (0.48) | (0.49) |
| # Children under 6 years | .63 | .51 | .59 |
| | (0.88) | (0.84) | (0.85) |
| Head of Household | 65.3 | 19.7 | 6.8 |
| | (0.47) | (0.39) | (0.25) |
| Education | | | |
| Years of Schooling | 7.6 | 8.7 | 7.1 |
| | (4.08) | (4.22) | (3.61) |
| Level of Education (%): | | | |
| No formal education | 2.6 | 1.8 | 4.4 |
| Incomplete primary | 16.3 | 13.3 | 18.6 |
| Primary | 20.5 | 16.5 | 19.5 |
| Incomplete secondary | 30.9 | 26.0 | 36.3 |
| Secondary | 17.0 | 24.0 | 13.7 |
| Incomplete university | 5.3 | 9.1 | 5.4 |
| University | 7.5 | 9.5 | 2.1 |
| Employment Status | | | |
| Weekly Earnings (pesos) | 10,727 | 9,078 | |
| | (13,114) | (9,766) | |
| Years of Experience | 20.5 | 18.0 | |
| | (12.47) | (11.25) | |
| Hours worked (weekly) | 49.9 | 46.1 | |
| | (12.07) | (11.44) | |
| N | 3,163 | 1,748 | 5,735 |

Notes:   Figures in parentheses are standard deviations.
          Female Participation Rate = 25 percent.
Source:   National Household Survey, 1988.

Working women have, on average, one and a half years more schooling than non-working women and approximately one year more schooling than working males. Working women are also more likely than working men to have completed secondary schooling and either attended or completed higher education. Despite this, working women's weekly earnings are, on average, only 84.6 percent of working men's (9,078 pesos compared to 10,727 pesos). This earnings differential is not completely explained by the slightly fewer hours worked per week by women; if we estimate average hourly income women still earn approximately 9 percent less than men.[3]

---

[3]   It is possible that gender differences in labor market experience may account for some part of this earnings differential. However, our variable "years of labor market experience" has been constructed by subtracting an individual's years of education plus six from his/her age, as per Heckman (1979) and is consequently not an accurate indicator of experience. It is likely to overestimate women's experience since they withdraw from the labor market more frequently than men and for longer periods because of childbearing.

**Table 8.2**
Occupational Distribution of Workers by Gender, Formal Sector, 1988

| Occupation Workers | Male (%) | Mean Weekly Wage (pesos) | Females (%) | Mean Weekly Wage (pesos) | Mean Weekly Wage (pesos) All |
|---|---|---|---|---|---|
| Professional/technical | 7.7 | 24,754 | 12.5 | 17,418 | 21,293 |
| Administrative | 1.3 | 38,440 | 0.9 | 25,751 | 34,979 |
| Clerical | 10.5 | 9,455 | 22.9 | 9,549 | 9,507 |
| Sales | 20.4 | 11,556 | 20.7 | 7,959 | 10,264 |
| Service | 9.7 | 8,829 | 21.1 | 6,744 | 7,682 |
| Agricultural | 2.1 | 14,991 | 0.7 | 13,643 | 14,784 |
| Laborer/Operative | 48.5 | 7,893 | 21.4 | 6,270 | 7,575 |
| All Occupations | | 10,726 | | 9,077 | 10,139 |

It is interesting to note in Table 8.2 that almost half of all male workers in the formal sector are employed in the lowest paid occupation (laborer/operative). Women are, however, more heavily represented than men in the next two lowest paying categories, service and clerical. Women's average earnings are lower than men's in all occupational categories except clerical.

## 4. The Determinants of Women's Labor Force Participation

Given that female workers average one more year of schooling than working men but that they earn, on average, only 84.6 percent of men's wages, we are interested in determining what part of the earnings differential is actually due to differences in human capital endowments and what part is "unexplained" by these factors. This "unexplained" component will largely reflect differences in the way employers reward male and female workers.[4]

However, we are faced with special problems in estimating earning functions for female workers. The problem arises because a woman's decision to participate in the formal labor market is influenced not only by her market wage, but also by the value she accords her work in the home (i.e., her reservation wage). In general, a woman's reservation wage is likely to be the highest (and hence her probability of participation in the labor market, lowest) when she has young children for whom to care.[5]

If we estimate earnings functions for working women we will be using a self-selected sample (women whose market wage exceeds the value of their time in the home) and our estimates will yield biased results. To correct for this selectivity we estimate a probit model in which the

---

[4] This "unexplained" component is generally taken to represent the "upper bound" to discrimination, since other factors are also likely to contribute to this "unexplained" component. If, for instance, we omit explanatory variables from the earnings equations the estimate of discrimination will be biased upwards.

[5] In this study we assume that prime-age males do not have the same options regarding labor force participation as females. Males have traditionally been viewed as providers for the family. Females, except where they are heads of households, have had the option of withdrawing from the labor market to undertake childrearing and home-care activities.

probability that a woman will participate is estimated given her parental status,[6] age, educational level, the size of the household in which she lives, and her status as head of household or otherwise.[7] These probit estimates are presented in Table 8.3. To illustrate the magnitude of the probit coefficients we estimate simulations predicting female participation rates for each condition while holding all other variables at the value of their sample mean (see Table 8.4).

### Table 8.3
### Probit Estimates for Female Participation

| Variable | Coefficient | t-ratio | Mean | Partial Derivative |
|---|---|---|---|---|
| Constant | -1.927 | -15.96 | 1.000 | |
| Age 20-25 | 0.685 | 11.55 | 0.234 | 0.207 |
| Age 26-30 | 0.862 | 13.55 | 0.151 | 0.261 |
| Age 31-35 | 0.842 | 12.18 | 0.103 | 0.255 |
| Age 36-40 | 0.884 | 12.09 | 0.103 | 0.252 |
| Age 41-45 | 0.705 | 8.92 | 0.067 | 0.213 |
| Age 46-50 | 0.562 | 7.01 | 0.068 | 0.170 |
| Age 51-55 | 0.382 | 4.14 | 0.051 | 0.115 |
| Children (0-6 yrs) | -0.134 | -3.53 | 0.393 | -0.040 |
| Household Size | 0.018 | 2.46 | 4.418 | 0.005 |
| Female Household Head | 0.763 | 14.07 | 0.111 | 0.231 |
| Incomplete Primary | 0.260 | 2.32 | 0.172 | 0.078 |
| Primary | 0.400 | 3.61 | 0.187 | 0.121 |
| Incomplete Secondary | 0.382 | 3.50 | 0.336 | 0.115 |
| Secondary | 0.833 | 7.43 | 0.162 | 0.252 |
| Incomplete University | 0.767 | 6.20 | 0.063 | 0.232 |
| University | 1.309 | 9.95 | 0.039 | 0.396 |

Notes: Dependent Variable: Labor Force Participation
 Sample: Women aged 15 to 60 years
 Mean Participation Rate: 25%
 Log-Likelihood = 3476.3

Schooling is entered as a series of dummy variables for each level of schooling. The probit coefficients in Table 8.3 show that the probability of participating increases steadily with each successive level of education successfully completed. The extent to which additional education increases the probability of participation is evident in Table 8.4. A woman with the mean values of all other characteristics and completed secondary schooling has a predicted probability of labor force participation 7 percent higher than a woman with completed primary school (probability = .34 versus .20). A woman with completed university has a predicted probability of participation

---

[6] It should be noted that our data only provide information on number of children aged 0 to 6 years by household. Where there is more than one women in a household, it is not possible to determine to which woman the children belong. We therefore lose some of the explanatory power of this variable.

[7] This method was developed by Heckman (1976) and has been widely used. See, for example, Gronau (1988).

56 percent higher than a woman with completed secondary schooling (probability = .53 versus .34).

Two variables controlling for household effects are included in the probit model, household size (a continuous variable) and whether the woman is the head of the household (entered as a dummy variable). Larger household size is shown to have a positive, but very small effect, on a woman's participation decision. By contrast, being a household head has a substantial impact. A woman with the mean values of the other characteristics but who is a household head has a predicted probability of participating of .47 compared to .21 for a woman who is not a household head.

Many studies have shown a woman's participation decision to be strongly influenced by family structure, particularly if she is the mother of young children.[8] This is also found to be true in Colombia where the presence of young children (aged 0 to 6 years) is shown to reduce the probability that a woman will participate. A woman has a predicted probability of participating of .20 if there are young children in the household and .25 if no young children are present.

### Table 8.4
Predicted Participation Probabilities by Characteristic

| Characteristic | Predicted Probability |
|---|---|
| **Education** | |
| Incomplete Primary | 0.11 |
| No Education | 0.16 |
| Primary | 0.20 |
| Incomplete Secondary | 0.19 |
| Secondary | 0.34 |
| Incomplete University | 0.32 |
| University | 0.53 |
| **Presence of Children (0-6 years)** | |
| No | 0.25 |
| Yes | 0.20 |
| **Female Headed Household** | |
| No | 0.21 |
| Yes | 0.47 |
| Overall Mean Participation Rate | 0.25 |

Note: Probability of participation while holding other variables constant at their sample mean.

---

[8]  See, for example, the chapters on Ecuador, Venezuela (1989), and Argentina in this volume.

## 5. Earnings Functions

We estimated earnings functions for men and the 1,748 women in our sample who were labor force participants. The regression estimates based on the standard human capital model where the dependent variable is the log of weekly earnings and the independent variables are experience, years of schooling and log weekly hours worked.[9] The experience proxy is entered as a squared term to test if the earnings function is parabolic in the experience term.

### Table 8.5
### Earnings Functions

| Variable | Men (1) | Women (Corrected for Selectivity)[a] (2) | Women (Uncorrected for Selectivity)[b] (3) |
|---|---|---|---|
| Constant | 5.662 | 6.115 | 5.66 |
| | (31.432) | (24.56) | (26.93) |
| Schooling (years) | .120 | .099 | .112 |
| | (35.415) | (17.15) | (25.37) |
| Log Hours | .426 | .447 | .457 |
| | (9.515) | (8.71) | (8.88) |
| Experience | .046 | .027 | .035 |
| | (11.941) | (5.12) | (7.58) |
| Experience squared | -.000 | -.000 | -.000 |
| | (-6.270) | (-2.64) | (-4.49) |
| Lambda[c] | | -.206 | |
| | | (-3.29) | |
| R2 | .304 | .299 | .294 |
| N | 3,161 | 1,748 | 1,748 |

a. Corrected for selectivity bias using probit equation for probability of labor market work in Table 8.3. Errors corrected for the use of an inverse Mills ratio.
b. Not corrected for selectivity bias. OLS using the subsample of working women.
c. Inverse Mills Ratio calculated using probit results for the probability of working in Table 8.3.
Notes: Dependent variable = log (weekly earnings).
   t-values are in parentheses

The first column of Table 8.5 presents the results for the male sample. The rate of return to schooling is estimated to be 12 percent which is consistent with previous research on Colombian urban labor markets.[10] The log earnings increase with experience but at a decreasing rate, as is expected in a normal age-earnings profile.

---

[9]  See Mincer (1974).

[10]  See Mohan (1986) and Psacharopoulos and Velez (1991).

## Table 8.6
### Decomposition of the Male/Female Earnings Differential

#### Percentage of Male Pay Advantage
#### Due to Differences in

| Specification | Endowments | | Wage Structure | | Male Pay Advantage | |
|---|---|---|---|---|---|---|
| **Corrected for Selectivity** | | | | | | |
| Evaluated at Male Means | 14.81 | (2.28) | 85.19 | (13.12) | 100 | (15.4) |
| Evaluated at Female Means | 8.02 | (1.23) | 91.98 | (14.16) | 100 | (15.4) |
| **Uncorrected for Selectivity** | | | | | | |
| Evaluated at Male Means | 22.14 | (3.41) | 77.86 | (11.99) | 100 | (15.4) |
| Evaluated at Female Means | 12.31 | (1.89) | 87.68 | (13.5) | 100 | (15.4) |

Notes: $W_m/W_f = 118\%$
   Figures in parentheses are percentages showing the male pay advantage.

We estimate two earnings functions for women. One uses the standard Mincerian model and the other "corrects" for potential selectivity bias by including the Lambda from the probit equation.

The selectivity corrected estimates in column 2 of Table 8.5 show the rate of return to schooling to be about 9 percent, less than the 11 percent from the uncorrected estimates. Hence, if we omit the selection term from the earnings function estimates we would be biasing the marginal rate of return upward. The significant and negative Lambda indicates that there is a strong positive correlation between the unobserved characteristics which are likely to make women highly productive in both the market and the home. These unobservables are, however, the characteristics likely to influence women to remain in the home.

## 6. Discrimination

As was noted in Section 2, working women in Colombia earn, on average, 15 percent less per week than working men. Using the Oaxaca decomposition method we are able to decompose this into a component due to differences in human capital endowments and a component due to "unexplained factors" (which principally includes differences in the labor market structure for men and women, i.e., discrimination).[11]

The standard Oaxaca decomposition method expresses the difference between the mean (log) wage rates of males and females as:

$$LnY_m - LnY_f = X_f(b_m - b_f) + b_m(X_m - X_f) \tag{1a}$$

or, alternatively as:

$$LnY_m - LnY_f = X_m(b_m - b_f) + b_f(X_m - X_f) \tag{1b}$$

---

[11]   See Oaxaca (1973).

There is an index number problem here but there is no advantage to choosing one equation over the other. Consequently we present the results of both in Table 8.6. The first term in both equations is the part of the log earnings differential attributable to differences in the wage structure between the sexes and the second term that is part of the log earnings differential attributable to differences in human capital endowments.

Although we estimate the decomposition for both the selectivity corrected and uncorrected samples, the former yields the more reliable estimate since it essentially uses women's offered wage (being estimated from the entire sample of women) rather than the paid wage (estimated using the sample of working women only).

The male pay advantage is 15.4 percent. Using the selectivity corrected estimates evaluated at the male means in Table 8.5, approximately 14.8 percent of this pay advantage is explained by observable factors, or differences in human capital endowments. The rest of the difference (approximately 85 percent) is due to differences in the way males and females are rewarded in the labor market.

## 7.    Discussion

Female labor force participation rates are shown in our study to be positively influenced by education. However, women are largely concentrated in occupations which are lower paying and have fewer opportunities for advancements. Prior studies in Colombia show that women pursue educational tracks which lead them to these occupations (Velez and Rodriguez, 1989). The findings also show that being the head of a household greatly increases the probability that a woman will participate.

The earnings differential of 15.4 found in our sample is surprisingly low, even when compared with those in many in industrialized countries.[12] This may be partly explained by the exclusion of non-formal workers from our sample. Tenjo (1990), in an analysis of Bogota's labor force in 1979, reported the wage differential to be closer to 30 percent when informal workers were included in the sample. The presence of minimum wage legislation, firmly enforced in the formal sector, may provide another explanation for this small earnings gap.

When explaining earnings, we found evidence of selectivity bias in the determination of weekly wages, pointing out that traditional ordinary least squares (OLS) coefficient estimates are biased upwards for women. Although human capital characteristics are relevant in explaining earnings, the Oaxaca decomposition suggests that differences in the labor market structure are more important than differences in human capital endowments in explaining male-female wage differentials. Hence much of the earnings differential can be attributed to discrimination.

Future research should study issues influencing women's choice of education field as this appears to be an important factor affecting their income levels and occupational opportunities. Another aspect that should be considered is the situation of female heads of household as they face more constraints to increase their participation.

---

[12]    Earnings differentials are typically around 25-30 percent. See Gunderson (1989), Tzannatos (1987), Zabalza and Tzannatos (1985) and Gregory and Duncan (1982).

# References

Departamento Administrativo Nacional de Estadística (DANE). *50 Años de Estadísticas Educativas*. Bogotá: Departamento Administrativo Nacional de Estadística, 1985.

Gregory, R.G. and R.C. Duncan. "Segmented Labour Market Theories and the Australian Experience of Equal Pay for Women." *Journal of Post-Keynesian Economics,* Vol. 3 (1982), pp. 403-428.

Gronau, R. "Sex-Related Wage Differentials and Women's Interrupted Labor Careers: The Chicken and Egg Question." *Journal of Labor Economics,* Vol. 6, no. 1 (1988), pp. 277-301.

Gunderson, M. "Male-Female Wage Differentials and Policy Responses." *Journal of Economic Literature,* Vol. 27, no. 1 (1989), pp. 46-117.

Heckman, J. "The Common Structure of Statistical Model Truncation, Sample Selection and Limited Dependent Variables and a Simple Estimator for such Models." *Annals of Economic and Social Measurement,* Vol. 5, no. 4 (1976), pp. 679-694.

Heckman, J. "Sample Selection Bias as a Specification Error." *Econometrica,* Vol. 47, no. 1 (1979), pp. 153-161.

International Labor Office. *Yearbook of Labor Statistics: Retrospective Edition, 1950-1990.* Geneva: International Labor Office, 1990.

Mincer, J. *Schooling, Experience and Earnings.* New York: Columbia University Press, 1974.

Mohan, R. *Work, Wages, and Welfare in a Developing Metropolis.* Consequences of Growth in Bogota, Colombia. New York: Oxford University Press, 1986.

Oaxaca, R. "Male-female Wage Differentials in Urban Labor Markets." *International Economics Review, Vol.* 14, no. 1 (1973), pp. 693-709.

Psacharopoulos, G. and E. Velez. "Schooling, Ability and Earnings in Colombia, 1988." *Economic Development and Cultural Change.* forthcoming, 1991.

Rico de Alonso, N. "Caraterísticas y Condiciones de la Participación Laboral Femenina a Nivel Urbano en Colombia." Paper presented at the Workshop on Mujer y Participación Laboral. Bogotá, April 1990.

Tenjo, J. "Labor Market, Wage Gap and Gender Discrimination: The Case of Colombia." Mimeograph. University of Toronto: Department of Economics, 1990.

Tzannatos, Z. "Equal Pay in Greece and Britain." *Industrial Relations Journal,* Vol. 18, no. 4 (1987), pp. 275-283.

Velez E. and P. Rodriguez, "Mujer y Educación en Colombia." Mimeograph. Instituto SER de Investigación. Bogotá, 1989.

Zabalza, A. and Z. Tzannatos, *Women and Equal Pay: The Effects of Legislation on Female Employment and Wages in Britain.* Cambridge: Cambridge University Press, 1985.

# 9

## Female Labor Force Participation and Earnings Differentials in Costa Rica

*Hongyu Yang*

### 1.    Introduction

Over the last decade interest in the treatment of women in the labor markets of developing countries has increased dramatically, and more attention is being paid to analyzing the labor force behavior of women and the returns to human capital, especially education.  Do women and men enjoy the same returns to human capital?  Is there an earnings differential between working men and women?  In the case of Costa Rica, the evidence shows that such a gap exists.  Figures 9.1 and 9.2 reveal the existence of significant male-female earnings differentials across schooling and age.  What factors cause this difference?  And how do these factors influence a woman's decision to participate in the labor force?  In this chapter we try to answer these questions.  First, we determine the earnings differential between male and female workers in Costa Rica.  Then we estimate the extent of wage discrimination against females.

In the following section we briefly review the economy and labor market in Costa Rica.  In Section 3 we discuss the data used in this study and present the main characteristics of male and female labor force participants.  In Section 4 we examine labor force participation and the factors influencing women's decision to participate.  In Section 5 we analyze the result of the male and female earnings functions and the decomposition is carried out in Section 6.  In the final section we discuss these findings and their implications.

### 2.    The Costa Rican Economy and the Labor Market

For most of the last twenty-five years economic growth in Costa Rica  has generated improved employment opportunities for workers.  However, during the economic recession in 1981-82, labor market conditions deteriorated countrywide.  Fortunately, recession was the exception rather than the rule in Costa Rica.  Gross domestic product grew by 6.5 percent per annum in the 1960s and by 4.5 percent per annum between 1970 and 1982.

Between 1963 and 1973 the Costa Rican labor force became markedly better educated.  The proportion without education fell from 15 percent to 10 percent, the proportion of illiterates fell by virtually the same percentage, and the proportion with only one to three years of primary education fell from 37 percent to 26 percent.  At the same time the proportion with four to six years of primary education increased from 37 percent to 45 percent, the proportion with secondary education from 9 percent to 16 percent, and the proportion with university education from 2  percent to  4  percent (Fields, 1988).  Between 1965 and 1988 the higher education

**Figure 9.1**
Schooling-Earnings Profiles by Gender
Costa Rica 1989

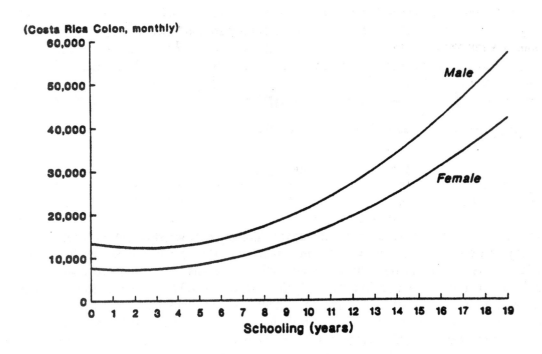

**Figure 9.2**
Age-Earnings Profiles by Gender
Costa Rica 1989

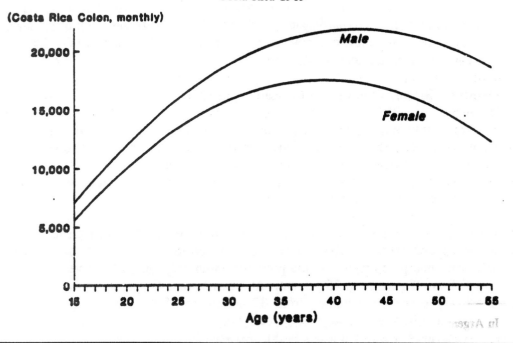

enrollment ratio rose from 6 percent to 24 percent and the secondary enrollment ratio increased from 24 percent to 41 percent; primary school enrollment was virtually 100 percent (UNESCO, Statistical Yearbook).

Economic growth has brought more employment opportunities and created enough new jobs to keep pace with the growth in the labor force.  Not only are more people employed, but the mix of jobs has improved in favor of the better-paying categories:  Wage-earners in place of unpaid family workers;  professional, technical, managerial, and office workers rather than manual workers;  manufacturing and other sectors in place of agriculture; public as opposed to private employment.

## 3.    Data Characteristics

The data used in this study come from the Encuesta de Hogares de Propositos Multiples (EHPM), a nationwide household survey that is conducted by the Statistics and Census Department of Costa Rica.  The data were collected in July 1989.  The data set contains 34,368 individual observations from 7,637 households.  Information is available on personal characteristics of the population such as age, sex, education and area of residence.  Employment variables include occupation, job category and hours worked per week.  Information exists on labor income, other income and family income.  From this data set, a total of 15,867 cases were used.  This sample included all individuals in the prime working age range (20 to 60 years) for whom relevant data were available.

Table 9.1 provides descriptive statistics for the main variables in the sample.  Working men and working women are defined as those who worked for more than one hour for pay during the reference week.  This definition excludes unpaid family workers.   As Table 9.1 shows, the female labor force participation rate (27 percent) is significantly lower than that for men (76 percent).  The marriage rate for working females is lower than for working males, and is much higher among non-working females.  Working women have less children than non-working women.  This suggests that marriage and family have a great influence on female participation.

Table 9.1 also shows great differences in the distribution of men and women by education level. Only 11 percent of working men had completed  secondary school compared to 22 percent of working women.  The largest gap in educational achievement occurs at the university level:  Only 5 percent of working men have university degrees compared to 11 percent of working women. Overall, the average years of schooling for working females is two years greater than that for their male counterparts.  This was confirmed elsewhere in a recent study (Gindling, 1991) which showed that from 1980  to 1985 the average years of schooling for working women was about one and half years more than that of working men.   This is typical in Latin America and Caribbean countries.[1]  However, despite the fact that women have more schooling than men, they earn less than males.

Tables 9.2A and 9.2B show the education and earnings differentials by occupation  and working sector in more detail. Women's schooling is higher than men's in all occupational categories except two: Managers and service workers.  Women's average earnings, however, are lower than men's in all occupational categories.  In the public sector females have an average of

---

[1]    In Argentina average schooling for working females is 9.4 years, while for working men it is 8.8 years; and in Venezuela, average years of schooling  are 8.5 and 6.9 for working females and males respectively.

**Table 9.1**
Means (and Standard Deviations) of Sample Variables

| Variable | Working Males | Working Females | Non-working Females |
|---|---|---|---|
| Hours worked/week | 47.64 | 40.53 | |
| | (13.33) | (16.29) | |
| Working experience (years) | 22.5 | 19.1 | |
| | (12.5) | (11.4) | |
| Primary income/month[a] | 18497.77 | 14942.14 | |
| | (18307.45) | (14525.66) | |
| Family income/month[a] | 30085.94 | 36826.81 | 23976.12 |
| | (28153.41) | (35964.48) | (23435.96) |
| Age (years) | 35.11 | 33.57 | 35.68 |
| | (10.76) | (9.68) | (11.49) |
| Head of household | 0.74 | 0.21 | 0.09 |
| | (0.44) | (0.41) | (0.28) |
| Household size | 5.10 | 5.23 | 5.20 |
| | (2.29) | (2.49) | (2.23) |
| No. of young children | 1.46 | 1.39 | 1.52 |
| | (1.38) | (1.35) | (1.42) |
| Urban | 0.42 | 0.61 | 0.42 |
| | (0.49) | (0.49) | (0.49) |
| Married | 0.73 | 0.46 | 0.76 |
| | (0.44) | (0.50) | (0.43) |
| Years of schooling | 6.66 | 8.47 | 6.18 |
| | (4.02) | (4.21) | (3.77) |
| No education | 0.07 | 0.03 | 0.08 |
| | (0.25) | (0.16) | (0.27) |
| Incomplete primary | 0.16 | 0.09 | 0.17 |
| | (0.36) | (0.29) | (0.38) |
| Completed primary | 0.43 | 0.35 | 0.43 |
| | (0.50) | (0.48) | (0.50) |
| Incomplete secondary | 0.13 | 0.13 | 0.11 |
| | (0.33) | (0.33) | (0.32) |
| Completed secondary | 0.11 | 0.20 | 0.12 |
| | (0.31) | (0.40) | (0.33) |
| University | 0.05 | 0.11 | 0.05 |
| | (0.22) | (0.31) | (0.22) |
| Graduate school | 0.03 | 0.06 | 0.004 |
| | (0.24) | (0.17) | (0.06) |
| Sample size | 5,463 | 2,126 | 5,892 |

a.   In current Costa Rica Colones
Notes: Labor Force Participation Rate: Female = 27%; Male = 76%
  Sample includes aged 20 to 60.  Working population consists of all those working.
  Excludes unpaid family workers.
  Numbers in parentheses are t-ratios.
Source:  Costa Rica 1989 Household Survey.

**Table 9.2A**
Mean Earnings and Education by Occupation and Sex

| Occupational Category | Earnings (Colon, monthly) | | Schooling (years) | |
| --- | --- | --- | --- | --- |
| | Males | Females | Males | Females |
| Professional/technical workers | 35,309 | 27,591 | 12.8 | 13.6 |
| Managers/Administrators | 43,883 | 31,656 | 12.0 | 9.7 |
| Office workers | 23,905 | 19,556 | 10.2 | 11.3 |
| Storekeepers/vendors | 22,176 | 12,763 | 7.7 | 7.9 |
| Agricultural workers | 12,112 | 8,506 | 4.5 | 4.7 |
| Porters/janitors | 17,260 | 10,434 | 6.4 | 6.7 |
| Service workers | 17,481 | 8,557 | 6.4 | 5.9 |
| Overall | 18,459 | 14,941 | 6.7 | 8.5 |
| N | 5,471 | 2,138 | 5,435 | 2,122 |

Source: Costa Rica Household Survey, 1989

**Table 9.2B**
Mean Earnings and Education by Sector of Employment and Sex

| Occupational Category | Earnings (Colon, monthly) | | Schooling (years) | |
| --- | --- | --- | --- | --- |
| | Males | Females | Males | Females |
| Public | 27,468 | 24,954 | 9.5 | 11.7 |
| Private | 16,584 | 10,928 | 6.1 | 7.2 |
| Overall Mean | 18,458 | 14,910 | 6.7 | 8.5 |
| N | 5,501 | 2,145 | 5,465 | 2,129 |

Source: Costa Rica Household Survey, 1989

two more years of schooling than males, and in private sector one year more. Nevertheless, women make 65.9 percent of men's earnings in the private sector and 90.8 percent in the public sector.

## 4. The Determinants of Female Labor Force Participation

As is commonly known, the major factors which influence women's labor market activity are educational attainment, marital status, fertility, "need" for income (which is measured by husband's income, family income excluding female's earnings, the number of earners in a family and the household status of women) and age.

Whether women participate in the labor force or not depends on those factors and their reservation wage. That is, when a woman searches in the labor market for a job, she will have some idea of the wage she desires or merits, based on her value at home or her previous wage. She can thus be viewed as setting a minimum standard for jobs she will find acceptable. She will accept a job that pays above this critical value and reject offers below this value.

This means that our sample of working women are self-selected. Therefore, if we use this non-random sample to estimate the earnings function for female workers, the result will be biased. Non-working women are unobserved. In order to correct for this selectivity bias, we use the well-known two-step method proposed by Heckman (1979). A probit equation is used to estimate the probability of a woman being in the work force and the inverse Mill's ratio (Lambda) is computed and added to the earnings function as an additional regressor.

In the probit work participation functions, age and schooling are entered as a series of dummy variables for each age group (in 5 years cohorts) and each level of schooling. This is to take into account any non-linearity in the effect of either age or schooling on participation. Other dummy variables in this model are marital status, residential area, and being a head of household. Number of young children and household size are continuous variables.

Table 9.3 presents the results of probit estimates for female work participation. Using those results we predict the probability of labor force participation for each characteristic (Table 9.4). As expected, women with incomplete primary education are less likely to participate in the labor force. At the completed primary level, however, educational attainment does not have a significant impact on participation. This is explained by the fact that about 50 percent of women are service workers and 30 percent are blue collar workers. This implies that the value of education credentials in the informal sector is limited. A similar situation exists in Bolivia.

The other education levels show a positive significant impact on participation. Secondary school graduates have an estimated participation probability that is 14 percentage points higher than incomplete primary school graduates. University graduates have a participation probability 21 percentage points higher than the graduates with some primary education. Graduate school graduates have the highest participation probability of all (54.2 percentage).

Married women participate less than unmarried women, 17.7 percent versus 40.4 percent. This reflects the fact that married women are likely to withdraw from the labor force if they have young children. The variable Presence of Children shows the difference among number of children. The more children a woman has, the less likely she is to participate in the labor force. Being a household head is also associated with a higher participation probability than that of non-household head.

## Table 9.3
### Probit Estimates for Female Labor Force Participation

| Variable | Coefficient | t-ratio | Mean | Partial Derivative |
|---|---|---|---|---|
| Constant | -1.241 | -10.10 | 1.000 | |
| Age 20 to 24 | 0.524 | 5.95 | 0.198 | 0.163 |
| Age 25 to 29 | 0.668 | 7.60 | 0.184 | 0.208 |
| Age 30 to 34 | 0.739 | 8.36 | 0.163 | 0.230 |
| Age 35 to 39 | 0.879 | 10.04 | 0.133 | 0.273 |
| Age 40 to 44 | 0.744 | 8.23 | 0.097 | 0.231 |
| Age 45 to 49 | 0.622 | 6.67 | 0.081 | 0.193 |
| Age 50 to 54 | 0.350 | 3.60 | 0.072 | 0.109 |
| Incomplete primary | -0.126 | -1.73 | 0.149 | -0.039 |
| Completed primary | 0.042 | 0.68 | 0.412 | 0.013 |
| Incomplete secondary | 0.160 | 2.14 | 0.116 | 0.050 |
| Completed secondary | 0.329 | 4.58 | 0.142 | 0.102 |
| University | 0.526 | 6.38 | 0.065 | 0.163 |
| Graduate School | 0.934 | 8.40 | 0.024 | 0.290 |
| Married | -0.684 | -15.63 | 0.680 | -0.213 |
| Number of young children | -0.027 | -1.71 | 1.487 | -0.009 |
| Urban | 0.289 | 7.63 | 0.473 | 0.090 |
| Household head | 0.340 | 5.67 | 0.120 | 0.106 |
| Household size | 0.019 | 2.10 | 5.200 | 0.006 |

Notes: Sample includes women aged 20 to 60 years.
Female labor force participation rate: 27%.

Log-Likelihood = -4062.8
Sample size = 8,039

The variable for residential area shows a positive and significant effect on participation. Women living in urban areas have a 45 percent greater participation probability than those living in rural areas. This suggests that urban areas provide more job opportunities and a more congenial environment for a woman to participate in market activities.

As expected, age has a positive and significant influence on participation and the relationship between the two variables is U-shaped. Women in their early 20s have a 21 percent probability of participating, and reach the peak of employment in their late 30s.

## 5. Earnings functions

In order to explain the variation in earnings in the sample by differences in the human capital characteristics of the individual, we use the standard Mincerian earnings functions (Mincer, 1974). The independent variables are years of schooling, years of working experience (Age-schooling-6), working experience squared (to account for the concavity of the earnings-experience profiles), and the log of hours worked per week. The inverse Mill's ratio, which was derived from the participation equation enters as an additional regressor to correct for sample selection bias.

## Table 9.4
### Predicted Female Labor Force Participation by Selected Characteristics

| Characteristic | Predicted Probability |
|---|---|
| Overall Mean Participation Rate | 27.0 |
| **Age** | |
| 20 to 24 | 21.3 |
| 25 to 29 | 25.7 |
| 30 to 34 | 28.0 |
| 35 to 39 | 32.9 |
| 40 to 44 | 28.2 |
| 45 to 49 | 24.2 |
| 50 to 54 | 16.6 |
| **Education** | |
| Incomplete Primary | 16.9 |
| Incomplete Secondary | 25.2 |
| Completed Secondary | 30.9 |
| Complete University | 38.1 |
| Complete Graduate School | 54.2 |
| **Female head of Household** | |
| Yes | 34.1 |
| No | 22.7 |
| **Marital Status** | |
| Married | 17.7 |
| Single | 40.4 |
| **Presence of children (0 to 12 years)** | |
| None | 25.2 |
| One | 24.4 |
| Two | 23.5 |
| Three | 22.7 |
| Four | 21.9 |
| Five | 21.0 |
| Six | 20.2 |
| **Residence** | |
| Urban | 28.9 |
| Rural | 19.9 |

Note:  Probability of participation holding other variables constant at their sample mean.
Simulations done only for variables whose coefficients are statistically significant.
Based on the results reported in Table 9.3

In Table 9.5 we see that the Lambda variable is insignificant.  This can be interpreted as evidence that there is no self-selection (Cogan, 1980) or that women as a group are more homogeneous than initially perceived. Since there is no statistical evidence on this point and the selectivity corrected and uncorrected points estimates are virtually identical, we will not differentiate between them in discussing the results below.

## Table 9.5
### Earnings Functions

| Variables | Men (uncorrected) | Women (corrected for selectivity) | Women (uncorrected for selectivity) |
|---|---|---|---|
| Constant | 4.528 (46.526) | 3.781 (28.549) | 3.693 (34.514) |
| Years of Schooling | 0.101 (40.707) | 0.129 (29.315) | 0.131 (31.946) |
| Experience | 0.035 (12.328) | 0.030 (6.431) | 0.031 (6.662) |
| Experience Squared | -0.000 (-8.243) | -0.000 (-3.144) | -0.000 (-3.382) |
| Ln(hours weekly) | 0.626 (26.898) | 0.714 (31.144) | 0.718 (31.641) |
| Lambda | | -0.050 (-1.128) | |
| R-Squared | 0.315 | 0.520 | 0.520 |
| Mean of dependent variable | 8.10 | 7.79 | 7.79 |
| N | 5,463 | 2,126 | 2,126 |

Notes: Corrected for selectivity bias using Probit equation in Table 9.3.
　　　Numbers in parentheses are t-ratios.
　　　Dependent Variable = Ln(weekly earnings).

Based on these results, the returns to investment in schooling for females is 3 percentage points higher than that for males, although women earn less on average than men. This apparently paradoxical fact is due to the lower foregone earnings of females (Psacharopoulos, 1985). In other words, the opportunity cost of women's time is lower. The rewards of market experience are slightly higher for men (3.5 percent) than women (3 percent), in part because women have more frequently interrupted careers.

## 6.    Discrimination

After estimating earnings functions for men and women we are able to address the key issue in this study: How much of the male-female earnings differential can be explained by observed factors (human capital endowments) and how much might be caused by discrimination?

The standard Oaxaca (1974) decomposition method was utilized to differentiate mean (log) wage rates of males and females. The equations are expressed as follow:

$$LnY_m - LnY_f = X_f(b_m-b_f) + b_m(X_m-X_f) \qquad (1)$$
$$= X_m(b_m-b_f) + b_f(X_m-X_f) \qquad (2)$$

Where $X_i$s denotes parameters of the earnings functions, $b_i$s are the corresponding estimates, and i=f (female) or m (male).   Equation 1 evaluates the earnings difference at male means characteristics while Equation 2 does so at the female means characteristics.  The first term on the right hand side of equation 1 and 2 measures the difference in earnings due to discrimination in the market place,  while the second term refers to the difference in the market evaluation of human capital endowments.

Table 9.6 presents the results of the decomposition.  For working women (uncorrected), we find that human capital differences produce a negative contributions to the male-female wage differentials.   That means the wage difference   cannot be explained by human capital endowments, but rather by the wage structure.  The wage differences due to discrimination account for more than 100 percent.  Using the selectivity estimates, the  wage gap due to human capital endowment is only 5.5 percent and up to 94.5 percent of earnings differentials may be explained by unobserved factors including discrimination.

### Table 9.6
#### Decomposition of the Male/Female Earnings Differential

| Specification | Percentage of Male Pay Advantage due to differences in | |
| --- | --- | --- |
| | Human Capital Endowments | Wage Structure |
| **Corrected for Selectivity** | | |
| Evaluated at Male Means | 6.7 | 93.3 |
| Evaluated at Female Means | 5.5 | 94.5 |
| **Uncorrected for Selectivity** | | |
| Evaluated at Male Means | -3.2 | 103.9 |
| Evaluated at Female Means | -3.6 | 103.6 |

Notes:  The decomposition is based on the results of Table 9.5, above.
$W_m/W_f$= 123.8%

## 7.    Discussion

The results of this study indicate that education has a powerful positive effect  on the probability of female labor force participation, with more educated women being more likely to participate in the market and more likely to be employed.   An increase in the level of education from primary to secondary increases the participation probability from 25.2 to 30.9 percent, and from secondary to graduate school education increases the participation probability from 30.9 to 54.2.

Marital Status is the most important determinant of female labor force participation.  Women with young children, or who are living in rural areas, or who are the head of a household, are also less likely to participate in market activities.

The earnings differential between working males and females is 19.2 percent. This result is consistent with other studies (see Gindling, 1991). It is worth noting that women make 65.9 percent of men's earnings in the private sector, and 90.8 percent of men's earnings in the public sector. This is partly due to the fact that the public sector in Costa Rica is the highest paid sector with significant protection being accorded by trade union activity.

Decomposition estimates suggest that the earnings differentials are not due to the lower rate of return to human capital of women. In fact, women, on average, have two more years of schooling than their male counterparts. Instead, unobserved characteristics, including discrimination, cause the earnings differentials in Costa Rica. Therefore, further studies should identify and analyze these unobserved characteristics for a better understanding of male-female wage differentials.

# Appendix 9
## Supplementary Figures

**Figure 9.3**
### Probability of Women Participating in the Labor Force by Level of Education

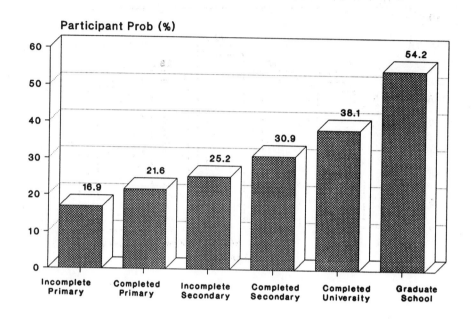

**Figure 9.4**
### Probability of Women Participating in the Labor Force by Marital Status, Area and Household Headship

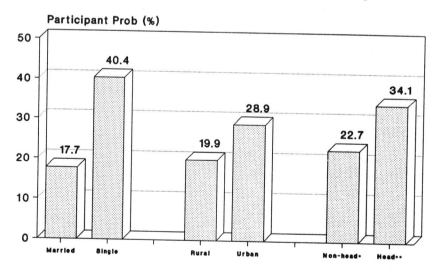

Note: • Not a household head
••• Household head

**Figure 9.5**
Probability of Women Participating in the Labor Force
by Age Group

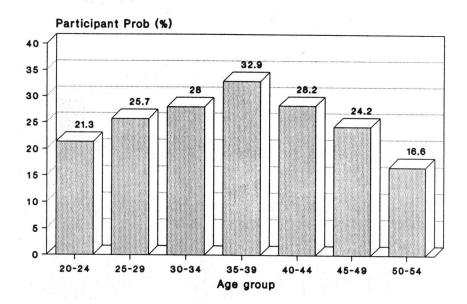

# References

Cogan, J. "Married Women's Labor Supply: A Comparison of Alternative Estimates" in J.P. Smith (ed.) *Female Labor Supply: Theory and Estimation.* Princeton, NJ: Princeton University Press, 1980.

Gindling, T.H. "Women Wage and Economic Crisis in Costa Rica." 1991 (Forthcoming), University of Maryland: Dept. of Economics.

Fields, G.S. "Employment and Economic Growth in Costa Rica." *World Development,* Vol. 16, no. 12 (1988). pp 1493-1507.

Hackman, J. "Sample Selection as a Specification Error." *Econometrica,* Vol. 47, no. 1 (1979). pp 153-161.

Mincer, J. *Schooling, Experience and Earnings.* New York: Columbia University Press, 1974.

Oaxaca, R.L. "Male-female Wage Differentials in Urban Labor Markets." *International Economic Review,* Vol. 14, no. 1 (1974). pp. 693-709.

Psacharopoulos, G. "Returns to Education: A Further International Update and Implications." *Journal of Human Resources*, Vol. 20, no.4 (1985). pp 583-604.

UNESCO, *Statistical Yearbook,* New York: UNESCO (1976, 1990).

# 10

# Why Women Earn Less Than Men in Costa Rica

*T. H. Gindling*

## 1.    Introduction

In Costa Rica, men earn higher wages than women on average.  In 1989, within the Central Valley (the focus of this chapter) men's wages were, on average, 3.5 percent higher than women's.[1]  The difference between the average wages of men and women in Costa Rica is lower than that for any other country reported in this volume.

In this chapter we measure the impact of differences in observable human capital endowments and different access to higher paying jobs for men and women on the male-female wage gap. These two potential sources of wage differences are not mutually exclusive.  For example, men could have access to higher paying jobs because they have higher levels of education, and higher paying jobs require more educated workers.  Therefore, we will explicitly measure the degree to which access to higher paying jobs is caused by differences in endowments.  In addition, we will measure that part of the male-female wage differential which is attributable to women being paid differently than men with the same endowments in similar jobs.  We will also measure the part of the differences in male and female wages unexplained by differences in observed human capital endowments.  While this difference is often used as a measure of labor market discrimination, we are unable to distinguish discrimination from unmeasured gender differences in tastes, human capital or ability.  Nor can we distinguish differences in wages due to discrimination from compensating differentials.  Similarly, we cannot distinguish which part of the differential unexplained by differences in observed endowments is due to pre-labor market discrimination or tastes.[2]

---

[1]    These data are from the Household Surveys of Employment and Unemployment for 1989.  For the country as a whole, an average man earned wages that were also 3.5 percent higher than an average woman's.  According to the Household Surveys of Employment and Unemployment for 1987 and 1988, in 1988 the male-female wage differential was 4.4 percent for the country as a whole and 9.8 percent for the Central Valley, and in 1987 the male-female wage differential was 8.6 percent for the country as a whole and 6.5 percent for the Central Valley.

[2]    This technique for measuring labor market discrimination is sometimes called the "residual difference" method.  Beginning with Oaxaca (1973) many studies of male-female earnings and wage differences have used this methodology.  In recent literature reviews,  Cain (1986) and Gunderson (1989) exhaustively list and discuss the difficulties with using this as a measure of labor market discrimination. Carvajal and Geithman (1983) and Gindling (1990, 1989a) have addressed the issue of male-female wage differentials in Costa Rica.  The present study extends these analyses.  We measure differences between male and female wages due to differences in human capital and differences in access to higher paying jobs.

## 2.   The Costa Rican Labor Market and Women

In Costa Rica the economic expansion of the late 1970's gave way, in the early 1980's, to the deepest recession since the 1930's.[3] GNP stagnated between 1979 and 1980 and fell in 1981 and 1982. Increased borrowing by the Central Government and Central Bank to finance increased spending and an overvalued exchange rate caused foreign public debt to more than double between 1978 and 1981. In December of 1980 the colon was devalued. This was followed by a dramatic increase in inflation (from 18.1 percent in 1980 to 90.1 percent in 1982) and a steep decline in real earnings (35 percent from July 1980 to July 1982). The unemployment rate rose steadily from 1979 and reached a peak of 9.4 percent in July 1982. Underemployment also increased, from 4.7 percent of the labor force in 1979 to 7.0 percent in 1982.

In mid-1982 the government instituted a package of policies intended to stabilize and revive confidence in the economy. By mid-1983 the economy had entered into a period of recovery. Rising terms of trade, increased foreign aid and the stabilization policies combined to bring about increases in the GDP, lower inflation and higher real earnings. By 1986, real earnings had nearly regained 1980 levels and GDP growth reached 5.5 percent. Between 1986 and 1989, GDP growth averaged 4.5 percent and unemployment and inflation rates remained low.

Gindling (1990, 1989a) notes that the male-female wage and earnings differentials increased between 1980 and 1982, but then fell to pre-recession levels by 1986. Results in Gindling (1990, 1989a) suggest that the increase in the male-female wage differential during the recession was primarily due to secondary family workers entering the labor force to compensate for the falling earnings of the family's primary worker (the "added worker" effect). These entrants were disproportionately female and had lower levels of education than women already in the labor force. After the recession, these secondary family workers left the labor force.

Starting in 1984 Costa Rica began a comprehensive structural adjustment program. The aim was to increase and diversify exports (Lizano, 1990). In particular, so-called "non-traditional" exports were encouraged through breaks, subsidies and technical assistance. "Non-traditional" exports included any export that was neither coffee, bananas, sugar or beef, and which was not exported to a Central American Common Market country. By 1990, the majority of Costa Rica's exports (by value) were "non-traditional exports." Most successful "non-traditional exports" have been agricultural goods (for example, flowers, ornamental plants and pineapples). However, some manufacturing products have become important exports, most notably textiles and electronic assembly. It is likely that women are disproportionately represented in this sector, particularly in the textile and electronic assembly industries. However, no data are available to verify this supposition.[4]

Recently, the legislature of Costa Rica passed the Law for the Promotion of the Social Equality of Women, the most comprehensive law of its kind in Latin America. The first article of this law states that "it is the obligation of the state to promote and guarantee the equality of rights between men and women in the political, economic, social and cultural arenas." However, by 1989, the year studied in this chapter, the law was not yet implemented.

---

[3]   The 1975-78 period was characterized by the rapid growth of Gross Domestic Product and Aggregate Demand, financed by a large increase in the price of coffee. In 1978 the terms of trade began declining from its "coffee boom" high. Driven largely by a fall in the price of coffee, terms of trade continued to fall until 1982.

[4]   See Gindling and Berry (1990) and Tardanico (1992) for a more comprehensive discussion of the Costa Rican labor market in the 1980's.

## 3. The Methodology

We will assume the mean natural logarithm of wages of men and women ($W_i$) can be represented by the wage equations:

$$W_i = \underline{B}_i' \underline{X}_i \tag{1}$$

where $i =$ Male (M) and Female (F), $\underline{B}_i$ is a vector of parameters to be estimated, and $\underline{X}_i$ is a vector of the average endowments (wage-determining personal characteristics) for men and women, including human capital endowments such as years of education, type of education, experience and other variables. The difference in mean natural logarithm of wages of men and women can be decomposed as follows:

$$W_M - W_F = \underline{B}_M'(\underline{X}_M - \underline{X}_F) + (\underline{B}_M - \underline{B}_F)'\underline{X}_F \tag{2}$$
$$= E + U$$

where $\underline{X}_M$ is a vector of average endowments for men and $\underline{X}_F$ is a vector of the average endowments for women. E is the part of difference between the average wages of men and the average wages of women explained by differences in endowments. U is the part not explained by differences in endowments; it is the difference between what women earn now and what women would earn if women faced the same wage-determination structure as men. U might be considered a rough measure of the difference in wages between men and women due to labor market discrimination. However, difficulties with interpreting U as the difference due to discrimination are well documented (for example, see Cain, 1986).[5] At this we will also explicitly measure the impact of each endowment on the male-female wage differential.

We also describe a method for measuring the part of the male-female wage differential due to differences between men and women in access to good jobs. This method was first developed by Brown, Moon and Zoloth (1980). Let the probability that a man or woman (i) is found working in a given job (j) be represented by $P_{ij}$. Assume that the mean natural logarithm of wages of men and women in each job can be represented by:

$$W_{ij} = \underline{B}_{ij}' \underline{X}_{ij} \tag{3}$$

The difference in average wages between men and women can be decomposed into:

$$W_M - W_F = \Sigma_j(P_{Fj}[\underline{B}_{Mj}'\underline{X}_{Mj} - \underline{B}_{Fj}'\underline{X}_{Fj}]) + \Sigma_j(\underline{B}_{Mj}'\underline{X}_{Mj}[P_{Mj} - P_{Fj}]) \tag{4}$$
$$= W + J$$

where J is the part of the average wage differential due to differences between men and women in access to jobs that pay higher wages, and W is the part due to differences in the pay that men and women earn within the same jobs.

---

[5] An alternative decomposition would be to measure U as the difference between the wages men earn now and the wages men would earn if men faced the same wage-determining structure as women. In this case equation one would be:

$$W_M - W_F = \underline{B}_F'(\underline{X}_M - \underline{X}_F) + (\underline{B}_M - \underline{B}_F)'\underline{X}_M \tag{2a}$$
$$= E + U$$

I also estimate this formulation of E and U. I report these in a footnote in Section 5. Cotton (1988) argues that to measure discrimination U should measure the difference in wages that would exist between men and women in the absence of discrimination. He argues that the best measure of discrimination would be:

$$W_M - W_F = \underline{B}_*'(\underline{X}_M - \underline{X}_F) + [(\underline{B}_M - \underline{B}_*)'\underline{X}_M + (\underline{B}_* - \underline{B}_F)'\underline{X}_F] \tag{2b}$$
$$= E + U$$

where $\underline{B}_* = \underline{B}_M P_M + \underline{B}_F P_F$ where $P_M$ and $P_f$ are the sample proportions of women and men. We do not present estimates of these statistics because they become cumbersome when we attempt to measure differences due to different access to high paying jobs.

Let $\hat{P}_{Fj}$ measure the probability that women in the sample would be found in sector j if faced with the same job-assignment structure as men. $\hat{P}_{Fj}$ is estimated by assuming that:

$$P_{Mjn} = \frac{\exp(\underline{K}_{Mj}'\underline{Z}_{Mn})}{\Sigma_k \exp(\underline{K}_{Mk}'\underline{Z}_{Mn})} \tag{5}$$

where $P_{Mjn}$ is the probability that each man, n, is found in job j, $\underline{Z}_{Mn}$ is a vector of endowments for each man, n, $\underline{K}_{Mj}$ is a vector of parameters to be estimated (for men) and k = all jobs. $\underline{K}_{Mj}$ is estimated using the logit technique and then:

$$\hat{P}_{Fjn} = \frac{\exp(\underline{K}_{Mj}'\underline{Z}_{Fn})}{\Sigma_k \exp(\underline{K}_{Mk}'\underline{Z}_{Fn})} \quad \text{is calculated for each female worker, n,}$$

and sector, j (where $\underline{Z}_{Fn}$ is a vector of personal characteristics for each woman, n.) The mean of $\hat{P}_{Fjn}$ in each sector is $\hat{P}_{Fj}$. Adding and subtracting $\underline{B}_{Mj}'\underline{X}_{Fj}\,\hat{P}_{Fj}$ and $\underline{B}_{Mj}'\underline{X}_{Fj}P_{Fj}$ from equation 3 one obtains:

$$W_M - W_F = \tag{6}$$

$$\Sigma_j(\hat{P}_{Fj}[\underline{B}_{Mj}'\underline{X}_{Fj}-\underline{B}_{Fj}'\underline{X}_{Fj}]) \quad + \quad \Sigma_j(P_{Fj}[\underline{B}_{Mj}'\underline{X}_{Mj}-\underline{B}_{Mj}'\underline{X}_{Fj}]) \quad +$$

$$\Sigma_j(\underline{B}_{Mj}'\underline{X}_{Mj}[\hat{P}_{Fj}-P_{Fj}]) \quad + \quad \Sigma_j(\underline{B}_{Mj}'\underline{X}_{Mj}[P_{Mj}-\hat{P}_{Fj}])$$

$$= \quad WU \qquad\qquad + \qquad WE \qquad +$$
$$\quad JU \qquad\qquad + \qquad JE$$

where WE is the part of the W explained by differences in endowments, WU is the part of W unexplained by differences in endowments, JE is the part of J explained by differences in endowments, and JU is the part of J unexplained by differences in endowments. WU can be considered a rough approximation of wage discrimination against women, while JU can be can be considered a rough approximation of job discrimination.[6]

---

[6] Job discrimination is considered to be the situation where qualified women are kept out of higher paying jobs. Wage discrimination is considered to be the situation where women are paid less than equally qualified men in the same jobs.

WU is a weighted average of the difference between what women earn now in each job and what women would earn in each job if they were paid according to the same wage structure as men. JU is the wage differential between what women earn now and what they would earn if women faced the same job assignment structure as men. An alternative measure, analogous to the measure discussed in the last footnote, is to construct WU as the difference between the wages men earn now in each job and the wages men would earn if they were paid according to the wage determining structure of women, and to construct JU as the wage differential between what men earn now and what men would earn if they faced the same job assignment structure as women. That is, estimate $\underline{K}_{Fj}$ using the logit technique calculate:

$$\hat{P}_{Mji} = \frac{\underline{K}_{Fji}'\underline{Z}_{Mji}}{\Sigma\underline{K}_{Fki}'\underline{Z}_{Mki}} \quad \text{for each male worker, i, and}$$

sector, j. The mean of $\hat{P}_{Mji}$ in each sector is $\hat{P}_{Mj}$. Then add and subtract $\underline{B}_{Fj}'\underline{X}_{Mj}P_{Mj}$ and $\hat{P}_{Mj}\underline{B}_{Fj}'\underline{X}_{Mj}$ from:

$$W_M - W_F = \Sigma(P_{Mj}[\underline{B}_{Mj}'\underline{X}_{Mj}-\underline{B}_{Fj}'\underline{X}_{Fj}]) + \Sigma(\underline{B}_{Fj}'\underline{X}_{Fj}[P_{Mj}-P_{Fj}]) \tag{4a}$$
$$= \qquad W \qquad\qquad + \qquad J$$

to obtain:

$$W_M - W_F = \Sigma_j(P_{Mj}[\underline{B}_{Mj}'\underline{X}_{Mj}-\underline{B}_{Fj}'\underline{X}_{Mj}]) \quad + \quad \Sigma_j(P_{Mj}[\underline{B}_{Fj}'\underline{X}_{Mj}-\underline{B}_{Fj}'\underline{X}_{Fj}]) \quad + \tag{6a}$$

$$\Sigma_j(\underline{B}_{Fj}'\underline{X}_{Fj}[P_{Mj}-P_{Mj}]) \quad + \quad \Sigma_j(\underline{B}_{Fj}'\underline{X}_{Fj}[\hat{P}_{Mj}-P_{Fj}])$$
$$= \quad WU \qquad\qquad + \qquad WE \quad +$$
$$\quad JU \qquad\qquad + \qquad JE$$

These estimates are presented in a footnote in Section 5.

## 4.    The Data and Specification of the Variables

The data used to estimate the decompositions described in Section 3 are from the Household Survey of Employment and Unemployment conducted by the Statistics and Census Department of the Costa Rican government. The Household Survey is conducted annually and we use the most recent survey available, 1989. The survey provides reliable data on wages, some job characteristics and some personal characteristics of workers. We use data from the Central Valley of Costa Rica to control for labor market conditions which may vary across regions and affect male-female differentials. The Central Valley includes the two largest cities in the country, San Jose and Alajeula, as well as two of the next four largest cities, Heredia and Cartago. The cities in the Central Valley are all within commuting distance of one another, and are expected to comprise a unified labor market. Over 60 percent of the Costa Rican labor force works in the Central Valley.

The literature on labor market segmentation (for example, Piore, 1971) justifies dividing the labor market into sectors. In segmented labor markets some workers are in "formal" sector jobs where working conditions are better and status and wages are higher than in the "informal" sectors. Access to formal sector jobs is limited and formal sector workers are protected from competition from informal sector workers by unions, labor protection legislation or internal labor markets. Wages in the formal sectors are higher than those in the informal sector for workers with identical human capital. Gindling (1991) argues that the labor market in the Central Valley of Costa Rica can be thought of as segmented into at least three distinct sectors. We consider two "formal" sectors where workers are "protected." The public (formal) sector is the highest paid sector, workers being protected by unions (the public sector is the only heavily unionized sector in Costa Rica) and government wage and hiring policies. Private-formal sector workers are protected by legislation (primarily minimum wage laws) and may be paid efficiency wages by large firms. On average, they earn lower wages than public sector workers. Workers in the informal sector are not protected by laws or unions (worker protection legislation is not enforced in the informal sector), and are paid the lowest wages of any sector.[7] (For a discussion of labor market segmentation in Costa Rica see Gindling, 1991 and 1989b.) Tenjo (1990) notes the importance of the domestic servant sector of the Colombian labor market in bringing about male-female earnings differentials. In this paper, we consider domestic servants as a separate sector. Unfortunately, we do not have reliable data on the value of payments in-kind to domestic servants. Because payments in-kind (for example, room, board, transportation, etc.) can be expected to be larger for domestic servants than for other workers, reported wages for domestic servants will probably under-estimate the actual returns to labor of domestic servants relative to other workers.

Work in the United States on discrimination and differential access of women to good jobs has focused on higher paying occupations (for example, Brown, Moon and Zoloth, 1980). In this paper we also measure the difference in wages between men and women due to different access to higher paying occupations within sectors. We are able to distinguish between four

---

[7]    If a worker is employed by the central government or a semi-autonomous (para-statal) enterprise then he/she is assigned to the public sector. If a worker is not assigned to the public sector, and he/she either works in a firm with more than five employees, or has more than high school education, or is classed as a professional or technical worker, he or she is assigned to the private-formal sector. If a worker is employed in a firm with five or fewer employee and does not have high school education, that worker is assigned to the informal sector. On average, the highest wages are paid in the public sector and the lowest in the informal sector.

occupational classes (in order of descending average wages): directors and managers, professionals and technical employees, administrative personnel, and laborers. These occupational differences are useful only for the two formal sectors.[8]

We thus divide the labor market into ten different sectors and occupations ("jobs") -- an informal sector, a domestic servant sector, and four different occupations within the public and private-formal sectors, respectively.

*The wage function.* The dependent variable in the wage function is the natural logarithm of hourly wages for the principal employment of the worker. The numbers presented in the results section will be the difference between the average logarithm of male and female wages. The difference in average wages in the Central Valley of Costa Rica between men and women is 3.5 percent of the female wage, while the difference between the average natural logarithms of wages is .05. There is a one-to-one correspondence between the percentage average difference and the difference in logarithms.[9]

The independent variables in the wage function include measures of human capital endowments. These are years of potential experience (age minus years of formal education minus five), EXP, experience squared, EXP2, and two measures of education: years of formal education (primary, secondary or university), ED, and a dummy variable which indicates whether or not a worker has had non-formal education, EXTRAED.

The independent variables also include an indicator of the location where the worker lives. Birdsall and Fox (1985), in a study of school teachers in Brazil, and Behrman and Wolfe (1984), in a study of women in Nicaragua, concluded that differences in the cost of living in different regions were important determinants of women's wages and male-female wage differentials. We include a dummy variable that is one if the worker lives in a rural area, RURAL, and another dummy variable which is one if a worker lives in an urban area that is not San Jose, URBAN. We expect that cost of living will be higher in San Jose, and higher in urban than rural areas outside San Jose.

We also control for two data problems. We expect the reported wages of self-employed workers will be over-estimated relative to salaried workers because they will include returns to capital and entrepreneurial input as well as labor. Therefore, we include a dummy variable which is one if

---

[8]   We use the International Occupational Classification (Clasificacion Internacional Uniforme de Ocupaciones) to classify workers into different occupations. We divide workers into professional and technical workers (one-digit classification 0), directors, and managers (including owners, one-digit classification 1), administrative personnel (one-digit classification 2), and laborers (one-digit classifications 3 through 9).

[9]   "Wages" are defined as the ratio of earnings to hours worked (data on hourly wages are not available). "Earnings" are defined as labor earnings from the principal job. The data on earnings and hours worked are not strictly comparable; reported earnings are "normal" monthly earnings while reported hours worked are the hours worked in the week prior to the survey. We estimate hourly wages by dividing monthly earnings by 4.3 divided by the hours worked per week. The household surveys do not sample all groups of people in the proportion that they are found in the population. For example, because households in rural areas are spaced farther apart than those in urban areas, people in rural areas are under-sampled relative to those in urban areas. The data contain weighing factors which allow the researcher to estimate population parameters from the sample data. The average wages reported in this paper are unweighted.

the worker is self-employed, SELFEMPL. A second data problem is that we do not have data on the value of payments in-kind. This problem is especially important for domestic servants. We attempt to address this problem by including a dummy variable which is one if a worker receives payments in-kind, INKIND.

*Job (sector and occupation) assignment functions.* The dependent variable is a qualitative variable that denotes the sector and occupation of the worker (see McFadden, 1984).

In these equations we want to control for any gender differences in human capital endowments which may affect access to higher paying sectors and occupations. Therefore we include, as independent variables, the same variables that were included in the wage function.[10] We also want to control for differences in tastes for different sectors and occupations. For example, a worker may prefer to work in the informal sector because of the more flexible working hours (even though pay is less than in the formal sectors). Included are dummy variables indicating whether a worker is married, single or divorced, MARRIED, whether a worker is the head of a household, JEFE, and the number of children in the household, CHILD.

Table 10.1 presents the means and standard deviations of the variables used in the estimation of the wage and job assignment functions for men and women. (Table 10A.1 in the Appendix presents the means and standard deviations of the variables used in the estimation of these functions for each sex and each sector and occupation.) Women average more years of formal education than men (8.7 versus 7.2 years). Employed women are also more likely to have had some non-formal education (30 percent of employed women have had some non-formal education compared to 15 percent of men). This may be because more highly educated women select to enter the work force than women with less education. On the other hand, most men may decide to work regardless of their education level. Also, younger workers are more likely to have higher levels of education in Costa Rica and the female work force is, on average, younger than the male work force. On average, potential experience is lower for employed women than employed men (18 years compared to 22 years for men). This is perhaps also a reflection of the age distributions of men and women in the work force. Employed women are less likely than men to be self-employed or to be heads of households.

Part B of Table 10.1 reports means and standard deviations for the variables used in this study using a sample which excludes domestic servants. As noted before, the wages of domestic servants are likely to be underestimated because they do not include the value of payments in-kind. This may artificially drive up the measured male-female wage differential. By excluding domestic servants from the sample, we can examine the effect of domestic servants on the male-female wage differential. If domestic servants are excluded from the sample, the average woman earns a higher wage than the average man. Also, the proportion of women reporting in-kind payments falls (from .068 to .018). This indicates that many domestic servants receive payments in-kind and that this data problem may be causing part of the observed male-female wage differential. However, care must be taken in interpreting this result. Domestic servants are almost always women. When domestic servants are excluded from the sample, the lowest paid

---

[10]    Several variables that were included in the estimation of the wage function are not included in the estimation of the job assignment functions because they do not exhibit any variation within at least one sector/occupation group. These are URBAN, RURAL, SELFEMPL and INKIND. These variables are also excluded from the estimates of the wage functions for each sex and sector/occupation. In addition to these variables, we exclude EXP2 from the estimate of the sector assignment function because the estimates will otherwise not converge.

### Table 10.1
### Means (and Standard Deviations) of Sample Variables by Gender
### Including and Excluding Domestic Servants
### Central Valley of Costa Rica

A.    <u>All Workers</u>

| Variable | Female | Male |
|----------|--------|------|
| Wage | 98.9 (100.3) | 102.3 (114.8) |
| Log of Wage | 4.29 (0.771) | 4.34 (0.728) |
| URBAN | 0.273 (0.446) | 0.226 (0.418) |
| RURAL | 0.272 (0.445) | 0.418 (0.493) |
| EXP | 18.0 (12.5) | 22.1 (14.6) |
| EXP2 | 481 (668) | 700 (876) |
| ED | 8.66 (3.94) | 7.22 (3.91) |
| EXTRAED | 0.301 (0.459) | 0.174 (.380) |
| INKIND | 0.0681 (0.252) | 0.040 (0.197) |
| SELFEMPL | 0.162 (0.368) | 0.237 (0.425) |
| MARRIED | 0.677 (0.468) | 0.685 (0.465) |
| JEFE | 0.161 (0.367) | 0.653 (0.476) |
| CHILD | 1.23 (1.30) | 1.326 (1.318) |
| N | 1,262 | 2,609 |

- Continued

## Table 10.1 (continued)
### Means (and Standard Deviations) of Sample Variables by Gender
### Including and Excluding Domestic Servants
### Central Valley of Costa Rica

**B.    Excluding Domestic Servants**

| Variable | Female | Male |
|---|---|---|
| Wage | 108.7 | 102.5 |
| | (105.2) | (114.8) |
| Log of Wage | 4.42 | 4.34 |
| | (0.705) | (0.728) |
| URBAN | 0.288 | 0.225 |
| | (0.453) | (0.420) |
| RURAL | 0.242 | 0.418 |
| | (0.429) | (0.493) |
| EXP | 17.7 | 22.0 |
| | (12.5) | (14.6) |
| EXP2 | 464 | 699 |
| | (653) | (875) |
| ED | 9.21 | 7.23 |
| | (3.94) | (3.91) |
| EXTRAED | 0.338 | 0.175 |
| | (0.473) | (0.380) |
| INKIND | 0.0178 | 0.0400 |
| | (0.132) | (0.196) |
| SELFEMPL | 0.182 | 0.238 |
| | (0.394) | (0.426) |
| MARRIED | 0.679 | 0.684 |
| | (0.467) | (0.465) |
| JEFE | 0.158 | 0.653 |
| | (0.365) | (0.476) |
| CHILD | 1.18 | 1.33 |
| | (1.25) | (1.32) |
| N | 1,065 | 2,599 |

Notes: The definitions of the variables are given in Section 6. The data used are from the 1989 Household Survey of Employment and Unemployment, conducted by the Census Department of the Government of Costa Rica. The data contain weighing factors which allow the researcher to estimate population parameters from the sample data. The estimates reported in this table are not weighted.

women are excluded from the sample. This will artificially lower the measured male-female wage differential. This illustrates the role of job segregation in driving the wedge between male and female wages.

While excluding domestic servants from the sample does not appreciably change the averages of the other variables used in this study for men, it has an important effect on the magnitudes of some of these variables for women. For example, the average level of education and the proportion of women who have had non-formal education rises (from 8.7 to 9.2 years and from 30 percent to 34 percent, respectively), indicating that domestic servants are among the lowest educated female workers. In the following section, we will estimate separate decompositions using samples which both include and exclude domestic servants.

## 5. Accounting for the Male-Female Wage Differential

The results of the estimation of the wage functions and the decompositions described in equation 2 are reported in Table 10.2. In the wage functions for both sexes, all coefficients but three are significantly different from zero at the five percent level of significance. The coefficient on the variable which is one if the worker receives payments in-kind (INKIND) is not significantly different from zero for men. For both men and women, the coefficients on the variable which is one if a worker lives in an urban area outside of San Jose (URBAN), and the coefficient on the variable which is one if the worker is self-employed (SELFEMPL) are not significantly different from zero at the five percent level.

The part of the male-female wage differential explained by differences in endowments, E, is negative (-0.123). This indicates that, after controlling for education, experience, location, payments in-kind and self-employment, the average wages of women are higher than men's. This is largely due to the fact that employed women have higher levels of formal and non-formal education than employed men. Differences in years of formal schooling (ED) between men and women account for most of the negative E (the effect of differences in years of formal schooling on E is -0.145). The differential explained by differences in endowments, E, would be more negative if it were not for the fact that men have higher levels of potential experience than women. The impact of differences in experience (EXP plus EXP2) on E is 0.058 (0.160 plus -0.102). Differences in average levels of the non-human capital explanatory variables (urban (URBAN) and rural (RURAL) location, self-employment (SELFEMPL) or payments in-kind (INKIND)) are not important in driving male and female wages apart.

The part of the male-female wage differential not attributable to differences in endowments, U, is almost three times the total male-female wage differential (U is 0.172 while the total differential is 0.05). This is driven mostly by the advantage men have in returns to experience and differences in the constant term in the wage functions (the impact of the two experience terms on U is 0.156, while the impact of differences in the constant terms is 0.124). Rates of returns to both formal and non-formal education are higher for women than men. (The impact of differences in the rates of return to formal education on U is -0.116.) The impact of all other variables on U is relatively small. These results suggest that women are discriminated against in the Costa Rican labor market. However, there are important qualifications. The experience variable measures potential experience--what experience would be if individuals began working when they left school and never stopped. Research indicates that women are more likely to leave the labor force (for example, to take care of children) and re-enter at a later date. This means that women's actual labor market experience will be overestimated relative to men's. One cannot

**Table 10.2**
Estimates of the Wage Functions, by Gender
And Estimates of E and U Including and Excluding Domestic Servants
Central Valley of Costa Rica

## A. All Workers

| Variable | Female | Male | $\underline{B}_{Mz}{}'(\underline{X}_{Mz}-\underline{X}_{Fz})$ | $(\underline{B}_{Mz}-\underline{B}_{Fz})'\underline{X}_{Fz}$ |
|---|---|---|---|---|
| CONSTANT | 3.02 (0.0738) | 3.15 (0.0517) | 0 | 0.124 |
| URBAN | -0.0322 (0.0409) | -.0236 (.0309) | 0.00111 | 0.00237 |
| RURAL | -0.163 (0.0425) | -0.183 (.0278) | -.0270 | -0.00561 |
| EXP | 0.0240 (0.00408) | 0.0396 (.00271) | 0.160 | 0.280 |
| EXP2 | -.000206 (0.000076) | -.000465 (.0000448) | -0.102 | -0.124 |
| ED | 0.114 (0.00500) | 0.101 (.00356) | -0.145 | -0.116 |
| EXTRAED | 0.0808 (0.0390) | 0.111 (0.0321) | -0.0141 | 0.00905 |
| INKIND | -.491 (0.0688) | -0.270 (0.0587) | 0.00754 | 0.0150 |
| SELFEMPL | -0.0367 (0.0505) | -.0430 (0.0286) | -0.00323 | -0.0129 |
| R-Squared | 0.405 | 0.364 | | |
| Std. Error of the Regression | 0.597 | 0.582 | | |
| N | 1,262 | 2,609 | | |

| Total | | | E: Explained by Endowments $\underline{B}_M{}'(\underline{X}_M-\underline{X}_F)$ -0.123 | U:Unexplained by Endowments $(\underline{B}_M-\underline{B}_F)'\underline{X}F$ 0.172 |
|---|---|---|---|---|

Notes: The dependent variable is the natural logarithm of wages. Standard errors of the coefficients are in parentheses.

$\underline{B}_{iz}$ is the coefficients for gender i on endowment variable z (for example, the coefficients on ED, EXP, etc.) (i = male, female).

$\underline{X}_{iz}$ is a the mean of endowment z for each gender i.

$B_i$ is a vector of the coefficients reported in this table.

$\underline{X}_i$ is a vector of mean wage determining characteristics for each gender.

Continued -

**Table 10.2** (continued)
Estimates of the Wage Functions, by Gender
And Estimates of E and U Including and Excluding Domestic Servants
Central Valley of Costa Rica

## B. Excluding Domestic Servants

| Variable | Female | Male | $\underline{B}_{Mz}'(\underline{X}_{Mz}-\underline{X}_{Fz})$ | $(\underline{B}_{Mz}-\underline{B}_{Fz})'\underline{X}_{Fz}$ |
|---|---|---|---|---|
| CONSTANT | 3.10 | 3.15 | 0 | 0.0522 |
| | (0.0769) | (0.0517) | | |
| URBAN | -0.0430 | -.0226 | 0.00142 | 0.00586 |
| | (0.0416) | (.0310) | | |
| RURAL | -0.113 | -0.181 | -.0319 | -0.0166 |
| | (0.0451) | (.0279) | | |
| EXP | 0.0256 | 0.0396 | 0.171 | 0.248 |
| | (0.00431) | (.00272) | | |
| EXP2 | -.000223 | -.000466 | -0.109 | -0.113 |
| | (0.0000808) | (.0000449) | | |
| ED | 0.108 | 0.101 | -0.198 | -0.0744 |
| | (0.00509) | (.00356) | | |
| EXTRAED | 0.0681 | 0.111 | -0.0181 | 0.0144 |
| | (0.0387) | (0.0321) | | |
| INKIND | -.180 | -0.273 | -0.00606 | -0.00168 |
| | (0.133) | (0.0589) | | |
| SELFEMPL | -.0278 | -.0453 | -0.00209 | -0.0336 |
| | (0.0501) | (0.0286) | | |
| R-Squared | 0.353 | 0.362 | | |
| Std. Error of the Regression | 0.569 | 0.582 | | |
| N | 1,065 | 2,599 | | |

| Total | | | E: Explained by Endowments $\underline{B}_M'(\underline{X}_M-\underline{X}_F)$ | U:Unexplained by Endowments $(\underline{B}_M-\underline{B}_F)'\underline{X}F$ |
|---|---|---|---|---|
| | | | -0.193 | 0.112 |

Notes: The dependent variable is the natural logarithm of wages.  Standard errors of the coefficients are in parentheses.

$\underline{B}_{iz}$ is the coefficients for gender i on endowment variable z (for example, the coefficients on ED, EXP, etc.) (i = male, female).

$\underline{X}_{iz}$ is a the mean of endowment z for each gender i.

$B_i$ is a vector of the coefficients reported in this table.

$\underline{X}_i$ is a vector of mean wage determining characteristics for each gender.

be sure if the gender difference in the coefficients on experience is due to differences in the rate of return to experience or to unmeasured differences in labor market experience. The fact that the rest of the difference is due to differences in intercept terms indicates that much of the difference in the wages between men and women is due to factors we cannot identify.[11]

The importance of domestic servants in driving the wedge between male and female wages has already been noted. When domestic servants are excluded from the sample used to estimate the wage equations the conclusions drawn above still hold (see Part B of Table 10.2). E is still negative (-0.193) and U positive (0.112). The most important variable causing E to be negative is still education and the most important variable causing U to be positive is potential experience. The biggest difference between parts A and B of Table 10.2 is the impact of the intercept term. The wage differential due to differences in the intercept terms is smaller (from .124 to .0522) in the estimates of the wage equations without data on domestic servants. This indicates that a part of the unexplained difference found in the first set of numbers is caused by the impact of domestic servants. With one exception, all coefficients are similar to those reported for the estimation where the full sample was used. The exception is the coefficient for the variable which is one if the worker receives payment in-kind for women; it is not significantly different from zero at the five percent level.

Table 10.3 presents the male-female wage differential for each sector and occupation, the proportion of men and women in each sector and occupation, and estimates of W (the part of the wage differential due to different wages paid to men and women in the same sectors and occupations) and J (the part of the differential attributable to different access to higher paying sectors and occupations-- see equation 4). Women are over-represented in the relatively higher paying sectors and occupations; specifically among professional and technical workers and administrative personnel in the public sector (see the last column of Table 10.3--the difference between the proportion of men and the proportion of women in these two sector/occupations is -.0.080 and -0.0302, respectively). There is no significant difference in the participation of men and women in the highest paying sector/occupation in the public sector, directors and managers. Women are also over-represented as domestic servants, the lowest paying sector/occupation (the difference between the proportion of men and the proportion of women in the domestic servant sector is -0.152). Women are under-represented in the other three of the four lowest paying sector/occupations; the informal sector, and among laborers in the public and private-formal sectors (see the last column of Table 10.3, the differences between the proportion of men and the proportion of women in these sectors are positive).[12] Despite women being over-represented in the lowest paying domestic servant sector, J, the part of the male-female wage difference attributable to different access to higher paying sectors and occupations, is a negative -0.0223, indicating that women are, on average, over-represented in the higher paying sectors and occupations.

W, the part of the wage differential due to different wages paid to men and women in the same sectors and occupations, is a positive 0.0723. This indicates that, on average, women are paid less than men in the same sectors and occupations. Women are paid more than men in only two

---

[11]    Using the decompositions described in equation 2a, the difference attributable to endowments, E, is -0.129, the difference not attributable to endowments, U, is 0.178.

[12]    On average, women are over-represented in the public sector and under-represented in the informal and private-formal sectors.

## Table 10.3
Average Natural Logarithm of Wages by Sector, Occupation and Gender,
Male-Female Differences in the Natural Logarithm of Wages by Sector and Occupation,
Male-Female Differences in Assignment to Sector and Occupation, Estimates of W and J

### A. All Workers

Sector and Occupation

| $W_j$ | $W_{Mj}$ | $W_{Fj}$ | $W_{Mj}-W_{Fj}$ | $P_{Mj}$ | $P_{Fj}$ | $P_{Mj}-P_{Fj}$ |
|---|---|---|---|---|---|---|
| **Informal** | | | | | | |
| 4.06 | 4.05 | 4.08 | -0.03 | 0.314 | 0.170 | 0.144 |
| **Private-Formal:** | | | | | | |
| *Professional and Technical* | | | | | | |
| 5.01 | 5.06 | 4.90 | 0.16 | 0.0422 | 0.0372 | 0.005 |
| *Directors and Managers* | | | | | | |
| 5.18 | 5.23 | 4.90 | 0.33 | 0.0261 | 0.00951 | 0.0165 |
| *Administrative Personnel* | | | | | | |
| 4.49 | 4.52 | 4.47 | 0.05 | 0.0356 | 0.0777 | -0.0420 |
| *Laborers* | | | | | | |
| 4.20 | 4.22 | 4.15 | 0.07 | 0.416 | 0.315 | 0.102 |
| **Public:** | | | | | | |
| *Professional and Technical* | | | | | | |
| 5.18 | 5.26 | 5.12 | 0.14 | 0.0448 | 0.124 | -0.080 |
| *Directors and Managers* | | | | | | |
| 5.34 | 5.30 | 5.42 | -0.12 | 0.00651 | 0.00634 | 0.00018 |
| *Administrative Personnel* | | | | | | |
| 4.80 | 4.85 | 4.74 | 0.11 | 0.0387 | 0.0689 | -0.0302 |
| *Laborers* | | | | | | |
| 4.52 | 4.54 | 4.47 | 0.07 | 0.0724 | 0.0357 | 0.0367 |
| **Domestic Servants** | | | | | | |
| 3.57 | 3.67 | 3.57 | 0.10 | 0.00383 | 0.156 | -0.152 |

$\Sigma_j P_{Fj}(W_{Mj}-W_{Fj}) = W$   0.0723

$\Sigma_j W_{Fj}(P_{Mj}-P_{Fj}) = J$   -0.0223

**Table 10.3** (continued)
Average Natural Logarithm of Wages by Sector, Occupation and Gender,
Male-Female Differences in the Natural Logarithm of Wages by Sector and Occupation,
Male-Female Differences in Assignment to Sector and Occupation, Estimates of W and J

### B. Excluding Domestic Servants

Sector and Occupation

| $W_j$ | $W_{Mj}$ | $W_{Fj}$ | $W_{Mj}-W_{Fj}$ | $P_{Mj}$ | $P_{Fj}$ | $P_{Mj}-P_{Fj}$ |
|---|---|---|---|---|---|---|
| Informal | | | | | | |
| 4.06 | 4.05 | 4.08 | -0.03 | 0.314 | 0.201 | 0.113 |
| Private-Formal: | | | | | | |
| Professional and Technical | | | | | | |
| 5.01 | 5.06 | 4.90 | 0.16 | 0.0423 | 0.0441 | -0.0018 |
| Directors and Managers | | | | | | |
| 5.18 | 5.23 | 4.90 | 0.33 | 0.0261 | 0.0113 | 0.0149 |
| Administrative Personnel | | | | | | |
| 4.49 | 4.52 | 4.47 | 0.05 | 0.0357 | 0.0920 | -0.0562 |
| Laborers | | | | | | |
| 4.20 | 4.22 | 4.15 | 0.07 | 0.418 | 0.373 | 0.045 |
| Public: | | | | | | |
| Professional and Technical | | | | | | |
| 5.18 | 5.26 | 5.12 | 0.14 | 0.0450 | 0.147 | -0.102 |
| Directors and Managers | | | | | | |
| 5.34 | 5.30 | 5.42 | -0.12 | 0.00654 | 0.00751 | -0.00097 |
| Administrative Personnel | | | | | | |
| 4.80 | 4.85 | 4.74 | 0.11 | 0.0389 | 0.0817 | -0.0428 |
| Laborers | | | | | | |
| 4.52 | 4.54 | 4.47 | 0.07 | 0.0727 | 0.0423 | 0.0305 |

$\Sigma_j P_{Fj}(W_{Mj}-W_{Fj}) = W$     0.0670

$\Sigma_j W_{Fj}(P_{Mj}-P_{Fj}) = J$                                         -0.148

Notes:   $W_j$ = average natural logarithm of wages in sector/occupation j.

   $W_{Mj}$ = average natural logarithm of wages for males in sector/occupation j.

   $W_{Fj}$ =   average natural logarithm of wages for females in sector/occupation j.

   $P_{Mj}$ = proportion of males in sector/occupation j.

   $P_{Fj}$ = proportion of females in each sector/occupation j.

sector/occupation groups: directors and managers in the public sector and in the informal sector (see column four in Table 10.3--the difference between the average natural logarithm of wages for men and the average natural logarithm of wages for women is -0.12 and -0.03 respectively for these sector/occupations).[13]

The second set of estimates in Table 10.3 excludes domestic servants from the sample. When this is done, W does not change appreciably while J falls (from -0.0233 to -0.148). This is expected because, with the exclusion of the lowest paid women from the sample, women are now even more over-represented in the higher paying sectors and occupations.[14] Estimates of the multinominal logit model by sector/occupation are presented in Table 10.4.

Tables 10.5 and 10.6 present the estimates of the decompositions described in equation 6.[15] In the last few paragraphs we concluded that women earn less than men with the same endowments, and that women are paid less than men in the same occupations and sectors. This is consistent with the decompositions presented in Table 10.6.

WU, the difference between the wages of men and women within sectors and occupations that is not explained by differences in endowments, is the only one of the decompositions reported in Table 10.6 which is positive (0.114). This indicates that the primary reason why women earn less than men is because women in the same sectors and occupations as (observably) equally qualified men are paid lower wages. In particular, men are paid more than women with the same endowments in every sector/occupation except among directors and managers in the public sector (see column 1 in Table 10.6--only among directors and managers in the public sector is the difference in the average natural logarithm of wages for men and women unexplained by differences in endowments negative, specifically it is -0.0610).

WE, the difference between the wages of men and women within sectors and occupations that is explained by differences in endowments is negative indicating that, on average, within each sector and occupation women have higher human capital endowments than men. Only among administrative personnel in the public sector are men paid more than women because they have higher levels of human capital endowments (see column 2 in Table 10.6--only among administrative personnel is the difference in the natural logarithm of wages between men and women due to differences in endowments positive, specifically 0.00313).

---

[13]   In the public sector as a whole, and in the informal sector as a whole, women are paid more than men.

[14]   Estimates of W and J using the decompositions described in equation 4a are 0.0521 for W and -0.00211 for J when domestic servants are included in the sample and 0.0519 for W and -0.132 for J when domestic servants are excluded from the sample.

[15]   In estimating the wage functions to calculate the decompositions described in equation 6 we use a smaller set of independent variables than was used to estimate the wage functions by gender. This is because the excluded variables have no variation in the sample for some jobs. We exclude the non-human capital variables; dummy variables for location, payments in-kind and self-employment. We include all human capital variables. The variables that we exclude had little impact on the measure of the difference in Table 16.3. We do not report decompositions using a sample which includes domestic servants in Table 16.5. This is because there were not enough men in the domestic servant sector to estimate a wage function. The results of the estimate of the multinomial logit estimates for men and women are reported in Table 16.4. The wage equations for each sex, sector and occupation are reported in Table A16.2 in the Appendix.

**Table 10.4**
Estimates of the Multinomial Logit Models by Gender
(Reference Sector is the Informal Sector)

| Variable and Sector/Occupation | Female | Male |
|---|---|---|
| **Private-Formal : Professional and Technical** | | |
| CONSTANT | -10.325 | -8.48227 |
| | (1.229) | (0.0115) |
| EXP | -0.0258 | 0.0338 |
| | (0.0226) | (0.0115) |
| ED | 1.004 | 0.683 |
| | (0.0884) | (0.0419) |
| EXTRAED | -0.0434 | 1.126 |
| | (0.404) | (0.262) |
| MARRIED | -0.158 | -0.290 |
| | (0.432) | (0.290) |
| JEFE | -0.0848 | -0.238 |
| | (0.607) | (0.342) |
| CHILD | -0.756 | -0.0359 |
| | (0.223) | (0.103) |
| **Private-Formal : Managers and Directors** | | |
| CONSTANT | -10.450 | -9.108 |
| | (1.935) | (0.719) |
| EXP | 0.0355 | 0.0219 |
| | (0.0313) | (0.0134) |
| ED | 0.757 | 0.630 |
| | (0.127) | (0.0465) |
| EXTRAED | 0.150 | 0.696 |
| | (0.631) | (0.308) |
| MARRIED | 0.546 | -0.0579 |
| | (0.839) | (0.384) |
| JEFE | -0.752 | 1.072 |
| | (1.138) | (0.486) |
| CHILD | -0.259 | -0.0575 |
| | (0.291) | (0.122) |
| **Private-Formal : Administrative Personnel** | | |
| CONSTANT | -3.681 | -4.927 |
| | (0.731) | (0.524) |
| EXP | -0.0727 | -0.0360 |
| | (0.0170) | (0.0135) |
| ED | 0.532 | 0.381 |
| | (0.0625) | (0.0418) |
| EXTRAED | 0.334 | 1.130 |
| | (0.303) | (0.270) |
| MARRIED | 0.0505 | 0.892 |
| | (0.318) | (0.334) |
| JEFE | -0.0238 | -0.0492 |
| | (0.482) | (0.321) |
| CHILD | -0.576 | -0.234 |
| | (0.142) | (0.110) |

- continued

**Table 10.4** (continued)
Estimates of the Multinomial Logit Models by Gender
(Reference Sector is the Informal Sector)

| Variable and Sector/Occupation | Female | Male |
|---|---|---|
| **Private-Formal : Laborers** | | |
| CONSTANT | 1.716 | 0.298 |
| | (0.442) | (0.193) |
| EXP | -0.0804 | -0.0339 |
| | (0.00977) | (0.00485) |
| ED | 0.123 | 0.108 |
| | (0.0428) | (0.0198) |
| EXTRAED | -0.793 | 0.359 |
| | (0.221) | (0.167) |
| MARRIED | -0.113 | -0.268 |
| | (-0.205) | (0.116) |
| JEFE | 0.237 | 0.224 |
| | (0.282) | (0.143) |
| CHILD | -0.0516 | 0.0795 |
| | (0.0730 | (0.0382) |
| **Public : Professional and Technical** | | |
| CONSTANT | -12.085 | -10.004 |
| | (1.040) | (0.657) |
| EXP | 0.0359 | 0.00895 |
| | (0.0174) | (0.0133) |
| ED | 1.121 | 0.801 |
| | (0.0759) | (0.0456) |
| EXTRAED | -0.922 | 0.627 |
| | (0.327) | (0.277) |
| MARRIED | -0.314 | 0.135 |
| | (0.358) | (0.338) |
| JEFE | 0.716 | 0.108 |
| | (0.441) | (0.365) |
| CHILD | 0.101 | 0.0330 |
| | (0.131) | (0.105) |
| **Public : Managers and Directors** | | |
| CONSTANT | -21.976 | -13.615 |
| | (3.628) | (1.733) |
| EXP | 0.101 | 0.0160 |
| | (0.0441) | (0.0252) |
| ED | 1.448 | 0.835 |
| | (0.210) | (0.0935) |
| EXTRAED | -0.530 | 1.009 |
| | (0.837) | (0.543) |
| MARRIED | 0.287 | -0.202 |
| | (0.992) | (0.729) |
| JEFE | 1.479 | 2.205 |
| | (0.995) | (1.179) |
| CHILD | 0.0692 | -0.505 |
| | (0.413) | (0.275) |

- continued

**Table 10.4** (continued)
Estimates of the Multinomial Logit Models by Gender
(Reference Sector is the Informal Sector)

| Variable and Sector/Occupation | Female | Male |
|---|---|---|
| **Public : Adminstrative Personnel** | | |
| CONSTANT | -5.490 | -5.864 |
| | (0.791) | (0.513) |
| EXP | -0.0414 | 0.00244 |
| | (0.0169) | (0.0117) |
| ED | 0.640 | 0.436 |
| | (0.0650) | (0.0406) |
| EXTRAED | -0.00821 | 1.507 |
| | (0.309) | (0.256) |
| MARRIED | -0.0494 | -0.178 |
| | (0.334) | (0.295) |
| JEFE | 0.0243 | 0.183 |
| | (0.473) | (0.342) |
| CHILD | -0.166 | 0.0588 |
| | (0.126) | (0.0930) |
| **Public : Laborers** | | |
| CONSTANT | -2.579 | -3.087 |
| | (0.818) | (0.361) |
| EXP | 0.0145 | 0.00148 |
| | (0.0143) | (0.00761) |
| ED | 0.196 | 0.143 |
| | (0.0740) | (0.0325) |
| EXTRAED | -1.303 | 0.659 |
| | (0.460) | (0.237) |
| MARRIED | -0.323 | -0.157 |
| | (0.350) | (0.205) |
| JEFE | 0.129 | 0.820 |
| | (0.422) | (0.0635) |
| CHILD | -0.117 | 0.114 |
| | (0.139) | (0.0635) |
| Log-Likelihood | -1320 | -3349 |
| Sample Size | 1065 | 2599 |

Notes: Standard errors of the coefficients are in parentheses.
Domestic Servants are excluded from the sample.

Recall that J, the part of the male female wage differential attributable to differences between men and women in access to higher paying sectors and occupations, is negative indicating that women are over-represented in the higher paying sectors. The most important reason why women are over-represented in higher paying sectors is differences in human capital endowments between men and women. The absolute value of JE, the difference between male and female wages attributable to women being assigned to lower paying sectors because they have lower levels of human capital endowments than men, is almost three times the absolute value of JU, the difference due to women being assigned to lower paying sectors not explained by differences in endowments (JE is -0.109 while JU is -0.0399).   In particular, higher levels of endowments

**Table 10.5**
Summary Tables of the Decompositions of the Male-Female Wage Differential
Across all Sectors/Occupations

| Endowments | Wage Structure | | | | | | |
|---|---|---|---|---|---|---|---|
| E | U | W | J | WE | WU | JE | JU |

Using the Sample Which Includes Domestic Servants ($W_M/W_F = 1.03$)

| | | | | | | | |
|---|---|---|---|---|---|---|---|
| -0.123 | 0.172 | 0.0723 | 0.0223 | na | na | na | na |

Using the Sample Which Excludes Domestic Servants ($W_M/W_F = 0.94$)

| | | | | | | | |
|---|---|---|---|---|---|---|---|
| -0.193 | 0.112 | 0.0670 | -0.148 | -0.0467 | 0.114 | -0.109 | -0.0399 |

Notes: E is the part of the wage difference explained by differences in human capital endowments.

U is the part of the wage difference unexplained by differences in human capital endowments.

W is that part of the wage difference due to different higher wages paid to men and women in the same sectors.

J is that part of the wage difference due to relatively less access by women (than men) to higher paid sectors.

WE is that part of W explained by differences in human capital endowments.

WU is that part of W not explained by differences in human capital endowments.

JE is that part of J explained by differences in human capital endowments.

JU is that part of J not explained by differences in human capital endowments.

cause women to be over-represented among the higher paying professional and technical workers in the private-formal and public sector, and under-represented among the lower paid workers, specifically among laborers in the private-formal and public sectors and in the informal sector (see the last column in Table 10.6, the difference between the proportion of men and women which is due to differences in endowments for professional and technical workers in the public sector is -0.0101, for professional and technical workers in the private-formal sector it is -0.0280; for laborers in the private-formal sector it is 0.0298; for laborers in the public sector is 0.0326; and for informal sector workers it is 0.0745).

JU is also negative, indicating that women are disproportionately represented in the higher paying occupations even when they do not have higher levels of endowments than men.   This is particularly the case in the public sector (see the third column of Table 10.6--the differences between the proportion of men and women which is not due to differences in endowments among professional and technical workers, directors and managers and administrative personnel in the pubic sector are -0.0623, -0.00123 and -0.0218 respectively) .[16]

## 6.   Discussion

The male-female wage differential in Costa Rica is smaller than that in the other countries studied in this volume.  The results presented in this chapter provide some explanation for this.

---

[16]   Estimates of WE, WU, JE and JU using the decompositions described in equation 6a are -0.0653, 0.115, -0.101 and -1.1308 respectively.

One explanation for the low male-female wage differential in Costa Rica is that employed women have, on average, higher levels of education than employed men. If women were paid the same as men with the same observed human capital endowments, women would earn, on average, substantially more than men in Costa Rica. This implies that policies which ensure equal access to education may cause male-female wage differentials to be lower than might be.

**Table 10.6**

Full Decompositon of the Difference in Average Male
and Female Natural Logarithm of Wages
Excluding Domestic Servants

**Sector and Occupation**

| $\underline{B}_{Mj}'\underline{X}_{Fj}-\underline{B}_{Fj}'\underline{X}_{Fj}$ | $\underline{B}_{Mj}'\underline{X}_{Mj}-\underline{B}_{Mj}'\underline{X}_{Fj}$ | $P_{Fj}-\hat{P}_{Fj}$ | $P_{Mj}-\hat{P}_{Fj}$ |
|---|---|---|---|
| **Informal** | | | |
| 0.0883 | -0.127 | 0.0358 | 0.0745 |
| **Private-Formal : Professional and Technical** | | | |
| 0.189 | -0.0358 | 0.0432 | -0.0480 |
| **Private-Formal : Directors and Managers** | | | |
| 0.284 | 0.0596 | 0.0147 | 0.000243 |
| **Private-Formal : Administrative Personnel** | | | |
| 0.112 | -0.0524 | -0.0283 | -0.0280 |
| **Private-Formal : Laborers** | | | |
| 0.0934 | -0.0229 | 0.0125 | 0.0326 |
| **Public : Professional and Technical** | | | |
| 0.179 | -0.0321 | -0.0623 | -0.0101 |
| **Public : Directors and Managers** | | | |
| -0.0610 | -0.0666 | -0.00123 | 0.000265 |
| **Public : Administrative Personnel** | | | |
| 0.104 | 0.00313 | -0.0218 | -0.0210 |
| **Public : Laborers** | | | |
| 0.112 | -0.0434 | 0.00449 | 0.0298 |

| **Total** | | | |
|---|---|---|---|
| WU | WE | JU | JE |
| $\Sigma_j P_{Fj}[\underline{B}_{Mj}'\underline{X}_{Fj}-\underline{B}_{Fj}'\underline{X}_{Fj}]$ | | $\Sigma_j\underline{B}_{Mj}'\underline{X}_{Mj}[P_{Fj}-\hat{P}_{Fj}]$ | |
| | $\Sigma_j P_{Fj}[\underline{B}_{Mj}'\underline{X}_{Mj}-\underline{B}_{Mj}'\underline{X}_{Fj}]$ | | $\Sigma_j\underline{B}_{Mj}'\underline{X}_{Mj}[P_{Mj}-\hat{P}_{Fj}]$ |
| 0.114 | -0.0467 | -0.0399 | -0.109 |

Notes: $P_{Mj}$ = proportion of males in sector/occupation j.

    $P_{Fj}$ = proportion of females in each sector/occupation j.

    $P_{Fj}$ = proportion of females in each sector/occupation j if females faced the same sector/occupation determining structure as men. This is defined in the text.

    $\underline{B}_{ij}$ are the coefficients of the earnings equations for sector j and gender i.

    $\underline{X}_{ij}$ is a vector of mean wage determining characteristics for gender i in sector j.

Another reason why male-female wage differentials are low in Costa Rica is that women are over-represented in the higher paying sectors and occupations. Specifically, women are over-represented in the highest paying public sector, and in higher paying occupations within the public sector. In part, this is because the public sector hires, more than any other sector, highly educated workers. In addition, the public sector hires women over men even if they have the same levels of human capital endowments.

The low male-female wage differential in Costa Rica does not necessarily imply that labor market discrimination against women is less in Costa Rica than in other Latin American countries. The most important reason that, on average, women are paid less than men in Costa Rica is that women are paid less than men with the same endowments and in the same sectors and occupations. If women were paid the same as men with the same human capital endowments in the same sectors and occupations, women would, on average, earn higher wages than men. This indicates that labor market discrimination may be an important phenomenon in Costa Rica.

Men are also paid more than women in Costa Rica because women are disproportionately represented in the lowest paying domestic servant sector. However, it is probable that the reported wages of domestic servants underestimate the actual returns to their labor; part of the payment to domestic servants is as payment in-kind, which is not reported. This would indicate that the "true" male-female wage differential in the Central Valley of Costa Rica is lower than the 3.5 percent reported at the beginning of this paper.

A final point regarding public policy in Costa Rica and male-female wage differentials: As part of the structural adjustment program currently being carried out in Costa Rica, the government has promised to reduce public sector employment (Lizano, 1990). The public sector plays an important role in keeping the male-female wage differential low in Costa Rica. If public sector employment does fall in Costa Rica, a rise in the male-female wage differential is likely.

### Appendix Table 10A.1
Mean (and Standard Deviations) of Sample Variables Used in the Wage
and Job Assignment Functions, by Gender and Sector and Occupation
Central Valley of Costa Rica

|  | Female Mean | Standard Deviation |  | Male Mean | Standard Deviation |
|---|---|---|---|---|---|
| **Informal** | | | | | |
| Wage | 90.928 | 135.239 | Wage | 75.730 | 75.250 |
| Logwage | 4.084 | 0.862 | Logwage | 4.045 | 0.748 |
| Urban | 0.280 | 0.450 | Urban | 0.208 | 0.406 |
| Rural | 0.271 | 0.446 | Rural | 0.540 | 0.499 |
| EXP | 27.374 | 15.371 | EXP | 27.626 | 17.070 |
| EXP2 | 984.495 | 1015.736 | EXP2 | 1054.203 | 1139.407 |
| ED | 5.991 | 2.197 | ED | 5.154 | 2.143 |
| EXTRAED | 0.322 | 0.469 | EXTRAED | 0.079 | 0.271 |
| INKIND | 0.023 | 0.151 | INKIND | 0.046 | 0.211 |
| SELFEMPL | 0.720 | 0.450 | SELFEMPL | 0.577 | 0.494 |
| Married | 0.678 | 0.469 | Married | 0.675 | 0.469 |
| Jefe | 0.220 | 0.415 | Jefe | 0.675 | 0.469 |
| Child | 1.243 | 1.303 | Child | 1.230 | 1.290 |
| **Private-Formal: Professional and Technical** | | | | | |
| Wage | 159.314 | 85.566 | Wage | 196.526 | 154.931 |
| Logwage | 4.904 | 0.633 | Logwage | 5.058 | 0.652 |
| Urban | 0.234 | 0.428 | Urban | 5.058 | 0.652 |
| Rural | 0.170 | 0.380 | Rural | 0.245 | 0.499 |
| EXP | 12.298 | 10.323 | EXP | 19.736 | 13.846 |
| ED | 13.766 | 3.184 | ED | 12.373 | 3.800 |
| EXTRAED | 0.468 | 0.504 | EXTRAED | 0.427 | 0.497 |
| INKIND | 0.021 | 0.146 | INKIND | 0.027 | 0.164 |
| SELFEMPL | 0.149 | 0.360 | SELFEMPL | 0.245 | 0.432 |
| Married | 0.660 | 0.479 | Married | 0.718 | 0.452 |
| Jefe | 0.128 | 0.337 | Jefe | 0.700 | 0.460 |
| Child | 0.532 | 0.856 | Child | 1.109 | 1.266 |
| **Private-Formal: Directors and Managers** | | | | | |
| Wage | 161.544 | 111.687 | Wage | 261.733 | 314.853 |
| Logwage | 4.887 | 0.646 | Logwage | 5.231 | 0.758 |
| Urban | 0.000 | 0.000 | Urban | 0.147 | 0.357 |
| Rural | 0.167 | 0.389 | Rural | 0.191 | 0.396 |
| EXP | 19.583 | 9.662 | EXP | 21.309 | 12.595 |
| EXP2 | 469.083 | 513.940 | EXP2 | 610.368 | 684.310 |
| ED | 11.583 | 3.872 | ED | 11.985 | 3.819 |
| EXTRAED | 0.583 | 0.515 | EXTRAED | 0.353 | 0.481 |
| INKIND | 0.083 | 0.289 | INKIND | 0.044 | 0.207 |
| SELFEMPL | 0.167 | 0.389 | SELFEMPL | 0.250 | 0.436 |
| MARRIED | 0.833 | 0.389 | MARRIED | 0.824 | 0.384 |
| JEFE | 0.083 | 0.289 | JEFE | 0.822 | 0.325 |
| CHILD | 1.000 | 0.853 | CHILD | 1.279 | 1.183 |

- Continued

### Appendix Table 10A.1 (continued)
#### Mean (and Standard Deviations) of Sample Variables Used in the Wage and Job Assignment Functions, by Gender and Sector and Occupation
#### Central Valley of Costa Rica

| | Female Mean | Standard Deviation | | Male Mean | Standard Deviation |
|---|---|---|---|---|---|
| **Private-Formal: Administrative Personnel** | | | | | |
| Wage | 100.312 | 68.665 | Wage | 102.630 | 47.212 |
| Logwage | 4.465 | 0.511 | Logwage | 4.525 | 0.487 |
| Urban | 0.224 | 0.419 | Urban | 0.204 | 0.405 |
| Rural | 0.204 | 0.405 | Rural | 0.140 | 0.349 |
| EXP | 11.837 | 9.727 | EXP | 14.935 | 11.736 |
| EXP2 | 233.755 | 491.137 | EXP2 | 359.323 | 559.321 |
| ED | 10.888 | 2.080 | ED | 9.989 | 2.701 |
| EXTRAED | 0.622 | 0.487 | EXTRAED | 0.398 | 0.492 |
| INKIND | 0.010 | 0.101 | INKIND | 0.043 | 0.204 |
| SELFEMPL | 0.000 | 0.000 | SELFEMPL | 0.011 | 0.104 |
| MARRIED | 0.694 | 0.463 | MARRIED | 0.839 | 0.370 |
| JEFE | 0.092 | 0.290 | JEFE | 0.602 | 0.492 |
| CHILD | 0.673 | 1.023 | CHILD | 1.000 | 1.011 |
| **Private-Formal: Laborers** | | | | | |
| Wage | 77.388 | 88.451 | Wage | 82.791 | 86.467 |
| Logwage | 4.151 | 0.520 | Logwage | 4.221 | 0.570 |
| Urban | 0.277 | 0.448 | Urban | 0.216 | 0.412 |
| Rural | 0.310 | 0.463 | Rural | 0.462 | 0.499 |
| EXP | 14.509 | 9.539 | EXP | 18.786 | 12.477 |
| EXP2 | 301.270 | 392.084 | EXP2 | 508.462 | 660.079 |
| ED | 7.673 | 2.948 | ED | 6.777 | 3.306 |
| EXTRAED | 0.242 | 0.429 | EXTRAED | 0.137 | 0.344 |
| INKIND | 0.020 | 0.141 | INKIND | 0.033 | 0.179 |
| SELFEMPL | 0.103 | 0.305 | SELFEMPL | 0.093 | 0.291 |
| MARRIED | 0.662 | 0.473 | MARRIED | 0.633 | 0.482 |
| JEFE | 0.103 | 0.305 | JEFE | 0.570 | 0.495 |
| CHILD | 1.378 | 1.352 | CHILD | 1.424 | 1.387 |
| **Public: Professional and Technical** | | | | | |
| Wage | 188.690 | 107.446 | Wage | 238.094 | 186.576 |
| Logwage | 5.116 | 0.482 | Logwage | 5.264 | 0.650 |
| Urban | 0.433 | 0.497 | Urban | 0.316 | 0.467 |
| Rural | 0.127 | 0.334 | Rural | 0.111 | 0.316 |
| EXP | 16.834 | 8.632 | EXP | 16.479 | 8.180 |
| EXP2 | 357.433 | 344.842 | EXP2 | 337.880 | 305.568 |
| ED | 14.134 | 2.524 | ED | 13.863 | 3.020 |
| EXTRAED | 0.299 | 0.459 | EXTRAED | 0.325 | 0.470 |
| INKIND | 0.000 | 0.000 | INKIND | 0.034 | 0.182 |
| SELFEMPL | 0.000 | 0.000 | SELFEMPL | 0.000 | 0.000 |
| MARRIED | 0.701 | 0.459 | MARRIED | 0.829 | 0.378 |
| JEFE | 0.248 | 0.433 | JEFE | 0.761 | 0.429 |
| CHILD | 1.197 | 1.190 | CHILD | 1.342 | 1.138 |

- Continued

## Appendix Table 10A.1 (continued)
### Mean (and Standard Deviations) of Sample Variables Used in the Wage and Job Assignment Functions, by Gender and Sector and Occupation
### Central Valley of Costa Rica

|  | Female Mean | Standard Deviation |  | Male Mean | Standard Deviation |
|---|---|---|---|---|---|
| **Public: Managers and Directors** | | | | | |
| Wage | 235.960 | 73.817 | Wage | 224.123 | 118.000 |
| Logwage | 5.425 | 0.291 | Logwage | 5.297 | 0.487 |
| Urban | 0.375 | 0.518 | Urban | 0.235 | 0.437 |
| Rural | 0.250 | 0.463 | Rural | 0.235 | 0.437 |
| EXP | 22.375 | 3.889 | EXP | 20.765 | 10.545 |
| EXP2 | 513.875 | 175.977 | EXP2 | 535.824 | 571.135 |
| ED | 15.375 | 2.615 | ED | 14.059 | 4.069 |
| EXTRAED | 0.375 | 0.518 | EXTRAED | 0.412 | 0.507 |
| INKIND | 0.000 | 0.000 | INKIND | 0.000 | 0.000 |
| SELFEMPL | 0.000 | 0.000 | SELFEMPL | 0.000 | 0.000 |
| Married | 0.750 | 0.463 | Married | 0.824 | 0.393 |
| Jefe | 0.500 | 0.535 | Jefe | 0.941 | 0.243 |
| Child | 0.875 | 1.126 | Child | 0.882 | 0.993 |
| **Public: Administrative Personnel** | | | | | |
| Wage | 122.141 | 47.077 | Wage | 137.081 | 57.770 |
| Logwage | 4.739 | 0.360 | Logwage | 4.847 | 0.378 |
| Urban | 0.230 | 0.423 | Urban | 0.347 | 0.478 |
| Rural | 0.149 | 0.359 | Rural | 0.168 | 0.376 |
| EXP | 13.621 | 7.785 | EXP | 19.139 | 10.917 |
| EXP2 | 245.437 | 283.155 | EXP2 | 484.287 | 515.488 |
| ED | 11.368 | 1.843 | ED | 10.119 | 2.910 |
| EXTRAED | 0.552 | 0.500 | EXTRAED | 0.495 | 0.502 |
| INKIND | 0.011 | 0.107 | INKIND | 0.020 | 0.140 |
| SELFEMPL | 0.000 | 0.000 | SELFEMPL | 0.000 | 0.000 |
| Married | 0.713 | 0.455 | Married | 0.752 | 0.434 |
| Jefe | 0.115 | 0.321 | Jefe | 0.723 | 0.450 |
| Child | 1.080 | 0.991 | Child | 1.356 | 1.316 |
| **Public: Laborers** | | | | | |
| Wage | 93.450 | 33.890 | Wage | 106.453 | 83.134 |
| Logwage | 4.467 | 0.401 | Logwage | 4.536 | 0.482 |
| Urban | 0.289 | 0.458 | Urban | 0.259 | 0.439 |
| Rural | 0.267 | 0.447 | Rural | 0.370 | 0.484 |
| EXP | 28.200 | 11.760 | EXP | 26.698 | 12.819 |
| EXP2 | 930.467 | 719.912 | EXP2 | 876.275 | 729.631 |
| ED | 6.622 | 2.855 | ED | 6.534 | 3.158 |
| EXTRAED | 0.156 | 0.367 | EXTRAED | 0.196 | 0.398 |
| INKIND | 0.044 | 0.208 | INKIND | 0.074 | 0.263 |
| SELFEMPL | 0.000 | 0.000 | SELFEMPL | 0.000 | 0.000 |
| MARRIED | 0.622 | 0.490 | MARRIED | 0.741 | 0.439 |
| JEFE | 0.244 | 0.435 | JEFE | 0.820 | 0.385 |
| CHILD | 1.067 | 1.214 | CHILD | 1.487 | 1.295 |

- Continued

**Appendix Table 10A.1 (continued)**
Mean (and Standard Deviations) of Sample Variables Used in the Wage
and Job Assignment Functions, by Gender and Sector and Occupation
Central Valley of Costa Rica

|  | Female Mean | Standard Deviation |  | Male Mean | Standard Deviation |
|---|---|---|---|---|---|
| **Domestic Servants** | | | | | |
| Wage | 46.022 | 37.374 | Wage | 46.678 | 28.248 |
| Logwage | 3.569 | 0.719 | Logwage | 3.665 | 0.655 |
| Urban | 0.193 | 0.396 | Urban | 0.400 | 0.516 |
| Rural | 0.431 | 0.497 | Rural | 0.600 | 0.516 |
| EXP | 19.624 | 13.634 | EXP | 26.700 | 17.607 |
| EXP2 | 570.061 | 740.029 | EXP2 | 991.900 | 1137.525 |
| ED | 5.711 | 2.324 | ED | 4.300 | 3.268 |
| EXTRAED | 0.102 | 0.303 | EXTRAED | 0.100 | 0.316 |
| INKIND | 0.340 | 0.475 | INKIND | 0.100 | 0.316 |
| SELFEMPL | 0.000 | 0.000 | SELLEMPL | 0.000 | 0.000 |
| Married | 0.670 | 0.471 | Married | 0.700 | 0.483 |
| Jefe | 0.178 | 0.383 | Jefe | 0.700 | 0.483 |
| Child | 1.503 | 1.521 | Child | 1.400 | 1.647 |

**Appendix Table 10A.2**
Estimates of the Wage Function for Each Sector, Occupation and Gender

Females
Sector and Occupation

| Variable | (1) | (2) | (3) | (4) | (5) | (6) | (7) | (8) | (9) |
|---|---|---|---|---|---|---|---|---|---|
| ONE | 3.044 (0.321) | 4.999 (0.513) | 4.215 (1.0742) | 3.501 (0.335) | 3.283 (0.102) | 3.247 (0.246) | 7.436 (1.685) | 3.87 (0.340) | 3.387 (0.361) |
| EXP | 0.021 (0.0135) | 0.0378 (0.0324) | 0.100 (0.0524) | 0.0264 (0.0130) | 0.0279 (0.00847) | 0.0281 (0.0131) | -0.403 (0.0156) | 0.0435 (0.0177) | 0.0287 (0.0199) |
| EXP2 | -0.000134 (0.000205) | -0.000134 (0.000880) | -0.00211 (0.00116) | -0.000201 (0.000250) | -0.000443 (0.000205) | -0.000215 (0.000336) | 0.00933 (0.000350) | -0.000839 (0.000481) | -0.000194 (0.000335) |
| ED | 0.0841 (0.0330) | -0.00436 (0.0302) | 0.0234 (0.0621) | 0.0561 (0.0259) | 0.0735 (0.00886) | 0.101 (0.0151) | 0.127 (0.0281) | 0.0421 (0.0239) | 0.0669 (0.0264) |
| EXTED | 0.244 (0.126) | -0.336 (0.185) | -1.000 (0.411) | 0.141 (0.103) | 0.125 (0.0587) | 0.112 (0.0734) | 0.663 (0.154) | 0.00918 (0.0786) | 0.0415 (0.156) |
| Std. Error of Regr. | 0.841 | 0.604 | 0.457 | 0.485 | 0.461 | 0.418 | 0.142 | 0.347 | 0.374 |
| $R^2$ | 0.643 | 0.166 | 0.680 | 0.134 | 0.221 | 0.262 | 0.896 | 0.110 | 0.207 |

- Continued

Notes: Standard Errors are in parentheses.
(1) is the Informal Sector
(2) is the Private-Formal: Professional and Technical
(3) is the Private-Formal: Directors and Managers
(4) is the Private-Formal: Administrative Personnel
(5) is the Private-Formal: Laborers
(6) is the Public: Professional and Technical
(7) is the Public: Directors and Managers
(8) is the Public: Administrative Personnel
(9) is the Public: Laborers

## Appendix Table 10A.2 (continued)
### Estimates of the Wage Function for Each Sector, Occupation and Gender

#### Males
#### Sector and Occupation

| Variable | (1) | (2) | (3) | (4) | (5) | (6) | (7) | (8) | (9) |
|---|---|---|---|---|---|---|---|---|---|
| ONE | 2.873 | 3.939 | 4.269 | 4.024 | 3.283 | 3.350 | 5.474 | 3.759 | 3.431 |
| | (0.106) | (0.261) | (0.519) | (0.296) | (0.0599) | (0.354) | (0.964) | (0.216) | (0.193) |
| EXP | 0.0457 | 0.0162 | 0.0339 | 0.00818 | 0.0348 | 0.0347 | 0.0155 | 0.0378 | 0.0305 |
| | (0.00528) | (0.0127) | (0.0299) | (0.0131) | (0.00410) | (0.0240) | (0.0499) | (0.0119) | (0.0111) |
| EXP2 | -0.000542 | -0.000176 | -0.00437 | -0.000272 | -0.000394 | -0.000547 | 0.000617 | -0.000536 | -0.000267 |
| | (0.0000791) | (0.000217) | (0.000545) | (0.000278) | (0.0000771) | (0.000639) | (0.000102) | (0.000257) | (0.0111) |
| ED | 0.0915 | -0.0644 | 0.0478 | 0.0474 | 0.0734 | 0.111 | 0.529 | 0.0637 | -0.000267 |
| | (0.0117) | (0.0156) | (0.0262) | (0.0241) | (0.00507) | (0.0182) | (0.0500) | (0.0148) | (0.000190) |
| EXTED | 0.100 | 0.239 | -0.189 | 0.466 | 0.227 | -0.0316 | -0.562 | 0.0406 | 0.0841 |
| | (0.0919) | (0.116) | (0.190) | (0.100) | (0.0454) | (.114) | (0.270) | (0.0709) | (0.0129) |
| Std. Error of Regr. | 0.692 | 0.599 | 0.0750 | 0.464 | 0.490 | 0.570 | 0.423 | 0.337 | 0.436 |
| $R^2$ | 0.145 | 0.186 | 0.772 | 0.129 | 0.262 | 0.255 | 0.432 | 0.231 | 0.197 |

Notes: Standard Errors are in parentheses.
(1) is the Informal Sector
(2) is the Private-Formal: Professional and Technical
(3) is the Private-Formal: Directors and Managers
(4) is the Private-Formal: Administrative Personnel
(5) is the Private-Formal: Laborers
(6) is the Public: Professional and Technical
(7) is the Public: Directors and Managers
(8) is the Public: Adminnistrative Personnal

## Appendix 10B

### Definitions of the Sectors

If a worker is employed by the central government or semi-autonomous (para-statal) enterprise they are assigned to the public sector. If a worker is not assigned to the public sector, and he or she either works in a firm with greater than five employees or has an education level above high school, or is classed as a professional or technical worker, he or she is assigned to the private-formal sector. If a worker is employed in a firm with five or fewer employees, and does not have an education level above high school, that worker is assigned to the informal sector. Highest wages are paid in the public sector, while lowest wages are found in the two informal sectors.

Within the private-formal and public sectors workers are further divided into four different occupations. We use the International Occupational Classification (Clasificacion Internacional Uniforme de Ocupaciones). We divide workers into professional and technical, directors, owners and general administrators, administrative employees, and other workers.

## Appendix 10.2

### Separating the Impact of Occupations and Sectors
### On the Male-Female Wage Difference

To separate the impact on wage differentials of different access to sectors from differences in wages due to different access to occupations within sectors we first estimate:

$$W_M - W_F = \Sigma(P_{Fj}[\underline{B}_{Mj}'\underline{X}_{Mj} - \underline{B}_{Fj}'\underline{X}_{Fj}]) \quad + \quad \Sigma(\underline{B}_{Mj}'\underline{X}_{Mj}[P_{Mj} - P_{Fj}]) \tag{3-4}$$

$$= \quad W \quad + \quad J$$

and

$$W_M - W_F = \Sigma(P_{Fj}[\underline{B}_{Mj}'\underline{X}_{Fj} - \underline{B}_{Fj}'\underline{X}_{Fj}]) \quad + \quad \Sigma(P_{Fj}[\underline{B}_{Mj}'\underline{X}_{Mj} - \underline{B}_{Mj}'\underline{X}_{Fj}]) + \tag{3-5}$$

$$\Sigma(\underline{B}_{Mj}'\underline{X}_{Mj}[P_{Fj} - P_{Fj}]) \quad + \quad \Sigma(\underline{B}_{Mj}'\underline{X}_{Mj}[P_{Mj} - P_{Fj}])$$

$$= \quad WU \quad + \quad WE \quad +$$

$$\quad JU \quad + \quad JE$$

where j indicates only the informal, private-formal and public sectors. We then desegregate the W's (W, WU and WE) further into that part due to differences in wages due to men and women being paid different wages within occupations and sectors and that part due to different access to occupations within sectors. Specifically, we again estimate 3-4 and 3-5 using subsets of the data used to estimate the decompositions described above; first, we estimate these decompositions using data that includes workers within the private-formal sector and second, using data on workers within the public sector (That is, let j in equations 3-4 and 3-5 indicate the occupation within each sector rather than the sector.)

We find that the difference in the wages between men and women due to different access to the informal, private-formal and public sectors, J in equation 3-5, is negative.[17]  This reflects the fact that women are over-represented in the higher-paid public sector.  Women are over-represented in the public sector both because they have higher levels of education than men and also because they have disproportionate access to the public sector than men with the same experience and education.  That is, JU and JE are both negative.

We find that the difference in wages between men and women due to different access to occupations within the private-formal sector, J, is also negative.  In the private-formal sector, this is because women have higher levels of human capital than men (JE is negative while JU is positive).  However, J is small (relative to the total difference in average wages between men and women) within the private-formal sector.

Within the public sector, women are over-represented among the higher paid occupations.  J is negative and in absolute value terms is larger than the J measured taking into account access to sectors.  We conclude that the public sector, by hiring women into higher paying occupations, is a factor keeping the wages of women high.

---

[17]    The independent variables used in the estimating of the wage equations at this step are the full set described in the text.  In estimating the wage equations in the next step, I use the more limited set of independent variables.

# References

Behrman, J., B. Wolfe and D. Blau. "Human Capital and Earnings Distribution in a Developing Country: The Case of Pre-Revolutionary Nicaragua." *Economic Development and Cultural Change*, (1985a). pp. 1-29.

-----. "Labor Force Participation and Earnings Determinants for Women in the Special Conditions of Developing Countries." *Journal of Development Economics*, Vol.15 (1985b). pp. 259-288.

Birdsall, N. and M. L. Fox. "Why Males Earn More: Location and Training of Brazilian Schoolteachers." *Economic Development and Cultural Change*, Vol. 33, no. 3 (1985). pp. 533-556.

Brown, R., M. Moon and B. Zoloth. "Incorporating Occupational Attainment in Studies of Male-Female Earnings Differentials." *Journal of Human Resources*, Vol. 15, no. 1 (1980). pp. 3-28.

Cain, G. "The Economic Analysis of Labor Market Discrimination: A Survey", in O. Ashenfelter and R. Leyard (eds.). *Handbook of Labor Economics*. North Holland, New York: North Holland, 1986. pp. 693-785.

Carvajal, M. and D. Geithman. "Human Capital and Sex Discrimination: Some Evidence from Costa Rica, 1963-1973", Florida International University Latin American and Caribbean Center, Discussion Paper No. 15, April, 1983.

Chapman, B. and J. Ross Harding. "Sex Differences in Earnings: An Analysis of Malaysian Wage Data." *Journal of Development Studies*, Vol. 21 (1985).

Cotton, J. "On the Decomposition of Wage Differentials." *The Review of Economics and Statistics*, (1988). pp. 236-243.

Gindling, T.H. "Labor Market Segmentation and the Determination of Wages in the Public, Private-formal and Informal Sectors in San Jose, Costa Rica." *Economic Development and Cultural Change*, Vol. 39, no. 3, (1991). pp. 585-606.

-----. "Ingresos de las Mujeres y Crisis Economica en Costa Rica." University of Costa Rica Institute for Research in Economic Science Working Paper #138. Costa Rica, 1990.

-----. "Women's Wages and Economic Crisis in Costa Rica." Paper presented at the 1989 Congress of the Latin American Studies Association. December, Miami, 1989a.

-----. "Crisis economica y segmentacion en el mercado de trabajo urbano en Costa Rica." *Revista de Ciencias Economicas,* Vol 9 (1989b). pp. 79-94.

Gindling T. H. and Berry, A. "Labor Market and Adjustment in Costa Rica", in S. Horton, R.Kanbur, and D. Mazumdar (eds.). *Labor Markets in an Era of Adjustment.* Washington D.C.: The World Bank, Economic Development Institute, 1990.

Gunderson, M. "Male-Female Wage Differentials and Policy Responses." *Journal of Economic Literature,* Vol 27, March (1989). pp. 46-72.

Koopman, J. *Review of Women in the Third World: Work and Daily Life* by J. Bisilliat and M. Fieloux, *Economic Development and Cultural Change,* Vol. 39, no. 2 (1991). pp.437-443.

Lizano. *Programa de Ajuste Estructural en Costa Rica.* Academia de Centroamericana Estudios 6, San Jose, Costa Rica.

McFadden, D. "Econometric Analysis of Quantitative Response Models" in Z. Griliches and M. Intriligator (eds.). *Handbook of Econometrics,* Vol. 2. New York: Elseveir Science Publishing, 1984. pp.136-145

Oaxaca, R. "Male-female Wage Differentials in Urban Labor Markets." *International Economic Review,* Vol. 14, no. 1 (1973). pp. 693-709.

Piore, M. "The Dual Labor Market: Theory and Implications", in D. M. Gordon, (ed.). *Problems in Political Economy: An Urban Perspective.* Lexington, Mass.: Heath, 1971.

Tardanico, R. "Economic Crisis and Structural Adjustment: The Labor Market of San Jose, Costa Rica, 1979-1987." *Comparative Urban and Community Research,* Vol. 4. forthcoming.

Tenjo, J. "Labor Markets, Wage Gap and Gender Discrimination: The Case of Colombia." Mimeograph. Toronto: University of Toronto, Department of Economics, 1990.

# 11

## The Effect of Education on Female Labor Force Participation and Earnings in Ecuador

*George Jakubson and George Psacharopoulos*

### 1. Introduction

An earlier analysis of women's labor force participation in Ecuador was undertaken by Finn and Jusenius (1975) using data for 1966. They found rather low rates of labor force participation among urban women, in the order of 25 percent, with participation rates being highest among women who had completed college (89 percent). Single women were more likely to work in the labor market, but earned substantially less than working wives, who also tended to be older and better educated.

Average earnings of employed women were approximately 55 percent of the average earnings of employed men. Controlling for age, education, and region, that differential drops to 20 percent. They speculate that the occupational distribution of men and women contributes to the remaining earnings differential.

### 2. Ecuador's Economy and Labor Market

Rapid development of the petroleum and service sectors during the 1970s meant that Ecuador had an average growth in GDP of 6.7 percent a year for the period 1970 to 1982. Social expenditures during that period produced major improvements in education and health, and literacy and school enrollment rates increased. The country developed a national network of health care facilities and registered decreases in infant and child mortality and a decline in birth rates. Urban development was also been significant. These improvements have had a positive effect on the social status of women in Ecuador; women constituted 16.3 percent of the economically active population in 1962 and 20.6 percent in 1982.

However, a decline in public sector revenues and expenditure since 1982, brought about in part by the sharp reduction in world oil prices in 1986 and the disruption of oil production, has caused serious problems for the education, health, housing and other social sectors, as well as for unemployment. Women, and especially poor women, have been affected by these economic crises.

Labor force participation rates among women have continued to rise, except among females aged 12 to 19 years who are remaining in school longer. Increased female labor force participation rates have been particularly high among women between ages 25 and 34 years. Participation rates have increased across all marital status categories and married women increased their labor force participation between 1974 and 1982 from 16.8 percent to 21.1 percent. It is reported that 61 percent of female heads of household were in the labor force in 1987 (World Bank, 1989).

Available evidence from several surveys suggests that female monthly earnings are lower than males across all educational levels and occupational categories. Even when adjustments are made for differences in average hours worked per week, women with similar levels of schooling and years of experience still earn less than men. This chapter investigates the causes of these earnings differentials.

## 3.   Data Characteristics

The data used in this chapter come from the 1987 Ecuador Household Survey which was conducted in the three largest cities, Quito, Cuenca, and Guayaquil. The sample therefore consists only of urban households. The reader should bear this in mind when interpreting the empirical findings.

The overall sample contains 21,855 individual observations. The sample used here consists of 4,876 households for which there are clean data on labor force participation and, where relevant, hours of work, earnings and other variables. Descriptive statistics appear in Table 11.1.

The sample was restricted to household heads and spouses between ages 12 and 64 at the time of the survey. There are 3,899 husband/wife pairs and 977 female heads of household.

Labor force participation was determined from responses to questions on recent activity. The questionnaire enabled us to distinguish not only those who were currently at work, but those who were temporarily away from work, on strike, on vacation, actively looking for work, etc., so that we could construct a very accurate measure of labor force participation. Forty-six percent of the 4,876 women were labor force participants. Of these women, 11 percent were not currently in a job at the time of the survey, so 41 percent of the female sample, or 1,975 women, were working in the labor market. All 3,899 men in the analysis sample were working in the labor market at the time of the survey.

The "years of schooling" variable was constructed using information on both the type of schooling completed (for example, primary) and the number of years in each school type. We added the number of grades in each schooling class completed (with the exception of the highest) to the number of years completed in the highest schooling class, so obtaining the number of years of schooling. Note that this really only approximates years of schooling. If an individual repeated a grade of primary school, or if (s)he skipped a grade, that will not be reflected in our measure. Nor does the variable measure number of grades of school completed. If an individual repeated a grade in the highest class of schooling, that will not be taken into account in our measure. Men averaged 9.7 years of schooling and women 8.54 years. Female workers had more years of schooling than women on average, 9.05 years.

Males averaged 39.7 years of age and women 37.7 years. There was little difference, on average, between female workers and non-workers, though there is somewhat less variation in age among female workers. Work experience was constructed as age minus years of schooling minus six.

**Table 11.1**
Mean (and Standard Deviations) of Sample Variables

| Variable | Male Workers | All Women | Working Women |
|---|---|---|---|
| Years of Schooling | 9.70 | 8.54 | 9.05 |
| | (4.90) | (4.36) | (4.85) |
| Age (years) | 39.7 | 37.7 | 37.9 |
| | (11.2) | (11.5) | (10.4) |
| Experience (years) | 23.6 | 23.2 | 22.8 |
| | (12.3) | (13.1) | (12.5) |
| Number of Persons in Household | 4.88 | 4.84 | 4.76 |
| | (1.99) | (2.02) | (2.00) |
| Number Children Aged 0-5 | .67 | .64 | .58 |
| | (.84) | (.84) | (.80) |
| Number Children Aged 6-11 | .76 | .73 | .75 |
| | (.94) | (.93) | (.93) |
| Number of Non-workers Aged 65+ | .04 | .05 | .06 |
| | .21 | .25 | .26 |
| Number of Non-workers Aged 12-64 | 1.62 | 1.66 | 1.08 |
| | (1.39) | (1.38) | (1.25) |
| Lives in Quito | .14 | .15 | .14 |
| | (.35) | (.35) | (.35) |
| Lives in Cuenca | .43 | .44 | .46 |
| | (.50) | (.50) | (.50) |
| Woman is a Spouse | | .80 | .71 |
| | | (.40) | (.45) |
| Labor Force Participant | 1.0 | .46 | 1.0 |
| | (0.0) | (.50) | (0.0) |
| Worker | 1.0 | .41 | 1.0 |
| | (0.0) | (.49) | (0.0) |
| Works in Formal Sector | .55 | | .41 |
| | (.50) | | (.49) |
| Works in Government Sector | .21 | | .19 |
| | (.41) | | (.39) |
| Temporary Worker | .06 | | .03 |
| | (.24) | | (.17) |
| Self-Employed | .37 | | .41 |
| | (.48) | | (.49) |
| Earnings per Month (sucres) | 35,077 | | 22,327 |
| | (54,216) | | (24,271) |
| Hours per Week | 42.5 | | 41.0 |
| | (19.2) | | (13.1) |
| Log Earnings | 10.2 | | 9.61 |
| | (.71) | | (.86) |
| Log Hours | 5.16 | | 4.87 |
| | (.37) | | (.63) |
| Log Average Hourly Earnings | 5.03 | | 4.74 |
| | (.78) | | (.92) |
| Sample Size | 3,899 | 4,876 | 1,975 |

Note:    Figures in parenthesis are standard deviations.
Source:    Ecuador Household Survey, 1987.

The survey records number of persons per household and the relationship of each person to the household head. Household servants living in the household are included in this count. We could also identify the number of individuals in the household by age and earning status. Households had an average of 1.6 adults between ages 12 and 64 who were neither head nor spouse and who were not working in the labor market. On average, the households contained .64 children between ages 0 and 5 and .73 children between ages 6 and 11. Twelve year olds were treated as "adults" in the analysis since labor force questions were asked of those twelve and older.

The sample was unevenly distributed among the three cities. Fifteen percent lived in Quito, 47 percent in Cuenca, and 38 percent in Guayaquil. Eighty percent of the women were either married or cohabiting with a male. The remaining 20 percent were female heads of household. Among married and cohabiting women, 92.5 percent of their male partners worked in the labor market, although only 66 percent of the husbands of working wives also worked.

Among male workers, 55 percent worked in the formal sector. Participation in this sector was determined on the basis of their coverage by the social security system. Twenty-one percent worked in the government sector, 37 percent were self-employed, and 6 percent were classed as temporary workers. On average, they worked 42.5 hours per week and earned 35,007 sucres per month. Of working women, 41 percent worked in the formal sector, 39 percent worked in the government sector, 49 percent were self-employed, and 17 percent were classed as temporary workers. On average, they worked 41 hours per week and earned 22,327 sucres per month.

Monthly earnings were constructed using information on earnings in the previous pay period. These were adjusted to reflect monthly earnings, assuming that earnings were the same in each of the pay periods needed to cover one month.[1]

The wage measure used in the analysis is the natural logarithm of average hourly earnings. Hours of work in the previous week were multiplied by 4 to reflect monthly hours. We thus assume that hours per week were constant. Average hourly earnings is the ratio of monthly earnings to monthly hours, and its logarithm is used as the wage measure below. On average, working women earned 27 percent less than working men.

We chose to use this wage measure rather than the logarithm of total earnings for the following reason. The logarithm of average hourly earnings is the difference between the logarithm of earnings and the logarithm of hours of work:

$$\log \text{avern} = \log \text{earn} - \log \text{hours}$$

Hence, in a regression of log earnings on log hours, the log hours variable should have a coefficient of unity:

$$\log \text{avern} = \log \text{earn} - \log \text{hours} = \text{ß'x} + u$$
$$\log \text{earn} = \text{ß'x} + \log \text{hours} + u$$

---

[1] For example, if the pay period was two weeks long, then monthly earnings are twice the earnings in the previous pay period.

For both men and working women, the coefficient of log hours in a log earnings regression was quite far from unity. This is most likely to be the result of measurement error in the hours variable.

In a regression equation this error simply becomes part of the disturbance term. While it reduces the precision with which the coefficients are estimated, it imparts no bias *per se* to the estimates. Measurement error in an explanatory variable, in contrast, *does* impart a bias. Using the logarithm of average hourly earnings as the dependent variable keeps all the measurement error on the left hand side of the estimating equation.

Experiments estimating hours equations are consistent with this analysis. The coefficient of average hourly earnings in a regression equation for hours of work is biased downwards if hours are measured with error. Essentially, a positive measurement error in hours induces a negative measurement error in average hourly earnings, and a negative measurement error in hours induces a positive measurement error in average hourly earnings, leading to a downward bias. For both the male and working female samples, the coefficient on average hourly earnings in an hours equation was either essentially zero or negative. This result is consistent with the measurement error hypothesis.

## 4.    Determinants of Female Labor Force Participation

We utilize a probit model to analyze the probability of labor force participation and labor market work for women in the sample. In the probit model we have:

$$P(y = 1 \mid x) = F(\beta'x) ,$$

where F() is the standard normal cumulative distribution function (cdf) and the dependent variable y takes on the values 0 or 1. We utilize maximum likelihood methods to estimate the coefficients ß. The inverse of the information matrix, evaluated at the maximum likelihood estimates, is used for inference. Standard errors are the square roots of the diagonal elements.

The derivative of the probability that y = 1, evaluated at $x = x_0$, is:

$$f(\beta'x_0) \beta$$

where f() is the standard normal probability density function (pdf). The derivative takes its maximum (absolute) value, for any given ß, at values of x where ß'x = 0, and decreases in (absolute) value as ß'x moves away from zero. Since the term f() is always positive, the sign of the derivative is the sign of ß.

In essence, the effect of a change in an explanatory variable on the probability of labor force participation (or labor market work) depends on that probability. When the probability of labor market participation is close to one or zero, changes in the explanatory variables have much smaller effects than when that probability is .5. Therefore, one must pick a point at which to evaluate the derivative.

We estimate the derivative by replacing the population parameter ß by its maximum likelihood estimate b. Two logical choices for points of evaluation of the derivative are (1) the sample mean values of the explanatory variables (xbar), and (2) the sample mean value of the dependent variable (ybar). In contrast to a linear model, the predicted value of the probability of labor force participation in a probit model, evaluated at the sample means of the explanatory variables, is *not* equal to the mean of the dependent variable. The former is:

$$f(b'xbar) \, b$$

while the latter is:

$$F^{-1}(ybar) \, b$$

where $F^{-1}()$ is the inverse of the standard normal cdf.

We use the latter point of evaluation, and evaluate the derivatives at the mean value of the dependent variable. For purposes of the simulation studies below, we adjust the constant term $b_0$ so that the predicted probability at the mean values of the explanatory variables is equal to the mean value of the dependent variable. The new constant term $b_0'$ is constructed as:

$$b_0' = b_0 + [ \, F^{-1}(ybar) - F(b'xbar) \, ] \, .$$

In cases in which the mean of the dependent variable is close to .5 the adjustment required is relatively small. That is the situation with these data. The labor force participation rate for these women is 46 percent and 41 percent. In cases in which the mean of the dependent variable is close to 0 or 1 the changes in the derivatives due to the adjustment can be more substantial.

Table 11.2 displays the results of probit equations for the probability of labor force participation and labor market work for the women in the sample. (Note that all men in the sample are working in the labor market.) The left hand panel of the table displays the results for labor force participation and the right hand panel displays the results for labor market work.

At the bottom of Table 11.2 we report the mean of the dependent variable followed by the maximized value of the log likelihood function. We display the chi-square statistic and degrees of freedom for testing the null hypothesis that all the slope coefficients in the model are zero. For both equations there is clear evidence against the hypothesis that the explanatory variables have no effect.

Years of schooling is a marginally significant determinant of female labor force participation and a significant determinant of labor market work. More highly educated women are more likely to participate and to work, but the effect is small.

Age is a significant determinant of both labor force participation and labor market work. We specified a quadratic in age to account for nonlinearities in the relationship and found clear evidence of curvature. Both probabilities increase with age to a peak at just over 40 years of age and then decline. Wives are significantly less likely to participate and work than female heads of household, and wives of working husbands are significantly less likely to participate and work than wives whose husbands do not work in the labor market.

Family structure has an important influence on the work and participation probabilities. The labor force participation decision, in theory, is made by comparing the value of market time (the wage) to the value of non-market time. Non-market time should be more valuable for women with larger families, other things equal.

**Table 11.2**
Probit Equations for Female Participation
and Labor Market Work

| Variable | Labor Force Participation | | Labor Market Work | |
|---|---|---|---|---|
| | Coefficient | Derivative[a] | Coefficient | Derivative[a] |
| Constant | -3.062 | | -3.729 | |
| | (1.27) | | (-14.57) | |
| Years of Schooling | .007 | .29 | .012 | .45 |
| | (1.49) | | (2.40) | |
| Age (years) | .220 | 8.73 | .247 | 9.59 |
| | (16.92) | | (-18.25) | |
| Woman is a Spouse | -.364 | -14.5 | -.00292 | -.11 |
| | (-4.0) | | (-18.25) | |
| Number Children Aged 0-5 | -.089 | -3.55 | -.094 | -3.64 |
| | (3.56) | | (-0.36) | |
| Number Children Aged 6-11 | -.029 | -1.13 | -.041 | -1.59 |
| | (1.32) | | (-1.78) | |
| Number Non-workers Aged 65+ | .004 | .16 | .063 | 2.45 |
| | (0.05) | | (0.77) | |
| Number Non-workers Aged 12-64 | -.417 | -16.5 | -.516 | -20.0 |
| | (-24.5) | | (-27.6) | |
| Husband Works | -.262 | -10.4 | -.298 | -11.6 |
| | (-3.19) | | (-3.51) | |
| Mean of the Dependent Variable | | .46 | | .41 |
| Log Likelihood | | -2864.0 | | -2658.6 |
| Chi-Square for $H_0$: slopes = zero | | 1004.1 | | 1265.4 |
| Degrees of Freedom | | 9 | | 9 |
| Sample Size | | 4,876 | | 4,876 |

a.   This is the derivative of the probability of labor force participation (or labor market work) with respect to the explanatory variable expressed in percentage points and evaluated at the mean value of the dependent variable. The constant term is adjusted so that predicted probability at mean values of explanatory variables equals the mean dependent variable.

Note:   Figures in parenthesis are t-ratios.

If we simply use number of persons in the household to control for family structure, we obtain the anomalous result that the number of persons in the household has a positive, rather than negative, effect on both work and participation probabilities. In part, at least, this effect is due to the fact that household servants are included in the count of people in the households. Families in which the wife and husband both work are wealthier, other things being equal, and hence are more likely to have servants.

Rather than control for family structure merely by using the number of persons in the household, we used a more detailed breakdown of the number of persons by age and earning status. We use four variables to control for family structure:

1.   The number of children under six years of age.  These children are not yet in school, and hence require substantial allocations of time.

2.   The number of children between six and eleven years of age.  These children are in school.  They require time for childrearing, but may also be available to care for younger siblings after school.

3.   The number of non-working adults over sixty five years of age.  These aged people may require some care, but may also be available for childcare.

4.   The number of non-working adults between twelve and sixty four years of age.  It is not clear who these people are.  They may be unemployed or disabled members of the extended family, etc.

There is a striking difference between these results as displayed in Table 11.2 and those in which we simply used the number of persons in the household.  Children under six years of age significantly reduce the probability of labor force participation and market work.  In contrast, school age children have no significant effect on labor force participation probability and a marginally significant (t = 1.8 in a sample of 4,876) effect on probability of labor market work.  Both point estimates are negative.[2]

The number of aged non-workers has no effect on either labor force participation or market work.  In part this is because there are very few households in the sample containing such people.  In contrast, the number of non-workers between 12 and 64 years of age has a large significant negative effect on both labor force participation and market work.  This effect is larger than the effect of young children in both equations.

In order to give a concrete idea of the magnitudes of the probit coefficients we conducted a number of simulation studies.  In each case we set the values of the explanatory variables to their sample means, and then varied a single dimension (except where noted below).  We adjusted the constant term so that the predicted probability, evaluated at the means of the explanatory variables, is equal to the mean of the dependent variable.  The results of these simulation studies appear in Table 11.3.

The first simulation concerns the effect of schooling.  A woman with the mean values of the other characteristics and 16 years of schooling has a predicted probability of labor force participation 11 percent higher than that of a woman with zero years of schooling (probability .49 versus .44) and a predicted probability of labor market work which is 13 percent higher (.44 versus .39).  Thus, while schooling has a positive effect on both labor force participation and market work, that effect is small.

The next simulation concerns the effect of age.  In performing these simulations, we adjusted both the value of age and the value of its square.  Age effects are substantively much larger than the schooling effect.  Other things equal (to their mean values), a 20 year old woman has a

---

[2]   Note, however, that cross section estimates of the effects of children on female labor force participation are biased upwards (in absolute value) as compared to panel data estimates in United States' data (Jakubson, 1988).  Essentially, if there are permanent components of tastes which lead a woman to have more children and to stay at home, the cross section estimate contains both the effects of children and (part of) the effect of these tastes.

predicted probability of participation of .18, in contrast to a 40 year old woman whose predicted probability of participation is .61. Participation probabilities increase with age to about 40 years and then decline, though a 50 year old has a higher predicted participation probability than a 30 year old. There are similar age effects on the probability of working in the labor market. At age 20 the predicted probability is .11, at age 30 it is .41, at age 40 it is .58, and at age 50 it is .52.

Female heads of household are much more likely to work and participate in the labor market than wives. The predicted participation probability for female heads is 50 percent higher than that of wives, and their predicted probability of working is almost twice that of wives. (In this simulation the value of the "husband works" variable is also adjusted so that a female head has no husband working.) Wives of working husbands are approximately 20 percent less likely to work or participate in the labor force than wives whose husbands do not work.

**Table 11.3**
Predicted Participation Probabilities by Characteristic

| Characteristic | Predicted Probability Participation | Working |
|---|---|---|
| Years of Schooling = 0 | .44 | .39 |
| Years of Schooling = 6 | .46 | .40 |
| Years of Schooling = 12 | .47 | .42 |
| Years of Schooling = 16 | .49 | .44 |
| Age = 20 | .18 | .11 |
| Age = 30 | .48 | .41 |
| Age = 40 | .61 | .58 |
| Age = 50 | .54 | .52 |
| Wife | .43 | .38 |
| Female Head of Household[a] | .65 | .61 |
| Husband Works[b] | .41 | .35 |
| Husband Does not Work[b] | .51 | .46 |
| Number of Children Aged 0-5 = 0 | .49 | .43 |
| Number of Children Aged 0-5 = 1 | .45 | .39 |
| Number of Children Aged 0-5 = 2 | .42 | .36 |
| Number Non-workers Aged 12-64 = 0 | .73 | .73 |
| Number Non-workers Aged 12-64 = 1 | .57 | .54 |
| Number Non-workers Aged 12-64 = 2 | .41 | .34 |
| Number Non-workers Aged 12-64 = 3 | .26 | .18 |

a.   Simulation also sets "Husband Works" equal to 0.
b.   Simulation also sets "Woman is a Spouse" equal to 1.

The last two simulation studies concern family structure effects. We first consider changes in the number of young children (under six years of age). A woman with mean characteristics with no young children has a predicted participation probability of .49. With two young children that probability drops to .42. The woman with no young children has a predicted probability of working of .43. With two young children that probability drops to .36.

The effects of changes in the number of non-workers aged 12-64 are even more dramatic. A woman with no non-workers between ages 12 and 64 in the household has a predicted probability of participation of .73 and a predicted probability of working of .73. With one non-aged adult non-worker those probabilities drop to .57 and .54, respectively. With two such people those probabilities drop to .41 and .34, respectively, and with three such people the probabilities are .26 and .18, respectively. Note that the mean number of non-aged adult non-workers is 1.66 with a standard deviation of 1.38, so that this range of values is not unreasonable.

## 5.    Earnings Functions

In this section we explore the determinants of average hourly earnings or the "wage" of men and women. We utilize a conventional human capital specification and specify the logarithm of the wage as a function of years of schooling, years of experience, and experience squared. In order to account for amenities available in the different cities we include dummy variables denoting residence in Quito or Cuenca. We also include dummy variables denoting work in the formal sector, work in the government sector, and temporary work. Finally, we include a dummy variable for self-employment since it may be difficult to separate returns to human capital from returns to capital for the self-employed.

The first column of Table 11.4 presents the results for the male sample. The rate of return to schooling is estimated to be 9.7 percent. Wage rates increase with experience to about 33 years of experience and then decline. Both coefficients of the quadratic are significantly different from zero. Men living in Quito have wage rates that are 13.4 percent lower than those living in Guayaquil, but in Cuenca there is no significant difference in wage rates. Formal sector workers earn 9 percent more, and there is no significant effect from working in the government sector or from being a temporary worker. Self-employed men earn 11.5 percent more than men who work for others.

The analysis of wage rates for women is more complicated than for men, women are less likely to work in the labor market. If the decision to work is a function of the wage rate (as well as other things), there is a potential "selectivity bias" in wage rate equations which do not also account for the decision to work. That is, the subsample of working women will be systematically truncated on the value of the dependent variable (wage).

The conventional solution to this potential problem is to estimate a two-equation system. The first equation specifies the probability of working, and the second specifies the (log) wage rate. One can then follow Heckman's (1979) procedure and use the results of the equation for the probability of working to "correct" the wage equation estimated from the subsample of workers by including the inverse Mill's ratio. That term is the conditional mean of the disturbance in the work/no work equation. This term (Lambda) is added as an additional regressor in the wage equation. Its coefficient is then an estimate of the covariance between the disturbances in the work/no work and wage equations. If that covariance is zero, then there is no bias resulting from focussing only on women workers.

Accordingly, we estimate the wage equation for the female sample both ways. In the second column of Table 11.4 we display the "selectivity corrected" estimates. The variable "Lambda" is the correction factor. The standard errors shown there are corrected for the use of an estimated Mill's ratio.

## Table 11.4
### Earnings Functions

| Variable | Men | Women[a] (Corrected for Selectivity) | Women[b] (Uncorrected for (Selectivity) |
|---|---|---|---|
| Constant | 3.579 | 3.449 | 3.480 |
| | (0.057) | (.109) | (.097) |
| Years of Schooling | .097 | .091 | .090 |
| | (.003) | (.005) | (.005) |
| Experience (years) | .031 | .015 | .014 |
| | (.003) | (.006) | (.006) |
| Experience-Squared (1000's of years) | -.428 | -.198 | -.185 |
| | (.060) | (.100) | (.098) |
| Lives in Quito | -.134 | -.087 | -.088 |
| | (.031) | (.054) | (.054) |
| Lives in Cuenca | -.016 | -.020 | -.021 |
| | (.022) | (.038) | (.038) |
| Works in Formal Sector | .090 | .265 | .264 |
| | (.028) | (.051) | (.051) |
| Works in Government Sector | .004 | .257 | .258 |
| | (.029) | (.055) | (.055) |
| Self-Employed | .175 | .255 | .256 |
| | (.028) | (.045) | (.045) |
| Temporary Worker | -.044 | .042 | .041 |
| | (.045) | (.102) | (.102) |
| Lambda[c] | | .027 | |
| | | (.042) | |
| $R^2$ | .333 | .304 | .303 |
| Mean of Dependent Variable | 5.03 | 4.73 | 4.37 |
| Sample Size | 3,899 | 1,975 | 1,975 |

a.  Corrected for selectivity bias using Probit equation for probability of labor market work in Table 11.2. Standard errors corrected for the use of an estimated inverse Mill's ratio.
b.  Not corrected for selectivity bias. OLS on the subsample of working women.
c.  Inverse Mill's ratio calculated using probit results for the probability of working in Table 11.2.
Notes: Dependent Variable: ln (hourly earnings)
Figures in parentheses are standard errors.

The point estimate of the coefficient on Lambda is positive, as it should be if high wage women are more likely to work in the labor market, *cet. par.* Under the null hypothesis that there is no selectivity bias, the coefficient on Lambda should be zero, and the standard errors produced by simple ordinary least squares (OLS) are correct. Those results (not shown) produce a "t-statistic" for Lambda of .63. Accordingly, one could fail to reject the hypothesis of selection and use uncorrected OLS estimates from the selected subsample. Those results appear in the third column of Table 11.4.

There is a too frequent tendency for this "two-step" procedure to fail to reject the null hypothesis. For this reason we also estimated the two equation system using maximum likelihood techniques (results not shown). There is virtually no difference between the results from the two methods. In fact, not only is there no statistical evidence for selection, but the selectivity corrected and uncorrected point estimates are virtually identical.  For this reason we will not differentiate between them in discussing the results below.

The rate of return to schooling for women is nine percent, slightly below that of men, and is precisely estimated.  Female wage rates increase with experience to about 40 years of experience and then decline, though their return to experience is somewhat below that of men.  Both coefficients of the quadratic are significantly different from zero.  There is no significant difference between female wage rates in Cuenca and Guayaquil, as is the case for men.  In contrast to the results for men, however, women's residence in Quito has no significant effect on female wage rates, though the point estimate is negative, as it was for men.

Women working in the formal sector have substantially higher wage rates.  The effect here is three times larger than the effect for men.  In contrast to men, women also gain from working in the government sector.  Government work pays women 25 percent higher wage rates, unlike the zero effect for men.  Similarly to the results for men, temporary work has no significant effect on female wage rates, and the self-employed have substantially higher wage rates.  The effect of self-employment for women is nearly 50 percent higher than the effect for men.

## 6.    Discrimination

As noted above, working women earn on average almost 30 percent less per hour than working men.  In this section we utilize conventional methods to decompose that differential into a component due to differences in the labor market structure faced by men and women ("prices") and differences in the characteristics of men and women ("endowments").

We first briefly review the decompositions used.  Least squares estimates go through the point of means, so we can write the difference between the mean (log) wage rates of men and women as:

$$\text{diff wage} = \text{ybar}_m - \text{ybar}_f = b_m'x_m - b_f'x_f$$

where $\text{ybar}_m$, $b_m$, and $x_m$ are the mean wage, coefficients, and mean values of the explanatory variables, respectively, for men, and similarly for women (with subscript "f").  By adding and subtracting the same quantity, we can arrive at four different decompositions of that difference with somewhat different interpretations.  Those decompositions are listed below and again at the bottom of Table 11.5.

Decompositions of the Wage Difference
Structure  +  Endowments  +  Interactions

Specification 1:  $x_f'(b_m - b_f)$  +  $b_m'(x_m - x_f)$
Specification 2:  $x_m'(b_m - b_f)$  +  $b_f'(x_m - x_f)$
Specification 3:  $x_f'(b_m - b_f)$  +  $b_f'(x_m - x_f)$ + $(b_m - b_f)'(x_m - x_f)$
Specification 4:  $x_m'(b_m - b_f)$  +  $b_m'(x_m - x_f)$ + $(b_m - b_f)'(x_f - x_m)$

Clearly, the decomposition is not unique.  Essentially, there is an index number problem in choosing a basis for comparison.  In Specification 1, we use the male subsample as the base.  The first term is the difference between what an average female would be paid on the basis of the male equation and what she would be paid on the basis of the female equation.  This reflects differences in the labor market structure facing men and women, i.e., differences in the "prices" of human capital characteristics. The second term is the difference between the pay to an average male and the pay to an average female, based on the male wage equation. This reflects differences in the characteristics (endowments) between men and women. Alternatively, one could do the same decomposition, but use the female subsample as the base. This is the decomposition in Specification 2.

Specifications 3 and 4 extend the analysis to allow for interaction effects. Specification 3 is an extension of Specification 1 and Specification 4 is an extension of Specification 2. In Specification 3, the labor market structure term is the same as in Specification 1, that is, the difference between the pay of an average female based on the male wage equation and based on the female equation. The endowment term is now the difference between the pay of an average male and an average female, based this time on the female wage equation. The last term consists of interaction effects between the differences in the wage equations and the differences in average characteristics. Specification 4 is a similar extension of Specification 2.

No specification is theoretically correct in all cases. If we assume that the labor market for men operates "correctly," then it is sensible to use the male labor market as the basis for the decomposition. Hence we have some preference for Specification 1 as the simplest case and Specification 3 as a more complicated case. We present the results for all four specifications in Table 11.5.

We must also deal with the question of what to use as the coefficients and characteristics of the "average" female. There are basically two possible choices for each. We could either use the wage equation estimates which have been corrected for selectivity bias or the uncorrected wage equation estimates. Similarly, we could either use the mean characteristics of all women or those of working women. The answers depend on the population about which we wish to make inference.

Suppose for the moment that wage rates could be observed for all women, whether or not they work in the labor market. One would then use the full sample of women to estimate the wage equation. Of course, we can only observe wage rates for those women who do work. The uncorrected wage equation, estimated on the subsample of working women, estimates the parameters of the conditional expectation of the (log) wage, given that the woman works, and (implicitly) given the current rule for deciding whether or not to work in the labor market. The purpose of the selectivity "correction" is to obtain estimates comparable to those which we would obtain if we could observe wage rates independently of labor force status. Hence the corrected wage equation estimates refer to the entire population, not just the working subsample.

We calculate the decomposition in two ways. In Table 11.5, the decompositions listed under the heading "Total Population" use the first interpretable method. Here we use the corrected female wage equation and the mean characteristics of all women. From this decomposition one could forecast the effects of policy changes. The decompositions listed under the heading "Workers Only" follow the second interpretable method. Here we use the uncorrected wage equation and the mean characteristics of working women.

For the population as a whole, women on average earn 50 percent less than men. Using Specification 1 where we use the experience of men as the basis for the decomposition, 31 percentage points of the wage differential are shown to be due to differences in labor market structure and 19 percentage points are due to differences in endowments. Of the difference due to labor market structure, 13 of the 31 percentage points are due to the differences in the

## Table 11.5
### Decompositions of the Male/Female Wage Differential
(Percent)

| | Total Population[a] | Workers Only[b] |
|---|---|---|
| Specification 1 | | |
| Labor Market Structure | 31.17 | 21.62 |
| Endowments | 18.96 | 7.76 |
| | | |
| Specification 2 | | |
| Labor Market Structure | 21.48 | 19.59 |
| Endowments | 28.64 | 9.78 |
| | | |
| Specification 3 | | |
| Labor Market Structure | 31.17 | 21.62 |
| Endowments | 28.64 | 9.78 |
| Interactions | -9.69 | -2.03 |
| | | |
| Specification 4 | | |
| Labor Market Structure | 21.48 | 19.59 |
| Endowments | 18.96 | 7.76 |
| Interactions | 9.69 | 2.03 |
| | | |
| Percentage Difference in Mean Average Hourly Earnings | 50.12 | 29.37 |

| | Structure | + | Endowments | + | Interactions |
|---|---|---|---|---|---|
| Specification 1: | $x_f{}' (b_m - b_f)$ | + | $b_m{}' (x_m - x_f)$ | | |
| Specification 2: | $x_m{}' (b_m - b_f)$ | + | $b_f{}' (x_m - x_f)$ | | |
| Specification 3: | $x_f{}' (b_m - b_f)$ | + | $b_f{}' (x_m - x_f)$ | + | $(b_m - b_f)' (x_m - x_f)$ |
| Specification 4: | $x_m{}' (b_m - b_f)$ | + | $b_m{}' (x_m - x_f)$ | + | $(b_m - b_f)' (x_m - x_f)$ |

a.  Total Population comparison uses female wage equation estimates corrected for selectivity and means for all women.

b.  Workers Only comparison uses female wage equation estimates not corrected for selectivity and means for working women.

intercepts of the two wage equations. Hence, 38 percent of the difference is due to different endowments, 36 percent of the difference is due to different "prices" for human capital characteristics, and 26 percent is from an unknown source (the difference in the intercepts), essentially a "fixed cost to being female."

From this decomposition, we would predict that if men and women had identical slope coefficients in the wage equation ("prices"), average female log wage would increase from 4.53

to 4.71. If, in addition, the mean characteristics were the same the average female log wage would rise to 4.90. Finally, if the intercepts were the same (no "fixed cost" to being female) there would be no wage differential.

If we use the female sample as the basis for the decomposition (Specification 2) the results are somewhat different. A much larger proportion of the wage differential (55 percent) is due to differences in endowments and only 17 percent is due to different returns to human capital characteristics. This is probably not the correct basis for comparison, however.

The expanded specifications (3 and 4) which include interaction terms tell much the same story. There is a difference in the sign of the interaction term. When we use male experience as the basis for comparison, the interaction effect is negative. That is, the interaction term tends to reduce the size of the predicted wage differential. In contrast, the interaction term is positive when we use the female experience as the basis of comparison.

The descriptive decompositions based only on working women are somewhat different. The mean difference in log wage rates is 29 percentage points. Using Specification 1, three-fourths of the difference is due to differences in labor market structure and only one-fourth is due to endowments. That pattern is maintained throughout all the specifications.

## 7. Discussion

Female labor force participation and earnings of employed women have increased, relative to men, since the 1966 survey analyzed by Finn and Jusenius (1975). Our sample shows the participation rate to be close to 50 percent, as opposed to 25 percent, and the average working woman earns 70 percent of average male earnings, in contrast to 55 percent.

Female labor force participation is positively related to education, with more educated women being more likely to participate in the market and more likely to be employed. At sample mean values, an increase in years of schooling from 6 to 12 increases the participation probability from .46 to .47 and increases the employment probability from .40 to .42.

Marital status and household status are the most important social determinants of both labor force participation and employment. Wives with working husbands are much less likely to work and participate than female heads of household. Women with young children are also less likely to participate and work.

We find no evidence of selectivity bias in the determinants of (log) average hourly earnings for women. That is, there is no evidence of systematic selection into the labor market based on unobservable variables which are correlated with the wage predictors. Therefore, wage equations estimated on the subsample of working women are no different than shadow wage relationships for all women.

Education is an important determinant of earnings for both men and women, and its effect is essentially the same for both groups. The return to labor market experience is higher for men, while sectoral differences are larger for women than men. In particular, women gain more from self-employment, government work, and formal sector work than do men. In contrast, men lose more in Quito (relative to the other cities) than do women.

In general, the decompositions of the wage rate differentials in Table 11.5 suggest that differences in labor market structure are more important than differences in labor market endowments in explaining the difference between average earnings of men and women. This is particularly true when one considers the subsample of working women. For these women, roughly twenty percentage points of the 30 percent differential can be attributed to differences in labor market structure, independent of the decomposition method employed. The most important difference appears to be the higher return to experience for men.

Differences in labor market endowments are more important when we consider all women. They account for almost one-half of the difference in average hourly earnings between men and women. This result is driven by the labor force participation and employment probabilities, which are functions of both social variables (marital status and household structure) as well as education.

Between ten and fifteen percentage points of the male-female earnings differential is due to the constant terms in the earnings equations. This represents an essentially unknown source of earnings differences. That effect is ameliorated when women work in the formal sector, the government sector, or are self-employed. These results suggest that women face a more serious wage disadvantage in the informal sector. Policies to extend formal sector coverage may be most effective in reducing the male-female earnings differential, at least for urban women.

# References

Finn, M. and C.L. Jusenius. "The Position of Women in the Ecuadorian Labor Force." Ohio State University: Center for Human Resource Research, 1975.

Gronau, R. "The Effect of Children on the Housewife's Value of Time" in T.W. Schultz (ed.). *Economics of the Family*. Chicago: University of Chicago Press, 1974.

Heckman, J.J. "Sample Selection Bias as a Specification Error." *Econometrica*, Vol. 47, no. 1 (1979). pp. 53-161.

Jakubson, G. "The Sensitivity of Labor Supply Parameter Estimates to Unobserved individual Effects: Fixed and Random Effects Estimates in a Nonlinear Model Using Panel Data." *Journal of Labor Economics*,, 1988.

Mincer, J. *Schooling, Experience and Earnings*. New York: Columbia University Press, 1974.

Oaxaca, R. "Male-Female Wage Differentials in Urban Labor Markets." *International Economic Review*, Vol. 14, no. 1 (1973). pp. 693-709.

World Bank. "Ecuador: Country Assessment of Women's Role in Development." Mimeograph. Washington, D.C.: Latin America and Caribbean Region, World Bank, 1989.

# 12

# Female Labor Force Participation and Earnings in Guatemala

*Mary Arends*

## 1.    Introduction

This chapter examines female labor force participation in Guatemala and attempts to explain the earnings differential between men and women using the human capital model.  Guatemala has unique development problems.  Its literacy rate is the lowest in Latin America, and there is a large schooling gap between men and women.   About 40 percent of its population are Amerindians, many of whom do not speak Spanish, and who have little access to social services or to formal labor markets.  About half the work force is employed in agriculture, much of it at the subsistence level.

Section 2 presents an overview of the Guatemalan economy, labor market, and schooling system. Section 3 presents the results of probit regressions for both men and women analyzing the characteristics which make an individual likely to be observed in the labor market.  Building on the results of Section 3, Section 4 presents the results of earnings regressions for men and women both corrected and uncorrected for selectivity.  There are separate earnings regressions for men and women who work in the formal sector.  Lastly, in Section 5, an upper bound on labor market discrimination is estimated and discussed.  Section 6 summarizes the findings and gives policy recommendations.

## 2.    The Guatemalan Economy and Labor Market

Guatemala had a GNP per capita of $910 in 1989, placing it only above Bolivia, the Dominican Republic and Honduras among Latin American countries.  The annual GNP per capita growth rate from 1965 to 1989 was .9 percent.[1]  Population growth rates between 1980 and 1989 were higher than average for Latin America at 2.8 percent per year. [2]  Ethnically, Guatemala is a very diverse country, with 23 different languages spoken, and 40 percent of the population Amerindian.  The Indians are marginalized from Guatemalan Spanish-speaking society, tend to be concentrated in rural areas, and tend to be subsistence farmers.

From 1980 to 1985, the country's GDP declined by an average of 1.1 percent per year.  A recovery started in 1986, and from 1988 to 1989, GDP grew by 4 percent in real terms.

---

[1]    *World Bank Development Report 1991*, Table 1.

[2]    Economist Intelligence Unit, p. 12 (1991).

According to the World Development report, in 1989 agriculture comprised 18 percent of GDP, industry 26 percent, and services 56 percent.

Rapid population growth and slow economic growth have led to unemployment and underemployment problems. Employment only increased by 2.1 percent per year from 1980 to 1989. Although officially the unemployment rate is low, many Guatemalans work in subsistence agriculture and are underemployed. In 1989, unemployment was estimated at 7.8 percent (down from 14 percent in 1986). In 1990, agriculture officially employed just over 30 percent of the work force, manufacturing 14 percent, trade, restaurants, and hotels 12 percent, and services 35 percent. Unofficially, however, agriculture is estimated to employ 60 percent of the economically active population.[3]   The service sector expanded greatly in the 1980s; the share of services in employment has increased from 23 percent of employment registered by IGSS in 1980 to 37 percent in 1989.[4]

Low productivity in the agricultural sector is manifested by wages that are about 50 percent of average wages in all sectors and 28 percent of wages in commerce. Guatemala has a dual agricultural sector, with subsistence and export farming. Wages are low in subsistence agriculture because of low prices for beans, corn and rice.[5]

Table 12.1 charts wage trends for the 1980s. Real wages declined from 1980 to 1986, but partially recovered from 1987 to 1989. The decline was especially severe in services, which declined to 58.6 percent of their 1980 level in 1986. In 1989, real wages in services recovered, but were still 25 percent below 1980 levels. Since women are concentrated in services, undoubtedly the decline hurt women. The drop in real wages was especially strong in the public sector where a wage freeze was in effect from 1981 to 1987.

## Table 12.1
### Real Wage Trends in Guatemala 1980-89 (1980=100)

|             | 1980-82 | 1983-84 | 1985  | 1986 | 1987  | 1988  | 1989  |
|-------------|---------|---------|-------|------|-------|-------|-------|
| All Sectors | 114.1   | 120.6   | 99.2  | 81.1 | 86.5  | 91.1  | 95.9  |
| Agriculture | 123.5   | 134.7   | 116.0 | 98.6 | 100.2 | 100.9 | 109.5 |
| Industry    | 108.6   | 114.6   | 105.9 | 86.1 | 85.5  | 85.1  | 91.0  |
| Services    | 96.8    | 91.8    | 71.6  | 58.6 | 69.0  | 70.5  | 75.0  |

Notes: Refers only to wages covered by the Guatemalan Institute of Social Security.
Services include public employees.

Source: World Bank, *Guatemala: Country Economic Memorandum,* Table IV.1

---

[3]   The Economist Intelligence Unit (1991), p. 16.

[4]   World Bank (1991a), p. 86.

[5]   World Bank (1991a), p. 84.

The Guatemalan government has not invested much in the human capital of its citizens. President Cerezo referred to "the social debt" of the country, and has vowed to compensate with social programs.[6] The government sector is very small, spending only 12 percent of GDP in 1989, compared to 28 percent in Costa Rica, and 32 percent in Panama. Government spending on social services amounted to an average of 3 percent of GDP in the 1980s, investing 2.3 percent of its GDP on education.[7] By way of comparison, Costa Rica spent about 15 percent of its GDP on the social sector and 8 percent on education. Honduras and El Salvador spent 3.5 percent of GDP on education and Mexico 4.5 percent.[8]

One of Guatemala's biggest problems is the low educational attainment levels of its economically active population, which results in low labor productivity and a high concentration of workers in low skilled occupations. Guatemala has an illiteracy rate which is higher than any other Central or South American country. Forty-five percent of the entire population and 53 percent of the female population is illiterate, compared to 20 percent and 19 percent respectively for Latin America as a whole. Only 77 percent of the relevant age group was enrolled in primary school in 1988, the lowest in Latin America, whose overall primary average enrollment is 107 percent.

The educational system in Guatemala is also inefficient. Almost two thirds of primary school children do not complete the primary school cycle. Because of high drop out and repeater rates, it takes 18 years of education rather than 6 to produce one primary school graduate. Rural children often do not finish the school year, resulting in a high repetition rate. Almost 50 percent of the children in grade 1 repeat the grade, and about 30 percent in other primary grades. Enrollment is skewed towards the lower grades.[9] Unlike most other Latin American countries, there is a large gap in education between males and females, which undoubtedly impedes women from participating in the labor market.

## 3. Sample Characteristics

The data come from a 1989 Encuesta Nacional Socio-Demografica (ENSD), carried out by the Instituto Nacional de Estadistica. The survey covers 9,270 households, comprising 33,262 cases. For the analysis, only individuals aged 14 to 65 were included, giving a sample of 26,284 individuals. Only people reporting positive hours and positive earnings were classified as working. Although 88.3 percent of men reported that they were employed, only 69 percent of the men reported positive hours and positive income. Ninety-two percent of the men who said they were employed but reported no hours or no income were employed in agriculture, presumably as family workers or self-employed subsistence farmers. This was not a problem for females; 28 percent reported that they were employed, and 23 percent reported positive hours and positive income. Undoubtedly, many of the women who were recorded as inactive were actually agricultural workers as well, but did not consider their labor to be employment.

Table 12.2A presents the means and standard deviations of the variables used in the analysis, with columns for working and non-working men and women. On the average, working women have

---

[6]    World Bank (1991a), p. 83.

[7]    World Bank (1991a), p. 90.

[8]    World Bank (1987), p. 9.

[9]    World Bank (1987), p. 4.

almost a year of schooling more than working men.[10]  Working women have higher educational attainments as well--16 percent have completed secondary education or above, as compared to 8 percent of the working men.  Non-working women have very low levels of schooling, so overall women have .84 years of schooling less than men.  A higher percentage of non-working women are illiterate than working women, while literacy rates for working and non-working men are about the same.

The survey has no variable for work experience, so a proxy is constructed where potential experience equals age minus schooling minus 6.  This variable will tend to overstate actual experience, especially for women, because they are likely to have interrupted their working lives to have children.  Working men have 2.83 more years of potential experience than working women.

Both men and women work over forty hours per week, with men working over 48 hours on the average.  Men worked almost 6 hours a week more than the women.

To compute the hourly wage, monthly earnings are divided by monthly hours, equal to weekly hours multiplied by 4.3.  Women have a very small pay disadvantage, earning on average 97 percent of male wages.  This is very low for Latin America, and for developed countries as well.[11]

The self-employed category includes domestic workers and excludes professionals.  Over half of the working women are self-employed, compared to 34 percent of working men.  Twenty-two percent of non-working men are classified as self-employed, again because of the missing data for men who are recorded as employed, but have no hours or no income.  Fifty-seven percent of working men work in the private sector, and 9 percent in the public sector.  Thirty-seven percent of working women work in the private sector and 11 percent in the public sector.

The analysis includes several household variables, including marital status, household size, number of children younger than 10 years old in the household, total household income, and the number of workers in the household.  Since the survey includes only children aged 10 and over, it is not possible to distinguish between children younger than 6 and older than 6, nor can the children be assigned to their actual parents or guardians.  For this reason, the child variable represents the number of children in the household.  Working women come from smaller-sized households, are less likely to be married, and have fewer children than non-working women.  Working men also come from smaller households, but have more children and are much more likely to be married than non-working men.

Table 12.2B presents the means and standard deviations of the variables used in the analysis, broken down by self-employed and formal sector.  Here, the formal sector is defined to include both private and public sector employees.  Self-employed males and females are older and have less education than males and females employed in the formal sector.  Women in the formal sector have about 4.5 more years of education than self-employed women, and for men the difference is 2.3 years.  Also, females and males with greater family responsibilities are more

---

[10]  In the data, only the years of schooling at the appropriate level was available.  It was not possible to determine whether the respondent was held back or whether the years of schooling indicate the highest grade actually completed.  Given Guatemala's high repeater rate, this is likely to overstate actual education.

[11]  See other chapters in this volume.  The pay ratio is 81 percent in Honduras, 75 percent in Uruguay, 70 percent in Venezuela, 85 percent in Panama, and 58 percent in Jamaica.

## Table 12.2A
### Means (and Standard Deviations) of Sample Variables

| Variable | Working Males | Non-Work Males | Total Males | Working Females | Non-Work Females | Total Females |
|---|---|---|---|---|---|---|
| Age | 34.88 (13.23) | 24.81 (13.28) | 31.87 (14.03) | 32.88 (12.75) | 31.44 (14.08) | 31.82 (13.79) |
| Married | .73 (.44) | .31 (.46) | .61 (.49) | .45 (.50) | .65 (.48) | .60 (.49) |
| Yrs. School | 3.90 (4.19) | 4.02 (3.68) | 3.87 (4.03) | 4.72 (4.83) | 2.66 (3.44) | 3.03 (3.88) |
| **School Level** | | | | | | |
| None | .32 (.46) | .30 (.46) | .31 (.46) | .33 (.47) | .51 (.50) | .47 (.50) |
| Incomplete Primary | .36 (.48) | .35 (.48) | .36 (.48) | .26 (.44) | .27 (.45) | .27 (.44) |
| Complete Primary | .16 (.36) | .15 (.35) | .15 (.36) | .14 (.35) | .10 (.30) | .11 (.31) |
| Incomplete Secondary | .09 (.28) | .16 (.36) | .11 (.31) | .11 (.31) | .09 (.28) | .09 (.29) |
| Secondary | .04 (.21) | .02 (.14) | .04 (.19) | .10 (.30) | .02 (.14) | .04 (.20) |
| University | .04 (.20) | .02 (.13) | .03 (.18) | .06 (.23) | .01 (.08) | .02 (.13) |
| Literate | .72 (.45) | .74 (.44) | .72 (.45) | .68 (.47) | .52 (.50) | .54 (.50) |
| Experience | 24.99 (14.68) | | | 22.16 (14.34) | | |
| Monthly Earnings(Q) Primary Job | 238.83 (357.02) | | | 183.51 (225.07) | | |
| Weekly Hours | 48.12 (11.45) | | | 42.27 (17.75) | | |
| Hourly Wage | 1.23 (1.98) | | | 1.19 (1.61) | | |

- continued

### Table 12.2A (Continued)
### Means (and Standard Deviations) of Sample Variables

| Variable | Working Males | Non-Work Males | Total Males | Working Females | Non-Work Females | Total Females |
|---|---|---|---|---|---|---|
| Self-Employed | .34 (.47) | .22 (.41) | .30 (.46) | .52 (.50) | .03 (.16) | .14 (.35) |
| Private Sector | .57 (.50) | .09 (.28) | | .37 (.50) | .05 (.22) | |
| Public Sector | .09 (.29) | | | .11 (.32) | | |
| Receive Some Pay in Kind | .13 (.34) | .16 (.37) | .15 (.36) | .21 (.41) | .01 (.12) | .06 (.24) |
| Household Size | 5.99 (2.57) | 6.76 (2.64) | 6.25 (2.63) | 5.69 (2.59) | 6.23 (2.61) | 6.17 (2.66) |
| # Employed in HHold | 2.21 (1.29) | 2.32 (1.31) | 2.24 (1.29) | 2.69 (1.33) | 1.84 (1.21) | 2.05 (1.28) |
| Total HHold Mo. Income | 468.50 (694.62) | 492.64 (1118.35) | 423.90 (746.12) | 729.65 (934.58) | 349.51 (673.67) | 419.89 (682.98) |
| # Children Aged <10 | 1.81 (1.56) | 1.73 (1.63) | 1.80 (1.58) | 1.46 (1.45) | 1.90 (1.59) | 1.82 (1.58) |
| Household Head | .70 (.46) | .24 (.43) | .56 (.50) | .19 (.39) | .07 (.26) | .10 (.30) |
| Indigenous | .32 (.47) | .38 (.49) | .36 (.48) | .23 (.42) | .36 (.48) | .36 (.48) |
| Rural | .60 (.49) | .67 (.47) | .64 (.48) | .36 (.48) | .65 (.48) | .61 (.49) |
| Live in Guatemala Province | .25 (.43) | .15 (.36) | .22 (.42) | .40 (.49) | .18 (.39) | .23 (.42) |
| N | 8,826 | 3,698 | 12,524 | 3,402 | 10,358 | 13,760 |

Notes: Participation rates are 90 percent for men, 29 percent for women.

Sixty-nine percent of the men and 24 percent of the women were classified as working, defined as having positive hours and positive income.

## Table 12.2B
### Means and Standard Deviations
### Formal Sector and Self-Employed

| Variable | Formal Males | Self-Employed Males | Formal Females | Self-Employed Females |
|---|---|---|---|---|
| Age | 32.54 (12.80) | 39.63 (12.79) | 29.95 (11.33) | 35.69 (13.40) |
| Married | .66 (.47) | .87 (.33) | .38 (.49) | .43 (.50) |
| Schooling (Yrs) | 4.65 (4.47) | 2.37 (3.06) | 7.06 (5.13) | 2.46 (3.19) |
| School Level | | | | |
| None | .25 (.43) | .45 (.50) | .17 (.38) | .48 (.50) |
| Incomplete Primary | .35 (.48) | .38 (.48) | .20 (.40) | .31 (.46) |
| Complete Primary | .18 (.39) | .10 (.30) | .16 (.36) | .13 (.33) |
| Incomplete Secondary | .10 (.30) | .05 (.22) | .17 (.38) | .05 (.23) |
| Secondary | .06 (.24) | .01 (.11) | .19 (.39) | .02 (.13) |
| University | .06 (.23) | .01 (.10) | .11 (.31) | .01 (.09) |
| Literate | .78 (.41) | .60 (.49) | .84 (.37) | .53 (.50) |
| Experience | 21.89 (14.06) | 31.26 (13.87) | 16.89 (12.45) | 27.23 (14.31) |
| Monthly Earnings Primary Job (Quetzals) | 266.95 (362.22) | 181.97 (339.20) | 267.48 (261.05) | 102.85 (143.46) |
| Weekly Hours | 47.91 (11.47) | 48.53 (11.41) | 43.09 (14.72) | 41.49 (20.21) |
| Hourly Wage (Quetzals) | 1.38 (1.97) | .93 (1.98) | 1.72 (1.89) | .68 (1.05) |
| Receive Some Pay In Kind | .11 (.31) | .18 (.38) | .11 (.31) | .31 (.46) |

- Continued

**Table 12.2B (Continued)**
**Means and Standard Deviations**
**Formal Sector and Self-Employed**

| Variable | Formal Males | Self-Employed Males | Formal Females | Self-Employed Females |
|---|---|---|---|---|
| Household Monthly Income (Quetzals) | 547.75 (698.09) | 308.20 (659.03) | 948.95 (1064.66) | 519.05 (730.17) |
| # Children Aged 0 to 9 | 1.72 (1.52) | 2.00 (1.60) | 1.31 (1.40) | 1.61 (1.48) |
| Own House | .59 (.49) | .82 (.39) | .55 (.50) | .66 (.47) |
| Household Head | .61 (.49) | .86 (.34) | .14 (.35) | .23 (.42) |
| Indigenous | .24 (.42) | .49 (.50) | .11 (.32) | .35 (.48) |
| Rural | .54 (.50) | .73 (.45) | .30 (.46) | .43 (.49) |
| Live in Guatemala Province | .31 (.46) | .13 (.34) | .47 (.50) | .32 (.47) |

likely to be self-employed than formal sector workers. Self-employed men and women are more likely to be married, to be a householdhead, and have more children than male and female employees. Also, the self-employed are more likely to live in a rural area and to belong to the indigenous population than formal sector workers. Women may choose to be self-employed because it is easier to combine activities like selling food in the market place with household responsibilities. This is evidenced also by the fact that self-employed females work fewer hours than women who are employees.

As for comparisons between men and women, females working in the formal sector have 2.4 years more schooling than males working in the formal sector. The self-employed have lower wages than formal sector employees, and females have a higher average wage than males in the formal sector. However, females that are self-employed earn on the average only 73 percent of what self-employed men earn. Females are concentrated in low paying self-employed labor. However, if women are choosing these occupations because of their flexibility and easy entry, the differential cannot simply be attributed to discrimination, because women gain non-pecuniary benefits.

Tables 12.3A, 12.3B, and 12.3C present male and female wages to better examine the pay differential. Table 12.3A shows male and female wages by schooling level by sector, whether public, private, or self-employed. Table 12.3B shows the wage by occupation for men and women, and Table 12.3C presents the wage by the industry. Table 12.3A shows that females do very well in the public sector, earning more than men in all but the highest and lowest educational level. However, only 9.5 percent of the entire work force is employed in the public sector. In the private sector, women with less than six years of schooling earn only about 65

## Table 12.3A
## Wage by Education Level by Sex
### (Quetzals per hour)

| Education Level | Private | | | | | Public | | | | | Self-Employed | | | | |
|---|---|---|---|---|---|---|---|---|---|---|---|---|---|---|---|
| | Male Wage | % | Female Wage | % | Ratio F/M | Male Wage | % | Female Wage | % | Ratio F/M | Male Wage | % | Female Wage | % | Ratio F/M |
| None | .69 | 11.4 | .45 | 2.3 | .65 | 1.40 | .6 | .57 | .03 | .41 | .63 | 11.1 | .51 | 6.8 | .81 |
| < Primary | .93 | 15.8 | .64 | 2.5 | .69 | 1.64 | 1.1 | 2.10 | .1 | 1.28 | .96 | 9.0 | .65 | 4.3 | .68 |
| Primary | 1.14 | 7.4 | 1.03 | 1.8 | .90 | 1.72 | 1.5 | 2.11 | .3 | 1.23 | 1.32 | 2.4 | .87 | 1.8 | .66 |
| < Second | 1.69 | 4.0 | 1.34 | 1.7 | .79 | 2.24 | 1.0 | 2.85 | .6 | 1.27 | 1.90 | 1.2 | 1.13 | .8 | .59 |
| Secondary | 2.30 | 1.7 | 2.03 | 1.3 | .88 | 3.35 | 1.2 | 4.07 | 1.2 | 1.21 | 1.48 | .3 | 1.66 | .2 | 1.12 |
| University | 5.45 | 1.6 | 3.90 | .7 | .72 | 4.46 | 1.1 | 4.26 | .8 | .96 | 4.08 | .3 | 4.24 | .1 | 1.04 |
| | | | | | | | | | | | | | | | |
| Sum | | 41.9 | | 10.3 | | | 6.5 | | 3.0 | | | 24.3 | | 14.0 | |

Note: Percentages refer to percentage of entire labor force comprised of each group.

## Table 12.3B
### Wages, Schooling, and Weekly Hours by Occupation by Sex
(Quetzals per Hour)

| Profession | Male | | | | Female | | | | Ratio Fem/Male Wage |
|---|---|---|---|---|---|---|---|---|---|
| | Wage | % of Work Force | Yrs. Ed. | Weekly Hours | Wage | % of Work Force | Yrs. Educ. | Weekly Hours | |
| Professionals | 3.51 | 5.1 | 11.89 | 40.6 | 3.57 | 11.3 | 12.01 | 32.3 | 1.02 |
| Administrators | 3.99 | 3.2 | 9.76 | 48.7 | 2.10 | 3.9 | 6.60 | 48.1 | .53 |
| Office Workers | 1.79 | 3.1 | 9.14 | 46.5 | 2.11 | 7.3 | 11.15 | 41.6 | 1.18 |
| Sales People | 1.64 | 7.1 | 5.21 | 52.4 | .99 | 21.3 | 4.11 | 47.1 | .60 |
| Agriculture | .73 | 48.4 | 1.76 | 47.4 | .48 | 9.9 | 1.30 | 41.3 | .66 |
| Miners | 1.00 | .2 | 1.72 | 46.3 | N/A | | | | |
| Transport | 1.64 | 3.9 | 4.71 | 54.3 | 1.16 | .1 | 3.51 | 34.3 | .71 |
| Artisans | 1.21 | 18.7 | 4.76 | 47.9 | .69 | 21.0 | 2.64 | 33.5 | .57 |
| Unclassified Workers | 1.05 | 6.9 | 3.41 | 47.8 | 1.06 | 2.2 | 4.29 | 47.8 | 1.01 |
| Personal Services | 1.13 | 3.3 | 4.71 | 57.1 | .54 | 23.1 | 2.77 | 49.9 | .48 |
| Overall | 1.23 | 100 | 3.90 | 48.1 | 1.19 | 100 | 4.72 | 42.3 | .97 |

percent of what men earn. The ratio improves for females with primary schooling and complete secondary schooling. Then, the ratio falls again for women with a university level education. At low levels of education, women who are self-employed are a little better off than women in the private sector; their earnings are higher and the ratio is more favorable. However, for women with primary and some secondary education, the ratio is very low in the self-employed sector, (.66 and .59 respectively) and wages are lower than in the private sector. Self-employed women with university education earn almost as much as working women in the public sector, and self-employed women with secondary and higher education actually earn more than men.

In Table 12.3B, women are shown to have a pay advantage when they work as professionals, office workers, or unclassified workers, occupations for which they have higher average years of schooling than men. Women are concentrated in personal services, sales, and artisans, which together account for 65 percent of female workers. They are also very low paying occupations; only agriculture has a lower wage. Also, the female to male wage ratio is very low in these occupations--from .6 to .48. Men are concentrated in agriculture (48.4 percent of male workers) and artisans (18.7 percent). Although agriculture is very low paying, male agricultural workers still receive a higher wage than female artisanal occupations and personal service workers receive.

Men work more hours than women in every occupation, and have more years of schooling in the occupations of administrator, sales person, agricultural worker, transporter, artisan, and personal services. This advantage in human capital endowments could help explain the wage differential, and will be discussed in Section 6.

Table 12.3C shows the wages for men and women by industry. Women have a pay advantage in construction and transport, but these two industries hire only 1.1 percent of working women. In both cases, the women have considerably higher schooling than the males. Men are concentrated in agriculture and manufacture, while women are concentrated in social services and commerce. Women in these sectors tend to be informal workers, selling goods on the street, or working as domestics.

**Table 12.3C**
Wages, Schooling and Weekly Hours by Industry by Sex
(Quetzals per Hour)

| | Male | | | | Female | | | | |
|---|---|---|---|---|---|---|---|---|---|
| Industry | Wage | % of Work Force | Yrs. Ed. | Weekly Hours | Wage | % of Work Force | Yrs. Educ. | Week Hours | Ratio Fem/Male Wage |
| Agriculture | .78 | 50.4 | 1.91 | 47.5 | .59 | 11.0 | 1.95 | 42.2 | .76 |
| Mining | 1.46 | .3 | 4.15 | 48.8 | N/A | | | | |
| Manufacture | 1.36 | 13.1 | 5.55 | 48.4 | .83 | 22.8 | 3.35 | 34.9 | .61 |
| Utilities | 2.32 | .7 | 6.25 | 45.9 | 2.26 | .2 | 9.17 | 43.3 | .97 |
| Construction | 1.28 | 7.0 | 3.61 | 47.0 | 1.53 | .2 | 9.26 | 43.0 | 1.20 |
| Commerce | 1.60 | 10.0 | 5.64 | 52.2 | 1.00 | 28.9 | 4.38 | 47.9 | .63 |
| Transport | 1.87 | 4.2 | 5.49 | 54.1 | 2.71 | .9 | 10.66 | 39.4 | 1.45 |
| Financial | 3.45 | 1.8 | 10.73 | 44.5 | 3.05 | 1.8 | 11.93 | 42.7 | .88 |
| Social Services | 2.01 | 12.6 | 7.29 | 46.4 | 1.63 | 34.2 | 6.21 | 42.5 | .81 |

## 4. The Determinants of Female Labor Force Participation

In this section, results of a probit equation estimation for both men and women are presented and discussed. It is necessary to estimate a probit equation to determine which characteristics influence whether an individual is observed in the labor force. Ordinary least squares (OLS) regression analysis assumes that the observations are a random sample of a population. However, the sample of working individuals in the population is not a random sample, but a truncated one. What is observed are people whose offered wage exceeded their reservation wage, and whose earnings could be reported. This is the selectivity problem discussed by Heckman (1979).

To correct for selectivity, Heckman's two-step method is used. First, the probit equation is estimated, and the inverse Mill's ratio (Lambda) is computed. The Lambda is a measure of unseen variables which affect the probability that an individual will be observed in the labor force. Then, Lambda can be included as a regressor in an OLS regression, correcting for selectivity. If Lambda is positive, the unseen factors which affect participation also earn a premium in the work force. If Lambda is negative, the factors which tend to increase earnings also tend to make the individual less likely to be observed in the labor force.

The probit equations include right hand side variables for educational levels, age splines, locality, marital status, household structure, and the "need for income" (proxied by the number of other employed people in the household and total household income excluding the respondent's income). Table 12.4A presents the results for men and Table 12.4B the results for women.

Looking at Table 12.4A, only two educational variables (no education and some secondary education) and four age variables are significant at the five percent level for men. Since male participation rates are already high (69 percent) the partial derivatives which represent the slope of the probit function are small.

The variables representing marital status, household headship, location, ethnic origin, and monthly household income are all significant. For men, being married increases the probability of working. Household headship also has a large positive effect on participation. The coefficients of the dummy variables representing ethnic origin and rural location are negative, as would be expected by the lack of access to formal labor markets. Also, many subsistence farmers and family workers did not have any earnings or hours reported and so were coded as "not-working." Most of the indigenous and rural population are subsistence farmers; 73 percent of indigenous men are agricultural workers. Also, of the indigenous men, 42 percent were self-employed and 21 percent were family workers.

Table 12.5 presents the results of a simulation to isolate the effect of each variable on the probability of participation. Other variables are held at the sample mean, while each dummy variable is set equal to 1. For men, looking at education, the probability of participation varies only by ten percentage points. Men who have completed secondary school have the highest probability of participation, while those with incomplete secondary schooling have the lowest. Those with incomplete secondary education could have a very high reservation wage as they try to complete secondary. Also, the expected participation rate could be low because of raised expectations. Those with incomplete secondary schooling perceive themselves as more qualified than those with primary education, so they want a better job, but they are not qualified for jobs requiring a secondary school degree. Completing secondary school appears to be an important qualification in the Guatemalan labor market. The secondary school diploma could be a signalling device that employers look for when hiring labor.

The effects of age on participation are notable for the 14 to 19 age group, where participation is at its lowest. Almost 70 percent are actually active, but of those working, about half are family workers in agriculture. Twenty-five percent of the men in the youngest age group are students. Participation peaks at the ages of 30 to 34 and is level until the ages of 50 and above. For older men, the probability declines steadily. There is not an abrupt falling off in participation levels.

In Table 12.4B, which presents the results of the probit estimation for females, it is apparent that schooling level is an important determinant of participation. It is significant at the 5 percent level for all schooling levels except university, and the partial derivatives are large compared to other variables. The number of children and marital status have the expected negative and significant impact on participation, indicating that women with more household responsibilities have a higher reservation wage than single or childless women.

All of the age splines are significant, except for age 50 to 54. Participation peaks between the ages of 30 and 34. However, in Guatemala, participation dips for women aged 35 to 39 and then rises again.

## Table 12.4A
### Probit Results for Male Participation

| Variable | Coefficient | T-Ratio | Partial Derivative |
|---|---|---|---|
| Constant | .625 | 7.40 | |
| **Education Levels** | | | |
| None | -.287 | 3.42 | -.095 |
| Some Primary | -.123 | 1.50 | -.040 |
| Complete Primary | -.075 | .89 | -.024 |
| Some Secondary | -.466 | 5.44 | -.154 |
| University | -.186 | 1.70 | -.062 |
| # of Children < 10 Years Old in Household | -.035 | 3.90 | -.011 |
| **Age Group** | | | |
| Age 14 to 19 | -.650 | 15.13 | -.215 |
| Age 25 to 29 | .102 | 1.93 | .033 |
| Age 30 to 34 | .137 | 2.33 | .045 |
| Age 35 to 39 | .047 | .77 | .015 |
| Age 40 to 44 | .104 | 1.51 | .034 |
| Age 45 to 49 | .090 | 1.22 | .030 |
| Age 50 to 54 | -.082 | 1.08 | -.027 |
| Age 55 to 59 | -.152 | 2.01 | -.050 |
| Age 60 to 65 | -.330 | 4.48 | -.109 |
| Married | .218 | 7.40 | .072 |
| Head of Household | .708 | 14.31 | .234 |
| Live in Guatemala Province | .273 | 7.11 | .090 |
| Live in Rural Area | -.170 | 5.01 | -.056 |
| Indigenous | -.293 | 9.92 | -.097 |
| Total Household Monthly Income (excludes respondent) | -.023 | 2.72 | -.007 |
| Number of Employed Persons in Household (excludes respondent) | .021 | 1.81 | .0071 |
| Log-likelihood | -6136.2 | | |

Notes: Base group is males aged 20 to 24 who have completed secondary education.

Dependent variable is "working" which is equal to 1 if individual reported positive hours and positive income.

## Table 12.4B
### Probit Results for Female Participation

| Variable | Coefficient | T-Ratio | Partial Derivative |
|---|---|---|---|
| Constant | .372 | 5.33 | |
| **Education Levels** | | | |
| None | .680 | 10.47 | -.193 |
| Some Primary | -.557 | 8.81 | -.158 |
| Complete Primary | -.524 | 7.82 | -.149 |
| Some Secondary | -.697 | 10.13 | -.198 |
| University | .164 | 1.59 | .046 |
| **# of Children < 10 Years Old in Household** | -.034 | 3.72 | -.009 |
| **Age Group** | | | |
| Age 14 to 19 | -.412 | 9.04 | -.117 |
| Age 25 to 29 | .197 | 3.98 | .056 |
| Age 30 to 34 | .387 | 7.52 | .110 |
| Age 35 to 39 | .366 | 6.96 | .104 |
| Age 40 to 44 | .374 | 6.59 | .106 |
| Age 45 to 49 | .230 | 3.68 | .065 |
| Age 50 to 54 | .087 | 1.28 | .024 |
| Age 55 to 59 | -.192 | 2.60 | -.054 |
| Age 60 to 65 | -.201 | 2.80 | -.057 |
| Married | -.6346 | 19.104 | -.183 |
| Head of Household | .339 | 7.29 | .096 |
| Live in Guatemala Province | .223 | 6.91 | .063 |
| Live in Rural Area | -.480 | 15.88 | -.136 |
| Indigenous | -.080 | 2.52 | -.022 |
| Total Household Monthly Income (excludes respondent) | .022 | 3.22 | .006 |
| Number of Employed Persons in Household (excludes respondent) | .006 | .56 | .001 |
| Log likelihood | -6338.3 | | |

Notes:   Base group are females aged 20 to 24 who have completed secondary education.
Dependent variable is "working" which is equal to 1 if individual reported positive hours and positive income.

Being the head of a household increases the probability of participation, as does living in Guatemala province and living in an urban area. A woman from an indigenous group is less likely to participate in the labor market. Household income has a positive effect on participation, which contradicts the "need for income" theory, which posits that women with less income are compelled to seek remunerated work. The number of other employed people in the household is not a significant variable.

Examining Table 12.5, it is apparent that education has a strong effect on participation--the probability increases from .18 for women with no education to .41 for women with completed secondary education. The lowest probability is for women with some secondary education, which further supports the belief that secondary education has a signalling effect. The probability of participating increases about 25 percent between no education and completed primary school, but the biggest jump in participation occurs with completed secondary schooling. The probability at that level is double what it is for primary school. In Guatemala, the effects of having completed secondary school are very similar to having attended the university level because of the very low schooling attainments for the population as a whole and women in particular.

The probability of participation drops by a percentage point, which is 5 percent of the participation rate with no children, when a woman has one child and further drops with additional children. That probability drops 13 percent between having no children and having three children. The effect is not as strong as has been presented in the other country case studies[12]; perhaps different results would be obtained if the number of children aged 0 to 6 and who in the household is primarily responsible for them could be determined.

Age is an important determinant of participation. The level stays about the same from age 30 to 44. Participation begins to drop off at age 45 to 49, and then continues to steadily decline, although for the oldest groups (age 55 to 59 and 60 to 65) it is higher than the youngest group (age 15 to 19). Surprisingly, participation stays relatively high at older ages. This was not the case in Uruguay and Panama, where participation fell off more abruptly.

An unmarried woman is twice as likely to be in the work force as a married woman. If a woman is a household head, she is about 50 percent more likely to work than a woman who is not a household head. A female household head is likely to be single, divorced, or widowed, and therefore has a responsibility to earn wage income. Even so, a household head has only a 30 percent probability of working, low compared to other countries.

Being of an indigenous group has a surprisingly small effect on participation, given the lack of access to labor market opportunities. The rural and indigenous variables are highly correlated. Thus, the rural coefficient may include the effects of the indigenous variables.

The effects of household headship, location, and ethnic group are similar for men and women, although household headship and location do not have as large an effect in percentage terms. For men, household headship increases the probability of participation by 24 percentage points. Ethnicity has a larger impact for men; indian men are 13 percent less likely to be observed in the work force than latinos, or Spanish-speaking men. For women, the corresponding decrease in probability is 10.5 percent.

---

[12] For example, see the chapters on Panama, Uruguay, and Venezuela in this volume.

**Table 12.5**
**Predicted Participation Probabilities by Characteristic**

| Characteristic | Male | Female |
|---|---|---|
| **Education** | | |
| No Education | .70 | .18 |
| Some Primary | .75 | .21 |
| Complete Primary | .78 | .22 |
| Some Secondary | .63 | .18 |
| Complete Secondary | .79 | .41 |
| University | .73 | .47 |
| **Number of Children Aged 0 to 9** | | |
| None | .75 | .22 |
| One | .74 | .21 |
| Two | .73 | .20 |
| Three | .71 | .19 |
| **Age** | | |
| 14 to 19 | .54 | .10 |
| 20 to 24 | .77 | .19 |
| 25 to 29 | .80 | .25 |
| 30 to 34 | .81 | .32 |
| 35 to 39 | .79 | .31 |
| 40 to 44 | .80 | .31 |
| 45 to 49 | .80 | .26 |
| 50 to 54 | .75 | .22 |
| 55 to 59 | .72 | .15 |
| 60 to 65 | .66 | .14 |
| **Married** | | |
| No | .68 | .33 |
| Yes | .76 | .14 |
| **Household Head** | | |
| No | .58 | .20 |
| Yes | .82 | .30 |
| **Live in Province of Guatemala** | | |
| No | .71 | .19 |
| Yes | .79 | .26 |
| **Live Rural Area** | | |
| No | .76 | .30 |
| Yes | .71 | .15 |
| **Of Indigenous Ethnicity** | | |
| No | .76 | .21 |
| Yes | .66 | .19 |
| **Number of Workers in Household Besides Respondent** | | |
| None | .72 | .20 |
| One | .73 | .20 |
| Two | .73 | .21 |
| Three | .74 | .21 |

## 5.    Earnings Functions

In this section, the returns to different human capital characteristics are estimated for men and women, in order to investigate the earnings gap between men and women. The standard Mincerian (1974) earnings function is used, where:

$$\log Y_i = a + b_1 \text{ Schooling}_i + b_2 \text{ Experience}_i + b_3 \text{ Experience Squared}_i + e_i$$

In the specification, the log of monthly earnings is the dependent variable, and the log of monthly hours is included as a regressor. To correct for selectivity, the inverse Mill's ratio (Lambda) is also included as a regressor.

Table 12.6 presents the results of separate earnings regressions for men and women, both correcting for selectivity and using the standard model. Examining the non-corrected model, females earn a higher return to education (16 percent versus 14 percent) and a slightly lower return to potential experience (.041 versus .045).[13] The experience squared term is significant and negative, indicating a concave shape. The elasticity of income to hours worked is higher for women; a one percent increase in monthly hours worked leads to a .48 percent increase in earnings. The R-squared is higher for females than males, suggesting that the earnings function has a better "fit" when explaining female earnings.

When Lambda is included as a regressor, the returns to schooling fall for both men and women, and the elasticity of earnings to hours falls also. Females have about a 2 percentage point higher return to a year of schooling than men. With selectivity, female returns to experience are higher than the male returns to experience (.034 versus .019). The coefficient of Lambda for both men and women is negative and significant, and is greater in absolute value for males. This indicates that unobserved characteristics that earn a premium in the labor market also make the individual less likely to be observed in the labor market. The significance of Lambda indicates that the uncorrected regression coefficients are biased.

In Table 12.7, the results of a regression including only those employed in the formal sector are presented. The probit estimates used to derive Lambda using formal sector participation as the dependent variable are presented in the Appendix Tables.

When only the formal sector is considered, in the selectivity equations, females have more than a 4 percentage point advantage in returns to schooling. The returns to schooling are lower in the formal sector than when all sectors are considered. For women, the return is only slightly lower. For males, returns to education in the formal sector are 2 percentage points less than for all sectors. The return to potential experience is higher in the formal sector for both men and women, but the gains drop more rapidly than for all sectors. The coefficient on Lambda becomes more negative for men while for women, it becomes less negative when going from Table 12.6 to Table 12.7. These findings are the opposite of Terrell's (1989), who found that returns to

---

[13]    Other studies have estimated returns to education in Guatemala. Sumner (1981) found a rate of return ranging from 5.9 percent to 10.8 percent. He examined the earnings of male farm workers compared to employees. Terrell (1989) estimated the rate of return to be only 2.2 percent. However, she included occupational and sectoral dummy variables in the regression. Terrell's study included women and looked at discrimination between male and female street vendors and shop assistants as representatives of the informal and formal sectors.

**Table 12.6**
**Earnings Functions**
**All Sectors**

| | Males | Males (Corrected for Selectivity) | Females | Females (Corrected for Selectivity) |
|---|---|---|---|---|
| Constant | 2.006 (10.822) | 2.755 (10.879) | .966 (6.928) | 1.615 (9.958) |
| Schooling (Years) | .143 (58.382) | .126 (42.034) | .164 (54.152) | .146 (36.690) |
| Log Monthly Hours | .344 (9.957) | .320 (9.269) | .475 (19.024) | .445 (17.761) |
| Experience | .045 (17.969) | .019 (5.370) | .041 (12.361) | .034 (9.248) |
| Experience Squared | -.001 (14.530) | -.000 (4.740) | -.001 (9.498) | -.001 (7.132) |
| Lambda | | -.501 (10.879) | | -.291 (7.526) |
| Adjusted R-Squared | .293 | .303 | .509 | .518 |
| N | 8,826 | 8,826 | 3,402 | 3,402 |

Notes: Numbers in parenthesis are t-ratios.
Dependent variable is log of monthly income.

education were higher in the formal sector and returns to experience higher in the informal sector. Given the relatively high educational attainments of women and men in the formal sector, it could be that there are decreasing returns to education at higher levels of schooling. As for experience, the nature of private and public sector formal jobs could be that there is more of a scope for job-specific human capital than for the self-employed, who tend to be in occupations that provide easy entry and exit into the labor market. Another reason is that the potential experience variable is a function of age, and self-employed workers are on the average older than formal sector workers.

The adjusted R-squared for the formal sector regressions is much higher than for all sector regressions. The human capital variables explain much more of the variation in earnings in the formal sector than the informal sector, which is expected. For the informal sector, a large part of earnings could be return on physical capital, which is not measured in the survey.

## Table 12.7
### Earnings Functions
### Formal Sector Only

|  | Males | Males (Corrected for Selectivity) | Females | Females (Corrected for Selectivity) |
|---|---|---|---|---|
| Constant | 1.845 | 2.906 | 1.284 | 1.6810 |
|  | (11.335) | (16.680) | (6.301) | (7.021) |
| Schooling (Years) | .129 | .101 | .159 | .1441 |
|  | (66.016) | (33.282) | (48.154) | (24.874) |
| Log Monthly Hours | .389 | .343 | .431 | .4148 |
|  | (12.811) | (11.415) | (11.647) | (11.124) |
| Experience | .056 | .036 | .052 | .0503 |
|  | (26.391) | (12.886) | (12.845) | (12.092) |
| Experience Squared | -.001 | -.000 | -.001 | -.0007 |
|  | (19.551) | (8.415) | (8.881) | (8.226) |
| Lambda |  | -.628 |  | -.153 |
|  |  | (14.267) |  | (3.093) |
| Adjusted R-Squared | .433 | .465 | .589 | .591 |
| N | 5,939 | 5,939 | 1,685 | 1,685 |

Notes: Numbers in parenthesis are t-ratios.
Dependent variable is log of monthly income.

## 6.     Discrimination

The upper bound on wage discrimination can be found using Oaxaca's (1973) equations:

$$\ln(\text{Earnings}_m) - \ln(\text{Earnings}_f) = X_m(b_m - b_f) + b_f(X_m - X_f) \quad (1)$$
$$= X_f(b_m - b_f) + b_m(X_m - X_f) \quad (2)$$

Where $X_m$ represents the means of the dependent variables for males, $X_f$ represents the means of the dependent variables for females, $b_m$ is the matrix of estimated coefficients for males, and $b_f$ is the matrix of estimated coefficients for females. Both equations give the differential between the predicted values of earnings for males and females, $b_m X_m - b_f X_f$. The first term on the right hand side in equation 1 gives the part of the differential that is explained by differences in how male and female human capital endowments are rewarded in the labor market (wage structure) evaluated at the male means. The second term calculates the part of the differential due to differences in the means of the dependent variables of men and women (endowments), multiplied by the female coefficients. Equation 2 is the same breakdown, but calculated at the female means rather than the male means. There is an index number problem with the two equations.

However, it makes more sense to evaluate the differential at the male means, since this paper is examining potential discrimination against women.

In calculating the percentage of the differential due to endowments and to wage structure, the means of the entire sample of men and women are used for schooling and experience, and the means of working men and women are used for log hours. Neither the Mill's ratio terms (Lambda) nor their coefficients are included in the equation because the parameter of interest is the mean for the whole sample, not just working men and women.[14]

In Table 12.8, the results of the Oaxaca decomposition are presented. They are calculated using the selectivity-corrected coefficients for schooling, experience, experience-squared, and log hours. In all sectors, 55 percent of the differential is explained by endowments when evaluated at the male means, and 45 percent of the differential is explained by endowments when calculated at the female means. The rest of the differential is an upper bound on discrimination, which amounts to about 50 percent of the measured differential.

**Table 12.8**
Decomposition of Sex Earnings Differential

| Specification | Percentage of the Differential Due to Differences in | | |
|---|---|---|---|
| | Endowments (%) | Wage Structure (%) | |
| Corrected for Selectivity | All Sectors | | |
| Equation 1 | 55.4 | 44.6 | Total Differential |
| Equation 2 | 45.3 | 54.7 | .37 |
| | Formal Sector Only | | |
| Equation 1 | 27.5 | 72.5 | Total Differential |
| Equation 2 | 20.3 | 79.7 | .70 |

Notes:  The decomposition is based on the results of Table 12.6 and Table 12.7.
All results are derived using selectivity-corrected coefficients.

When looking at only the formal sector, less of the total differential is explained by the difference in endowments. Twenty-eight percent of the differential measured at the male means can be attributed to endowments, while 73 percent represents an upper bound on discrimination in the formal sector. Based on this information, it appears that there is more discrimination in the formal sector compared to all sectors.

It is important to keep in mind that the wage structure part of the decomposition represents an upper bound on discrimination. If there are unmeasured characteristics in which men have an advantage, and these characteristics earn a premium, the upper bound is upwardly biased.

---

[14]   See the chapter in this volume by Psacharopoulos on Venezuela.

However, if there is discrimination which impedes women from obtaining the schooling they desire or from entering a lucrative occupation, discrimination will be downwardly biased.

## 7.  Discussion

One of the biggest problems Guatemalan women face is the lack of schooling opportunities. There is a large schooling gap that favors men.  Increasing quantity and quality of schooling, especially at the primary and secondary level, would undoubtedly increase women's labor force participation, allow more opportunity to enter into formal labor markets, and increase earnings.

Although the overall difference between male and female wages appears small, it masks important distinctions between the formal and informal sector.  Most women workers are self-employed workers.  On the average, they make 75 percent of what men earn.  Female workers in the public sector, to contrast, have higher wages than males in the same sector.  In the formal sector, females have a higher average wage, although males have an earnings advantage when predicting wages for the entire sample.  The high ratio of female to male wages does not rule out labor market discrimination.  The Oaxaca decomposition shows that between 73 and 80 percent of the differential between male and female earnings in the formal sector is due to differences in how male and female human capital characteristics are rewarded in the market.  It appears that discrimination is greater in the formal sector than in all sectors.

Occupational choice appears to be an important factor in determining wages.  Another question is whether females are constrained by societal factors from entering many occupations, or whether women choose to work in certain jobs because of their compatibility with household work.

### Appendix Table 12A.1
### Probit Results for Male Formal Sector Participation

| Variable | Coefficient | T-Ratio |
|---|---|---|
| Constant | .642 | 8.50 |
| **Education Levels** | | |
| None | -.555 | 7.55 |
| Some Primary | -.428 | 6.02 |
| Complete Primary | -.318 | 4.33 |
| Some Secondary | -.679 | 8.97 |
| University | -.125 | 1.31 |
| # of Children < 10 Years Old in Household | -.021 | 2.48 |
| **Age Group** | | |
| Age 14 to 19 | -.443 | 10.53 |
| Age 25 to 29 | .044 | .93 |
| Age 30 to 34 | -.060 | 1.16 |
| Age 35 to 39 | -.107 | 1.99 |
| Age 40 to 44 | -.093 | 1.59 |
| Age 45 to 49 | -.175 | 2.82 |
| Age 50 to 54 | -.303 | 4.59 |
| Age 55 to 59 | -.442 | 6.57 |
| Age 60 to 65 | -.504 | 7.35 |
| Married | .103 | 2.48 |
| Head of Household | .141 | 3.07 |
| Live in Guatemala Province | .352 | 10.76 |
| Live in Rural Area | -.163 | 5.49 |
| Indigenous | -.478 | 17.66 |
| Total Household Monthly Income (excludes respondent) | -.010 | 1.16 |
| Number of Employed Persons in Household (excludes respondent) | .004 | .36 |
| Log-likelihood | -7801.4 | |

Note:   Base group is males aged 20 to 24 who have completed secondary education.

## Appendix Table 12A.2
### Probit Results for Female Formal Sector Participation

| Variable | Coefficient | T-Ratio |
|---|---|---|
| Constant | .285 | 3.82 |
| **Education Levels** | | |
| None | -1.389 | 19.77 |
| Some Primary | -1.199 | 18.05 |
| Complete Primary | -.975 | 14.03 |
| Some Secondary | -.889 | 12.70 |
| University | .182 | 1.80 |
| # of Children < 10 Years Old in Household | -.032 | 2.69 |
| **Age Group** | | |
| Age 14 to 19 | -.354 | 6.61 |
| Age 25 to 29 | .162 | 2.70 |
| Age 30 to 34 | .266 | 4.21 |
| Age 35 to 39 | .211 | 3.21 |
| Age 40 to 44 | .091 | 1.25 |
| Age 45 to 49 | .018 | .22 |
| Age 50 to 54 | -.248 | 2.60 |
| Age 55 to 59 | -.361 | 3.51 |
| Age 60 to 65 | -.564 | 5.13 |
| Married | -.639 | 15.57 |
| Head of Household | .163 | 2.78 |
| Live in Guatemala Province | .179 | 4.61 |
| Live in Rural Area | -.214 | 5.45 |
| Indigenous | -.339 | 7.51 |
| Total Household Monthly Income (excludes respondent) | .006 | .81 |
| Number of Employed Persons in Household (excludes respondent) | .063 | 4.61 |
| Log likelihood | -3778.3 | |

Note: Base group are females aged 20 to 24 who have completed secondary education.

## Appendix Table 12A.3
### The Oaxaca Decomposition
### Guatemala--All Sectors

### A.  Evaluated at Male Means

| Variable | Selectivity | | | Non-Selectivity | | |
|---|---|---|---|---|---|---|
| | (1) (Xm-Xf) *bfs | (2) (bms-bfs) *Xm | (3) (bmsXm- bfsXf) | (4) (Xm-Xf) *bf | (5) (bm-bf) *Xm | (6) (bmXm- bfXf) |
| Schooling | -.1194 | -.0749 | -.1943 | -.1343 | -.0796 | -.2139 |
| Log Hours | .0921 | -.6661 | -.5739 | .0983 | -.6947 | -.5963 |
| Experience | .0953 | -.3777 | -.2824 | .1170 | .0777 | .1947 |
| Exp. Sq. | -.0642 | .1704 | .1062 | -.0797 | -.0312 | -.1109 |
| Constant | 0 | 1.1403 | 1.1403 | 0 | 1.0393 | 1.0393 |
| Lambda | .2007 | -.0837 | .1170 | ---- | ---- | ---- |
| | | | | | | |
| Total | .2044 | .1084 | .3128 | .0013 | .3115 | .3128 |
| Percentage | .6536 | .3464 | 1 | .0042 | .9958 | 1 |

### B.  Evaluated at Female Means

| Variable | Selectivity | | | Non-Selectivity | | |
|---|---|---|---|---|---|---|
| | (1) (Xm-Xf) *bms | (2) (bms-bfs) *Xf | (3) (bmsXm- bfsXf) | (4) (Xm-Xf) *bm | (5) (bm-bf) *Xf | (6) (bmXm- bfXf) |
| Schooling | -.1036 | -.0907 | -.1943 | -.1176 | -.0963 | -.2139 |
| Log Hours | .0661 | -.6401 | -.5739 | .0712 | -.6675 | -.5963 |
| Experience | .0525 | -.3349 | -.2824 | .1258 | .0689 | .1947 |
| Exper Sq. | -.0355 | .1417 | .1062 | -.0849 | -.0260 | -.1109 |
| Constant | 0 | 1.1403 | 1.1403 | 0 | 1.0393 | 1.0393 |
| Lambda | .3455 | -.2285 | .1170 | ---- | ---- | ---- |
| | | | | | | |
| Total | .3250 | -.0122 | .3128 | -.0055 | .3183 | .3128 |
| Percentage | 1.0391 | -.0391 | 1 | -.0176 | 1.0176 | 1 |

## Appendix Table 12A.4
### The Oaxaca Decomposition
### Guatemala--Formal Sector

### A. Evaluated at Male Means

| Variable | Selectivity | | | Non-Selectivity | | |
|---|---|---|---|---|---|---|
| | (1) (Xm-Xf) *bfs | (2) (bms-bfs) *Xm | (3) (bmsXm-bfsXf) | (4) (Xm-Xf) *bf | (5) (bm-bf) *Xm | (6) (bmXm-bfXf) |
| Schooling | -.3477 | -.1993 | -.5471 | -.3830 | -.1394 | -.5224 |
| Log Hours | .0609 | -.3812 | -.3203 | .0634 | -.2242 | -.1608 |
| Experience | .2518 | -.3054 | -.0536 | .2592 | .0813 | .3406 |
| Exp. Sq. | -.1644 | .1876 | .0231 | -.1717 | -.0062 | -.1779 |
| Constant | 0 | 1.2246 | 1.2246 | 0 | .5608 | .5608 |
| Lambda | .0794 | -.3660 | -.2866 | ---- | ---- | ---- |
| | | | | | | |
| Total | -.1200 | .1603 | .0403 | -.2321 | .2724 | .0403 |
| Percentage | -2.9813 | 3.9813 | 1 | -5.7648 | 6.7648 | 1 |

### B. Evaluated at Female Means

| Variable | Selectivity | | | Non-Selectivity | | |
|---|---|---|---|---|---|---|
| | (1) (Xm-Xf) *bms | (2) (bms-bfs) *Xf | (3) (bmsXm-bfsXf) | (4) (Xm-Xf) *bm | (5) (bm-bf) *Xf | (6) (bmXm-bfXf) |
| Schooling | -.2442 | -.3029 | -.5471 | -.3106 | -.2118 | -.5224 |
| Log Hours | .0504 | -.3706 | -.3203 | .0571 | -.2179 | -.1608 |
| Experience | .1820 | -.2356 | -.0536 | .2778 | .0627 | .3406 |
| Exper Sq. | -.0988 | .1220 | .0231 | -.1739 | -.0040 | -.1779 |
| Constant | 0 | 1.2246 | 1.2246 | 0 | .5608 | .5608 |
| Lambda | .3265 | -.6130 | -.2866 | ---- | ---- | ---- |
| | | | | | | |
| Total | .2159 | -.1756 | .0403 | -.1495 | .1898 | .0403 |
| Percentage | 5.3627 | -4.3627 | 1 | -3.7135 | 4.7135 | 1 |

# References

Economist Intelligence Unit. *Guatemala, El Salvador, Honduras: Country Profile 1991-92.* London: Economist Intelligence Unit Limited, 1991.

Heckman, J.J. "Sample Selection Bias as a Specification Error." *Econometrica,* Vol. 47, no. 1 (1979). pp. 153-161.

Killingsworth, M.R. and J.J. Heckman. "Female Labor Supply: A Survey" in O. Ashenfelter and R. Layard (eds.) *Handbook of Labor Economics.* Amsterdam: North Holland, 1986, pp. 103-204.

Mincer, J. *Schooling, Experience, and Earnings.* New York: Columbia University Press, 1974.

Oaxaca, R. "Male-female Wage Differentials in Urban Labor Markets." *International Economic Review,* Vol. 14, no. 1 (1973). pp. 693-701.

Rodriguez, Aida and Susana Schkolnik. *Chile y Guatemala: Factores que afectan la participacion feminina en la actividad economica.* Santiago, Chile: Centro Latinoamericano de Demografia, 1974.

Sumner, Daniel. "Wage Functions and Occupational Selection in a Rural Less Developed Country Setting." *Review of Economics and Statistics,* Vol. 63, (1981) pp. 513-519.

Terrell, Katherine. "An Analysis of Wage Structure in Guatemala City." *The Journal of Developing Areas,* Vol. 23 (April 1989) pp. 405-423.

World Bank. *Guatemala: Basic Education Sector Memorandum.* Projects Department, Latin America and the Caribbean Regional Office, Report No. 6248-GU, June 6, 1986.

World Bank. *Guatemala: Country Economic Memorandum.* Country Department II, Latin America and the Caribbean Region, Report No. 9378-GU, June 19, 1991.

World Bank. *Second Basic Education Project: Staff Appraisal Report.* Country Department II, Latin America and the Caribbean Regional Office, Report No. 7004-GU, November 10, 1987.

World Bank. *Social Indicators of Development 1990.* Baltimore, MD: Johns Hopkins University Press, 1990. p. 124-5.

World Bank. *World Development Report 1991.* New York: Oxford University Press, 1991.

# 13

# Women's Labor Force Participation and Earnings in Honduras

*Carolyn Winter and T.H. Gindling*

## 1. Introduction

Honduras, with a per capita GNP of US$598 in 1990, is one of the poorest countries in Latin America. Beset by economic crises, it is in the midst of a structural adjustment program that is, in the short term, increasing unemployment, reducing real wages and imposing additional hardships on an already poor population. Women's labor force participation rates are relatively low; in 1989 just over 30 percent of women aged 15 to 65 years were working in the labor market compared to 72 percent of men in the same age group. The earnings differential between men and women is surprisingly low in Honduras, with women earning just over 81 percent of men's weekly average earnings.[1]

The objectives of this paper are to examine (1) what factors influence a woman's decision to participate in the labor market and (2) whether working men and women with similar observable human capital endowments are rewarded equally in the labor market. In examining these issues, however, it is important to recognize that labor markets in Honduras are not homogenous. Like most Latin American countries, the labor market consists of a formal waged and salaried sector, subject to government regulations and trade union activities, and an informal sector composed of self-employed workers and merchants and traders. More than half of all working women are self-employed workers while two thirds of men work in formal sector employment.

Simple univariate models are used to examine the determinants of the decision to work and the decision to work in either the formal sector or in self-employment. The participation probit equations are of interest in that they explain what factors influence a woman's decision to enter the labor market and what factors are principally responsible for their concentration in the informal sector. The results of the probit regressions are used in estimating selectivity-corrected wage equations for female and male workers by economic sector. We determine how much of the earnings differential is due to gender differences in human capital endowments using the Oaxaca decomposition method.

---

[1] This differential is low not only relative to other Latin American countries, but also relative to many industrialized countries. In Bolivia and Jamaica, for instance, women earn 63 percent and 58 percent of men's earnings, respectively (see the relevant chapters in this volume). In industrialized countries such as Britain, Australia and the United States, women earn close to three quarters of men's earnings. (Gunderson, 1989).

The following section of the paper, Section 2, briefly outlines the economic situation in Honduras and describes the main features of the labor market. Section 3 presents the mean characteristics of the working and non-working populations as derived from the Encuesta de Hogares. Section 4 describes the methodology used and presents the empirical results of the participation equations and in Section 5 we present the selectivity corrected earnings functions estimates. Section 6 presents the results of the Oaxaca decomposition. The policy implications of these findings are discussed in Section 7.

## 2.     The Honduran Economy and Labor Market

Honduras' economic progress has been slow over the past two decades. Major structural imbalances in the economy have compounded problems caused by the extremely limited diversification of the productive sectors. Agriculture continues to be the most important sector of the economy accounting for almost one quarter of GDP in 1990 and generating close to two-thirds of merchandise exports. Agricultural exports are, however, limited to three or four crops (coffee, bananas and sugar), making the economy very vulnerable to drops in commodity prices. Sharp falls in the market prices of these products in the 1980s has slowed economic growth and a real GDP growth of 2.3 percent in 1989 fell to an estimated -1.1 percent in 1990.[2]

Estimates of unemployment vary widely, but it is clear that the rate of labor market absorption has declined markedly with the economic downswing.[3] Rapid population growth has also meant that employment opportunities have not been able to keep pace with the increase in the labor force.[4] Underemployment of workers is also reportedly high in all sectors of employment, affecting as much as 60 percent of the economically active population.[5]

Male and female workers exhibit very different patterns of employment in Honduras. Table 13.1 shows the ratio of male to female earnings by economic sector (public, private and self-employment). Over half of working women are working in the lowest paying economic sector, self-employment, where they earn only 62 percent of men's earnings. While men work predominantly in the private sector, it is interesting to note that women have a pay advantage over men in this sector. In the public sector the differential is very low, with women earning 95 percent of men's wages. Overall, women in the formal sector (private and public sectors combined) have a pay advantage of almost 6 percent.

Economically active men work predominantly in the agricultural sector as Table 13.2B shows. The majority of these agricultural workers (59 percent) are self-employed. Average weekly earnings are lowest in this sector and are particularly low among self-employed agricultural workers. By contrast, only 2.8 percent of women work in the agricultural sector and are predominantly in the higher paying private sector (see Table 13.2A).

---

[2]     Economist Country Report, (1991).

[3]     Estimates of unemployment in the late 1980s vary from 12 to 25 percent. See Economist Country Profile (1990) and World Bank (1987).

[4]     The World Bank (1990) reports that the total fertility rate was 5.6 children per woman in 1987. A 1987 World Bank report estimated that 10,000 new work positions were being created annually for an estimated 30,000 new labor force entrants.

[5]     Nyrop (1987).

**Table 13.1**
Average Wages by Employment Sector and Gender
(Lempiras per Week)

| Sector | Females | | | Males | | | Ratio Female/Male Earnings |
|---|---|---|---|---|---|---|---|
| | Average Earnings | Females Educ. (years) | Distrib. of Workers (%) | Average Earnings | Males Educ. (years) | Distrib.of Workers (%) | |
| Self-Employment | 37.68 | 3.81 | 54 | 60.59 | 3.09 | 35 | 62 |
| Public Sector | 156.09 | 11.12 | 17 | 164.02 | 8.85 | 13 | 95 |
| Private Sector | 91.27 | 8.20 | 28 | 89.82 | 5.24 | 51 | 101 |
| Formal Sector[a] | 120.57 | 9.25 | 46 | 113.96 | 6.01 | 65 | 106 |

a. Formal sector data reflect average earnings of both public and private sector employees.

Source: Encuestra Permanente de Hogares (EPHPM), September 1989.

Economically active women are principally employed in the social service and commerce sectors. Employment opportunities have grown fastest in these sectors in recent years, but many of these new positions are reportedly unstable, marginal occupations such as domestic service and selling on the streets.[6] As Table 13.2A shows, 42 percent of all working women are in the service sector and are predominantly self-employed. Thirty percent of working women are in the commerce sector and over two-thirds of them are self-employed. Women's average earnings in these two economic sectors are very low relative to other sectors and are well below men's. Self-employed women in the commercial sector, for example, earn only 49 percent of self-employed men's earnings. Working women are also concentrated in the manufacturing sector which has contracted during the economic crisis. The creation of free zones in 1987, however, has given rise to a growing force of maquiladora workers and has become an important source of employment for women. It is notable that women have a pay advantage in the transport and construction sectors and in private agricultural employment.

Public sector employment in many Latin American countries provides women with better employment opportunities and working conditions. For this reason, women in the formal sector tend to be more heavily represented in public employment. This is not the case in Honduras, however. Sixty-two percent of female formal sector workers are employed in the private sector.

This preliminary review indicates that the male/female earnings differential is, in large part, the result of women's propensity to work in self-employment. In the formal sector, women's average earnings are actually higher than men's. The major policy question is why women work principally as self-employed workers in lower paying occupational sectors, especially given their higher average educational attainments.

## 3. Sample Characteristics

The data used in this analysis come from the 1989 national survey, the Honduras Encuestra Permanente de Hogares de Propósitos Múltiples (EPHPM). This survey includes 8,648

---

[6] Economist Country Profile, (1990).

## Table 13.2A
### Distribution and Average Earnings by Industry Group
### and Economic Sector
### Women

| Industry Group | Self-Employment | | Private Employment | | Public Employment | | All Economic Sectors | |
| | Worker Distrib.[a] (%) | Average Earnings (weekly) | Worker Distrib.[a] (%) | Average Earnings (weekly) | Worker Distrib.[a] (%) | Average Earnings (weekly) | Worker Distrib.[b] (%) | Average Earnings (weekly) |
|---|---|---|---|---|---|---|---|---|
| Agriculture | 32.0 | 29.13 | 68.0 | 58.16 | 0 | 0 | 2.8 | 49.82 |
| Mining | 0 | 0 | 0 | 0 | 0 | 0 | 0 | 0 |
| Manufacturing | 56.9 | 28.31 | 42.4 | 75.24 | .6 | 129.21 | 20.9 | 49.54 |
| Utilities | 0 | 0 | 0 | 0 | 100 | 144.47 | 0.2 | 144.47 |
| Construction | 17.6 | 90.31 | 23.5 | 125.00 | 58.8 | 130.12 | 0.5 | 140.95 |
| Commerce | 69.7 | 53.74 | 30.2 | 79.96 | 0 | 0 | 30.3 | 62.36 |
| Transport | 0 | 0 | 27.5 | 126.53 | 72.5 | 158.73 | 1.1 | 163.23 |
| Financial | 5.0 | 237.21 | 80.0 | 170.69 | 15.0 | 185.19 | 2.6 | 176.19 |
| Social Services | 49.0 | 25.61 | 15.0 | 110.21 | 36.0 | 156.06 | 41.5 | 85.30 |

a.   This column shows the proportion of workers in this sector relative to workers in the other economic sectors (self-, private and public employment).

b.   This column shows the distribution of workers by Industry Grouping.

Source:   Encuestra Permanente de Hogares (EPHPM), September 1989.

## Table 13.2B
### Worker Distribution and Average Earnings by Industry Group
### and Economic Sector
### Men

| Industry Group | Self-Employment | | Private Employment | | Public Employment | | All Economic Sectors | |
| | Worker Distrib.[a] (%) | Average Earnings (weekly) | Worker Distrib.[a] (%) | Average Earnings (weekly) | Worker Distrib.[a] (%) | Average Earnings (weekly) | Worker Distrib.[b] (%) | Average Earnings (weekly) |
|---|---|---|---|---|---|---|---|---|
| Agriculture | 58.8 | 39.7 | 41.0 | 45.78 | 0.2 | 113.48 | 42.2 | 46.57 |
| Mining | 40.0 | 48.34 | 60.0 | 169.86 | 0 | 0 | 0.3 | 121.25 |
| Manufacturing | 9.9 | 83.24 | 88.4 | 111.65 | 1.3 | 87.79 | 12.4 | 108.46 |
| Utilities | 0 | 0 | 4.4 | 79.07 | 95.6 | 187.65 | 1.4 | 182.88 |
| Construction | 8.9 | 81.29 | 75.7 | 75.75 | 15.3 | 110.04 | 9.4 | 83.74 |
| Commerce | 48.3 | 108.62 | 51.0 | 111.34 | 0.6 | 96.28 | 11.7 | 115.52 |
| Transport | 19.2 | 145.51 | 57.4 | 111.77 | 23.4 | 224.89 | 5.0 | 129.17 |
| Financial | 5.3 | 253.23 | 79.4 | 202.40 | 15.3 | 224.89 | 2.2 | 209.21 |
| Social Services | 15.0 | 93.06 | 36.0 | 120.85 | 49.0 | 170.89 | 15.0 | 143.08 |

a.   This column shows the proportion of workers in this sector relative to workers in the other economic sectors (self-, private and public employment).

b.   This column shows the distribution of workers by Industry Grouping.

Source:   Encuestra Permanente de Hogares (EPHPM), September 1989.

households and 46,672 individuals and has information on labor force participation, earnings, hours worked and employment by occupational sector. It also contains information on individual characteristics such as age, years of education, and marital status, and on household characteristics such as number of children in the household, ownership status, number of household members, and total income of the household.

As the focus of our study is prime-aged workers we restricted our sample to individuals aged 15 to 65 years. Our sample thus consisted of 23,388 individuals, which included 12,498 women and 10,890 men.

Tables 13.3A and 13.3B show the mean characteristics of the sample by gender and work status. Individuals were considered to be working if they reported positive earnings from public, private or self-employed work and if they reported working positive hours during the week prior to the survey. Individuals seeking employment were not included in the sample. The female participation rate in our sample was just over 30 percent, which is low but comparable to the average female participation rate for all Latin American countries. The male participation rate, 72 percent, is relatively low as would be expected given the existing high levels of unemployment.

Women work slightly fewer hours per week than men on average and, across all economic sectors, earn approximately 81 percent of men's average earnings. However, as Tables 13.3A and 13.3B show, the significantly lower earnings of self-employed women account for much of this differential; self-employed women earn only 62 percent of self-employed men's earnings although they report working the same number of hours per week. The earnings differential is very small in the public sector where women earn 95 percent of men's earnings and in the private sector women actually have a pay advantage over men. Women's average earnings in the formal sector are higher than men's.

As the data do not provide information on individuals' years of experience in the labor force, we constructed this variable in the standard way as age minus years of education minus six. Clearly, this measure will tend to overestimate experience, especially for women who generally withdraw from the labor market when they have young children to care for. Estimated years of experience are considerably higher for self-employed men and women than for workers in the formal sectors.

Although women workers average one and a half years more schooling than men, women's educational advantage widens if we consider only formal sector workers. Here, women have 3.2 years more schooling than men. In the private sector women have almost three more years of schooling than men and in the public sector they have over two years more schooling. Working women have 1.6 years more schooling than non-working women. Non-working men, however, have 1.2 years more schooling than their working counterparts which may partly reflect the reported high levels of education unemployment among men. (World Bank, 1990b).

Working women have fewer pre-school age children (under 7 years) than non-working women. Among working women, self-employed working women have more young children than women in the formal sector.

## 4.    The Determinants of Labor Force Participation

In this section we try to identify the major determinants of individuals' labor force participation decisions. It is assumed that the decision to work is made simultaneously with the decision

## Table 13.3A
### Means (and Standard Deviations) of Variables by Gender and Economic Sector

| Variable | Women | | | | | |
|---|---|---|---|---|---|---|
| | Private Sector | Public Sector | Formal Sector[a] | Self-Employment | All Working | Non-Working |
| Weekly Earnings (Lempiras) | 91.27 (97.19) | 156.09 (100.6) | 120.57 (121.32) | 37.68 (48.15) | 73.54 (88.31) | |
| Hours Worked (Weekly) | 45.15 (12.45) | 40.09 (8.28) | 43.31 (11.69) | 44.25 (20.83) | 43.75 (17.22) | 1.68 |
| Experience (Years) | 15.51 (11.25) | 17.56 (10.05) | 16.62 (11.04) | 25.27 (13.97) | 21.33 (13.45) | |
| Education (years) | 8.20 (4.24) | 11.12 (3.83) | 9.25 (4.35) | 3.81 (3.08) | 6.29 (4.61) | 4.63 (3.86) |
| Age (years) | 29.72 (9.81) | 34.68 (9.22) | 31.87 (9.99) | 35.09 (12.61) | 33.62 (11.60) | 30.67 (13.47) |
| Married (percent) | .44 | .43 | 45.0 | .44 | .44 | .57 |
| Children:0-6 Years (Number) | 0.58 (0.83) | 0.58 (0.83) | 0.58 (0.83) | 0.75 (0.99) | .67 (.92) | .89 (1.11) |
| Children:7-14 Years (Number) | 0.79 (1.07) | 0.81 (1.00) | 0.81 (1.05) | 1.16 (1.23) | 1.00 (1.16) | 1.12 (1.27) |
| Household Size (Number of Members) | 5.72 (2.62) | 5.55 (2.29) | 5.65 (2.49) | 5.91 (2.44) | 5.78 (2.47) | 6.38 (2.70) |
| Workers in Household (Number) | 2.45 (1.32) | 2.20 (0.99) | 2.36 (1.20) | 2.30 (1.08) | 2.33 (1.14) | 1.70 (1.09) |
| Urban Residence (percent) | 87.1 | 76.0 | 8.25 | 60.4 | 70.4 | 46.6 |
| N | 1,050 | 642 | 1,692 | 2,112 | 3,804 | 8,694 |

a. Formal Sector is Private and Public Sector combined.
Note: Female Labor Force Participation Rate = 30.4%.

## Table 13.3B
### Means (and Standard Deviations) of Variables by Gender and Economic Sector

| Variable | Men | | | | | |
| --- | --- | --- | --- | --- | --- | --- |
| | Private Sector | Public Sector | Formal Sector[a] | Self-Employment | All Working | Non-Working |
| Weekly Earnings (Lempiras) | 89.92 (117.13) | 164.02 (150.49) | 113.96 (150.32 | 60.59 (88.66) | 90.46 (121.63) | |
| Hours Worked (Weekly) | 47.25 (12.04) | 43.52 (8.69) | 46.59 (11.91) | 44.39 (13.68) | 45.73 (12.39) | |
| Experience (Years) | 19.90 (13.10) | 21.78 (12.92) | 20.62 (13.19) | 29.26 (13.10) | 23.81 (14.11) | |
| Education (years) | 5.24 (4.22) | 8.88 (5.11) | 6.01 (4.68) | 3.09 (3.10) | 4.89 (4.35) | 6.11 (4.23) |
| Age (years) | 31.14 (11.89) | 36.63 (11.06) | 32.63 (12.07) | 38.36 (12.7) | 34.7 (12.63) | 24.72 (12.20) |
| Married (percent) | .63 | .77 | 64.6 | .80 | .70 | .19 |
| Children:0-6 Years (Number) | 0.88 (1.09) | 0.76 (0.95) | 0.85 (1.06) | 1.09 (1.20) | .95 (1.12) | .58 (.94) |
| Children:7-14 Years (Number) | 1.00 (1.20) | 0.93 (1.10) | 0.99 (1.18) | 1.23 (1.36) | 1.09 (1.26) | 1.22 (1.30) |
| Household Size (Number of Members) | 6.03 (2.83) | 5.65 (2.44) | 5.94 (2.74) | 6.02 (2.60) | 6.02 (2.70) | 6.80 (2.71) |
| Workers in Household (Number) | 2.16 (1.17) | 1.97 (1.17) | 2.11 (1.13) | 1.98 (1.11) | 2.07 (1.13) | 2.13 (1.33) |
| Urban Residence (percent) | 60.6 | 73.9 | 63.2 | 26.8 | 49.0 | 52.6 |
| N | 3,881 | 926 | 4,807 | 3,063 | 7,870 | 3,020 |

a. Formal Sector is Private and Public Sector combined.

Note: Male Labor Force Participation Rate = 72.3%

regarding which economic sector to enter (formal or self-employment). Thus, much the same factors will affect the work participation decision as affect the choice of sector of employment --the value of the offered market wage, which is based on the individual's investments in human capital (in education, job training, etc.), and the value the individual places on his/her household activities, such as caring for young children and other family members (i.e., his/her reservation wage). There may, however, be additional unobservable factors influencing individuals' participation decisions which will be reflected in the error terms of univariate probit estimates run for the work/no work decision and the work in the formal sector/in self-employment decision.

The degree of correlation between the error terms obtained in these univariate probit estimations is indicative of the extent to which these unobservables influence the participation decision. In cases where the correlation is found to be high, the determinants of labor force participation are most accurately estimated using a bivariate probit analysis. However, where the correlation between the error terms in the separate univariate probits is close to zero, the observables have little effect on the work decision and univariate probits will yield the same results as the bivariate probit model. Our univariate probit estimates showed the correlations between the error terms to be very close to zero in both the female and male estimates. We thus present the results of the simple univariate probits in this paper.

**Table 13.4A**
Probit Estimates for Labor Force Participation
Women

| Variable | Coefficient | t-ratio | Mean | Partial Derivative |
|---|---|---|---|---|
| No Education | 0.206782 | -2.079 | 0.20299 | -0.0698 |
| Incomplete Primary | -0.011000 | -0.115 | 0.31309 | -0.0037 |
| Primary | 0.113128 | 1.190 | 0.21859 | 0.0382 |
| Incomplete Secondary | -0.148105 | -1.530 | 0.14186 | -0.0500 |
| Secondary | 0.504869 | 5.103 | 0.085214 | 0.1706 |
| Tertiary[a] | 0.327910 | 2.729 | 0.021203 | 0.1108 |
| Age | 0.118956 | 20.274 | 31.575 | 0.0402 |
| Age squared | -0.001464 | -18.411 | 1166.0 | -0.0004 |
| Children: Aged 0-6 | -0.096133 | -7.304 | 0.82789 | -0.0324 |
| Children: Aged 7-14 | 0.012629 | 1.054 | 1.0875 | 0.00426 |
| Household Size | -0.039571 | -7.182 | 6.2029 | -0.0133 |
| Household Income | 0.0002010 | 3.653 | 144.08 | 0.00006 |
| Urban Residence | 0.462375 | 16.253 | 0.5388 | 0.1562 |
| Constant | -2.59976 | -19.122 | 1.0000 | |

Log Likelihood = -6837.0
N = 12,498

a.   The omitted education category is "incomplete tertiary."
Notes: Dependent Variable: Labor Force Participation (1 = work/0 = not work).
       Sample: Women aged 15 to 65 years
       Mean Participation Rate: 30.4%

***Results of the work participation probit.*** Tables 13.4A and 13.4B report the results of the work participation probits for women and men. The dependent variable is labor force participation (1 if the individual works, 0 if not) and the independent variables include age, education level (dummy variables), two proxies for household wealth (total household income and household size), the number of children under seven years of age and between ages seven and fourteen, and a dummy variable denoting urban or rural residence. Simulated probabilities of participation for each condition are presented in Table 13.5.

## Table 13.4B
### Probit Estimates for Labor Force Participation
### Men

| Variable | Coefficient | t-ratio | Mean | Partial Derivative |
|---|---|---|---|---|
| No Education | 0.638304 | 6.769 | 0.18503 | 0.1972 |
| Incomplete Primary | 0.643799 | 7.208 | 0.33361 | 0.1989 |
| Primary | 0.651321 | 7.323 | 0.22158 | 0.2012 |
| Incomplete Secondary | 0.235611 | 2.631 | 0.13921 | 0.0728 |
| Secondary | 0.459933 | 4.562 | 0.05877 | 0.1421 |
| Tertiary[a] | 0.304603 | 2.780 | 0.03544 | 0.0941 |
| Age | 0.190997 | 30.445 | 31.939 | 0.0590 |
| Age squared | -0.0020931 | -25.953 | 1196.7 | -0.0006 |
| Children: Aged 0-6 | 0.169899 | 11.019 | 0.84949 | 0.05250 |
| Children: Aged 7-14 | -0.074029 | -5.560 | 1.1289 | -0.0228 |
| Household Size | -0.030312 | -4.955 | 6.2414 | -0.0093 |
| Household Income | -0.000714 | -8.079 | 95.983 | -0.0002 |
| Urban Residence | 0.0794300 | 2.415 | 0.5002 | 0.0245 |
| Constant | -3.15155 | -22.535 | 1.0000 | |

Log Likelihood = -5036.5
N = 10,890

a.    The omitted education category is "incomplete tertiary."
Notes:  Dependent Variable: Labor Force Participation (1 = work/0 = not work).
        Sample: Men aged 15 to 65 years
        Mean Participation Rate: 72.3%

The effects of higher educational attainment on women's participation are particularly interesting. Table 13.5 shows that, holding all other variables at their mean values, the probability of participation increases substantially with each additional level of education completed. A woman with completed primary education has a 67 percent greater probability of participating that a woman with no education (probabilities = 31.66 versus 21.32). The probability of participation is as great again for women having completed secondary education rather than completed primary (probability = 31.66 versus 46.61). Women with completed higher education, however, actually have a lower probability of participation than women with completed secondary education (probability = 39.81 versus 46.61). This may, in part, reflect the high levels of unemployment existing among individuals with university level education.[7] Men also have lower probabilities

---

[7]  World Bank, 1990b.

**Table 13.5**
Predicted Probability of Labor Force Participation

| Characteristic | Predicted Probability | |
| --- | --- | --- |
| | Women (%) | Men (%) |
| Education | | |
| No education | 21.32 | 78.96 |
| Incomplete Primary | 27.41 | 78.93 |
| Primary Education | 31.66 | 79.33 |
| Incomplete Secondary | 23.21 | 65.63 |
| Secondary Education | 46.61 | 73.45 |
| Incomplete Tertiary | 27.17 | 56.62 |
| Tertiary Education | 39.81 | 68.13 |
| | | |
| Age Group[a] | | |
| Years: 15-19 | 14.77 | 38.89 |
| 20-24 | 24.66 | 71.48 |
| 25-29 | 31.16 | 82.23 |
| 30-34 | 36.29 | 86.29 |
| 35-39 | 42.17 | 87.33 |
| 40-44 | 42.14 | 88.69 |
| 45-49 | 37.98 | 88.67 |
| 50-54 | 33.59 | 87.93 |
| 55-59 | 27.33 | 82.95 |
| 60-65 | 19.25 | 80.95 |
| | | |
| Presence of Children (0-6 years) | | |
| No children | 30.98 | 71.57 |
| One child | 27.68 | 77.04 |
| Two children | 24.55 | 81.86 |
| Three children | 26.33 | 85.99 |
| | | |
| Urban Residence | | |
| Yes | 35.84 | 76.46 |
| No | 20.47 | 75.01 |

a.  Predicted probabilities for age splines were calculated in separate probit estimates reported in Appendix Tables 13A.2a and 13A.2b.

Note:  Probability of participation is estimated for each variable while holding all other variables at their means.

of participation with incomplete or completed tertiary education than with completed secondary education.[8]   Participation probabilities for men decline as higher levels of education are completed.   Among females, there is some evidence that incomplete programs of study are associated with lower levels of participation; a woman's probability of participation is 23.21 if she has incomplete secondary education versus 31.66 if she has completed primary education.

---

[8]   Actual labor force participation rates by education level, derived from the Encuestra de Hogares, are reported in Appendix Table A19.1 and show the same pattern.

**Table 13.6A**
Probit Estimates for Formal Sector Participation
Women

| Variable | Coefficient | t-ratio | Mean |
|---|---|---|---|
| No Education | -2.23845 | -10.257 | 0.14117 |
| Incomplete Primary | -1.93825 | -9.330 | 0.28233 |
| Primary | -1.53930 | -7.452 | 0.23580 |
| Incomplete Secondary | -0.721031 | -3.408 | 0.11278 |
| Secondary | 0.0526476 | 0.247 | 0.16693 |
| Tertiary[a] | 0.239748 | 0.936 | 0.040747 |
| Age | 0.0427856 | 3.428 | 33.628 |
| Age squared | -0.000709 | -4.094 | 1265.6 |
| Children: Aged 0-6 | -0.10547 | -3.797 | 0.67508 |
| Children: Aged 7-14 | -0.069173 | -3.172 | 1.0008 |
| Urban Residence | 0.238599 | 4.273 | 0.70426 |
| Constant | 0.586040 | 2.005 | 1.00000 |

Log Likelihood = -1808.1
N = 3,804

a. The omitted education category is "incomplete tertiary."
Notes: Dependent Variable: Formal Sector Worker = 1, Self Employed Worker = 0.
Sample: Women aged 15 to 65 years

Women's participation rates by age group show the typical inverse U-shape. Women's participation peaks between ages 35 and 45 and then declines. Men's participation by age group does not follow the typical pattern. Although participation probabilities are lower for men aged below age 25, they are fairly consistent between ages 25 to 54 and drop only slightly for the two oldest age groups. The reasons for these differences are not clear, but it is possible that severe economic conditions and limited access to social security mean that most men must continue to work past retirement age.

Having young children aged six years or less reduces the probability that a woman will work. Having one young child reduces the probability by 11 percent (probability = 27.68 versus 30.98) and with two children the probability is greatly reduced (by 26 percent). As would be expected, increasing numbers of young children increase the probability that a man participates.

The effects of the two proxy measures for household wealth are as expected. The coefficients for household size are significant and negative for both women and men indicating that individuals in larger households are less likely to work. Higher household income is significant and positive for women indicating that women from wealthier homes are more likely to work. This possibly reflects the fact that women from wealthier homes are better educated and better able to afford child care if they have young children.

Women are much more likely to participate in the labor market if they live in urban areas. Holding all else equal, women in urban areas have a participation probability 15 percentage points higher than women in rural areas (probability = 35.84 versus 20.47). Indeed, as Table 13.2A shows, women work predominantly in three industrial groups that are largely urban based, social services, commerce and manufacturing. Men are equally likely to participate if they are in urban or rural areas (probability 76.46 versus 75.01).

*Results of the sector choice probit.* The sector choice probits identify the principal factors influencing individuals' decisions to enter formal sector employment or self-employment. The results reported in Tables 13.6A and 13.6B show that higher levels of education increase the probability that a person works in the formal sector. The effect is considerably stronger for women with completed secondary education than men. With lower levels of education, however, women are much more likely to work in the informal sector than men.

## Table 13.6B
### Probit Estimates for Formal Sector Participation
### Men

| Variable | Coefficient | t-ratio | Mean |
|---|---|---|---|
| No Education | -0.774975 | -4.663 | 0.20584 |
| Incomplete Primary | -0.778168 | -4.748 | 0.35591 |
| Primary | -0.621599 | -3.781 | 0.22173 |
| Incomplete Secondary | -0.474562 | -2.802 | 0.09834 |
| Secondary | -0.073145 | -0.417 | 0.064803 |
| Tertiary[a] | 0.221414 | 1.144 | 0.03659 |
| Age | -0.070252 | -9.310 | 34.706 |
| Age squared | 0.0006043 | 6.199 | 1364.1 |
| Children: Aged 0-6 | -0.052095 | -3.598 | 0.95184 |
| Children: Aged 7-14 | 0.0082884 | 0.655 | 1.0915 |
| Urban Residence | 0.760121 | 21.854 | 0.49022 |
| Constant | 2.249 | 10.738 | 1.00000 |

Log Likelihood = -4410.7
N = 7,870

a.    The omitted education category is "incomplete tertiary."
Notes: Dependent Variable: Formal Sector Worker = 1, Self Employed Worker = 0.
       Sample: Men aged 15 to 65 years

Women with young children (0-6 years old) are much more likely to work in the informal sector. Interestingly, having young children has the same effect among men, although it is much weaker. This result may reflect that self-employed workers are generally from poorer families which also tend to have more children. Having older children (7-14 years old) also raises the likelihood that a woman will work in self-employment, but the effect is not as strong as for younger children.

The age variable shows that women are more likely to work in the formal sector as they get older. This may occur because younger women are more likely to have pre-school age children and, lacking access to child care facilities, may turn to self-employment where the more flexible work hours permit them to combine work and childcare activities. The effect is reversed among men; older men are more likely to be working in self-employment.

Living in an urban area significantly increases the probability that both women and men will work in the formal sector. The effect is especially high for men.

## 5.    Earnings Functions

In this section we estimate standard Mincerian earnings functions for men and women workers to explain what factors account for male/female earnings differentials. We estimate the earnings functions for all workers and separately for formal sector and self-employed workers.

In proceeding with these estimates, however, we are faced with problems of selectivity bias at two levels. First, there is a potential selectivity bias problem in examining the causes of the earnings differential between male and female workers. If we use samples consisting only of working males and working females we will in effect have a self-selected sample including only individuals whose market wage exceeds their reservation wage. This is generally a more serious problem among women since their reservation wage rises when they have young children to care for. Given the relatively low participation rate among men in Honduras, however, we cannot discount the possibility that certain groups of men may have high reservation wages too. To correct for potential selectivity bias in this instance we use Heckman's (1979) procedure and include the Lambda (the inverse Mill's Ratio) estimated in the labor force participation probit regressions in the earnings functions as an independent variable. The coefficients of the Lambdas in the earnings functions provide an estimate of the covariance between the disturbances in the work/no work and wage equations.

The second potential selectivity bias problem occurs in the earnings functions estimated for formal sector and self-employed workers. Here again we have self-selected samples of workers. We thus introduce two selectivity correction Lambdas in this set of earnings functions, one which corrects for selectivity in the work/no work decision and one correcting for the formal/self-employment decision.

*Earnings functions estimates for all workers.* Earnings functions, corrected and uncorrected for selectivity bias, were estimated with the dependent variable being the log of weekly wages. Independent variables included years of education, experience and experience squared and the log of hours worked. The results are shown in Table 13.7.

In the selectivity corrected female earnings functions the Lambda is significant and negative at the 5 percent level, indicating that the sample of female workers is indeed not a random sample. Thus, we choose to interpret the selectivity corrected estimates although we also report the uncorrected estimates.

**Table 13.7**
**Earnings Functions Estimates**
**All Sectors**

| Variable | Corrected for Selectivity | | Uncorrected for Selectivity | |
|---|---|---|---|---|
|  | Women | Men | Women | Men |
| Schooling | 0.140065 | 0.153006 | 0.178335 | 0.15357 |
| (Years) | (35.195) | (70.165) | (59.62) | (72.44) |
| Log Hours | 0.41405 | 0.33953 | 0.443998 | 0.340209 |
|  | (18.786) | (13.607) | (19.770) | (13.633) |
| Experience | 0.024446 | 0.048364 | 0.050428 | 0.051944 |
|  | (6.345) | (12.113) | (16.067) | (22.703) |
| Experience | -0.00020 | -0.00057 | -0.000592 | -0.00065 |
| Squared | (-3.107) | (-9.443) | (-10.226) | (-16.10) |
| Constant | 1.54986 | 1.32357 | 0.333006 | 1.25063 |
|  | (10.703) | (11.119) | (3.415) | (12.677) |
| Lambda | -0.58644 | -0.061413 |  |  |
|  | (-11.252) | (-1.094) |  |  |
| R2 | 0.548 | 0.41 | 0.533 | 0.418 |
| N | 3,804 | 7,870 | 3,804 | 7,870 |

Notes: Wf/Wm=81%
         Dependent Variable: Log(weekly earnings)
         t-values are in parentheses

The returns to schooling are slightly higher than those reported for other Latin American countries, being 14 percent for women and 15 percent for men.[9] The corrected estimates for women are almost 4 percent lower than the uncorrected estimates indicating the extent of the potential selectivity bias.

Following the expected age-earnings profiles for both sexes, the log earnings increase with experience but at a decreasing rate. The returns to experience are twice as high for men as for women, a difference which is larger than that found in most countries in the region.[10]

---

[9]    Rates of return to education in Chile, for example, are 12 percent for women and 10 percent for men. In Venezuela they are 10 percent and 9 percent for women and men, respectively. See the relevant chapters in this volume.

[10]    In Venezuela and Costa Rica the returns to experience are 3 percent and 2 percent for men and women, respectively. In Argentina they are 4 percent and 3 percent. (See the relevant chapters in this volume.)

**Table 13.8A**
**Earnings Functions**
**Women**
**Formal Sector**

| Variable | Corrected for Selectivity | | Uncorrected for Selectivity | |
|---|---|---|---|---|
| | Formal Sector | Self-Employed | Formal Sector | Self-Employed |
| Schooling | 0.14467 | 0.07183 | 0.105166 | 0.122433 |
| (Years) | (19.58) | (6.620) | (45.746) | (19.875) |
| Log Hours | 0.16867 | 0.464540 | 0.175992 | 0.503134 |
| (weekly) | (4.353) | (17.731) | (4.502) | (18.759) |
| Experience | 0.04219 | 0.023624 | 0.051491 | 0.0564288 |
| | (9.383) | (3.733) | (13.634) | (11.898) |
| Experience | -0.00056 | -0.00019 | -0.00069 | -0.000686 |
| Squared | (-6.123) | (-1.998) | (-8.118) | (-8.47) |
| Constant | 2.18014 | 1.46655 | 1.82304 | 0.094762 |
| | (10.628) | (6.504) | (11.512) | (0.747) |
| Lambda | 0.07314 | -0.18079 | | |
| (Sector | (0.989) | (-1.665) | | |
| Choice) | | | | |
| Lambda | -0.24861 | -0.62508 | | |
| (Work/No | (-3.697) | (-7.568) | | |
| Work Choice) | | | | |
| R2 | 0.569 | 0.308 | 0.566 | 0.28 |
| N | 1,692 | 2,112 | 1,692 | 2,112 |

Notes:  In the formal sector wf/wm=106%
For self-employment wf/wm=62%
Dependent Variable: Log(weekly earnings)
t-values are in parentheses

Earnings functions estimates for formal sector and self-employed workers. Tables 13.8A and 13.8B report the corrected and uncorrected estimates for male and female formal and self-employed workers. In discussing the results we again focus on the selectivity corrected estimates which are negative and highly significant for both formal sector and self-employed men. In the female estimates, the Lambdas are negative and significant for the work/no work choice but are not significant for the sector of employment choice.

The returns to schooling are significantly higher for women than men in the formal sector, being 14 percent for women and close to 12 percent for men. While the sample selectivity correction increases the returns to schooling for women it lowers the returns for men. The returns to education for self-employed men and women are substantially lower than those for workers in the formal sector. The returns are, however, almost the same for both sexes, being 8 percent for men and 7 percent for women.

### Table 13.8B
### Earnings Functions
### Men
### Formal Sector

| Variable | Corrected for Selectivity | | Uncorrected for Selectivity | |
|---|---|---|---|---|
| | Formal Sector | Self-Employed | Formal Sector | Self-Employed |
| Schooling | 0.119711 | 0.0878 | 0.149912 | 0.139821 |
| (Years) | (47.611) | (14.066) | (76.165) | (25.321) |
| Log Hours | 0.278491 | 0.195870 | 0.341647 | 0.26377 |
| (weekly) | (10.193) | (4.774) | (11.759) | (6.215) |
| Experience | 0.061424 | 0.067102 | 0.059671 | 0.0492847 |
| | (15.357) | (7.531) | (25.706) | (9.413) |
| Experience | -0.00062 | -0.00069 | -0.00072 | -0.00057 |
| Squared | (-10.303) | (-5.325) | (-16.905) | (-7.05) |
| Constant | 2.18050 | 0.685204 | 1.26325 | 1.444042 |
| | (16.64) | (3.004) | (11.084) | (0.172) |
| Lambda | -0.92244 | -1.09904 | | |
| (Sector | (-25.234) | (-16.046) | | |
| Choice) | | | | |
| Lambda | -0.276831 | -0.369725 | | |
| (Work/No | (-4.982) | (-2.678) | | |
| Work Choice) | | | | |
| R2 | 0.59 | 0.25 | 0.558 | 0.19 |
| N | 4,807 | 3,063 | 4,807 | 3,063 |

Notes: In the formal sector wf/wm=106%
For self-employment wf/wm=62%
Dependent Variable: Log(weekly earnings)
t-values are in parentheses

The returns to experience for women, at 4 percent, continue to be lower than the returns for men (6 percent) in the formal sector. The gap in returns to experience between the sexes increases for self-employed workers where the returns are almost 4 percent higher for men.

## 6. Examining the Earning Differential

Efforts to explain male/female earnings differentials have typically been estimated using the relative earnings of all male and female workers. Some more recent studies, however, have shown that earnings differentials can differ markedly across different segments of a country's labor market.[11] This is clearly the case in Honduras where women in the formal sector have

---

[11] See, for example, Alderman and Kozel (1989).

a pay advantage of 6 percent, but earn only 62 percent of men's earnings in self-employed work. Given these differences we examine the causes of the earnings differentials separately for formal and self-employed workers as well as for all workers.

The Oaxaca (1973) decomposition method enables us to estimate what proportion of the earnings differential can be explained by differences in human capital endowments (education and experience) and what proportion remains "unexplained" by these endowments. We are unable to determine what factors contribute to this "unexplained" proportion; it is really a catch-all reflecting differences in the way the labor market structure rewards female and male workers (i.e., discrimination) as well as the effects of omitted variables. However, it is generally taken to be representative of the "upper bound" of discrimination and to reflect the way in which the labor market rewards the attributes of male and female workers.

The Oaxaca decomposition expresses the difference between the mean (log) wage rates of males and females as:

$$BmXm-BfXf \quad = Xm(Bm-Bf) + Bf(Xm-Xf) \tag{1}$$
$$= Xf(Bm-Bf) + Bm(Xm-Xf) \tag{2}$$

Where:  Bm,Bf are the estimated coefficients of the earnings functions.
Xm,Xf are the means of the explanatory variables in the earnings functions.

Equations 1 and 2 estimate the same thing but the weighting of each is different; one is estimated using the male means and the other using the female means. There is theoretically no advantage to using one equation over the other, so both estimates are reported. We present the decompositions using the selectivity corrected estimates.

Table 13.9 presents the Oaxaca estimates for all workers and by economic sector. The estimates show that the earnings differential is not explained by women's lower human capital endowments. In fact, the negative sign for the endowments estimates show women to have the advantage in terms of endowments. The size of the endowments advantage differs substantially by economic sector, being large in the formal sector and relatively small in among self-employed workers. These estimates reflect actual differences in educational attainment between women and men in the different sectors as shown in Tables 13.2A and 13.2B. Women average two and a half years more schooling than men in the formal sector and .72 of a year more schooling in self-employment

Working women as a whole average almost one and a half years more schooling than working men. Any advantage which women have in terms of endowments, however, is canceled out by the fact that the wage structure is so favorable to men in all sectors. The large advantage which female formal sector workers have in terms of endowments (-610.66), for instance, is canceled out by the way the wage structure rewards women for these attributes (710.44). These estimates thus indicate that wage discrimination in Honduras, imposed either informally by employers or formally by labor legislation, greatly reduces women's potential earnings. This is true in both economic sectors, but is more severe in the formal sector.

Table 13.9
Decomposition of the Male/Female Earnings Differential
(Corrected for Selectivity)

| Specification | Percentage of the Earnings Differential due to differences in | |
| --- | --- | --- |
| | Endowments | Wage Structure |
| **All Workers** | | |
| Evaluated at Male Means | -40.68 | 140.68 |
| Evaluated at Female Means | -37.48 | 137.48 |
| **Formal Sector Workers** | | |
| Evaluated at Male Means | -610.44 | 710.44 |
| Evaluated at Female Means | 189.87 | 81.01 |
| **Self Employed Workers** | | |
| Evaluated at Male Means | -15.53 | 115.53 |
| Evaluated at Female Means | -125.22 | 225.22 |

Notes:  For all workers wf/wm=81%
        In the formal sector wf/wm=106%
        For self-employment wf/wm=62%

## 7.    Discussion

The examination of male/female earnings differentials in Honduras is complex and requires further study.  However, the findings of this study suggest the following policy recommendations:

1.   **Improve school retention rates and educational quality:** The relationship between higher educational attainment, occupational attainment and higher earnings is very evident in this study.  Individuals with fewer years of schooling are less likely to work and, when they do work, are more likely to be in lower-paying self-employment (See Appendix Table 13A.1).  This is particularly so for women -- self-employed women average 3.81 years of schooling compared to the average 9.6 years of women in the formal sector. (See Tables 13.3A and 13.3B).   Although access to primary school is no longer a serious problem in Honduras, repetition and dropout rates are exceptionally high; only 30 percent of school entrants complete primary school and sixth grade graduates have completed, on average, 10.3 years of schooling.  The quality of education provided is also poor(World Bank, 1990b). Reducing the dropout and repetition rate and improving educational quality will improve the employment and earnings prospects of students.  Improving educational quality is likely to be especially important for girls since this is recognized to be important in influencing poorer parents' decisions to keep young girls in school rather than having them work in the home.

2. **Primary and secondary education should be given priority in educational spending:** This study shows that the probability of participation among women increases substantially if they have completed primary and secondary education. Both female and male secondary school graduates have higher (predicted and real) participation rates than individuals with incomplete or complete tertiary education (See Appendix Table 13A.1 and Table 13.5), indicating that public investments will yield higher returns if invested in lower educational levels.

3. **Labor and commercial legislation should be reviewed** to determine whether there are laws which prevent women from participating in certain sectors or which limit women entrepreneurs' access to credit. This study indicates that women in the formal sector are affected by wage discrimination. The reasons for this are not clear but in many Latin American countries legislation regulates women's participation in various industries and occupations, thereby limiting their productivity and earnings potential. A study of existing legislation and its implementation would help to identify whether this is the case in Honduras. It is also not clear why self-employed women earn so much less on average than self-employed men. Limited access by self-employed women to credit could be a contributing factor. Legislation also regulates women's access to credit in many Latin American countries, a factor which could also be clarified in a review of the country's labor and commercial laws.

4. **Review textbooks to remove gender stereotyping and provide incentives for girls to pursue non-traditional courses of study:** Women in Honduras work predominantly in the lowest paying economic sector (self-employment) and are concentrated in the lowest paying occupations (social services, commerce and manufacturing) in both economic sectors (See Tables 13.2A and 13.2B). The reasons why women choose to enter lower-paying occupations even when they have higher education is not clear, but these occupations have traditionally been considered "women's work." The removal of gender stereotyping in school textbooks may be one way to change these attitudes and to encourage women to enter more productive occupations with higher rewards. Another approach would be to encourage girls to pursue non-traditional courses of study, such as the sciences. However, the way in which these incentives could be provided would have to be given careful consideration.

5. **Stimulate private sector provision of childcare:** This study shows that the probability that a woman will participate in the labor force declines sharply when she has young children to care for. Having one pre-school aged child reduced the probability that a woman will work by 11 percent, and having two young children reduced the probability by 21 percent (See Table 13.5). Improved access to adequate childcare services would permit more women to work. In cases where women enter self-employment because childcare responsibilities make it difficult for them to adhere to the set working hours of the formal sector, access to childcare would permit them to move into the formal sector.

6. **Macroeconomic adjustment measures will clearly continue to be important in** stimulating economic growth and in increasing the capacity of the labor market to absorb new entrants to the work force.

## Appendix Table 13A.1
### Labor Force Participation Rates and Average Earnings
### by Education Level and Gender

| Education Level | Women | | Men | |
|---|---|---|---|---|
| | Participation Rate (percent) | Average Earnings (weekly) | Participation Rate (percent) | Average Earnings (weekly) |
| No Education | 21.2 | 28.06 | 80.4 | 43.89 |
| Incomplete Primary | 27.4 | 38.46 | 77.1 | 60.63 |
| Primary Education | 32.8 | 51.59 | 72.3 | 84.12 |
| Incomplete Secondary | 24.2 | 77.09 | 51.1 | 111.44 |
| Secondary Education | 59.6 | 134.85 | 79.7 | 186.38 |
| Incomplete Tertiary | 36.9 | 159.76 | 45.0 | 174.05 |
| Tertiary Education | 58.5 | 298.22 | 74.64 | 311.52 |

Source: Encuestra Permanente de Hogares (EPHPM), September 1989.

**Appendix Table 13A.2a**
Probit Estimates for Labor Force Participation
Women

| Variable | Coefficient | t-ratio | Mean | Partial Derivative |
|---|---|---|---|---|
| No Education | -0.202482 | -2.035 | 0.20299 | -0.06849 |
| Incomplete Primary | -0.009142 | -0.096 | 0.31309 | -0.00392 |
| Primary | 0.115780 | 1.216 | 0.21859 | 0.039166 |
| Incomplete Secondary | -0.148358 | -1.529 | 0.14186 | -0.05018 |
| Secondary | 0.505177 | 5.106 | 0.085214 | 0.170891 |
| Tertiary[a] | 0.331862 | 2.760 | 0.021203 | 0.112262 |
| | | | | |
| Age (years) | | | | |
| 20 to 24 | 0.361003 | 8.188 | 0.16939 | 0.12212 |
| 25 to 29 | 0.554827 | 12.038 | 0.14306 | 0.18768 |
| 30 to 34 | 0.695527 | 14.385 | 0.11746 | 0.23528 |
| 35 to 39 | 0.848591 | 16.895 | 0.10002 | 0.28706 |
| 40 to 44 | 0.847938 | 15.559 | 0.07505 | 0.28683 |
| 45 to 49 | 0.740173 | 12.627 | 0.06313 | 0.25038 |
| 50 to 54 | 0.622538 | 9.765 | 0.05112 | 0.21059 |
| 55 to 59 | 0.443165 | 5.884 | 0.03576 | 0.14991 |
| 60 to 65[b] | 0.177309 | 2.239 | 0.036646 | 0.05998 |
| | | | | |
| Children: Aged 0-6 | -0.095233 | -7.080 | 0.82789 | -0.03221 |
| Children: Aged 7-14 | 0.012520 | 1.000 | 1.0875 | 0.00423 |
| | | | | |
| Household Size | -0.039867 | -7.203 | 6.2029 | -0.01348 |
| Household Income | 0.0001980 | 3.596 | 144.08 | 0.000066 |
| | | | | |
| Urban Residence | 0.462566 | 16.264 | 0.5388 | 0.15647 |
| | | | | |
| Constant | -1.02162 | -9.901 | 1.0000 | |

Log Likelihood = -6844.6
N = 12,498

a.   The omitted education category is "incomplete tertiary".
b.   The omitted age category is 15 to 19 years.
Notes: Dependent Variable: Labor Force Participation
   Sample: Women aged 15 to 65 years
   Mean Participation Rate: 30.4%

## Appendix Table 13A.2b
### Probit Estimates for Labor Force Participation
### Men

| Variable | Coefficient | t-ratio | Mean | Partial Derivative |
|---|---|---|---|---|
| No Education | 0.70908 | 7.485 | 0.18503 | 0.22083 |
| Incomplete Primary | 0.71145 | 7.916 | 0.33361 | 0.22157 |
| Primary | 0.72186 | 8.060 | 0.22158 | 0.22481 |
| Incomplete Secondary | 0.30361 | 3.366 | 0.13921 | 0.09455 |
| Secondary | 0.52531 | 5.205 | 0.05877 | 0.16360 |
| Tertiary[a] | 0.38020 | 3.473 | 0.03544 | 0.11841 |
| | | | | |
| Age (years) | | | | |
| 20 to 24 | 0.84964 | 19.619 | 0.1573 | 0.2646 |
| 25 to 29 | 1.20642 | 23.776 | 0.1343 | 0.3757 |
| 30 to 34 | 1.37585 | 24.506 | 0.11938 | 0.4284 |
| 35 to 39 | 1.42424 | 23.756 | 0.09687 | 0.4435 |
| 40 to 44 | 1.49276 | 22.47 | 0.076492 | 0.4649 |
| 45 to 49 | 1.49144 | 21.311 | 0.064922 | 0.4644 |
| 50 to 54 | 1.45389 | 19.944 | 0.055739 | 0.4527 |
| 55 to 59 | 1.23433 | 15.766 | 0.039945 | 0.3844 |
| 60 to 65[b] | 1.15815 | 14.968 | 0.040129 | 0.3606 |
| | | | | |
| Children: Aged 0-6 | 0.17482 | 11.229 | 0.84949 | 0.0544 |
| Children: Aged 7-14 | -0.0457 | -3.310 | 1.1289 | -0.0142 |
| | | | | |
| Household Size | -0.0336 | -5.467 | 6.2414 | -0.0104 |
| Household Income | -0.0007 | -8.291 | 95.983 | -0.0002 |
| | | | | |
| Urban Residence | 0.08363 | 2.543 | 0.5002 | 0.0260 |
| | | | | |
| Constant | -0.7554 | -7.649 | 1.0000 | |

Log Likelihood = -5036.6
N = 10,890

Notes: a. Omitted variable in the education category is "incomplete tertiary"
     b. Omitted variable in the age category is age 15 to 19.
     Notes: Dependent Variable: Labor Force Participation (1 = work/0 = not work).
     Sample: Men aged 15 to 65 years
     Mean Participation Rate: 72.3%

# References

Alderman, H. and V. Kozel. "Formal and Informal Sector Wage Determination in Urban Low-Income Neighborhoods in Pakistan." Living Standards Measurements Working Paper No. 65. Washington D.C.: World Bank.

Danes, S.M., M. Winter and M.B. Whiteford. "Informal and Formal Market Participation of Rural Honduran Women." Working Paper No. 82. Michigan State University: Women in International Development Institute, 1985.

Gronau, R. "Sex-Related Wage Differentials and Women's Interrupted Labor Careers: The Chicken and Egg Question." *Journal of Labor Economics,* Vol. 6, no. 3 (1988). pp. 277-301.

Gunderson, M. "Male-Female Wage Differentials and Policy Responses." *Journal of Economic Literature,* Vol. 27 (1989). pp. 46-72.

Heckman, J.J. "Sample Selection Bias as a Specification Error." *Econometrica,* Vol. 47, no. 1 (1979). pp. 53-161.

Nyrop, R. (ed.). *Honduras: A Country Study.* American University: Foreign Areas Studies, 1987.

Oaxaca, R.L. "Male-female Wage Differentials in Urban Labor Markets." *International Economic Review,* Vol. 14, no. 1 (1973). pp. 693-709.

The Economist Intelligence Unit. *Guatemala, El Salvador, Honduras. Country Report.* No. 3. New York, 1991.

The Economist Intelligence Unit. *Guatemala, El Salvador, Honduras. Country Profile 1989-90.* New York, 1991.

Tunali, I. "A General Structure for Models of Double-Selection and an Application to a Joint Migration/Earnings Process with Remigration." *Research in Labor Economics,* Vol. 8, Part B (1986). pp. 235-282.

World Bank. "Social Investment in Guatemala, El Salvador and Honduras." Workshop on Poverty Alleviation, Basic Social Services and Social Investment Funds within the Consultative Group Framework. Latin America and Caribbean Regional Office, June, 1990a.

World Bank. "Honduras Social Sector Programs." Country Department II. Latin America and Caribbean Regional Office, November, 1990b.

World Bank. "Honduras: Country Economic Memorandum." Latin American and Caribbean Regional Office, April, 1987.

World Bank. "Honduras: A Review of Selected Key Problems of the Agricultural Sector." Projects Department, Latin American and Caribbean Regional Office, October, 1981.

# 14

# Female Labor Force Participation and Earnings: The Case of Jamaica

*Katherine MacKinnon Scott*

## 1.    Introduction

On average, women's weekly earnings in Jamaica are only 57.7 percent of men's earnings. In Jamaica this has serious social ramifications as one-third of all households are headed by women. The observed wage differential helps to explain why female heads of households and their dependents are more likely to live in poverty than male heads of households and their dependents. From both the viewpoint of equity and social well-being, understanding the causes of this wage differential is important. This study is an empirical investigation of gender-based wage differentials in Jamaica. The specific issue to be addressed is the extent to which observed differences between male and female earnings are a function of different human capital characteristics or the different values placed on male and female labor in the market.

Labor force survey data from October 1989 are used in the analysis. Specifically, earnings functions for men and women are compared and the wage differential that exists is decomposed into two components: The portion due to different endowment levels between men and women (the explained differential) and that due to discrimination in the labor market (or the unexplained differential). The earnings function for women is corrected for selectivity through the use of the inverse Mill's ratio obtained from the relevant labor force participation function.

Section 2 provides background information on Jamaica and its labor market characteristics. A description of the data and the sample used is presented in Section 3. Section 4 contains the results of the participation function for women and Section 5 the results of the earnings functions for men and women. The extent of gender-based labor market discrimination is presented in the sixth section and Section 7 discusses the findings and recommendations.

## 2.    The Jamaican Labor Market

Jamaica is a small country with only 2.3 million inhabitants. In 1987, agriculture employed one quarter of the population but contributed just over 6 percent of GDP. In contrast, manufacturing employed close to 15 percent of the population and comprised over 22 percent of GDP. The other large employment sectors are services and commerce (representing 26 and 13 percent of employment respectively) with the remainder of employment being primarily in construction and transport (Statistical Institute of Jamaica, 1989). The economy is heavily dependent on bauxite and alumina exports and the fall in bauxite prices in the 1980s had a serious impact on the economic situation of the country. In addition, the primary agricultural crop is sugar, which faces a highly stagnant international market.

High rates of economic growth were recorded in the 1950s and 1960s but fell in the 1970s. In the last ten years, average GDP growth has been negative due to the international economic crisis, the fall of bauxite prices, and government policies which have aggravated the situation (World Bank, 1990). Unemployment rates have been high historically and peaked in 1980 at 27 percent.[1] Some recovery in the economy has taken place during the last decade and, in spite of a reorganization in the public sector which decreased employment there, job creation in the other sectors has occurred.

The labor force in Jamaica has several characteristics of interest for the present study. The first, mentioned above, is the high rate of unemployment. This rate is higher given the definition of unemployment used by the Government of Jamaica (which includes people as unemployed even if they are not actively seeking employment). It is argued that this is a more accurate measure of Jamaican unemployment due to the few positive incentives for job-search that exist and the fact that, in rural areas, information about jobs is relatively well known so there is little to be gained by actively searching for a job (McFarlane, 1988; ILO, 1982). The Appendix provides information on unemployment using both the extended and restricted definition.

Another characteristic of Jamaica which affects the labor force is the high number of female-headed households. One third of all households in Jamaica have a female head of household (Sinclair, 1988), which is higher than for Latin America at large, but is fairly typical of the Caribbean (Powell et al., 1988). More female-headed households exist in the eastern region of the country and in Kingston than in rural areas (Powell, 1976) and some evidence exists that in the Kingston Metropolitan Area this figure is as high as 50 percent. A 1989 study shows that people in the poorest quintile in Jamaica were, among other things, more likely to live in female-headed households (Anderson, 1990). Additionally, unemployment affects female-headed households more often than male-headed households. Over half of the unemployed household heads in the labor force are female and, as can be seen in Table 14.1, female heads of households are three times as likely to be unemployed as their male counterparts.

**Table 14.1**
Jamaica: Unemployment of Heads of Households
by Gender
(percent)

|                                     | 1985 | 1986 | 1987 |
|-------------------------------------|------|------|------|
| Male Households<br>Heads Unemployed | 7.7  | 6.4  | 5.8  |
| Female Households<br>Heads Unemployed | 21.7 | 20.3 | 15.2 |

Source: STATIN 1987.

---

[1]   This figure is the official one and is based on the extended definition of unemployment which includes all people wanting work and available to work. The unemployment figure would be 13 percent if the restricted definition of unemployment (i.e., only those actively seeking work) were used (McFarlane, 1988).

A third characteristic of the labor force is the large proportion who are self-employed. The increase in self-employment began in the 1970s (Klinov, 1987) and by the early 1980s almost one-half of all male workers and one-third of all female workers were self-employed (Doeringer, 1987). It is argued that half of the self-employed are actually in the informal sector (Lisk, 1987), a higher proportion than in Latin America and the Caribbean as a whole (ILO, 1988). The fall in formal sector employment coincided with a rise in employment in the informal sector with a subsequent fall in the informal sector's productivity (Doeringer, 1987). There is evidence that the informal sector in Jamaica works to absorb the excess supply of labor (Klinov, 1987; Doeringer, 1987) and may well be a form of disguised unemployment (Villarreal Gonda, 1983).

The final point concerning the labor force that is of interest for this study is the lack of training received by workers. Ninety percent of the labor force in Jamaica has had no specialized or vocational training (Lisk, 1987). In essence, the only training received by Jamaican workers is on-the-job training. In addition to this lack of training, the quality of the formal educational system is presumed to be low; few companies rely on the schooling system for skill training (Doeringer, 1987) and employers in both public and private sectors have indicated that the basic level of knowledge of school leavers, and particularly people with three years of secondary education, is so low that "many of them are almost untrainable" (UNESCO, 1983:119).

The characteristics of the Jamaican labor market outlined above have an impact on both the decision to participate in the labor force and the productivity of the labor force. First, women who are heads of households can be expected to have participation rates similar to those of men. Second, the labor absorption role of the informal sector leads to low productivity which may decrease the impact of human capital investments on earnings. Finally, the absence of training and the lack of articulation between formal education and the needs of the labor market also influence human capital and earnings.

## 3.   The Data

The data used in this paper are from a random sample of the 1989 Labor Force Survey carried out by the Statistical Institute of Jamaica. This is a bi-annual survey carried out in April and October of each year. In the October 1989 round the survey covered 6,000 households. The data used in the present analysis is a random sample of this October, 1989 data set and includes 5,219 households for a total of 18,657 individuals. Of these individuals, 5,654 are in the prime age for working (between ages 20 and 59).

Table 14.2 presents some summary information on this prime age group. The working population is defined as all those with positive earnings and hours worked. This definition omits unpaid family workers but it does include the self-employed. Almost 62 percent of the sample population is defined as working.

The sample is a fairly young one with the average age of working men and women being 35 years, slightly higher than the age of the sample population as a whole. Working women have the highest education levels, having completed an average of 7.8 years of schooling. Working men have, on average, approximately half a year less schooling than their female counterparts. Only at the university level do men have more schooling, although the difference is slight.

Thirty-eight percent of the sample of working women are heads of households compared to 54 percent of working males. Working women live in slightly larger households than working men.

The difference in size is primarily due to the fact that working women live in households with more children under age 14.

Experience, as used here, is potential experience, not actual experience.[2] Potential experience closely approximates actual experience for those individuals who have worked steadily since leaving school. This potential experience may be a good approximation of real experience for men but for women, who traditionally move in and out of the labor force, the experience variable will overstate actual experience.[3]

As is the case in many other Latin American and Caribbean countries (see other chapters in this volume), the greatest difference between male and female workers is found in earnings. The difference in weekly earnings between men and women in Jamaica is substantial. As can be seen in Table 14.2, working women earn only 57.7 percent of what men earn even though women work, in hourly terms, only six percent less per week than men.[4] The minimum wage in Jamaica in 1988 for a forty hour week was J\$80. Thus, if the weekly earnings in Table 14.2 are adjusted to a forty hour week both men and women are, on average, still making less than the minimum wage. Men, however, earn an average of 70 percent of the minimum wage while working women, on average, earn only 43 percent. Correcting for the difference in hours worked shows women earning 61.4 percent of men's earnings.

## 4.    Determinants of Female Labor Force Participation

For women, unlike men, there is assumed to be a reservation wage which will affect a woman's decision to participate in the labor force.[5] When the reservation wage is higher than market wages, women will remain outside the labor market. Only when this unobserved reservation wage, or the non-market value of women's labor, is lower than the market wage will women choose to participate in the labor market. As the reservation wage is not observed for non-working women, the female earnings function will produce biased results if an ordinary least squares earnings estimation technique is used. In order to correct for this selectivity bias it is necessary to estimate a participation function for women which regresses women's demographic and human capital characteristics on their probability of participating in the labor market (Heckman, 1979). From this equation, the inverse Mill's ratio can be calculated and included in the earnings function.

---

[2]    This is calculated as "age minus number of years of schooling minus 6." This definition follows Mincer, 1974.

[3]    A 1988 study of female-headed households in Jamaica showed that one-third of the women who worked did so intermittently [Powell, 1988].

[4]    The earnings variable was constructed from information on annual earnings and number of months worked. The earnings variable used here is annual earnings divided by the number of months worked divided by 4.2. The information on both hours worked per week and months worked per year collected in the survey is not continuous. Continuous variables were created by taking the midpoint of the ranges provided for each.

[5]    There is some evidence in Jamaica that men may also have a reservation wage as male labor force participation rates in Jamaica are lower than those in other countries. For the purposes of the present study, however, the reservation wage for men is considered to be zero.

**Table 14.2**
Jamaica
Means (and Standard Deviations) of Sample Variables

| Variable | Total Sample[a] | Working Men | Working Women |
|---|---|---|---|
| Age | 34.06 (11.12) | 35.01 (11.09) | 35.21 (10.43) |
| Schooling (years) | 7.71 (2.43) | 7.37 (2.41) | 7.84 (2.41) |
| Education | | | |
| No formal education | 0.004 (0.06) | 0.003 (0.06) | 0.002 (0.04) |
| Incomplete Primary | 0.02 (0.15) | 0.03 (0.18) | 0.01 (0.12) |
| Finished primary school | 0.58 (0.49) | 0.64 (0.48) | 0.58 (0.49) |
| Some secondary school | 0.17 (0.37) | 0.14 (0.35) | 0.16 (0.37) |
| Finished secondary school | 0.26 (0.44) | 0.20 (0.40) | 0.27 (0.45) |
| University | 0.005 (0.07) | 0.009 (0.10) | 0.006 (0.08) |
| Experience | 21.35 (12.42) | 22.64 (12.24) | 22.37 (11.77) |
| Earnings (weekly) | --- --- | 57.39 (149.28) | 33.09 (90.60) |
| Hours worked per week | --- --- | 41.16 (7.13) | 38.62 (8.25) |
| N | 5,654 | 1,939 | 1,550 |

a.  Sample includes all those between ages 20 and 59.
Note:  Numbers in parentheses are standard deviations.

Labor force participation is defined here as all those who work for pay.  While it would, perhaps, be more appropriate to use the broader definition of labor force participation (i.e., including the unemployed) there are serious problems with using definitions of unemployment.[6]  As employment is a more straightforward and easily measured concept it will be used here.  Thus,

---

[6]  As noted above, Jamaica uses two definitions of unemployment (McFarlane, 1988).

a woman is considered to participate in the labor force if she reports hours worked and has positive earnings. Women who are self-employed are considered to be participating although unpaid family workers and the unemployed are excluded. Of the 3,212 women between ages 20 and 59 included here, 1,550 were working for pay (48.3 percent of all women and 27.4 percent of the sample). Given the dichotomous nature of the dependent variable, a probit model is used to estimate the probability of participation.

The regressors in the participation function take into account family, geographic location, and personal characteristics of the individual women. Family variables include number of children and adults in the household. Children in the household are divided into two groups, those under six and those aged 6 to 14 years. In general, it is predicted that the presence of children under age six will increase the value of a woman's time in the house in terms of household production and hence lower her probability of participating in the labor force. Heckman (1974) found that the effect of having one child under six is to raise the asking price (the wage at which a woman will work) by 15 percent, which thus lowers the probability of participation.

It should be noted that it is not possible to determine to whom the children in the sample "belong." In other words, in any given household there may be more than one woman with children. The way in which the data were collected makes it impossible to determine how many children each of these women has. The inability to match children with their mothers may not, however, be a serious problem in the present analysis. Some evidence from Jamaica indicates that the responsibilities of childcare fall to all females in the household regardless of who the actual mother is (World Bank, 1985; Powell et al, 1988). If all women in a given household share in childcare responsibilities, then the expected sign of the coefficient for the presence of very young children will still be negative.

It is expected that the presence of non-earning adults in a woman's household would increase her probability of participating. On the one hand, if these adults take over childcare responsibilities, as has been shown to be the case in Jamaica (Powell et al., 1988), they will free the children's mother to work outside the home. On the other hand, each adult with zero income represents a drain on family resources that might force females within the household to work. Thus, while the sign of the coefficient is expected to be positive, it will not be possible to determine which effect has the greater impact. The presence of income earning adults is expected to have the opposite effect, decreasing the need for further income.

Also included in the model is a variable which addresses the status of the individual woman in the household. A large percentage of women in the sample are heads of households. These women will be more likely to be primary workers, working full time and having less choice about labor market participation. It is expected that they will be more likely to participate in the labor force.

The geographic area, and specifically the parish in which a woman lives, is also expected to influence her decision to participate. It would be expected that urban dwellers would be more likely to participate given the (1) more "liberal" attitudes towards women's participation in the urban areas, and (2) the high rates of migration experienced in Jamaica, especially among woman to urban areas (World Bank, 1985).[7] Kingston and St. Andrews are the two parishes with the

---

[7]   The cause of migration is typically to find work (Ankar & Knowles, 1978). To the extent that women who migrate do find work, it is expected that the coefficients on the urban variables will be positive.

greatest degree of urbanization. Unfortunately, however, there are also some rural areas in Kingston and St. Andrews as well as urban areas in other parishes; this mixture of rural/urban may confound the effects of parish on participation in the analysis.

The only information contained in the data about the characteristics of the individual women are age and schooling. Information on health and nutritional status was unavailable in the labor force survey.[8] Some evidence exists showing that these factors affect participation more in the urban formal sector than in rural areas or the informal sector (Behrman and Wolfe, 1984). The omission of health and nutrition variables may bias estimates of participation for urban women.

Age is represented by a series of dummy variables, broken down into five-year age groups. The base group is the youngest (ages 20 to 24). Educational achievement is also broken down into dummy variables. (The use of dummy variables is designed to take into account any non-linearity in the effect of either age or schooling on participation). The first level is "no formal schooling or incomplete primary" and is the base group. Some primary, finished primary, some secondary and finished secondary are the other groups. No one in the sample has completed a university degree. Unfortunately there is no information as to whether people attended university without earning a degree. It is expected that the value of the coefficient for all the schooling variables will be positive as it has been shown (Heckman, 1974) that the increase in the market (offered) wage will increase more than the increase in the woman's asking (shadow) wage.

The results of the probit equation are presented in Table 14.3. The effect of education is particularly interesting. Only finishing secondary school (five or six years) has a significant impact on the probability of employment. The finding that lower levels of schooling do not have a significant impact on participation may reflect the low quality of the educational system or may be a function of the "degree inflation" that has occurred as education levels have risen (UNESCO, 1983).

Geographic location does not appear to play a significant role in a woman's decision to participate in the labor force. None of the parishes included in the equation have a significant impact at the 5 percent level, although at the 10 percent level women in St. Andrews are more likely to work than women in Kingston. The greater probability of working for women in St. Andrews than in Kingston may reflect the fact that most female migration is not to Kingston but to other urban areas (World Bank, 1985).

Female heads of households are more likely to participate than other women which gives credence to the assumption that these women have a labor market behavior more like their male counterparts than other women. In other words, by nature of being the head of their household, they take on the characteristics of primary workers and have fewer choices about working.

The effect of age on participation is somewhat counter-intuitive. As can be seen in the table, the probability of participation increases with age. It could be expected that the youngest group of women, aged 20 to 25 would have lower participation rates as they are at reproductive age and/or are still in school. The variable measuring the number of children, however, should capture the effect of fertility (in fact, the coefficient on children under six is indeed significant and negative).

---

[8]    Note that several rounds of a Living Standards Measurement Survey have been carried out in Jamaica in the past two years. These surveys do have such information. Due to various constraints, this information was not incorporated in this study.

## Table 14.3
### Probit Estimates for Female Participation

| Variable | Coefficient | t-ratio | Partial Derivative |
|---|---|---|---|
| Constant | -0.584 | -3.30 | |
| | | | |
| Age 25-29 | .161 | 1.95 | 64.18 |
| Age 30-34 | .406 | 4.44 | 6.17 |
| Age 35-39 | .650 | 6.24 | 25.88 |
| Age 40-44 | .650 | 5.48 | 25.88 |
| Age 45-49 | .546 | 4.45 | 21.75 |
| Age 50-55 | .294 | 2.43 | 11.71 |
| Age 55-59 | .278 | 2.20 | 11.09 |
| | | | |
| Education | | | |
| Finish Prim. | .148 | 1.31 | 5.90 |
| Some Second. | .130 | .99 | 5.16 |
| Finish Second. | .314 | 2.57 | 12.52 |
| Finish Univers. | 5.518 | .01 | 219.75 |
| | | | |
| Area of Residence | | | |
| St. Andrew | .218 | 1.67 | 8.70 |
| St. Thomas | -.020 | - .11 | - .79 |
| Portland | -.293 | -1.51 | -11.68 |
| St. Mary | -.174 | -.93 | -6.95 |
| St. Ann | -.197 | -1.20 | - 7.84 |
| Trelawny | .106 | .51 | 4.20 |
| St. James | .080 | .53 | 3.20 |
| Hanover | -.311 | -1.64 | -12.37 |
| Westmoreland | -.202 | -1.30 | -8.04 |
| St. Elizabeth | -.246 | -1.55 | -9.81 |
| Manchester | -.038 | -.24 | -1.51 |
| Clarendon | -.137 | -.90 | -5.47 |
| St. Catherine | .193 | 1.47 | 7.68 |
| | | | |
| Head of House | .379 | 6.13 | 15.08 |
| Children 0-6 | -.155 | -5.77 | -6.16 |
| Children 6-14 | .072 | 3.34 | 2.86 |
| Adult No Income | -.344 | -17.34 | -13.69 |
| Adult w/income | .585 | 22.79 | 23.29 |

Notes:   Dependent Variable: Labor Force Participation
Sample: Women aged 20 to 59.
N = 3212
Mean Participation Rate: 48.3
Log-likelihood = -1495.1

Also, fewer than one percent of all Jamaican women have a university degree which indicates that women aged 20 to 24 are not in school.[9] Running a probit which has overall participation (i.e., including the unemployed) as the dependent variable shows that the two youngest groups have the highest rates of participation. Clearly, the negative coefficients in the present equation are indicative of the extremely high unemployment rates among these age groups.

The composition of the family has a significant impact on female participation. As expected, the number of children under age six has a negative impact on the probability of participation. The number of children aged six to fourteen has a positive impact on participation.

The signs of the coefficients on the number of adults, income earners and non-earners in the household are the reverse of the expected ones. A greater number of non-wage earning adults in the household lowers the probability of participation while the more earning adults there are in the household, the higher the participation. If the non-earning adults are elderly or males who will not take over household duties, it may well be that the effect of having more of these non-earning adults is to raise the value of the woman's non-market labor. It is not, however, clear why an increase in earning adults increases the probability of participation.

Simulations based on the above equation show the impact of various characteristics of women. As can be seen in Table 14.4, the probability of participating in the labor force increases with age up until a woman reaches age 45 when participation starts to decline. Women in age ranges 35 to 40 and 40 to 45 have the highest participation rates (61.4 percent). The difference is quite large -- twenty-five percentage points between a 20 year old and a 40 year old.

A completed secondary degree is the only educational level which significantly affects the probability of participation. Women who complete secondary school have a three percentage point higher probability of working than a woman with the average level of education (less than eight years of schooling).

Other simulations show the change in participation based on status in the household and the composition of the household. Heads of households are shown to be much more likely to participate than woman who are not heads of households (15 percentage points higher). Having two children under age 6 lowers the probability of participation below the average level and having two or more children between ages six and fourteen raises the level of participation above the average level.

Both the number of adults with income and those without affect the probability of participation to a great extent. Notice that a woman in a household with one non-earning adult has a 48.6 percent probability, but that a woman in a household with two non-earning adults has only a 35.3 probability of participating. The same type of impact on participation can be seen in the number of income earning adults.

---

[9]    Unless of course large groups of people attend the university without completing degrees. The data do not provide information on this.

**Table 14.4**
Predicted Participation Probabilities by Characteristic (%)

| Characteristic | Predicted Probability |
|---|---|
| **Age:** | |
| 20 to 24 | 35.9 |
| 25 to 29 | 42.1 |
| 30 to 34 | 51.8 |
| 35 to 39 | 61.4 |
| 40 to 44 | 61.4 |
| 45 to 49 | 57.4 |
| 50 to 54 | 47.3 |
| 55 to 59 | 46.7 |
| **Education** | |
| Finished Secondary School | 51.8 |
| **Head of Household** | |
| Head of household | 57.8 |
| Not head of household | 42.8 |
| **Family Composition** | |
| Children under six | |
| Zero | 53.3 |
| One | 47.2 |
| Two | 41.1 |
| Three | 35.2 |
| **Adults with No Income** | |
| Zero | 62.1 |
| One | 48.6 |
| Two | 35.2 |
| **Children 6 to 14** | |
| Zero | 44.0 |
| One | 46.8 |
| Two | 49.7 |
| Three | 52.6 |
| **Adults with Labor Income** | |
| Zero | 35.8 |
| One | 58.7 |
| Two | 79.0 |

Notes:   Overall Mean Participation Rate = 48.3%
Simulations done only for variables whose coefficients are significant.

## 5. Earnings Functions

The standard earnings function uses the Mincerian formulation of experience, experience squared, and schooling regressed on the natural log of earnings:

$$LnY = b_0 + b_1S + b_2EX + b_3EX^2 \qquad (1)$$

where:

$LnY$ = the natural log of weekly earnings
$EX$ = experience (potential; defined as age-school-6)
$EX^2$ = experience squared
$S$ = years of schooling

To standardize for hours worked, the natural log of weekly hours was entered on the right-hand side of the equation.

As the question of interest for this paper is the effect of human capital on men's and women's wages, the proper specification of female earnings functions must take into account the selectivity factor (the inverse Mill's ratio from the probit model). This variable is added to the standard Mincerian specification for the female earnings function.

The sample used to calculate the earnings functions specified above consists of all working individuals. The results of the equations are presented in Table 14.5. As can be seen, regardless of the specification, schooling has a significant, positive impact on earnings for both men and women. The return to education is high, with women experiencing a much greater return to education than men (20 percent for women compared to 12.3 percent for men).

The impact of experience on earnings is significant for both men and women. The impact is similar for men and women although men have a slightly higher return than do their female counterparts in the corrected general equation. Experience squared is also significant.

The inverse Mill's ratio in the female earnings function is significant and negative. This indicates that the dispersion of rewards in non-market work is greater than that in the market, and that attributes which increase productivity in non-market and market work are highly correlated. Thus women who are less productive in the home are more likely to be in the labor force.

## 6. Discrimination

From the sample characteristics it can be seen that there is a rather large difference between male and female earnings. Subtracting the two equations and reordering the terms allows an estimate to be made of the discrimination in the labor market (this is the standard Oaxaca (1973) decomposition procedure). The initial equation is:

$$LnY_m - LnY_f = X_m b_m - X_f b_f \qquad (2)$$

Algebraic manipulations leave the following equation:

$$LnY_m - LnY_f = b_m(X_m - X_f) + X_f(b_m - b_f) \qquad (2a)$$

where the second term on the right-hand side measures potential discrimination through the difference in prices or the way in which endowments are valued in the market. The first term measures the effect from endowments of the two groups and, as such, does not necessarily indicate discrimination.[10]

**Table 14.5**
**Earnings Functions**

|  | Male | Female (corrected for selectivity) | Female (not corrected for selectivity) |
|---|---|---|---|
| Constant | 1.605 | 0.101 | -0.435 |
|  | (2.27) | (0.20) | (-0.86) |
| Schooling | 0.123 | 0.202 | 0.215 |
|  | (6.76) | (9.86) | (10.50) |
| Experience | 0.077 | 0.067 | 0.082 |
|  | (5.45) | (4.33) | (5.44) |
| Experience Squared | -0.001 | -0.001 | -0.001 |
|  | (-3.48) | (-3.08) | (-4.04) |
| Log hours | -0.268 | -0.091 | -0.091 |
|  | (-3.46) | (-0.74) | (-0.63) |
| LAMBDA |  | -0.389 |  |
|  |  | (-4.32) |  |
| R-squared | 0.042 | 0.079 | 0.068 |
| N | 1,935 | 1,550 | 1,550 |

Notes:  Numbers in parentheses are t-ratios.
Dependent variable = log (weekly earnings)

Table 14.6 presents the results of the Oaxaca decomposition. Two specifications are presented to take into account the index problem. The decomposition in the second line is simply:

$$LnY_m - LnY_f = b_f(X_m-X_f) + X_m(b_m-b_f)$$ (2b)

Both specification are shown here. It should be noted that the unexplained portion of the earnings differential is the upper bound of discrimination. It is clear that additional characteristics of men and women which affect productivity can lower this upper bound if men have greater endowments.

Decomposing the male and female earnings functions shows that women actually have superior endowments. Both education levels and experience (as defined here) are higher for women than for men. Depending on the specification used, the size of the advantage to women varies from 13 to 19 percent. This higher package of endowments is offset by the very strong effect of different valuations of male and female labor in the marketplace. The unexplained portion of

[10]  The difference in endowments may, however, reflect pre-market discrimination.

**Table 14.6**
Decomposition of the Male-Female Earnings Differential

| Specification | Percentage Due to | |
| --- | --- | --- |
| | Endowments[a] | Rewards |
| Equation 2a | -13.7 | 113.7 |
| Equation 2b | -19.1 | 119.1 |
| ($Wage_m/Wage_f = 173\%$) | | |

a.  Note that the negative sign indicates an advantage to women.

the differential is so strong that it not only explains the wage gap but negates the effect of women having higher endowments. In short, wage differentials in Jamaica are not a function of different levels of human capital between men and women but are, instead, due to the pricing mechanism.

## 7.  Discussion

In 1987 the Government of Jamaica issued a National Policy Statement on Women which states that "...sustained progress in the economic and social development of Jamaica...necessitates the full participation of the women of Jamaica." It is also states that "(Women's) participation in development is ... on inequitable terms..." which represent costs to both the women themselves and Jamaica as a whole (Sinclair, 1988:2).   The results of the present study bear witness to the inequitable terms of women's participation in the labor force and also provide information on how the goal of full participation by women, at least in the labor force, can be reached.

Increasing women's participation in the labor market is an important first step in helping women to become full participants in the development process in Jamaica.  Increasing the number of women who complete high school is a solution with long lasting effects for participation.  In addition, the returns to women's education are much higher than men's and any additional education provided to women will have a large, positive impact on their earnings.

But increasing participation, regardless of how it is done, will not by itself enable women to participate on an equitable basis in Jamaica.  The earnings differential between men and women is not due to women's lack of human capital.  On the contrary they have greater endowments of human capital than their male counterparts.  As was shown in Section 6, anywhere from 113 percent to 119 percent of the differential is due to women's work being valued at a lower rate than men's.

What can be concluded from the present study is that, while there are policy options which exist to increase women's participation in the labor market in Jamaica, the study does not show what specific policies can be used to decrease the existing labor market inequities.  The most important finding of this study is that gender-based discrimination in Jamaica is high and that this is a critical issue that must be addressed if woman are to be equal partners with men in the Jamaican economy.

### Appendix 14A.1
#### Unemployment Rates in Jamaica (%)

| Year (April) | Extended Definition | Restricted Definition |
| --- | --- | --- |
| 1943[a] | 22.7 | 11.4 * |
| 1953[a] | 23.4 | 12.0** |
| 1960 | 24.0 | 13.0** |
| 1970 | 20.3 | 12.2 |
| 1975 | 19.9 | 9.1 |
| 1980 | 27.9 | 14.9 |
| 1981 | 26.2 | 10.8 |
| 1982 | 27.0 | 13.0 |
| 1983 | 25.8 | 13.0 |
| 1984 | 25.5 | 11.5 |
| 1985 | 24.4 | 11.7 |
| 1986 | 25.0 | 11.0 |
| 1987 | 21.2 | 8.6 |

*-Modified
**-Estimated
a. -December

Note:   The Extended definition of unemployment includes all those who want work and are available for work. The restricted definition includes those who want and are available to work and who are actively seeking work.

Source: McFarlane, 1988, p. 14.

# References

Anderson, P. "Levels of Poverty and Household Food Consumption in Jamaica in 1989." Paper presented at the Workshop on Food and Nutrition Policies: Issues and Recommendations for the 1990s and Beyond. Jamaica: Jamaica and Caribbean Food and Nutrition Institute, 1990.

Anker, R. and R.C. Knowles. "Female Labor Force Participation in Kenya" in G. Standing, and G. Sheehan (eds.). *Labor Force Participation in Low-Income Countries*. Geneva: International Labor Office, 1978.

Behrman, J. and B.L. Wolfe. "Labor Force Participation and Earnings Determinants for Women in the Special Conditions of Developing Countries." *Journal of Development Economics*, Vol. 15 (1984). pp. 259-288.

Doeringer, P. B. "Market Structure, Jobs and Productivity: Observations from Jamaica." Report No. DRD285. Washington, D.C.: World Bank, 1987.

Heckman, J. "Sample Selection Bias as a Specification Error." *Econometrica*, Vol. 47, no. 1 (1979). pp. 153-161.

-----. "Shadow Prices, Market Wages, and Labor Supply." *Econometrica*, Vol. 42, no. 4 (1974). pp. 679-694.

International Labor Office. *World Employment Review*. Geneva: International Labor Office, 1988.

-----."Employment and Economic Growth: Labor Force, Employment and Unemployment." Report No. II. Geneva: International Labor Office, 1982.

Klinov, R. "Costs and Returns to Liberalization: The Jamaican Case." Report No. DRD297. Washington, D.C.: World Bank, 1987.

Lisk, F. " An Action Programme for Jamaica, 1987/89, to Sustain the Incomes and Living Standards of the Poor During Adjustment: Employment Policies and Programmes for the Non-Rural Poor." Port-of-Spain: International Labour Office, 1987.

McFarlane, C. "Measurement of Unemployment with Special Reference to the Jamaican Experience." *Journal of the Statistical Institute of Jamaica*, Vol. 1. (1988). pp. 43-59.

Oaxaca, R.L. "Male-female Wage Differentials in Urban Labor Markets." *International Economic Review,* Vol. 14, no. 1 (1973). pp. 693-709.

Powell, D. et al. "Women's Work, Social Support Resources and Infant Feeding Practices in Jamaica". Mimeograph. Washington D.C.: International Center for Research on Women, 1988.

Powell, D. "Female Labour Force Participation and Fertility: An Exploratory Study of Jamaican Women." *Social and Economic Studies,* Vol. 25, no. 3 (1976). pp. 234-258.

Statistical Institute of Jamaica (STATIN). *The Labour Force, October 1987.* Kingston: Statistical Institute of Jamaica, 1989.

Statistical Institute of Jamaica. *The Labour Force, April 1987.* Kingston: Statistical Institute of Jamiaca, 1987.

Sinclair, P.A. "The Jamaican Situation." Vienna: United Nations Interregional Seminar on Women and the Economic Crisis, 1988.

Tokeman, V.E. and A. Uphoff. " A Note of the Labour market in Jamaica, 1980-85." Kingston: PREALC, International Labor Office, 1986.

UNESCO. *Jamaica: Development of Secondary Education.* Paris: UNESCO, 1983.

Villarreal Gonda, R.I. "An Econometric Forecasting Model of Employment for Jamaica." Mimeograph. 1983.

World Bank. *World Development Report, 1990.* Washington, D.C.: World Bank, 1990.

World Bank. "Jamaica: A Survey of Female Headed Low Income Households." Washington, D.C.: Office of the Adviser on Women in Development, World Bank, 1985.

# 15

# Women's Participation Decisions and Earnings in Mexico

*Diane Steele*

## 1. Introduction

The purpose of this study is to examine the factors which influence women's decisions to participate in the labor force in Mexico. Using data from the 1984 Encuesta Nacional de Ingreso-Gasto de los Hogares, we focus on factors which have been shown in previous studies to influence the decision to enter the workforce such as age, education level, presence of young children, marital status, and household wealth. The scope of the analysis is limited by the use of this survey since information on several key factors, including hours worked per week, participation in the public sector or the private sector, participation in the formal or informal labor market, and tenure on the job, is not available. Where possible, proxies for these variables have been created using existing information.

Following a brief description of the Mexican labor market, we discuss, in Section 3, the characteristics of the sample used in this analysis. Section 4 examines factors influencing women's labor force participation. In Section 5 we derive earnings functions estimates for working men and working women. Using the standard human capital model we also perform the analyses controlling for selectivity bias in our sample of working women. Section 6 decomposes the earnings differential and considers what proportion of this differential is attributable to discrimination in the labor market.

## 2. The Mexican Economy

Mexico experienced high rates of economic growth between 1950 and 1974. Social welfare and general standards of living improved substantially over these two decades. Welfare programs brought about declines in infant mortality, malnutrition and morbidity, and the illiteracy rate fell from 40 percent in 1950 to 18 percent in 1980. Between 1960 and 1980, infant mortality declined from 74 to about 50 deaths per 1,000 live births, and life expectancy at birth increased almost 10 years from 59 to 68 years.

The economy experienced a serious, albeit brief, financial crisis in 1976 which was terminated by major oil discoveries in 1977. This prosperity, however, was short lived.

During the decades of economic growth, Mexico made great improvements in the quality of and access to public education. Primary education coverage increased from 17.6 percent to 79.8 percent between 1950 and 1980. Nationwide, the number of schools tripled, the number of teachers quintupled, and school enrollment increased sevenfold. Since the crisis in 1982, provision of educational services has slowed.[1]

Since 1982, an economic crisis has existed in Mexico. The crisis, caused by rising interest rates and falling oil prices, has caused severe hardships for the poor, and many of the gains of the previous two decades have been threatened. Real wages have declined by 40 percent and social sector spending has declined from 20 percent of total government expenditures in 1982 to around 12 percent in 1991.

## 3.   Data Characteristics

This analysis is based on data collected for the 1984 Encuesta Nacional de Ingreso-Gasto de los Hogares. The survey data include 7,536 individuals in the third quarter of 1984. The data include information for all individuals aged 12 years and older.

In the survey, wage information was reported by quarter. In order to determine weekly wages, the quarterly wage was divided by 3 to give monthly wage, and the resulting monthly wage was divided by 4.3 to give weekly wages.

Although participation is commonly defined to include those currently employed and those seeking employment, these data do not permit the identification of job seekers. It was only possible to identify individuals as currently employed or not currently employed. In addition, income from wage information was not reported for all workers. The sample was limited to respondents between the ages of 15 and 65, and to workers reporting positive income. This resulted in a sample of 3,360 working men, 1,217 working women, and 450 non-working women. Ninety-six percent of all men and 73 percent of all women in the sample were reported to be working.

Because the survey variables were limited, it was necessary to construct variables for use in the analyses. The amount of experience in the labor market was estimated as age minus years of schooling minus six. This overestimates actual experience because it does not take into account voluntary or involuntary absences from the labor force. This is especially true for women who are more likely to withdraw from the labor force for childrearing.

Most studies indicate that the presence in the household of young children influences the decision to enter the labor market. The data did not, however, provide information on children aged under 12 years. Consequently, we were only able to include a variable for children aged 12 to 14 years.

Table 15.1 gives means and standard deviations of the sample variables by gender. Working women are, on average, two and a half years younger than working men, but non-working women are more than seven years older. Working women have one and a third years more schooling than working men, and working men have almost two years more schooling than non-working women.

Women earn almost 86 percent of men's weekly wages. There is no information on the number of hours worked, making it impossible to determine whether this difference is driven by number of hours worked. The experience variable indicates that working women have almost four years less experience than men, but it should be remembered that this is a constructed variable.

---

[1]   See Carlson and Prawda (1991).

**Table 15.1**
Means (and Standard Deviations) of Sample Variables

| Characteristics | Working Men | Working Women | Non-Working Women |
|---|---|---|---|
| Age | 33.01 | 30.47 | 40.32 |
| | (12.02) | (11.20) | (14.45) |
| Years of Schooling | 6.26 | 7.56 | 4.36 |
| | (4.25) | (4.02) | (3.64) |
| Experience (years) | 20.76 | 16.91 | |
| | (13.70) | (12.85) | |
| Weekly Wages (pesos) | 6590.90 | 5643.70 | |
| | (6295.60) | (4026.80) | |
| | | | |
| Education (%) | | | |
| No Education | 10 | 6 | 19 |
| | (30) | (24) | (40) |
| Primary Incomplete | 30 | 18 | 42 |
| | (46) | (38) | (50) |
| Primary Complete | 22 | 24 | 19 |
| | (42) | (43) | (39) |
| Junior High Incomplete | 6 | 5 | 3 |
| | (24) | (22) | (16) |
| Junior High Complete | 14 | 23 | 7 |
| | (35) | (42) | (26) |
| High School Incomplete | 4 | 3 | 2 |
| | (19) | (17) | (15) |
| High School Complete | 4 | 12 | 2 |
| | (20) | (33) | (12) |
| University Incomplete | 4 | 3 | 3 |
| | (19) | (18) | (18) |
| University Complete | 5 | 5 | 1 |
| | (22) | (23) | ( 9) |
| | | | |
| Married (%) | 18 | 31 | 32 |
| | (38) | (46) | (47) |
| Urban (%) | 70 | 83 | 55 |
| | (46) | (38) | (50) |
| Children (%) | 2 | 3 | 1 |
| | (14) | (17) | (11) |
| Self-Employed (%) | 5[a] | 1 | |
| | (21) | ( 9) | |
| | | | |
| N | 3,360 | 1,217 | 450 |
| | | | |
| Labor Force Participation Rate (%) | 96 | 73 | |

Notes:    a.    Based on only 3,334 men.
          Figures in parentheses are standard deviations.  Sample includes respondents between ages 15 and 65.
Source:    Encuesta Nacional de Ingreso-Gasto de los Hogares, 1984.

Proportionately more women, working or non-working, are married than men. More working women reside in urban areas than working men or non-working women. In this sample, a relatively small proportion of working men or working women are self-employed.

## 4.   Determinants of Female Labor Force Participation

There are many factors which influence the decision to participate in the labor market. For women, these factors include productive skills (human capital) such as schooling and job market skills; personal characteristics such as age, marital status, the presence of children in the home; and other factors such as area of residence (urban or rural), and availability of childcare services.

In our sample, working women have more years of schooling than working men but less experience in the labor market than men, and earn only 86 percent of men's wages. The purpose of this analysis is to determine what part of the difference in wages is due to real differences in human capital endowments, and what part is due to "unexplained" factors. These "unexplained" factors can be loosely defined as discrimination against women in the workforce.

The probit model that we use includes both working and non-working women. However, because working women have chosen to participate in the labor market, we must assume that their market wage exceeds their reservation wage (labor in the job market is more valuable than labor in the home). To correct for this selectivity effect when running the earnings functions, we use the selectivity correction procedure developed by Heckman.[2] This model estimates the probability that a woman will participate in the labor market based on her human capital endowments, personal characteristics, and other factors.

In our probit model, the independent variables include age, educational level, relative household wealth, area of residence and parental status. Age is entered into the equation as age splines (by five year groupings). Education is similarly entered as a series of dummy variables indicating the highest level of education attempted. Total household income is used as a surrogate for total household wealth. As explained above, the measure for a woman's parental status is a poor one, given that the data provide information only on the number of children between ages 12 and 14 years residing in the household. Consequently, this parental status variable is not expected to be significant. Because previous studies have also shown that women's labor force participation is higher in urban areas, we included a dummy variable set to one if the woman resides in an urban area and zero if she resides in a rural area.

Table 15.2 presents the results of the probit model. The probit coefficients show that probability of participation in the labor market decreases as women become older although it remains relatively high even at older ages. The extent to which increased age decreases the probability of participation is shown in Table 15.3. Table 15.3 also shows that with completion of each level of education, the probability of participating increases.

Table 15.3 shows that with increased levels of education, women are more likely to participate in the labor market. For example, women who have completed Junior High are 9 percent more likely to participate than those who have only completed Primary level (probability = .81 versus .74). It can also be seen, however, that at higher levels of education, completion is an important factor. For example, women who attempt High School, but do not complete are less likely to participate than women who complete Junior High (probability = .62 versus .81).

---

2    See Heckman (1979).

## Table 15.2
### Probit Estimates for Women's Participation

| Variable | Coefficient | T-ratio | Mean | Partial Derivative |
|---|---|---|---|---|
| Constant | -1.190 | -6.67 | 1.000 | |
| Age 15-19 | 1.599 | 7.82 | .119 | .467 |
| Age 20-24 | 1.313 | 7.04 | .206 | .384 |
| Age 25-29 | 1.277 | 6.73 | .165 | .373 |
| Age 30-34 | 1.066 | 5.57 | .116 | .311 |
| Age 35-39 | 1.085 | 5.59 | .098 | .317 |
| Age 40-44 | 1.015 | 5.21 | .089 | .297 |
| Age 45-49 | .594 | 2.76 | .050 | .173 |
| Age 50-54 | .494 | 2.38 | .056 | .144 |
| Age 55-59 | .541 | 2.52 | .044 | .158 |
| Children (aged 12-14) | .563 | 2.20 | .025 | .164 |
| Urban Residence | .564 | 6.55 | .754 | .165 |
| Primary Incomplete | -.170 | -1.36 | .244 | -.049 |
| Primary Complete | .149 | 1.05 | .227 | .043 |
| Junior High Inc | .271 | 1.20 | .043 | .000 |
| Junior High Com | .390 | 2.19 | .187 | .114 |
| High School Inc | -.179 | -.72 | .029 | -.052 |
| High School Com | 1.041 | 4.75 | .092 | .304 |
| University Inc | -.365 | -1.55 | .034 | -.106 |
| University Com | .973 | 3.44 | .042 | .284 |
| Tech Ed/Primary[a] | .469 | 3.06 | .098 | .137 |
| Tech Ed/Secondary[b] | .399 | 2.39 | .134 | .116 |
| Household Income (pesos) | .000 | 2.61 | 186,780 | .000 |

a.   Technical Education and Primary Incomplete or Complete.
b.   Technical Education and Junior High or High School.
Notes: Dependent Variable - Labor Force Participation.
       Sample: Women Aged 15 to 65.
       Mean Participation Rate: 73 percent.

Predicted probabilities for participation steadily decrease as women's ages increase. While women aged 15 to 19 years have a 90 percent probability of participating in the labor market, women aged 55 to 59 years have only a 60 percent probability of participating.

The presence of children (aged 12 to 14 years) in the household, as expected, does not appreciably reduce a woman's probability of participating. Our analysis shows that when there are children in the household aged 12 to 14 years, women have a 91 percent probability of participating. In fact, our study shows that women are less likely to participate when there are no children in the household. Most studies indicate that it is pre-school aged children that reduce the probability of participation.

Urban residence does increase the probability of a woman's participation in the labor market. Women residing in urban areas have a 28 percent greater probability of participating than those residing in rural areas (probability = .82 versus .64).

**Table 15.3**
Predicted Participation Probabilities by Characteristic

| Characteristic | Predicted Probability |
|---|---|
| **Education** | |
| Primary Incomplete | .63 |
| Primary Complete | .74 |
| Junior High Incomplete | .78 |
| Junior High Complete | .81 |
| High School Incomplete | .62 |
| High School Complete | .94 |
| University Incomplete | .55 |
| University Complete | .93 |
| | |
| **Age** | |
| 15 - 19 years | .90 |
| 20 - 24 years | .85 |
| 25 - 29 years | .84 |
| 30 - 34 years | .78 |
| 35 - 39 years | .79 |
| 40 - 44 years | .76 |
| 45 - 49 years | .62 |
| 50 - 54 years | .58 |
| 55 - 59 years | .60 |
| | |
| **Presence of Children (12-14 years)** | |
| No | .78 |
| Yes | .91 |
| | |
| **Urban Residence** | |
| No | .64 |
| Yes | .82 |

Notes:    Probability of participation holding other variables constant at their sample mean.

## 5.    Earnings Functions

Earnings functions are estimated for males and for the 1,217 females from our sample who were participating in the labor force. Two estimates of the earnings functions are estimated for females. The first corrects for selectivity by including the Lambda estimated in the probit. The second is uncorrected for selectivity. No corrected estimates are made for men. Typically men are not viewed as having to choose between labor in the home and labor in the market place because they do not traditionally take on the childrearing and home-care activities.

We use the standard human capital model where the dependent variable is the log of weekly wages and the independent variables are experience, experience squared, years of schooling, and self-employment. This model is expressed as:

$$LnY = b_0 + b_1S + b_2EX + b_3EX^2 + b_4SE$$

where:

LnY = the natural log of weekly wages,
EX = experience (potential: defined as age-years of school-6),
EX2 = experience squared,
S = years of schooling, and
SE = self-employed (one if self-employed).

A serious shortcoming in the estimation was the lack of information on the hours worked by each worker. Lacking this information, we were forced to assume that all workers supplied the same amount of labor. This assumption is clearly invalid, given existing knowledge about women's typical work patterns, but there was no way to derive estimates from the existing data.[3] A broad surrogate for sector of employment, paid or self-employment, is also included as an independent variable, but because so few of the survey respondents are self-employed, the results from this variable should be interpreted with caution. The survey did provide information on the respondents' occupation. However, when dummy variables indicating which occupational sector the respondent belonged to were added to the equation, they provided no additional information.

The results of these earnings functions are shown in Table 15.4. The first column presents results for the male sample. The rate of return to schooling for males is estimated to be 13 percent. Log earnings increase with experience but, as expected in a normal age-earnings profile, they decrease with age. The broad occupational sector variable, self-employment, is highly significant and negative indicating that earnings are lower among the self-employed.

The correction for selectivity in the female earnings functions is shown to be important. The equation which corrects for selectivity shows the rate of return to schooling to be close to 11 percent, substantially below the 15 percent estimated in the uncorrected equation. Lambda itself is significant and negative. Similarly, the experience variable in the corrected equation is below that in the uncorrected equation. In both cases the self-employment variable is significant and negative showing that earnings are lower among the self-employed.

## 6. Discrimination

Working women in this survey earn 86 percent of male weekly wages. Using the Oaxaca method we are able to decompose this earnings differential into a component attributable to differences in human capital endowments, and a component which is largely attributable to wage discrimination. The difference between the mean (log) wage rates of males and females in the Oaxaca decomposition method is expressed as:

$$B_m X_m - B_f X_f = X_f(b_m - b_f) + b_m(X_m - X_f) \tag{1a}$$
$$= X_m(b_m - b_f) + b_f(X_m - X_f) \tag{1b}$$

There is always an index number problem experienced here. Theoretically, there is no advantage to estimating the results using male means or female means, so we present both. The first term in both equations is the part of the log earnings differential that can be ascribed to differences in the wage structures between the sexes and the second term is that part of the log earnings differential that can be ascribed to differences in human capital endowments.

---

[3]    See Gronau (1988), pp 277-301. See also Ng, Scott, and Velez and Winter in this volume.

## Table 15.4
### Earnings Functions

| Variable | Men Uncorrected | Women (Corrected for Selectivity) | Women (Uncorrected for Selectivity) |
|---|---|---|---|
| Constant | 6.665 (127.85) | 7.285 (40.88) | 6.585 (65.60) |
| Years of schooling | .132 (36.76) | .109 (8.85) | .147 (19.85) |
| Experience | .086 (24.84) | .056 (5.56) | .067 (9.71) |
| Experience squared | -.001 (-19.78) | -.001 (-2.52) | -.001 (-8.49) |
| Self-employed | -1.217 (-19.84) | -1.313 (-4.87) | -1.480 (-5.32) |
| Lambda | | -1.487 (-6.70) | |
| $R^2$ | .391 | .362 | .303 |
| N | 3,334 | 1,217 | 1,217 |

Notes: T-ratios are in parentheses.

Dependent variable = log (weekly wages).

Table 15.5 presents the results of the decomposition using the selectivity corrected sample since it yields a more credible estimate.

## Table 15.5
### Decomposition of the Male/Female Earnings Differential

| Specification | Percentage of Earnings Differential Due to Differences in | |
|---|---|---|
| | Endowments | Wage Structure |
| Evaluated at Male Means | 20.0 | 80.0 |
| Evaluated at Female Means | 28.1 | 71.9 |

Note: $W_m/W_f = 117\%$

Using the equation evaluated at the male means we see that only 20 percent of the differential is due to differences in human capital endowments, and 80 percent is due to unobservable factors. The equation evaluated at the female means shows that approximately 28 percent of the differential is due to differences in human capital endowments and 72 percent due to differences in the way men and women are rewarded in the labor market.

## 7.    Discussion

As has been shown, women's participation rates are positively influenced by the amount of education.  Urban residence has a positive effect on participation, and the presence of teenaged children in the household does not appear to influence women's decision to work.

A wage differential of 14 percent is low in comparison with other Latin American countries, and with some industrialized countries.[4]  This may be explained in part by our inability to identify several of the important factors in the decision making process, such as hours worked, public versus private sector and formal versus informal sector.

The small differential may also be due to several factors that we can identify in the existing data. Working women have, on average, one and a third more years of schooling than working men. Working women are also more likely to complete higher levels of education than working men. Twenty-eight percent of the working women attempted Junior High with 23 percent completing, compared to only 20 percent of working men who attempted Junior High with 14 percent completing.  Similarly, 15 percent of working women attempted High School with 12 percent completing, compared to 8 percent of working men who attempted with 4 percent completing.

Despite the low earnings differential between men and women, this study has shown that only a small proportion of the differential can be explained by differences in human capital endowments.  The "upper bound" estimate of discrimination is 72 or 80 percent, depending on the equation used. Given the nature of the survey data used in these analyses, males may have had endowments which were superior to women's but of which we are not aware.  If this is the case, the lack of information will bias the estimate of the component due to wage discrimination upwards.

Clearly, further research into the factors influencing women's participation decisions needs to be done.  Further research should include those human capital factors that were missing or had to be estimated in this study.  Especially important are hours worked per week and tenure in the job market.

---

[4]    In Britain, women earn 74 percent of men's wages.  Khandker reports women's wages as being about two-thirds of men's in Peru while Chu Ng found women's wages in Argentina to be 65 percent of men's (both in this volume).  See also Gunderson (1989), Tzannatos (1987), Zabalza and Tzannatos (1985), and Gregory and Duncan (1982).

# References

Carlson, S. and J. Prawda. *Basic Education in Mexico: Trends, Issues and Policy Recommendations*. Washington, D.C.: World Bank, June 1991.

Gregory, R.G. and R.C. Duncan. "Segmented Labour Market Theories and the Australian Experience of Equal Pay for Women." *Journal of Post-Keynesian Economics*. Vol.3 (1982). pp. 403-428.

Gronau, R. "Sex-Related Wage Differentials and Women's Interrupted Labor Careers: The Chicken and Egg Question." *Journal of Labor Economics*. Vol. 6, no. 1 (1988). pp 277-301.

Gunderson, M. "Male-Female Wage Differentials and Policy Responses." *Journal of Economic Literature*. Vol. 21, no.1 (1989). pp 46-72.

Heckman, J. "Sample Selection Bias as a Specification Error." *Econometrica*. Vol. 47, no. 1 (1979). pp. 153-161.

Tzannatos, Z. "Equal Pay in Greece and Britain." *Industrial Relations Journal*. Vol. 18, no. 4 (1987). pp. 275-283.

World Bank. *Mexico, Selected Policy Papers*. Washington, D.C.: World Bank, June 20, 1989.

World Bank. *Staff Appraisal Report, Mexico, Water, Women and Development Project*. Washington, D.C.: World Bank, May 24, 1989.

Zabalza, A. and Z. Tzannatos. *Women and Equal Pay: The Effects of Legislation on Female Employment and Wages in Britain*. Cambridge: Cambridge University Press, 1985.

# 16

# Female Labor Force Participation and Wages: A Case Study of Panama

*Mary Arends*

## 1. Introduction

This chapter examines the differential in earnings between males and females in Panama. In the sample, female wages are 85 percent of male wages, a very high percentage for Latin America. What are the reasons for this high percentage? How does Panama's low participation rate for women affect female earnings? The country is also interesting because of its extensive Labor Code, which has many sections pertaining specifically to women. Because of long standing structural problems in the labor market, Panama has a high unemployment rate, especially for women.

In Section 2, the economic and labor market situation in Panama are discussed. Section 3 pertains to the data and includes descriptive statistics. Section 4 presents the results of a univariate probit model for both men and women that attempts to determine which characteristics make an individual likely to be observed in the work force. The results of the probit are used to correct for selectivity in earnings regressions. Section 5 discusses the results of earnings regressions for men and women, both correcting for selectivity and without correcting for selectivity. A decomposition of the earnings differential is calculated to estimate how much of the differential is due to differences in endowments and how much could be attributed to labor market discrimination. Lastly, there is a discussion of the policy implications of the findings.

## 2. The Panamanian Economy and Labor Market

The population growth rate was 2.2 percent from 1980 to 1989, which is average for Latin America as a whole. Thirty-five percent of the population was aged from 0 to 14 years in 1989, while 60 percent of the population was aged from 15 to 64 years, about average for Latin America. The labor force growth rate was 2.9 percent in the 1980s, averaging 3.3 percent for women.[1]

Panama had a GNP of $1,760 per capita in 1989. Growth was high from 1965 to 1980 at 5.5 percent, but the economic problems of Latin America in the 1980s affected Panama also, and

---

[1]    Economist Intelligence Unit (1991), p.55.

growth was only .5 percent from 1980 to 1989. The economy was very heavily oriented towards services, which accounted for 74 percent of GDP in 1989, while industry accounted for 15 percent and agriculture for 11 percent.[2]    Recent political problems strongly impacted the economy.    In 1988, United States' sanctions and massive capital flight led to 16 percent contraction of GDP.  In 1989, the economy did not recover and GDP fell again by .9 percent.[3]

However, the most chronic problem in Panama is persistent unemployment.  A 1985 World Bank country study stated that unemployment was, without a doubt, the gravest economic and social problem.[4]  In the study, the 1983 unemployment rate was estimated at 9.5 percent.  The situation steadily worsened during the 1980s.  Unemployment estimates for 1989 ranged from 16.0 percent to 20.1 percent.[5]  In the sample used in this study, the male and female unemployment rates were 14 percent and 22 percent, respectively.

To confront Panama's unemployment problem, one strategy was to increase the public sector. The Torrijos regime, which governed from 1969 to 1981, used this strategy throughout its tenure, and enacted the Emergency Employment Program in 1977.  When the Emergency Program ended in 1980, 25 percent of workers were in the public sector.[6]  Because of budget constraints, the public sector could not continue to provide employment, and the percentage of workers in the public sector steadily declined throughout the 1980s.  However, the percentage of workers in the public sector remained high at 21.9 percent in 1989.[7]

The participation rate declined from over 60 percent in early 1970s to just over 50 percent in 1982 and 1983.  This happened because of greatly increased enrollment in secondary and tertiary education, a reduction in the voluntary retirement age from 62 to 55, and a falling female participation rate.[8]  However, according to one official source, female participation rates rose during the 1980s from 17.8 percent in 1980 to 20.8 percent in 1989.[9]    The total labor force participation rate was estimated at 58 percent in 1989.[10]

An important contributing factor to unemployment was Panama's labor code. Instituted in 1972, it substantially increased the cost of hiring labor for employers.  Workers were given more job security, benefits, and bargaining power.  It required employers to pay high severance pay which increases with the length of service, discouraging temporary hires.   The total burden on

---

[2]    World Bank (1991), Tables 1 and 3.

[3]    Economist Intelligence Unit (1991), p. 54.

[4]    World Bank (1985), p.9.

[5]    The estimates come from the Economist Intelligence Unit and the World Bank Panama Operations Desk respectively.

[6]    World Bank (1985), p. 19.

[7]    World Bank, Latin America and the Caribbean, Country Department II, unpublished table, (1991).

[8]    World Bank (1985), p. 11.

[9]    World Bank (1990), p. 238-239.

[10]    The Economist Country Profile, 1991-92.

employers including a thirteen-month bonus and paid vacations was estimated by the World Bank to be 40 percent.[11] Employers could not reduce a worker's salary, so piecework could not be paid on the basis of productivity. As a result of these regulations, Panama's labor costs were among the highest in the Caribbean Basin. The World Bank recommended changes in 1985 as conditions for a structural adjustment loan. The reforms were finally accepted in March 1986, despite a ten-day work stoppage by the unions and fierce political opposition. The modifications permitted piecework, encouraged rewards for productivity, and rationalized overtime provisions for some firms.[12] Whether these changes have had a great impact remains to be seen.

Many aspects of Panamanian law apply directly to women in the labor force. There are provisions in Panama's Constitution (Article 62) and in the Labor Code (Section 10) that employers must provide equal pay for equal work. Legal redress is available, but the burden of proof is on the employee. No real attempt has been made in Panama to address the issue through the courts. Low female labor force participation rates and women's willingness to be self-employed are two explanations why this is so.[13]

There are provisions in the Labor Code which may add to the female unemployment problem. Employers are required to provide 14 weeks of maternity leave, with the employer making up the difference between regular pay and social security payments. It is unlawful to dismiss a woman during pregnancy and five months thereafter without judicial approval. New mothers are entitled to a paid hour break each day in order to breast feed their babies. If a company employs over 20 females, it is required to provide a nursery. Also, the Code forbids women from working in dangerous occupations, such as mines and civil construction. In a Labor Code survey, Spinanger interviewed employers in various sectors of the economy. Two-thirds said that maternity protection laws discouraged them from hiring women. Employers were willing to increase wages by 25 percent to have more flexible maternity arrangements.[14] Such laws may encourage employers to discriminate against all women, including those who have no intention to have a child or older women who do not plan to have more children.

Another characteristic of Panama's labor market is regional disparity in earnings. Heckman and Hotz (1986) found evidence that the Panamanian labor market was segmented by regions, with less developed regions showing higher rates of return to education than developed regions. Rural regions such as Darien, Veraguas, and Cocle had high rates of return, while the Canal Zone and Panama City showed rates of return comparable to the United States.[15] Also, in the Canal Zone, wages are about three times higher than in the rest of the country.[16] Only 2.6 percent of workers are employed in the Canal Zone, but their salaries, which are raised in real terms in accordance with United States cost of living changes, may have prevented other wages in the

---

[11]  World Bank (1985), p. 17.

[12]  Tollefson (1989), p. 135.

[13]  Spinanger (1984), p. 21.

[14]  Spinanger (1984), p. 29.

[15]  Heckman and Hotz (1986), p. 540.

[16]  Because of the Panama Canal treaty, former Canal Zone employees who became employees in Panama were guaranteed wages and conditions similar to those their position had commanded when employed by the U.S. (see Tollefson, p. 142).

Canal areas of Colon and Panama from falling, which would help solve the unemployment problem.[17]

Panama has a long-standing, strong commitment to education. Adult illiteracy was 12 percent in 1989. Schooling is compulsory for 9 years, and begins at age 5. Enrollments were higher than average for Latin America, given Panama's per capita income. Primary school enrollments as a percentage of the relevant age group were 102 percent in 1965 and 106 percent in 1988. Secondary school enrollments were 34 percent in 1965 and 59 percent in 1988, compared to an average in Latin America of 48 percent in 1988. Twenty-eight percent of the relevant age group was enrolled in tertiary education in that year, a percentage that was only surpassed by three Latin American countries, all with higher per capita income--Argentina, Venezuela, and Uruguay.[18]

## 3.    Data Characteristics

The data for this study were taken from the Encuesta de Hogares-Mano de Obra of August 1989, by the Office of Statistics and Census of Panama (DEC). The survey consisted of 8,817 households, comprised of 38,416 individuals. Out of this sample, the individuals of economically active age (ages 15 to 65) were selected, giving a sample of 23,196 individuals. The survey covered both urban and rural households, and the data were weighted to give an accurate representation of the population.

One limitation of the data was that about 30 percent of employed males had no hours and/or no income reported. Over 90 percent of the males that were recorded as "employed" but had no hours or no income were either family workers or self-employed workers in agriculture. Table 16.1 summarizes the problem. Labor force participation includes employed and unemployed workers. Work force participation includes only those who were recorded as "employed" in the survey. The third column labelled "+Hours, +Income" consists only of workers who reported positive hours and positive income. The table breaks down these rates by province. Overall, a wage rate could be calculated for only 71 percent of the male workers. The problem is severest for the rural provinces of Darien and Bocas del Toro. Because of the low percentages of male workers with positive hours and positive income, there is a selectivity problem when examining the male wage functions. The males for whom hours and income are available are a special subset of the male workers. Therefore, in Section 4, the results of separate probit equations for both the males and females are presented.

For females, most rural women were classified as "housewives" and therefore inactive. It is likely that many of them are actually unremunerated family workers. Unfortunately, there is no way to determine the kind of work these women do.

In Table 16.2, the means of the sample variables for the working and non-working samples of males and females are shown. For the table and the subsequent regressions, working was defined as having positive hours and positive income. About 50 percent of the men and 30 percent of the women in the sample of individuals aged 15 to 65 were classified as working. Schooling was calculated by taking the number of years completed at the highest level and adding the number of years required to finish preceding levels. Because it was not known if the individual

---

[17]    World Bank (1985), p. 19.

[18]    World Bank, (1990), pp. 238-239, and World Bank (1991), Table 29.

**Table 16.1**
**Participation Rates**

| Province | Male | | | Female | | |
|---|---|---|---|---|---|---|
| | Labor Force | Work Force | +Hours +Income | Labor Force | Work Force | +Hours +Income |
| Bocas del Toro | .88 | .81 | .78 | .21 | .19 | .19 |
| Cocle | .88 | .79 | .36 | .36 | .29 | .23 |
| Colon | .80 | .64 | .54 | .40 | .30 | .29 |
| Chiriqui | .84 | .72 | .52 | .34 | .26 | .25 |
| Darien | .94 | .94 | .19 | .32 | .31 | .18 |
| Herrera | .84 | .80 | .40 | .33 | .29 | .28 |
| Los Santos | .89 | .86 | .43 | .30 | .24 | .23 |
| Panama | .79 | .65 | .57 | .48 | .37 | .37 |
| Veraguas | .89 | .85 | .29 | .28 | .23 | .20 |
| Country Wide | .83 | | .47 | .41 | | .28 |

Notes: Labor Force includes individuals reported as employed and unemployed.
Work Force includes only individuals reported as employed.
+ Hours +Income includes only employed individuals reported with positive
hours and positive income. It excludes most self-employed and family
workers in agriculture.

completed his or her degree, or how many years were repeated, the measure of schooling is subject to bias. For both men and women, individuals who worked had higher education and were older than those of the same gender who were not working. Working females had one more year of education than working men on the average, and were less than a year younger. Five percent more working women had 4 to 6 years of university level education than working men. Sixty-one percent of working women lived in the province of Panama, compared to 47 percent of the non-working women and 56 percent of the working men. Fifty-six percent of the non-working men lived in a rural area, compared to only 37 percent of the working men. Only 24 percent of the working women lived in a rural area, while 47 percent of the non-working women did.

Working men had higher monthly earnings, more weekly hours and higher tenure than working women. The overall ratio of female to male hourly wage was .85. Working women were much more likely to work in the public sector (36 percent versus 28 percent), less likely to be self-employed (15 percent versus 21 percent), and more likely to work in a small firm (38 percent versus 34 percent) compared to working men.

**Table 16.2**
**Means (and Standard Deviations) of Sample Variables**

|  | Working Males | Non-Working Males | Working Females | Non-Working Females |
|---|---|---|---|---|
| **Age** | 35.57 (11.78) | 31.17 (15.46) | 34.81 (10.74) | 32.95 (14.85) |
| **Education (Years)** | 9.21 (4.40) | 7.33 (4.02) | 10.45 (4.35) | 7.76 (4.03) |
| **Education Level** |  |  |  |  |
| No Education | .03 (.17) | .07 (.25) | .02 (.13) | .07 (.25) |
| Incomplete Primary | .10 (.31) | .19 (.39) | .07 (.25) | .15 (.36) |
| Primary | .25 (.43) | .26 (.44) | .20 (.40) | .24 (.42) |
| Incomplete Secondary | .23 (.42) | .28 (.45) | .21 (.40) | .31 (.46) |
| Secondary | .18 (.39) | .11 (.32) | .22 (.42) | .13 (.34) |
| Less than 4 yrs. | .06 (.24) | .05 (.22) | .11 (.31) | .05 (.22) |
| 4 yrs. and above | .11 (.31) | .03 (.16) | .16 (.36) | .03 (.17) |
| Technical | .03 (.18) | .02 (.14) | .03 (.16) | .02 (.14) |
| **Region** |  |  |  |  |
| Bocas del Toro | .04 (.19) | .01 (.10) | .01 (.11) | .02 (.15) |
| Cocle | .05 (.23) | .10 (.30) | .05 (.22) | .08 (.27) |
| Colon | .07 (.26) | .06 (.25) | .07 (.26) | .08 (.27) |
| Chiriqui | .15 (.36) | .14 (.35) | .12 (.32) | .16 (.37) |

- continued

## Table 16.2
### Means (and Standard Deviations) of Sample Variables

| | Working Males | Non-Working Males | Working Females | Non-Working Females |
|---|---|---|---|---|
| Darien | .00 (.06) | .02 (.13) | .00 (.07) | .01 (.10) |
| Herrera | .04 (.19) | .06 (.23) | .04 (.20) | .05 (.22) |
| Los Santos | .03 (.18) | .05 (.21) | .03 (.17) | .04 (.20) |
| Panama | .56 (.50) | .43 (.50) | .61 (.49) | .47 (.50) |
| Veraguas | .05 (.22) | .14 (.34) | .05 (.22) | .09 (.29) |
| Rural | .37 (.48) | .56 (.50) | .24 (.43) | .47 (.50) |
| Primary Monthly Earnings (Balboas) | 341.86 (395.94) | | 274.15 (266.96) | |
| Weekly Hours | 42.76 (12.66) | | 40.14 (12.39) | |
| Primary Wage (Balboas/Hour) | 1.97 (2.43) | | 1.67 (1.60) | |
| Self Employed | .21 (.41) | .29 (.45) | .15 (.35) | .00 (.06) |
| Public Sector | .28 (.45) | | .36 (.48) | |
| Private Sector Employee | .49 (.40) | | .48 (.40) | |
| Employer | .02 (.15) | | .01 (.09) | |
| Small Firm | .34 (.47) | .46 (.50) | .38 (.49) | .07 (.25) |
| Tenure | 7.92 (8.01) | | 7.30 (7.15) | |

- continued

**Table 16.2**
Means (and Standard Deviations) of Sample Variables (continued)

|  | Working Males | Non-Working Males | Working Females | Non-Working Females |
|---|---|---|---|---|
| # People in Household | 5.10 (2.45) | 5.52 (2.63) | 4.96 (2.35) | 5.55 (2.52) |
| # of Children Aged 0 to 6 | .72 (.98) | .56 (.93) | .64 (.91) | .79 (1.05) |
| # of Children Aged 7 to 12 | .64 (.92) | .68 (.91) | .67 (.98) | .73 (.99) |
| Household Head | .65 (.48) | .36 (.48) | .22 (.42) | .10 (.31) |
| Household Monthly Primary Income (Balboas) | 581.98 (603.39) | 235.70 (422.08) | 710.95 (709.71) | 310.27 (445.45) |
| Total Monthly Household Income (Balboas) | 657.62 (695.60) | 340.51 (509.54) | 819.33 (814.20) | 413.20 (535.24) |
| # of Employed in Household | 1.96 (1.06) | 1.70 (1.27) | 2.11 (.99) | 1.45 (1.09) |
| N | 5,446 | 6,205 | 3,190 | 8,355 |

Notes:   Participation rate is .83 for men, .41 for women. Forty-seven percent of men and 28 percent of women have positive hours and positive income and are defined as "working."

Regarding household characteristics, both working women and men came from smaller households than non-working individuals. In the sample, there was not enough information to determine which adults were the actual parents of the children in the household. Therefore, as a proxy, the number of children in the household was used. Working men had more children aged 0 to 6 than non-working men, while working women had fewer children than non-working women. Working men and women were more likely to be household heads than non-working men and women. Also, working women had significantly higher household primary income and household income than working men. Non-working women had higher household income than non-working men. There was no variable in the survey for marital status.

Table 16.3A presents the wage differentials between men and women, broken down by sector and level of education. In every case except in the employer sector for workers with primary education (which includes only 9 women), the male wage rate exceeds the female wage rate. The employers' wage rates tend to be highest for both men and women. For men and women, the public sector is better paid than both the private sector and the self-employed sector. In every sector except employers, the ratio tends to be low for both primary and less educated and for university educated. It is interesting to note that self-employed women with some secondary or completed secondary education do well compared with men with similar education; the ratio is .89. For the public sector and self-employed categories, the university-educated women actually have the lowest wage ratio in the sector.

**Table 16.3A**
Wage by Schooling Level
(Balboas per hour)

| | Public | | | Private Employee | | |
|---|---|---|---|---|---|---|
| | Male | Female | F/M Ratio | Male | Female | F/M Ratio |
| Some Primary | 1.57 | 1.14 | .73 | .94 | .60 | .63 |
| Primary | 1.66 | 1.28 | .77 | 1.10 | .62 | .56 |
| Some Secondary | 2.03 | 1.80 | .87 | 1.34 | .86 | .64 |
| Secondary | 2.75 | 2.13 | .77 | 1.79 | 1.52 | .85 |
| University | 4.57 | 3.22 | .70 | 3.34 | 2.43 | .73 |
| Technical | 2.59 | 1.83 | .71 | 1.73 | 1.03 | .58 |

| | Employer | | | Self-Employed | | |
|---|---|---|---|---|---|---|
| | Male | Female | F/M Ratio | Male | Female | F/M Ratio |
| Some Primary | 2.51 | .93 | .37 | 1.11 | .72 | .65 |
| Primary | 2.18 | 2.44 | 1.12 | 1.16 | .89 | .77 |
| Some Secondary | 2.49 | 2.41 | .97 | 1.37 | 1.22 | .89 |
| Secondary | 6.26 | 3.30 | .53 | 1.58 | 1.41 | .89 |
| University | 7.31 | 6.45 | .88 | 3.11 | 1.75 | .56 |
| Technical | N/A | .83 | | 1.02 | .85 | .83 |

Wages for women with little education are significantly higher if self-employed than if a private sector employee. For women with secondary school level education and above, private sector employees earn more than the self-employed. For men, the pattern is similar with self-employed workers earning more than private sector workers at low levels of education, and vice versa at higher levels of education, but the difference is not as great as for women. This implies that access to the formal sector is difficult for those with low education.

Table 16.3B presents the wage differentials by region and education level. The ratio of the female wage to the male wage tends to be highest at the secondary school level across regions. Also, for all levels of schooling, the ratio is lower for Panama and Colon, the most urbanized regions of the country and the two regions with the highest average hourly wage. Women have higher overall average wages than men in Bocas del Toro, Chiriqui, Los Santos, and Veraguas, which, with the exception of Veraguas, are middle income provinces.[19] Darien, the poorest province, has very low female to male wage ratios for those with less than primary education, some secondary education, and a university education. The ratio of female to male wages tends to be more favorable in middle income provinces for workers with intermediate levels of education.

---

[19] The classifications of regions as high, middle, and low income are from Heckman and Hotz (1986), p. 521.

**Table 16.3B**
Wages by Region, Sex, and Schooling Level
(Balboas per hour)

| | Overall | Less than Primary | Primary | Some Secondary | Secondary | University | Technical |
|---|---|---|---|---|---|---|---|
| **Bocas del Toro** | | | | | | | |
| Male (2.4%) | 1.58 | 1.30 | 1.53 | 1.53 | 2.19 | 2.43 | N/A |
| Female (.5%) | 1.60 | 1.08 | 1.40 | 1.36 | 1.93 | 1.89 | N/A |
| Ratio F/M | 1.01 | .83 | .92 | .89 | .88 | .78 | |
| **Cocle** | | | | | | | |
| Male (3.3%) | 1.23 | .86 | .95 | 1.11 | 1.63 | 3.24 | 1.29 |
| Female (2.0%) | 1.06 | .48 | .51 | 1.07 | 1.75 | 2.47 | 1.40 |
| Ratio F/M | .86 | .56 | .54 | .96 | 1.07 | .76 | 1.09 |
| **Colon** | | | | | | | |
| Male (4.6%) | 2.07 | 1.07 | 1.65 | 1.68 | 2.69 | 2.82 | 1.19 |
| Female (2.8%) | 1.52 | .56 | .79 | 1.12 | 1.88 | 2.20 | 1.08 |
| Ratio F/M | .73 | .52 | .48 | .67 | .70 | .78 | .91 |
| **Chiriqui** | | | | | | | |
| Male (9.1%) | 1.27 | .97 | 1.05 | 1.09 | 1.38 | 3.03 | 1.97 |
| Female (4.6%) | 1.44 | .77 | .86 | .97 | 1.96 | 2.59 | .87 |
| Ratio F/M | 1.13 | .79 | .82 | .89 | 1.42 | .85 | .44 |
| **Darien** | | | | | | | |
| Male (.3%) | 1.88 | 1.43 | 1.59 | 1.96 | 1.86 | 5.54 | 1.22 |
| Female (.2%) | 1.21 | .60 | 1.15 | .98 | 1.59 | 1.45 | N/A |
| Ratio F/M | .64 | .42 | .72 | .50 | .85 | .26 | |
| **Herrera** | | | | | | | |
| Male (2.4%) | 1.43 | .79 | 1.08 | 1.15 | 1.83 | 3.54 | 1.19 |
| Female (1.7%) | 1.33 | .60 | .52 | .93 | 1.73 | 2.87 | .79 |
| Ratio F/M | .93 | .76 | .48 | .81 | .95 | .81 | .66 |
| **Los Santos** | | | | | | | |
| Male (2.1%) | 1.26 | .78 | .87 | 1.30 | 1.86 | 4.03 | 1.62 |
| Female (1.1%) | 1.34 | .54 | .58 | 1.05 | 1.79 | 3.16 | 1.72 |
| Ratio F/M | 1.06 | .69 | .67 | .81 | .96 | .78 | 1.06 |
| **Panama** | | | | | | | |
| Male (34.3%) | 2.35 | 1.27 | 1.40 | 1.70 | 2.38 | 4.47 | 1.87 |
| Female (23.6%) | 1.83 | .83 | .88 | 1.25 | 1.79 | 3.05 | 1.23 |
| Ratio F/M | .78 | .65 | .63 | .74 | .75 | .68 | .66 |
| **Veraguas** | | | | | | | |
| Male (3.3%) | 1.39 | .70 | 1.05 | .95 | 1.78 | 3.17 | 2.37 |
| Female (2.0%) | 1.48 | .54 | .71 | 1.25 | 1.63 | 2.71 | .42 |
| Ratio F/M | 1.06 | .77 | .68 | 1.32 | .92 | .85 | .18 |

Note:   Percentages in parentheses represent percentage of all workers in each group.

Wage differentials between men and women by occupation are shown in Table 16.3C. Men are concentrated in artisanry, agriculture, and personal services, while over half of the females are employed as professionals and teachers or personal service providers. Education levels are lowest in agriculture, personal services, and artisans. The ratio of female to male wage is low (less than 65 percent) for personal services, sales people, and artisans. These professions make up about 50 percent of the female labor force. Professions with a very high ratio (agriculture and transport) make up a very small share of the female work force. The wage for female office workers and unclassified workers is higher than for male workers in the same categories. In each case where the female wage is higher than the male wage, females in that category also have more years of schooling than the males. In some of the categories, males make more than females, but also have higher schooling, such as personal services, sales, artisanry, and personal services, which could explain the differential. For the categories of professionals and administrators, where there is little difference in schooling or females have more schooling, the male wage rate is higher, and that is not readily explained. However, the grouping "professionals" includes school teachers, who are low paid compared to others with university degrees. The differential has a large impact on women with university education and very low education.

## Table 16.3C
### Wage Differentials by Occupation

| Profession | Male as a percentage of | | | Female as a percentage of | | | |
| | Wage | Work Force | Yrs. Ed. | Wage | Work Force | Yrs. Ed. | Ratio Fem/ Male Wage |
|---|---|---|---|---|---|---|---|
| Professionals | 4.46 | 11.3 | 14.84 | 3.05 | 20.8 | 14.80 | .69 |
| Administrators | 3.83 | 7.8 | 12.39 | 3.38 | 3.7 | 13.48 | .88 |
| Office Workers | 1.79 | 6.2 | 11.29 | 1.89 | 24.2 | 12.32 | 1.06 |
| Sales People | 1.71 | 9.4 | 9.24 | .99 | 10.0 | 8.52 | .58 |
| Agriculture | .92 | 14.2 | 5.38 | 1.72 | .5 | 5.52 | 1.87 |
| Transport | 1.63 | 9.5 | 8.62 | 2.98 | .1 | 11.51 | 1.83 |
| Artisans Clothing, Furniture | 1.70 | 18.6 | 8.80 | .89 | 5.7 | 8.62 | .52 |
| Other Artisans | 1.34 | 3.6 | 7.43 | 1.48 | 1.2 | 9.10 | 1.10 |
| Unclassified Workers | 1.22 | 6.7 | 7.43 | 1.26 | 1.2 | 8.09 | 1.03 |
| Personal Services | 1.26 | 12.6 | 7.82 | .78 | 32.5 | 7.04 | .62 |
| Overall | 1.97 | 100 | 9.21 | 1.67 | 100 | 10.45 | .85 |

## 4.  Determinants of Work Force Participation

In this section, the results of a univariate probit regression are discussed.  The probit was estimated separately for men and women.  The need to estimate the probits arises because the working men and women are a selected subset of all men and women.  They are people who obtained wage offers higher than their reservation wage.  Reservation wages are affected by tastes, age, and schooling.  For example, an individual with high education would have a higher reservation wage because of raised expectations and would be less willing to take a lower paying job than someone with low education.  A woman who has young children would be less likely to work than a woman who has no children because her time in the household is more valuable to her.  An individual in his or her teens would be less likely to be in the work force because of opportunities for schooling, and a long work life ahead to earn a return on schooling.  A man in an urban area may have a lower reservation wage than a man in a rural area because in urban areas, goods that may have been readily available from a small plot of land in a rural area must be bought.  For example, an urban worker may have to buy the fruits, subsistence food or firewood which he could gather or cultivate easily if he lived in the countryside.

In order to obtain unbiased estimates for the return to schooling, experience, hours, and tenure, it is necessary to correct for selectivity.  This is done using Heckman's (1979) two-step procedure.  The probit includes as independent variables schooling levels, age levels, regions, and variables that represent the structure of the household.  The inverse Mill's ratio (Lambda) is computed in order to account for the unseen variables that affect the decision to work.  Then, Lambda can be included as a regressor in an ordinary least squares (OLS) regression.  A positive value of the Lambda coefficient implies that characteristics that make an individual more likely to be in the work force also lead to higher earnings, while a negative value means that characteristics associated with staying out of the work force imply higher earnings.  An example of a characteristic that would explain a negative Lambda coefficient is higher education, because it increases the reservation wage, decreasing the probability of work force participation, while higher schooling also earns a compensating differential in earnings.

Because such a high percentage of men do not have hours or income reported, a probit regression is estimated for men as well as women.  The probit for men includes the same independent variables as the probit for women in order to make comparisons between them.  A priori, the researcher would expect that the number of children would have a strong negative effect on the female participation decision, because females traditionally carry more responsibility in the household for child care.  Living in a rural area would be likely to decrease participation for both males and females.  One would expect the age group to have less of an effect on male participation rates than female rates because male participation rates are consistently high, while females have more elastic labor supply.

Tables 16.4A and 16.4B present the results for the probits for men and women.  Table 16.5 presents a simulation where the effect of each characteristic on the probability of work force participation is examined.  All other values are held at the sample mean, so that the effect of only the relevant characteristic can be determined.  First, it is evident for every characteristic that the probability of a given male being in the work force is higher than for a given female.  Looking at education levels, for females the likelihood of working increases with higher education levels.  In Table 16.5, participation rates increase from 10 percent for those with no education to 48 percent for those with over 4 years of university education.  These results contrast with the results for males, where those with technical education have the highest likelihood of participation

## Table 16.4A
### Probit Results for Male Work Force Participation

| Variable | Coefficient | T-Ratio | Partial Derivative |
|---|---|---|---|
| Constant | -2.808 | -29.08 | |
| **Education Levels** | | | |
| Some Primary | .200 | 2.80 | .079 |
| Complete Primary | .560 | 8.06 | .223 |
| Some Secondary | .651 | 8.80 | .259 |
| Secondary | .737 | 9.47 | .294 |
| Technical | .812 | 7.42 | .324 |
| less than 4 Yrs. Univ. | .453 | 4.93 | .181 |
| 4+ Yrs. Univ. | .683 | 7.32 | .272 |
| # of Children 0 to 6 | .041 | 2.81 | .016 |
| # of Children 7 to 12 | -.034 | -2.35 | -.013 |
| **Age Group** | | | |
| Age 20 to 24 | .902 | 18.71 | .360 |
| Age 25 to 29 | 1.158 | 21.88 | .462 |
| Age 30 to 34 | 1.186 | 20.05 | .473 |
| Age 35 to 39 | 1.210 | 19.11 | .482 |
| Age 40 to 44 | 1.150 | 17.28 | .458 |
| Age 45 to 49 | 1.014 | 14.70 | .404 |
| Age 50 to 54 | .826 | 11.44 | .329 |
| Age 55 to 59 | .649 | 8.26 | .259 |
| Age 60 to 65 | -.030 | -.39 | -.012 |
| **Region** | | | |
| Bocas del Toro | 1.358 | 12.81 | .541 |
| Cocle | .182 | 2.78 | .072 |
| Colon | .632 | 9.15 | .252 |
| Chiriqui | .675 | 11.88 | .269 |
| Darien | -.338 | -2.28 | -.135 |
| Herrera | .243 | 3.23 | .097 |
| Los Santos | .469 | 6.00 | .187 |
| Panama | .493 | 9.54 | .196 |
| Rural | -.276 | -8.32 | -.110 |
| Head of Household | .900 | 23.30 | .359 |
| Total Household Income | .000 | 13.69 | .000 |
| Number of workers in Household | .270 | 21.13 | .107 |

Notes:   Dependent Variable for probit is whether individual reported positive hours and positive income. Base group is no education, age 15 to 19, living in Veraguas.

### Table 16.4B
#### Probit Results for Female Work Force Participation

| Variable | Coefficient | T-Ratio | Partial Derivative |
|---|---|---|---|
| Constant | -2.740 | -24.57 | |
| **Education Levels** | | | |
| Some Primary | .206 | 2.28 | .064 |
| Complete Primary | .609 | 7.10 | .191 |
| Some Secondary | .489 | 5.56 | .153 |
| Secondary | .857 | 9.51 | .269 |
| Technical | .649 | 5.44 | .204 |
| less than 4 Yrs. Univ. | .837 | 8.43 | .263 |
| 4+ Yrs. Univ. | 1.224 | 12.15 | .384 |
| # of Children 0 to 6 | -.098 | -6.27 | -.030 |
| # of Children 7 to 12 | -.047 | -2.97 | -.014 |
| **Age Group** | | | |
| Age 20 to 24 | .460 | 8.28 | .144 |
| Age 25 to 29 | .850 | 14.71 | .267 |
| Age 30 to 34 | 1.151 | 19.43 | .361 |
| Age 35 to 39 | 1.206 | 20.13 | .379 |
| Age 40 to 44 | 1.010 | 16.13 | .317 |
| Age 45 to 49 | .826 | 12.26 | .259 |
| Age 50 to 54 | .426 | 5.78 | .134 |
| Age 55 to 59 | .056 | .65 | .017 |
| Age 60 to 65 | -.113 | -1.24 | -.035 |
| **Region** | | | |
| Bocas del Toro | -.109 | -.86 | -.034 |
| Cocle | .110 | 1.40 | .034 |
| Colon | .190 | 2.46 | .059 |
| Chiriqui | .035 | .52 | .011 |
| Darien | .057 | .31 | .018 |
| Herrera | .161 | 1.86 | .050 |
| Los Santos | .181 | 1.95 | .057 |
| Panama | .125 | 2.06 | .039 |
| Rural | -.388 | -10.87 | -.122 |
| Head of Household | 1.008 | 22.91 | .316 |
| Total Household Income | .000 | 9.94 | .000 |
| Number of workers in Household | .450 | 32.05 | .141 |

Notes:    Dependent variable for probit is whether individual reported positive hours and positive income. Base group is no education, age 15 to 19, living in province of Veraguas.

**Table 16.5**
Predicted Participation Probabilities by Characteristic

| Characteristic | Male | Female |
|---|---|---|
| **Education** | | |
| No Education | .30 | .10 |
| Some Primary | .37 | .14 |
| Complete Primary | .51 | .25 |
| Some Secondary | .55 | .21 |
| Complete Secondary | .58 | .34 |
| Technical | .61 | .26 |
| 1 to 3 Yrs. University | .47 | .33 |
| 4 to 6 Yrs. University | .56 | .48 |
| **Number of Children Aged 0 to 6** | | |
| None | .49 | .27 |
| One | .51 | .24 |
| Two | .53 | .21 |
| Three | .54 | .18 |
| **Number of Children Aged 7 to 12** | | |
| None | .51 | .26 |
| One | .50 | .24 |
| Two | .49 | .23 |
| Three | .47 | .21 |
| **Age** | | |
| 15 to 19 | .22 | .10 |
| 20 to 24 | .55 | .20 |
| 25 to 29 | .65 | .33 |
| 30 to 34 | .66 | .44 |
| 35 to 39 | .67 | .46 |
| 40 to 44 | .64 | .39 |
| 45 to 49 | .59 | .32 |
| 50 to 54 | .52 | .19 |
| 55 to 59 | .45 | .11 |
| 60 to 65 | .21 | .08 |
| **Region** | | |
| Bocas del Toro | .82 | .18 |
| Cocle | .40 | .25 |
| Colon | .57 | .27 |
| Chiriqui | .59 | .22 |
| Darien | .22 | .23 |
| Herrera | .42 | .26 |
| Los Santos | .51 | .27 |
| Panama | .52 | .25 |
| Veraguas | .33 | .21 |
| **Live Rural Area** | | |
| No | .55 | .30 |
| Yes | .45 | .18 |
| **Household Head** | | |
| No | .33 | .20 |
| Yes | .67 | .57 |
| **Number of Workers in Household** | | |
| None | .31 | .08 |
| One | .41 | .16 |
| Two | .52 | .30 |
| Three | .63 | .47 |

at 61 percent. For men, this could reflect very high reservation wages for those who attended the university due to raised expectations, while women with university education have a low reservation wage due to a strong preference to work outside the home.

Another contrast is the effect of the number of children on work force participation. Women with children aged 0 to 6 are less likely to be in the labor force than women with no children, while men with young children are more likely to be in the labor force than men without children. The probability of participation for females drops from 27 percent for women with no children aged 0 to 6 to 18 percent for women with three children in that age group. For men, the probability increases as the number of young children increases from 49 percent with none to 54 percent with three small children. Women are caring for children in the home, while men are earning outside the home to support the family financially. The number of children aged 7 to 12 affects men and women about equally. The effect is small; for both men and women the probability drops about 4 percent when the number of older children is raised from none to three.

As for the effects of age, both men and women have peak work force participation rates between 35 and 39 years of age. The female pattern is more concave than the male pattern, with female participation rates dropping at a younger age than male participation. The probability for women drops from 32 percent to 19 percent between the 45 to 49 and the 50 to 54 age groups. For men, a drop of this magnitude occurs between the 55 to 59 and 60 to 65 age group, where the participation drops 14 percentage points. This is expected given the discussion above, and given econometric labor supply studies, which find that female labor supply is more elastic than male labor supply.[20]

The regional variables affect male participation rates strongly, while for females, only 2 of the 8 regional variables are significant at the 5 percent level. The two significant variables, Panama and Colon, are the most urbanized provinces in Panama. For males, every regional variable is significant at the 5 percent level, with probability of participation the highest at 82 percent in Bocas del Toro, a middle income province, and the lowest at 22 percent in Darien, a low income province. This can be explained by the fact that men in the poorer regions are more likely to be self-employed agricultural workers, and therefore excluded from the sample of working men. Both male and female participation is affected by whether the individual lives in an urban or rural area; for both the coefficient is negative and significant, and the effect is larger for women. Living in an urban area implies for men an 11 percent greater probability of working and for females, a 12 percent greater probability of working than living in a rural area. This is consistent with the prediction made above.

The variables which proxy household structure, total household income, whether the individual is the head of the household, and the number of occupied people in the household, are all positive and significant determinants of both male and female participation rates. For women, the probability of working increases from 20 percent to 57 percent if she is a household head. For males, the corresponding percentages are 33 percent and 67 percent. For both men and women, with more workers in the household, the probability of the individual working increases, and the increase is more for women than men.

What effect do these variables representing household structure have on labor force participation? A member of a richer household is more likely to be working than a member of a poorer household. The richer have greater access to the formal labor market. Once again, this could

---

[20]   See Killingsworth and Heckman, (1986).

be due to the missing data for poorer farmers and their families. As for the females, there are probably interactions between high education level and high household income, since well-educated women tend to marry well-educated men with high earning potential. Household headship is an important determinant because household heads bear more of the financial responsibilities in the family. Lastly, it is not self-evident why the number of occupied people in the household has a positive effect. With more employed members of the household, a given individual has less need to work, but families with many workers may be poorer families that must send children and women into the work force in order to maintain their living standard. It could also mean that there is a family "work ethic" with members preferring to work outside the home.

There are important differences between men and women in how characteristics affect work force participation. The differences are greatest with respect to number of small children, education levels, and regions. In the next section, the results of these probit regressions are used in earnings functions to correct for selectivity.

## 5.    Earnings Functions

In Mincer's (1974) model to estimate earnings regressions, the log of earnings is regressed on schooling, experience, and experience squared. The earnings function is concave and increasing in schooling and experience. In this section, the model is used to estimate separate male and female earnings functions, both correcting for selectivity and using the most basic model.

In the case of Panama, it is possible to use tenure instead of potential experience as the regressor. The latter experience variable is usually calculated by taking age, subtracting the years of schooling and subtracting six, which is the age when schooling is assumed to begin. This proxy is likely to be upwardly biased, especially for women, because it does not take into account years spent out of the work force since the completion of schooling, nor the deterioration of experience when a person stops working for an extended period of time. Women are likely to have interrupted careers if they have had children. For this reason, tenure, which is the amount of time spent at the present job, is a better proxy for women of human capital acquired on the job than the estimate of experience. The drawback of using tenure is that if workers change jobs frequently, it discounts accumulated experience which transfers between jobs. In Panama this presents less of a problem than in the United States where workers are mobile and change jobs readily. There is a high unemployment problem, which makes workers less likely to quit jobs and search for better ones.

Log of monthly earnings is the dependent variable, while years of schooling, tenure, tenure squared, and the log of monthly hours are the independent variables. Including the log of hours on the right hand side of the equation rather than using the log of hourly wage as the left hand side variable allows the value of the elasticity of earnings to hours to differ from one. To correct for selectivity, according to the Heckman procedure, the inverse Mill's ratio (Lambda) is included as an independent variable in the earnings regression. Table 16.6 presents the results of the regressions for males and females, both including Lambda and excluding Lambda.

From the table, it is evident in the uncorrected regressions that females earn a higher return to schooling and tenure, while men have a higher elasticity of log earnings to log hours. Both exhibit a concave earnings profile, with decreasing returns to tenure. The rate of return to education for females is almost 3 percent higher than for males, and the rate of return to tenure

### Table 16.6
### Earnings Functions

| | Males | Males (Corrected for Selectivity) | Females | Females (Corrected for Selectivity) |
|---|---|---|---|---|
| Constant | .722 | 1.951 | .455 | 1.098 |
| | (6.130) | (16.771) | (3.982) | (9.018) |
| Schooling | .097 | .072 | .119 | .098 |
| (Years) | (47.692) | (27.312) | (46.360) | (30.363) |
| Log Monthly | .659 | .561 | .599 | .589 |
| Hours | (29.187) | (27.366) | (26.741) | (27.169) |
| Tenure | .079 | .056 | .103 | .089 |
| | (27.688) | (19.729) | (25.384) | (21.578) |
| Tenure | -.002 | -.001 | -.003 | -.002 |
| Squared | (-16.866) | (-11.016) | (-17.131) | (-14.594) |
| Lambda | | -.679 | | -.389 |
| | | (-20.586) | | (-12.276) |
| Adjusted R-Squared | .456 | .524 | .605 | .629 |
| N | 5,445 | 5,445 | 3,189 | 3,189 |

Notes: Numbers in parenthesis are t-ratios.
Dependent variable is log of monthly income.

is about 2.5 percent higher. A one percent increase in hours leads to a .66 percent increase in earnings for men, and a similar increase in hours leads to a .60 percent increase in earnings for females. The fit of the regression is better for females than males--the R squared is .61 for the female regression and .46 for the male regression.

When Lambda is added to the male regression, the return to schooling drops from 9.7 percent to 7.2 percent. Similarly, the return to tenure decreases from 7.9 percent to 5.6 percent. The elasticity of earnings to hours also decreases. The coefficient on Lambda is negative and significant, which means that characteristics that earn a higher return also make a man less likely to be in the work force. This could occur because men with high educational levels are less likely to work due to a high reservation wage and lack of jobs which meet their qualifications.

For females, when Lambda is included in the regression, returns to schooling drop 2 percentage points from 11.9 percent to 9.8 percent. Returns to tenure drop from 10.3 percent to 8.9 percent. The elasticity of wages to hours worked falls marginally from .6 to .59. The coefficient on Lambda is also negative and significant, but the value of the coefficient is much less negative than for the men. Again, the characteristics women have which allow them to earn a higher return make it less likely that they will be observed in the work force. Women with qualifications that earn high returns in the work force have a high reservation wage and prefer to stay at home. The negative Lambda could also be caused by high unemployment rates, which are higher for women than men.

In Table 16.7, unemployment rates for men and women by education levels are shown. They are based on what the person reported in the household survey, and indicate the proportion of those who say they are unemployed over the total who report being employed plus the unemployed. Unemployment rates are highest for those who have secondary school level education. They are very high for women and reach 29 percent for those with a secondary school level education. Surprisingly, they are lowest for those with low education, but these workers are likely to be self-employed, or family workers, and therefore report themselves as being employed, while they may not have reported hours or income.

**Table 16.7**
Unemployment Rates by Education Levels

| Education Level | Males | Females |
|-----------------|-------|---------|
| Less than Primary | 6.4 | 13.7 |
| Primary | 9.6 | 15.3 |
| Incomplete Secondary | 21.6 | 28.3 |
| Secondary | 20.1 | 29.0 |
| University | 14.5 | 16.7 |
| Technical | 24.9 | 21.6 |

Notes:    Unemployment rates are based on respondents' answers, and are the ratio of unemployed to the labor force participants. Participants include both those reported as employed and as unemployed.

In Table 16.8, the results of an alternative earnings specification including the sector of employment are presented. Including the variables self-employed, employer, and public sector worker does not have a large effect on the coefficients of the other variables. Compared with Table 16.6, returns to education fall by about one percentage point for men and women without correcting for selectivity, while they fall about two percentage points for women when correcting for selectivity. Returns to tenure are about one percentage point lower for males and two percent lower for females. For men, those who are self-employed earn between 23 and 25 percent less than private sector employees, while working in the public sector increases wages by between 27 and 26 percent. Employers earn the highest wages, earning 51 to 58 percent more than the base group. When Lambda is included in the regression, it decreases the coefficient on the sectors slightly. For women, being self-employed implies 35 to 36 percent lower earnings, while working in the public sector earns a 34 percent premium compared to private sector employees. Again, the highest earnings are gained by employers, ranging from a 57 to 62 percent premium. In regressions both corrected and uncorrected for selectivity, the sector choice has a larger impact on women than men.

### Table 16.8
### Alternative Earnings Functions

| | Males | Males (Corrected for Selectivity) | Females | Females (Corrected for) Selectivity |
|---|---|---|---|---|
| Constant | 1.098 | 2.322 | 1.2489 | 1.912 |
| | (9.447) | (20.374) | (9.875) | (9.875) |
| Schooling | .087 | .062 | .1011 | .080 |
| (Years) | (42.355) | (23.831) | (38.880) | (24.985) |
| Log Monthly | .611 | .513 | .4828 | .469 |
| Hours | (27.678) | (25.783) | (20.351) | (20.656) |
| Tenure | .0640 | .042 | .0799 | .066 |
| | (22.161) | (14.753) | (19.484) | (16.043) |
| Tenure | -.001 | -.001 | -.0020 | -.002 |
| Squared | (-13.056) | (-7.205) | (-13.099) | (-10.553) |
| Public Sector[a] | .275 | .261 | .3444 | .339 |
| | (12.313) | (12.169) | (13.218) | (13.281) |
| Employer[a] | .586 | .507 | .6233 | .566 |
| | (10.275) | (8.767) | (5.621) | (5.167) |
| Self-Employed[a] | -.231 | -.249 | -.3455 | -.358 |
| | (-10.178) | (-11.803) | (-9.800) | (-10.486) |
| Lambda | | -.673 | | -.389 |
| | | (-20.926) | | (-12.791) |
| Adjusted R-Squared | .497 | .564 | .6463 | .670 |
| N | 5,445 | 5,445 | 3,189 | 3,189 |

a.   Base group is private sector employees.
Notes: Numbers in parenthesis are t-ratios.
       Dependent variable is the log of monthly earnings.

## 6.   Discrimination

The upper bound on wage discrimination can be found using Oaxaca's (1973) equations:

$$\ln(\text{Earnings}_m) - \ln(\text{Earnings}_f) = X_m(b_m - b_f) + b_f(X_m - X_f) \tag{1}$$
$$= X_f(b_m - b_f) + b_m(X_m - X_f) \tag{2}$$

Where $X_m$ represents the means of the dependent variables for males, $X_f$ represents the means of the dependent variables for females, $b_m$ is the matrix of estimated coefficients for males, and

$b_f$ is the matrix of estimated coefficients for females. Both equations give the differential between the predicted values of earnings for males and females, $b_m X_m - b_f X_f$. The first term on the right hand side in equation 1 gives the part of the differential that is explained by differences in how male and female human capital endowments are rewarded in the labor market (wage structure) evaluated at the male means. The second term calculates the part of the differential due to differences in the means of the dependent variables of men and women (endowments), multiplied by the female coefficients. Equation 2 is the same breakdown, but calculated at the female means rather than the male means. There is an index number problem with the two equations. However, it makes more sense to evaluate the differential at the male means, since this paper is examining potential discrimination against women.

In calculating the percentage of the differential due to endowments and to wage structure, the means of the entire sample of men and women are used for schooling, and the means of working men and women are used for log hours and tenure. Both working and non-working individuals have reported schooling, but only working men and women have positive hours and years of tenure. Neither the Mill's ratio terms (Lambda) nor their coefficients are included in the equation because the parameter of interest is the mean for the whole sample, not just working men and women.[21]

Table 16.9 shows the calculations of the Oaxaca decomposition using the regression coefficients correcting for selectivity. There is not a large difference between the calculations evaluated at the male means (equation 1) and at the female means (equation 2). From 14 to 15 percent of the differential between male and female wages can be explained by endowments, while 85 to 86 percent are explained by the wage structure.

However, it should be noted that the differential due to wage structure is an upper bound on discrimination. If there are attributes not measured here that are valuable in the labor market, and men have these attributes in greater quantity or quality than women, the upper bound on discrimination will be upwardly biased. However, if there are societal characteristics that are not measured here preventing women from entering the labor force or inhibiting women from acquiring human capital, the measure of discrimination will be underestimated.

**Table 16.9**

Decomposition of Sex Earnings Differential

| Specification | Percentage of the Differential Due to Differences in | | |
| --- | --- | --- | --- |
| | Endowments | Wage Structure | Total |
| Corrected for Selectivity | | | |
| Equation 1 | 14.7 | 85.3 | 37 |
| Equation 2 | 13.9 | 86.1 | 37 |

Note: The decomposition is based on the results of Table 16.6.

---

[21]   See the chapter in this volume by Psacharopoulos on Venezuela.

## 7. Discussion

Despite high educational attainments for women, Panama's female participation rate is low. A very important impediment to equality is difficulty in finding a job indicated by the incredibly high unemployment rate women face. This is especially a problem for women with secondary level education.

The overall ratio of female to male wage in Panama is favorable compared with other Latin American countries, such as Uruguay, Venezuela and Peru.[22] However, at the minimum 85 percent of the differential cannot be explained by differences in endowments between men and women, and can be attributed to wage structure discrimination.

A topic of further study would be whether the Labor Code has impacted female wages favorably. The evidence presented here indicates that for women who have jobs, the wage gap is small relative to other countries, but that the labor code also discourages employers from hiring women because they must provide benefits that are specific to women. Employers perceive that it is cheaper to hire men. The code could be reformed to provide more flexibility to employers for providing maternity benefits. Laws designed to help women may actually hurt them.

The choice to work as an employee or to be self-employed has an important implication for earnings for both men and women. Individuals with lower levels of education seem to earn higher wages as self-employed workers than as employees. To alleviate high unemployment, credit could be extended to women who would like to be self-employed. However, in the long run, sound economic growth would provide private sector jobs. In the sample, only a small percentage of working women are self-employed (15 percent) and with a big increase in the number of self-employed women, undoubtedly their wages would decrease. With high enough economic growth, employment in the private sector would increase and wages would increase to reflect productivity growth.

Labor market discrimination seems to be more of a factor for women with very low educational levels and relatively high educational levels. This could be because given the high unemployment rates for women with secondary education, only very qualified or determined women can get jobs, and, therefore, their wages are a higher percentage of men's wages. Better enforcement of anti-discrimination laws would help those women that are private and public sector employees earn a wage more equal to male employees.

---

[22] See Khandker, Arends, and Winter (in this volume) who report the ratio to be about .67, .75 and .78 in Peru, Uruguay, and Venezuela, respectively.

# References

Economist Intelligence Unit. *Nicaragua, Costa Rica, Panama: Country Profile 1991-92*. London: Economist Intelligence Unit Limited, 1991.

Heckman, J.J. "Sample Selection Bias as a Specification Error." *Econometrica*, Vol. 47, no. 1 (1979). pp. 153-161.

Heckman, J.J. and V.J. Hotz, "An Investigation of the Labor Market Earnings of Panamanian Males: Evaluating the Sources of Inequality." *Journal of Human Resources*, Vol. 21 (1986) pp. 507-42.

Killingsworth, M.R. and J.J. Heckman, "Female Labor Supply: A Survey" in O. Ashenfelter and R. Layard (eds.) *Handbook of Labor Economics*. Amsterdam: North Holland, 1986, pp. 103-204.

Mincer, J. *Schooling, Experience, and Earnings*. New York: Columbia University Press, 1974.

Oaxaca, R. "Male-female Wage Differentials in Urban Labor Markets." *International Economic Review*, Vol. 14, no. 1 (1973). pp. 693-701.

Spinanger, D. "Labor Market in Panama: an Analysis of the Employment Impact of the Labor Code." *Kiel Working Papers*, No. 221, December 1984.

Tollefson, S. "The Economy" in S. Meditz and D. Hanratty (eds.) *Panama: a Country Study*. Washington, DC: United States Government, Department of the Army, 1989. pp. 123-171.

World Bank. *Panama: Structural Change and Growth Prospects*. Washington, DC: World Bank, 1985.

World Bank. *Second Structural Adjustment Project--Panama*. Latin America Division, Panama Desk, 1986.

World Bank. *Social Indicators of Development 1990*. Baltimore, MD: Johns Hopkins University Press, 1990. p. 238-9.

World Bank. *World Development Report*. New York: Oxford University Press, 1991.

# 17

# Women's Labor Market Participation and Male-Female Wage Differences in Peru

*Shahidur R. Khandker[1]*

## 1. Introduction

This study uses Peruvian Living Standard Survey (PLSS) data to estimate women's labor market (i.e., wage) participation, and male-female differences in productivity (measured by wages). The purpose is to (1) identify those characteristics that enable some women, though not as many men, to participate in the wage sector, (2) determine the private economic returns to education by gender, and (3) evaluate how much of the male-female wage gap is due to differences in human capital. Identifying the constraints to women's labor market participation and productivity is an important policy exercise in Peru where female participation rates are below the average for the region (Suarez-Berenguela, 1987).

Results indicate that gender differences in human capital, such as education and experience, account for some of the observed differences in labor market participation and productivity. Estimates of the returns to education show the private rate to be generally higher for women, especially for secondary school level and rural areas. However, school enrollment rates for females are lower than for males, indicating that parents invest less in female than male children.

The study uses a household model framework (Becker, 1965) that provides an estimable labor market participation equation. This equation can help estimate the relative effect of individual, household, and market factors in influencing an individual's labor market participation. The study uses, in addition, a human capital model as per Becker (1964) and Mincer (1974) to analyze wages in the wage sector. The focus here is on human capital variables such as education and experience as determinants of productivity. Wage estimates provide measures of the private rates of returns to education for men and women and can be used to identify how much variation in male-female wages is due to gender differences in education and other job-related characteristics.

The human capital model, however, may not satisfactorily explain variations in wages since productivity is likely to be determined by a number of factors including, but not limited to, human capital variables. A satisfactory analysis, therefore, requires identifying potentially

---

[1] Comments on an earlier draft by George Psacharopoulos, Zafiris Tzannatos, and Indermit Gill are gratefully acknowledged. I am also indebted to Jorge Castillo who provided excellent assistance in analyzing the data. The usual disclaimer applies.

observable characteristics other than human capital that can affect an individual's wage. Unfortunately, these are not clearly understood and are thus difficult to incorporate in the analysis. There are, however, ways to reduce the impact of unobserved characteristics. This study uses a sample selection correction technique to estimate the severity of sample selection bias in the wage estimates that may arise because the analysis is restricted to wage earners. This procedure determines whether sample selection correction significantly alters the wage estimates and hence the estimates of the returns to education and gender differences in productivity.

The chapter is structured as follows. Section 2 briefly describes the Peruvian economy and labor market to illustrate women's position in the overall economy. Section 3 discusses the data and highlights the differences between males and females in terms of wage-related characteristics. Section 4 discusses the determinants of female labor force participation and Section 5 the wage determinants and returns to education. Section 6 discusses the extent to which male/female earnings differentials can be attributed to differences in the way the market structure rewards male and female workers. Policy implications are in the concluding section.

## 2.    Peru:  Economic Background and Women's Status in the Labor Market

Peru is a middle income country with a per capita income of US$1300 in 1988. The economy is heavily dependent on mineral resources which are its major export goods. It also has considerable potential for fishing and hydrocarbon resource development. The country is geographically divided by the Andean mountains into three regions--the highlands (Sierra), the rain forest (Selva) and the coast regions. About half of Peru's 20 million (1987 estimates) population lives in the coastal regions, 40 percent in the Andean highlands, and the remainder in the Selva (i.e., Amazon) region.

Table 17.1 presents data relating to employment, unemployment, and labor productivity in Peru during the period 1970-85. Between 1970 and 1985 the labor force increased from 4.2 million to 6.6 million, of which about 88 percent were employed. During this time the employed labor force increased by 46 percent with 28 percent of that increase being employed in agriculture. Unemployment increased by about 7 percentage points over the same period.

Column 4 in Table 17.1 gives figures on adequate employment for the labor force who are employed. According to these figures, the rates of underemployment in Peru ranged between 46 and 54 percent of the labor force in 1970 and 1985, respectively. Thus, underemployment is more serious than open unemployment in Peru. Labor productivity, defined as value added per employed person, is also a problem in Peru. As column 5 indicates, labor productivity declined in Peru between 1981 and 1985. Increasing labor productivity and adequate employment opportunities are significant problems in Peru.

In Peru women's labor force participation rates are below those in many Latin American countries (Suarez-Berenguela, 1987), but it has increased between 1970 and 1985. For example, women's labor force participation increased from 34 to 43 percent in urban Peru.[2] Women's all-Peru participation rate is 57 percent for 1985 (Schafgans, 1990), their participation being much higher in rural than urban areas. Of all economically active women, about 18 percent work in the wage sector, 55 percent are farmers, and 27 percent work in the informal (non-farm) activities. Women are thus predominantly in agriculture and self-employed non-farm activities. Table 17.2 shows that women are predominantly employed in the informal sector; in 1985 about

---

[2]    See Table 23.2. The figures are calculated as: Column 3 x Column 1/100.

**Table 17.1**
Peru - Employment and Labor Productivity, 1970-1985

|  | Total Labor Force[a] | Unemployment Rate (Percent of the Labor Force) | Employment | | | Adequate Employment[b] | Labor Productivity[c] |
|---|---|---|---|---|---|---|---|
|  |  |  | Total | Agriculture | Non-Agriculture |  |  |
|  | (1) | (2) |  | (3) |  | (4) | (5) |
| 1970 | 4,167.3 | 4.7 | 3,971.4 | 1,873.6 | 2,097.8 | 2,058.0 | 613.4 |
| 1975 | 4,817.5 | 4.9 | 4,581.3 | 1,950.0 | 2,631.3 | 2,537.7 | 676.2 |
| 1980 | 5,607.2 | 7.0 | 5,210.7 | 2,046.0 | 3,164.7 | 2,341.4 | 680.3 |
| 1981 | 5,779.0 | 6.8 | 5,377.5 | 2,272.2 | 3,105.3 | 2,613.7 | 684.2 |
| 1982 | 5,958.0 | 7.0 | 5,540.0 | 2,328.1 | 3,211.9 | 2,567.5 | 666.7 |
| 1983 | 6,136.7 | 9.2 | 5,585.7 | 2,355.1 | 3,230.6 | 2,306.9 | 585.5 |
| 1984 | 6,351.3 | 10.5 | 5,684.4 | 2,374.9 | 3,309.5 | 2,242.0 | 603.2 |
| 1985 | 6,555.5 | 11.8 | 5,781.9 | 2,392.7 | 3,389.2 | 2,235.4 | 609.0 |

a. Thousands of persons.
b. The Ministry of Labor classifies a person as underemployed if weekly working hours are less than 35 and/or the income is less than the 1967 minimum wage adjusted for inflation.
c. Value Added (Intis of 1979) per employed person.
Sources: Ministry of Labor and National Statistical Institute, 1970-1985.

**Table 17.2**
Sectoral Distribution of the Economically Active Population (EAP)
in Urban Peru by Gender, 1970-85

| Sector | (1) Distribution of EAP | | (2) Distribution of Female EAP | | (3) Women as % of Sectoral Labor Force | |
|---|---|---|---|---|---|---|
|  | 1970 | 1985 | 1970 | 1985 | 1970 | 1985 |
| Informal | 58.7 | 66.4 | 71.9 | 62.4 | 46.0 | 49.9 |
| Self-employed | 36.0 | 51.7 | 23.1 | 19.8 | 54.4 | 54.8 |
| Employees | 16.5 | 13.1 | 9.3 | 9.0 | 22.0 | 24.9 |
| Domestic worker | 6.2 | 1.6 | 39.5 | 33.6 | 93.0 | 92.9 |
| Formal | 41.3 | 33.6 | 28.1 | 37.6 | 18.0 | 30.1 |
| White-collar employees | 9.7 | 8.0 | 10.7 | 16.1 | 22.0 | 38.2 |
| Blue-collar employees | 18.4 | 9.1 | 3.4 | 7.6 | 7.0 | 18.0 |
| Government employees | 13.2 | 16.4 | 14.1 | 13.9 | 29.0 | 32.8 |

Note: Includes unpaid workers.
Sources: Suarez-Berenguela 1987 and PLSS data.

33 percent of the economically active population in urban Peru were women employed in the informal sector compared to 10 percent in the formal sector.

Women's wages in the formal sector are lower than men's. Women's employment options and productivity perhaps reflect their low education and employment opportunities. Peruvian women have about five years of schooling on average compared to seven years for men. Only 8 percent of men did not attend school compared to 25 percent of women (King and Bellew, 1990). This paper attempts to account for differences in women's labor market participation and wages using household survey data from Peru.

## 3.    Data Characteristics

The data are drawn from the Peruvian Living Standard Survey (PLSS) household data collected jointly by the World Bank and the Peruvian Instituto Nacional de Estadistica (INE). These data provide detailed socio-economic information on over 5,100 households and 26,000 individuals. The samples were drawn from a self-weighted national probability sample of Peruvian households and represent an approximate 1/100 sample of the population. The sampling frame is based on a 1984 National Health and Nutrition Survey. About 25 percent of the households in the PLSS were in metropolitan Lima, 28 percent in other urban areas, and 47 percent in rural areas. The data were collected between June 1985 and July 1986 (see Grootaert and Arriagada, 1986).

The sample includes workers aged 14 to 60. The wage earner participation equation is estimated using information for all potential workers. The wage equation in Section 5, however, is estimated only for men and women reporting wage and remuneration and hours worked and who list this as their main occupation in the week prior to data collection. Self-employed and unpaid family workers are thus excluded. This reduced sample consists of 2,255 men from 1,856 households and 898 women from 783 households, drawn from a total of 6,429 men from 4,142 households and 6,942 women from 4,387 households. The wage labor market participation rate is 13 percent for women and 35 percent for men. Table 17.3 gives the means and standard deviations of the variables by gender.

Women wage earners have one more year of education on average than men wage earners. Employed women also have more vocational training -- 52 percent of women have training compared to 31 percent of men. Despite this, women receive about half of men's wages.[3] This suggests that there are significant differences in wage structures between men and women. Occupational segregation may cause this male-female wage gap. Women also come from relatively wealthier households (in terms of landholding and unearned income). The data suggest that more married (or cohabiting) men participate in the labor market than married (or cohabiting) women. Employed women are also younger on average than employed men.

## 4.    Determinants of Female Labor Force Participation

What influences women's participation in the labor market? Do women differ from men in responding to labor market opportunities? Does human capital (for instance, education) help women, more than men, to participate in the wage sector? Do women face different market

---

[3]    The real hourly wage rate, i.e., nominal hourly wages deflated at 1985 consumer price indices (RHW) is defined as RHW = AC/AH where:  AC = annual compensation = monthly pay x months worked in the past year;  AH = annual hours = weekly hours x months worked in the past year x 4.33. Note that the above male-female wage difference is adjusted for male-female sample differences.

**Table 17.3**
**Means (and Standard Deviations) of Sample Variables**

| Variables | Females | | Males | |
|---|---|---|---|---|
| | Working for wage | All | Working for wage | All |
| Number of observations | 898 | 6,942 | 2,255 | 6,429 |
| Real hourly wage rate[a] | 3.184 | 1.162 | 3.820 | 1.601 |
| | (1.684) | (2.545) | (2.330) | (2.627) |
| Education | | | | |
| Years of schooling | 9.013 | 5.606 | 8.212 | 6.991 |
| | (4.272) | (4.327) | (4.143) | (4.059) |
| Primary | 0.226 | 0.321 | 0.343 | 0.390 |
| | (0.419) | (0.467) | (0.475) | (0.488) |
| Secondary | 0.423 | 0.222 | 0.345 | 0.270 |
| | (0.494) | (0.416) | (0.476) | (0.444) |
| Post-Secondary | 0.189 | 0.049 | 0.132 | 0.074 |
| | (0.392) | (0.215) | (0.339) | (0.262) |
| Vocational Training | 0.518 | 0.239 | 0.309 | 0.195 |
| | (0.500) | (0.427) | (0.462) | (0.396) |
| Secondary technical diploma | 0.031 | 0.012 | 0.024 | 0.014 |
| | (0.174) | (0.109) | (0.153) | (0.118) |
| Post-Secondary diploma | 0.074 | 0.019 | 0.032 | 0.017 |
| | (0.261) | (0.135) | (0.177) | (0.130) |
| University diploma | 0.117 | 0.025 | 0.082 | 0.042 |
| | (0.322) | (0.156) | (0.274) | (0.200) |
| Attended public school | 0.758 | 0.691 | 0.847 | 0.838 |
| | (0.428) | (0.462) | (0.360) | (0.368) |
| Age | 30.871 | 32.056 | 33.432 | 31.057 |
| | (9.816) | (12.566) | (11.354) | (12.718) |
| Married or cohabiting | 0.408 | 0.556 | 0.624 | 0.542 |
| | (0.492) | (0.497) | (0.485) | (0.498) |
| Unearned real income (x1000) | 2.980 | 1.796 | 2.164 | 1.800 |
| | (8.555) | (6.904) | (11.433) | (9.185) |
| Landholding (hectares) | 1.673 | 3.663 | 1.624 | 1.899 |
| | (35.328) | (49.515) | (19.770) | (51.717) |
| OUA residence | 0.313 | 0.305 | 0.324 | 0.302 |
| | (0.464) | (0.460) | (0.468) | (0.459) |
| Rural residence | 0.147 | 0.397 | 0.235 | 0.402 |
| | (0.354) | (0.489) | (0.424) | (0.490) |

a.    Intis at June 1985 prices.
Notes:    Numbers in parentheses are standard deviations.
Source:    Peru Living Standard Survey, 1986.

structures than men? Answers to these questions will help policy makers promote women's participation in the labor market.

This section outlines a theoretical framework to address women's labor market participation and reports the results from Peru.

The decision to join in the labor market, given the constraints, is based on an individual's income-leisure trade-off. A household model framework can help identify the constraints that affect an individual's allocation of time (Becker, 1965). This model identifies individual characteristics such as education and experience, household characteristics, including landholding and unearned income, and market conditions, such as wages, which may influence an individual's allocation of time. Thus the time allocated to different activities, including leisure, can be written as a function of individual, household, and market characteristics. The time allocation data can produce a discrete choice structure of whether or not individuals participate in the wage market. The decision can be estimated using a probability function independently for males and females as follows:

$$Y_m = \tau_{om} + X_m\tau_{1m} + Z_m\tau_{2m} + e_m \tag{1}$$
$$Y_f = \tau_{of} + X_f\tau_{1f} + Z_f\tau_{2f} + e_f \tag{2}$$

where: $Y_i (i=m,f)$ are binary dependent variables with 1 if the ith individual participates in the wage labor market and 0 otherwise; X is a vector of individual characteristics that influences an individual's time allocation; Z is a vector of household and market factors which also explains why an individual participates in the labor market; $\tau$ is the vector of coefficients to be estimated, and e is an error term.[4]

Different reasons can justify the inclusion of individual (X), and household and market (Z) factors as explanatory variables in labor market participation equations 1 and 2. An individual characteristic, such as the level of education, can be treated as an explanatory variable that may indicate the potential productivity of an individual at home and in market production. Holding market wages constant, an increase in the level of an individual's education can increase his or her probability of labor market participation if it increases the opportunity costs of staying at home. The household's constraints include such household asset variables as landholding, which may act as a proxy for productive household assets. The productive assets exert a price effect and an income effect on an individual's labor market participation. The price effect would raise the marginal product or "shadow price" of an individual's labor, while the income effect would encourage an individual to consume more of his or her leisure -- even at its given opportunity cost. The household's unearned income -- another household characteristic -- can influence labor market participation via a pure income effect. Market factors such as market wages exert an income and a substitution effect on an individual's time allocation. These factors may also include community variables, such as the household's proximity to community services (schooling, health, and banking services). These variables measure the impact on time allocation

---

[4]   $Y_j$ equal to zero includes individuals who are either self-employed in family business and farming or exclusively engaged in non-market home production. Including self-employment and home production in one category assumes that the degree of independence between participation in these two activities is almost zero (Khandker, 1987). No test is done to assess the validity of this assumption, but for simplicity we assume that these activities can be jointly undertaken with low transactions cost for switching from one job to the other and hence in this sense, the participation decisions are not independent.

of implicit prices of many goods and services the household uses for production and consumption.[5]

How do we estimate the labor market participation equation? Because the dependent variable takes the value of 1 or 0 in both equations 1 and 2, the error structures yield heteroscedasticity; hence ordinary least squares produces inconsistent estimates. A maximum likelihood method such as the probit technique which takes care of heteroscedasticity problem can produce efficient estimates (Maddala, 1983). I shall use this technique to estimate both equations, 1 and 2.[6]

Table 17.4 reports probit equation results that examine the probability that a woman will join the wage labor market. A similar probit equation is run for the male sample and is also reported in Table 17.4 for comparing the response pattern between men and women in Peru. Based on the Likelihood Ratio test, the hypothesis that marital status has no effect on the participation of men or women is rejected. Table 17.4 is then based on the preferred specification that includes marital status, landholding and unearned income as identifying variables in the labor market participation equation.

Consider first a woman's decision to join the labor market. Both general and technical education affect her decision just like they affect a man's participation decision. However, the response coefficient differs between men and women. Vocational training and secondary education increase women's labor market participation more than men's. In Peru as a whole, the probability that a woman will join the wage market is about 10 percent higher if both men and women have vocational training. Additionally, the probability that a woman will join the wage market is at least 5 percent higher if both women and men complete secondary school. This suggests that improving women's education can increase their labor market participation faster than a similar increase in men's education would affect their participation. Public school attendance seems to be an important determinant of both women's and men's labor market participation. Both unearned income and landholding (which measure the income effect on leisure) generally decrease the probability of being in the labor market for men and women. Landholding significantly reduces men's participation in the wage market, but only affects women's participation in rural areas. Labor market participation for both genders is lower outside Lima, 32 and 53 percent lower for women and 33 and 74 percent lower for men, respectively, in other urban areas and rural areas. There is a higher probability that women will work for wages than men in rural Peru.

Using the above probit results, we predict the effect of changing certain characteristics on women's labor market participation. Two types of predictions are made, one using the women's probit equation and the other using the men's probit equation. The second predicted category

---

[5]    No information on any of these market factors is available except for rural areas. Thus Z variables include only household-level variables.

[6]    A single probit which estimates separately 1 and 2 may produce inefficient estimates if the errors $e_m$ and $e_f$ are correlated. The errors are likely to be correlated if men and women participate in the wage market from the same household. A bivariate probit is necessary to estimate the labor market participation equations, 1 and 2, to obtain efficient estimates. However, for our sample of 898 women and 2,255 men, only 6 percent of men and women belong to the same household that participate in the labor market. We assume, therefore, that the correlation between errors is zero.

**Table 17.4**
Probit Estimates for Female and Male Participation

| Variables | Females | Males |
|---|---|---|
| Constant | -1.452 (-15.190) | -0.753 (-9.504) |
| Gen. Experience | 0.062 (8.918) | 0.058 (10.231) |
| Education | | |
| Primary | -0.013 (-0.195) | 0.023 (0.450) |
| Secondary | 0.399 (5.052) | 0.187 (2.993) |
| Post-Secondary | 0.743 (5.595) | 0.355 (3.283) |
| Vocational Training | 0.363 (7.034) | 0.261 (5.808) |
| Secondary technical diploma | 0.300 (1.977) | 0.213 (1.520) |
| Post-Secondary diploma | 0.704 (5.376) | 0.432 (3.125) |
| University diploma | 0.818 (5.559) | 0.291 (2.374) |
| Attended public school | 0.080 (1.495) | 0.079 (1.634) |
| Unearned real income | -0.0058 (-2.011) | -0.0024 (-1.259) |
| Landholding | -0.00003 (-0.053) | -0.0016 (-1.685) |
| Married or cohabiting | -0.556 (-10.968) | 0.125 (2.555) |
| OUA residence | -0.320 (-6.300) | -0.329 (-7.684) |
| Rural residence | -0.530 (-8.301) | (-15.364) (-15.364) |
| Selected sample (sample size) | 6,942 | 6,429 |
| Log-likelihood | -2145.155 | -3686.749 |

Note: Numbers in parentheses are t-statistics.

explains women's predicted probability of being in the wage sector if women behave in the same way as men in responding to market incentives to participate in the wage market. With other sample characteristics remaining the same, we predict the probability of women's labor market participation for different educational levels (including general and technical education), public-private school attendance, marital status and regions where they live. The information is given in Table 17.5. The mean predicted probability of women's being in the wage sector is 9 percent against a 13 percent actual participation. This suggests that the participation model works well in explaining variations in women's labor market participation decision. However, the mean predicted probability of women's market participation almost quadruples if women behave the same way as men in responding to market incentives (column B). This is an interesting finding that suggests that the labor market response pattern is different for women than men in Peru. In particular, there may be structural differences in men's and women's job specialization which may produce these large variations in their response behavior.

The predicted probability for changing an individual job characteristic is given by the predicted individual probability for each characteristic. As expected, an increase in educational attainment leads to an increase in women's labor market participation. Note that women's participation does not change substantially if women have primary instead of less than primary education. However, women's participation increases more as women attain higher education and the gain is the highest if they attain post-secondary level of education. It is interesting to note that the increases in labor market participation are even much higher for the same level of education if women were to respond in the same way as men to changes in market incentives. For instance, a woman with secondary education increases her probability of participation by an additional 23 points if she follows men's response behavior rather than women's response pattern. Women with vocational training have a 6 percent higher probability of being in the wage market than women with no vocational training. However, women with vocational training can do even better if they follow men's response behavior. Thus, a woman with vocational training has a 26 percent higher probability if she follows a man's response pattern. Women gain substantially in labor force participation if they have a university rather than secondary or post-secondary diploma.

However, the gain is only marginal if they attended public rather than private school. A woman's gain does not vary by whether or not she follows women's or men's response patterns in this respect. Single women participate more by about 9 percent compared to married women and their probability is 15 percent higher if they follow single men's response pattern. In contrast, a married woman's participation rate is 29 percent higher if she follows a married man's response behavior. The predicted participation rate for women is highest in Lima (15 percent) followed by other urban areas (9 percent) and rural areas (6 percent). The predicted probability of being in the wage market increases if women follow men's response pattern: 48 percent in Lima, 35 percent in other urban areas, and 21 percent in rural areas.

## 5.   Wage Determinants and Returns to Education

Following Becker (1964) and Mincer (1974), assume that variations in wages arise from differences in the stock of human capital such as schooling and experience. This assumption can be formally represented in an estimable equation form 3 below:

$$\ln W_i = \alpha_{0i} + \beta_{1i}S_i + \beta_{2i}K_i + \beta_{3i}K^2_i + \epsilon_i \tag{3}$$

where $\ln W_i$ is the natural log of the hourly wage rate of the ith individual (i=m for male, i=f for female wage worker); S is the individual's years of schooling, K is the individual's postschool

## Table 17.5
### Predicted Female Participation Probabilities
### by Characteristic (%)

| Characteristics | Predicted Probability (A) | (B) |
|---|---|---|
| **Education** | | |
| Less than primary | 7.07 | 30.57 |
| Primary | 6.89 | 31.39 |
| Secondary | 14.21 | 37.40 |
| Post Secondary | 23.36 | 43.91 |
| **Vocational Training** | | |
| No | 7.54 | 30.70 |
| Yes | 14.14 | 40.40 |
| **Secondary Tech. Diploma** | | |
| No | 8.79 | 32.84 |
| Yes | 25.48 | 49.50 |
| **Post Secondary Diploma** | | |
| No | 8.64 | 32.64 |
| Yes | 25.48 | 49.30 |
| **University Diploma** | | |
| No | 8.53 | 32.67 |
| Yes | 29.03 | 43.72 |
| **Attended public school** | | |
| No | 8.00 | 30.97 |
| Yes | 9.25 | 33.82 |
| **Marital Status** | | |
| Single | 14.90 | 30.45 |
| Married | 5.52 | 34.96 |
| **Residence** | | |
| Lima | 14.87 | 48.14 |
| Other Urban areas | 8.65 | 35.34 |
| Rural areas | 5.80 | 21.51 |
| **Predicted Mean Participation** | 8.87 | 32.93 |

Note:  (A) calculates the predicted probability using coefficient of female participation and (B) is based on the coefficients of the male participation equation of Table 17.2.

experience (defined as age - S - school entry age, say, 6); $K^2$ is the individual's experience squared; $\alpha_o$ and $\beta_j$ (j=1,2,3) are, respectively, the intercept and slope coefficients to be estimated; and $\epsilon_i$ is the individual specific unobserved error. If the error is normally and independently distributed, an ordinary least squares (OLS) technique can be applied to estimate the wage equation. The estimated coefficient $\beta_1$ measures the proportional increase in the wages associated with each additional year of education.

As postschool experience increases, productivity and wages tend to rise. But further increases in postschool experience may lead to a decline in wages and productivity because of diminishing marginal returns. The concavity of the wage profile is thus captured by the quadratic experience terms.[7] According to human capital theory, education and experience are likely to have major effects on productivity.

Two possible interpretations of wage equation 3 are found in the literature. The first is due to Rosen (1974) who interprets the equation as an hedonic index on characteristics which affect the price of the individual's time. The more dominant interpretation is given by Mincer (1974) who views equation 3 as a generalization of the equilibrium relation between wages and education, where the coefficient $\beta_1$ is the estimate of the private rate of return to the time spent in school instead of in the labor market. Mincer's interpretation is widely applied in the empirical literature and is derived as follows. Assume that: (1) the only cost of schooling for an individual is his or her forgone earnings; (2) individuals enter the labor force immediately after completion of schooling; and (3) each individual's working life of N years is independent of his years of education. Given the additional assumption of a steady state with no productivity growth, one can write the present value of the life earnings of an individual with S years of schooling as:

$$V(S) = \int_{S}^{N} W(S) \frac{1}{r} e^{-rt dt} = W(S) \frac{1}{r}(ep^{-rs}-e^{-rN}) \tag{4}$$

where r is the rate of discount indicating people's time preference. If r is the same for everyone (and N is large), the equation becomes:

$$V(S) = W(S)\frac{1}{r}e^{-rs} = V_o, \text{ for all } S; \tag{5}$$

and the present value of income streams are equalized among individuals. The above can then be rewritten as:

$$W(S) = W_o e^{rs}, \text{ where } W_o = V_o r. \tag{6}$$

Taking log on both sides, we have:

$$\ln W = W_o + rS, \tag{7}$$

where $W_o$ may be interpreted as the permanent labor income of a worker. Individuals facing a given market interest rate, r, choose that level of schooling that maximizes the present value of

---

[7]    Although information on job-specific experience is available, we cannot include it in the wage equation because it is an endogenous variable. In contrast, post-school experience is exogenous to the extent that the individual's education is parentally determined and hence predetermined.

their lifetime earnings. Thus r also represents the internal rate of return. Specification 7 then justifies using a semilogarithmic wage function, as in equation 3 to estimate the economic returns to education, (the estimated coefficient of S). Note that as Mincer's assumptions may not hold in the real world, the estimated schooling coefficient, $\beta_1$ in equation 3, is only an approximation of the internal rate of return. Thus, if S takes the value of years of schooling in 3, then its coefficient $\beta_1$ measures an average economic rate of return to an additional year of schooling.

Equation 3 may be too simple to estimate an individual's productivity in the wage market when factors other than human capital influence the wages and hence the economic returns to education. Moreover, education quality may not be homogenous as assumed in equation 3. Thus, the basic wage model needs to be adjusted to reflect reality. Three adjustments in the functional form of equation 3 are undertaken in this paper.[8] First, there is a possibility that regional labor markets may behave differently and hence yield quite different estimates. Three distinct markets (metropolitan Lima, other urban areas, and rural areas) have already been identified (Stelcner *et. al.*, 1988). The wage rate and labor market participation equations are thus estimated separately for men and women in these three regions. While this method is preferred where there is no interregional migration, such migration does occur as educated workers move to higher wage markets.

But interregional migration may bias estimates of the returns to education as well as to labor market participation. In Latin American countries, as much as half the life-cycle returns to schooling of rural residents result from migrating to urban centers (Schultz, 1988). This bias could not be reduced even if the migrants' original location were known, because migration is a self-selection process. Using regional "shifters" in the wage equation fitted for the country as a whole, one can illustrate the potential severity of interregional migration on the estimated returns to schooling and labor market participation. In particular, because high-wage urban regions have more and better schooling, introducing regional shift variables in the wage or participation equations reduces the estimated returns to schooling, or the influence of schooling on participation in the labor market.

Second, since different levels of schooling impart different skills and wages, an adjustment is necessary to quantify the effect of the quality of different categories of education on wages. There are at least three ways one can quantify the effect of heterogenous quality of education. The first method is by including schooling squared, $S^2$, as an additional variable. In this case the derivative of the dependent variable (log wage) with respect to S gives us an estimate of $(\beta_1 + 2pS)$, where p is the estimated coefficient of $S^2$. By inserting different values of schooling levels, say, 5 for primary level, 10 for secondary, and 14 for post-secondary education in this expression, we can estimate the private rate of return for each category of schooling. The drawback of this method is that it gives equal weight to each category of education in the sense that only the incremental return varies by the level of education, but not the basic return to education. The second method requires an introduction of different education dummies for different levels of schooling where an education dummy is defined as a value of 1 if the individual belongs to a particular schooling level and 0 otherwise. In this second case, the educational-level-specific economic rate of return is calculated by deflating the estimated coefficient of a particular schooling dummy with the difference in years of schooling between this particular schooling level and the reference or control school group. The problem with this approach is that it understates the returns to primary education (Psacharopoulos, 1981). The third

---

[8]    Note that these adjustments are also applied to the labor market participation equations 1 and 2.

method is a more direct way of estimating the economic returns to various categories of education, and it involves using splines of schooling years in the wage equation 3. For example, if an individual has 9 years of schooling, the value for his or her education takes 5 years in primary schooling, 4 years in secondary and 0 years in post-secondary education. This method is better in the sense that it estimates directly the economic returns to different quality education. This paper employs all three methods to estimate and compare the school returns for three categories of education -- primary, secondary, and post-secondary.

Third, an adjustment is necessary to control for the effect on wages of the quality of education across schools, particularly between private and public schools. Attendance or non-attendance in public school is included in the wage and participation functions to control for the influence of unobserved school quality. Parental characteristics also often contribute to children's unobserved ability by giving them a better education (Schultz, 1988). Thus, by including this school quality variable in the wage function, we may reduce the impact of parental characteristics on an individual's productivity and hence returns to education.[9]

With these three adjustments in equation 3, the extended wage equation can be written as:

$$\ln W_i = \alpha_{0i} + \sum_{j=1}^{3} \beta_{1ji} S_{ji} + \beta_{2i} K_i + \beta_{3i} K^2_i + \sum_{h=1}^{2} \beta_{4hi} REG_h + \beta_{5i} PUBSCL + \epsilon_i \qquad (8)$$

where $S_{ji}$ is the jth-level education of the ith individual, REG represents regional dummies such as Lima, other urban areas, and rural areas, and PUBSCL indicates whether or not an individual attended a public school. Again, like equation 3, we may assume that the errors are independently and normally distributed in which case an OLS can yield unbiased estimates.

An adjustment is, however, essential in our OLS strategy to estimate either model 3 or 8 free from sample selection bias. The sample selection bias arises for endogeneity if the decision to participate in the labor market is conditioned by the worker's labor-leisure choice. Thus the estimates of either equation will be biased if it is estimated by including only wage-earners -- thus excluding persons not reporting a wage yet who are part of the potential labor force. The decision to join the labor market influences wages because the characteristics that affect labor market participation may also interact with wages. Thus the wage estimates need to be independent of the possible impact of these characteristics.

Estimating model 3 or 8 in conjunction with labor market participation equation 1 or 2 may reduce sample selection bias from the wage estimates. Heckman (1979) has suggested a two-step procedure to estimate the wage and labor market participation equations. In the first stage the expected values of the residuals of equation 3 or 8 that are truncated are obtained by estimating the labor market participation equation 1 or 2 by the probit method. By introducing the estimated values of residuals from the participation equation into wage equation 3 or 8, we can use ordinary

---

[9]    One may include parents' characteristics directly in the wage regression. But parents may influence children's earnings only via children's school attainment. Thus, by including parental characteristics in the wage equation one would only reduce the returns to individual's education (see Stelcner *et.al.*, 1988.)

**Table 17.6**
Earnings Functions for Wage Equation (3)

| Variables | Females | | Males | |
| --- | --- | --- | --- | --- |
| | OLS | Adj. OLS | OLS | Adj. OLS |
| Constant | -0.583 | -0.779 | -0.159 | 1.359 |
| | (-5.366) | (-2.965) | (-2.305) | (5.597) |
| Years of Schooling | 0.124 | 0.131 | 0.115 | 0.081 |
| | (16.674) | (8.584) | (11.287) | (0.304) |
| Gen. Experience | 0.076 | 0.079 | 0.055 | 0.003 |
| | (9.291) | (8.584) | (11.287) | (0.304) |
| Gen. Exper. Squared (x100) | -0.129 | -0.136 | -0.068 | 0.031 |
| | (16.746) | (-6.448) | (-6.392) | (1.676) |
| OUA Residence | -0.125 | -0.144 | -0.170 | 0.035 |
| | (-2.131) | (-2.281) | (-4.513) | (0.718) |
| Rural Residence | -0.339 | -0.369 | -0.358 | 0.164 |
| | (-4.127) | (-4.096) | (-7.887) | (1.786) |
| Lambda | | 0.085 | | -1.019 |
| | | (0.815) | | (-6.52) |
| R-Squared | 0.355 | 0.355 | 0.331 | 0.343 |
| N | 898 | 898 | 2,255 | 2,255 |

Note: Numbers in parentheses are t-statistics.

least squares to estimate the wage function in the second stage. Heckman's two-step procedure yields consistent estimates.[10]

An identification problem emerges, however. The variables that explain wages may also explain individual labor market participation. That is, the vector X and Z in equation 1 or 2 contains the variables included in the wage equation 3 or 8. Thus we need some identifying variables in equation 1 or 2 not included in the wage equation to help distinguish a participant from a non-participant.

Three variables are considered here as potential candidates for identifying the labor market participation equation from the wage equation. The first two variables are included in vector Z: landholding and unearned income. Both are expected to influence the likelihood that a person will work for wages by affecting the person's reservation wage. If an individual has a considerable amount of land or unearned income, he or she will be less likely to work for wages

---

[10]   Note that sample selection correction does not predict a priori the direction in which this would alter the wage estimates.

because the returns in other activities are higher. These two variables are expected to influence only labor market participation -- not wages. The third identifying variable is marital status which is included in the X vector of the participation equation 1 or 2. Married couples can specialize more easily than unmarried individuals, which usually encourages married men to work for wages and married women to work in the home (Schultz, 1988). Marital status thus can influence labor market participation, but not an individual's market productivity.[11]

The wage models -- equations 3 and 8-- are estimated by the OLS method with and without sample selectivity bias. The results of these wage regressions for men and women are shown in Tables 17.6 and 17.7, respectively. The basic wage model explains about 36 percent and 33 percent of the wage variations among women and men. The extended model, on the other hand, explains about 37 percent of women's and 34 percent of men's wage variations. This suggests that the human capital model explains more than one-third of wage variations among men and women in Peru. Either model's explanatory power does not change very much if we use Heckman's approach to correct for the endogeneity of labor market participation decisions.

Nevertheless, sample selection bias correction has an important influence on women's as well as men's productivity in the wage sector. The sign of the coefficients of the correlation between wage earner and wage rate errors (i.e., Lambda) determines the type of selection that generates the group of men and women workers. Tables 17.6 and 17.7 suggest that the most able men select non-wage employment, since men who work for wages earn less than an average man in Peru. Among women, on the other hand, the most able individuals seem to select wage employment. The results thus indicate that unobserved characteristics that influence labor market participation also influence an individual's productivity.

Among the important determinants of productivity according to wage equation 8, education and experience are crucial; returns to experience, however, are higher for women than for men. Education on average has an important influence on both men's and women's productivity. Furthermore, education at all levels influences both men's and women's productivity in Peru.

Technical education increases labor market productivity among men and women in Peru. Women's wages increase by 15 percent and men's wages by 19 percent if they have had vocational training. But when sample selection correction is introduced, women's wage gains increase to 28 percent, while men's gains drop to 4 percent. In contrast, the wage changes of both men and women with secondary diplomas are not significant as a result of changes in secondary diploma holdings among men and women. Conversely, the wages of male university graduates are about 32 percent higher for men than for women before selectivity correction. The adjusted OLS increases women's returns to university diploma by 22 percent but reduces men's returns by 12 percent.

In comparison with private schooling, the returns to public school attendance are lower for both male and female productivity. Wages are 20 percent lower for women and about 4 percent lower for men who attended public school than for those who attended private school. When sample selection correction is made, the wage differences fall to 17 percent for women but increase to 10 percent for men. The difference in the productivity of public versus private school graduates indicates that the public school system should be improved. This finding is consistent with other studies (Stelcner *et.al.*, 1988; King, 1988).

---

[11]    Marital status, however, can influence an individual's productivity if we assume that married people are healthier than non-married people and health affects productivity.

**Table 17.7**
Earnings Functions for Wage Equation 8

| Variables | Females | | Males | |
|---|---|---|---|---|
| | OLS | Adj. OLS | OLS | Adj. OLS |
| Constant | -0.030 | -0.861 | -0.377 | 1.606 |
| | (-0.245) | (-3.079) | (4.766) | (3.770) |
| Gen. Experience | 0.072 | 0.083 | 0.048 | 0.007 |
| | (8.601) | (9.248) | (9.635) | (0.473) |
| Gen. Exper. Squared (x100) | -0.131 | -0.162 | -0.064 | 0.016 |
| | (-6.815) | (-7.607) | (-5.915) | (0.556) |
| Education | | | | |
| Primary | 0.311 | 0.300 | 0.270 | 0.256 |
| | (3.254) | (3.163) | (4.904) | (4.637) |
| Secondary | 0.874 | 0.990 | 0.696 | 0.577 |
| | (8.434) | (9.094) | (11.246) | (7.832) |
| Post-Secondary | 1.224 | 1.432 | 0.977 | 0.763 |
| | (8.415) | (9.076) | (10.389) | (6.417) |
| Secondary technical diploma | -0.133 | -0.038 | -0.030 | -0.087 |
| | (-0.873) | (-0.244) | (0.276) | (-0.757) |
| Post-secondary diploma | 0.324 | 0.528 | 0.365 | 0.134 |
| | (2.741) | (3.977) | (3.601) | (1.043) |
| University diploma | 0.153 | 0.372 | 0.484 | 0.343 |
| | (1.169) | (2.541) | (5.184) | (3.262) |
| Attended public school | -0.195 | -0.171 | -0.043 | -0.098 |
| | (-3.078) | (-2.700) | (-0.927) | (-1.964) |
| OUA Residence | -0.089 | -0.185 | -0.176 | 0.098 |
| | (-1.492) | (-2.795) | (-4.462) | (0.106) |
| Rural Residence | -0.381 | -0.567 | -0.420 | 0.051 |
| | (-4.447) | (-5.551) | (-9.014) | (0.305) |
| Lambda | | 0.456 | | -1.909 |
| | | (3.302) | | (-2.935) |
| R-Squared | 0.372 | 0.380 | 0.339 | 0.341 |
| N | 898 | 898 | 2,255 | 2,255 |

Note: Numbers in parentheses are t-statistics.

**Table 17.8**
Estimates of Private Rates of Return to Schooling
by Gender Using Alternative Estimation Procedures

| Method of Estimation | Private Rates of Return by School Level | | | | | |
| | Primary | | Secondary | | Post-secondary | |
| | Male | Female | Male | Female | Male | Female |
|---|---|---|---|---|---|---|
| 1.  Schooling Squared[a] | | | | | | |
| OLS | 0.09 | 0.11 | 0.09 | 0.11 | 0.08 | 0.11 |
| OLS with selectivity | 0.08 | 0.13 | 0.07 | 0.14 | 0.06 | 0.14 |
| 2.  Schooling Dummy[b] | | | | | | |
| OLS | 0.05 | 0.05 | 0.12 | 0.15 | 0.16 | 0.20 |
| OLS with selectivity | 0.04 | 0.05 | 0.10 | 0.17 | 0.13 | 0.24 |
| 3.  Schooling Splines | | | | | | |
| OLS | 0.09 | 0.09 | 0.09 | 0.13 | 0.09 | 0.09 |
| OLS with selectivity | 0.09 | 0.09 | 0.09 | 0.15 | 0.09 | 0.10 |

a.     Schooling Squared means schooling squared is added to the regression equation 8.
b.     Schooling Dummy means we use school dummies in the regression.

Workers in Lima are paid more than their counterparts with the same education in other urban and rural areas. According to the extended model, female workers in Lima earn 9 percent more than workers in other urban areas, and 38 percent more than workers in rural areas. When selectivity bias is corrected, the wage differences increase to 19 percent in other urban areas and 57 percent in rural areas. For men the wage differences are, respectively, 18 percent and 42 percent without selectivity correction. When sample selection bias is corrected, the differences seem to disappear.

*Estimates of returns to schooling.* Table 17.8 presents three sets of estimates of returns to education based on the three methods outlined earlier. Each set contains two types of results, one is the OLS and the other is the OLS corrected for sample selectivity bias. They are reported for both men and women. A comparison of regular and adjusted OLS results suggests that the estimates are sensitive to sample selection correction. Moreover, they are sensitive to the method used for estimating the returns to education of various categories. Men lose from education because of sample selection correction. This is true for each method except for the splines method. Thus for males the returns decrease from 9 to 7 percent at the secondary level, and from 8 to 6 percent at the postsecondary level if we look at the schooling squared method. The decrease is from 12 to 10 and 16 to 13, respectively, at the secondary and postsecondary levels with the schooling dummy approach. Women, on the other hand, gain in almost all approaches used for calculating the school returns. For women the returns increase from 11 to 14 both at secondary and postsecondary levels when the schooling squared technique is used. For women the gain is the largest at the postsecondary level under the dummy schooling method, i.e., the increase is from 20 to 24 percent when sample selection correction is made.

The differences among three alternative methods for calculating the returns to education of different categories are substantial. As expected, the return to schooling is biased downward at the primary level with the dummy variable method. The OLS estimate of the returns to primary education is 5 percent for both men and women under the dummy schooling method, while it is 9 percent for both men and women with the splines method. In contrast, the returns are 9 percent for men and 11 percent for women using the schooling squared method. As the schooling squared method gives equal weight to both primary and post-primary education it seems to overestimate the returns to primary education. The schooling dummy method registers a much higher return for both secondary and postsecondary education than any other method for both men and women. Thus the return to postsecondary education for women is 24 percent compared to 14 and 10 percent under squared and splines methods, respectively. The results, therefore, show that the estimates of the returns to education vary remarkably with the kind of method used for calculating these estimates.

The differences in returns to schooling for men and women are also worth noting. The returns to schooling are higher for women than for men, especially at the secondary and postsecondary level. This is true for all three methods used for calculating the returns to schooling. This finding contrasts with studies from other countries that suggest that the returns to schooling are similar for men and women (Schultz, 1989). The return to schooling is higher for women at the secondary level than at any other level with the splines method, a result which is consistent with other Latin American and Asian countries (Schultz, 1988; Mohan, 1986). However, with the dummy and squared methods, the return to schooling is higher for women at the postsecondary level than at any other level.

## 6. Male-Female Wage Differences

A large number of studies based on United States' data and a few studies from developing countries attempt to identify the extent of male-female wage differences that is explained by differences in human capital and other observed job-related characteristics (Becker, 1985; Birdsall and Fox, 1985; Gronau, 1988; Mincer and Polachek, 1974; Oaxaca, 1973; Gannicott, 1986). One standard procedure to measure the male-female wage gap is to fit equation 3 or 8 by ordinary least squares separately to a sample of male (m) and female (f) workers as follows:

$$\ln W_m = X_m \, \beta_m + \epsilon_m \tag{9}$$

and

$$\ln W_f = X_f \, \beta_f + \epsilon_f \tag{10}$$

where: $\beta_m$ and $\beta_f$ are the vectors of unknown coefficients, including the intercepts; $X_m$ and $X_f$ which are, respectively, the vector of males' and females' observed characteristics; and $\epsilon_m$ and $\epsilon_f$ are, respectively, the males' and females' individual specific error. A property of ordinary least squares is that the regression lines pass through the mean values of the variables so that:

$$\ln W_m = X_m \, \hat{\beta}_m \tag{11}$$

$$\ln W_f = X_f \, \hat{\beta}_f \tag{12}$$

The hats denote the estimated values of the coefficients.

By simple manipulation of equations 11 and 12 the male-female wage gap function can be written as:

$$\ln \bar{W}_m - \ln \bar{W}_f = (\bar{X}_m - \bar{X}_f) \, \hat{\beta}_m + \bar{X}_f \, (\hat{\beta}_m - \hat{\beta}_f)$$
$$= (\bar{X}_m - \bar{X}_f) \, \hat{\beta}_f + \bar{X}_m \, (\hat{\beta}_m - \hat{\beta}_f) \qquad (13)$$

where the first part of the right-hand side of equation 13 measures the wage gap due to male-female differences in wage-related characteristics and the second part measures the gap explained by the differences in male-female wage structures for the same observed job-related characteristics. Thus, one can measure the wage gap in two ways: Using the male wage structure or, alternatively, using the female wage structure.[12] Both the basic and extended wage models are used here to measure and compare the wage gap that is explained by the job-related characteristics.

*Determinants of male-female wage differences.* As Table 17.3 showed, men earn more than women in Peru. In fact, women earn about half of men's wages, when the log wage differences are adjusted for male-female sample size differences. What explains the male-female wage differences? Table 17.9 shows the wage variations between males and females that are explained by the wage equations 3 and 8 under the OLS estimation method, with and without sample selection correction.

**Table 17.9**
Male-Female Wage Gap Decomposition Estimates
for All Peru By Alternative Sample Selection Methods

| Earnings Function Type | Sample Size | | Percentage Explained By Human Capital Variables Using OLS Method | | | |
|---|---|---|---|---|---|---|
| | | | Without Sample Selection Correction | | With Sample Selection Correction | |
| | Men | Women | (A) | (B) | (A) | (B) |
| Basic | 2,255 | 898 | -24 | -40 | 218 | -62 |
| Extended | 2,255 | 898 | -71 | -89 | 167 | -232 |

Note:   Two wage structures are used: (A) male wage structure, and (B) female wage structure.

The OLS results of the basic and extended equations explain nothing in terms of male-female differences in human capital variables. That means the wage differences are not explained by

---

[12]   Note that the second component of equation 13 is often taken as relecting wage discrimination. Because it is difficult to remove the effects of all possible wage-determining factors, including those that may reflect female discrimination outside the labor market, it is indeed difficult to attribute the second component as a measure of sex-discrimination in the wage market (Gunderson, 1989).

male-female differences in job-related characteristics, but by differences in the wage structures. In fact, wage structures for men and women are so different that women are not paid consistently according to their human capital endowment. Thus, human capital differences produce even negative contributions in the calculation of male-female wage differences. However, when the sample selection correction is applied and male wage structure is used to calculate the wage gap, the model explains more than 100 percent of the differences in wages in terms of the differences in job-related characteristics. This method includes, in addition with the standard variables, a correlation factor that measures the relationship between the errors of the wage equation and the labor market participation. This result suggests that the unobserved characteristics that influence both the labor market participation and productivity explain fully the male-female wage differences in Peru.[13]   However, when female wage structure is used to calculate the wage gap, even sample selection correction does not help the human capital model to explain the wage gap that exists in Peru. If the unobserved characteristics explain the wage gap, it follows that we need to identify more observable characteristics of a worker other than his or her human capital variables to explain the male-female wage differences that exist in Peru.[14]

## 7.    Discussion

This paper addresses four critical questions. First, what influences men and women to participate in the labor market? Although education and training raise labor market participation of both men and women, vocational training and secondary school increase the labor market participation of women more than that of men. Thus, improving education for women can increase their participation faster than a similar increase in men's education would affect the participation of men. Unearned income and landholding reduce the participation of both men and women. The probability of being in the wage sector is high for married men and low for married women, indicating an expected job specialization after marriage.

Second, what determines the productivity of men and women in the wage market? Experience, education, and training are all effective. The quality of education is also significant: Those employees educated in private schools are more productive than those with a public school education. Moreover there are sharp regional differences in productivity. Men and women from other urban areas and rural areas are paid less than their counterparts in Lima. The extent of male-female differences in productivity depends on the impact of sample selectivity bias.

Third, is there any systematic gender bias in the estimated returns to schooling if we ignore the possible sample selection rule of who is a wage earner? The results suggest that sample selection correction decreases the returns to schooling for men but increases them for women. Sample selection bias is substantial for both men and women, showing that the selected wage earners are not a random sample. The magnitude and direction of the bias, however, vary by method used

---

[13]    This is an interesting finding because it does not include any controversial control variable such as occupational status in the wage regression. The wage function includes an additional variable--the sample selection correction factor--that accounts for the unobserved characteristics influencing labor market participation.

[14]    Even controlling the wage equation for occupational differences which may imply some variations in unobserved characteristics does not solve the puzzle of why men earn more than women in Peru. Although occupational status is a choice variable, we control for it's effect in the wage equation by including a number of occupational dummies. This method still does not alter the conclusion of this study.

for the calculation of these returns. The returns to schooling are higher for women at the primary school level. The results confirm that sample selection bias is an important factor in labor market participation. The most able men select non-wage employment, while the most able women select wage employment.

And finally, why do men earn more than women? Although there are some differences in human capital, the extent to which these differences explain the wage gap depends critically on sample selection correction factors and the wage structure used to calculate the wage gap. Thus when sample selection correction is not included in the wage regression of a random sample of males and females, the human capital model does not explain any portion of the wage gap that exists in Peru. This is true no matter whether we use the male or female wage structure to calculate the wage gap. When the correction factor is included and the male wage structure is used, the model explains 100 percent of the wage gap. This suggests that the unobserved characteristics that influence labor market participation and productivity also affects the productivity differences between males and females. Clearly it would be useful to identify other observable characteristics that affect wage differences.

Two policy implications that result from our answers to these questions should be mentioned. First, since public schools are less effective than private schools in raising productivity and reducing the wage gap, policymakers should take steps to make the public school system more effective.

Second, as the school returns are higher for women than for men, parents should invest equally, if not more, in female education. However, the PLSS survey data indicate that parents enroll more male than female children in schools, especially at the secondary level (Schafgans, 1990). This clearly supports the notion that school investment in children is not gender neutral, nor is it governed by the private rate of returns to schooling for men and women. Apart from equity reasons, there is a strong case for an efficiency-based argument for investing more equally in male and female children. The results of this paper indicate that investments in education and training for women raise their participation and productivity in the labor market more than a similar investment in men's education. In addition, these investments reduce fertility, improving the education of children and the health and nutrition of all family members. Thus human capital investment in women is a high return activity and at least as good as an equivalent investment in men. The government, therefore, must identify ways to channel more resources toward women's education.

# References

Becker, G.S. *Human Capital*. New York: Columbia University Press, 1964.

----. "A Theory of the Allocation of Time." *Economic Journal,* Vol. 75 (1965). pp. 493-517.

----. "Human Capital, Effort and the Sexual Division of Labor." *Journal of Labor Economics,* Vol. 3 (1985). pp. 533-558.

Behrman, J.R. and N. Birdsall. "The Quality of Schooling." *American Economic Review,* Vol. 73, no. 5 (1983). pp. 928-946.

Birdsall, N. and M.L. Fox. "Why Males Earn More." *Economic Development and Cultural Change,* Vol. 33, no. 3 (1985). pp. 533-556.

Dagsvik, J. and Aaberge, R. 1990. "Household Production, Time Allocation, and Welfare in Peru." PRE Working Paper No. 503. Washington, D.C.: World Bank, 1990.

Gannicott, K. "Women, Wages and Discrimination: Some Evidence from Taiwan." *Economic Development and Cultural Change,* Vol. 39, no. 4 (1986). pp. 721-730.

Grootaert, C. and A.M. Arriagada. "The Peruvian Livings Standards Survey: An Annotated Questionnaire." Washington, D.C.: World Bank, 1986.

Griliches, Z. "Estimating Returns to Schooling: Some Econometric Problems." *Econometrica,* Vol. 45, no.1 (1977). pp. 1-22.

Gronau, R. "Sex-related Wage Differentials and Women's Interrupted Labor Careers - The Chicken or the Egg." *Journal of Labor Economics,* Vol. 6 (1988). pp. 277-301.

Gunderson, M. "Male-female Wage Differentials and Policy Responses." *Journal of Economic Literature,* Vol. 27 (1989). pp. 46-72.

Heckman, J. "Sample Selection Bias as a Specification Error." *Econometrica,* Vol. 47, January (1979). pp. 153-161.

Khandker, S.R. "Labor Market Participation of Married Women in Bangladesh." *Review of Economics and Statistics,* Vol. 71 (1987). pp. 536-541.

King, E.M. "Does Education Pay in the Labor Force." PHREE Working Paper. Washington, D.C.: World Bank, 1988.

King, E.M. and R. Bellew. "Gains in the Education of Peruvian Women, 1940 to 1980." PRE Working Paper No. 472. Washington, D.C.: World Bank, 1990.

Maddala, G.S. *Limited-dependent and Qualitative Variables in Econometrics*. New York: Cambridge University Press, 1983.

Mincer, J. *Schooling, Experience and Earnings*. New York: Columbia University Press, 1974.

Mincer, J. and S. Polachek. "Family Investments in Human Capital: Earnings of Women." *Journal of Political Economy*, Vol. 82 (1974). pp. S76-S108.

Mohan, R. *Work, Wages and Welfare in a Developing Metropolis*. New York: Oxford University Press, 1986.

Newman, J. "Labor Market Activitiy in Cote d'Ivoire and Peru." LSMS Working Paper No. 36. Washington, D.C.: World Bank, 1987.

Oaxaca, R. "Male-female Wage Differentials in Urban Labor Markets." *International Economic Review*, Vol. 14, no. 1 (1973). pp. 693-709.

Psacharopoulos, G. "Returns to Education: An Updated International Comparison." *Comparative Education*, Vol. 11, no. 3 (1981). pp. 321-341.

Robb, R. "Earnings Differentials between Males and Females in Ontario, 1971." *Canadian Journal of Economics*, Vol. 11, no. 2 (1978). pp. 350-359.

Rosen, S. "Hedonic Functions and Implicit Markets." *Journal of Political Economy*, Vol. 82 (1974). pp. 34-55.

Schafgans, M.M.A. "A Comparison of Men and Women in the Labor Force in Peru." in B. Herz and S. Khander (eds.). *Women's Work, Education and Welfare in Peru*. Forthcoming.

Schultz, T.P. "Women and Development: Objectives, Framework, and Policy Interventions." PHR Working Paper. Washington, D.C.: World Bank, 1989.

-----. "Educational Investment and Returns." in H. Chenery and T.N. Srinivasan (eds.). *Handbook of Development Economics*, Vol. 1. Amsterdam: North Holland, 1988.

Stelcner, M., A.M. Arriagada, and P. Mook. "Wage Determinants and School Attainment Among Men in Peru." LSMS Working Paper No. 41. Washington, D.C.: World Bank, 1988.

Suarez-Berenguela, R. "Peru Informal Sector, Labor Markets, and Returns to Education." LSMS Working Paper No. 32. Washington, D.C.: World Bank, 1987.

World Bank. "Peru, Politices to Stop Hyperinflation and Initiate Economic Recovery." Mimeograph. Country Study Series. Washington, D.C.: World Bank, 1989.

# 18

# Is there Sex Discrimination in Peru?
# Evidence from the 1990 Lima Living Standards Survey

*Indermit A. Gill*

## 1.    Introduction

Allegations of imperfectly functioning labor markets have been commonplace in the literature for many years. Researchers have struggled to provide reliable estimates of discrimination against women, racial and ethnic minorities, of the degree of segmentation in labor markets by occupation and location, and the effects of government intervention on these "market failures." For example, it has been argued that while the government often creates jobs that are protected from market forces, it also -- sometimes simultaneously -- serves as an employer for "unfairly" disadvantaged groups such as women.

This chapter readdresses these issues using a somewhat novel approach: It combines analysis of one form of alleged labor market failure -- gender discrimination -- with the examination of another facet -- segmentation of the labor market by type of employer. More precisely, I examine if the degree to which similar observed skills of men and women are differentially rewarded depends upon whether an individual works in the wage sector or as a self-employed worker. This provides crude indicators of two forms of market imperfection: First, it throws up first-round estimates of the differences in returns to human capital (schooling, general work experience, and job-specific skills) of the self-employed and wage workers. Since in Peru these classes roughly correspond to the informal and formal sector, respectively, the results can be used to determine whether the pecuniary rewards to human capital differ across sectors, i.e., whether the labor market is occupationally segmented. Second, it provides a preliminary measure of gender biases in remuneration under differing employment regimes, indicating whether the gender gap in earnings is driven by market structure or skill differentials.

Uncovering differences by employment type and gender is just the first step, though. There are good reasons to believe that while self-employment is often harder to initiate than paid employment (because it may require high startup costs), it provides workers with relatively flexible work schedules. Married and cohabiting women (who, facts indicate, often balance two careers -- household and market work) are very likely to benefit from this flexibility.[1]  The upshot of the discussion is that while married women are better suited for self-employment or informal market work, single women and men constitute relatively "fungible" human capital. Standard measures of skills must be augmented by considerations of gender and marital status in studying the effectiveness of skill accumulation (investment in human capital) as a welfare enhancing device. Not realizing this will lead to inefficient policy design.

A number of studies have been written on the Peruvian labor market in the years since the 1985-86 Peruvian Living Standards Survey results were made available. Labor market participation of Peruvian men and women, their schooling decisions and earnings determinants, and other forms of market segmentation have been examined by a battery of capable researchers. In other words, all the favorite areas of labor economists have been explored. Why another study on Peru? While repetition in scientific inquiry rarely needs to be justified, this study more than just duplicates past efforts: First, while human capital effects on work participation and earnings have been repeatedly explored for men (e.g., Stelcner, Arriagada, and Moock, 1988) and for women (e.g., King, 1990; Khandker, 1992), explicit gender comparisons of these phenomena are relatively rare. This study does just that. Second, as discussed above, while allegations of market imperfection (referred to as "labor market segmentation," "duality" or "sex discrimination") are implicit in many studies of labor markets in Latin America, there has been no comprehensive examination of these aspects of market failure in a unified analytical setting. Finally, since this study uses the 1990 Living Standards Survey, it is worthwhile examining whether the market structure revealed by these data differs substantially from that indicated by the 1985-86 survey.

To sharpen the discussion, consider the following facts:

1.  While about half of the women who worked in the market were self-employed, only about a third of men were self-employed.

2.  Both wage and self-employed males worked about 48 hours per week, while self-employed women worked about 7 hours less than wage and salaried women (35 and 42 hours respectively).

3.  The variance of hours worked in the salaried sector is less than half the value of the variance of hours worked per week by the self-employed for both men and women.

4.  About 62 percent of self-employed women were married or cohabiting, as compared with 37 percent of wage and salaried women. For men, the ratio is 62 percent for both classes.

5.  While the female-male ratio of monthly earnings is roughly the same for wage workers and the self-employed (about 0.62 and 0.66 respectively), the ratio for hourly earnings is much lower in the wage sector than among the self-employed (0.71 and 0.92 respectively).

---

[1]    The other main beneficiaries from this hours flexibility are likely to be workers with large market skills. Wage and salaried employment generally have hour restrictions, and able workers (who have a high marginal cost of leisure) may be forced into corner solutions. It is likely that men with unusually large entrepreneurial skills will choose self-employment for this reason, and work longer than the median worker.

Using standard techniques, this study tries to explain these facts. First, the determinants of the decision to work in the market are examined using simple univariate probit procedures.[2] The aim of the exercise is two-fold: To obtain an understanding of gender differences in the decision to work, and to obtain a summary measure of the difference in unobserved work-choice related characteristics of workers and non-workers by computing the Mill's ratio. Then the factors affecting sector choice (wage work or self-employment) are examined, again using univariate probit procedures. The aims of this exercise are to isolate the effects of marital status on sector choice, and to obtain summary measures differences in sector-choice related unobserved attributes of working women and men.

Second, Mincerian human capital earnings functions are estimated for all workers with and without sample selectivity corrections proposed by Heckman (1979), using the results of work participation probit regressions. Also, separate earnings functions are estimated for wage and salaried workers and for the self-employed using a simple two-step sample selectivity correction based on the results of both work participation and sector choice probit procedures.

Third, using Oaxaca's (1973) technique, the explained gender gap in earnings is decomposed into two parts: The gap in earnings due to observed skill differences, and the differential due to a gender gap in returns to similar observed skills, which constitutes the theoretical upper bound to sex discrimination in the marketplace. I also briefly examine whether industrial and occupational segregation by sex explains some of the observed earnings differential.

Finally, I examine the key policy implications of the analysis. The main policy implication that emerges is that, given the nature of female work histories, policies that increase access to education for women may not be adequate to improve the welfare of women. These measures must be supplemented by encouraging female entrepreneurship (e.g, by credit subsidization), which allows women to obtain gainful employment which is more compatible with their traditional roles as homemakers. This does not mean that education subsidization is useless, because schooling fundamentally changes the occupations that women choose for themselves: It increases participation in market activities, especially in the wage sector.

## 2. Background

Summary statistics are presented (Table 18.1) separately for wage and salaried workers and for the self-employed. There are compelling reasons to expect differences in levels of earnings, effort and human capital across sectors. First, self-employed earnings confound the returns of non-human capital -- for which the data are poor -- and the returns to human capital --which are the primary concern of this paper. Second, differences in levels of earnings for equally skilled male and female workers may exist in the wage sector if employers discriminate against women -- as is commonly alleged --but not in the self-employed sector. Third, schooling as a signal of work-related ability is valuable only in the wage sector. If returns to schooling are higher in the wage and salaried sector than among the self-employed, this would be evidence consistent with the view that schooling serves at least in part as a signalling device.

---

[2]    Henceforth, for the sake of brevity, "work" refers to work other than household activities such as housekeeping, childbearing and childcare, and nursing relatives. The intention is not to minimize the importance of these functions, but simply to keep sentences short.

**Table 18.1**

Means (and Standard Deviations) of Variables: By Employment Category

| Variable | Females | | | Males | | |
| --- | --- | --- | --- | --- | --- | --- |
| | All | Wage and Salary | Self-Employed | All | Wage and Salary | Self-Employed |
| LF Participation Rate (Fraction) | 0.38 (0.44) | | | 0.69 (0.50) | | |
| Average Hours Worked (Hours/Week) | 38.70 (19.35) | 42.03 (14.79) | 34.72 (23.37) | 48.51 (17.96) | 48.40 (14.73) | 48.70 (21.16) |
| Income from Main Job (Intis/Month) | 7493 (23012) | 6368 (17522) | 8913 (28664) | 11417 (36192) | 10284 (35572) | 13606 (37296) |
| Hourly Earnings (Intis/Hour) | 46.10 (233.0) | 36.07 (133.3) | 61.12 (321.1) | 56.03 (204.6) | 50.59 (219.8) | 66.52 (166.5) |
| Schooling (Years) | 7.41 (4.08) | 10.69 (4.16) | 7.42 (3.91) | 8.01 (4.42) | 10.11 (4.01) | 9.05 (3.85) |
| Age (Years) | 31.78 (13.50) | 32.00 (10.94) | 36.46 (11.32) | 32.36 (13.56) | 34.87 (11.80) | 36.51 (12.36) |
| Tenure (Years on Current Job) | 5.14 (6.53) | 5.35 (7.03) | 4.87 (5.85) | 7.97 (8.77) | 8.01 (8.92) | 7.88 (8.49) |
| Fraction Married | 0.37 (0.48) | 0.30 (0.46) | 0.47 (0.50) | 0.39 (0.49) | 0.50 (0.50) | 0.45 (0.50) |
| Fraction Cohabiting | 0.10 (0.30) | 0.07 (0.25) | 0.15 (0.36) | 0.11 (0.31) | 0.13 (0.34) | 0.17 (0.38) |
| Fraction Separated | 0.07 (0.25) | 0.10 (0.30) | 0.11 (0.31) | 0.03 (0.16) | 0.03 (0.17) | 0.04 (0.19) |
| Fraction Single | 0.43 (0.49) | 0.51 (0.50) | 0.20 (0.40) | 0.47 (0.50) | 0.33 (0.47) | 0.33 (0.47) |
| Fraction Household Head | 0.08 (0.27) | 0.11 (0.31) | 0.19 (0.37) | 0.47 (0.50) | 0.59 (0.49) | 0.68 (0.47) |
| Household Size (Number of Members) | 6.52 (3.08) | 6.29 (2.90) | 5.91 (2.76) | 6.47 (3.07) | 6.08 (2.86) | 6.13 (3.04) |
| Workers in Household (Number) | 2.14 (1.36) | 2.93 (1.42) | 2.73 (1.31) | 2.17 (1.35) | 2.46 (1.42) | 2.49 (1.38) |
| # Children: 0-5 Years (Number) | 0.82 (1.01) | 0.65 (0.97) | 0.62 (0.86) | 0.83 (1.02) | 0.68 (0.91) | 0.75 (1.01) |
| # Children: 6-13 Years (Number) | 1.15 (1.19) | 0.78 (1.01) | 1.10 (1.09) | 1.17 (1.19) | 0.89 (1.08) | 1.03 (1.11) |

Note: "All" includes non-workers.

The numbers in Table 18.1 indicate that:

1.  Female labor force participation is about half of the rate for men: 38 percent to 69 percent. The average hours worked per week by women are about 10 hours less than men. The male-female difference is about 6 hours per week for wage and salaried workers, but about 14 hours for the self-employed. The coefficient of variation (standard deviation divided by the mean) for hours worked by self-employed women is 0.67, compared with 0.45 for self-employed men.[3] This seems to indicate greater flexibility in terms of hours of self-employment, which could be especially valuable for married and cohabiting women.

2.  This last inference is confirmed by the observation that while only about 35 percent of working men were self-employed, 45 percent of working women are self-employed. While 62 percent of self-employed women were married or cohabiting, 61 percent of wage and salaried women were single or separated.

3.  The level of schooling among the self-employed is lower for both males and females than for wage sector workers. The gender gap in schooling among the self-employed is greater (1.6 years, favoring men) than for the wage sector (0.6 years, favoring women).

4.  Self-employed workers are generally older than wage workers, but the intersectoral differences in tenure (years at current job) are insignificant. Men have been at their current jobs about 3 years more than their female counterparts.

5.  The male-female gap in average hourly earnings is greater in the wage sector (14 intis per hour) than among the self-employed (5 intis per hour). Hourly earnings are higher in the self-employed sector, even though schooling and tenure levels are higher among salaried workers. Since part of self-employed workers' earnings are the returns to non-human capital, this finding is not surprising.

## 3.  Occupational Choice Decisions

The aim of this section is to analyze the determinants of the decision to choose market work, and to obtain a measure of sample selectivity that can be used (in the next section) to study the determinants of earnings. The central concerns are the existence and interpretation of reported wages. For these purposes, the occupational choice of men and women can be classified into three categories:

1.  Non-market activities (household work, investment in non-job-specific human capital, or leisure),

2.  Wage and salaried employment, and

3.  Self-employed market activities.

---

[3]    The coefficient of variation is 0.35 and 0.31 for wage and salaried women and men respectively.

This classification allows us to study two aspects of gender difference in work histories: The decision whether or not to participate in market work, and the choice of occupation when hours flexibility is a desirable attribute of a job.[4]

*The determinants of work participation.* The decision to participate in market work depends upon the offered market wage, W, and the reservation wage, W*. The market wage depends upon stocks of human capital (schooling, training, job-specific skills, etc.). Reservation wages depend upon the productivity of labor at home (in bearing and rearing children, looking after older relatives, etc.), or returns to pre-employment investment in human capital (e.g., earning a diploma) or the taste for leisure (which could depend upon the age and unearned income of the person). Thus we can write:

$$P = P (W, W^*) \quad (1)$$
$$\phantom{P = P (} + \quad -$$

where P equals 1 if the person works in the market, and 0 if the person does not. We can write this as:

$$P = P (E, X, T; \ R, A, D; \ others) \quad (2)$$

where E is the education level, X is previous work experience, T is job training -- factors affecting market wage, R is unearned income, A is age, and D is the number of dependents (young children and old or infirm relatives) -- factors affecting reservation wage. The signs of the derivatives $P_E$, $P_X$, $P_T$, $P_R$, $P_A$ and $P_D$ can be inferred from standard consumer theory.

*The choice of market sector.* The choice of occupation in the market sector -- wage employment or self-employment -- is generally made simultaneously with the decision whether or not to work in the market sector. That is, some of the factors affecting the work participation decision also affect the choice of sector of employment. Represent the sector choice decision as:

$$T = T (W^s, W^w) \quad (3)$$
$$\phantom{T = T (} + \quad -$$

where T equals 1 if the person is self-employed, and 0 if the person is a wage worker, $W^s$ is self-employed sector earnings, and $W^w$ is the wage sector earnings.

If employment in the wage sector requires more, or relatively rigid, hours, workers who value hours flexibility more will prefer self-employment. Married women tend to fall into this category. But self-employment also usually requires greater non-human capital than wage employment. So age will, in general, be positively correlated with the decision to be self-employed, both because of its obvious association with marital status, and because older workers have more accumulated wealth.

The role of education in the choice of type of employment is relatively less clearcut. If schooling serves only as a signal of innate ability to potential employers, then schooling will be more

---

[4]    It is not necessary that only one alternative be chosen.  In fact, it is likely that household work is combined with self-employment by many women.

valued in the wage sector. Education levels among the self-employed will be lower than among wage and salaried workers.[5]

***Estimation technique.***  In any case, variables such as education, marital status and age, which influence P, also may influence T. If there are common observable influences, it is reasonable to expect that there are common unobserved variables that affect both P and T. That is, if equations 1 and 3 are written as:

$$P = \beta_1 Z_1 + \epsilon_1 \tag{4}$$
$$T = \beta_2 Z_2 + \epsilon_2 \tag{5}$$

then,  $\epsilon_1$ and  $\epsilon_2$ are likely to be correlated, so that probit or ordinary least squares (OLS) estimators of $\beta_1$ and $\beta_2$ are inefficient. The solution is to estimate equations 4 and 5 using a bivariate probit regression procedure. On the other hand, if the covariance between $\epsilon_1$ and $\epsilon_2$ is zero, then a stepwise probit procedure (in which equation 4 is estimated using data on both workers and non-workers, and then the sector choice probit equation is estimated using data only on workers) yields reliable estimates of $\beta_1$ and $\beta_2$ .

To see whether a stepwise probit procedure is adequate, i.e., to test if:

$$\text{Correlation } (\epsilon_1, \epsilon_2) = 0 \tag{6}$$

I estimated equations 4 and 5 separately, and tested the hypothesis that:

$$\text{Correlation } (\hat{\epsilon}_1, \hat{\epsilon}_2) = 0. \tag{7}$$

This is not a rigorous test for deciding that a bivariate probit estimation yields the same results as a stepwise probit procedure. If correlation $(\epsilon_1, \epsilon_2)$ is not equal to zero, then  $\hat{\epsilon}_1$ and  $\hat{\epsilon}_2$ computed by estimating equations 4 and 5 separately are not reliable. But if equation 7 holds, the stepwise probit provides a good approximation to the bivariate probit results without any of the additional distributional restrictions required by this procedure.

The results showed that correlation $(\hat{\epsilon}_1, \hat{\epsilon}_2)$ was .0056 for females, and -0.0044 for males, so the hypothesis that correlation $(\epsilon_1, \epsilon_2) = 0$ cannot be rejected. In this paper, then, I report the results of stepwise probit estimations.[6]  It should not be surprising, though, to find that these correlations are insignificant, even though there are (observed) common influences. If all the common influences are observable, then the error terms of the two equations will be uncorrelated. There are good reasons to believe that education, age, and marital status are (or closely proxy) the common factors in both the work participation and the sector choice decision.

---

[5]    There may be other reasons for this differential in schooling levels: Self-employed sector work may require job-specific skills more than general human capital (schooling), while wage sector jobs value general skills more due to relatively rapid changes in the nature of jobs in the wage sector.

[6]    For bivariate probit estimations of work participation and sector choice equations for Santiago (Chile) in 1987 and Lima (Peru) in 1990, see Gill (1991b).

**Table 18.2**
Work Participation Probit Estimates: All Males & Females
*Dependent Variable: Did you work last week? (Yes=1, No=0)*

| | Females | | | Males | | |
|---|---|---|---|---|---|---|
| | Coeff. | Standard Error | % Deriv. | Coeff. | Standard Error | % Deriv. |
| Schooling: 5 Years[a] | -0.146 | 0.100 | -5.7 | -0.011 | 0.161 | -0.4 |
| Schooling: 6-9 Years | 0.001 | 0.096 | 0.1 | -0.050 | 0.143 | -1.7 |
| Schooling: 10 Years | 0.023 | 0.089 | 0.9 | 0.141 | 0.139 | 4.8 |
| Schooling: 11-16 Years | 0.178 | 0.113 | 6.9 | -0.251 | 0.156 | -8.4 |
| Schooling: 17+ Years | 0.628 | 0.135 | 24.3 | 0.130 | 0.180 | 4.4 |
| Age: 21-30 Years[a] | 0.971 | 0.909 | 37.7 | 1.206 | 0.092 | 40.5 |
| Age: 31-40 Years | 1.453 | 0.113 | 56.3 | 1.581 | 0.140 | 53.1 |
| Age: 41-50 Years | 1.227 | 0.123 | 47.6 | 1.448 | 0.177 | 48.7 |
| Age: 51-65 Years | 0.648 | 0.134 | 25.1 | 0.452 | 0.161 | 15.2 |
| Married[a] | -0.369 | 0.099 | -14.3 | 0.230 | 0.145 | 7.7 |
| Cohabiting | -0.238 | 0.120 | -9.3 | 0.550 | 0.192 | 18.5 |
| Widowed | -0.227 | 0.195 | -8.8 | -0.035 | 0.328 | -1.2 |
| Separated | 0.006 | 0.148 | 0.3 | 0.336 | 0.243 | 11.3 |
| Household Head | 0.484 | 0.136 | 18.8 | 0.667 | 0.133 | 22.4 |
| Household Income | 1.3e-9 | 1.1e-9 | 0.0 | 1.8e-9 | 3.1e-9 | 0.0 |
| # Household Workers | 0.686 | 0.021 | 2.7 | 0.026 | 0.025 | 0.9 |
| Boys: 0-5 Years | -0.129 | 0.053 | -5.0 | 0.116 | 0.085 | 3.9 |
| Girls: 0-5 Years | -0.093 | 0.053 | -3.6 | 0.136 | 0.086 | 4.6 |
| Boys: 6-13 Years | -0.041 | 0.044 | -1.6 | -0.014 | 0.069 | -0.5 |
| Girls: 6-13 Years | 0.049 | 0.046 | 1.9 | -0.043 | 0.075 | -1.5 |
| Constant | -1.099 | 0.115 | -42.6 | -0.703 | 0.151 | -23.6 |
| Log Likelihood | | -1500.8 | | | -937.8 | |
| Chi-Square | | 395.5 | | | 894.1 | |
| Sample Size | | 2,518 | | | 2,344 | |
| Mean of Dependent Variable | | 0.4039 | | | 0.7223 | |

a. The omitted schooling group is "0-4 years," the omitted age group is "14-20 years," and the omitted marital status class is "Single."

## 4. Results of Work Participation Probit Regressions

Table 18.2 reports the results of probit regressions for about 2,500 females and about 2,300 males aged between 14 and 65 years in 1990. Education, Age and Marital Status variables are all included as dummies. The results show that:

1. Schooling has a relatively stronger influence on the female decision to participate in market work. There is some evidence that incomplete programs of study (6-9 years,

and 11-16 years) are associated with lower male participation, probably because the reservation wage is increased by the expected wage gains obtained by acquiring a diploma. This result is also found for Chile (Gill, 1991a).

2.  The age profile of work participation is inverse U-shaped, with women entering the market later and staying longer. Late entry of women into the labor market is probably due to childbirth and childrearing. Late departure may be because of the lower retirement benefits in jobs traditionally held by women, the pure income effect of lower lifetime savings of women relative to men, or the longer lifespans of women.[7]

3.  Married and cohabiting women have a labor force participation rate of about 33 percent compared to a rate of 47 percent for single women (see Table 18.3). Other things equal, married and cohabiting men are more likely to be working in the market than single men. Being a household head significantly increases the likelihood of being a labor market participant for both women and men.

4.  The number of workers in the household marginally, but significantly, raises the probability of working outside the home for women. This is the opposite of what we expected to find. The influence of household income (other than the individual's) is also inexplicably positive but insignificant. The number of young children (aged 0-5 years) -- conditional upon the person being married or cohabiting -- is negatively associated with work participation for women. There is some evidence that the presence of older girls (potential substitutes for adult females in household work) increases the probability of female market participation.

***Reasons for not working.*** Table 18.4 and Appendix Table A24.1 report reasons for not working by marital status. Married women who are not working cite "household work" and "physically unable to work" as the main reasons, single women cite "studying" and "household work." Married men who don't work list "retired," "sick" or "unable to work", or "job-related factors" as the reason. Single non-working men are generally attending school.

The sample of working men therefore differs from the male population: Male workers are relatively old, or more experienced, and more likely to be married or cohabiting than male non-workers. The sample of working women differs from the female population: Ceteris paribus, working women are older, more likely to be unmarried, and are likely to have more education than non-working women.

Heckman's (1979) sample selectivity correction uses a measure of the covariance of errors in the work participation regressions and the earnings regressions to adjust for differences in unobserved characteristics of workers and non-workers. Working men seem to be relatively more able to acquire job experience (finding and holding onto jobs), and working women are more able than non-workers in acquiring schooling. In analyzing the determinants of male and female earnings, it is likely that the sample selectivity correction for men will affect the coefficients measuring the returns to experience, while for women it is likely to alter the returns to schooling.

---

[7]    This last reason is unlikely because, even though life expectancy at birth in 1988 was 65 and 61 for Peruvian women and men respectively, it is very likely that life expectancy at age 14 is relatively uniform (and considerably higher than 65 years) for the two sexes.

**Table 18.3**
**Predicted Probability of Female Labor Force Participation**

| Characteristic | Predicted Probability[a] (Percentage) |
|---|---|
| 0. Mean Participation Rate | |
| All Women | 40.39 |
| Married Women Only | 31.22 |
| 1. Completed Schooling | |
| 0 to 4 Years | 38.64 |
| 5 Years | 33.17 |
| 6 to 9 Years | 38.70 |
| 10 Years | 39.55 |
| 11 to 16 Years | 45.60 |
| 17 and More Years | 63.29 |
| 2. Age | |
| 14 to 20 Years | 14.18 |
| 21 to 30 Years | 46.00 |
| 31 to 40 Years | 64.85 |
| 41 to 50 Years | 56.15 |
| 51 to 65 Years | 33.57 |
| 3. Marital Status | |
| Married | 33.05 |
| Single | 47.25 |
| 4. Female Head of Household | 57.94 |
| 5. Number of Children Aged 0 to 5 Years[b] | |
| 0 Children | 42.55 |
| 1 Child | 38.19 |
| 2 Children | 34.02 |
| 6. Number of Children Aged 6 to 13 Years[b] | |
| 0 Children | 42.55 |
| 1 Child | 42.64 |
| 2 Children | 42.78 |

a. Intercept is adjusted to make predicted probability equal to mean probability.
b. Simulation conditional on being married, cohabiting or widowed.

## 5.   Results of the Sector Choice Probit Regressions

Before we go on to examine the determinants of earnings we must analyze the determinants of career choice. This is a valuable exercise for two reasons: First, it may be important to adjust for sample selectivity in occupational choice while estimating earnings equations. Second, knowledge of determinants of occupational choice could be pivotal for designing policy. If it is discovered that women do worse in wage employment than as self-employed workers, then policy that aims to promote female entrepreneurship (e.g., by providing subsidized credit for female

**Table 18.4**
Reasons for Not Working: By Sex and Marital Status (%)

| | Married, Cohabiting & Widowed | | Separated & Single | | Total | |
|---|---|---|---|---|---|---|
| | Women | Men | Women | Men | Women | Men |
| 1. Studying | 0.93 | 3.41 | 83.22 | 91.16 | 50.62 | 79.64 |
| 2. Household Work | 75.47 | 4.55 | 8.92 | 1.20 | 35.28 | 1.64 |
| 3. Retired, Renter, etc. | 5.00 | 46.02 | 0.38 | 0.69 | 2.21 | 6.64 |
| 4. Unable to Work | 8.95 | 15.34 | 1.30 | 0.69 | 4.33 | 2.61 |
| 5. Sick | 5.58 | 12.50 | 1.45 | 1.89 | 3.09 | 3.28 |
| 6. Job Related Reasons[a] | 0.81 | 13.64 | 1.98 | 2.49 | 1.52 | 3.95 |
| 7. Other Reasons | 3.26 | 4.55 | 2.75 | 1.89 | 2.95 | 2.24 |
| Total Observations | 860 | 176 | 1,311 | 1,165 | 2,171 | 1,341 |

a.   Job Related Reasons Include paid or unpaid vacation, waiting to hear from employer, strike at work, waiting to start new job, and waiting for harvest.

entrepreneurs) will be more effective in improving the economic status of women than measures to provide skills (such as schooling and vocational training) that make women better paid employees. An understanding of the determinants of occupational choice helps in identifying barriers to profitable employment, and in evaluating the effectiveness of alternative policy measures.

Table 18.5 reports the determinants of the decision to work as self-employed instead of working as wage or salaried employees. The main findings are:

1.   For both sexes, increased schooling makes it more likely that the person works in the wage and salaried sector. For women the effect is stronger. For men, completed programs of study (10 years, or 17 and more years) are more important influences than the years of completed schooling per se.

2.   Age has a statistically insignificant but perceptible positive influence on the probability of choosing self-employment for both women and men.

3.   Tenure at current job has nonlinear effects on the probability of being self-employed. For both women and men, the effect is inverted U-shaped: Workers who are short-stayers in the market choose self-employment while those who expect to be long-stayers at their jobs tend to be in the wage and salaried sector. The downturn is sooner for women (between 5 and 10 years) than for men (after 11 years at the current job).

**Table 18.5**
Sector Choice Probit Estimates
*Dependent Variable: Self-Employed = 1, Wage or Salaried = 0*

| | Females | | Males | |
|---|---|---|---|---|
| | Coefficient | t-statistic | Coefficient | t-statistic |
| Schooling: 5 Years | 0.03 | 0.19 | -0.082 | -0.55 |
| Schooling: 6-9 Years | 0.18 | 1.18 | -0.043 | -0.32 |
| Schooling: 10 Years | -0.42 | -2.92 | -0.236 | -1.81 |
| Schooling: 11-16 Years | -1.02 | -5.46 | -0.207 | -1.36 |
| Schooling: 17+ Years | -0.99 | -5.05 | -0.207 | -1.36 |
| Age: 21-30 Years | 0.07 | 0.42 | -0.302 | -2.30 |
| Age: 31-40 Years | 0.15 | 0.79 | 0.077 | 0.53 |
| Age: 41-50 Years | 0.20 | 0.95 | 0.102 | 0.62 |
| Age: 51-65 Years | 0.21 | 0.85 | 0.261 | 1.48 |
| Tenure: 2-3 Years | 0.12 | 1.01 | 0.004 | 0.05 |
| Tenure: 3-5 Years | 0.17 | 1.29 | 0.186 | 1.68 |
| Tenure: 5-10 Years | -0.20 | -1.44 | 0.221 | 2.13 |
| Tenure: 11+ Years | -0.21 | -1.73 | -0.130 | -1.20 |
| Married | 0.74 | 5.52 | -0.545 | -4.70 |
| Cohabiting | 0.79 | 4.63 | -0.201 | -2.28 |
| Widowed | 0.58 | 2.14 | 0.219 | 0.65 |
| Separated | 0.22 | 1.17 | -0.208 | -1.07 |
| Household Head | 0.17 | 0.96 | 0.378 | 3.34 |
| Household Income | 1.6e-9 | 0.75 | 9.8e-8 | 0.98 |
| # Household Workers | 0.00 | 0.21 | 0.023 | 0.87 |
| Children: 0-5 Years | 0.08 | -1.69 | 0.064 | 1.73 |
| Children: 6-13 Years | 0.05 | -1.32 | 0.047 | 1.54 |
| Constant | -0.40 | -1.79 | -0.268 | -1.49 |
| Log Likelihood | | -575.8 | | -1037.8 |
| Chi-Square | | 238.2 | | 116.0 |
| Sample Size | | 1,011 | | 1,686 |
| Mean of Dependent Variable | | 0.4461 | | 0.3541 |

4.    Single women overwhelmingly choose salaried sector employment, and married, cohabiting and previously married women choose self-employment. On the other hand, married, cohabiting and separated men are more likely to choose wage sector employment.

5.    While being a household head raises the likelihood of being self-employed, the effect is significant only for men. Other household income has a positive but insignificant effect on the probability of being self-employed. The number of children (conditional on being married or cohabiting) only weakly influences the probability of being self-employed.

## 6.    Earnings Regressions

*The problem of sample selectivity.*    Earnings data are available only for men and women who were working during the survey period. Inferences drawn from these data may be biased, since the sample (working women and men) may not be randomly drawn from the population (all women and men). For example, we know that the average woman who works is more educated than a woman who does not. If women are being sorted (into workers/non-workers) on the basis of observable attributes such as education, then it is likely that they are also sorted by unobserved characteristics. Because of this nonrepresentativeness of the studied sample, the earnings equation:

$$W = \alpha_0 + \alpha_1 E + \alpha_2 X + \alpha_3 X^2 + \alpha_4 T + \alpha_5 T^2 + \beta D + \epsilon \qquad (8)$$

(where E is education, X is potential work experience, T is tenure at current job, and D is a marital status variable) yields biased estimates of the coefficients.

Heckman (1979) has proposed that estimating equation 9 below instead of the above earnings function at least partially corrects for this sampling bias.

$$W = \alpha_0 + \alpha_1 E + \alpha_2 X + \alpha_3 X^2 + \alpha_4 T + \alpha_5 T^2 + \beta D + \gamma \lambda_1 + \epsilon \qquad (9)$$

Equation 9 includes a new variable, $\lambda_1$, which is called the selectivity correction factor. Heuristically, this is a summary measure of the comparative advantage of workers over non-workers in market activities. Theory cannot ex ante tell us what sign $\gamma$ should be, though it is relatively easy to interpret the coefficient. If $\gamma$ is negative, this implies that the unobserved attributes that make workers earn more (than their observed skills would justify) are the same attributes that make it less likely that the person would work in the first place. Put another way, market wage offers are positively correlated with reservation wages. If $\gamma$ is positive, then the sample of workers have a comparative advantage in market work.

Estimates of returns to human capital based on equation 9 above are more reliable for policy purposes. To illustrate this point, consider proposals to subsidize training as a welfare increasing device. These proposals are of necessity based on data for workers, which show that trained workers earn more than untrained workers who seem otherwise identical. Using simple statistical methods to evaluate that returns to training may result in biased estimators of the effectiveness of training for not just for non-workers, but even for workers. The reason is that there may be trained workers who do not participate in market work, so that the earnings data are truncated.[8] Sample selectivity correction is required to obtain a reliable evaluation of the effectiveness of this policy.

---

[8]    While on this subject of policy effectiveness and non-random assignment, it is worthwhile to distinguish between three questions listed by Heckman and Robb (1985):

  1. What would be the impact of a proposed policy on earnings if people were randomly chosen to be its beneficiaries?

  2. How do the post-policy earnings of the beneficiaries compare to what they would have been in the absence of the policy measure?

  3. What would be the effect of this policy on the earnings of the beneficiaries if the future selection rule differs from the past selection rule?

Question 1 is a special case of question 3. Both these questions are much harder to answer than question 2, because they ask to forecast the increment in the earnings of beneficiaries over their prepolicy earnings when no selection bias characterizes enrollment while selection bias characterizes the available data.

**Table 18.6**
**Female Earnings Regressions**

| | Dependent Variable: Log (Hourly Earnings from Main Job) | | | | | |
|---|---|---|---|---|---|---|
| | (1) | (2) | (3) | (4) | (5) | (6) |
| Schooling | 0.0821 | 0.0772 | 0.0764 | 0.0711 | 0.0740 | 0.0538 |
| | (9.02) | (7.49) | (7.89) | (6.53) | (7.70) | (4.79) |
| Age-School-6 | 0.0684 | 0.0641 | 0.0613 | 0.0568 | 0.0458 | 0.0221 |
| | (7.51) | (6.41) | (6.24) | (5.30) | (4.35) | (1.77) |
| (Age-School-6)$^2$ | -0.0010 | -0.0010 | -0.0009 | -0.0009 | -0.0007 | -0.0004 |
| | (-5.51) | (-4.82) | (-4.72) | (-4.09) | (-3.53) | (-1.52) |
| Tenure | | | 0.0265 | 0.0269 | 0.0271 | 0.0287 |
| | | | (1.88) | (1.90) | (1.93) | (2.06) |
| Tenure$^2$ | | | -0.0009 | -0.0009 | -0.0008 | -0.0008 |
| | | | (-1.68) | (-1.69) | (-1.63) | (-1.65) |
| Married & Cohabiting Dummy | | | | | 0.2976 | 0.4383 |
| | | | | | (3.97) | (5.15) |
| Work Participation Selectivity ($\lambda_1$) | | -0.0511 | | -0.0536 | | -0.1931 |
| | | (-1.02) | | (-1.07) | | (-3.43) |
| Constant | 1.7762 | 1.9684 | 1.8298 | 2.0328 | 1.8764 | 2.6299 |
| | (12.11) | (8.24) | (12.20) | (8.41) | (12.58) | (9.93) |
| F-Statistic | 38.38 | 29.01 | 23.77 | 19.98 | 22.78 | 21.43 |
| Adjusted R$^2$ | 0.1151 | 0.1152 | 0.1167 | 0.1168 | 0.1316 | 0.1424 |
| Sample Size | 863 | 863 | 863 | 863 | 863 | 863 |

**Means of Variables**

| | | | | | | |
|---|---|---|---|---|---|---|
| Log (Hourly Earnings) | | 3.2897 | | 3.2897 | | 3.2897 |
| Schooling | | 9.4085 | | 9.4085 | | 9.4085 |
| Age-Schooling-6 | | 18.4850 | | 18.4580 | | 18.4580 |
| Tenure | | | | 5.1315 | | 5.1315 |
| Married & Cohabiting | | | | | | 0.5040 |
| Average Hours Per Week | | 34.3500 | | 34.3500 | | 34.3500 |
| Lambda (Workers/Non-workers) | | 0.7075 | | 0.7075 | | 0.7075 |

Notes:   t-statistics in parenthesis.
Schooling is Highest Grade Attained (in Years).
Tenure is Number of Years Worked at Current Job.

## Table 18.7
### Male Earnings Regressions

#### Dependent Variable: Log (Hourly Earnings from Main Job)

|  | (7) | (8) | (9) | (10) | (11) | (12) |
|---|---|---|---|---|---|---|
| Schooling | 0.0915 | 0.0910 | 0.0941 | 0.0936 | 0.0930 | 0.0933 |
|  | (15.72) | (15.26) | (15.77) | (15.33) | (15.48) | (15.27) |
| Age-School-6 | 0.0344 | 0.0311 | 0.0376 | 0.0348 | 0.0338 | 0.0346 |
|  | (5.67) | (3.82) | (5.71) | (4.10) | (4.80) | (4.07) |
| (Age-School-6)$^2$ | -0.0004 | -0.0003 | -0.0004 | -0.0003 | -0.0003 | -0.0003 |
|  | (-3.01) | (-1.99) | (-2.91) | (-2.05) | (-2.45) | (-2.14) |
| Tenure |  |  | -0.0070 | -0.0072 | -0.0082 | -0.0082 |
|  |  |  | (-0.090) | (-0.093) | (-1.06) | (-1.06) |
| Tenure$^2$ |  |  | 0.0000 | 0.0000 | 0.0001 | 0.0001 |
|  |  |  | (0.10) | (0.15) | (0.21) | (0.21) |
| Married & Cohabiting Dummy |  |  |  |  | 0.0831 | 0.0869 |
|  |  |  |  |  | (1.55) | (1.46) |
| Work Participation Selectivity ($\lambda_1$) |  | -0.0219 |  | -0.0188 |  | 0.0078 |
|  |  | (-0.58) |  | (-0.50) |  | (0.19) |
| Constant | 2.0977 | 2.1515 | 2.0649 | 2.1121 | -2.0763 | -2.0570 |
|  | (23.36) | (16.49) | (22.66) | (16.00) | (22.72) | (14.98) |
| F-Statistic | 94.24 | 70.53 | 57.49 | 47.77 | 48.35 | 41.28 |
| Adjusted R | 0.1472 | 0.1468 | 0.1484 | 0.1479 | 0.1491 | 0.1485 |
| Sample Size | 1,622 | 1,622 | 1,622 | 1,622 | 1,622 | 1,622 |

#### Means of Variables

| | | | | | | |
|---|---|---|---|---|---|---|
| Log (Hourly Earnings) |  | 3.4672 |  | 3.4672 |  | 3.4672 |
| Schooling |  | 9.7475 |  | 9.7475 |  | 9.7475 |
| Age-Schooling-6 |  | 19.8175 |  | 19.8175 |  | 19.8175 |
| Tenure |  |  |  | 8.0600 |  | 8.0600 |
| Married & Cohabiting |  |  |  |  |  | 0.6485 |
| Average Hours Per Week |  | 46.6455 |  | 45.6455 |  | 45.6455 |
| Lambda (Workers/Non-workers) |  | 0.3505 |  | 0.3505 |  | 0.3505 |

Notes:   t-statistics in parenthesis.
Schooling is Highest Grade Attained (in Years).
Tenure is Number of Years Worked at Current Job.

*Results of earnings regressions.*   This subsection discusses the results of fitting equations 8 and 9 to the data for about 863 women and 1,622 men aged 15 to 65. Ideally, hourly earnings should be used as the dependent variable, since it is earnings "potential" that the human capital earnings function tries to explain. Since hourly earnings are obtained by deflating monthly earnings by hours worked per month (actually, average hours worked per week multiplied by 4.3), and because the assumption of a constant wage-elasticity of hours supplied may not necessarily be legitimate, I experimented with both hourly and monthly earnings.[9]

Table 18.6 presents the results of hourly earnings regressions for all women, and Table 18.7 for all men. Odd-numbered columns are results of fitting equation 8, and even-numbered columns are estimations of selectivity corrected equation 9. Monthly earnings regressions are reported in Appendix Tables A24.2 and A24.3.

The main results are:

1.   The return to schooling in Lima is about 1 to 3 percentage points higher for men than for women. While the sample selectivity correction affects the return to schooling for women, it leaves the return to schooling for men unaltered. Hourly and monthly earnings regressions yield roughly the same rate of return to schooling.

2.   The return to potential work experience (age - schooling - 6 years) is generally higher for women, being higher for men only when tenure at current job and marital status are included as independent variables. For women, the rate of return to potential experience falls when tenure at current job is included. For men, it remains unchanged. Sample selectivity correction lowers the returns to experience for both men and women.

3.   Tenure at current job is always insignificant for men when potential experience is included in the regression, but is always significant for women, especially in the monthly wage regressions. This is because, while for men potential experience is a good continuous, interrupted careers make potential experience a poor proxy of job skills for women. Tenure at current job contains information on job skills for women, but for men it is redundant when potential experience is included in the regression.

4.   Married and cohabiting women and, to a lesser extent, men, are paid more than single and separated women and men. This result is consistent with the hypothesis

---

9   Suppose that the monthly earnings equation to be fitted is:

$$\text{Log } W = \alpha + \beta Z + \gamma \text{ Log } H + \delta \lambda + \epsilon$$

where W is monthly earnings, Z is the set of human capital variables, H is the number of hours worked per month, and l is the sample selectivity correction factor. Then the estimated hourly equation is:

$$\text{Log } W/H = \alpha + \beta Z + d \lambda + \epsilon_h, \quad \text{or}$$

$$\text{Log } W - \text{Log } H = \alpha + \beta Z + d \lambda + \epsilon_h.$$

This roughly amounts to assuming that $\gamma = \delta W/\delta H = 1$. That is, the inverse of the supply elasticity of hours of work is one.

that unobserved social ability is positively associated with unobserved professional ability.[10] Including a marital status variable reduces the coefficient on potential experience considerably for women; for men it does not alter this coefficient at all.

5. The coefficient for sample selectivity is negative for women, but insignificant for men in the hourly earnings regressions. For monthly earnings, the sample selectivity coefficient is negative for both women and men, but more important for women. This implies that sample selectivity is a more severe problem when studying female earnings and labor supply than for males. The negative sign of this coefficient implies that the unobserved attributes that make women more prolific in market work also make them less likely to be in the market (and stay at home or be in school). For men, it implies that the unobserved characteristics that make men better paid also make it more likely that the worker be in school or retired.

6. The coefficient of logarithm of average hours worked per week is close to 0.4 for women, and about 0.3 for men. But this estimate is not reliable, since hours worked are jointly determined with wages, and this endogeneity implies that the ordinary least equares (OLS) estimator is biased.[11]

*Wage workers versus the self employed.* Tables 18.8 and 18.9 report the results of hourly wage equations for self-employed and waged and salaried women and men respectively, and Appendix Tables A24.4 and A24.5 report the results of monthly wage regressions. These are the results of fitting the equation:

$$W = \alpha + \alpha_1 E + \alpha_2 X + \alpha_3 X^2 + \alpha_4 T + \alpha_5 T^2 + \beta D + \gamma \lambda_1 + \delta \lambda_2 + \epsilon \tag{10}$$

where E is education, X is potential work experience, T is tenure at current job, D is a marital status dummy that takes the value 1 if the worker is married or cohabiting, $\lambda_1$ is the sample selectivity index (inverse of Mill's ratio) obtained from the work participation probit regression, and $\lambda_2$ is the sector choice selectivity correction factor (inverse of Mill's ratio obtained from the sector choice probit estimation).

The main results are:

1. The return to schooling for self-employed women is about 4-6 percent, considerably lower than the 8-10 percent return for salaried women. The return to schooling for men is about 9-10 percent. It seems that self-employed women operate in a relatively segmented market.

2. The return to general experience (age adjusted by years of schooling) for men is about 2 percent per year in both the self-employed and the wage sector. For women, the rate of return to experience (in both sectors) drops considerably when a marital

---

[10] That is, the ability to find and sustain a relationship with a mate is positively correlated with the ability to find and keep a job.

[11] To correct for the endogenous nature of hours worked, I used Instrumental Variables techniques. Hours worked are instrumented by using schooling, age, marital status, and number of children and dependent relatives. Since the numbers of children and old or sick relatives are likely to affect hours worked but not wages, the equations are identifiable. The results will be reported in future work.

status variable is included in the regression. The likely reason is that marital status contains information about the work history of women (apart from potential experience and current tenure), since it may be correlated with frequency and duration of absence from the labor market. Since men generally participate in the market work continuously, marital status will not add to the information on accumulated job skills already provided by work experience and tenure.

3.  The return coefficients for tenure are generally insignificant. The only exception is the case of self-employed women, for whom the coefficient is about 4 percent but statistically insignificant in the hourly wage regression, and 7 percent and significant in the monthly wage regression. Again, salaried women and men display similar characteristics, while self-employed women seem to be in a relatively distinct market.

4.  Married and cohabiting women earn significantly higher hourly wages than women who are single or separated, especially in the self-employed sector. This evidence is consistent with the argument that being married provides a source of financing for self-employment among women. In the wage sector, the premium to being married may be due to the greater specialization afforded by marriage. However, it is puzzling that married and cohabiting men earn higher wages in the wage sector, while there is no premium to being married for self-employed men.

5.  Firm size, included in the estimations for self-employed workers as a proxy for the amount of non-human capital, always has a positive coefficient. The effect of firm size on earnings is larger for women than for men.

6.  Unionization has a statistically insignificant effect on wages for women and for men the effect is positive but weak. The magnitude of the union coefficient is larger for women than men, indicating that collective bargaining raises women's wages more than men's. But the statistical insignificance of the union coefficient refutes claims that unionization systematically raises the earnings of workers, and that the decline of unionization has worsened the position of the working class.

7.  Work participation selectivity is negative for both men and women. This implies that the unobserved attributes that make some workers earn higher wages than their observed human capital would justify, are also the attributes that make it less likely that the female or male worker works. For women, this can be interpreted to mean that the unobserved characteristics that make women better earners in the market (relative to what their observed skills would lead us to expect) also make them more productive in household work or in accumulating pre-job human capital. For men, it can be interpreted to mean that attributes associated with high earnings are likely to make them attend more school and retire earlier.

8.  Sector choice selectivity is generally insignificant, which means that while self-employed and wage workers differ in their earnings-related observed attributes such as schooling, age and marital status, they do not differ in their earnings-related unobserved characteristics.

## Table 18.8
### Female Earnings Regressions: By Employment Status

#### Dependent Variable: Log (Hourly Earnings from Main Job)

| | Self-Employed | | | Wage & Salaried Workers | | |
|---|---|---|---|---|---|---|
| | (13) | (14) | (15) | (16) | (17) | (18) |
| Schooling | 0.0633 | 0.0671 | 0.0411 | 0.1098 | 0.1013 | 0.0765 |
| | (3.46) | (2.97) | (1.62) | (10.73) | (7.36) | (4.05) |
| Age-School-6 | 0.0446 | 0.0447 | 0.0158 | 0.0491 | 0.0482 | 0.0345 |
| | (2.30) | (1.79) | (0.60) | (5.06) | (4.08) | (2.35) |
| (Age-School-6)$^2$ | -0.0007 | -0.0007 | -0.0004 | -0.0008 | -0.0007 | -0.0006 |
| | (-2.11) | (-1.69) | (-0.78) | (-3.45) | (-2.98) | (-1.96) |
| Tenure | | | 0.0367 | | | 0.0133 |
| | | | (1.28) | | | (0.78) |
| Tenure$^2$ | | | -0.0008 | | | -0.0002 |
| | | | (-0.68) | | | (-0.41) |
| Married & Cohabiting Dummy | | | 0.4644 | | | 0.2228 |
| | | | (2.32) | | | (1.71) |
| Firm Size | 0.0453 | 0.0492 | 0.0388 | | | |
| | (0.84) | (0.89) | (0.71) | | | |
| Union | | | | 0.0894 | 0.0866 | 0.0478 |
| | | | | (1.21) | (1.16) | (0.62) |
| Work Participation Selectivity ($\lambda_1$) | | 0.0260 | -0.1363 | | -0.0369 | -0.0944 |
| | | (0.26) | (-1.17) | | (-0.65) | (-1.56) |
| Sector Choice Selectivity ($\lambda_2$) | | -0.0209 | 0.0778 | | 0.0254 | 0.0924 |
| | | (-0.18) | (0.56) | | (0.51) | (1.26) |
| Constant | 2.5182 | 2.4683 | 2.7924 | 1.4615 | 1.5596 | 1.7651 |
| | (7.37) | (4.24) | (4.70) | (9.66) | (6.15) | (5.43) |
| F-Statistic | 4.18 | 2.79 | 2.95 | 37.99 | 25.42 | 17.57 |
| Adjusted R$^2$ | 0.0363 | 0.0309 | 0.0495 | 0.2394 | 0.2376 | 0.2409 |
| Sample Size388 | 388 | 388 | 388 | 471 | 471 | 471 |

#### Means of Variables

| | | | | | | |
|---|---|---|---|---|---|---|
| Log (Hourly Earnings from Main Job) | | | 3.5944 | | | 3.1713 |
| Schooling | | | 7.4378 | | | 11.1423 |
| Age-Schooling-6 | | | 24.0976 | | | 14.5053 |
| Tenure | | | 5.0099 | | | 5.3786 |
| Average Weekly Hours | | | 27.8853 | | | 39.2519 |
| Firm Size | | | 1.6213 | | | |
| Union | | | | | | 0.3737 |

Notes: t-statistics in parentheses.

## Table 18.9
### Male Earnings Regressions: By Employment Status

#### Dependent Variable: Log (Hourly Earnings from Main Job)

| | Self-Employed | | | Wage & Salaried Workers | | |
|---|---|---|---|---|---|---|
| | (19) | (20) | (21) | (22) | (23) | (24) |
| Schooling | 0.0945 | 0.0971 | 0.1006 | 0.0914 | 0.0932 | 0.0938 |
| | (7.96) | (7.52) | (7.75) | (14.44) | (13.19) | (13.11) |
| Age-School-6 | 0.0154 | 0.0209 | 0.0281 | 0.0341 | 0.0224 | 0.0200 |
| | (1.29) | (1.23) | (1.63) | (5.12) | (2.47) | (2.07) |
| $(\text{Age-School-6})^2$ | -0.0000 | -0.0001 | -0.0002 | -0.0004 | -0.0002 | -0.0002 |
| | (-0.17) | (-0.46) | (-0.69) | (-2.85) | (-1.10) | (-0.98) |
| Tenure | | | 0.0315 | | | 0.0019 |
| | | | (-2.09) | | | (0.22) |
| Tenure$^2$ | | | 0.0007 | | | 0.0001 |
| | | | (1.47) | | | (-0.50) |
| Married & Cohabiting Dummy | | | 0.0498 | | | 0.1592 |
| | | | (0.44) | | | (2.36) |
| Firm Size | 0.0093 | 0.0094 | 0.0101 | | | |
| | (1.99) | (2.00) | (2.17) | | | |
| Union | | | | 0.0846 | 0.0872 | 0.0886 |
| | | | | (1.72) | (1.77) | (1.78) |
| Work Participation Selectivity ($\lambda_1$) | | 0.0399 | 0.0454 | | -0.0731 | -0.0258 |
| | | (0.52) | (0.55) | | (-1.75) | (-0.56) |
| Sector Choice Selectivity ($\lambda_2$) | | -0.0251 | 0.0175 | | 0.0660 | 0.1871 |
| | | (-0.30) | (-0.20) | | (-1.33) | (-1.68) |
| Constant | 2.4444 | 2.3999 | 2.3585 | 1.9690 | 2.3111 | 2.2665 |
| | (13.52) | (6.93) | (6.57) | (20.49) | (11.47) | (10.88) |
| F-Statistic | 18.92 | 12.65 | 9.13 | 66.18 | 44.65 | 30.54 |
| Adjusted $R^2$ | 0.1170 | 0.1144 | 0.1192 | 0.1983 | 0.1966 | 0.2020 |
| Sample Size | 542 | 542 | 542 | 1,055 | 1,055 | 1,055 |

#### Means of Variables

| | | |
|---|---|---|
| Log (Hourly Earnings from Main Job) | 3.6362 | 3.3710 |
| Schooling | 9.0738 | 10.1047 |
| Age-Schooling-6 | 21.9686 | 18.7878 |
| Tenure | 8.1274 | 8.0542 |
| Average Weekly Hours | 44.7459 | 44.8355 |
| Firm Size | 2.5134 | |
| Union | | 0.3815 |

Notes:   t-statistics in parenthesis.

## 5. Accounting for the Earnings Differential

*The Oaxaca decomposition.*   Table 18.10 below provides the results of the Oaxaca decomposition of earnings into the part due to endowed skill differences and the part due to differences in the returns to these skills. The evidence broadly indicates that much of the earnings differences are because of the latter. That is, skill differences between men and women explain only about 10 to 15 percent of the difference in earnings; the rest is attributable to differential rewards to human capital. The choice of index type does not seem to affect this result very much.

The results for salaried sector decomposition need clarification. The estimated intercept for men is much larger than that for women, so that wage offers calculated by netting out the intercept (and selectivity bias) from mean wages yield a negative discrimination against women, or discrimination against men. This indicates poor choice of functional form or omission of strongly relevant variables. Experimenting with variables such as firm size, occupation and industry dummies did not eliminate this problem. Fortunately, this changes when marital status is included in the regression, and the results are then consistent with the results for all men and women.

*Possible explanations.*   Before the earnings differential between men and women is specifically attributed to labor market discrimination, it is useful to examine the labor market further. One argument against the discrimination view is that having the same amount of market skills is not sufficient to result in the same earnings for men and women; women may choose low wage work for several reasons. The criterion that immediately comes to mind is hours flexibility. To examine this question, the non-pecuniary characteristics of jobs need to be examined. A preliminary solution is to study gender differences in the industrial and occupational composition of employment.

Table 18.11 lists the industrial composition of female and male employment and their mean earnings. Lima's women are concentrated in non-government services, retail and non-retail commerce. Services are the only extraordinarily low paying sectors, but these sectors are generally thought to afford greater hours flexibility. Males are relatively more dispersed across industries, though about a quarter of males in Lima work in manufacturing. Except in industries where they are scantily represented (transportation, government services, and construction), females earn less than their male counterparts in all sectors, with the largest differentials existing in household services and manufacturing (one dominated by women and the other by men). These results are very similar to the ones obtained in Gill (1991a) for Chile.

Table 18.12 lists industry means of schooling, tenure at current job and age. Working women are marginally less schooled than men, they have considerably less tenure at their current job, and are about a year and a half younger. Given the differences in levels of human capital across sectors, the large earning differentials in manufacturing, finance and real estate, services and non-retail commerce seem to be reasonable: These sectors also have the largest gender gaps in schooling, tenure and age.

The occupational distribution of female and male employment ratios and earnings ( Table 18.13) clearly shows the occupations in which women are concentrated (office workers, service workers, self-employed traders, and professionals). Among these occupations, only professionals and self-employed traders are also those that have unusually low female-to-male earnings ratios. Table 18.14 shows that these occupations have the largest differences in schooling, tenure and/or age. Much of the lower wages of women in Lima can therefore be attributed to segregation (unequal work), not discrimination (unequal pay for the same work).

## Table 18.10
### Accounting for Earnings Differentials: The Oaxaca Decomposition[a]
#### (All Numbers are Percentages)

| Norm: | Male Wage Function | | Female Wage Function | | |
|---|---|---|---|---|---|
| Components: | Coefficients | Endowments | Coefficients | Endowments | Total |
| **I.   All Women and Men** | | | | | |
| Using Equations without Tenure | 80.5 | 19.5 | 84.9 | 15.1 | 82.5 |
| Using Equations with Tenure | 89.6 | 10.4 | 84.3 | 15.7 | 82.5 |
| Using Equations with Tenure & Marital Status | 90.9 | 9.1 | 85.4 | 14.6 | 82.6 |
| **II.   Salaried Women and Men** | | | | | |
| Using Equations without Tenure | 112.5[b] | -12.5[b] | 105.8[b] | -5.8 | 81.9 |
| Using Equations with Tenure | 117.7[b] | -17.7[b] | 120.0[b] | -20.0 | 81.9 |
| Using Equations with Tenure & Marital Status | 54.3 | 45.7 | 39.4 | 60.6 | 81.9 |
| **III. Self-Employed Women and Men** | | | | | |
| Using Equations without Tenure | 84.0 | 16.0 | 95.9 | 4.1 | 95.9 |
| Using Equations with Tenure | 88.4 | 11.6 | 86.6 | 13.4 | 95.9 |
| Using Equations with Tenure & Marital Status | 88.5 | 11.5 | 87.2 | 12.8 | 95.9 |

a.    All equations include log of average hours worked per week; the regressions for salaried workers include union status and the regressions for self-employed workers included firm size.

b.    Denotes that the earnings differential to be explained is negative.

Notes: Male Wage function as Discriminatory Norm:

Coefficients Component = $X_f(\beta_m-\beta_f)$, Endowments Component = $\beta_m(X_m-X_f)$.

Female Wage function as Discriminatory Norm:

Coefficients Component = $X_m(\beta_m-\beta_f)$, Endowments Component = $\beta_f(X_m-X_f)$.

**Table 18.11**
Labor Force and Earnings by Sex and Industry

| Industry | Percentage Labor Force | | | Earnings | | |
|---|---|---|---|---|---|---|
| | Females | Males | F/M | Females | Males | F/M |
| Agriculture & Fishing | 0.89 | 2.19 | 0.41 | 2.81 | 13.45 | 0.21 |
| Mining | 0.22 | 0.43 | 0.51 | 11.00 | 12.26 | 0.90 |
| Manufacturing:  Non-Textiles | 8.46 | 17.17 | 0.49 | 5.35 | 12.19 | 0.44 |
| Manufacturing: Textiles | 8.91 | 7.25 | 1.23 | 4.09 | 8.24 | 0.50 |
| Construction | 0.22 | 9.68 | 0.02 | 13.20 | 11.60 | 1.14 |
| Commerce: Non-Retail | 10.80 | 9.81 | 1.10 | 10.03 | 15.34 | 0.65 |
| Commerce: Retail | 28.51 | 14.43 | 1.98 | 9.17 | 8.91 | 1.03 |
| Transport & Communication | 1.89 | 7.98 | 0.24 | 19.66 | 11.43 | 1.72 |
| Finance & Real Estate | 3.79 | 6.39 | 0.59 | 9.24 | 21.67 | 0.43 |
| Services: Community & Other | 3.79 | 8.28 | 2.25 | 5.92 | 10.78 | 0.55 |
| Services: Government | 4.90 | 8.65 | 0.57 | 14.12 | 8.47 | 1.67 |
| Services: Household | 12.69 | 7.25 | 1.75 | 3.01 | 6.86 | 0.44 |
| Total Number in Sample | 898 | 1,642 | | 898 | 1,642 | |

Notes: Earnings are Monthly Earnings in Thousands of 1990 Intis.

**Table 18.12**
Average Schooling, Tenure and Age by Industry

| Industry | Schooling | | Tenure | | Age | |
|---|---|---|---|---|---|---|
| | Female | Male | Female | Male | Female | Male |
| Agriculture & Fishing | 4.80 | 7.22 | 23.28 | 9.44 | 45.63 | 39.67 |
| Mining | 13.50 | 11.43 | 2.25 | 10.46 | 24.50 | 42.43 |
| Manufacturing: Non-Textiles | 10.05 | 9.58 | 5.42 | 8.23 | 30.01 | 34.39 |
| Manufacturing: Textiles | 8.45 | 9.77 | 3.98 | 7.10 | 34.45 | 33.43 |
| Construction | 11.50 | 7.66 | 3.75 | 7.16 | 29.50 | 35.30 |
| Commerce: Non-Retail | 8.82 | 10.09 | 5.01 | 8.13 | 35.41 | 37.02 |
| Commerce: Retail | 7.49 | 8.21 | 4.90 | 6.59 | 36.88 | 33.32 |
| Transport & Communication | 12.44 | 9.31 | 6.57 | 7.52 | 35.52 | 36.72 |
| Finance & Real Estate | 11.41 | 12.10 | 4.27 | 7.55 | 29.24 | 36.55 |
| Services: Community & Other | 12.99 | 13.08 | 6.20 | 7.90 | 33.40 | 36.48 |
| Services: Government | 11.51 | 11.70 | 6.43 | 11.35 | 34.16 | 37.48 |
| Services: Household | 6.92 | 8.25 | 4.61 | 8.60 | 33.80 | 37.37 |
| All Workers | 9.26 | 9.60 | 5.25 | 8.03 | 34.46 | 35.97 |
| All Non-Workers | 6.70 | 6.10 | 0.00 | 0.00 | 27.31 | 20.64 |
| Total Number in Sample | 3,202 | 3,155 | 1,033 | 1,737 | 3,942 | 3,752 |

Notes:  Schooling is Highest Grade Attained (in Years).
Tenure is Number of Years Worked at Current Job.
Age is in Years.

**Table 18.13**
Labor Force and Earnings by Sex and Occupation

| Occupation | Percentage Labor Force | | | Earnings | | |
|---|---|---|---|---|---|---|
| | Females | Males | F/M | Females | Males | F/M |
| Professional: Non-Teachers | 9.91 | 11.91 | 0.84 | 9.02 | 19.06 | 0.47 |
| Professional: Teachers | 8.69 | 2.80 | 3.10 | 4.65 | 9.56 | 0.49 |
| Managers & Proprietors | 0.67 | 1.83 | 0.37 | 16.22 | 42.26 | 0.38 |
| Office Workers | 17.26 | 10.90 | 1.58 | 8.05 | 8.09 | 1.00 |
| Traders: Sales & Others | 5.23 | 6.03 | 0.87 | 13.55 | 10.40 | 1.30 |
| Traders: Self-Employed | 14.03 | 7.19 | 1.95 | 11.95 | 24.86 | 0.48 |
| Traders: Vendors & Hawkers | 12.47 | 7.13 | 1.75 | 6.79 | 6.34 | 1.07 |
| Service Workers | 17.04 | 10.41 | 1.64 | 5.53 | 6.93 | 0.80 |
| Farm Workers | 1.00 | 1.52 | 0.66 | 3.06 | 5.11 | 0.60 |
| Industry Workers: Non-Precision | 9.24 | 6.15 | 1.50 | 3.53 | 5.92 | 0.60 |
| Industry Workers: Precision | 1.22 | 15.47 | 0.08 | 3.13 | 7.18 | 0.44 |
| Construction & Other Workers | 3.23 | 18.70 | 0.17 | 3.93 | 11.80 | 0.34 |
| Total Number in Sample | 898 | 1,642 | | 898 | 1,642 | |

Note:   Earnings are Monthly Earnings in Thousands of 1990 Intis.

**Table 18.14**
Average Schooling, Tenure and Age by Occupation

| Occupation | Schooling | | Tenure | | Age | |
|---|---|---|---|---|---|---|
| | Female | Male | Female | Male | Female | Male |
| Professional: Non Teachers | 12.89 | 14.01 | 6.43 | 8.91 | 32.21 | 37.33 |
| Professional: Teachers | 14.57 | 15.65 | 5.90 | 7.35 | 34.64 | 36.07 |
| Managers & Proprietors | 15.33 | 14.10 | 6.96 | 12.41 | 36.33 | 44.87 |
| Office Workers | 11.75 | 11.45 | 5.00 | 9.03 | 29.90 | 35.78 |
| Traders: Sales & Others | 10.28 | 9.94 | 5.12 | 8.62 | 32.11 | 36.57 |
| Traders: Self-Employed | 6.99 | 9.38 | 5.06 | 7.23 | 38.70 | 36.60 |
| Traders: Vendors & Hawkers | 6.70 | 7.61 | 4.90 | 6.85 | 35.91 | 33.37 |
| Service Workers | 5.67 | 8.39 | 5.08 | 7.11 | 36.14 | 34.84 |
| Farm Workers | 5.67 | 6.09 | 20.91 | 9.57 | 44.33 | 39.84 |
| Industrial Workers | 7.98 | 8.41 | 4.33 | 8.10 | 35.39 | 33.67 |
| Industrial Workers: Precision | 8.20 | 8.88 | 4.26 | 8.61 | 29.64 | 35.22 |
| Industrial Workers: Other | 8.41 | 7.81 | 4.17 | 7.14 | 28.86 | 34.95 |
| All Workers | 9.16 | 9.60 | 5.25 | 8.03 | 34.46 | 35.97 |
| All Non-Workers | 6.70 | 6.10 | 0.00 | 0.00 | 27.31 | 20.64 |
| Total Number in Sample | 3,202 | 3,155 | 1,033 | 1,737 | 3,942 | 3,752 |

Notes:   Schooling is Highest Grade Attained (in Years).
Tenure is Number of Years Worked at Current Job.
Age is in Years.

The earnings differentials between men and women seem to be more closely related to their tenure differences, rather than differences in schooling levels. These tables suggest that there are large positive interactions between schooling and work experience (both job-specific and general). The nature of female human capital seems to prevent it from obtaining market returns equal to those for men, since average tenure is generally smaller for women, both across sectors and occupations. It bears repeating that these results are remarkably similar to those for Santiago (see Gill, 1991b), so that these patterns seem to be at least a Latin American and not just a Peruvian phenomenon.

## 6.   Summary and Policy Implications

To provide a summary statement of the policy lessons of this paper, we charted the returns to schooling for self-employed and salaried men and women. Figure 18.1 shows that hourly earnings levels are higher for self-employed workers regardless of gender and that male-female patterns within sectors differ remarkably. Returns to schooling for salaried men and women, and self-employed men are about the same, and considerably higher than returns to schooling for self-employed women.

**Figure 18.1**
Schooling-Earnings Profiles Self-employed & Wage Workers
Lima, 1990

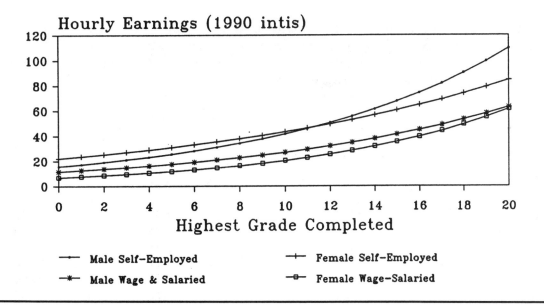

Suppose that the aim of policy is to improve the economic position of women. This means that we want women to move vertically (along the Y-axis). According to the graph, there are two vehicles for this movement: The first is an increase in the education of women, which moves women along either the self-employed or the wage sector schooling-earnings profile. The second is a movement of women from the wage sector (where, aside from lower earnings relative to the self-employed, the male-female earnings gap is large) to the self-employed sector (where mean hourly earnings are roughly the same for men and women). Naturally, the relative effectiveness of these policies depends upon their costs and not just the benefits illustrated above. But there seems to be evidence that a policy of education subsidies will encourage women to work in the wage sector, where there are higher returns to schooling but where average earnings are lower than in the self-employed sector.

Given the difference in levels, there are clearly obstacles to being self-employed. One likely obstacle is startup capital. Improving access to credit would help to remove this barrier. If women (especially mothers) obtain greater overall benefits from flexibility in work schedules, a policy of credit subsidization would be more compatible with the objective of improving the economic status of women than education subsidies. There are probably still good arguments for schooling subsidies. However, this paper provides some evidence that increased schooling, by lowering fertility, can make women choose work patterns similar to those of males only up to a point. Women will always choose to have some children, and childcare will always remain a relatively female-intensive activity. Policy design must recognize that women need more flexibility in work schedules than men.

If there are positive externalities associated with the improved status of women, credit subsidization for women may be the more effective instrument in attaining these benefits, at least in urban areas where schooling has already reached reasonable levels. The discussion above seems to justify subsidization of work schedule flexibility primarily for women with children. This creates a targeting problem, because a policy of credit subsidization for mothers will lead to fertility that is higher than optimal as women try to qualify for this subsidy. Subsidized credit for women without children (younger, unmarried women) can be rationalized if returns to sector-specific experience among the self-employed are high, so that there are advantages to early entry.

The evidence in this study indicates high returns to sector-specific experience for self-employed women. A simpler policy implication emerges as a result of this: Education policy must be supplemented by a policy that facilitates the transition of women from the wage to the self-employed sector, for example, through credit subsidization.

## Appendix Table 18A.1
### Reasons for Not Working: Females, by Marital Status and Age

| Age Group (Years) | 14-20 | 21-30 | 31-40 | 41-50 | 51-65 | All |
|---|---|---|---|---|---|---|
| **Married, Cohabiting & Widowed Women** | | | | | | |
| 1. Studying | 3.85 | 1.83 | 1.12 | 0.00 | 0.00 | 0.93 |
| 2. Household Work | 80.77 | 90.37 | 86.59 | 86.62 | 68.54 | 75.47 |
| 3. Retired, Rentier etc. | 0.00 | 0.00 | 0.00 | 2.82 | 12.92 | 5.00 |
| 4. Unable to Work | 0.00 | 0.46 | 0.00 | 0.70 | 7.87 | 8.95 |
| 5. Sick | 3.85 | 3.67 | 5.03 | 6.34 | 7.30 | 5.58 |
| 6. Job Related Reasons | 0.00 | 0.00 | 3.35 | 0.70 | 0.00 | 0.81 |
| 7. Other Reasons | 11.54 | 3.67 | 3.91 | 2.82 | 3.37 | 3.26 |
| Total Observations | 26 | 218 | 179 | 142 | 178 | 860 |
| **Single & Separated Women** | | | | | | |
| 1. Studying | 87.80 | 46.90 | 15.00 | 5.56 | 0.00 | 83.22 |
| 2. Household Work | 6.21 | 27.59 | 55.00 | 50.00 | 56.25 | 8.92 |
| 3. Retired, Rentier etc. | 0.00 | 0.00 | 0.00 | 0.00 | 6.25 | 0.38 |
| 4. Unable to Work | 0.22 | 1.38 | 0.00 | 11.11 | 15.63 | 1.30 |
| 5. Sick | 1.11 | 4.83 | 10.00 | 11.11 | 9.38 | 1.45 |
| 6. Job Related Reasons | 1.33 | 9.66 | 15.00 | 11.11 | 3.13 | 1.98 |
| 7. Other Reasons | 3.33 | 9.66 | 5.00 | 11.11 | 9.38 | 2.75 |
| Total Observations | 451 | 145 | 20 | 18 | 32 | 1,311 |
| **Married, Cohabiting & Widowed Men** | | | | | | |
| 1. Studying | .. | 38.46 | 0.00 | 8.33 | 0.00 | 3.41 |
| 2. Household Work | .. | 23.08 | 0.00 | 16.67 | 1.54 | 4.55 |
| 3. Retired, Rentier etc. | .. | 0.00 | 0.00 | 16.67 | 60.00 | 46.02 |
| 4. Unable to Work | .. | 7.69 | 0.00 | 0.00 | 3.08 | 15.34 |
| 5. Sick | .. | 15.38 | 0.00 | 16.67 | 18.46 | 12.50 |
| 6. Job Related Reasons | .. | 15.38 | 83.33 | 16.67 | 12.31 | 13.64 |
| 7. Other Reasons | .. | 0.00 | 16.67 | 25.00 | 4.62 | 4.55 |
| Total Observations | * | 13 | 13 | 12 | 65 | 176 |
| **Single & Men** | | | | | | |
| 1. Studying | 90.30 | 64.36 | .. | .. | .. | 91.16 |
| 2. Household Work | 0.81 | 2.97 | .. | .. | .. | 1.20 |
| 3. Retired, Rentier etc. | 0.00 | 0.99 | .. | .. | .. | 0.69 |
| 4. Unable to Work | 0.00 | 0.99 | .. | .. | .. | 0.69 |
| 5. Sick | 1.62 | 8.91 | .. | .. | .. | 1.89 |
| 6. Job Related Reasons | 4.04 | 12.87 | .. | .. | .. | 2.49 |
| 7. Other Reasons | 3.23 | 8.91 | .. | .. | .. | 1.89 |
| Total Observations | 371 | 101 | * | * | * | 486 |

Note: * Indicates fewer than 7 observations.

## Appendix Table 18A.2
### Female Monthly Earnings Regressions

#### Dependent Variable: Log (Monthly Income from Main Job)

|  | (25) | (26) | (27) | (28) | (29) | (30) |
|---|---|---|---|---|---|---|
| Schooling | 0.0733 | 0.0628 | 0.0618 | 0.0500 | 0.0609 | 0.0383 |
|  | (8.77) | (6.62) | (6.95) | (5.00) | (6.87) | (3.71) |
| Age-School-6 | 0.0589 | 0.0497 | 0.0465 | 0.0362 | 0.0384 | 0.0119 |
|  | (7.04) | (5.40) | (5.15) | (3.68) | (3.99) | (1.04) |
| $(\text{Age-School-6})^2$ | -0.0009 | -0.0007 | -0.0007 | -0.0006 | -0.0006 | -0.0002 |
|  | (-5.08) | (-3.92) | (-4.00) | (-2.89) | (-3.28) | (-0.94) |
| Tenure |  |  | 0.0451 | 0.0465 | 0.0449 | 0.0471 |
|  |  |  | (3.49) | (3.60) | (3.48) | (3.68) |
| $\text{Tenure}^2$ |  |  | -0.0012 | -0.0013 | -0.0012 | -0.0012 |
|  |  |  | (-2.66) | (-2.72) | (-2.61) | (-2.66) |
| Married & Cohabiting Dummy |  |  |  |  | 0.1618 | 0.3157 |
|  |  |  |  |  | (2.33) | (4.04) |
| Log (Hours/Week) | 0.3932 | 0.3816 | 0.3707 | 0.3571 | 0.3875 | 0.3798 |
|  | (8.38) | (8.11) | (7.87) | (7.57) | (8.16) | (8.06) |
| Work Participation Selectivity ($\lambda_1$) |  | -0.1080 |  | -0.1162 |  | -0.2145 |
|  |  | (-2.35) |  | (-2.55) |  | (-4.18) |
| Constant | 5.5340 | 5.9845 | 5.7271 | 6.2208 | 5.6869 | 6.5539 |
|  | (24.68) | (20.39) | (24.99) | (20.86) | (24.81) | (21.36) |
| F-Statistic | 39.81 | 33.00 | 29.17 | 26.02 | 25.90 | 25.21 |
| Adjusted $R^2$ | 0.1526 | 0.1567 | 0.1639 | 0.1690 | 0.1682 | 0.1837 |
| Sample Size | 862 | 862 | 862 | 862 | 862 | 862 |

#### Means of Variables

|  |  |  |  |  |  |  |
|---|---|---|---|---|---|---|
| Log (Monthly Income) |  | 8.2610 |  | 8.2610 |  | 8.2610 |
| Schooling |  | 9.4030 |  | 9.4030 |  | 9.4030 |
| Age-Schooling-6 |  | 18.4850 |  | 18.4580 |  | 18.4580 |
| Tenure |  |  |  | 5.1286 |  | 5.1286 |
| Married & Cohabiting |  |  |  |  |  | 0.5041 |
| Average Hours Per Week |  | 34.3635 |  | 34.3635 |  | 34.3635 |
| Lambda (Workers/Non-workers) |  | 0.7074 |  | 0.7074 |  | 0.7074 |

Note:   t-statistics in parenthesis.

## Appendix Table 18A.3
### Male Monthly Earnings Regressions

**Dependent Variable: Log (Monthly Income from Main Job)**

|  | (31) | (32) | (33) | (34) | (35) | (36) |
|---|---|---|---|---|---|---|
| Schooling | 0.0850 | 0.0815 | 0.0866 | 0.0831 | 0.0838 | 0.0824 |
|  | (15.53) | (14.53) | (15.41) | (14.24) | (14.83) | (14.32) |
| Age-School-6 | 0.0513 | 0.0365 | 0.0524 | 0.0383 | 0.0442 | 0.0379 |
|  | (8.85) | (4.79) | (8.38) | (4.81) | (6.68) | (4.77) |
| $(Age-School-6)^2$ | -0.0007 | -0.0004 | -0.0007 | -0.0004 | -0.0005 | -0.0004 |
|  | (-5.77) | (-2.82) | (-5.36) | (-2.75) | (-4.43) | (-2.93) |
| Tenure |  |  | -0.0015 | -0.0024 | -0.0041 | -0.0041 |
|  |  |  | (-0.32) | (-0.33) | (-0.56) | (-0.57) |
| $Tenure^2$ |  |  | -0.0001 | -0.0000 | -0.0000 | -0.0000 |
|  |  |  | (-0.22) | (-0.21) | (-0.16) | (-0.08) |
| Married & Cohabiting Dummy |  |  |  |  | 0.1907 | 0.1564 |
|  |  |  |  |  | (3.77) | (2.80) |
| Log (Hours/Week) | 0.3171 | 0.2983 | 0.3197 | 0.2994 | 0.2955 | 0.2888 |
|  | (6.93) | (6.40) | (6.98) | (6.46) | (6.41) | (6.22) |
| Work Participation Selectivity ($\lambda_1$) |  | -0.1059 |  | -0.1029 |  | -0.0562 |
|  |  | (-2.96) |  | (-2.87) |  | (-1.42) |
| Constant | 6.0386 | 6.3790 | 6.0071 | 6.3404 | 6.1226 | 6.2834 |
|  | (32.14) | (28.93) | (31.73) | (28.51) | (32.05) | (28.34) |
| F-Statistic | 99.07 | 81.00 | 66.47 | 58.11 | 59.48 | 52.04 |
| Adjusted $R^2$ | 0.1948 | 0.1984 | 0.1951 | 0.1983 | 0.2016 | 0.2017 |
| Sample Size | 1,622 | 1,622 | 1,622 | 1,622 | 1,622 | 1,622 |

### Means of Variables

|  |  |  |  |
|---|---|---|---|
| Log (Monthly Income) | 8.7233 | 8.7233 | 8.7233 |
| Schooling | 9.7477 | 9.7477 | 9.7477 |
| Age-Schooling-6 | 19.8175 | 19.8175 | 19.8175 |
| Tenure |  | 8.0601 | 8.0601 |
| Married & Cohabiting |  |  | 0.6486 |
| Average Hours Per Week | 45.6457 | 45.6457 | 45.6457 |
| Lambda (Workers/Non-workers) | 0.3505 | 0.3505 | 0.3505 |

Note:    t-statistics in parenthesis.

**Appendix Table 18A.4**
Female Earnings Regressions: By Employment Status

**Dependent Variable: Log (Monthly Income from Main Job)**

| | Self-Employed | | | Wage & Salaried Workers | | |
|---|---|---|---|---|---|---|
| | (37) | (38) | (39) | (40) | (41) | (42) |
| Schooling | 0.0439 | 0.0430 | 0.416 | 0.0998 | 0.0916 | 0.0872 |
| | (2.64) | (2.09) | (2.03) | (9.88) | (6.80) | (6.35) |
| Age-School-6 | 0.0526 | 0.0416 | 0.0172 | 0.0471 | 0.0495 | 0.0378 |
| | (3.00) | (1.85) | (0.74) | (5.00) | (4.31) | (2.70) |
| $(\text{Age-School-6})^2$ | -0.0008 | -0.0006 | -0.0004 | -0.0008 | -0.0008 | -0.0007 |
| | (-2.64) | (-1.63) | (-0.90) | (-3.54) | (-3.29) | (-2.33) |
| Tenure | | | 0.0712 | | | 0.0232 |
| | | | (2.75) | | | (1.43) |
| $\text{Tenure}^2$ | | | -0.0018 | | | -0.0004 |
| | | | (-1.61) | | | (-0.75) |
| Log (Average Hours | 0.4168 | 0.4054 | 0.3702 | 0.5380 | 0.5361 | 0.5212 |
| Worked) | (6.29) | (6.02) | (5.53) | (6.31) | (6.25) | (6.06) |
| Firm Size | 0.1313 | 0.1286 | 0.1239 | | | |
| | (2.64) | (2.57) | (2.48) | | | |
| Union | | | | 0.0931 | 0.0882 | 0.0530 |
| | | | | (1.72) | (1.77) | (1.78) |
| Work Participation | | -0.0986 | -0.1413 | | -0.0125 | -0.0291 |
| Selectivity ($\lambda_1$) | | (-1.08) | (-1.55) | | (-0.23) | (-0.52) |
| Sector Choice | | -0.0353 | -0.1358 | | 0.0415 | 0.0130 |
| Selectivity ($\lambda_2$) | | (-0.34) | (-1.28) | | (0.86) | (0.26) |
| Constant | 5.7773 | 6.2218 | 6.7557 | 4.7280 | 4.7079 | 4.9707 |
| | (15.56) | (10.62) | (11.30) | (12.81) | (10.89) | (10.97) |
| F-Statistic | 13.08 | 9.38 | 8.98 | 30.41 | 21.80 | 17.46 |
| Adjusted $R^2$ | 0.1516 | 0.1482 | 0.1757 | 0.2383 | 0.2365 | 0.2396 |
| Sample Size | 338 | 338 | 338 | 471 | 471 | 471 |

**Means of Variables**

| | | |
|---|---|---|
| Log (Monthly Income from Main Job) | 8.3596 | 8.2750 |
| Schooling | 7.4378 | 11.1423 |
| Age-Schooling-6 | 24.0976 | 14.5053 |
| Tenure | 5.0099 | 5.3786 |
| Average Weekly Hours | 27.8853 | 39.2125 |
| Firm Size | 1.6213 | |
| Unionization | | 0.3737 |

Note:    t-statistics in parenthesis.

## Appendix Table 18A.5
### Male Earnings Regressions: By Employment Status

Dependent Variable: Log (Monthly Income from Main Job)

| | Self-Employed | | | Wage & Salaried Workers | | |
|---|---|---|---|---|---|---|
| | (43) | (44) | (45) | (46) | (47) | (48) |
| Schooling | 0.0970 | 0.0930 | 0.0945 | 0.0808 | 0.0794 | 0.0792 |
| | (8.98) | (7.94) | (8.00) | (13.10) | (11.48) | (11.31) |
| Age-School-6 | 0.0453 | 0.0287 | 0.0318 | 0.0458 | 0.0293 | 0.0290 |
| | (4.06) | (1.86) | (2.02) | (7.03) | (3.36) | (3.12) |
| $(\text{Age-School-6})^2$ | -0.0005 | -0.0002 | -0.0003 | -0.0006 | -0.0003 | -0.0003 |
| | (-2.44) | (-0.81) | (-0.91) | (-4.56) | (-1.92) | (-1.74) |
| Tenure | | | 0.0142 | | | 0.0037 |
| | | | (-1.03) | | | (0.45) |
| $\text{Tenure}^2$ | | | 0.0003 | | | -0.0003 |
| | | | (0.77) | | | (-0.69) |
| Log (Average Hours Worked) | 0.2842 | 0.2577 | 0.2687 | 0.3743 | 0.3565 | 0.3565 |
| | (4.22) | (3.74) | (3.85) | (5.70) | (5.39) | (5.39) |
| Firm Size | 0.0102 | 0.0102 | 0.0043 | | | |
| | (2.41) | (2.41) | (2.49) | | | |
| Union | | | | 0.0421 | 0.0410 | 0.0435 |
| | | | | (0.89) | (0.87) | (0.91) |
| Work Participation Selectivity $(\lambda_1)$ | | -0.1178 | -0.1201 | | -0.1144 | -0.1104 |
| | | (-1.67) | (-1.68) | | (-2.84) | (-2.72) |
| Sector Choice Selectivity $(\lambda_2)$ | | 0.0163 | 0.0205 | | -0.0416 | -0.0355 |
| | | (0.22) | (0.26) | | (-0.87) | (-0.73) |
| Constant | 6.2339 | 6.5856 | 6.5413 | 5.8188 | 6.2711 | 6.2420 |
| | (22.61) | (16.26) | (15.67) | (21.58) | (19.39) | (19.04) |
| F-Statistic | 29.56 | 21.58 | 16.91 | 54.82 | 40.31 | 31.38 |
| Adjusted $R^2$ | 0.2088 | 0.2103 | 0.2093 | 0.2034 | 0.2077 | 0.2066 |
| Sample Size | 542 | 542 | 542 | 1,055 | 1,055 | 1,055 |

### Means of Variables

| | | |
|---|---|---|
| Log (Monthly Income from Main Job) | 8.8725 | 8.6422 |
| Schooling | 9.0738 | 10.1045 |
| Age-Schooling-6 | 21.9686 | 18.7878 |
| Tenure | 8.1274 | 8.0542 |
| Average Weekly Hours | 44.7459 | 46.3467 |
| Firm Size | 2.5134 | |
| Unionization | | 0.3810 |

Notes: t-statistics in parenthesis.

# References

Cornwell, Christopher and Peter Rupert. "Unobservable Individual Effects, Marriage and the Earnings of Young Men," working paper, State University of New York at Buffalo, 1990.

Gill, Indermit. "Is there Sex Discrimination in Chile? Evidence from the CASEN Survey," in *Female Employment and Pay in Latin America,* A Regional Study, edited by George Psacharopoulos, Human Resources Division, Technical Department, Latin America and the Caribbean Region, The World Bank, 1991a.

Gill, Indermit. "Gender, Occupational Choice, and Earnings in Latin America: The Cases of Lima and Santiago," Human Resources Division, Technical Department, Latin America and the Caribbean Region, The World Bank, 1991b.

Glewwe, Paul. "The Distribution of Welfare in Peru in 1985-86," Living Standards Measurement Study Working Paper No. 42, The World Bank, 1988.

Heckman, James J. "Sample Selection Bias as a Specification Error," *Econometrica,* Volume 47: pages 153-161, 1979.

Heckman, James J. and Richard Robb. "Alternative Methods for Evaluating the Impact of Interventions," in Longitudinal Analysis of Labor Market Data, edited by J. Heckman and B. Singer. Cambridge University Press: pages 156- 245, 1985.

Killingsworth, Mark R. and James J. Heckman. "Female Labor Supply: A Survey," in *Handbook of Labor Economics,* Volume 1, edited by O. Ashenfelter and R. Layard. Elsevier Science Publishers: pages 103-204, 1986.

Khandker, Shahidur. "Women's Labor Force Participation and Male-Female Wage Differences in Peru." This volume, 1992.

King, Elizabeth M. "Does Education Pay in the Labor Market? The Labor Force Participation, Occupation, and Earnings of Peruvian Women," Living Standards Measurement Study Working Paper No. 67, The World Bank, 1990.

Mincer, Jacob. *Schooling, Experience and Earnings.* Columbia University Press, New York, 1974.

Moock, Peter, Philip Musgrove and Morton Stelcner. "Education and Earnings in Peru's Informal Nonfarm Family Enterprises," Living Standards Measurement Study Working Paper No. 64, The World Bank, 1990.

Oaxaca, Ronald. "Male-female Wage Differentials in Urban Labor Markets," *International Economic Review:* pages 693-709, 1973.

Stelcner, Morton, Ana-Maria Arriagada, and Peter Moock. "Wage Determinants and School Attainment among Men in Peru," Living Standards Measurement Study Working Paper No. 38, The World Bank, 1988.

United Nations Development Programme. *Human Development Report,* New York: Oxford University Press, 1990.

World Bank. *World Development Report.* Washington, D.C. Oxford University Press, 1990.

# 19

# Women's Labor Force Participation and Earnings: The Case of Uruguay

*Mary Arends*

## 1. Introduction

Women's wages are about 75 percent of men's wages in Uruguay. This study investigates this differential using econometric analysis. Uruguay is an interesting country to study because of its high female labor force participation rate (about 50 percent of females between the ages of 14 and 65 participate) and because of a long-standing commitment to public education. There is a wide scope for investigation of human capital characteristics and their effect on female earnings.

A description of the Uruguayan labor market is given in the next section. Section 3 discusses the sample used in the analysis. Section 4 looks at the characteristics that influence a woman's decision to participate in the labor force. It examines the selectivity problem, which arises because working women are a self-selected group out of the entire female sample. Section 5 uses a Mincerian earnings function to estimate returns to human capital endowments in the labor market and considers how returns differ between men and women, taking into account the selectivity problem. Section 6 breaks down the earnings differential to determine how much can be explained by differences in endowments and what is the upper bound of possible labor market discrimination.

## 2. The Uruguayan Economy and Labor Market

Uruguay's demographics are characterized by low growth rates, a high emigration rate, an aging population, and a high degree of urbanization. The average annual population growth rate from 1965 to 1980 was .4 percent, and was .6 percent from 1980 to 1988. Of the total population in 1988, 26.2 percent was aged 0 to 14, 62.7 percent was aged 15 to 64, and 11.1 percent was over 65. Eighty-five percent of the population lived in an urban area, and about 52 percent lived in Montevideo. Due to higher emigration rates among men, in 1989, 53 percent of the population of 2,747,800 people were women. Considering the population aged 14 to 65 the disparity was even greater; 55 percent of a total of 2,116,200 people in this age group were female.

Economically, although Uruguay has one of the highest GNP per capita in Latin America at US$2,620 in 1989, the country has experienced stagnation since the mid-1950s due to import-substitution policies in the fifties and sixties, and stabilization policies in the late seventies and eighties. The annual growth rate was 1.3 percent from 1965 to 1988, and -.4 percent from 1980 to 1988. The share of industry in the economy has declined from 32 percent in 1965 to 29 percent in 1988. Sixty percent of the country's GNP in 1988 came from the service sector. In addition, the country has suffered political upheaval. In 1973, there was a military coup, and a dictatorship ruled the country until March 1, 1985. This period coincided with a fall in real wages, which had fallen to 62 percent of their 1968 level by 1984.[1]

The stagnation, coupled with the recent military regime, has led to high emigration rates as Uruguayans move to Brazil and Argentina. Emigration was concentrated in the years 1973 to 1977 and reached its peak in 1974, when 62,400 people left the country. There were approximately 300,000 emigrants from 1963 to 1981, which represents about 10 percent of the current Uruguayan population. Emigrants tended to be males, in their early or late twenties, and married. They also tended to be workers in the private industrial sector. Because of the age and educational attainment of emigrants, the impact of the emigration on the labor market was strong and lasting. For example, Aguiar (1984) estimates that Uruguay lost 20.7 percent of its population between the ages of 20 and 29, 10.8 percent of its economically active population, 20 percent of its salaried workers, 22.6 percent of its artisans and day workers, and 27.9 percent of its employees in industry.[2]

This has provided opportunities for women to enter the labor force, as the female economically active population has grown relative to the male population. In addition to the decrease in qualified males in the work force, declining family living standards have encouraged a high level of female labor force participation. Sending women and young people into the paid labor force who would otherwise be at home is a survival strategy to maintain family living standards.[3] Fortuna and Prates (1989) report evidence that between 1971 and 1979 real wages fell 45 percent, and between 1973 and 1979 90 percent of the population in Montevideo maintained its level of family earnings due to the incorporation of more of its members into the labor force.[4] Women's participation rate increased from 27 percent in 1967 to 36.9 percent in 1979.[5] The growth in female participation has continued throughout the 1980s. In 1989, it reached 47 percent.

Another characteristic of the Uruguayan labor market is the long hours worked. Besides increasing the number of workers in the family to maintain living standards, workers increase their hours, especially in the public sector, and take on extra jobs, often in the informal sector. In the sample, 10 percent of the workers reported having more than one job. Labor supply increases because hours increase and participation levels increase even though real wages have declined. Apparently the income effect of lower wages (which makes leisure less affordable) outweighs the substitution effect (which would decrease labor supply because leisure is less expensive). These responses, which represent a shift in the labor supply curve outward, will tend to decrease real wages further, holding the labor demand curve constant.[6]

The work week also tends to be long because of expensive labor market laws requiring employers to pay a one month bonus, social security benefits, health insurance, accident insurance, and two

---

[1]   Weinstein (1988), p. 94.

[2]   Aguiar (1984), p. 22.

[3]   Taglioretti (1983), p. 30.

[4]   Fortuna and Prates (1989), p. 81.

[5]   Aguiar (1984), p. 38.

[6]   Aguiar (1984), p. 34.

weeks' leave to each employee. Employers who face an upturn in demand are likely to require existing hires to work more hours, rather than expand the labor pool. Another consequence of the laws is the expansion of the informal sector in the Uruguayan labor market. By World Bank estimates, from 16 to 28 percent of the labor force was employed in the informal sector in 1987.[7] Employers may subcontract tasks to the informal sector, and women play a role as an expendable labor force, as documented by Fortuna and Prates (1989) in the textile and recycling sectors.[8]

Uruguay has traditionally had an extensive public schooling system. Enrollments in secondary school, as a percentage of the relevant age group, was higher than for any other Latin American country in 1965 at 44 percent, and in 1987 it was 73 percent, second only to Argentina. Tertiary enrollments were also the highest in Latin America in 1987 at 42 percent. The economically active population with incomplete primary education has declined from 20.1 percent in 1969 to 10.1 percent in 1989, while the percentage with secondary and university education has increased from 31.2 percent to 58.5 percent.[9] The system includes teaching schools, a "labor university" which provides secondary technical education, and one national university. However, the Uruguayan economy has had difficulties finding suitable employment for highly educated graduates with raised expectations, and consequently, unemployment rates are higher than average among college graduates.[10]

## 3.   Data Characteristics

The data used in this study are drawn from the 1989 Encuesta Nacional de Hogares conducted by the General Administration of Statistics and the Census (DGEC) in Uruguay. It is a household survey of 31,766 individuals in 9,648 households. The survey only includes urban households, and thus excludes the 15 percent of the population in rural areas. For the analysis in this chapter, only individuals aged 14 to 65 were included, providing a sample of 20,502 individuals.

An individual was classified as working if he or she reported positive earnings and positive hours worked in a primary occupation. Excluded were those who reported no hours because they were on vacation or sick because no regular hours could be estimated for them. An individual was classified as a labor force participant if he or she was classified as employed (whether remunerated or not), laid off, looking for work for the first time, or on strike.

Descriptive statistics for the working male, working female, and non-working female samples are presented in Table 19.1. The female participation rate is 52 percent. Working females have a higher level of education than working men. Schooling was calculated using information about the highest level of education attained and the number of years completed at that level, adding the number of years in each previous level to the number of years at the highest level. For some individuals, the schooling in years could not be estimated because the level was unknown. Since the schooling system was changed in 1977, the measure for schooling is an estimate, and subject to inaccuracies. Experience was estimated using the proxy of age minus years of schooling minus 6. This measure is very likely to overestimate experience because there is no way to measure

---

[7]   World Bank (1991), p. 33.

[8]   Fortuna and Prates (1989), pp. 82-93.

[9]   World Bank (1991), p. 34.

[10]   World Bank (1991), p. 39.

## Table 19.1
### Means and (Standard Deviations) of Sample Variables

| Females | Working Males | Working Females | Non-Working |
|---|---|---|---|
| Age | 38.81 (13.29) | 37.54 (12.43) | 38.63 (16.96) |
| **Marital Status** | | | |
| Married | .71 (.46) | .54 (.50) | .60 (.49) |
| Education (Yrs) | 8.34 (3.59) | 9.06 (3.92) | 7.53 (3.38) |
| **Education Level** | | | |
| None | .01 (.08) | .01 (.11) | .02 (.14) |
| Some Primary | .14 (.35) | .11 (.31) | .18 (.38) |
| Complete Primary | .28 (.45) | .25 (.43) | .29 (.45) |
| 1st Cycle Secondary | .24 (.42) | .26 (.44) | .29 (.45) |
| 2nd Cycle Secondary | .09 (.28) | .14 (.35) | .09 (.29) |
| University | .08 (.27) | .10 (.30) | .04 (.19) |
| Technical | .16 (.37) | .07 (.25) | .06 (.23) |
| Teacher | .01 (.08) | .05 (.23) | .03 (.19) |
| Other | .00 (.06) | .01 (.12) | .01 (.09) |
| Monthly Primary Earnings (Pesos) | 187,390 (168,550) | 106,870 (95,390) | |
| Primary Job--Hourly Wage (Pesos) | 980 (2,360) | 730 (800) | |
| Years of Experience | 24.64 (14.55) | 22.60 (13.97) | |

- continued -

**Table 19.1** (continued)
**Means and (Standard Deviations) of Sample Variables**

| Females | Working Males | Working Females | Non-Working |
|---|---|---|---|
| Primary Job--Hours Worked Weekly | 48.44 (16.23) | 37.31 (16.05) | |
| Work in Public Sector | .24 (.43) | .21 (.41) | |
| Work in Private Sector (Wage Earners) | .50 (.50) | .58 (.49) | |
| Work in Informal Sector | .16 (.39) | .36 (.48) | |
| Employer | .06 (.25) | .02 (.14) | |
| Self-Employed | .18 (.39) | .20 (.40) | |
| Household Size | 4.15 (1.86) | 3.99 (1.90) | 4.14 (2.00) |
| # Children Aged 0 to 3 | .26 (.54) | .23 (.51) | .25 (.54) |
| # Children Aged 4 to 6 | .20 (.45) | .18 (.44) | .18 (.44) |
| # Children Aged 7 to 12 | .47 (.76) | .44 (.74) | .44 (.75) |
| Head of Household | .71 (.45) | .16 (.37) | .10 (.30) |
| Total Household Monthly Income (Pesos) | 364,820 (465,240) | 373,480 (320,640) | 310,370 (389,900) |
| Number of Employed in Household | 2.02 (1.00) | 2.21 (.96) | 1.41 (1.02) |
| Lives in Montevideo | .52 (.50) | .55 (.50) | .49 (.50) |
| N | 6,646 | 4,484 | 6,494 |

Notes:  Female Participation rate = 52%
          Male Participation rate = 84%

the time individuals may have spent out of the labor force. The bias is likely to be greater for females, who typically interrupt their working lives during childbearing years. Working males on average have more experience and work longer hours than working females.

All female observations were included in the probit regression, while only those females classified as working, and for whom schooling and experience could be calculated with some accuracy, were included in the wage regression.

Wages were calculated by taking the monthly income in the participant's primary job, and dividing it by the hours worked in a week times 4.3 to approximate monthly hours.

Unemployment rates in the sample are much higher for women than men (10 percent versus 5.7 percent).[11] The unemployment rate is higher for those who have a university education--8 percent for men and 11 percent for women. For both sexes, about half of the unemployed with a university education are first time job seekers.

One question in examining wage differentials between men and women is whether the two groups choose different occupations, with women either choosing or being forced by lack of opportunity into the lower paid occupations. Table 19.2A presents the distribution of occupations by gender; 17 percent of the females working are professionals, technicians and teachers, while only 7 percent of the men are in this category. Thirty-two percent of working women work in personal services and 18 percent in office work (corresponding figures for men are 1 percent and 13 percent). For each occupation except transport, females make considerably less than males. The lowest paid occupation is agriculture, but a very small percentage of either males and females are employed in this sector. The next lowest paid group is personal services and 32 percent of the women are employed in this occupation. Men are more heavily represented in artisan and non-classified occupations which are also low paying. Taglioretti (1983) notes that most of the increase in women's labor supply has been absorbed by state and social services. Personal services have also played a large role in absorbing the increase.[12]

In Table 19.2B, the breakdown of employment by sector is shown. Males are more likely to work in the public sector or to be employers than females. Females tend to work in the informal sector; 36 percent of working females and 19 percent of working males are employed there. The informal sector is defined here as including the self-employed who either have or do not have a regular work place in firms of less than five people. Self-employed professionals and technicians are considered to be formal sector workers. The informal sector also includes workers receiving a regular wage in the private sector providing personal services, while working for enterprises of less than five people. It includes most domestics, thus the high female participation rate in this sector. Looking at average education levels, employers, public sector workers, and formal sector workers tend to have the most years of schooling. In every sector, women have more education than men, with the exception of the informal sector.

---

[11]   Unemployment rates are defined as the percentage of the labor force categorized as laid off workers or first time job seekers.

[12]   Taglioretti (1983), p. 49.

**Table 19.2A**
Occupational Distribution and hourly wages (pesos) by Gender

| | Male % | Hourly Wage | Female % | Hourly Wage | Ratio F/M Wage | Hourly Wage-- All Workers |
|---|---|---|---|---|---|---|
| Professionals | 7 | 2,192 | 17 | 1,273 | .58 | 1,605 |
| Administrators | 4 | 2,114 | 2 | 1,213 | .57 | 1,930 |
| Office Workers | 13 | 1,055 | 18 | 872 | .83 | 967 |
| Sales People | 14 | 1,085 | 13 | 630 | .58 | 907 |
| Agricultural Workers | 1 | 515 | 0 | 495 | .96 | 514 |
| Transport Workers | 6 | 857 | 0 | 1,282 | 1.50 | 862 |
| Artisans of Cloth Furniture, Etc. | 23 | 756 | 13 | 417 | .55 | 664 |
| Other Artisans | 8 | 770 | 3 | 657 | .85 | 749 |
| Not Elsewhere Classified | 13 | 661 | 2 | 623 | .94 | 657 |
| Personal Services | 11 | 693 | 32 | 520 | .75 | 576 |

Note: Mean wage for entire population is 882 pesos.

**Table 19.2B**
Hourly Wage for Working Men and Women by Type of Employment
(in Pesos)

| | Females | | | Males | | | Ratio of Female to Male Wage |
|---|---|---|---|---|---|---|---|
| | Wage | Number | Yrs. Educ. | Wage | Number | Yrs. Educ. | |
| Self-Employed | 662 | 881 | 8.26 | 1,023 | 1,219 | 7.71 | .75 |
| Employee | 738 | 3,515 | 9.22 | 905 | 4,997 | 8.38 | .82 |
| Employer | 1,389 | 88 | 10.10 | 1,825 | 430 | 9.22 | .76 |
| Public Sector | 990 | 932 | 11.69 | 901 | 1,633 | 8.63 | 1.10 |
| Private Sector | 670 | 3,552 | 8.36 | 1,013 | 5,013 | 8.21 | .66 |
| Formal Sector | 883 | 2,851 | 10.43 | 1,051 | 5,381 | 8.62 | .84 |
| Informal Sector | 480 | 1,633 | 6.65 | 709 | 1,265 | 7.01 | .68 |

Note: Wage is calculated by taking primary job monthly income and dividing it by weekly hours worked in primary job, multiplied by 4.3 to estimate monthly hours.

**Table 19.2C**
**Hourly Wages by School Levels**
**(in Pesos)**

|  | Self-Employed | | | Informal Sector | | | Employer | | |
|---|---|---|---|---|---|---|---|---|---|
|  | Male | Female | Ratio | Male | Female | Ratio | Male | Female | Ratio |
| Less than Primary | 563 | 348 | .62 | 552 | 396 | .72 | 1111 | 903 | 0.81 |
| Primary | 700 | 480 | .69 | 669 | 500 | .75 | 1376 | 1142 | 0.83 |
| Secondary | 1275 | 614 | .48 | 807 | 501 | .62 | 1951 | 1120 | 0.57 |
| University | 2169 | 1737 | .80 | 1193 | 761 | .64 | 2588 | 2499 | 0.97 |

|  | Public Sector | | | Private Worker | | |
|---|---|---|---|---|---|---|
|  | Male | Female | Ratio | Male | Female | Ratio |
| Less than Primary | 717 | 665 | .93 | 687 | 451 | 0.66 |
| Primary | 760 | 695 | .91 | 696 | 551 | 0.79 |
| Secondary | 910 | 853 | .94 | 914 | 646 | 0.71 |
| University | 1431 | 1268 | .89 | 2151 | 1211 | 0.56 |

Notes:   Definition of Informal:

1. Must work in enterprise employing 5 persons or less.
2. Includes self-employed and wage workers in personal service sector.
3. Excludes professionals and technicians, and employers.

Private workers are those who work for a wage, excluding employers, the self-employed, and public sector employees. It includes some informal sector employees.

In Table 19.2C, the male-female wage differential is evident. The table presents wage rates broken down by schooling level and sector of employment. In every sector, women earn less than men. However, in some sectors the differential is smaller than others; in the public sector, women make about 90 percent of the men's wage, while the ratio is much smaller for the private sector, especially at higher levels of education. The high ratio in the public sector is probably due to the emigration of educated men and to anti-discrimination laws for Uruguayan women.

## 4.   Determinants of Female Labor Force Participation

Table 19.3 presents the results of a probit regression to determine which characteristics influence a woman's decision to participate in the labor force. The partial derivative is computed at the means of the independent variables.

It is necessary to run the probit in order to correct for selectivity bias using Heckman's (1979) two-step procedure. In effect, women who report positive earnings are a special subset of the women in the sample. They have decided to work because the wage they earn exceeds their reservation wage. The reservation wage is affected by education, age and family structure. When children are very young, a mother places more value on time spent in the home, and therefore, her reservation wage is higher. Similarly, a woman who is in school and has not completed her degree would be likely to have a high reservation wage, because of her desire to complete the degree rather than work. With higher education, expectation of a higher salary results which tends to increase the reservation wage. The reservation wage also reflects tastes--

## Table 19.3
### Probit Results for Female Work Force Participation

| Variable | Coefficient | T-ratio | Partial Derivative |
|---|---|---|---|
| Constant | -2.199 | -18.66 | |
| **Education Levels** | | | |
| Some Primary | -.185 | -1.70 | -.070 |
| Completed Primary | -.025 | -.23 | -.009 |
| First Cycle Secondary | .042 | .38 | .016 |
| Second Cycle Secondary | .292 | 2.58 | .111 |
| Technical | .075 | .64 | .028 |
| Teacher | .430 | 3.46 | .164 |
| University | .473 | 3.97 | .180 |
| Other Education Level | .247 | 1.51 | .094 |
| # of Children 0 to 3 | -.193 | -7.09 | -.073 |
| # of Children 4 to 6 | -.115 | -3.57 | -.043 |
| # of Children 7 to 12 | -.107 | -5.43 | -.040 |
| **Age Group** | | | |
| Age 20 to 24 | .846 | 14.34 | .322 |
| Age 25 to 29 | 1.240 | 20.34 | .472 |
| Age 30 to 34 | 1.453 | 24.47 | .553 |
| Age 35 to 39 | 1.281 | 21.43 | .487 |
| Age 40 to 44 | 1.288 | 21.44 | .490 |
| Age 45 to 49 | 1.065 | 17.33 | .405 |
| Age 50 to 54 | .779 | 12.34 | .296 |
| Age 55 to 59 | .575 | 8.70 | .219 |
| Age 60 to 65 | .312 | 4.51 | .119 |
| Head of Household | .813 | 18.41 | .309 |
| Live in Montevideo | .050 | 1.78 | .019 |
| Total Household Income | -.000 | -4.50 | -.000 |
| Number of Occupied Persons in Household | .607 | 39.98 | .231 |

Notes:  Dependent variable for probit is whether individual is in work force defined by reporting positive hours and positive income.
Base group is individuals with no education, aged 14 to 19.

for example a "taste" for work inside the home rather than outside the home.  It could be that two women with similar characteristics are offered the same wage, but one of the women has a higher reservation wage so only one woman is observed in the labor force.  For those who do not work, a wage is not observed.  Therefore, a participation equation is estimated using characteristics observed for everyone in the sample, such as age, education, and family size.

This equation is used to determine work. When this ratio, or Lambda, is included in the earnings function it eliminates the bias due to selectivity.

A factor tending to decrease the reservation wage is the need for income. Standing (1982) explained how having a higher need for income would tend to increase labor force participation.[13] For example, in the probit the number of people employed, the total household income, and whether the woman is the head of the household are all proxies for the need for income. If many household members are employed, that would reduce the need for a female to work outside the home. Likewise, higher household income would be expected to have a negative effect on labor force participation. On the other hand, if a woman is the head of the household, this increases her responsibility to earn money.

The dependent variable in the probit is a dummy variable equal to 1 if the woman is working and if she reports positive earnings and positive hours worked for the previous week and equal to 0 otherwise. Dummy variables are used to represent various levels of schooling and age splines. Other dummy variables include whether the woman is the head of the household and whether the woman lives in Montevideo. Variables that proxy the structure of the household include the number of children aged 0 to 3, 4 to 6, and 7 to 12, and the number of employed people in the household. It was not possible to determine in every case which children belonged to which female in each household, so the number of children in the household is used as a proxy. The number of children were grouped in this manner because Uruguay has a very well developed preschool program and primary school begins at age 6. Preschool education covers about 40 percent of children aged 3-5; 75 percent of 5 year olds attend school. Sixty-nine percent of the children in the sample aged 4 to 6 attend school. This would help women with their childcare duties, and therefore enable them to participate in the labor force when the children reach a younger age than in other Latin American countries, where schooling might begin at age six. However, about 60 percent of children without access to preschool education are from the poorest households. Women that have more of a need for income may not have the opportunity to send their young children to school. The other variables used in the probit are total household income and the number of working people in the household.[14]

Table 19.4 presents the results of a simulation testing for each characteristic while holding all other characteristics at the value of their sample mean. It is apparent that education plays a role in predicting whether a female works. For example, the probability ranged from .28 for women with some primary education to .54 for women with university level education. Also, at lower levels of education the effect is not as significant as for higher levels; looking at the t-statistics, they are insignificant at the 5 percent level for all education levels except the second cycle of secondary school, the university, and teacher school. Apparently, the opportunity cost of staying out of the labor market is higher for women with more education, and the opportunity cost effect outweighs the positive effect that education has on the reservation wage. The net effect is that higher education is associated with higher participation rates in the labor force.

---

[13]   Standing, (1982), p. 55.

[14]   As shown in the other chapters in this book, being married had a significant negative effect on the probability of working in an earlier equation, but was left out in the final probit equation because of correlation effects with the number of children.

## Table 19.4
### Predicted Working Probabilities by Characteristic

| Characteristic | Predicted Probability |
| --- | --- |
| **Education Levels** | |
| No Education | .35 |
| Some Primary | .28 |
| Completed Primary | .34 |
| First Cycle Secondary | .37 |
| Second Cycle Secondary | .46 |
| Technical | .38 |
| Teacher | .52 |
| University | .54 |
| Other Education Level | .45 |
| **# of Children 0 to 3** | |
| None | .39 |
| One | .32 |
| Two | .25 |
| Three | .20 |
| **# of Children 4 to 6** | |
| None | .38 |
| One | .34 |
| Two | .30 |
| Three | .26 |
| **# of Children 7 to 12** | |
| None | .39 |
| One | .35 |
| Two | .31 |
| Three | .28 |
| **Age Group** | |
| Age 14 to 19 | .12 |
| Age 20 to 24 | .38 |
| Age 25 to 29 | .54 |
| Age 30 to 34 | .62 |
| Age 35 to 39 | .55 |
| Age 40 to 44 | .55 |
| Age 45 to 49 | .47 |
| Age 50 to 54 | .35 |
| Age 55 to 59 | .28 |
| Age 60 to 65 | .20 |
| **Head of Household** | |
| Yes | .65 |
| No | .34 |

-continued-

**Table 19.4** (continued)
Predicted Working Probabilities by Characteristic

| Characteristic | Predicted Probability |
|---|---|
| Live in Montevideo | |
| Yes | .55 |
| No | .49 |
| | |
| Number of Occupied Persons in Household | |
| None | .08 |
| One | .22 |
| Two | .44 |
| Three | .67 |
| Four | .85 |

As for age effects, participation is high at all ages compared to other Latin American countries, and peaks at the age of 30 to 34. This indicates that Uruguayan women have a high dedication to the work force throughout their life cycle. Age is a highly significant determinant of participation at all levels, and the age splines have the highest-valued partial derivatives of all the explanatory variables. Participation is lowest at ages 14 to 19, which is expected given Uruguay's high enrollment rates in secondary and tertiary education.

The number of children is also a negative and significant determinant of labor force participation. With no children aged 0 to 3 and other things being equal, the participation rate would be .39. With one child aged 0 to 3, the probability drops to .32, with two to .25 and with 3 to .20. There is also a significant difference in the effect of 0 to 3 year old children compared with 4 to 6 year old children. The number of children aged 7 to 12 has less of an impact than the number of younger children.

Being the head of a household also significantly increases the probability that a woman will work from .34 to .65. This makes sense because female headed households are likely to be poorer than male headed households, increasing the woman's necessity to work. The number of employed persons in the household has a significant, positive effect on the probability that a female will be working. The explanation for the sign is not immediately obvious. This may show that wealthier households tend to divide up labor, with women working at home and men working outside the home, while poorer households have to send more members, including children, into the wage earning market. It may also show a kind of family "work ethic" with members preferring to work outside the home. The coefficient on household income is small and negative, which is as expected. Lastly, living in Montevideo had a small, positive, but not very strong effect on the decision to work.

## 5.   Earnings Functions

Regression results for men and for women, both corrected for selectivity and uncorrected for selectivity, are presented in Table 19.5. Obviously, the sample for the earnings regression includes only working men and working women who reported positive income, positive hours,

## Table 19.5
### Earnings Functions

| | Males | | Females | | Females (Corrected for Selectivity) | |
|---|---|---|---|---|---|---|
| | basic | alternate | basic | alternate | basic | alternate |
| Constant | 1.112 (14.362) | 1.545 (20.492) | .421 (5.467) | 1.092 (13.766) | .351 (4.139) | .990 (11.610) |
| Schooling (Years) | .098 (41.524) | .085 (36.974) | .110 (36.244) | .076 (23.347) | .112 (35.532) | .078 (23.468) |
| Experience | .057 (29.110) | .042 (19.712) | .042 (16.152) | .036 (13.758) | .044 (15.866) | .039 (14.028) |
| Experience Squared | -.001 (-20.582) | -.001 (-14.737) | -.001 (-11.576) | -.001 (-10.110) | -.001 (-11.518) | -.001 (-10.584) |
| Log Hours | .586 (31.298) | .516 (28.620) | .685 (39.653) | .628 (37.709) | .684 (39.656) | .626 (37.674) |
| Married | | .274 (14.310) | | .040 (1.987) | | .037 (1.806) |
| Informal | | -.277 (-14.284) | | -.427 (-18.007) | | -.432 (-18.216) |
| Public Sector | | -.075 (-4.270) | | .152 (5.704) | | .151 (5.688) |
| Employer | | .421 (13.891) | | .509 (7.269) | | .507 (7.258) |
| Lambda | | | | | .060 (2.001) | .093 (3.243) |
| Adjusted R-squared | .352 | .397 | .401 | .464 | .402 | .465 |
| N | | 6,646 | | 4,484 | | 4,484 |

Note:   Base group for regressions including sectors and marital status are unmarried individuals, either self-employed or wage-earners in the private sector, who are not employers.

and for whom the years of schooling and experience could be estimated. The model estimated is the standard Mincer wage-earnings equation, where the log of wage is regressed on years of schooling, experience, and experience squared. In these regressions, the dependent variable is the log of the primary monthly earnings, and the independent variables include the log of weekly hours. The log of the hourly wage is not used as the dependent variable because then the elasticity of the wage with respect to hours would be constrained to be one. In the final results, this elasticity is always significantly different from 1.

The earnings functions are corrected for selectivity using Heckman's two-stage procedure (1979). By computing the probit equation, it is possible to compute the inverse Mill's ratio (Lambda) for each working woman in the sample. The Lambda is then included in the explanatory variables for the female regression, and the results are compared with the uncorrected regression.

In the uncorrected regression, the return on education for women is seen to be about 11.1 percent. A one percent increase in weekly hours worked is associated with a .7 percent increase in monthly earnings. The return on experience is 4 percent, and the sign on experience squared is negative, implying a concave earnings function. When Lambda is added to the regression determining women's earnings, the return to schooling increases very slightly to 11.2 percent and a one percent increase in hours worked is still associated with a .7 percent increase in wages. There is very little difference in the results when Lambda is included. Lambda is positive and barely significant at the 5 percent level. This indicates that those characteristics that are associated with high earnings also increase the probability that the woman will be in the labor force. Another way of saying this is that working women have a comparative advantage in work outside the home. Those women who earn higher wages are also likely to have lower reservation wages.

The return to schooling is higher for women than men (11.1 percent versus 9.9 percent), but men have a higher return to experience at about 5.8 percent. The elasticity of earnings to hours worked is about the same for both groups. There is no selectivity correction for men because their participation rate is high at 84 percent.

Interesting results occur when dummy variables representing sectors and marital status are added to the wage equation. The rate of return for education to women declines to 7.7 percent from 11.1 percent in the uncorrected regression, and the return to experience also declines to 3.7 percent. The increase in adjusted R-squared implies that these variables were omitted variables in the first regression and perhaps some of the return to education should be attributed to sectoral choice. It is apparent that working in the informal sector is associated with a 43 percent decline in earnings when compared to the reference group of those employed in the private formal sector, while working in the public sector or being an employer implies earnings premiums of 15 percent and 51 percent, respectively, compared to the reference group. The sector effects are significant. When Lambda is added to the equation, its coefficient is larger and more significant than when the sectors are not included in the regression. There must be interactions between the decision to work and the choice of sector. Again, the other coefficients are not affected much when Lambda is added to the right hand side of the equation, although the returns to schooling and experience increase slightly. Being married, *ceteris parabis* increases wages by about 4 percent, but the effect is barely significant at the 5 percent level when Lambda is not in the equation, and is insignificant when correcting for selectivity.

For men, adding the marital status and sectoral dummies decreases the return to schooling by about 1.3 percent and reduces the return to experience by about 1.5 percent. The return to schooling becomes higher for men than women. For the men, working in the informal sector or the public sector is associated with lower wages than the reference group by 28 percent and 8 percent respectively, while employers earn a 42 percent premium. This implies that the sectoral choice is more important in determining female earnings than male earnings. However, married males earn approximately 27 percent more than single men, and the effect is significant. The rationale for including marital status in the regression is that it is often observed that married people earn more than single people across countries. One explanation could be that skills valued in the household are also beneficial in the work place. Another explanation is that marriage allows male workers to increase their efficiency through specialization of labor, with the female concentrating on household tasks and the men concentrating on outside work.

The experience profile for all specifications peaks later for men than women. For the women's regressions with selectivity, it peaks at about 35 years of age; for women's regressions without selectivity, it peaks at about 36 years of age; and for men, the profile peaks at about 38 years of age.

## 6.    Discrimination

Having estimated the coefficients for males and females, the Oaxaca decomposition can be determined. Oaxaca (1973) devised a method to break down the earnings differential into two parts; differences explained by differentials in human capital endowments (endowments) and differences caused by variations in returns to human capital in the labor market (the wage structure). The latter represents the upper bound to discrimination.

In symbols, the difference between males and females is the following:

$$\ln (\text{Earnings}_m) - \ln (\text{Earnings}_f) = X_b b_m - X_f b_f$$

$X_i$ represents the means of the sample parameters, and $b_i$ their corresponding coefficients. There are two equations that can be used to do the decomposition, and they will give different results. One equation measures the differential using the female means and the other measures it using the male means.

$$X_b b_m - X_f b_f = X_f(b_m - b_f) + b_m(X_m - X_f) \tag{1}$$
$$X_b b_m - X_f b_f = X_m(b_m - b_f) + b_f(X_m - X_f) \tag{2}$$

The first term in both equations on the right side refer to the differences in earnings due to difference in wage structure, while the second term refers to the differences due to the differences in endowments. The two equations present a base number problem, and there is no economic reason to use one of the two equations over the other. Table 19.6 includes the results using both equations.

Using the earnings coefficients from the selectivity corrected ordinary least squares (OLS) estimates for the regression including only experience, schooling and log hours, 23 percent of the difference in earnings can be attributed to differences in endowments and 77 percent to the difference in wage structure between men and women. The percentages are coincidentally the same whether evaluated at the male or female means. The OLS estimates uncorrected for selectivity imply that a higher percentage of the difference can be explained by the differences in endowments. For the regressions with the dummy variables for sectors and marital status included, the percentage explained by endowments is higher, whether the estimates are corrected for selectivity or not. A higher percentage is explained by endowments with the uncorrected OLS equations than the corrected OLS equations. The upper bound on discrimination is estimated at about 55 to 60 percent for the equations including the sectoral and marital status dummy variables.

**Table 19.6**
Decomposition of the Male/Female Earnings Differential

| Specification | Percentage of Male Pay Advantage Due to Differences In | |
|---|---|---|
| | Endowments (%) | Wage Structure (%) |
| Corrected for Selectivity | | |
| | | |
| Evaluated at Female Means (Equation 1) | | |
| Simple Regression | 23 | 77 |
| Regression with Sectors | 35 | 65 |
| | | |
| Evaluated at Male Means (Equation 2) | | |
| Simple Regression | 23 | 77 |
| Regression with Sectors | 40 | 60 |
| | | |
| Uncorrected for Selectivity | | |
| | | |
| Evaluated at Female Means (Equation 1) | | |
| Simple Regression | 24 | 76 |
| Regression with Sectors | 39 | 61 |
| | | |
| Evaluated at Male Means (Equation 2) | | |
| Simple Regression | 26 | 74 |
| Regression with Sectors | 44 | 56 |

## 7.   Discussion

What conclusions can be made about discrimination against women in Uruguayan labor markets? Overall, Uruguayan women earn about 75 percent of what men earn, and in some sectors that ratio is higher than in others. Specifically, women in the public sector earn about 90 percent of what their male colleagues make, while women in the informal sector earn between 65 to 75 percent of male earnings.

The relatively strong position of females in Uruguayan labor markets can be attributed to high educational attainments and to the recent emigrations. The exodus of educated, prime working age men in the 1970s provided labor market opportunities to women who were prepared to take advantage of them, specifically those with higher educational levels.

However, there are market forces working against women, especially those with lower educational levels. Declining standards of living have pushed more women out into the labor market, and this has tended to decrease women's real wages in the sectors that women with little education and little work experience are likely to enter, and especially in the informal sector. The greatest expansion in absorbing the female labor force has come in social and personal services, traditionally female occupations. They also happen to be among the lowest paying occupations.

Looking at the earnings regressions, it seems that the choice of sector has a larger impact on women's than men's earnings. It could be that the pay in informal sector activities is lower because of non-pecuniary advantages, such as proximity to the home or flexible working hours, in which case there would not be labor market discrimination, but lower wages as the result of trade-offs made by working women.

From the decomposition, it is true that in every case differences in wage structure are more important in explaining the differential than differences in endowments. However, the difference in coefficients could be biased upwards. For example, the proxy for experience in the female regression is likely to be overestimated, because women typically have interrupted careers in order to raise children. This will bias the return to experience downward, since the wage experience profile is concave. This will also increase the percentage of the differential attributed to wage structure, and therefore, discrimination. Also, it would be helpful to have measurements of job tenure, or uninterrupted time in the labor force. This is a proxy for dedication to labor market activities, and could be a missing variable that is higher for men than women and which is desirable to employers. It is important to note also that adding the sectoral variables increases the percentage attributable to endowments; the choice of sector is obviously an important factor in examining discrimination.

Uruguayan women could benefit from policies that would make it easier to combine household work and work in the formal sector, such as expanded provision of daycare. Coverage of the already-existing preschool program could be expanded to poorer families. Pay is low in the informal sector, and the ratio of female to male wage is also low. The same is true of the self-employed sector. The state has already done much in the area of preschool education. Also, further work should be done to determine why the wage structure is different between men and women, and whether women are constrained by custom or habit from more highly paid occupations.

# References

Aguiar, C. *El Impacto de las Migraciones Internacionales en el Mercado de Empleo del Pais de Origen: El Caso Uruguayo.* Montevideo: Centro Interdisciplinario de Estudios Sobre el Desarrollo Uruguay, 1984.

Aldrich-Langen, C. *The Admission and Academic Placement of Students from Selected South American Countries.* Washington, DC: National Association for Foreign Student Affairs, 1978.

Fortuna, J. C. and S. Prates, "Informal Sector versus Informalized Labor Relations in Uruguay." in A. Portes, M. Castells, and L. Benton (eds.) *The Informal Economy: Studies in Advanced and Less Developed Countries.* Baltimore: The Johns Hopkins University Press, 1989.

Heckman, J. "Sample Selection Bias as a Specification Error." *Econometrica,* Vol. 47 (1979). pp. 153-161.

Lubell, H. *The Informal Sector in the 1980s and 1990s.* Paris: Development Centre of the Organisation for Economic Co-operation and Development, 1991.

Mann, A. and C. Sanchez, "Labor Market Responses to Southern Cone Stabilization Policies: The Cases of Argentina, Chile, Uruguay." *Inter-American Economic Affairs,* Vol. 38 (Spring 1985) pp. 19-39.

Mincer, J. *Schooling, Experience and Earnings.* New York: Columbia University Press, 1974.

Oaxaca, R. "Male-female Wage Differentials in Urban Labor Markets." *International Economic Review.* Vol. 14, no. 1 (1973) pp. 693-701.

Portes, A., S. Blitzer, and J. Curtis, "The Urban Informal Sector in Uruguay: Its Internal Structure, Characteristics, and Effects." *World Development,* Vol. 14, no. 6 (1986) pp 727-741.

Solari, A. "Analysis of Educational Financing and Administration in a Context of Austerity: the Case of Uruguay." *Major Project in the Field of Education in Latin America and the Caribbean (Chile).* No. 21, April 1990, pp. 34-56.

Standing, G. *Labor Force Participation and Development*. Geneva: International Labor Organization,1982.

Taglioretti, G. *Women and Work in Uruguay*. Paris: UNESCO, 1983.

Weil, T. *Area Handbook for Uruguay*. Washington, DC: American University, 1971, pp. 117-144.

Weinstein, M. *Uruguay: Democracy at the Crossroads*. Boulder, CO: Westview Press, 1988.

World Bank, "Uruguay: Employment and Wages." Country Operations, Division 4. Report No. 9608-UR, May 1991.

# 20

## Female Participation and Earnings, Venezuela 1987

*Donald Cox and George Psacharopoulos*

### 1.    Introduction

In 1987, the average earnings of Venezuelan working women were 70 percent of the average earnings of Venezuelan working men.  What accounts for the pay gap?  Are human capital indicators lower for women?  Or is the gap due in part to labor market discrimination?  This chapter sheds some light on these questions by analyzing Venezuelan household survey microdata.

Simple comparisons of differences in average earnings can be misleading when making inferences about possible discrimination because skill indicators can differ between men and women.  So we seek to estimate earnings differences while controlling for earnings determinants.

### 2.    The Venezuelan Labor Market

Modernization, improved access to education, the growth of the public sector, and long term declines in fertility rates have all contributed to significant increases in female labor force participation rates in Venezuela and by 1989, women accounted for 30 percent of the labor force.  Women's participation rates have increased in both public and private sectors, although the increase has been most pronounced in the public sector.

A number of studies (World Bank, 1990) show that women earn lower wages than men in Venezuela.  While the wage differentials are partly explained by women's concentrations in lower-paying industries and in the informal sector, there is some evidence suggesting that women earn less than men even when they have similar levels of education, years of experience in the labor force, and when they hold similar jobs.  This study uses 1987 Household Survey data to determine what proportion of the male/female earnings differential is due to differences in human capital endowments and how much of the differential can be attributed to differences in the way employers value male and female labor.

### 3.    Data Characteristics

We use data from the Encuesta de Hogares, a survey covering a representative cross-section of households in Venezuela.  The survey was conducted by the Oficina Central de Estadistica e Informatica (OCEI) in the second semester of 1987.  The data set contains observations from 131,032 households covering 681,328 persons and contains information about labor market earnings and individual characteristics such as age, schooling, gender, and place of residence.

From the large data set we selected a random sample of 10 percent of the individuals. Since we are interested in the behavior of prime-age individuals, we restricted our sub-sample to individuals aged between 20 and 55 years. Further, we dropped persons with inconsistent labor-market information: Those who reported having earnings but no hours worked or vice versa. These sample-selection criteria result in an aggregate sample of 17,725 individuals: 8,375 working males, 4,131 working females and 5,219 non-working females. (The reasons for including non-working females in our analysis is explained in a later section.)

Table 20.1 displays means and standard deviations (S.D.) of selected variables from the sample. The average age of working men and women is about the same, but average schooling among working women exceeds that of working men by almost a year. Eleven percent of working women attended university, compared with 8 percent of men. And half of the working women attended secondary school compared with 41 percent of men.

A higher proportion of men were self-employed--28 percent compared to 22 percent for working women. But female workers were better represented in the public sector than men--31 versus 17 percent. The earnings of women are 70 percent those of men (2,700/3,827).

Non-working women are slightly older than their working counterparts, and have approximately 2 years less schooling. The variable "years of experience" is computed in the standard way by subtracting years of schooling plus 6 from age. Note that we do not have measures of actual labor market experience in our data set. So we must use potential years of labor market experience as a proxy. We recognize, of course, that women frequently experience interruptions in their careers, so that our experience measure is an imperfect proxy for actual years spent working.

## 4.   Determinants of Female Labor Force Participation

We seek to estimate earnings functions for men and women, but our analysis for women poses a special problem because of the intermittency of female labor force participation. Hence we are estimating earnings functions for self-selected samples of women. That is, we estimate earnings functions for women whose market wage exceeds the value of time spent at home.

Our analysis is based on the occupational choice model of Roy (1951) that has been explored by Heckman (1979), Lee (1978), Willis and Rosen (1979), Borjas (1987) and others.

Suppose the market wage of woman "i" is given by the equation:

$$w(m) = bX + e(m), \tag{1}$$

where X denotes a vector of wage determinants, b measures the returns to those determinants, and e(m) is the error term for woman "i." (The subscript "i" applies to the terms w(m), X, and e(m) and is suppressed for convenience.) The value of time spent at home for woman "i" is expressed as:

$$w(h) = aZ + e(h). \tag{2}$$

The vector Z denotes the determinants of the woman's productivity at home. We assume the vector Z contains all of the elements of X, plus other determinants. This assumption makes sense since variables such as being a household head would affect productivity at home but not in the

## Table 20.1
### Means (and Standard Deviations) of Sample Variables

| Variable | Working Men | Working Women | Non-Working Women |
|---|---|---|---|
| Age | 33.6 | 33.50 | 34.15 |
| | (9.78) | (9.00) | (10.56) |
| Years of Schooling | 6.97 | 7.86 | 5.50 |
| | (3.79) | (4.02) | (3.64) |
| Years of Experience | 20.65 | 19.64 | 22.65 |
| | (11.00) | (10.03) | (12.40) |
| Education Level | | | |
| No Education | 0.06 | 0.06 | 0.16 |
| | (0.24) | (0.24) | (0.36) |
| Primary | 0.47 | 0.34 | 0.51 |
| Secondary | 0.41 | 0.50 | 0.34 |
| University | 0.08 | 0.11 | 0.04 |
| Self-Employed | 0.28 | 0.22 | -- |
| | (0.45) | | |
| Public-Sector Worker | 0.17 | 0.31 | -- |
| | (0.37) | | |
| Weekly earnings (bols.) | 3,826.5 | 2,700.2 | -- |
| | (3,523.6) | (2,060.6) | |
| Earnings of Others | 4,909.8 | 6,734.7 | -- |
| | (4,496.3) | (5,763.7) | |
| N | 8,375 | 4,131 | 5,219 |

Notes:   Mean Female Participation = .4418.
         Figures in brackets are standard deviations.
Source:  Encuesta de Hogares, 1987.

market. On the other hand, it is hard to think of personal attributes that affect the market wage but not the value of time spent at home.

The vector a denotes the returns to attributes Z and e(h) is the error term associated with the value of time at home. (The subscript "i" applies to the terms w(h), Z, and e(h) and is suppressed for convenience.)

The error terms e(.) are assumed to be normal with expectation 0 and covariance matrix of full rank.

A woman chooses to work if, and only if:

$$I = w(m) - w(h) = bX - aZ + e(m) - e(h) > 0, \tag{3}$$

where I denotes an index of labor force participation. The variable I, which differs for each individual in the cross-section, is a continuous variable that indexes the propensity for a woman to enter the labor force. If the variable I crosses a certain threshold, the woman enters the labor force (otherwise she does not). We do not lose anything essential by normalizing this threshold to 0, as in expression (3).

Consider the expected value of women's wages, conditional on working in the market and on X.

$$E(w(m)) = bX + E(e(m)|I > 0). \tag{4}$$

"E" denotes the expectations operator. This is the standard sample-selection problem considered by Heckman (1974, 1979). The expected value of the wage is conditional on the sample-selection rule, which in this case is that the women work (I > 0). Focus on the last term in 4, the expectation of the error term. That expression can be written as:

$$E(e(m)|I > 0) = c(f(I)/F(I)) = cL, \tag{5}$$

where f(I) denotes the ordinate of the standard normal density evaluated at the index I, F(I) the standard normal distribution function evaluated at (I), and the ratio of the two (rewritten as L) is the inverse Mill's ratio term.

It can be shown that the variable c can be written as:

$$c = s(h)(s(m)/s(h) - r(m,h)), \tag{6}$$

where s(.) denotes the standard deviation of e(.), (e.g., s(m) is the standard deviation of the error term associated with market wage offers) and r(m,h) is the correlation between e(m) and e(h) (-1 <= r <= 1).

The derivation in equation 6 is useful for determining the sign of the coefficient of the Mill's ratio, or selectivity term. The sign of c can be positive, negative, or zero, depending on the dispersion and covariance of the error terms e(.). For example, if e(m) and e(f) are inversely correlated (r < 0), so that unobserved characteristics that raise market productivity (e.g., aggressiveness) lower productivity in the home, and the dispersion of market wages (captured by s(m)) is low relative to that of home production (s(h)), then the coefficient of the selection term will be positive. In this case positive self-selection will occur; women sort themselves into the sectors in which they are most productive.

On the other hand, if s(m) and s(h) are roughly equal and r is approximately 1, the coefficient c will be close to zero. In this case, there is a strong positive correlation between unobserved market and home traits and the dispersion in the market and home error terms is the same. It makes sense that self-selection effects are minimal in this case because unobservables in each sector are strongly correlated and their dispersion is the same.

Now consider the case in which r = 1 but s(h) > s(m). Unobservables that help boost the payoff to home production boost the payoff to market work as well. And the dispersion of rewards in the home sector is higher than that of the market. The most productive women will be attracted to the sector with the greater dispersion. The reason is that if they are going to be at the top, they might as well be at the top of a wide distribution--this strategy maximizes the reward from sector choice. On the other hand, women whose e(.) terms are lowest will be attracted to the sector with the lesser dispersion (in this case the market sector). The reason is that if they are going to be at the bottom of the distribution, they might as well choose the sector with the smaller dispersion so that their reward, which will be smallest, will at least not be too small. In this instance, then, the market sector attracts the women who are least productive in terms of their unobservables, so that the selection effects in the market wage equation are negative.

The first step in estimating selectivity-adjusted earnings functions is to estimate the index function 3 using probit. The vector Z contains age dummies, schooling dummies, dummies for region of residence, dummies for whether the woman was a wife or partner of the household head, and earnings of other household members, and a rural residence dummy.

The dependent variable in the probit analysis is labor force participation, which is defined as earning at least 200 bolivares per month in 1987. This definition is not strictly comparable with the official one, which counts both the unemployed and employed as members of the labor force. But the concept of unemployment is complicated; experts disagree on exactly who is unemployed. The concept of employment is unambiguous; it is easy to identify those who have earned over a threshold amount.

The estimation results are presented in Tables 20.2 and 20.3. The probability of participating in the labor force steadily rises with age until women reach their late forties, then it declines. The age effects are large. For example, the probit coefficients indicate that, controlling for other factors, the probability of participation is about 30 percentage points higher for women in their early 40's than for those in their early 20's. Education has powerful effects on participation too. All else being equal, secondary school graduates have an estimated participation probability that is 30 percentage points higher than primary school graduates. University graduates have a participation probability 70 percentage points higher than primary school graduates. But graduating from a technical secondary school results in a lower participation probability than graduating from an academic secondary school. This result is puzzling, but also likely to be imprecise--less than 2 percent of the sample attended technical school. Those with some university education are less likely to participate in the labor force than secondary school graduates. Part of the reason might be that attending a university raises reservation wages leading to longer spells of unemployment. The marital status and headship variables are very large, precisely estimated and have the anticipated sign in the participation probit. Being a wife or partner reduces the probability of participation by 22 percentage points, so family responsibilities compete for time spent in the market. Being a household head raises the participation probability by 23 percentage points. Income of other family members reduces the probability of working. This is most likely due to income effects which raise the demand for time spent at home (Mincer, 1962). A 15,000 bolivare increase in other income reduces the probability of working by 4 percentage points.

Finally, participation probabilities follow distinct regional patterns. Women from Caracas are more likely to work than those from Guayana. A 9 percentage point difference in participation probabilities exists between the two regions. And living in a rural area reduces the probability of participating by 13 percentage points.

**Table 20.2**
Probit Estimates for Female Participation

| Variable | Coefficient | t-value | Mean | Partial derivative |
|----------|------------|---------|------|--------------------|
| Constant | -.861 | -10.80 | 1.000 | |
| Age < 25 | -.153 | -2.33 | .211 | -.064 |
| Aged 25-29 | .346 | 5.49 | .187 | .136 |
| Aged 30-34 | .473 | 7.51 | .170 | .186 |
| Aged 35-39 | .526 | 8.36 | .143 | .207 |
| Aged 40-44 | .605 | 9.17 | .103 | .239 |
| Aged 45-49 | .452 | 6.64 | .086 | .179 |
| Some primary | .191 | 3.52 | .172 | .075 |
| Primary grad. | .265 | 5.08 | .258 | .104 |
| Some secondary | .778 | 14.34 | .250 | .306 |
| Secondary grad. | .991 | 15.56 | .115 | .390 |
| Technical | .531 | 4.36 | .015 | .209 |
| Some university | .735 | 8.74 | .039 | .289 |
| University grad. | 1.809 | 16.24 | .031 | .712 |
| Wife or partner | -.561 | -16.18 | .563 | -.221 |
| Household head | .587 | 9.42 | .085 | .231 |
| Other earnings | -.674E-oS | -2.59 | 6492.1 | -.000 |
| Caracas | .443 | 6.10 | .055 | .174 |
| Central | .303 | 6.16 | .282 | .119 |
| W Central | .325 | 6.75 | .318 | .129 |
| Guayana | .226 | 4.38 | .222 | .0897 |
| Rural | -.338 | -7.25 | .142 | -.133 |

Notes: Sample: Women aged 20 to 55 years.
   Observations          9350
   Mean Participation    .4418
   Log-Likelihood        -5457.3
   Chi-Squared Statistic 1920.3

## 5.   Earnings Functions

The next equation to explore is the selectivity-adjusted earnings function for women. Rather than deflate monthly log earnings by hours worked, we include the log of hours worked as a separate regressor. This functional form is more flexible than using log (earnings/hours), which restricts the elasticity of earnings with respect to hours to be unity.

We estimate the standard Mincerian earnings function, which includes years of education, experience and experience squared as regressors, in addition to the log of hours worked. The regression results are given in Table 20.4. This table displays the earnings function adjusted for selection bias. The estimated rate of return to schooling for women is about 12 percent, which is high by United States' standards but lower than that found in other Latin American countries (see other chapters in this volume). The log earnings increase with experience at a decreasing rate, which is a familiar result for earnings equations of this sort. Recall that it is potential experience that is measured here, since most women have interruptions in their careers. At

## Table 20.3
### Predicted participation probabilities by characteristic

| Characteristic | Predicted Probability |
|---|---|
| **Age** | |
| 20-24 | .27 |
| 25-29 | .45 |
| 30-34 | .50 |
| 35-39 | .53 |
| 40-44 | .56 |
| 45-49 | .50 |
| 50-55 | .32 |
| | |
| Education | |
| No education | .25 |
| Some primary | .31 |
| Primary grad | .34 |
| Some secondary | .54 |
| Secondary grad | .62 |
| Technical | .44 |
| Some university | .52 |
| University grad | .87 |
| | |
| Wife or partner | |
| No | .56 |
| Yes | .34 |
| | |
| Household head | |
| No | .41 |
| Yes | .64 |
| | |
| Region and location | |
| Caracas | .50 |
| Central | .45 |
| W Central | .46 |
| Guayana | .42 |
| Other region | .33 |
| | |
| Urban | .45 |
| Rural | .32 |

sample means, the rate of return to experience is 1.8 percent. The peak of the earnings-experience profile implied by the estimates is 50, which means that the estimated peak in earnings occurs at about age 64. So earnings do not turn down until women are well into their potential retirement years. The estimated elasticity of earnings with respect to hours worked is significantly different from unity. The coefficient in Table 20.4 indicates that a one percent increase in weekly hours worked is associated with about a half a percent rise in monthly earnings.

Finally, the coefficient of the selectivity variable (inverse Mill's ratio) is negative and significant at the .05 level. Multiplying the coefficient of the selectivity variable with its sample mean gives the average error term conditional on being in the labor force, which is about 5 percent.

**Table 20.4**
Earnings Functions

| Variable | Men | Women (Corrected for Selectivity) | Women (Uncorrected for Selectivity) |
|---|---|---|---|
| Constant | 3.986 (38.369) | 4.425 (38.878) | 4.302 (43.623) |
| Schooling (years) | .106 (63.587) | .117 (35.725) | .121 (47.657) |
| Experience | .052 (25.568) | .030 (10.051) | .031 (10.841) |
| Experience squared | -.0006 (-14.806) | -.0003 (-4.924) | -.0003 (-5.329) |
| Ln (hours) | .682 (25.327) | .535 (21.863) | .541 (22.210) |
| Lambda (Selectivity Variable) | | -.064 (-2.164) | |
| $R^2$ | .379 | .426 | .426 |
| N | 8,375 | 4,131 | 4,131 |

Notes: Figures in parenthesis are t-ratios.
Dependent variable = log (hourly earnings)

Analysts are sometimes puzzled by negative selection effects, but they are consistent with one of the scenarios discussed in the theoretical section--namely, (1) a strong positive correlation between unobservables in market and home productivity and (2) a greater dispersion in rewards to hometime compared to market work.

To see whether adjustment for sample-selection bias makes a difference for rates of return to schooling and experience we re-estimated the earnings function by simple ordinary least squres (OLS) (Table 20.4). The estimated rate of return to schooling is a fraction of a percentage point higher for the corrected estimate. Both the slope and concavity of the earnings profile increase a bit in absolute value. The net effect is a 1.9 percent rate of return to experience at sample means, compared with a 1.8 figure. The effect of omitting the selection terms from the earnings-function estimates is to bias upward the marginal rate of return to human-capital indicators by about 5 percent (not percentage points).

The earnings function for men is also given in Table 20.4. Note that we do not correct for selection bias in the male earnings functions. The reason is that labor force participation for prime-aged males should be exogenous. If we were to include males that are close to school age or retirement age the decision would be endogenous, but recall that our samples are for people aged 20 to 55. Some males might have earnings below the threshold of 200 bolivares, but for reasons that are likely to be exogenous to the model; illness, unemployment caused by deficient demand, or search unemployment.

The estimated rate of return for schooling is slightly lower for males than females. But the returns from labor market experience are a lot higher for men than women. At sample means the rate of return to experience is 2.4 percent for men, a third higher than the comparable figure for women. This result is consistent with human-capital-investment theory, which predicts that workers with long horizons will invest in skills more than those with short ones. And men are likely to have much longer horizons than women who drop out of the labor force to raise children.

How is the investment effect reflected in the experience-earnings profile? Investing a lot early in the career entails foregone earnings, which lowers starting wages. But as skills accumulate with experience investment declines. The latter occurs because it pays to invest the most when young. The two effects combine to steepen the earnings profile.

## 6. Discrimination

Now that we have estimated earnings functions for men and women, we can address the question posed at the beginning: how much of the male-female earnings differential can be explained by observed factors? How much might be caused by discrimination?

The technique used to answer this question is the widely-used Oaxaca (1973) decomposition. The idea is to split the difference in log wages into that accounted for by differences in observed variables, and that accounted for by differences in the way those variables are rewarded. We can write the difference in log earnings of men and women as:

$$B_m X_m - B_f X_f \quad = (B_m - B_f)X_m + B_f(X_m - X_f) \tag{7a}$$
$$= (B_m - B_f)X_f + B_m(X_m - X_f), \tag{7b}$$

where $B_i$ $i = m,f$ are the estimated coefficients of the earnings functions and $X_i$ $i = m,f$ are the averages of the explanatory variables in the earnings functions. Focus on expression 7a. The first term is the difference in rewards, for those having mean attributes of men. The second term is the differential due to differences in attributes, weighted by the vector of female coefficients. Expression 7b does the same job as 7a, but the weights are different. (We discuss this below.)

Before we proceed further in calculating the "explained" component of the wage gap, we need to address three further issues. First, what sample means should we use for women--workers only or the entire sample? The answer is that we should use the entire sample, because the selectivity corrected equations gives us an estimate of the population regression function when we base our predictions on the estimate of b in equation 1. Second, we do not include the Mill's ratio terms or their coefficients in making our predictions because we seek to measure the conditional mean for the population, not just the sample of working women. Third, though we use entire-sample means for female schooling and experience, we use the working-sample mean for log hours, since hours for non-working women equal zero because they do not participate in the labor force.

Second, note that the Oaxaca-decomposition can be done two ways, hence expressions 7a and 7b. Which way is best? Economic theory gives little guidance; this is an example of the index-

**Table 20.5**
Decomposition of the Male/Female Earnings Differential

| | Percentage of Male Advantage Due to Differences in | | Male Pay Advantage |
| --- | --- | --- | --- |
| | Endowments | Wage Structure | |
| Estimated at Male Means (7a) | 12.87 (30.5) | 29.33 (69.5) | 42.20 (100.0) |
| Estimated at Female Means (7b) | 14.96 (35.4) | 27.24 (64.6) | 42.20 (100.0) |

Notes:   Figures in parentheses are percentages
Male pay advantage = 42.2%

number problem which arises in many problems in applied economics. So we will do the decomposition both ways.

The male pay advantage is 42.2 percent. This is the empirical analogue of expression 7. How much of the advantage is explained by observable factors? The answer is 12.9 percentage points. This is the empirical analogue of the expression $B_f(X_m - X_f)$. The rest of the advantage is due to the way attributes are rewarded. So observables explain a little less than a third of the pay advantage for men. If we do the calculations according to expression 7b instead (to explore the index number problem) the amount of the pay advantage explained is 15 percentage points, or a little over a third of the actual pay advantage.

A couple of caveats about the Oaxaca decomposition technique should be noted. First, the right-hand-side variables do not capture every skill component that affects earnings. So if we attribute all of the unexplained pay gap to discrimination, we must recognize that it is an upper bound. After all, some of the unexplained advantage could be due to male skill advantages that we did not measure. Left-out variables bias measures of discrimination upward. On the other hand, the right-hand-side variables themselves could be affected by discrimination. Suppose discrimination led women to go to school for fewer years than they would have liked. If discrimination affects right-hand-side variables, this could bias discrimination measures downward.

# References

Borjas, G.J. "Self-selection and the Earnings of Immigrants." *American Economic Review*, Vol. 77 (1987). pp. 531-555.

Heckman, J. "Sample Selection as a Specification Error." *Econometrica*, Vol. 47, no. 1 (1979). pp. 153-161.

-----. "Shadow Prices, Market Wages, and Labor Supply." *Econometrica*, Vol. 42, no. 4 (1974). pp. 679-694.

Lee, L. "Unionism and Wage Rates: A Similtaneous Equations Model with Qualitative and Limited Dependent Variables." *International Economic Review*, Vol. 19 (1978). pp. 415-433.

Mincer, J. "Labor Force Participation of Married Women: A Study of Labor Supply" in National Bureau of Economic Research. *Aspects of Labor Economics*. Princeton, New Jersey: Princeton University Press, 1962.

Oaxaca, R.L. "Male-female Wage Differentials in Urban Labor Markets." *International Economic Review, Vol.* 14. no. 1 (1973). pp. 693-709.

Roy, A.D. "Some Thoughts on the Distribution of Earnings." *Oxford Economic Papers*, Vol. 3 (1951). pp. 135-146.

Willis, R. and S. Rosen. "Education and Self-selection." *Journal of Political Economy*, Vol. 87, no. 5, part 2 (1979). pp. S7-S36.

World Bank. "Venezuela: A Country Assessment on the Role of Women in Development." Mimeograph. Washington, D.C.: Latin American and Caribbean Region, World Bank. 1990.

# 21

# Female Earnings, Labor Force Participation and Discrimination in Venezuela, 1989

*Carolyn Winter*

## 1. Introduction

In this chapter we try to determine (1) what factors are most likely to influence female labor force participation and (2) what factors account for existing male-female wage differentials in Venezuela. The 1989 household survey data show working female monthly earnings to be approximately 78 percent of male earnings. Although this differential is not as large as that reported in many other Latin American countries, it is still substantial.[1] It is important to determine whether this differential is the result of different endowments in productivity-related characteristics between the sexes, such as education and work experience, or whether it is a consequence of labor market discrimination. If men and women in Venezuela are paid according to the same wage structure differences in endowments should account for all the observed earnings differentials. If, however, we adjust for differences in endowments between the sexes and we continue to find a wage gap, this can be interpreted as evidence of wage discrimination between the sexes. Following Oaxaca's (1973) approach, we decompose sex-specific earnings into an "endowment" component and a "discrimination" component and attempt to estimate the extent to which wage differentials result from discrimination.

The following section provides a brief description of the Venezuelan labor market, its fluctuating fortunes since the end of the "oil boom," and general factors affecting women's labor force participation. Section 3 describes the data base used in the analysis and some basic features of the data. In Section 4 we present probit estimates showing the determinants of women's labor force participation and in Section 5 we consider earnings functions estimates for working males and females and include corrections for possible selectivity bias among women. Section 6 presents the estimate of the extent to which earnings differentials can be explained by discrimination.

## 2. The Setting: The Venezuelan Economy and Labor Market

The discovery and widespread exploitation of oil meant that Venezuela changed rapidly from an agriculture-based economy to one of the largest oil exporters by mid-century. Although the oil industry itself has never been a large employer of labor (in 1989 it employed only 0.7 percent

---

[1]   Many of the other studies reported in this volume (Brazil and Peru, for example), report women's earnings to be about two-thirds of men's. Birdsall & Fox (1985) report that female teachers in Brazil earn less than 55 percent of male teacher's earnings.

of the labor force) it fueled the growth and expansion of the economy which is now predominantly urban-based. In 1989 approximately 82 percent of the population lived in urban areas, principally in the northern industrialized states.

The rapidly growing population and the economic windfalls of the "oil boom" during the sixties and seventies prompted the government to give priority to the expansion of education, particularly tertiary education where enrollments increased by 9.1 percent per annum between 1975 and 1984 (Psacharopoulos and Steier, 1988). Improved access to schooling has especially benefitted females who now have, on average, 1.6 years more schooling than males.

Increased access to education has meant that women's labor force participation has increased significantly, from 22 percent in the 1970s, to 29 percent in 1982, and to 38 percent in 1989 (de Planchart, 1988; Psacharopoulos and Alam, 1991). The proportion of women holding professional and technical jobs grew from 15.2 percent in 1961, to 22.1 percent in 1987, and 21.1 percent in 1989 (de Planchart, 1988). In terms of earnings, however, women continue to be concentrated in lower paying occupations. The proportion of women in the highest paying category, managerial occupations, has changed little over the past two decades (see Appendix table) and in professional occupations, women are predominantly found in the lower paying areas, such as nursing and teaching.

Economic growth halted abruptly in 1979 with the end of the "oil boom" and labor shortages were replaced by rising unemployment which peaked at 14 percent in early 1985, stabilized around 6.9 percent in 1988 and began to rise sharply again in 1989. Workers in low-paid, low skills jobs have been most immediately affected and women are often heavily represented among these groups.

Women's labor force participation has also been affected by "protective" labor legislation laws introduced in the seventies which inadvertently work to exclude women from certain sectors of the labor market. These laws prohibit employers from hiring women for "physically and morally" dangerous work, for night work, or in industries with numerous daily shifts. It is also illegal for women to work in most occupations in the mining sector. In addition, legislation stipulating generous maternal leave privileges at full pay makes female labor potentially more costly to employers than male labor.

Recorded incidents of discrimination against female workers are few, but there is evidence that employers seek not to hire women and actively discriminate against hiring married women (Rakowski, 1985). Clauses supporting equal pay for equal work have really only been enforced in the public sector which possibly accounts for the high proportion of women (more than twice as many women as men) employed in this sector.

Venezuela's rapid population growth rate, averaging 3.5 percent in the previous two decades and 2.8 percent in the 1980s, means that 40 percent of the population is now under 15 years of age. To keep unemployment at its current levels, a real annual growth rate in the GDP of 5 percent would have to be achieved and maintained. This is not expected (Economist Intelligence Unit, 1989). Changes in women's labor force participation and the extent to which discrimination affects their earnings will thus be a real concern in any poverty alleviation efforts; women are more heavily represented among lower income groups than men and the proportion of female headed households, already accounting for over 20 percent of all households, is continuing to increase.

## 3.    Data Characteristics

The analysis is based on data from the 1989 Venezuela Household Survey conducted by the Oficina Central de Estadisticas e Informatica (OCEI).  Such Household Surveys were conducted twice yearly between 1968 and 1983, and quarterly from 1984.  The survey covers nine political administrative regions, Caracas Metropolitan area, Capital, Central, West-central, Zuliana, Los Andes, Southern, Non-eastern, and Guyana.  Data from the Guyana region were collected independently in the 1989 survey and technical difficulties with the data prevented its inclusion in this analysis.  The available survey data included 159,818 individual observations from which a 10 percent random sample was drawn for use in this analysis.

The survey provides detailed information on labor issues including employment status, weekly hours worked, occupation and industry category, and monthly income.  Data on socio-economic characteristics such as age, educational attainment, marital status, number of children and household size is also available.

Labor participation, as commonly defined, includes those employed and those seeking employment.  However, because a large informal sector exists in Venezuela, it was difficult to identify  individuals as unemployed or as being employed in the formal sector in the data base. Consequently, only actively employed individuals, identified by their positive responses to questions concerning employment status, weekly hours worked and monthly income, were defined as participating in the labor force.  Individuals with incomplete or inconsistent labor market information were excluded from the sample.  This included unpaid family workers and workers who did not report hours worked.  Income was reported erratically by younger and older respondents.  Consequently the sample was restricted to prime-age working males (20-60 years) and prime-age females (20-55 years).  Within the samples of working males and females, individuals who reported earning less than 10 percent of the mean hourly wage for their sex or more than 15 times the mean hourly wage were excluded.  Fifteen cases, reporting either extremely high or low earnings, were excluded in this way.  This resulted in a sample of 2,408 working males and 3,143 females, of whom 1,181 were working in either the public or private sector.  The proportion of employed men and women were 76 and 38 percent respectively.

A proxy for labor force experience was constructed as age minus years of schooling minus six years.  This proxy measure will almost certainly overstate experience since no adjustments can be made for periodic absences from the labor force.  Overestimates will be most severe for women since they are more likely to withdraw during childrearing.

Table 21.1 gives means and standard deviations of the sample variables by gender.  Working women earn approximately 78 percent of men's weekly earnings but, on average, work fewer hours per week (38.48 compared to 43.71 hours).  After adjusting for differences in weekly hours worked, women's hourly earnings are 12 percent less than men's.  The proxy measure for labor force experience is lower for women.

As in most Latin American countries, female workers in Venezuela have, on average, approximately one and one half years more schooling than male workers.  This educational advantage holds true at all education levels beyond primary school, even at tertiary levels. Working women are also more likely than men to be studying while they are working. Married/cohabiting women are less likely to participate than married/cohabiting men.

**Table 21.1**
Venezuela - Means (and Standard Deviations) of Sample Variables

| Variable descriptions | Working Men | Working Women | Non-working Women |
|---|---|---|---|
| Age (years) | 35.97 | 34.07 | 33.6 |
| | (10.68) | (8.90) | (10.25) |
| Years of schooling | 6.93 | 8.52 | 6.31 |
| | (4.14) | (4.23) | (3.85) |
| Experience | 23.05 | 19.55 | |
| | (12.17) | (10.8) | |
| Earnings[a] (weekly) | 1518.23 | 1179.91 | |
| | (1292.81) | (773.07) | |
| Hours worked (per week) | 43.71 | 38.48 | |
| | (8.37) | (9.73) | |
| | | | |
| Distribution by Education (percent): | | | |
| No education | 0.08 | 0.05 | 0.11 |
| | (0.27) | (0.21) | (0.31) |
| Incomplete primary | 0.19 | 0.11 | 0.19 |
| | (0.39) | (0.31) | (0.39) |
| Primary | 0.27 | 0.22 | 0.27 |
| | (0.44) | (0.41) | (0.44) |
| Incomplete secondary | 0.23 | 0.27 | 0.22 |
| | (0.42) | (0.45) | (0.41) |
| Secondary | 0.11 | 0.16 | 0.09 |
| | (0.32) | (0.37) | (0.29) |
| Secondary technical | 0.02 | 0.02 | 0.01 |
| | (0.13) | (0.14) | (0.10) |
| Incomplete university | 0.04 | 0.09 | 0.07 |
| | (0.21) | (0.28) | (0.26) |
| University | 0.06 | 0.1 | 0.01 |
| | (0.23) | (0.30) | (0.08) |
| Currently a student | 0.03 | 0.09 | 0.09 |
| | (0.18) | (0.29) | (0.29) |
| Marital Status (percent): | | | |
| Married (or cohabiting) | 0.73 | 0.55 | 0.71 |
| | (0.44) | (0.50) | (0.45) |
| | | | |
| Distribution by Employment Status (percent): | | | |
| Public Sector | 0.15 | 0.36 | |
| | (0.36) | (0.48) | |
| Private Sector | 0.74 | 0.61 | |
| | (0.44) | (0.49) | |
| | | | |
| Number of Observations | 2408 | 1181 | 1962 |

a.     Bolivars
Notes:   - Standard deviations are given in parentheses
        - Sample includes working males aged 20 to 60 years and working and non-working females aged 20 to 55 years.
        - Female labor force participation rate = 38%
        - Male labor force participation rate = 76%
Source: Venezuela Household Survey, 1989.

## 4.    Determinants of Female Labor Force Participation

Numerous factors influence a woman's decision to participate in the labor market -- her investments in human capital, personal characteristics such as her marital status and whether she has young children, and other factors such as the availability of suitable childcare options. Ultimately, her decision to participate will rest upon the comparison of her market wage with the value of her time in the home (i.e., her reservation wage).

This means that if we estimate earnings functions using data from our sample of working women, the sample will include only women whose market wage exceeds their reservation wage. Consequently, we will be estimating earnings functions for a self-selected sample of women.

To correct for this we follow Heckman's (1979) widely adopted procedure and estimate a probit equation for the full sample of women (working and non-working) in which the probability that a woman will participate is estimated given various conditions, in this case whether she has young dependent children, her age, region of residence and educational attainment. The dependent variable in this model is a dummy variable for labor force participation (1 if a participant and 0 if not). The inverse Mill's ratio (Lambda) is estimated in this equation and entered in the earnings equations to adjust for the possible selectivity bias inherent in our sample of working women. The probit estimates are shown in Table 21.2. Table 21.3 estimates predicted participation rates for each characteristic while the values of other characteristics is held at their sample mean.

In line with the general human capital literature, education is found to have a powerful effect on participation. The probit coefficients in Table 21.2 show that the probability of participating rises steadily with each successive level of education. The predicted probabilities in Table 21.3 makes this very evident. A woman with mean values of all other characteristics and completed university education has a predicted probability of labor force participation 37 percentage points higher than a woman with completed secondary education (probability = .87 versus .50). Similarly, a woman with completed secondary education has a predicted probability of participation 21 percentage points higher than a woman who has only completed primary education (probability = .50 versus .29).

The effects of age on participation are as expected, with women's probability of working increasing steadily from their mid-twenties and peaking between ages 41 and 45. Low participation rates among women in their early twenties are consistent with the high enrollment (44 percent) of women in this age group in higher education.

It is widely posited that being the mother of young children (under 6 years of age) significantly increases the opportunity costs of women's labor force participation and increases the probability that they will withdraw from the labor force.[2] Our estimates support this finding. Table 21.3 shows that a woman has a predicted probability of participation of .32 if she has young children and .41 if she does not.

---

[2]    See Behrman and Wolfe (1984) and Gronau (1988).

## Table 21.2
### Probit Estimates for Female Participation

| Variable | Coefficient | t-ratio | Variable Mean | Partial Derivative |
|---|---|---|---|---|
| Constant | -1.054 | -8.78 | 1.000 | |
| Age 20 to 25 | -.052 | -.47 | .253 | -.019 |
| Age 26 to 30 | .320 | .81 | .185 | .120 |
| Age 31 to 35 | .438 | 3.78 | .153 | .164 |
| Age 36 to 40 | .448 | 3.93 | .153 | .168 |
| Age 41 to 45 | .495 | 4.12 | .098 | .186 |
| Age 41 to 50 | .208 | 1.67 | .084 | .078 |
| | | | | |
| Education | | | | |
| Incomplete primary | .103 | 1.01 | .160 | .038 |
| Primary | .270 | 2.81 | .254 | .101 |
| Incomplete secondary | .607 | 6.11 | .240 | .228 |
| Secondary | .814 | 7.31 | .119 | .306 |
| Secondary Technical | .259 | 1.31 | .013 | .097 |
| Incomplete university | .782 | 5.57 | .078 | .294 |
| University | 1.925 | 11.15 | .041 | .724 |
| | | | | |
| Children | -.254 | -8.01 | .461 | -.095 |
| Student | -.284 | -2.66 | .091 | -.107 |
| Urban Residence | .164 | 2.37 | .818 | .062 |

Notes:   Dependent Variable: Labor Force Participation
Sample :Women aged 20 to 55
N: 3143
Log-Likelihood  -1867.7
Mean Participation Rate: 38%

Many studies have shown that participation rates are strongly affected by the woman's area of residence.[3]   In Venezuela, urban residents have an estimated probability of participating 6 percentage points higher than rural residents.

## 5.   Earnings Functions

In estimating the earnings functions (Table 21.4) we utilize a conventional human capital specification and specify the logarithm of the wage as a function of years of schooling, years of experience and experience squared.  The experience proxy is entered as a squared term to test if the earnings function is parabolic in the experience term.  Earnings functions are estimated for males and the 1,181 working women.[4]   The inverse Mill's ratio, derived from the probit estimate,

---

[3]   See Birdsall and Fox (1985), Behrman and Wolfe (1984) and Khandker in this volume.

[4]   No correction is made for selection bias in the male sample since we treat labor force participation as an exogenous variable.  It is assumed that prime-age males do not have the same options regarding labor force participation as do females.  Males are traditionally viewed as providers for the family while females may have the option of leaving the labor market to undertake childrearing and homecare activities.

## Table 21.3
### Predicted Participation Probabilities by Characteristic

| Characteristics | Predicted Probability[a] |
|---|---|
| **Education** | |
| No education | .21 |
| Incomplete primary | .24 |
| Primary | .29 |
| Incomplete secondary | .42 |
| Secondary | .50 |
| Secondary technical | .29 |
| Incomplete university | .49 |
| University | .87 |
| **Presence of Young Children** | |
| No | .41 |
| Yes | .32 |
| **Student** | |
| No | .38 |
| Yes | .27 |
| **Area** | |
| Rural | .32 |
| Urban | .38 |
| Overall Mean Participation Rate | .38 |

a. Probability of participation is reported for each condition, holding other conditions constant at their mean values.

is entered as a regressor to correct for sample selection bias. Its coefficient will provide an estimate of the covariance between the disturbances in the work/no work and wage equations.

The rates of return to schooling are 9 percent for men which is comparable with the earlier findings of Psacharopoulos and Alam (1991). The rate of return for the "corrected" and "uncorrected" estimates for women are 10 percent and 11 percent, respectively. This shows that, had we omitted the selection term from the earnings equation, the marginal rate of return would have been biased upward.

The log earnings increase with experience at a decreasing rate in accordance with the expected age-earnings profiles. It is important to remember that it is potential experience that is measured here, and that most women have interruptions in their careers. Hence, the experience variable is likely to be an overestimate. With respect to hours worked, the coefficient indicates that a one

## Table 21.4
### Earnings Functions

| Variable | Men Uncorrected | Women (Corrected for Selectivity) | Women (Uncorrected for Selectivity) |
|---|---|---|---|
| Constant | 3.91812 | 3.81234 | 3.51945 |
| | (20.692) | (14.456) | (17.993) |
| Schooling | .090507 | .101094 | .111062 |
| | (30.701) | (13.237) | (24.406) |
| Ln Hours | .541290 | .545487 | .554462 |
| | (11.127) | (11.103) | (11.307) |
| Experience | .034726 | .023371 | .028033 |
| | (9.705) | (3.725) | (5.078) |
| Experience squared | -.000389 | -.000205 | -.000283 |
| | (-5.925) | (-1.575) | (-2.376) |
| Lambda | | -.137366 | |
| | | (-1.640) | |
| $R^2$ | .321 | .397 | .395 |
| N | 2,408 | 1,181 | 1,181 |

Notes: T-ratios are in parentheses
Dependent variable = log (weekly earnings)

percent increase in weekly hours worked is associated with just over a half percent rise in monthly earnings. Finally, the coefficient of the selectivity variable (the inverse Mill's ratio) is negative and significant only at the 10 percent level. Multiplying the coefficient of Lambda with its sample mean gives the average error term conditional on being in the labor force, which is about 12 percent. The negative and significant Lambda (at the 10 percent level) indicates that there is some correlation, although weak, between the unobserved characteristics that make women highly productive in the market and at home.

Comparing the estimates for men and women, the coefficient on education is higher for females than men, indicating that additional schooling adds more to female than male earnings. The returns to experience rise faster for males in their earlier working years than for women. Multiplying out the coefficients and sample means for experience and experience squared we find that male earnings peak at 43.7 years, while for females (using corrected data) they peak at 50 years. This difference may be partly explained by the fact that most women's labor force experience is interrupted by absences during childbearing.

## 6. Discrimination

The standard Oaxaca (1973) decomposition permits us to estimate what proportion of the male-female earnings differential is attributable to differences in observed characteristics (i.e., different human capital endowments) and that which is attributable to "unexplained" factors, including discrimination.

We write the difference in log weekly earnings of males and females as:

$$B_m X_m - B_f X_f \qquad = X_f(b_m - b_f) + b_m(X_m - X_f) \qquad (1a)$$
$$= X_m(b_m - b_f) + b_f(X_m - X_f) \qquad (1b)$$

In both equations, the first term is the part of the log earnings differential attributable to differences in the wage structures between the sexes and the second term is that part of the log earnings differential attributable to differences in human capital endowments. An index number problem means that we can estimate discrimination in two ways. There is no reason to choose one method over the other, so we present results for both.

The first expression 1a estimates discrimination based on the supposition that women are paid on the same wage scale as men. In this case (see Table 21.5), differences in endowments account for 14 percent of wage differences and up to 86 percent of earnings differentials may be due to discrimination[5].

### Table 21.5
#### Decomposition of the Wage Differential[a]

| Specification | Difference due to Endowments | | Difference due to unexplained factors | | Male Pay Advantage | |
|---|---|---|---|---|---|---|
| Using expression 1a | 14 | (1.1) | 86 | (18.9) | 100 | (22) |
| Using expression 1b | 5 | (1.1) | 95 | (21.0) | 100 | (22) |

a.   Means of Working Women Only — Uncorrected.
Notes: Figures in parentheses are percentages showing the male pay advantages.
(Wm/Wf=128.6%).

Choosing the second expression 1b, we find that only 5 percent of wage differences can be explained by differences in endowments if all workers are paid as if they are females. As much as 95 percent of earnings differentials are explained by discrimination if females have the same endowments as males.

## 7.   Discussion

The wage differential between men and women in Venezuela is surprisingly low with working women earning, on average, 78 percent of men's wages. This differential is low even for industrialized nations (in Britain and Greece women earn 74 and 73 percent of men's wages, respectively) and is among the lowest in Latin America.[6]

---

[5]   It should be noted that this represents the "upper bound" to discrimination, i.e., that various factors other than discrimination can account for the wage differential. For instance, if we have omitted variables from the earnings equations this will bias the estimate of discrimination upwards.

[6]   Khandker reports women's wages as being about two-thirds of men's in Peru while Ng found women's wages in Argentina to be 65 percent of men's (both in this volume). See also Gunderson (1989).

There are two factors that may partly explain this low differential:

First, women average more years of schooling than men and have significantly higher attendance rates at tertiary education -- in 1989, 10 percent of women had tertiary education compared to 6 percent of men. Given existing acute shortages of managerial personnel, skilled workers, and technicians in Venezuela, this must have provided women with some advantage in the labor market. Indeed, women in three industry groups (mining, construction and transport) earn more than men on average, being employed mostly in higher skill occupations.

Second, equal pay legislation enacted in the 1970s, although only enforced in the public sector, seems to have played a role in increasing women's wages. Certainly, there is evidence that adherence to equal pay legislation by the public sector has attracted women employees; more than one third of all working women were employed in this sector in 1989.

Our estimates show only a small proportion of the earnings differential to be the result of differences in human capital endowments. Much of the earnings differential can thus be ascribed to employer discrimination between the sexes.[7] This discrimination may take various forms -- women may be required to have higher levels of education and more experience than men to qualify for the same job, or they may be paid lower wages for the same work. Further studies are necessary to determine what forms discrimination takes in Venezuela.

This study suggests that factors influencing women's participation in the labor force are also deserving of further investigation. The probability that a woman will participate in the labor force is shown to decrease significantly if she has children under six years of age. To date, little consideration has been given to the provision of childcare facilities in Venezuela. Access to these services is likely to be important in enabling women to participate, particularly women in poorer areas who need to supplement household incomes.

---

[7]   We cannot, however, discount the fact that there may be male skill advantages which have not been included in our estimates. If this is the case, our estimate of discrimination will be biased upwards.

## Appendix Table 21A.1

### Occupational Characteristics of Employed Women

| Occupational Group | Percent in occupation who are women | | | Percent of employed women in occupation | | | Average monthly earnings (bolivars) 1989 | Average Age 1989 | Av. Hrs. worked per week 1989 | Av. Ed. in years 1989 |
|---|---|---|---|---|---|---|---|---|---|---|
| | 82 | 87 | 89 | 82 | 87 | 89 | | | | |
| Professional | 55 | 54 | 67.2 | 19.8 | 22.1 | 22.1 | 7161.81 | 34.5 | 35.7 | 12.2 |
| Managerial | 10 | 14.2 | 14.7 | 1.6 | 2 | 1.4 | 9379.41 | 36.4 | 46.1 | 10.6 |
| Office | 55 | 61 | 64.7 | 23.1 | 20.7 | 19.5 | 5015.16 | 30.8 | 39.8 | 9.8 |
| Sales | 29 | 30 | 34 | 13.7 | 14.8 | 13.5 | 4624.2 | 35.1 | 38.3 | 7.1 |
| Farmer | 3 | 4 | 4.2 | 1.6 | 1.8 | 1.8 | 3454.52 | 39.8 | 37.6 | 2.2 |
| Transport | 2 | .7 | 1.6 | .6 | .4 | .4 | 5978 | 28.4 | 40.2 | 7.8 |
| Crafts | 13 | 14 | 14.7 | 11.6 | 11.9 | 9.7 | 4009.99 | 34.3 | 36.8 | 6.2 |
| Service | 57 | 54 | 41.8 | 27 | 26.1 | 25.7 | 3226.35 | 35.1 | 40.8 | 5.4 |
| Miner | 0 | n/a | n/a | 0 | n/a | n/a | n/a | n/a | n/a | n/a |

Sources:    1982 and 1987 from Perez de Planchart, United Nations Interregional Seminar, Sept. 1988.
1989 from OECI Household Survey, 1989.

# References

Birdsall, N. and N. Fox. "Why Males Earn More: Location and Training of Brazilian Schoolteachers." *Economic Development and Cultural Change,* Vol. 33, no. 3 (1985). pp. 533-556.

Behrman, J. R. and B. L. Wolfe. "Labor Force Participation and Earnings Determinants for Women in the Special Conditions of Developing Countries." *Journal of Development Economics,* Vol. 15 (1984). pp. 259-288.

Gannicott, K. "Women, Wages and Discrimination: Some Evidence from Taiwan." *Economic Development and Cultural Change,* Vol. 39, no.4 (1986) pp. 721-730.

Gronau, R. "Sex-Related Wage Differentials and Women's Interrupted Labor Careers: The Chicken and Egg Question." *Journal of Labor Economics,* Vol.6, no. 3 (1988). pp. 277-301.

Gunderson, M. "Male-female Wage Differentials and Policy Responses." *Journal of Economic Literature,* Vol. 21, no. 1 (1989). pp. 46-72.

Heckman, J.J. "Sample Selection Bias as a Specification Error." *Econometrica,* Vol. 47, no. 1 (1979).pp. 53-161.

Khandker, S.R. "Labor Market Participation, Returns to Education, and Male-Female Wage Differences in Peru." In this volume.

Knight, J.B. and R.H. Sabot. "Labor Market Discrimination in a Poor Urban Economy." *The Journal of Development Studies,* Vol. 19, no. 1 (1982). pp. 67-87.

McCoy, J.L. "The Politics of Adjustment: Labor and the Debt Crisis." *Journal of InterAmerican Studies and World Affairs,* Vol. 28 (1986/87). pp. 103-38.

Oaxaca, R.L. "Sex Earning Differentials" in G. Psacharopoulos (ed.). *Economics of Education: Research and Studies.* New York: Pergamon Press, 1987.

Oaxaca, R.L. "Male-female Wage Differentials in Urban Labor Markets." *International Economic Review,* Vol. 14, no.1 (1973). pp. 693-709.

Perez de Planchart, M.C. *Case Study of Venezuela: Women and the Economic Crisis.* Vienna: United National Interregional Seminar on Women and the Economic Crisis, 1988.

Psacharopoulos, G. and A. Alam. "Earnings and Education in Venezuela: An Update from the 1987 Household Survey." *Economics of Education Review,* Vol. 10, No. 1 (1991).

Psacharopoulos, G. and F. Steier. "Education and the Labor Market in Venezuela, 1975-1984." *Economics of Education Review,* Vol. 7, no. 3 (1988). pp. 321-332.

Psacharopoulos, G. and E. Velez. "Does Training Pay Independent of Education?  Some Evidence from Colombia." *International Journal of Educational Research,* forthcoming, 1991.

Rakowski, C.A. *Women in Nontraditional Industry: The Case of Steel in Ciudad Guayana, Venezuela.* Working Paper No. 104. Michigan: Michigan State University, 1985.

Rakowski, C.A. *Production and Reproduction in a Planned Industrial City: The Working- and Lower-Class Households of Ciudad Guayana, Venezuela.* Working Paper No. 61. Michigan: Michigan State University, 1984.

The Economist Intelligence Unit. *Venezuela to 1993. A Change in Direction?* Special Report No. 2003. London: The Economist Intelligence Unit, 1989.

United Nations. *Five Studies on the Situation of Women in Latin America.* Santiago: United Nations,1983.

Urdaneta, L. *Participation Economica de la Mujer Y La Distribucion del Ingreso.* 1986. Caracas: Banco Central de Venezuela, 1986.

# Appendix A

## Contents of Companion Volume

Acknowledgments
Foreword

# Appendix B

## The Authors

**Mary Arends** is a Consultant for the World Bank's Latin America and Caribbean Technical Department, Human Resources Division.

**Jon A. Breslaw** is Associate Professor in the Department of Economics, Concordia University, Montreal.

**Donald Cox** is Associate Professor of Economics, Economics Department, Boston College at Chesnut Hill, Massachusetts.

**Indermit Gill** is Assistant Professor in the School of Management at the State University of New York at Buffalo.

**T.H. Gindling** is Assistant Professor in the Department of Economics, University of Maryland, Baltimore County.

**George Jakubson** is Associate Professor in the School of Industrial Labor Relations at Cornell University.

**Shahidur Khandker** is a Research Economist in the Women in Development Division, Population and Human Resources Department, The World Bank.

**Thierry Magnac** is associated with INRA, ESR Paris, France and the Department of Economics, University College of London, United Kingdom.

**Georges Monette** is Associate Professor in the Department of Mathematics, York University, Toronto.

**Ying Chu Ng** is Assistant Professor at Hong Kong Baptist College.

**George Psacharopoulos** is Senior Human Resources Advisor, Technical Department, Latin America and the Caribbean Region, The World Bank.

**Katherine Scott** is a Consultant for the World Bank's Latin America and Caribbean Technical Department, Human Resources Division.

**J. Barry Smith** is Associate Professor in the Department of Economics, York University, Toronto.

**Diane Steele** is an Analyst at the American Institutes for Research, Washington D.C.

**Morton Stelcner** is a Professor in the Department of Economics at Concordia University, Montreal.

**Jaime Tenjo** is Assistant Professor in the Department of Management and Economics at the University of Toronto, Scarborough Campus.

**Jill Tiefenthaler** is Assistant Professor in the Department of Economics at Colgate University.

**Zafiris Tzannatos** is a Labor Economist in the Education and Employment Division, Population and Human Resources Department of the World Bank.

**Eduardo Velez** is an Education Specialist in the Human Resources Division of the Latin American and Caribbean Region of the World Bank.

**Carolyn Winter** is a Human Resources Specialist in the Women and Development Division, Population and Human Resources Department of the World Bank.

**Hongyu Yang** is a Consultant in the Human Resources Division of the Latin American and Caribbean Region of the World Bank.